WHO OWNS IR€LAND

WHO OWNS IRELAND

THE HIDDEN TRUTH OF LAND OWNERSHIP IN IRELAND

KEVIN CAHILL

The History Press

This book is dedicated to
Ros, Jane, Kay and Stella
And to
Ian, Jen and Ed
And to
Ivo, Arlo and Rona

First published 2021

The History Press
97 St George's Place, Cheltenham,
Gloucestershire, GL50 3QB
www.thehistorypress.co.uk

© Kevin Cahill, 2021

The right of Kevin Cahill to be identified as the Author
of this work has been asserted in accordance with the
Copyright, Designs and Patents Act 1988.

All rights reserved. No part of this book may be reprinted
or reproduced or utilised in any form or by any electronic,
mechanical or other means, now known or hereafter invented,
including photocopying and recording, or in any information
storage or retrieval system, without the permission in writing
from the Publishers.

British Library Cataloguing in Publication Data.
A catalogue record for this book is available from the British Library.

ISBN 978 0 7509 8445 4

Typesetting and origination by The History Press
Printed and bound in Great Britain by TJ Books Limited, Padstow, Cornwall.

CONTENTS

Introduction   7

Antrim	21	Leitrim	237
Armagh	32	Limerick	247
Carlow	40	Londonderry or Derry	260
Cavan	52	Longford	273
Clare	65	Louth	282
Cork	76	Mayo	291
Donegal	91	Meath	313
Down	104	Monaghan	326
Dublin City	113	Roscommon	335
County Dublin	126	Sligo	346
Fermanagh	139	Tipperary	356
Galway	150	Tyrone	368
Kerry	168	Waterford	379
Kildare	189	Westmeath	390
Kilkenny	201	Wexford	401
Offaly (King's County)	214	Wicklow	413
Laois (Queen's County)	226		

Context   424
Appendix   446
End Note   448
Special Bibliography   449
General Bibliography   456
Acknowledgements   462

INTRODUCTION

An Irish Childhood – The 'Why and the Tao' of This Book

There are worse places to be born in than Ireland – but, if you are lucky, there are few better. I was lucky and this book is a sort of generalised thanks to a providence I don't believe in, for the peculiar good fortune of being born in the Republic and not in one of the planet's war zones or famine-stricken places.

It is easy to define a good childhood. It is one in which the impact of each day, wet or dry, is neither dimmed nor enhanced by memory; just held there, crystal clear, and with the water that got into your wellies as uncomfortable as it was at the time, sockie, smellie, slushie, cold. A child's day is defined by immediate things: the walk to school; the staring at the sun, past the holy nun, out the classroom windows; the golden red pinkeens caught in the shiny waters of the local river. But as childhood edges forward, other things enter the frame.

The biggest one in my childhood was land. The two elderly relatives in Tipperary had a 120-acre farm, with three fine horses in the last far field, for what purpose no one seemed to know. Unrideable, they neither raced nor worked at the plough. Maybe some things should just be left to live?

The cousins, however, were women of substance and it was the land that made them so, as even a child could see. Their land was grand to explore and walk across, with always new things to be found. On Mayday there was the circumambulation of the farm boundaries with the parish priest, the rain streaming up the leg of your trousers, filling the incense turible, dousing the charcoal and plastering your altar boy's white surplice to your black soutane. The poor priest read from a swamped book of Latin verse, unintelligible to us and maybe to him, too. But we knew what the Catholic juju was meant to do: keep the pishogues and other demons off the land and out of the farm. It may have been the 1950s but the ancient evil of the secret curse still stalked the place.

And it was the evenings, before all fifteen decades of the Rosary, every night, that brought the land into focus. Where these rich green fields that surrounded us had come from, endlessly retold. How the Mahers, the cousins' family, had wrested it from the hands of English usurpers, even if it was four or five hundred years since the English did the usurping.

The name of the usurpers are in this book, their descendants from the wars of Cromwell and Elizabeth I still clinging to the land booty of conflict in Tipperary, hundreds of years later. But, finally giving way to the native Irish – us.

Halfway on the walk from the farm into Golden there was a cross set on a concrete plinth in the ditch. Men of the old IRA, fresh from their breakfast in the farm's kitchen, had been ambushed by the Black and Tans, and died on that roadside. As a child, you only get the edge of it; the excitement of ancient gunfire, never the horrors of violent death. But it made us cling around the valve radio with ferverous intent, as the Hungarians battled their Soviet masters during our sun-ravaged, hazelnut autumn of 1956.

We may not have actually understood it, but we knew intuitively what those strange people, in a far-off land of which we knew 'terribly little', were trying to do. Then, the first strangers for many years, refugees arrived. Ireland was ungenerous to the Jews of Europe in the 1930s, unaware that Ireland, too, got an ominous mention in the Wansee document setting out the Holocaust plan, and with my home county then headed by a TD (MP) who was a rabid admirer of Hitler, the Hungarians were treated slightly better than the pre-war Jews.

Nothing, however, then prepared Ireland for the payback for the missionary Catholic Irish piety that clung to the coat-tails of Britain's Empire and pervaded that Empire; the penny-black babies of our childhood coming home to the 'religious motherland', to a far better welcome – I hope – than the Jews of the pre-war continent got. Every country in Europe owes the Jewish people a debt that can never be repaid, for their sufferings in the Holocaust. One way of repaying it is to welcome, now, all those threatened by conflict and oppression.

The end of my childhood, which coincided with my going to Rockwell, was filled, every evening in that Tipperary farmhouse, with the stories of how each bit of the surrounding farms had been wrested from foreigners and strangers who shared neither our all-smothering religion nor our distant past as another people. Oddly, I have no recollection of the Land Commission, the body that did the actual wresting and resettling, ever being mentioned.

The Irish now live in a new-found land, with the liberal young dictating the culture of the place – as they should. The past is another planet. The future, the only thing the young have, is best in their possession. But forgetting the past is never safe, it may rise like a ghoul from the grave and bite your behind. And not all the pishogues are quite dead, yet. Some, the worst, live on in government still.

A Few Facts About Modern Ireland – North and South – and the UK Too

The island of Ireland is situated, according to the poet Desmond O'Grady, 'on the dark edge of Europe'. It has a long, wild Atlantic wave-etched coastline to its west.

The Republic of Ireland is an avid member of the European Union, especially now that the UK has departed the European project. It's the last English-speaking country in the EU, except maybe for Malta. It is No. 119 in size, in the world acreage listing of 193 countries, with 17,342,080 acres (Kevin Cahill, *Who Owns the*

World, pp. 270–81). Together with Northern Ireland, the island is 20,862,755 acres and ranks equal to a notional No. 114 in the full list of countries by size. The population of the Republic for 2020 is estimated at 4,937,786 people, from figures provided by the Central Statistics Office of Ireland. The population of Northern Ireland for 2020 is estimated at 1.87 million people. Both figures together are still less than the pre-famine population of 1841 – the famine that chopped Irish history in half.

Gross Domestic Product (GDP) per Capita

GDP per capita is a curious, little-understood number that tells you more about how history is working than do most other numbers. This is the total output of a country's economy, divided by its population. It is a good, but not absolute, pointer towards how the benefits of progress are reaching ordinary people. Northern Ireland is rated with the UK while the Republic of Ireland is rated separately.

GDP per capita for the Republic of Ireland in 2019, the year before Covid-19 struck, was given by the World Bank at $78,661 and the country was ranked fourth in the world in these terms. The International Monetary Fund estimated the Republic's GDP per capita at $77,771 and with the same fourth-place ranking. This book does not use the world economic figures widely touted by the CIA, an espionage organisation.

The United Kingdom: Ireland's Nearest Neighbour

The United Kingdom's economic rankings are strikingly different. For 2019, the World Bank gives the country, the Republic's neighbour with a population thirteen times greater than that of the Republic, a figure of $42,300 for GDP per capita and a ranking in the world of No. 23. The International Monetary Fund estimates UK GDP per capita in 2019 at $41,030 and ranks the country No. 21 in the world.

These are not the kinds of figures with which to be sailing free from the massive EU trading bloc to the east, nor to be setting out into the stormy waters of the post-Covid-19 world – not that the Brexiteers ever mentioned these figures. All was ideology for the departure into the economic unknown, led by a convicted constitutional gangster as prime minister, who lied to his sovereign and misled Parliament, according to the unanimous judgements of two supreme courts, those of the UK and Scotland.

The 'How' of this Book – The Return of Owners of Land for Ireland 1872–76

History, Stephen said, is a nightmare from which I am trying to awake.

These are probably the thirteen most famous words in *Ulysses*, that day out in Dublin on 16 June 1904 made into a masterful monument by Jimmy Joyce, aka James Joyce. *Ulysses* towers over the wastelands of modern literature, as it towers over Dublin, the city it immortalised. Now, those words may appear to slightly contradict the sense of the introduction. They don't. They complement it.

And, as the good Jimmy wanted, they raise, by implication, the issue of what Irish history actually is. Is it the almost theatrical – if it weren't for the dead and injured – triumph of the armed nationalist heroes of 1916, when some Irish men and Irish women, again in 'durty' Dublin's streets, challenged the armed might of the largest empire the world had every known? Or is it something else, more prosaic in the telling, though far more powerful in the execution and the result, and for that reason, all but suppressed?

There are more than 8 million Land Commission records, dating from 1881 and earlier, for which no public access is available. They are lodged in a warehouse in Portlaois, in God knows what kind of order. The Irish state's secrecy about its own people's records is as obsessive as the culture of secrecy in the UK now, and wholly of a piece with the secrecy in the time of the landlords. In his prescient article in the *Irish Times* on 23 September 2013, John Grenham asks the question that this book is mostly about: 'How long can it possibly take to decontaminate this part of our history?'

History, however, is above all slow, and the events that really affect its course are usually slow, too. Ireland is no exception. But what actually changed Ireland, what forced the slothful process of snail's pace change into action, was the famine of 1845 to 1850. This catastrophe set in motion a process of land reform the like of which has not occurred almost anywhere else in the world. And that process, of which the 1916 rebellion was indeed a part, was what changed the people of the island forever.

From being uniquely landless, as we shall see, the people of Ireland became the first peasant people to evict their landlords and eventually take possession of the bulk of the island's land. That took time, from the first Land Sale Acts of 1870, arranged while the Republic was still part of the United Kingdom, to the closure of the Land Commission in Dublin in 1999.

And although there are as many versions of Irish history as there are narrators to tell it, this is a version based on the factual identification of who the Irish people – the people who actually inhabit the island of Ireland – are and were; what land they actually owned in 1876, and for all of history before that; and what they own now, which is most of their portion of the island.

The words of Joyce also invoke that crucial observation by George Santayana, often mistakenly attributed to Sir Winston Churchill, that those who do not learn history are bound to repeat it. And we are repeating it, if indirectly.

About 90,000 families in Ireland face potential eviction from their homes as a result of the reckless negligence of Irish bankers and the Irish state in 2008. These families now face an aspect of the same fate, minus the troops with guns, that the famine victims faced – eviction. Eviction may not now kill as it did in famine times, but it splits families and not infrequently causes suicide after years of intolerable misery – ultimately, through little fault of the home owners themselves. Evictions are now the result of chronic government failure. In this matter, the modern Irish state stands like the landlords of old, inflicting injury without acknowledging responsibility, or indeed duty.

The Irish state has a duty to keep the roofs over the heads of its citizens, especially when they are under threat of being ripped off by carpetbaggers from foreign tax havens, supported by Irish laws inherited from the time of the landlords. The landlords were the people who made the land waste for its inhabitants because they owned the land, the law, the military, and ultimately the state. And as for modern 'law' and those clinging to its archaic skeleton, they often forget the words of that eminent doctor of the Catholic Church, Thomas Aquinas, who tells us, following Aristotle, 'There is no obligation to obey bad laws.'

Laws, as most lay people will tell you, are mostly unintelligible nowadays. This isn't an accident. It's the modern way of concealing skulduggery, injustice, fraud and a raft of other crimes. If it was anything else, laws would be transparent and accessible, not opaque and unintelligible.

Where you detect obscurity, drive through it to the crime that lies behind it, the commonest of which is, like the famine, state irresponsibility. The thread, more like the rotten rope that links the famine, is irresponsibility by those with power – and unaccountability.

On the night of 28 September 2008, as the banking crisis came to a head in the Irish Republic, the Irish Government put the nation in hock for a subsequent thirty years, to the tune of $64 billion, without proper explanation, then or later. The investigation into the event didn't start until 2015, seven years on. And guess what? No one had any written records of events that night. The governors of probably the most literate nation on earth didn't find the time to make even a note on the back of an envelope.

Renting is a Valuable Part of a Mixed Economy in a Well-Governed State

Now, there is a place in every economy for people who rent land and buildings to others. But they should not be the same people who are governing the state, making the laws of the state and controlling the police, the judiciary and the military in the state. That was why the time of the landlords, of which I write, was not the best of times, but was the worst of times for most (meaning 99 per cent), though not quite all (meaning less than 1 per cent), of the people of Ireland.

Where This Book is Coming From: The Numbers, Big Empires and Little Empires

The story in this book begins with a long-forgotten survey of landownership, the first ever Irish Domesday. (England had the first one in 1086 and none thereafter until the Return.) It's called the Return of Owners of Land and started life in Imperial Great Britain, in the second house of that countries bicameral Parliament, the House of Lords. It was an attempt by the landowners – the landlords – who totally dominated the House of Lords, to head off a raucous reformer in the House of Commons, John Bright MP. The time was 1872 and Great Britain was the imperial heart of the largest land empire the world had ever known, an expanse of land encompassing over a quarter of the planet and about a fifth of the planetary population. This vast expanse of territory and population was governed from London by the Parliament of Great Britain, an inner union of just four countries: England, Ireland, Scotland and Wales. The Empire itself ran to about 6,600,000,000 acres, out of the earth's total land acreage of 33,558,000,000 acres, excluding Antarctica, most of which is currently a legal possession of the British Crown. Out on the dark edge of Europe, this small agglomeration of just four countries, England, Ireland Scotland and Wales, with a total land surface of about 77,686,209 acres, had its own internal landownership problems at the time of the Return of Owners of Land in 1872.

The origins of the problems in Ireland were historic. Beginning with an extension of the Norman Conquest of England in 1066, the descendants of the same Norman landgrabbers turned up on the neighbouring island, Ireland, between 1169 and 1171, there to attempt to impose what they had so successfully imposed in England. This was absolute ownership of all land by the reigning monarch, and that monarch's divine right to decide who held tenure on any land within the sovereign's dominions.

At its core, then, the main issues of Irish history subsequent to 1169 were an issue of the English Crown's right to the ownership and allocation of land within its declared domains. Ireland was persistently treated as a dominion of the reigning monarch in England for most of the period 1169 to 1922. Issues of nationality affected this underlying reality, but were diffused by the partial acquiescence of the native Irish aristocracy – and landowners themselves – to the Crown's claim.

The issue of land was an issue of power and wealth amongst aristocrats, some English and some born in Ireland. Beneath the squabbles of the powerful, however, there was a native Irish population, almost entirely landless and, as with all peasants everywhere until modern times, with virtually no access to the law and virtually no legal rights, which were reserved for landowners.

The Native Irish: Nationality, Identity, Power and Land

The native Irish, aristocratic chieftans excluded, were a mass of people who were called Irish because they were born on the island. They shared the historic condition of the bulk of populations everywhere on the planet – they were landless. They fairly consistently numbered between 98 and 99 per cent of the population of the island. They lived, as did most of the planet's population, without the benefit of law, with their lives, like the land, entirely in the hands of their landlords, in the same way that the mass of the population in England, Scotland and Wales also lived, if under slightly milder regimes. Irish history, in the sense of the history of the people on the island after 1169, is, in one narrative, an issue of Irish national resistance to foreign occupation.

But in practice it is also a story of resistance by one bunch of landowners born in Ireland to the English, later British Crown, and the Crown's landowners who had been sent to Ireland to enforce Crown landownership there. Had the rebel Irish landlords ever defeated the English Crown decisively between 1169 and 1922, the lot of the Irish peasantry would, almost certainly, have changed but little. They would have remained de facto serfs and landless, just paying rent to local-born land thieves instead of foreign ones.

Skipping, then, the periodic local aristocratic Irish opposition to English (later British) landownership in Ireland, at its most turbulent between the Elizabethan and Cromwellian period, we arrive at two unusual occurrences. The first was the population explosion on the island between 1800 and 1840, when the numbers of people living on the island rose from about 4 million to either 6.5 million or 8.5 million (both figures are cited in the main sources). The 1841 Census was for the whole island, including that portion now described as Northern Ireland, and the 8.5 million is the more commonly accepted figure for the 1841 population.

Within that figure, and not disclosed by the census, was an economic bombshell that would start killing the native Irish by the hundreds of thousands from 1845 onwards. This was the nature of landownership and the scale of landlessness on the island. Using the 1872 figures from the Return of Owners of Land, we can say that about 99 per cent of this population possessed no means of independent economic survival if the main food staple of this huge group of human beings, the potato, failed.

Coin or ordinary currency was also almost unknown amongst this group, who were the overwhelming majority of the population. They mostly paid rent in kind, with the crops they grew, retaining potatoes as a dietary staple on the plots they held at the will of their landlord. It was this discretion on the part of the Irish landlords and government in London that turned a natural disaster – potato blight – into a lethal, killer famine.

Figures from the Return of Owners of Land for 1872

Out of a total rateable acreage for the island of 20,159,768 acres, there were 32,614 owners of more than 1 acre of land, whose total holdings came to 20,150,612 acres. There were 36,144 owners of less than 1 acre, whose total holdings came to 9,605 acres. Together, all the people who owned land in

Ireland came to 68,758. What's missing from the summary in the Return of Owners of Land for the island as a whole is the population of the island. The population figure for 1872 is given with each of the thirty-two counties in the Return, but not repeated in the summaries. It comes to approximately 4,989,919 people. If this figure is correct, the population of the island fell from 8.5 million in 1841 to 4.9 million just over thirty years later. The official figure given by the government for famine deaths between 1845 and 1850, is 21,720. This figure has never been officially corrected.

It is reasonable to believe that the failure to summarise the population figures in the Return was a further official attempt to conceal the sudden, apparently inexplicable, halving of the population of the island over a period of just thirty years. It also conceals something else, however, which is the scale and nature of landownership on the island, something that had not changed in recorded Irish history up to that point.

A maximum of 68,000 people owned all of the land on the island, out of a population of 4.89 million. The percentage of landowners to landless was 1.3 per cent owning every acre of the island, and 98.7 per cent owning not a blade of grass. If the cottagers with up to 1 acre are removed, the ratio moves to 0.6 per cent of the population owning over 99 per cent of all land on the island and 99.4 per cent of the population owning nothing at all.

Because almost no historic discussion has ever taken these basic figures into account, and most historic discussions fail to identify or address the actual population of the island and the real status of that population, most historic narratives about Ireland come close to fiction, and do, however accidentally, falsify the reality. The reality was best addressed when the American reformer Henry George visited Ireland in 1879. He described the condition of the Irish population, almost twenty years after the famine, as one of 'abject slavery'. Elsewhere, he compared the Irish rural population to that of the Russian serfs.

But it was his economic comment that is most important of all. He wrote that it was not, as English economists asserted, 'the imprudence of the Irish peasants that made them make the potato the staple of their food … they lived on the potato because rack rents stripped everything else from them'.

The morally barbaric and economically absurd system of rent and tenure in Ireland was an economic decision of the ruling government in London, dominated by landlords, and the landlords in Ireland, many of whom were members of the House of Lords in the British Parliament. Faced with a catastrophe entirely of their own construction over time, the average solution of the average owner of land to the famine was to hunt the tenants out onto the side of the road, where over a million of them died, and tear down what little shelter they had, so that even more died. It was, in the words of Lord Clarendon, the British Viceroy in Ireland, 'a policy of extermination'. His words – not those of any apologist or critic.

That history is recounted here. Not for any moral reason – history has no morality and the primary beneficiaries of history, the landowners, to judge by their conduct in the face of famine in Ireland and equally regularly in India, had no morality either.

This is not primarily an issue of morality, then, but an issue of unaccountable power and how it behaves. And of the powerlessness of those it affects. There were native Irish members in the House of Commons during the famine; people like Daniel O'Connell. Their voices were drowned out by the elegant 'yahoos' in the House of Lords, who preferred the trappings of wealth in London and shopping in Mayfair to the care of their fellow human beings and tenants in Ireland.

Henry George, already mentioned, made the other key economic and governance point about the famine when he wrote, 'The potato blight might have come and gone without stinting a single human being of a full meal' if the government had halted or modified food exports from the island and not sent in 100,000 soldiers (many of them Irish) to exacerbate the food shortages and add hugely to costs that would have been more humanely spent on saving people's lives. Indeed, it is often mentioned in famine literature that soldiers sometimes gave part of their pay to the tenants they were helping to evict, to try and alleviate the misery they were being ordered to cause.

Officialdom in London sought, as Hitler was later to do with the Jews, to blame the victims for their own deaths. Indeed, the last word on those same imperial civil servants goes to the historian Simon Schama in his *History of Britain* (2002), 'While there had been some handwringing over the loss of an eighth of the Irish population during the hunger of 1845–49, the equivalent of nearly the entire population of Ireland had died (of famine) in India in 1877–78.' And it was, as Schama shows, virtually the same imperial civil servants and their immediate successors who had improved their kill rate by 800 per cent on the meagre results of their administrative murders in Ireland thirty years earlier.

So, how did the famine affect the underlying issue of landownership? The famine cut Irish history in half. There was a 'before', where 99 per cent of the population muddled along in a survival mode. And then there was an 'after'. The after was simple enough – the landless Irish population, as enumerated above, had learned, in the worst possible of ways, that the only security for human life, for a natural term of life, lay in the possession of land. Tenants were at the mercy of landlords and died in their hundreds of thousands when the landlords threw them out.

This understanding was almost entirely subconscious. It achieved its conscious expression in political activity, but the real truth, the real deep desperation that drove the Irish population into that political activity, was the trauma of the famine itself. Perhaps the most extraordinary outcome is the stable parliamentary democracy that is the Irish Republic. The tipping of the famine into 'a policy of extermination' was government and landlord inspired, in the presence of a

Parliament that totally ignored what was happening in Ireland and did nothing effective to stop it.

The Irish population were not the first nor the only people this has happened to, but they were the only ones to achieve something between an 85 and 95 per cent conversion from landlords to small peasant farmers. A great deal of the prosperity of modern Ireland, north and south, originated with that event, notwithstanding episodic financial disasters such as that of 2008 or Taoiseach (Prime Minister) Eamon De Valera's fantastical economic war against the UK in the 1930s.

Land Redistribution

But is there a way to measure the effect of this land redistribution that is perhaps partly objective? Here is a suggestion.

The Republic of Ireland occupies a very unusual and little commented upon place in the modern world. In 2019, it was ranked fourth in the world by the World Bank in its league of countries by GDP per capita. The figure was $78,661 per person. GDP per capita is a measure of a country's economic output. It divides the country's GDP by its total population. That makes it a reasonably good measure of a country's standard of living. According to one think tank, 'It tells you how prosperous a country feels to each of its citizens.' (Doesn't seem to work in Ireland though, despite this fact.)

The two key world financial institutions, the World Bank and the International Monetary Fund, publish the annual GDP of most of the world's countries and territories each year. Wikipedia also publishes the two institutions' lists each year. There are no World Bank figures for 2020 available yet, but in the equally prestigious International Monetry Fund rankings, the Republic of Ireland comes fourth again, with an average per capita figure of $77,771. The two institutions create their tables in slightly different ways, of which the IMF is reckoned to be the tougher and more rigid. But these are not league tables. This is not a competition. This method is the closest to showing how well economies are actually functioning that the world has so far established.

Here is a table that shows where Ireland sat in the rankings in 2018 and 2019:

GDP per capita (World Bank 2018 and International Monetary Fund 2019)

Country/ Area	World Bank 2018 ($)	Rank	IMF 2019 ($)	Rank	Population
Qatar	126,898	1	69,687	5	2,687,871
Macau	123,892	(2)	81,151	(–)	623,000
Luxembourg	113,337	2	113,196	1	613,894
Singapore	101531	3	63,987	8	5,700,000

Country/ Area	World Bank 2018 ($)	Rank	IMF 2019 ($)	Rank	Population
Ireland (Republic)	83,203	4	77,771	4	4,830,000
Brunei	80,920	(5)	(–)	(–)	451,970
UAE	75,075	6	(–)	(–)	9,680,000
Kuwait	72,897	7	(–)	(–)	4,700,000
Switzerland	68,060	8	83,716	2	8,570,000
Norway	65,510	9	77,975	3	5,357,000
Hong Kong	64,596	(–)	49,334	(–)	7,436,154
San Marino	63,037	10	(–)	(–)	33,376
United States	62,794	11	65,111	7	329,450,000
Iceland	57,303	12	67,037	6	362,860
Netherlands	56,238	13	52,367	11	17,000,000
Denmark	55,671	14	59,795	9	5,800,000
Austria	55,454	15	50,022	13	8,795,000
Saudi Arabia	55,335	16	(–)	(–)	34,140,000
Sweden	53,208	17	51,241	12	10,120,000
Germany	53,074	18	46,563	16	82,900,000
Australia	51,663	19	53,825	10	25,115,000
Belgium	51,408	20	45,175	18	11,400,000
Finland	48,416	21	48,868	14	5,520,000
Canada	48,130	22	46,212	17	37,590,000
Bahrain	47,303	23	(–)	(–)	1,442,659
United Kingdom	45,973	24	41,030	21	66,870,000

The more natural home for Ireland as a country is in the IMF 2019 rankings. It is No. 4, with Switzerland at No. 2 and Norway at No. 3. Both these latter countries have small populations and have substantial agricultural sectors. Norway has oil and Switzerland has finance, as has Ireland. This suggests that small countries, with a balance between industry sectors in the domestic economy, do best economically in the modern world.

While the full role of land distribution in economic structures remains to be properly documented by historians and economists, a final glance towards Asia further indicates its importance. In 1980, the GDP per capita of India was $263, and its estimated ranking in either of the lists was around No. 120. In 2020, forty years later, India ranked No. 126 in the world lists, with a GDP per capita of $2,041 in the 2019 IMF list. In 1980, China ranked a little above India with a GDP per capita of $317. It was one of the world's poorest countries. In 2020, China has a GDP per capita of $7,755 and ranks No. 73 in the IMF list. This is the fastest rise in prosperity ever seen on planet earth, through all of history.

One factor that clearly contributed was China's redistribution of rural land. All land up to the 1990s in China was held by the state in various forms of collectives. But in the late 1990s China granted families leases of up to thirty years on their holdings. These leases are now being extended in practice. Despite its extraordinary technological success, this one move has probably done more to end poverty in China than anything else occurring in the economic spectrum. India, on the other hand, has remained marooned in a land-holding structure that is corrupt and wholly inequitable, much of which predates even the British Raj (Empire) with some land debts going back centuries, into medieval times.

But the most striking figure of all in the table is the position of the United Kingdom, at No. 24 in the 2018 World Bank list and No. 21 in the 2019 IMF list. The UK has almost fourteen times the population of the Republic, but has only a little under half of the Republic's GDP per capita. Most critically, what the UK has never done is redistribute land.

The bulk of UK freehold land is in the hands of the same tiny 'counsinhoods' that have held it for generations, many related to the Irish landlords of old. The table also demonstrates the economic mountain the newly elected Conservative Government in the UK will have to climb to make good on the core economic promises it made to win the vote in December 2019 and to leave the EU. If it cannot shift GDP, it cannot keep its promises.

One of the Conservative promises was about a new emphasis on science and technology post Brexit. There, too, the UK will have to overtake its small neighbouring republic, which has remained in the EU. In the November 2019 list of the world's 500 top supercomputers, the Republic of Ireland ranked seventh in the world, with fourteen supercomputers in the country – all Chinese, and mostly installed in American corporations. The UK ranked eighth in the world with just eleven supercomputers. Small may not always be beautiful, but it certainly seems to work economically.

An Objective Way to Examine Irish and UK Economics After the Land Reforms That Transferred Landownership to the People of the Republic

The World Gross Domestic Product Per Capita Rankings

One purpose of this book is to apply history to the present. One very simple way to do that is to take the three countries involved in our story – Britain, Ireland and India, and see how they are doing now. Two eminent organisations (and one dubious one) produce GDP per capita figures: the International Monetary Fund, the World Bank and the CIA, the US espionage organisation. Here are the rankings for our three key countries for 2018 and 2017:

GDP Per Capita and Rank Out of 193 Countries and Territories

Country	The International Monetary Fund 2018	The World Bank 2017
Ireland	$78,785, 5th	$76,305, 5th
UK	$45,705, 26th	$43,877, 24th
India	$7,874, 119th	$7,056, 120th

Noting that this is Ireland after the financial crash of 2008, there is only one other characteristic that Ireland shares with almost no other country in the world – between about 1870 and 1960, it cleared its murderous landlords, domestic and foreign, out of the part of the island that constitutes the Republic. It is not a major oil producer (yet) and it is not entirely an offshore banking centre, either. It remains a place still largely living off the land bought by its own people, for themselves – if with huge mortgage assistance from the very same British Government that let them down so badly during the famine years. History is nothing if not repetitive, lethally ironic, and mostly misguided by incompetence in government. It seems as though government inflicts a hit on its occupants, driving their collective IQ down to that of a severely challenged infant.

The international media have made much of a modern economic boom in India, but much less of how that boom is distributed on the subcontinent. About 20 per cent of the Indian population are inside the boom tent. But 80 per cent of the population are not. They remain in the clutches of landlords, with perpetual loan bondage being commonplace. That 80 per cent of the excluded Indian population still live on $2 a day, the equivalent of what their ancestors were living, or, dying, on in 1872.

The Irish, contrary to the opinion of their landlords of old, are neither feckless nor lazy. But they are no more hardworking than the people of most other countries. Their extraordinary ranking in the modern economic world has to be attributable to something else, and the only thing Ireland has that makes it different from most countries is possession of its own land, by its own people, in plots sufficiently large to be economic. An Indian peasant's day is as long now as it was in 1872, and hugely onerous, for the same awful reward as in 1872.

China

In 2007 a small delegation visited the author in Devon from the Chinese Embassy in London to chat about the forthcoming book, *Who Owns the World*. A central question from the Chinese, whose own government had recently begun to grant leases to peasant families, was how the figures had worked in Ireland. They were given an early version of this chapter. They were then shown the roadblock created in India by the hereditary loans and landlords, and the 80 per cent of the Indian population that was excluded from modern economic progress.

The author forecast that Chinese growth, if leases were extended to give peasant farming families security (as the Chinese Government was doing anyhow), would enable China to hugely outstrip India's growth, as indeed it has. In 2000, China was approximately No. 169 in the world economic rankings, with a GDP per capita of $2,932, while India was much where it is now at No. 119. But in just twenty years, between 2000 and 2020 China has risen to No. 73 in the world economic ranking, with a GDP per capita of $9,769, having in the meantime created long-term inheritable and tradable leases for family farms.

The Republic of Ireland may be a small country on the dark edge of Europe, but its history in relation to what land reform can mean is both unique and capable of powering those countries prepared to engage in it way up the economic ladder – and leaving stagnant those that retain the landlord system.

So, it would help to let the Irish people see that the issue of who bought 2 acres from the pre-Land Commission landlords in 1870 is not an issue of Irish national security in 2019. Set the records free.

Kevin Cahill, Fellow of the Royal Historical Society and Fellow of the British Computer Society,

Exeter,
August 2020.

A final footnote or, maybe, heel note. Jimmy Joyce was a very fine Irish fellow, as fine Irish fellows go. But behind the jokes was serial seriousness, and seldom more serious than when he comments on history. In *Ulysses*, he 'tin-canned' Irish history into a single day, securely encapsulating a great deal of Irish history. All of Dublin is there in all its 'durty' glory.

Right now certain things in Ireland feel like famine things: 90,000 people in the Republic live in imminent fear of repossession of their homes; they fear the arrival of an agent, always Irish, but representing absentee tax dodgers mostly. You can make land mystical, mythical even, but it's always mundane in the end. In Ireland we've done all three to it, without noticing that we're still here and it's still here and we remain its occupants …

ANTRIM

INCLUDING CARRICKFERGUS

	1876	2020 est
Population in County Antrim plus Carrickfergus	404,070	615,364
All owners of land	5,570	–
Percentage of the population	1.37	–
Owners of nothing at all	398,500	–
Percentage of the population	98.63	–
Size of County	708,405 acres	715,520 acres
Number of dwellings (of which rented)	71,229 (65,659)	Figures not available
Number of owned farm holdings over one acre	2,249	4,285

County Comparisons

	Acreage 1876	Population 1876
County Antrim, Ireland	708,405 acres	404,070
Gloucestershire, England	733,640 acres	534,640
Ayrshire, Scotland	721,947 acres	220,908
Carmarthenshire, Wales	510,574 acres	115,714

The Rt Hon. Lord O'Neill of Shane's Castle had 64,153 acres in the county in 1876, with a valuation of £44,947 about £3,775,548 in current money. By the time Bateman makes his entry in *The Great Landowners of Great Britain and Ireland* for this musical aristocrat, the acreage is amended to 65,919 acres, and the valuation to £44,000. By 1883 Lord O'Neill had become a reverend. This title is still extant and is held by Raymond Arthur Clanaboy O'Neill, the 4th Baron. He was educated at Eton and was an honorary colonel in the North Irish Horse. He was Lord Lieutenant of Antrim from 1994 to 2008. His ancestor in 1876 inherited the estates of the Earl O'Neill when that title became extinct in 1855. He also changed his name to O'Neill, having been born William Chichester. He was made a baron in the peerage of the United Kingdom in 1868. These O'Neills are descendants of the Rev. Edward Chichester, a relative of the Marquis of Donegal. The seat is still Shane's Castle. According to Timothy William Ferres, a blogger from Belfast, the estate is still over 3,000 acres in extent.

Sir Richard Wallace Bart MP of Antrim Castle, County Antrim, had 58,365 acres in the county in 1876, with a valuation of £67,954 about £5,708,136 in current money. Sir Richard sat for Lisburn as an MP and was one of the richest men in Ireland in 1876. He outranked the Marquis of Downshire by over £100,000 p.a. in modern money. Bateman gives the Baronet's home as Sudbourne Hall, Wickham Market. He was a man of huge means with 11,224 acres in Suffolk, 25 acres in Cambridge, and 2,693 acres in County Down, which – with the Antrim estate – gave him a total of 72,307 acres, with a valuation of £85,737. He was the seventy-third largest landowner in the United Kingdom, and the twenty-fourth richest man in the country based on his land valuation. The estate, slightly confusingly, is referred to as the Hertford Estate. It originated with Sir Fulke Conway, the Hertford ancestor in the 1600s. Sir Richard was the illegitimate son of the 4th Marquis and inherited the estates when his father died. The title went to a cousin. Sir Richard had a son but Ferres tells us nothing about him and the Baronetcy became extinct when Sir Richard died.

Sir Richard's enduring mark on the United Kingdom is the Wallace art collection at Manchester Square in London. No details of what happened to the estate are publicly available but the estate of the 4th Marquis's cousin, who got the Marquisate, came to 12,289 acres in Warwick and Worcester with about 1,700 acres in Antrim and Down. He was Queen Victoria's Lord Chamberlain.

The Earl of Antrim of Glenarm Castle, Glenarm, had 34,292 acres in the county in 1876, with a valuation of £20,837 about £1,750,308 in current money. The Eton-educated Earl had, alongside the Antrim acres, 112 acres in Londonderry for a total estate of 34,404 acres with a valuation of £20,910. The title is the Earldom of Antrim of the second creation, the previous Earldom – which had advanced to a Marquisate – having become extinct. The title is still extant and is held by Alexander Randal Mark McDonnell, the 9th Earl. The estate is now down to the demesne around the castle, which is lived in by the Earl's son, Viscount Dunluce, and his family. The family history is romantic and goes back to Scotland in the thirteenth century. The occupant of the estate in 1876 was the 6th Earl.

The Rev. Arthur Hercules Pakenham of Langford Lodge, Crumlin, County Antrim, had 14,629 acres in the county in 1876, with a valuation of £15,601 about £1,310,484 in current moeny. Bateman merely notes this huge estate and its clerical owner, who acquired it in 1854. The Pakenham family are directly connected to the Earls of Longford (*see* Longford) but were also related to the highest levels of the land-owning British aristocracy, a daughter of the family having married the Duke of Wellington. The estate was created for Roger Langford from confiscated O'Neill lands by Chichester in the 1600s, alongside grants for Hugh Clotworthy and Henry Upton. The family were military and sold the estate to the Air Ministry in 1940. It became first an airfield, then a site for the Martin-Baker aircraft company. The house was blown up by the British army in 1959. There is a Neolithic site near the lodge.

George Carthenac Macartney of Lissanoure Castle, had 12,532 acres in the county in 1876, with a valuation of £6,355 about £533,820 in current money. Bateman gives no biographical details of the George Macartney who inherited the estate in 1874, just as the Returns were commencing. Bateman records him having 310 acres in County Meath and 276 acres in County Londonderry for a total estate of 13,118 acres, with a valuation of £6,783. The site is beautiful and it was held in the eighteenth century by Sir George Macartney, who became successively a Baron in 1770 and an Earl and Viscount in 1792. He was Chief Secretary of Ireland from 1769 to 1772, Ambassador to Russia and Governor of Madras. He also headed the first British mission to China in 1772. He married a daughter of the Earl of Bute but died in 1806 without heirs and all the titles became extinct.

The estate at Lissanure was a grant made at the end of the Cromwellian settlement in 1649 to Captain Macartney, who became Mayor of Belfast and an MP, but later lost the estates when he sided with William of Orange in 1689. He did not get them back until after the Battle of the Boyne in 1690. At the beginning of the Second World War, the Mackie family of Belfast bid for the estate but had to wait until 1946 to take possession. During the war it was used as a military base, hospital and prisoner of war camp. The Mackie family still live at the castle, which they have restored.

Viscount Massereene and Ferrard of Oriel Temple, County Louth, had 11,777 acres in the county in 1876, with a valuation of £8,649 about £726,516 in current money. Lord Massereene is more properly described in Bateman as Viscount Massereene and Ferrard, Oriel Temple, County Louth.

Bateman records the then Viscount – having 11,777 acres in Antrim, 2,045 acres in Meath and 9 acres in Monaghan, together with the Louth land – possessed a total of 21,024 acres with a valuation of £15,031. The address given in *Debrett's Peerage and Baronetage* is Antrim Castle, which was burnt down by the IRA in 1922. The Massereenes had an estate in Kent in Yorkshire at the time of the Returns.

The title and confirmation of the estates in Ireland were a gift from Charles II when the Restoration occurred in England in 1660. The children of the 3rd Viscount then made the classic Irish landowner moves. The eldest daughter Jane married a landowner, Sir Hans Hamilton Bart, of Mount Hamilton in Armagh. The next daughter, Rachel, married the 4th Earl of Antrim, whose descendants had over 34,000 acres in 1876, and the third daughter, Mary, married the Bishop of Down and Connor. The 4th Viscount married Lady Catherine Chichester, the eldest daughter of the 4th Earl of Donegall, who had almost 23,000 acres in 1876. In 1756 the then Viscount was made the Earl of Massareene, although this title became extinct in 1816. The other titles were inherited by his daughter, Harriett, Viscountess Massereene. She married the Viscount Ferrard, which is where the merged titles come from. Ferres tells us:

> In 1668, the Massereenes owned about 45,000 acres in Ireland; however, by 1701, the land appears to have shrunk to 10,000 acres; and, by 1713, the County Antrim estates comprised 8,178 acres.
>
> Land acquisition through marriage etc. meant that the land-holdings amounted to 11,778 acres in 1887. In the 1600s the Massereene's possessed the lucrative fishing rights to Lough Neagh by means of a 99-year lease and they were also accorded the honour *Captains of Lough Neagh* for a period.

The current peer, the 14th Viscount Massereene John David Clotworthy Whyte-Melville Foster, is one of the hereditaries dispossessed from the House of Lords in 1999. He lives in Yorkshire, served in the Grenadier Guards and has been a stockbroker. He further describes himself as a landowner.

Lieutenant General the Viscount Templetown of Castle Upton, Templepatrick, County Antrim, had 10,239 acres in the county in 1876, with a valuation of £8,902 about £747,768 in current money. This Eton-educated Guards officer represents the third allocation of land by Chichester in 1649, being a member of the Upton family. He commanded the Coldstream Guards in the Crimea. General the Viscount Templetown, Knight Commander of the Bath, of Castle Upton, Templepatrick, County Antrim, had 12,845 acres in County Monaghan in 1876, to give him a total estate of 24,769 acres, with a valuation of £19,217. Afterwards he commanded the 60th Rifles and the 2nd Life Guards, and finished his military career as a general in command of Western and Southern districts. He sat as MP for County Antrim before he succeeded.

The 3rd Marquis of Donegall KP, GCH, CB, the Castle Belfast, had 14,011 acres in Antrim in 1876, with a valuation of £14,011 about £1,176924 in current money. The 3rd Marquis of Donegal was a descendant of Sir Arthur Chichester (*see* Londonderry) who arrived in Ulster in the seventeenth century and, while creating great estates for others, also created a huge one for himself and his descendants. At the time of the Returns he had, together with the Antrim acreage, 8,155 acres in Donegal, 193 acres in Londonderry and 31 acres in Down, a total estate of 22,996 acres with a valuation of £41,649. He was certainly rich enough to have the Palace appointments that Bateman records for him. He was educated at Eton and was a cavalry officer. Bateman notes that he was an aide de camp to Queen Victoria, Vice Chamberlain of the Royal Household and Captain of the Yeoman of the Guard. These were critical appointments in the power structure of Great Britain at the time. The Empire was at its peak, the largest the world had ever known in terms of land held, and Victoria was Empress of India, the largest country in the Empire. He would have had access to unlimited influence, and perhaps more importantly, all the key financial information of the time. It cost to be in Royal service, but it also conferred advantages.

Bateman makes an interesting note about the Donegal acreage: 'The above rental partly arises from nearly 140,000 acres, chiefly in Donegal, let on leases forever.'

The 3rd Marquis was also MP for Carrickfergus, Belfast and for County Antrim.

The title is still extant and is held by Arthur Patrick Chichester, the 8th Marquis. He gives his residence as Dunbrody Park, County Wexford. This estate is still owned by the Chichester family and the records of the Antrim and Donegal estates are held in the Public Records Office of Northern Ireland.

William Agnew of Kilwaughter Castle, Larne, County Antrim, had 9,770 acres in the county in 1876, with a valuation of £5,845 about £490,980 in current money. According to Ferres, the Agnews started out as the King's rent collectors in County Antrim and built a castle at Kilwaughter in 1622. They were Presbyterians (dissenters) and no titles came their way. But by the time we get to the Returns there is a question as to who owned the estate and castle. Ferres gives us a last Agnew owner by the name of William Agnew, but the dates are wrong. Bateman's William was born in 1799, Ferres was born in 1824, but died unmarried and the estate passed to his niece, the Countess Balzani (an Agnew who married her music teacher, an Italian Count). In 1916 on the death of the Count the estate went to his two daughters, who lived in Italy. The estate was seized at the beginning of the Second World War as 'enemy property'. It became an American military base. The castle was bought for scrap by a Belfast company in 1951, but is now owned by an Agnew descendant in Australia and there are moves by local historians to have it restored. There is no record of what happened to the land in the public domain.

Mrs Legge of Malone House, Belfast had 8,565 acres in the county in 1876, with a valuation of £4,844 about £406,896 in current money. There is no Bateman entry for Mrs Legge but Ferres tells us that in 1868 the property was acquired by Viscount Harberton. According to Bateman, the Viscount lived at Lyston Court Ross in Hereford. However, Bateman only gives an estate of 5,223 acres in County Kildare; no mention of Antrim or Belfast. The Legge family were sugar merchants in Belfast in the eighteenth century and leased land from the Earl of Donegall around what is now Legge Lane and the Malone Road.

Top 121 owners of land in County Antrim in 1876 ranked by acreage

		Acreage	Valuation 1876 (£)	Current Valuation Est(£)
1	O'Neill, The Rt Hon. the Lord, Shane's Castle, Antrim	64,163	44,947	3,775,548
2	Wallace, Sir Richard Bart, Antrim Castle, Co. Antrim	58,365	67,945	5,707,380
3	Antrim Earl of, Glenarm Castle, Glenarm	34,292	20,837	1,750,308
4	Pakenham Rev. A.H., Longford Lodge, Crumlin	14,629	15,601	1,310,484
5	Macartney, George T., Lisanoure Castle	12,532	6,355	533,820
6	Massereene and Ferrard, Viscount, Oriel Temple, Co. Louth	11,777	8,649	726,516
7	Templetown, Lieutenant General Lord, Templepatrick, Co. Antrim	10,239	8,902	747,768
8	Donegall, Marquess of, Grosvenor Sq., London	9,788	14,011	1,176,924
9	Agnew William, Kilwaughter, Larne	9,770	5,845	490,980
10	Legge, Mrs, Malone House, Belfast	8,565	4,844	406,896
11	Moore, James Stewart, Ballydinnity, Dervock	8,242	3,334	280,056
12	Crommelin, Samuel D., Carrowdore Castle, Donghadee	7,549	967	81,228
13	Leslie, James E., Leslie Hill, Ballymoney	7,428	5,449	457,716
14	Macnaghten, Sir E.C.W., Bart, Dundarave, Bushmills	7,134	7,062	593,208
15	M'Neill Henry H., Parkmount, Belfast	7,011	4,300	361,200
16	Magenis, R.H., Finvery House	6,816	3,698	310,632
17	Montgomery, John, Benvarden, Ballymoney	6,792	3,481	292,404
18	Waveny, Lord, The Castle, Ballymena	6,546	6,810	572,040
19	White, Major, -	5,996	1,535	128,940
20	Fullerton, Alex G., Bournmouth and London	5,611	2,919	245,195
21	Smyth, Robert, Gaybrook, Mullingar	5,592	2,641	221,844

		Acreage	Valuation 1876 (£)	Current Valuation Est(£)
22	Cuppage, Alexander, -	5,560	1,962	164,808
23	Dobbs, Conway Edward, Leeson St, Dublin	5,348	539	45,276
24	Boyd, Sir Harley Hugh Bart, The Mansion, Ballycastle	5,304	3,501	294,084
25	Coey, Sir Edward, Merville Whitehouse, Belfast	5,257	5,183	435,372
26	Dobbs, Conway Richard, Castle Dobbs, Carrickfergus	5,060	5,065	452,460
27	Chaine, James, Ballycraigy, Antrim	5,010	4,972	417,648
28	Gray, George, Graymount, Belfast	4,531	3,985	334,740
29	Alexander, Robert J., Portglenone House, Portglenone	4,215	3,576	300,384
30	Cramsie James, Ballymoney	4,036	2,173	182,532
31	Hill-Trevor, Lord A.E., Brynkinalt, Chirk, N. Wales	3,949	2,669	224,196
32	Montgomery, H. Reps, Ballydrain, Belfast	3,909	2,295	192,780
33	M'Gildowney, John, Clarepark, Ballycastle	3,811	2,449	205,716
34	Cromie, John, Cromore	3,756	2,912	244,608
35	Montgomery, Alexander, Potters Walk Antrim	3,736	2,511	210,924
36	Downshire Marquess of, Hillsborough, Co. Down	3,717	3,501	294,084
37	Wardlaw, General, Dublin	3,696	3,094	259,896
38	Greg, Thomas, Ballymenock and London	3,546	4,683	393,372
39	M'Garel, Charles, Belgrave Square, London	3,541	4,083	342,972
40	Rowan, Rev. R.W., Mount Davey's, Ballymena	3,423	3,299	277,116
41	Benn George, Glenraville, Ballymena	3,393	1,115	93,660
42	Hutchinson, Thomas L., Ballymoney	3,390	1,891	158,844
43	Casement, John, Churchfield, Ballycastle	3,312	1,824	153,216
44	Gage, Robert, Rathlin Island, Ballycastle	3,311	869	72,996

		Acreage	Valuation 1876 (£)	Current Valuation Est(£)
45	Halliday, A.H. Reps, Dublin	3,228	3,054	256,536
46	Watson, William, Co. Wicklow	2,991	938	78,792
47	Macauley, Alexander, Willmount, Blessington, Co. Wicklow	2,965	1,033	86,772
48	White, John, Whitehall, Broughshane	2,897	821	68,964
49	Thompson, Samuel, Muckamore Abbey, Antrim	2,853	2,497	209,748
50	Hutchinson, W.F., Stranocum	2,730	2,219	186,396
51	Dyott, Richard and others, -	2,714	1,767	148,428
52	Owens, James, Holestone, Doagh	2,571	2,548	214,032
53	Cuppage Adam, Glenbank, Ballycastle	2,424	883	74,172
54	Clarke, George J,, The Steeples, Antrim	2,422	2,313	194,292
55	Fulton, Captain, Braidjule, Lisburn	2,297	1,189	99,876
56	Henry, Captain Fred H., Lodge Park, Straffan, Co. Kildare	2,289	2,008	168,672
57	Donegall, Marquess of, The Castle, Belfast	2,275	2,923	245,532
58	Smith, John, Belfast	2,219	1,005	84,420
59	Hamilton-Jones, Thos, Moneyglass House, Toombridge	2,212	2,306	193,704
60	Fergueson, Thomas Reps, -	2,204	824	69,216
61	Fitzsimmons, George, Dunsona, Belfast	2,144	2,244	188,496
62	Commissioners, Carrickfergus Municipal	2,136	715	60,060
63	Orr, Wm Reps, Hugomont, Ballymena	2,083	716	60,144
64	Casement, Thomas, Ballee House, Ballymena	2,073	2,143	180,012
65	Adair, Henry, Carnlough	2,071	1,930	162,120
66	Downshire, Marquess, Hillsborough, Co. Down	2,070	1,424	119,616
67	Ferguson, John F., Donegall Place, Belfast	1,992	1,292	108,528
68	Lanyon, Sir Charles, The Abbey, Whiteabbey	1,951	2,158	181,272
69	Hassard, Robert, Parkmore, Cushendall	1,830	160	13,440

		Acreage	Valuation 1876 (£)	Current Valuation Est(£)
70	Stewart, Alexander, Ballyedmond, Rostrevor	1,806	786	66,024
71	Casement, Rev. Robert, Ballymena	1,763	486	40,824
72	Jackson, A. Wray, Somerset, Coleraine	1,723	1,344	112,896
73	Wiley, Mrs, Bray, Co. Wicklow	1,692	270	22,680
74	Patrick, John, Ballymena	1,664	971	81,564
75	Getty, Samuel G., -	1,657	308	25,872
76	Young, John, Galgorm Castle, Ballymena	1,649	2,027	173,880
77	Miller, Campbell, Gilgad, Ballymena	1,642	1,720	144,480
78	Hunter, James, Dunnaney	1,640	325	27,300
79	Bruce, Edward S., 39th Regiment	1,622	824	69,216
80	Dalway, Marriott R., Bellahill, Carrickfergus	1,617	1,216	102,144
81	Montgomery, Thomas, Birdhill, Antrim	1,610	622	52,248
82	Dunseath, Mrs, Knockanure, Ballymona	1,596	1,061	89,124
83	Cuppage, Frances, Silverwood, Lurgan	1,502	821	68,964
84	Graham, George, Ballymena	1,493	371	31,164
85	Leckey, Hugh Junior, Berdivelle, Coleraine	1,492	959	80,556
86	Lyons, William T.B., Brookhill, Lisburn	1,491	2,070	173,880
87	Fisher, John, Cleggan, Ballymena	1,489	192	16,128
88	Moore, William, Merrion Square, Dublin	1,470	965	81,060
89	Allen, Henry E., Kingstown	1,454	1,045	87,780
90	Batt, Robert A., -	1,438	938	78,792
91	Traill, William, Ballylough, Bushmills	1,402	1,177	98,868
92	Hannay, Raymond A., Portrush	1,400	1,231	103,404
93	Gage Marcus, Ballynacree, Ballymoney	1,396	1,080	90,720
94	Anderson, J.C., -	1,392	75	6,300
95	Caruth, Robert, Craigywarren, Ballymena	1,350	169	14,196
96	Tome, Rev. Henry Joy, Co. Wicklow	1,334	547	45,948
97	Langtry, Charles Reps, Co. Antrim	1,329	779	65,436

		Acreage	Valuation 1876 (£)	Current Valuation Est(£)
98	Murray, Alexander, Drumadoon	1,281	661	55,524
99	Boyd, Jane C., Ballycastle	1,249	416	34,944
100	Beers, J. Leslie, Balleymoney	1,244	782	65,688
101	M'Donnell, John m.d., 32 Fitzwilliam St, Dublin	1,235	496	41,664
102	Casement, George, Ballymena	1,233	847	71,148
103	Torrens, James, Greenesland, Belfast	1,232	1,961	164,724
104	Coates, William, Glentoran, Belfast	1,198	1,646	138,264
105	Cornwall, Mrs, -	1,196	514	43,176
106	Owens, John, Holestone, Doagh	1,195	434	36,456
107	Greer, Mrs, -	1,148	315	26,430
108	M'Neilly, D. Reps, Glenhead, Glenwhirry	1,136	295	24,780
109	Bennett, Thomas, Castleroe	1,121	862	72,408
110	Joy, George, Co. Wicklow	1,107	1,214	101,976
111	Lyle, James, Portstewart	1,107	667	56,028
112	Sayers, William, Oaklands, Broughshane	1,088	445	37,380
113	Young, Samuel R., Farm Lodge, Ballymena	1,084	773	64,932
114	Boomer, Miss, Lisburn	1,077	597	50,148
115	Scott, Thomas, Wilisboro', -	1,040	626	52,584
116	Moore, John S., Moyarget, Ballycastle	1,027	491	41,244
117	M'Cance, Finlay, Suffolk, Dunmurry	1,011	2,094	175,896
118	M'Curdy, Hugh, Breene Armoy	1,011	133	11,172
119	Bruce, Henry S.B., Liverpool	1,009	424	35,616
120	Montgomery, Captain, Benvarden, Ballymoney	1,005	683	57,372
121	Ross, William, Falls Road, Belfast	21	2,047	171,948

Top 20 owners of land in County Antrim in 1876 ranked by valuation (income)

		Acreage	Valuation 1876 (£)	Current Valuation Est (£)
1	Wallace, Sir Richard Bart, Antrim Castle, Co. Antrim	58,365	67,945	5,707,380
2	O'Neill, The Rt Hon. the Lord, Shane's Castle, Antrim	64,163	44,947	3,775,548
3	Antrim, Earl of, Glenarm Castle, Glenarm	34,292	20,837	1,750,308
4	Pakenham, Rev. A.H., Longford Lodge, Crumlin	14,629	15,601	1,310,484
5	Donegall, Marquess of, Grosvenor Sq., London	9,788	14,011	1,176,924
6	Templetown, Lieutenant General Lord, Templepatrick, Belfast	10,239	8,902	747,768
7	Massereene and Ferrard, Viscount, Oriel Temple, Co. Louth	11,777	8,649	726,516
8	Macnaghten, Sir E.C.W., Bart, Dundarave, Bushmills	7,134	7,062	593,208
9	Waveny, Lord, The Castle, Ballymena	6,546	6,810	572,040
10	Macartney, George T., Lisanoure Castle	12,532	6,355	533,820
11	Agnew, William, Kilwaughter, Larne	9,770	5,845	490,980
12	Leslie, James E., Leslie Hill, Ballymoney	7,428	5,449	457,716
13	Coey, Sir Edward, Merville, Whitehouse, Belfast	5,257	5,183	435,372
14	Dobbs, Conway Richard, Castle Dobbs, Carrickfergus	5,060	5,065	452,460
15	Chaine, James, Ballycraigy, Antrim	5,010	4,972	417,648
16	Legge, Mrs, Malone House, Belfast	8,565	4,844	406,896
17	Greg, Thomas, Ballymenock and London	3,546	4,683	393,372
18	M'Neill, Henry H., Parkmount, Belfast	7,011	4,300	361,200
19	M'Garel, Charles, Belgrave Sq., London	3,541	4,083	342,972
20	Gray, George, Graymount, Belfast	4,531	3,985	334,740

ARMAGH

	1876	2020 est
Population in County Armagh	179,221	176,754
All owners of land	2,467	–
Percentage of the population	1.37	–
Owners of nothing at all	177,679	–
Percentage of the population	98.63	–
Size of County	309,561 acres	309,760 acres
Number of dwellings (of which rented)	34,426 (31,659)	N/A from NI authorities
Number of owned farm holdings	2,467	3,346

County Comparisons

	Acreage 1876	Population 1876
County Antrim, Ireland	309,561	404,070
Westmorland, England	335,160	65,010
Wigtownshire, Scotland	309,087	38,830
Brercknock	302,237	59,901

The 3rd Earl of Charlemont, James Molyneux Caulfield of Roxburg Castle, Moy, County Tyrone, had 20,695 acres in Armagh in 1876, with a valuation of £18,591 about £1,561,644 in current money. The 3rd and last Earl of Charlemont, who died in 1892, and the earldom with him, was an MP for Armagh and sat in the House of Lords in London as a representative Irish peer. He was Lord Lieutenant of Tyrone. The Charlemont Estate, which he inherited in 1863, was large and rich. He had, with the Armagh acreage, 5,903 acres in Tyrone and 222 acres in Dublin, for a total estate of 26,820 acres with a valuation of £26,334.

Before the Caulfields became Earls they had been Viscounts. That title still exists and is held by John Dodd Caulfield, the 15th Viscount, who lives in Canada. When the titles 'devolved' to his ancestor, a cousin of the 3rd Earl, the family remained in Northern Ireland and were leading politicians in the Northern Ireland Parliament. It is not clear when they moved to Canada and there is no accessible record of the fate of the estate, though some of it may have gone to the National Trust.

The 2nd Baron Lurgan of Brownlow House, Lurgan, had 15,166 acres in County Armagh in 1876, with a valuation of £20,424 about £1,715,616 in current money. The family name is Brownlow and this title has been extinct since 1991. The estate was held by the 2nd Baron Brownlow at the time of the Return in 1876 and Bateman appears to have missed his death in 1882 when the title and the estate went to the 3rd Baron.

The 2nd Baron was active in British politics and was a Lord in Waiting in the 1st Gladstone administration. He was also Lord Lieutenant of Armagh.

The estate in 1876, with the Armagh acreage, included 110 acres in County Down, with a valuation of £20,589. Distant relatives still live in Northern Ireland.

The 7th Duke of Manchester, William Drogo Montague of Kimbolton Castle, St Neots, and the Castle Tandragee, had 12,298 acres in County Armagh in 1876, with a valuation of £17,164 about £1,441,776 in current money. There are only twenty-five Dukes in the UK, of which only one, the Duke of Norfolk, the hereditary Marshal of England, still has a permanent seat in the House of Lords. Three other Dukes, Wellington, Montrose and Somerset, have been elected to sit amongst the ninety-nine hereditary peers still in the House, the only Parliament on earth where such an arrangement persists.

In landowning terms, the Dukes as a group were the dominant owners in the 1876 Return, with nine of the twenty-five appearing in the top twenty landowners. Two of them, Sutherland and Buccleuch, were respectively number 1 and 2 in the list.

The 7th Duke of Manchester – the title still exists – was the last of that title to have a relatively normal life. He went to the Military Academy at Sandhurst, was a captain in the Grenadier guards, an ADC in South Africa and an MP. He died in 1890. The subsequent two Dukes, the 8th and the 9th, went bankrupt and the 12th Duke did time in prison in America for a sporting fraud. The current Duke, the 13th, lives in California.

In 1876 the 7th Duke had, with the Armagh acreage, 13,835 acres in Huntingdon, 1,124 acres in Cambridge and 55 acres in Bedford, a total holding of 27,312 acres, with a valuation of £40,360.

The 4th Earl of Gosford of Gosford Castle, Markethill, had 12,177 acres in County Armagh in 1876, with a valuation of £13,705 about £1,151,220 in current money. This Harrow-educated peer had 6,417 acres in Cavan, which, together with the Armagh land, gave him a total acreage of 18,594 with a valuation of £17,934.

Unusually, Bateman does not cite his biography but he was a significant courtier as the Victorian era came to an end. He was a Lord of the Bedchamber to the Prince of Wales and Vice Chamberlain to the household of HM Queen

Alexandra. He carried the Queen Consort's Ivory Rod at the coronation of Edward VII. He married Lady Louisa Montague, a daughter of the 7th Duke of Manchester (*see* above). The title is held at the time of writing by Charles David Nicholas Alexander John Sparrow Acheson, the 7th Earl. Like his ancestor, he was educated at Harrow.

Francis Cope of the Manor House, Loughall, County Armagh, had 9,367 acres in the county in 1876, with a valuation of £12,463 about £1,046,892 in current money. The estate originated in the early seventeenth century in the reign of James I. He granted the two Manors of Loughall and Carrowbrack in Armagh to the Lord Saye and Seale, who sold them to Sir Anthony Cope, the 1st Baronet Cope. The Cope family married senior clergymen, including the Lord Bishop of Kilmore and Ardagh, and the Dean of Elphin. They are relatives of the Brownlow Barons of Lurgan.

Ferres gives a very interesting update on the estates. The Manor of Loughall was sold to the Northern Ireland Ministry of Agriculture in 1947 by Field Marshal Gerald Templer, who defeated the Communist insurgency in Malaya, but who was never elevated to the House of Lords. There are no pubs in Loughall although the area is a centre for cider apple growing. Ferres says the estates have never been broken up and are still there.

The Church Temporalities Commissioners of Upper Merrion Street, Dublin, had 8,548 acres in County Armagh in 1876, with a valuation of £12,032 about £1,010,688 in current money. For the Church Temporalities Commissioners, *see* Dublin City and Wicklow.

Granville Henry Jackson Alexander of Forkhill, Dundalk, had 8,324 acres in County Armagh in 1876, with a valuation of £5,151 about £432,684 in current money. This infantry officer, who served with the 83rd Regiment of Foot, gets no further footnote in Bateman. The land he had, while considerable, was all that he had. However, what he did have scattered around Armagh and nearby counties was cousins. Bateman lists no fewer than four Alexanders, as follows.

Robert Jackson Alexander of Portglenone House, Ballymena, had 4,215 acres in Antrim, 2,866 acres in Londonderry and 1,769 acres in Tyrone, for a total of 8,850 acres with a valuation of £6,272.

Robert Quin Alexander of Acton, Poyntspass, Co. Armagh, had 192 acres in Armagh and 2,973 acres in County Dublin, for a total estate of 3,165 with a valuation of £3,192, the acreage and valuation just getting him into Bateman.

Samuel Maxwell Alexander of Roe Park, Limavady, Co. Derry, had 5,229 acres in Londonderry and 504 acres in Donegal for a total estate of 5,733 acres with a valuation of £4,236.

Finally, Bateman mentions J. Alexander of Milford House Antrim, who had 2,375 acres with a valuation of £2,809.

Captain Mark Seton Synnot of Ballymoyer House, Newtown-Hamilton, County Armagh, had 7,321 acres in the county in 1876, with a valuation of £4,682 about £393,288 in modern money. This estate began as a property of the 1st Baronet Synnot, a wealthy linen merchant, who leased it from the dioceses of Armagh. By 1876 it was in the hands of Mark Seton Synnott of Ballymoyer. He was a captain in the Armagh Light Infantry and a justice of the peace. The estate eventually went to Susanna Synnott, who married Major General Arthur Fitzroy-Hart. Their son, a brigadier general, sold part of the estate to the tenants under the Land Acts, later donating the remaining land to the National Trust in 1938.

Robert John M'Gough of Silverbridge, Newtown-Hamilton, had 7,213 acres in Armagh in 1876, with a valuation of £4,079 about £342,636 in modern money This landowner is likely to be a relative of the Macgeough-Bonds of the Argory, County Tyrone, but there is nothing in the available public record to expand the entry.

Top 100 owners of land in County Armagh in 1876 ranked by acreage

		Acreage	Valuation (£) 1876	Valuation Current Est (£)
1	Charlemont, Earl of, The Moy Charlemont	20,695	18,591	1,561,644
2	Lurgan, Rt Hon. Lord, Brownlow House, Lurgan	15,166	20,424	1,715,616
3	Manchester, Duke of, The Castle, Tandragee	12,298	17,164	1,441,776
4	Gosford, The Earl of, The Castle, Markethill	12,177	13,705	1,151,220
5	Cope, Francis, Loughall	9,367	12,463	1,046,892
6	Close, Maxwell C., Drumbanagher, Newry	9,087	10,865	912,660
7	Church, Temporalities Commissioners of, Upper Merrion Street, Dublin	8,548	12,032	1,010,688
8	Alexander, Henry, Forkhill, Dundalk	8,324	5,151	432,684

		Acreage	Valuation (£) 1876	Valuation Current Est (£)
9	Synnot, Marcus, Ballymoyer House, Newtownhamilton	7,321	4,682	393,288
10	M'Gough, Robert John, Silverbridge, Newtownhamilton	7,213	4,079	342,636
11	Richardson, John G., Moyallon, Gilford	5,974	8,183	687,372
12	Verner, Sir William Bart, of Churchill, Verner's Bridge, Moy	5,436	4,053	340,452
13	Crawford, Andrew J., Dublin	5,258	4,040	339,360
14	Ball, Thomas P. Reps, Castleblaney	5,085	4,071	341,964
15	Stronge, Sir J.M. Bart, Tynan Abbey, Tynan	4,404	5,568	467,712
16	Wilson, Joseph, Dublin	4,049	4,679	393,036
17	Bond, J.W. M'Gough, Drumsill House, Armagh	3,992	3,567	299,628
18	De Salis, Count, London	3,663	5,392	452,928
19	Molyneux, Sir Capel, Castledillon, Armagh	3,416	4,598	386,232
20	Synge, Alexander H., England	3,275	2,315	194,460
	Kilmorey, Earl of, Woburn Park, Chertsey, Surrey	3,061	3,320	278,880
	Hamilton, Jones, Thos M., Moneyglass House, Toome	3,027	1,897	159,348
	Caledon, Earl of, Caledon House, Caledon	2,877	3,236	271,824
	Reed, John, Carrickmacross	2,722	1,769	148,596
	Hall, Major William T., Narrowater, Warrenpoint	2,656	3,581	300,804
	Armstrong, Henry Bruce, Killylea House, Killylea	2,279	2,704	227,136
	Slack, John G. Reps, -	2,187	1,075	90,300
	Cope, John, Drumilly, Loughall	1,897	2,283	191,772
	Daly, Ptolemy, Newry	1,889	1,243	104,412
	Keene, Augustine, France	1,747	2,048	172,032
	Parnell, John, Dublin	1,641	2,060	173,040
	Johnston, James, Carrickbreeds, Dundalk	1,639	1,162	97,608
	Wakefield, Thomas C., -	1,570	1,346	113,064

	Acreage	Valuation (£) 1876	Valuation Current Est (£)
Dartry, Earl of, Dartry House, Monaghan	1,565	2,005	168,420
Irwin, William Arthur, Carnagh, Keady	1,516	1,117	93,828
Blacker, Stewart, Carrickblacker, Portadown	1,466	2,216	186,144
Harden, Richard James, Harrybrook, Tandragee	1,436	1,752	147,168
Bond, William M'G, The Argory, Moy	1,421	1,424	119,616
Trustees of Bishop Storm's Charities, Armagh	1,365	2,173	182,532
Murphy, James (Red), Newry	1,353	758	63,672
Chambre, Meredith, Hawthorn Hill, Newry	1,281	854	71,736
Commissioner of Education for Endowed Schools, Dublin	1,275	1,469	123,396
Bigger, Mrs Charlotte, Falmore Hall, Dundalk	1,274	582	48,888
Quin, John J., Newry	1,255	1,124	94,416
Levington, John G., Coombe House, Westbury-on-Tyne	1,243	715	60,060
Coulter, Joseph, Dundalk	1,207	608	51,072
Harris, Hugh, Ashford, Middleton	1,193	1,282	107,688
Obre, Ralph S., Clantilaw, Tartaraghan	1,152	1,241	104,244
Trustees of Woodward Estate, Bath, England	1,124	1,292	108,528
Dobbbin, Leonard, Armagh and Dublin	1,097	1,947	163,548
Cross, Colonel William, Dartan, Killylea	1,090	1,169	98,196
Atkinson, Joseph, Crowhill, Loughall	1,052	1,454	122,136
Douglas, John, Mountain Lodge, Keady	1,025	798	67,032
Hassard, Messers, -	992	1,113	93,492
Foxall, William, Dublin	978	711	59,724
M'Noughten, Sir Edmund, Bushmills, Co. Antrim	920	1,379	115,836

		Acreage	Valuation (£) 1876	Valuation Current Est (£)
	Wickham, M.B., Benlighthill, Norwood, Surrey	920	1,281	107,604
	M'Can, T.A., Elslow, Bedford	901	492	41,328
	Bell, James Reps, Aughnacloy	886	583	48,972
	Eastwood, Louisa C, Castletown Castle Dundalk	877	500	42,000
	Bigger, J.J. Reps, Dundalk	865	622	52,248
	Huston, Mary, Oranghill, Belfast	860	1,036	87,024
	Hill-Trevor, Lord, Brynkinalt, Chirk, Denbigshire	844	1,471	123,564
	Scott, John, Annaclare, Armagh	802	1,278	107,352
	Douglas, George, Lisburn	772	927	77,868
	Thornton, Major J.H.T., -	766	1,325	113,568
	Clermont, Lord, Ravensdale, Flurrybridge	758	522	43,848
	Jordan Ralph, Bray	743	540	45,360
	Burgess, John Y., Parkmaur, Dungannon	729	742	62,328
	Jeffers, James, Rosshall, Drogheda	724	322	27,048
	Kelly, Peter Jas m.d., Heathall, Newry	720	461	38,724
	Allan, Richard, Dublin	706	405	34,020
	Kelly, Denis, Dundalk	651	391	32,844
	Balfour, B.T., Townly Hall, Drogheda	645	827	69,468
	Kirke, John Reps, Annvale, Keady	594	1,470	123,480
	Stanley, Charles, Roughan Park, Dungannon	569	508	42,672
	Thompson, Margaret, Greenwood Park, Newry	562	444	37,296
	Littleldale, William E., Dublin	530	317	25,628
	Ashmore, Jas Reps, Armagh	529	652	54,768
	Macartney, J.W.E., The Palace, Clogher, Co. Tyrone	506	540	45,360

Top 20 landowners in County Armagh in 1876 ranked by valuation (estimated income)

		Acreage	Valuation 1876 (£)	Valuation Current (£)
1	Lurgan, Rt Hon. Lord, Brownlow House, Lurgan	15,166	20,424	1,715,616
2	Charlemont, Earl of, The Moy, Charlemont	20,695	18,591	1,561,644
3	Manchester, Duke of, The Castle, Tandragee	12,298	17,164	1,441,776
4	Gosford, The Earl of, The Castle, Markethill	12,177	13,705	1,151,220
5	Cope, Francis, Loughall	9,367	12,463	1,046,892
6	Church Temporalities, Commissioners of, Upper Merrion Street, Dublin	8,548	12,032	1,010,688
7	Close, Maxwell C., Drumbanagher, Newry	9,087	10,865	912,660
8	Richardson, John G., Moyallon, Gilford	5,974	8,183	687,372
9	Stronge, Sir J.M. Bart, Tynan Abbey, Tynan	4,404	5,568	467,712
10	De Salis, Count, London	3,663	5,392	452,928
11	Alexander, Henry, Forkhill, Dundalk	8,324	5,151	432,684
12	Synnot, Marcus, Ballymoyer House, Newtownhamiliton	7,321	4,682	393,288
13	Wilson, Joseph, Dublin	4,049	4,679	393,036
14	Molyneux, Sir Capel, Castledillon, Armagh	3,416	4,598	386,232
15	M'Gough, Robert John, Silverbridge, Newtownhamilton	7,213	4,079	342,636
16	Ball, Thomas P. Reps, Castleblaney	5,085	4,071	341,964
17	Verner, Sir William Bart, Churchill, Verner's Bridge, Moy	5,436	4,053	340,452
18	Crawford, Andrew J., Dublin	5,258	4,040	339,360
19	Hall, Major William T., Narrowater, Warrenpoint	2,656	3,581	300,804
20	Bond, J.W. M'Gough, Drumsill House, Armagh	3,992	3,567	299,628

CARLOW

	1876	2020 Est
Population in County Carlow	51,650 (1871)	54,612 (2017)
All owners of land	1,576 (1871)	28,243
Percentage of the population	3.05	51.7
Owners of nothing at all	50,074	21,441-
Percentage of the population	96.95	-
Size of County	221,572 acres	221,440 acres
Number of dwellings (of which rented)	9,701 (8,125) (1871)	28,057 (27,916)
Number of owned farm holdings	1,576 (1871)	1,802

County Comparisons

	Acreage 1876	Population 1876	Population 2020 Est
County Carlow, Ireland	221,572	51,650 (1871)	54,612
Huntingdonshire, England	225,613	63,708	169,508 (2011)
Radnorshire, Wales	207,394	25,430	25,821
Peebleshire, Scotland	232,410	12,330	8,376

This county, unusually, still retains a portion of an 1876 estate, with the main residence Borris House still lived in by Sarah and Morgan Kavanagh, descendants of the owners at that time. This particular estate, that of the McMurrough Kavanaghs, in turn, links into the origin of the central originating strand of the history of landownership in Ireland. This was the Norman invasion in the second half of the twelfth century, more than a century after the predecessors of the same group had invaded and conquered England. Those two invasions, of both England and then Ireland, points towards the key issue raised by Professor John Powelson in his book *The Story of Land*. Why, he asks, did people who had plenty of land persist in killing others to obtain more of it? The Normans had a half-empty European continent behind them, before they Channel-hopped to England and stole the place. The same belligerent land grabbers brought back with them to England in 1066 the Imperial Roman concept of the Emperor or monarch owning all land, which had ceased to apply in England when the Romans left in about AD 410.

The Normans then installed that principle in Ireland and, as we know, it persists in Northern Ireland where the Queen owns all land, and in the Republic where the state owns all land.

All those long centuries ago Carlow lay in the direct path of the Normans as they advanced up country from their landing point on Bannow Strand in Wexford in 1169. They didn't have to fight that much of the way. The then chief of the McMurrough clan, Dermot, the ousted King of Leinster, had made an alliance with Richard de Clare, the Earl of Pembroke, known as Strongbow, and promised his daughter, Aoife, to him in marriage, if Strongbow would help restore Dermot to the local throne. A somewhat romanticised version of the story can be found on the website of Borris House, the current home of the McMurrough Kavanagh descendants, as it was in 1876 and long before that. The house is magnificent in the English style and the restoration exquisite. It is still surrounded by 650 acres of the 1876 estate. Those in search of the Pembroke legacy won't find it in Carlow, but might look at the richest landowner in Dublin in 1876, a successor Earl of Pembroke (there were many creations of this title) earning no less than the equivalent of over £6 million from his slums and ground rents in the city.

The county is hugely agricultural and fertile. This probably explains the large quantity of religious foundations dating from Gaelic and pre-Norman Ireland and afterwards, in Carlow. There are over 800 ancient sites in what is a relatively small county. Among those remains are at least six sites – Athkillan, Ballymoon, Dunleckney, Killerig, Ballin Temple and Leighlinbridge – linked to the Knights Templar, an enormously rich Catholic military order. They had a curious full name, the Poor Fellow-Soldiers of Christ and of the Temple of Solomon, sometimes known as the Order of Solomon's Temple. There is no biblical reference to Christ as a soldier, indeed he is known as the Prince of Peace. And he was no fan of the traders in the Temple, whom he banished. Founded in 1119, the Templars were suppressed in 1312 by the Pope at the request of King Philip of France, who owed the Order immense sums of money. The Templars more or less invented international banking in Europe and the concentration of sites in Carlow suggests that the county was as valuable then as it is now. The Templers were the most efficient European fighting force in the twelfth century and were closely linked to the Normans, who were Europe's premier marauders and land grabbers at the time. The Normans often had a lot of cash on hand from the lands they usurped and the cities and towns they sacked and plundered. The Wikipedia account of the Norman invasion of Ireland is full of the kind of interesting details about how they behaved in Ireland, which often appears in school histories, but seldom examines what being besieged or occupied by the Normans meant; cruel and violent death, usually. The great French historian De Juvenal, though writing about William the Bastard's invasion of England, might just as easily have been referring to Strongbow's invasion of Ireland:

We have often seen them in the imagination – the greedy horde embarking at St Valery-sur-Somme and then, arrived at London, having the country carved up amongst themselves by a victorious bandit chief, seated on his throne of stone. (*Who Owns the World*, P20.)

Because so much of history is used to sanctify evil acts, this might be the moment to give the judgement of St Augustine in his AD 432 work *The City of God*, on the activities of people such as William and Strongbow:

> And if these ragamuffins grow but up enough to keep forts, build habitations, possess cities and conquer adjoining nations, then their government is no longer called thievish, but graced with the eminent name of kingdom.

While all this was happening, where were the landless peasants of Carlow? They were where they usually were: unknown, unnamed, at the bottom of the heap. And, as we show, that was where they still were over seven centuries later. Nothing had changed, just the names and nationalities of the landowners. Not that medieval Carlow was safe for the Normans. They had to build over 150 castles in this small county, just to keep themselves out of harm's way.

In the modern county of Carlow there are 1,802 farms, with ninety-nine of those over 250 acres in extent. The total number of farms is not that much greater than the number of holders of over 1 acres in 1876, which was 581. The difference lies in the average farm size. In 2020 it is 94 acres, back in 1876 it was 381 acres. One of the features of modern rural Carlow are the number of registered stud farms. There are seven and, interestingly, the average size is around 200 acres. The largest farmer to be identified in Carlow, via the EU subsidy payments, is that of Richard Cope in the north of the county. The chroniclers of the European payments, Darragh McCullough and Sean Duffy at the *Independent* newspaper, reckon Mr Cope and his three sons farm about 1,500 acres, much of which, they note, is rented. This recognises two realities, one economic, one individual. To farm successfully in the modern world you need to produce food on a scale that is competitive with farms in Europe and America, many of which are effectively between 10,000 and 100,000 acres (*See Who Owns the World*). The personal reality is that, having won possession of some land, families are loath to give it up, and so they rent it.

Through the county flows the Barrow, a good salmon and great trout river.

Rt Hon. Henry Bruen, of Oak Park, Carlow, had 16,477 acres, valuation £14,097 about £1,184,148. The Rt Hon. Henry Bruen was the MP for Carlow, a member of the Privy Council of Ireland and a considerable owner of land outside Carlow. He had 6,932 acres at Coolbawn in Wexford and 218 acres in Kildare, giving him a high enough personal valuation to lead the list of richest landowners by county in 1876. He was the descendant of soldiers who arrived in Ireland with Oliver Cromwell in the 1640s. The family first acquired land in the western counties, in Galway and Roscommon, but moved east in the 1700s. The military tradition stayed in the family and the estate in Carlow was purchased by a Colonel Henry Bruen in the 1770s with money made from fighting in America. The last two Bruens of record were military men. Captain Edward Bruen, grandson of Henry, was a captain in the Royal Navy during the First World War, and Henry Bruen was a lieutenant in the Royal Artillery. The last male Bruen, the fifth Henry, died in 1954. By then the estate had been reduced to about 1,500 acres. He left nothing to his estranged daughter, Gladys, who had several years earlier married Prince Milo of Montenegro. The remainder of the estate was bequeathed to a cousin in England, minus a weekly income for life of £6 to his daughter, Patricia. In 1957, the estate was purchased at auction for £50,555 by Brownes Hill Estates, However, within three years the property was back on the market after fierce protest from local smaller farmers. The estate was bought by the Irish Land Commission for £68,000, and 700 acres were divided up among smallholders, while the house and the remaining land were taken over as a research centre for the Irish Agricultural Institute (Teagasc). The last member of the Bruen family to be buried in the family's private burial ground at the Mausoleum was Gladys, the estranged wife of Henry (d. 1969).

The Rt Hon. Arthur McMorrough Kavanagh MP, Borris House, Borris, owned 16,051 acres, valued at £7,905 about £664,020 in modern money. To write about the MacMorrough (or McMurrough in Bateman) Kavanaghs is to write about much of history of Ireland for the last 850 years. It was in 1167 that the ancestor, Dermot, the deposed King of the province of Leinster, entered negotiations with the then Earl of Pembroke, Richard de Clare aka Strongbow, to get himself back on the throne. Dermot baited the pitch with his daughter Aoife's hand in marriage, a promise he later kept. In 1169 a force of Normans arrived at Bannow strand in Wexford. Strongbow followed and went to war on Dermot's behalf. The countryside was not left in a good state and many of the locals wound up dead. When Dermot died, Strongbow claimed the throne of Leinster, in right of his wife, which was not how you did things in Ireland at the time. In 1171 Henry II, the King of England, worried about Strongbow creating a separate kingdom in Ireland, turned up with another army; armies are always expensive undertakings and a great deal of plunder is needed to maintain them. Once more, plunder occurred. But the die was cast. In 1177 Henry made his son, John, Lord of Ireland. Until 1921 the Sovereigns of England sought to enforce this claim. At its core lay the Norman-introduced concept of the sovereign owning all land. That claim was used to persistently dispossess the local landowners of their lands and hand them over to settlers from Great Britain. There were three major 'settlements' or 'plantations' in Ireland between the mid-1500s and the late seventeenth century, and many minor ones based on the sovereign's right to all land. The MacMurrough-Kavanaghs lost land in most of them. Nonetheless, by 1876 they had managed to hold on to a grand total of 29,025 acres, with a valuation of £15,608. Arthur had 16,051 acres in Carlow, 7,341 acres in Kilkenny, 5,013 acres in Wexford and 620 acres in Meath. Arthur was, by any reckoning, an extraordinary man. He was almost limbless but learned to ride aged 3, spent time in a harem, and sat in Parliament with his manservant propping him up. He was a protestant and a conservative but was widely respected by his tenants. He died in 1880.

The Earl of Bessborough, Piltown, County Kilkenny, had 10,578 acres, valuation £5,522 about £463,848 in modern money. In his biography of this peer the author Bateman gives no biographical details. The Earl was the 5th Earl and had died between the Returns being published in 1876 and the publication of Bateman's summary from the Returns in 1883. The Earl was a distinguished but very British politician, serving in a whole string of London administrations between 1848, when he was made master of the buckhounds in the Russell administration, until he became Lord Stewart of the Household in Gladstone's government in 1874. He doubled up as Lord Lieutenant of Carlow from 1838 until his death in 1880.

The additional acreage, 694 acres in Leicester, 23,967 acres in Kilkenny, 200 acres in Tipperary and 1 acre in Waterford, gave him a valuation of £22,384. This would have made him very comfortable in the high society of Victoria's London. He died childless and the title passed to his brother. The title still exists and is held by Myles Ponsonby, the 12th Earl, who lives in West Sussex. The house at Piltown was sold by the 9th Earl in the 1930s and became Kildalton Agricultural College. He was Governor General of Canada from 1931 to 1935.

The Earl of Courtown, Gorey, had 7,395 acres, valued at £2,756 about £231,504 in modern money. The present Earl of Courtown, the 9th, James Patrick Montague Burgoyne Winthrop Stopford, is an elected hereditary peer and a government minister in the House of Lords. His title is Lord in Waiting. He went to Eton, as did his ancestor who held the lands in 1876. The Stopfords have been English aristocrats since the tenth century. Legend has it that the first Baron de Stopford, or Baron of Stockport, was granted the title by Hugh Lupus, who came to England with William the Bastard in 1066. Lupus was made Earl of Chester and with it given all the lands of Cheshire, save those of the bishop. William enforced the sovereign's right to all land, from the beginning. What happened to Lupus was predictable. He was William's nephew. In turn Lupus had a nephew, Gilbert Grosvenor, to whom it is said, he granted lands in Cheshire that the Grosvenors still hold, but now as the estate of the Duke of Westminster. What the Grosvenors did not get was the Earldom of Chester, which is held by the Prince of Wales. A check on the Earldom quickly shows its huge importance in medieval England, but there is no mention of Hugh Lupus or the Grosvenors!

The Stopford ancestor came to Ireland as a senior officer in Cromwell's army in 1641 but extended his lands after the restoration of royal rule in 1660. Perhaps as a mark of unfulfilled ambition, his first home was on Tara Hill in County Meath, the traditional seat of Irish High Kings.

The 5th Earl, who held the lands the Carlow in 1876, also had 14,426 acres in Wexford and 1,493 acres in Cheshire. The valuation was £12,092.

Sir Thomas Pierce Butler Bt, Ballin Temple, Tullow, had 6,455 acres with a valuation of £4,139 about £347,647 in current money. This estate, which is still partly extant and in the Butler family, takes us back, as with the McMurrough-Kavanagh estate, to the Norman invasion and the first creation of the post-Gaelic Ireland landowning system.

The 1876 estate evolved from the huge tracts of land taken by Strongbow after his deal with Dermot McMurrough and marriage to his daughter, Aoife. One of Strongbow's daughters married William Marshall, one of the most aggressive land acquirers of the twelfth century and the first Earl Marshall of England, a title now held by the Duke of Norfolk. Marshall was the second of the holders of the Earl of Pembroke title, which was recreated for different families, on a total of ten occasions. The land stayed within the Anglo–Norman aristocracy and was in the hands of the Butlers of Cloughgrenan when Thomas was made a first knight in 1628, later becoming an MP. An earlier legend has it that the house was named Ballin Temple because of a link to the Knights Templar.

Sir Thomas, the 10th Baronet and holder of the estate in 1876, was a soldier in the infantry, serving in the 56th and 24th Regiments of Foot in the Crimea. He was also High Sheriff of Carlow and Deputy Lieutenant of the County.

The estate still owns the fishing rights on the River Slaney and the present holder of the knighthood, the 13th, is Eton-educated Sir Richard Pierce Butler, a former banker with Paine Webber International, who has restored the house and the fishing.

Robert Westley Hall Dare, Newtownbarry House, Newtown, Barry, County Wexford, had 5,627 Acres in Carlow, valued at £1,757 about £147,588 in current money. The Hall Dares were post-famine buyers of land in Ireland, but were linked by marriage to the Farnham peerage in Co. Cavan. The slightly smaller part of the 1876 land was in Wexford and stood at 5,239 acres, with a valuation of £2,894. The total Hall Dare holdings came to 12,336 acres with 1,470 acres in Essex. Robert was 10 when he inherited in 1876 and a descendant, Clody Norton, still lives in the Newtownbarry House.

Denis Beresford, in Bateman Pack-Beresford, of Fenagh House, Bagnalstown, had 7,697 acres in Carlow with a valuation of £6,936 about £582,624 in current moeny. The Beresfords were one of the most successful land acquirers in the post-Norman occupation, putting a Marquisate in their family knapsack as they went. (*See* Waterford) The holder of the land in 1876 died in 1881 and his biography is omitted in Bateman's *Great Landowners* of 1883. His obituary, however, tells you a good deal about him and a little about the Beresfords. He was the second son of the distinguished Peninsular officer, the late Major-General Sir Denis Pack, KCB (who five times received the thanks of Parliament for his military services). His mother was the Lady Elizabeth Louisa la Poer Beresford, daughter of George, 1st Marquis of Waterford. Denis was born on 7 July 1818 and assumed, by Royal Licence, the additional name of Beresford in March 1854, in compliance with the will of his godfather and relative William Carr, Field Marshal Viscount Beresford, GCB, by virtue of which he had succeeded to that nobleman's estates in Carlow. In 1858 he was appointed Deputy Lieutenant and Justice of the Peace, and served the office of High Sheriff for Carlow county. In 1862, on the retirement of Capt. W.K. McClintock Bunbury, he was elected Member of Parliament for Carlow in the Conservative interest; he was re-chosen at the General Election of 1865. On 12 February 1863 he married Annette Caroline, only daughter of Robert Clayton Browne, Esq. Deputy Lieutenant of the County of Browne's Hill, by whom he left a youthful family of seven sons and two daughters.

Philip Jocelyn Newton, Dunleckney, Bagnalstown, had 5,134 acres, valued at £4,026 about £338,184. The Eton-educated Philip Newton was a descendant of a soldier who came to Ireland with William of Orange in 1688. The estate was originally part of land acquired by Sir Nicholas Bagnal, who was Marshal of Queen Elizabeth I's army in Ireland. The Newtons acquired the estate through marriage to the Bagnal heiress Sarah Bagnal in 1785. The house was sold in 1942 by Philip Newton's daughter. It has since been restored by Helen and Derke Sheane.

Thomas Bunbury, Lisnevagh, Carlow, owned 4,960, acres, with a valuation of £3,667 about £308,028 in modern money. It seems likely that Thomas Bunbury was either the nephew or son of Thomas Bunbury, a Royal Navy captain and local politician. Unusually, there is no entry for Bunbury in Bateman, although he qualified for entry on both acreage and valuation. He is almost the only politically active landowner whose name does not appear on the local Knot of the Society of the Ancient and most benevolent order of the

Friendly Brothers of Saint Patrick. At a meeting in Samuel Whitmore's Club House Hotel in Carlow in 1839 the Brothers discussed the Bible, the New Testament and passed a resolution that no person should be allowed to 'swear an Oath on the Holy Evangelists whilst their head was covered by any type of head covering'. They also discussed tree planting, tolls on roads and bridges, customs charged at fairs and base coinage, food and wine, putting a stop to duelling, faction fights and cock fighting, the drinking of spirits among the 'lower class of persons' in the county, charitable donations, and amalgamating with the Freemasons. At this time many of the Knot members were also members of the Freemasons. A significant number of landowners, especially smaller ones, together with many of the Church of Ireland Clergy, were members of the Freemasons and kept in touch through the Society.

William Fitzwilliam Burton, Burton Hall, Carlow. Acres in Carlow 5,964. Valuation £2,922 about £245,448 in current money. This Eton-educated cavalry officer of the 4th Light Dragoons had small holdings in several other counties; in Kildare 577 acres, in Queen's County 155 acres, in Dublin 55 acres, in Wicklow 32 acres and in King's County 597 acres. Each of these holdings probably gave him voting rights under the pre-reform landholding qualification. He was High Sheriff of the County in 1849. Burton Hall was sold by his grandson in 1927 and demolished in 1932.

Owners of 1,000 acres or more in Carlow in 1876 (plus owners of up to 800 acres)

		Acreage	Valuation 1876 (£)	Valuation current est (£)
1	Bruen Henry, Oak Park, Carlow	16,477	14,097	1,184,148
2	Kavanagh, Arthur McMorrough, Borris House, Borris	16,051	7,905	664,020
3	Bessborough, Earl of, Piltown Co., Kilkenny	10,578	5,522	463,848
4	Courtown, Earl of, Gorey	7,395	2,756	231,504
5	Butler, Sir Thomas P. Bt, Ballintemple, Tullow	6,455	4,139	347,676
6	Hall, Dare R.W., Newtownbarry	5,627	1,757	147,588
7	Beresford, Denis W.P., Fenagh Lodge	5,567	4,687	393,708
8	Newton, Philip J., Dunleckney	5,037	3,946	331,464
9	Bunbury, Thos KMC, Lisnevagh	4,960	3,667	308,028

		Acreage	Valuation 1876 (£)	Valuation current est (£)
10	Burton, William F., Burton Hall	4,422	2,922	245,448
11	Browne, John F., Browne's Hill	4,410	5,094	427,896
12	Newton, Philip C., Mount Leinster	4,294	715	60,060
13	Ossory, Bishop of Reps, The Palace, Kilkenny	3,769	2,474	207,816
14	Duckett, William, Duckett's Grove, Carlow	3,441	2,687	225,708
15	Doyne, C.M., Wells, Gorey	3,203	2,561	215,124
16	Bunbury, Colonel Kane Reps, Moyle	3,098	2,741	230,244
17	Kerry, Knight of, Glanleam, Valentia	2,694	1,643	138,012
18	Chancery, Court of, Dublin	2,617	1,557	130,788
19	Wolseley, Sir Clement T., Mount Wolseley, Tullow	2,547	1,982	166,488
20	Tighe, Rt Hon. W.F. Woodstock Park, Co. Kilkenny	2,185	1,316	110,544
21	Eustace, Hardy, Castlemore	2,087	1,933	162,372
22	Alexander, John, Ballygowan	2,015	1,264	106,176
23	Clonmel, Earl of, Bishop's Court, Straffan	1,945	1,230	103,320
24	Hatchell, John, Ballypierce, Newtownbarry	1,836	1,022	85,848
25	Tighe, Robert, Agent Mr Elliott, Johnstown, Carlow	1,652	592	49,728
26	Rochfort, Horace, Clongrennane	1,623	1,231	103,404
27	Keogh, Colonel John H., Kilbride	1,579	1,082	90,888
28	Lecky John J, Ballykealey	1,449	1,249	104,916
29	Paul, Sir Robert J., Ballyglan, Waterford	1,401	1,136	95,424
30	Roberts, Sarah, -	1,331	551	46,284
31	Bagnall, Beauchamp, Bennekerry	1,309	1,210	101,640
32	Guize, Lieutenant Colonel, St Waleran, Gorey	1,283	652	54,768
33	Hutchinson, Joseph, Roscrea	1,282	1,053	88,452
34	Hagerty, Edmund, Borris	1,256	792	66,528
35	Eustace James, Newtown	1,255	857	71,988
36	Singleton, Thos Reps, -	1,249	858	72,072
37	Duckett, Stewart, Russelstown Park	1,232	1,076	90,384
38	Elliot, Nicholas G., Johnstown, Carlow	1,199	1,027	86,268

		Acreage	Valuation 1876 (£)	Valuation current est (£)
39	Brady John, Myshall Lodge	1,198	659	55,356
40	Davis, Charles Reps of, Coolmanagh, Hackettstown	1,174	794	66,696
41	Seaton, Lord, Bert House, Athy	1,167	711	59,724
42	Connolly, Eugene, Artane	1,128	596	50,064
43	Durdin, Rev. Alex, 88 Lower Mount, St Dublin	1,121	324	27,216
44	O'Ferrall, Rt Hon. R.M., Balyna House, Enfield, Co. Meath	1,106	446	37,464
45	Doherty, John, -	1,105	690	57,960
46	Bonham, John Rev., Hacketstown	1,091	519	43,596
47	Watson, Sarah, Kilconnor	1,087	1,068	89,712
48	Doyne, James W.C., Seapoint, Gorey	1,026	1,923	161,532
49	Betty, William, Ballyedmond, Hackettstown	1,024	264	22,176
50	Vaughan, P.W., Goldenfort	980	742	62,328
51	Connolly, John, Kinnegad	926	578	48,552
52	Gray, Mary, -	900	515	43,260
53	Murphy, Jane, -	881	799	67,116
54	Garrett, Rev. Jas, Kellistown	874	739	62,076
55	Arthur, Colonel Thomas, -	866	571	47,964
56	Hartstronge, Lorenzo, -	855	646	54,264
57	Corcoran, Mary, Enniscorthy	836	298	25,032
58	Mills, Arthur, Glasnevin, Dublin	785	609	51,156
59	Watson, Robert G., Ballydaiton	776	562	47,208
60	Byrne, E.A., Rosemount, New Ross	757	349	29,316
61	Blackney, Hugh, -	750	792	66,528
62	Cooper, Darby H., Carlow	748	801	67,284
63	Des Veux, Sir Chas Bt, -	722	685	57,540
64	Lecky, W.H.E., -	721	649	54,516
65	Watson, Robert L., Kilconnor, Fenagh	687	210	17,640
66	Carlingford, Viscount Reps of, -	686	583	48,972
67	Bunburry, Thomas Reps, -	652	362	30,408
68	Stewart, Eliza D., -	651	1,053	88,452
69	Cogan, Rt Hon. William H.F., Tinode Co., Wicklow	651	575	48,048
70	Hamilton, Douglas, -	649	559	46,956

		Acreage	Valuation 1876 (£)	Valuation current est (£)
71	Cooper, H.H., Shrule	644	418	35,112
72	Frankfort, Viscount, -	636	493	41,412
73	Elliott, William, Kilmeany	632	539	45,276
74	Foote, Elinor Reps, -	624	386	32,424
75	Mahon, Jane, -	621	490	41,160
76	Pike -, Kilnock	616	623	52,332
77	Bailey, John M., Sherwood Park	603	435	36,540
78	Hardy, Thomas H. Reps, Borough, Hackettstown	602	499	41,916
79	Dowse, Samuel, Friarstown	599	536	42,024
80	French-Brewster, R.A., 26 Merrion Sq., Dublin	586	521	43,764
81	Alcock, Edward, Ballynoe	570	365	30,660
82	Butler, Edward H., -	547	416	34,944
83	Guiness, Thomas H., Haroldstown, Tobinstown, Tullow	543	396	33,364
84	Browne, John F., Brown's Hill, Carlow	543	385	32,340
85	Howard, Sir Ralph Reps, 6 Bellgrove Mansion, London	543	238	19,992
86	Cramer, Maurice, -	521	507	42,588
87	Hutchinson Anne, -	503	422	35,448
88	Kennedy, C.P., Castletown, Carlow	493	467	39,228
89	Byrne, Thomas, Hackststown	481	310	26,040
90	Lyons, Ed Reps, -	475	373	31,332
91	Walsh, Marcella, -	470	354	29,736
92	Walker, Lawrence Rep, -	470	293	24,612
93	Maher, Joseph, Carlow	450	371	31,164
94	Aylward, James, Rathhwade	435	331	27,084
95	De Montmorency, Fredrick H., Broughilltown	428	339	28,476
96	Morgan, Hon. E.D.G.	419	326	27,384
97	Thompson, Elizabeth D. Reps	391	259	21,756
98	Stopford, Hon. and Ven H.S., Clonmore, Hacketstown	388	307	25,788
99	White, Michael, Boolyvannan	383	139	11,676

The 20 richest landowners in Carlow in 1876 based on valuation

Rank	Name and address	Acreage	Valuation 1876 (£)	Equivalent current est (£)
1	Bruen, Henry, Oak Park, Carlow	16,477	14,097	1,184,148
2	Kavanagh, Arthur MacMorrough, Borris House, Borris	16,051	7,905	664,020
3	Bessborough, Earl of, Piltown, Co. Kilkenny	10,578	5,522	463,848
4	Browne, John F., Browne's Hill	4,410	5,094	427,896
5	Beresford, Denis W.P, Fenagh Lodge	5,567	4,687	393,708
6	Butler, Sir Thomas P. Bt, Ballintemple, Tullow	6,455	4,139	347,676
7	Newton, Philip J., Dunleckney	5,037	3,946	331,464
8	Bunbury, Thos K.M.C., Lisnevagh	4,960	3,667	308,028
9	Burton, William F., Burton Hall	4,422	2,922	245,448
10	Courtown, Earl of, Gorey	7,395	2,756	231,504
11	Bunbury, Colonel Kane Reps, Moyle	3,098	2,741	230,244
12	Duckett, William, Duckett's Grove, Carlow	3,441	2,687	225,708
13	Doyne, C.M., Wells, Gorey	3,203	2,561	215,124
14	Ossory, Bishop of Reps, The Palace, Kilkenny	3,769	2,474	207,816
15	Wolseley, Sir Clement T., Mount Wolseley, Tullow	2,547	1,982	166,488
16	Eustace, Hardy, Castlemore	2,087	1,933	162,372
17	Doyne, James W.C., Seapoint, Gorey	1,026	1,923	161,532
18	Hall, Dare R.W., Newtownbarry	5,627	1,757	147,588
19	Kerry, Knight of, Glanleam, Valentia	2,694	1,643	138,012
20	Chancery, Court of, Dublin	2,617	1,557	130,788

CAVAN

	1876	2020 Est
Population in County Cavan	140,555	73,183
All owners of land	1,044	51,391
Percentage of the population	0.74	-
Owners of nothing at all	139,511	23,286
Percentage of the population	99.26	-
Size of County	454,048 acres	467,200 acres
Number of dwellings (of which rented)	26,372 (25,358)	25,720
Number of owned farm holdings	1,483	5,282

Key Cavan land facts

	1876	2020 Est
Total acreage	454,048	467,200
Population	140,555	76,092
Owners of nothing at all	139,511	(23,739)
Total dwellings	26,372	25,869
Small holdings 1876 owners of less than 1 acre	328	66
Landowners of over 1 acre 1876	716	5,216
Acres and percentage of county owned by owners of over 1,000 acres	197,800 46.6%	

County Comparisons

	Acreage 1876
Buckinghamshire, England	456,210
Roxburghshire, Scotland	423,463
Glamorganshire, Wales	428,386

The county became part of the province of Ulster in 1650, having been the independent or semi-independent kingdom of Breifne prior to that. By 1876 the county reflected, as did most other counties in this survey, the effect of three specific 'plantations' or, as they are now termed 'ethnic cleansings'. These were the Elizabethan plantation of Ulster in (1500s), the post-1641 seizure of Gaelic landlord acreage, and finally the Cromwellian and post-Boyne settlements. Not a single Gaelic-style name occurs in the top twenty landowners, or even the top 100.

The 10th Lord Farnham of Farnham Hall, Cavan, had 29,455 acres in the county in 1876, with a valuation of £20,938 about £1,758,792 in current money. Lord Farnham was the MP for Cavan in the House of Commons. Bateman adjusts the acreage to 25,920 acres and the valuation to £18,250.

The family name is Maxwell and they arrived in Ireland during the plantations of Elizabeth I. They started out life as churchmen, first as Dean of Armagh with considerable estates attached, later as Bishop of Kilmore and Ardagh. The title was created in 1756 in the peerage of Ireland for John Maxwell, who had sat as MP for Cavan since 1727. His successor, the 2nd Baron, was advanced to Viscount in 1761 and to Earl in 1763. When he died, the title of Earl expired with him but was recreated in 1785 for his brother. The second Earldom expired in 1823 but the Barony continued.

By 1823 Baron Farnham was preaching to his tenants. He employed a 'moral agent' and told the tenants to keep the Sabbath, be responsible towards the education of their children, imbuing within their children a strict moral sense, and to ensure that they abstained from all evil habits, including cursing and the distillation or consumption of alcohol. By 1923 a large part of the estate had been taken over by the Land Commission. In 1931 the family moved to England. The 12th Baron Farnham died in March 2001 and his wife, Diana, Baroness Farnham, now resides in England, where she is a current Lady in Waiting to Queen Elizabeth II. The Farnham House estate was sold to a local entrepreneur after 2001, who developed it into a hotel resort.

The 5th Earl of Annesley of Castlewellan, County Down, had 24,221 acres in County Cavan in 1876, with a valuation of £8,802 about £739,368. This Eton-educated peer had a sizable estate, with 24,350 acres in County Down and 2,489 acres in Queen's County (Laois) bringing the total to 51,060 acres with a valuation of £29,539.

According to Ferres, the family are of great antiquity, having acquired land in Oxfordshire at the time of the Norman Conquest in 1066, and later in Nottinghamshire. Robert Annesley came to Ireland in the time of Elizabeth I (1558–1603). He was a naval officer and later a captain in the army that came to suppress the Earl of Desmond's rebellion and to plant Munster. He held high office in the government, being created first a knight, then Viscount Valentia in Kerry and finally Baron Mount Norris of County Armagh. Ferres makes an important point here. From the marriage of this new peer to a daughter of Sir Francis Phillips of Picton Castle originated three lines of titled aristocratic landowners; that of the Earl of Anglesea, of Altham and of Mountmorris. He further consolidated his position as a landowner and aristocrat by marrying, when widowed, Jane, daughter of Sir John Stanhope and sister of the 1st Earl of Chesterfield, landowners all, the latter a big one. This was when the family settled at Castlewellan. His grandson, Francis Annesley, was appointed to the Commission for the sale of estates in Ireland by William III (winner of the Battle of the Boyne) and sat in both the Irish and English Parliaments.

In 1758 a descendant, William Annesley, was made Baron Annesley and married the eldest daughter of Marcus Beresford, the 1st Earl of Tyrone, a major landowner. Later, a descendant would marry a daughter of the 2nd Earl of Howth, another major aristocratic landowner. (*See* Dublin)

These various marriages and title acquisitions are cited to demonstrate how huge landholdings were consolidated through marriage and retained within families by the same process. The 7th Earl held the estates at the time of the Returns. In 1967 the Northern Ireland Government bought the estate, which now consists of 1,114 acres. The estate records are retained in the Northern Ireland Record Office.

The 3rd Marquis of Headfort of Headfort House, Kells, had 7,443 acres in County Meath in 1876, with a valuation of £7,433 about £624,372 in modern money. This title still exists and is held by Thomas Michael Taylour, the 7th Marquis. The estates of the 3rd Marquis, some of which were legally held in his son's name, ran to 14,251 acres in County Cavan, 12,851 acres in Westmorland, 4,534 acres in Yorkshire, 3,393 acres in Lancashire, 3 acres in Cumberland and 178 acres in Glamorgan. Including the Meath acreage, the total landholdings was 42,754 acres with a valuation of £39,606. The Taylours were more English than even Anglo–Irish. The first of the family in Ireland came in the 1650s and, having assisted the Government with the survey of confiscated lands in Down (the Down survey) following the Cromwellian war in Ireland, he bought land from that survey.

In 1704 Thomas Taylour (the spelling has varied) picked up a Baronetcy, and in 1726 joined the Privy Council, the Crown's official advisors, becoming a Rt Hon. in the process. This is the normal launchpad for higher things. One of his descendants became Dean of Clonfert, another a general in the army. In 1760 the 3rd Baronet, Sir Thomas, was made Baron Headfort. In 1762 he was made a Viscount and in 1766 he was made Earl of Bective, which is still the courtesy title used by the eldest son of the Marquis of Headfort. The 2nd Marquis became an MP before succeeding and then Lord Lieutenant of Cavan. The accumulation of offices and influence continued with the 3rd Marquis, who was High Sheriff of Meath and of Cavan,

State Stewart to the Lord Lieutenant of Ireland and, prior to succeeding, an MP for Westmorland, thus retaining the English link. The 4th Marquis was a Senator in the first senate of the Irish Free State. The estate started to be dissolved as far back as the 1890s and the House was sold to a Canadian, together with about 1,000 acres. The current Marquis, a Harrow-educated estate agent, lives in Oxfordshire.

The Rt Hon. Colonel Edward J. Saunderson of Saunderson, Castle Belturbet, County Cavan, had 12,367 acres in County Cavan with a valuation of £7,370 about £619,080 in modern money. A great deal is known about this man politically, but little as a landowner. Bateman adds no acreage other than the land in Cavan at the address of Belturbet. Although a younger son, he inherited the estates in 1857 from his father, Colonel Alexander Saunderson. In 1865 he married a daughter of the Kerry landowner, Baron Ventry. He was an officer in the army and eventually a colonel in the Royal Irish Fusiliers, a militia regiment. He started out as a Gladstonian Liberal MP but became a vehement proponent of the Unionist cause in Ireland, becoming the Conservative MP for North Armagh, master of the Orange order in Belfast in the early 1900s and a member of the Privy Council. He was a justice of the peace and a Deputy Lieutenant of the County. There is a statute of him in Portadown. The estate was sold by his son, Captain Alexander Saunderson, in 1977 and is now owned by Scouting Ireland, who bought it in 1997 and who have built one of the world's five international scouting centres there.

The Church Temporalities Commissioners of 24 Merrion Square, Dublin, held 10,751 acres of Cavan in 1876, with a valuation of £6,763. The Church Temporalities were the landholding arm of the Church of Ireland, holding the land on behalf of the Church, and administering it, mainly on behalf of the clergy and for the upkeep of churches and buildings. They had land in most Irish counties but, not being an individual, do not appear in Bateman. A table of their registered holdings is included below. They were hugely influential after the mid 1600s and at the restoration, but they lived in a parallel universe to the population. They exercised fairly rigid sectarian prejudice against non-Protestants, i.e. about 90 per cent of the population.

County	Temporalities acres	Valuation 1876 (£)	Valuation Current, est (£)
Carlow	None shown		
Dublin County	615	1,494	125,496
Dublin City	15	4,095	233,980

County	Temporalities acres	Valuation 1876 (£)	Valuation Current, est (£)
Kildare	628	911	76,524
Kilkenny	2,014	1,763	148,092
Kings County (Offaly)	7,647	4,000	336,000
Longford	1,735	1,366	114,744
Louth	679 + 2	984 +113	92,148
Meath	2,919	3,874	325,416
Queens County (Laois)	3,738	2,524	212,016
Westmeath	1,116	1,395	117,180
Wexford	746	927	77,868
Wicklow	None shown		
Antrim	634	1,061	89,154
Armagh	8,548	12,032	1,010,688
Down	5,354	6,501	546,084
Tyrone	28,002	13,462	1,130,808
Londonderry	13,413	9,642	809,928
Fermanagh	10,357	6,341	532,644
Donegal	21,489	6,840	574,560
Monaghan	1,519	1,272	106,848
Cavan	10,751	6,763	569,772
Galway	2,931	1,663	139,692
Leitrim	11,950	4,539	381,276
Mayo	782	593	49,812
Roscommon	813	1,123	94,332
Sligo	868	739	62,076
Clare	825	1,238	103,992
Cork	1,914	2,335	196,140
Kerry	1,500	694	58,296
Limerick	2,202+23	2,811+298	261,156
Tipperary	2,240	2,582	216,888
Waterford	657	667	56,028

Harriett Sophia Parker was the dowager Countess of Morley in Devon, who held 10,504 acres in County Cavan in 1876 with a valuation of £2,734 about £229,656 in current money. Sophia Parker lived at Whiteway, Chudleigh in Devon, where she owned 1,924 acres. With her Cavan acres she had a total estate of 12,464 acres, with a valuation of £5,199. Because she was entered in the Returns without her title, she was something of a mystery in Ireland at times. The family and estate records are held at the Plymouth and West Devon Records Office and not at the National Records Office. The title still exists and the current holder is Mark Lionel Parker, the 7th Earl, who lives in Devon. The 6th Earl was a soldier who for many years was Lord Lieutenant of Devon. He died in 2015. The original family seat at Saltram was gifted to the National Trust in 1957.

Alexander Nesbitt of Lismore, Crossdoney, County Cavan, had 9,735 acres in 1876, with a valuation of £5,981 about £502,404 in current money. Bateman gives Nesbitt 1,482 acres in King's County (Offaly) and 280 acres in Sussex, for a total of 11,497 acres with a valuation of £6,444. The Nesbitts came from the borders of Scotland and England at Annandale and were assignees in Donegal of the Earl of Annandale. They first appear in the Cavan area after the Cromwellian wars in Ireland in the seventeenth century. By 1876 the estate was in the hands of Alexander Nesbitt, who was a Deputy Lieutenant and High Sheriff of the County. When he died the estate passed to his sister, whose son inherited in 1886, slightly after both Bateman and the Return. His name was Thomas Cosby Burrowes (*see* next entry), who was High Sheriff of the County and married Anna, a sister of the 10th Baron Farnham (*see* Franham, above). Members of the family still lived in the area until the 1970s. The estate records appear to be privately held.

Robert Burrowes of Stradone House, Stradone, County Cavan, had 9,572 acres in the county in 1876, with a valuation of £5,426 about £455,784 in modern money. This officer in the 1st Dragoons cavalry regiment links the dominant owner in Cavan, Baron Farnham, with the Nesbitts, above, giving the three families control of 48,762 acres in a county of just over 454,000 acres. The family obtained the estate from James I as part of the plantation of Ulster. Ownership was confirmed by Charles I in 1638. Robert Burrowes was the son of Robert Burrowes, who was MP for Cavan, justice of the peace and Deputy Lieutenant.

Admiral the Lord Charles Beresford MP of Curraghmore, Waterford, held 8,817 acres of Cavan in 1876, with a valuation of £2,113 about £177,492 in modern money. Bateman gives this son of the 4th Marquis of Waterford and brother of the 5th Marquis, all members of probably the largest landowning cousinhood in Ireland in 1876, the Beresfords. As the son of a Marquis, Charles Beresford had the courtesy title of 'Lord' but was created Baron Beresford in the peerage of the United Kingdom in 1916 and was given a state funeral at St Paul's Cathedral in London when he died in 1919. Admiral the Lord Charles

William De La Poer Beresford, to give him his full title, inherited his Cavan estate from the Most Reverend the Right Honourable John De La Poer Beresford, Archbishop of Armagh and Primate of All Ireland (Church of Ireland). He was enormously wealthy and made huge gifts to mainly Church of Ireland foundations. There is an extensive Wikipedia entry for Charles Beresford, who managed to be an MP for much of his naval career and this was coloured by a number of affairs, which officers of the period did not have, unless they were Peers.

Lord Lisgar of Lisgar House, Bailleborough, County Cavan, had 8,503 acres in the county in 1876, with a valuation of £5,619 about £471,996 in modern money. This Old Etonian peer's family name was Young and as the Rt Hon. Sir John Young he was Governor-General of Canada, Governor of New South Wales and Chief Secretary for Ireland. He was MP for Cavan for twenty-four years. His father was a director of the East India Company, the great Imperial carpetbaggers in the Far East during the eighteenth and nineteenth centuries. He married Annabella, a daughter of the 2nd Marchioness of Headfort, another landowner, by her first husband, Edward Tuite Dalton.

Bateman amends the entry quite significantly, attributing the lands to Lady Lisgar and her second husband, Sir Francis Charles Fortescue, who had been Lord Lisgar's private secretary in the Ionian Islands, New South Wales and Canada. Lord Lisgar died in 1876 and the title became extinct. The lady and her husband had, as well as the Cavan acreage, 1,498 acres in Oxford, 699 acres in Leicester and 292 acres in Northampton, totalling 11,413 acres with a valuation of £11,458. Ferres amends this further, by changing Sir Francis Fortescue into Sir Francis Fortescue Turville of Bosworth Hall, Leicestershire.

Most of the estate was sold off at the end of the nineteenth century and the 'great house' burnt down in 1918.

Top 20 landowners in Cavan in 1876

		Acreage	Valuation 1876 (£)	Valuation Current Est (£)
1	Farnham, Lord, Farnham Hall, Cavan	29,455	20,938	1,758,792
2	Annesley, Earl, Castlewellan, Co. Down	24,221	8,802	739,368
3	Headfort, Marquis of, Headfort, Kells	14,220	9,013	757,092
4	Saunderson, Edward J., Saunderson Castle, Belturbet	12,362	7,370	619,080

		Acreage	Valuation 1876 (£)	Valuation Current Est (£)
5	Church Temporarities, Commissioners of, Dublin	10,751	6,763	558,092
6	Parker, Harriett, Devon, England*	10,540	2,734	229,656
7	Nesbitt, Alexander, Lismore and Mincing Lane, London	9,735	5,981	502,404
8	Burrowes, Robert, Stradone House, Stradone	9,572	5,426	458,808
9	Beresford, Lord Charles, Curraghmore, Waterford	8,817	2,113	177,492
10	Lisgar, Lord, Castle, Bailieborough	8,503	5,619	471,996
11	Pratt, Mervyn, Cabra Castle, Kingscourt	8,095	5,295	444,780
12	Lanesborough, Earl of, Lanesborough, Belturbet	7,946	6,240	524,160
13	Singleton Henry Sydenham, Hasley Heath, Hants, England	6,609	3,633	305,172
14	Gosford, Earl of, Markethill	6,417	4,229	355,236
15	Beresford, Rt Hon. and most Rev., Palace, Armagh	6,218	3,910	328,440
16	Garvagh, Lady, Garvagh, Londonderry	5,803	2,804	235,536
17	Coote, Richard, Bellamont Forest, Coothill	5,321	6,504	546,336
18	Humphreys, William, Ballyhaise, Co. Cavan	5,146	4,010	336,840
19	Dease, Gerald (a minor), Turbotson, Castlepollard	4,647	2,829	237,636
20	Finlay, John, Brackley House, Bawnboy	4,337	976	81,984

* Harriett Sophia Parker, Dowager Countess of Morley of Chudleigh, Devon.

Top 20 landowners in Cavan by rental valuation

		Acreage	Valuation 1876 (£)	Valuation Current Est (£)
1	Farnham, Lord, Farnham Hall, Cavan	29,455	20,938	1,758,792
2	Headfort, Marquis of, Headfort, Kells	14,220	9,013	757,092
3	Annesley, Earl, Castlewellan, Co. Down	24,221	8,802	739,368

4	Saunderson, Edward J., Saunderson Castle, Belturbet	12,362	7,370	619,080
5	Church Temporariities, Commissioners of, Dublin	10,751	6,763	558,092
6	Coote Richard, Bellamont Forest, Coothill	5,321	6,504	546,336
7	Lanesborough, Earl of, Lanesborough, Belturbet	7,946	6,240	524,160
8	Nesbitt, Alexander, Lismore and Mincing Lane, London	9,735	5,981	502,404
9	Lisgar, Lord, Castle, Bailieborough	8,503	5,619	471,996
10	Burrowes, Robert, Stradone House, Stradone	9,572	5,426	458,808
11	Pratt Mervyn, Cabra Castle, Kingscourt	8,095	5,295	444,780
12	Gosford, Earl of, Markethill	6,417	4,229	355,236
13	Humphreys, William, Ballyhaise, Co. Cavan	5,146	4,010	336,840
14	Beresford, Rt Hon. and most Rev., Palace, Armagh	6,218	3,910	328,440
15	Singleton, Henry Sydenham, Hasley Heath, Hants, England	6,609	3,633	305,172
16	Clements, H. Theolopilus, Ashfield Lodge, Coothill	3,908	2,924	245,616
17	Dease, Gerald (a minor), Turbotson, Castlepollard	4,647	2,829	237,636
18	Garvagh, Lady, Garvagh, Londonderry	5,803	2,804	235,536
19	Parker, Harriett, Devon, England*	10,540	2,734	229,656
20	Saunderson, Lewelyn T.R., Drumkeen, Cavan	4,160	2,644	222,096

* Harriett Sophia Parker, Dowager Countess of Morley of Chudleigh, Devon.

Landowners of over 1,000 acres in Cavan in 1876

		Acreage	Valuation 1876 (£)	Valuation current (£)
1	Farnham, Lord, Farnham Hall, Cavan	29,455	20,938	1,758,792
2	Annesley, Earl, Castlewellan, Co. Down	24,221	8,802	739,368
3	Headfort, Marquis of, Headfort, Kells	14,220	9,013	757,092

		Acreage	Valuation 1876 (£)	Valuation current (£)
4	Saunderson, Edward J., Saunderson Castle, Belturbet	12,362	7,370	619,080
5	Church Temporariities, Commissioners of, Dublin	10,751	6,763	558,092
6	Parker, Harriett, Devon, England	10,540	2,734	229,656
7	Nesbitt, Alexander, Lismore and Mincing Lane, London	9,735	5,981	502,404
8	Burrowes, Robert, Stradone House, Stradone	9,572	5,426	458,808
9	Beresford, Lord Charles, Curraghmore, Waterford	8,817	2,113	177,492
10	Lisgar, Lord, Castle, Bailieborough	8,503	5,619	471,996
11	Pratt, Mervyn, Cabra Castle, Kingscourt	8,095	5,295	444,780
12	Lanesborough, Earl of, Lanesborough, Belturbet	7,946	6,240	524,160
13	Singleton, Henry Sydenham, Hasley Heath, Hants, England	6,609	3,633	305,172
14	Gosford, Earl of, Markethill	6,417	4,229	355,236
15	Beresford, Rt Hon. and most Rev., Palace, Armagh	6,218	3,910	328,440
16	Garvagh, Lady, Garvagh, Londonderry	5,803	2,804	235,536
17	Coote, Richard, Bellamont Forest, Coothill	5,321	6,504	546,336
18	Humphreys, William, Ballyhaise, Co. Cavan	5,146	4,010	336,840
19	Dease, Gerald (a minor), Turbotson, Castlepollard	4,647	2,829	237,636
20	Finlay John, Brackley House Bawnboy	4,337	976	81,984
21	Fay, John, Moyne Hall, Cavan	4,179	2,566	215,544
22	Saunderson, Lewelyn T.R., Drumkeen, Cavan	4,160	2,644	222,096
23	Hodson, Sir George, Hollybrook, Bray	4,121	2,269	190,596
24	Clements, H. Theolopilus, Ashfield Lodge, Coothill	3,908	2,924	245,616
25	Hassard, Richard, 1 Westminster Chambers, London	3,749	622	52,248

		Acreage	Valuation 1876 (£)	Valuation current (£)
26	Hassard, Jason Alext Reps of, Gardenhill	3,610	578	48,552
27	Saunders, Richard, Dartford, Kent	3,588	816	68,544
28	Beresford, J.D. Reps of, Dublin	3,356	2,160	181,440
29	O'Reilly, Anthony Reps of, Baltrasna, Oldcastle	3,053	2,098	176,232
30	Sitator, Colonel, -	2,944	1,861	156,324
31	Crofton, Parsons, 6 Sprawl St, London	2,741	504	42,336
32	Saunderson, Samuel, Cloverhill, Belturbet	2,560	1,736	145,824
33	Venebles, Rev. E.B. White, Redhills Demesne, Redhills	2,532	1,667	140,028
34	Smith, William Reps of, Drumkeel, Bellananagh	2,431	1,449	121,716
35	Clements, Theopilus H., Rakenny, Coothill	2,426	1,815	152,460
36	Storey, Joseph, Bingfield, Crossdoney	2,415	1,383	116,172
37	Moore, Samuel, -	2,402	1,345	112,980
38	Dobbin, Leonard, 27 Gardiner's Place, Dublin	2,364	737	61,908
39	Leslie, William, Coothill	2,354	1,440	120,960
40	Stuart, Viscountess, Stuart Hall, Stuartstown, Co. Tyrone	2,260	1,345	112,980
41	Southwell, Viscount Reps of, -	2,252	1,432	120,288
42	Coote, Colonel George Charles Henry, -	2,235	900	75,600
43	Jones, John Copeland, Nahillah Belturbet, Co. Cavan	2,235	1,518	127,512
44	Townley, Charlotte, Tullyoin, Coothill	2,180	1,437	120,708
45	Dunlop, Mrs D., Monsterboice, Drogheda	2,051	1,225	102,900
46	Greville, Lord, Clonyn, Delvin	1,970	1,182	99,288
47	Fleming, Edward Reps of, Limerick	1,917	1,908	160,272
48	Nugent St George, Bobsgrove	1,832	1,389	116,676
49	Hutton, Caroline, Putney Park, Surrey, England	1,806	625	52,500
50	Saunders, Richard, Dublin	1,773	1,037	87,108

		Acreage	Valuation 1876 (£)	Valuation current (£)
51	Vernon, John Edward, Mount Merrion House, Booterstown	1,766	1,165	97,860
52	Marley, Brinsby, Mullingar and England	1,668	929	78,036
53	Fox, Charles D., 6 Leinster St, Dublin	1,667	955	80,220
54	Hamilton, James, Castle, Hamilton	1,649	1,875	157,500
55	Bredin, Edgar R., Hamilton, Ontario, Canada	1,629	886	74,424
56	Newburgh, Arthur R.C., -	1,563	1,091	91,644
57	Adams, Benjamin Samuel, Shinan House, Shercock	1,548	1,153	96,852
58	Stephenson, John M., England	1,505	390	32,760
59	Leslie, John, Kiltybegs, Carrickmacross	1,503	901	75,684
60	Waring, Rev. Charles, Benburb, Moy	1,468	1,017	85,428
61	Adams, Ambrose G., Northlands, Carrickmacross	1,446	913	76,692
62	O'Reilly-Dease, Matthew, Ravensdale, Bray	1,417	892	74,928
63	Annesley, Hon. William O'B. Beresford, London	1,412	843	70,812
64	Leslie, John, Glasslough, Co. Monaghan	1,375	718	60,312
65	Mackarness, Rev. George R., Home Vicarage, Ashbourne, Derbyshire	1,370	726	60,984
66	Nixon, William, Thornhill	1,346	251	21,084
67	Erskine, Robert, Cavan	1,328	1,281	107,604
68	Sankey, A.W.G, Fortfredrick, Virginia	1,324	713	59,892
69	Armstrong, Elliott, Bristle Road, Bath, England	1,308	745	52,580
70	Rotheram, Edward, Crossdrum, Oldcastle	1,290	940	78,960
71	Adams, Chas Stuart, Glynch House, Newbliss	1,287	705	57,316
72	Lloyd, Bartholomew C Reps of, Dublin	1,277	725	60,900
73	Finlay, Sir Thomas Bt (Reps of) Hampstead Road, London	1,231	471	39,564

		Acreage	Valuation 1876 (£)	Valuation current (£)
74	Magee, William, Killashandra, Co. Cavan	1,228	85	7,140
75	Thompson, Theopilus, Cavan	1,187	731	61,404
76	Talbot, De Malahide Lord, Malahide	1,133	641	53,844
77	Annesley, Hon. Arthur, Castlewellan, Co. Down	1,131	828	69,552
78	Rathburne, William H., Finglas, Dublin	1,127	690	57,960
79	Cuming, Robert John, Crover, Mount Nugent	1,118	1,479	124,236
80	Dawson, Robert Peel, Londonderry	1,116	440	36,960
81	O'Brien, Robert F., Killashandra	1,091	208	17,472
82	Annesley, Hon. George, Castlewellan, Co. Down	1,057	621	52,164
83	Gresson, George, 10 Fredrick St S., Dublin	1,050	525	44,100
84	Kennedy, Edward, Cavan	1,046	514	43,176
85	Frankfort, Viscount, -	1,045	536	45,024
86	Cooke, James Richard, 73 Blessington Street, Dublin	1,042	577	48,468
87	O'Reilly, Thomas, Drumbannow, Bazllyheelin	1,029	593	49,812
89	Montgomery, Nathaniel, Riversdale, Swanlinbar	1,027	733	61,572
90	Phillips, Michael, Bawnboy, Co. Cavan	1,024	689	57,876
91	Finlay, Alfred (a minor), Ballyshannon	1,023	358	30,072
92	Johnston, William, Bawnboy House, Bawnboy	1,016	686	57,624
93	Grattan, Henry, Dublin	1,004	604	50,736

CLARE

	1876	2020 Est
Population in County Clare	147,864	118,817
All owners of land	1,025	73,272
Percentage of the population	1.025	–
Owners of nothing at all	146,859	36,323
Percentage of the population	98.975	–
Size of County	759,775 acres	807,680 acres
Number of dwellings (of which rented)	26,069 (25,044)	42,534
Number of owned farm holdings	1,767	6,550

County comparisons

	Acreage 1876	Population 1876
Clare	759,775	147,864
Cornwall, England	758,961	362,343
Ayrshire, Scotland	721,947	220,908
Carmarthen, Wales	510,574	115,710

Lord Leconfield of Petworth Hall, Sussex, England, had 37,292 acres in County Clare in 1876, with a valuation of £15,699 about £1,318,716 in modern money. This title originated with the Barons of Egremont in Cumbria in 1449. The family now hold both the Leconfield title and that of Egremont, although neither seat bring a place in the House of Lords. The current holder of the title is John Max Henry Scawen Wyndham, 7th Baron Leconfield, who still lives at Petworth Castle.

The holder of the title and the acreage in 1876 was the 2nd Baron Leconfield. Eton educated, and an officer in the Life Guards, he had 30,221 acres in Sussex, 24,733 acres in Yorkshire, 11,147 acres in Cumberland, 37,292 acres in Clare, 6,292 acres in Limerick and 273 acres in Tipperary. His total was 109,935 acres, making him thirty-eighth largest landowner in the United Kingdom in 1876, with a valuation of £88,112.

The Marquis of Conyngham of Slane Castle, County Meath, held 27,613 acres of Clare in 1876 at a valuation of £10,808 about £907,872

in modern money. This Eton-educated peer, like Lord Leconfield, was an officer in the Life Guards. Like the Leconfield title, the Conyngham one is still extant, with the 8th Marquis, Henry Vivian Pierpoint Conyngham, still recording Slane Castle as the family seat. During the famine years both of these landlords eventually resorted to mass evictions in Clare, which occurred in an atmosphere that was totally poisoned. The rule of law evaporated and the landlord's agents went about with loaded revolvers and a personal armed bodyguard in some cases. It is hard to know what the ultimate principal in the matter, Major General the Marquis, thought of it all, as rents dried up while he strode about Buckingham Palace as an extra equerry to Queen Victoria. But the situation of these two proved a key point: you cannot run a civil society on the basis of unfair laws and of monopoly control of the key commodity, land, enforced by armed men.

Bateman records the Conyngham acreage as 9,737 acres in Kent, 122,300 acres in Donegal, with 7,060 acres in Co. Meath. Together with the Clare acreage, Conyngham had 166,710 acres, with a valuation of £50,076.

His acreage made him the seventeenth largest landowner in the four countries of Great Britain in 1876.

Edward P. Westby of Roebuck, Castle Dondrum, County Dublin, had 25,799 acres in Clare in 1876, with a valuation of £7,691 about £646,044 in modern money. Here is what the National University of Ireland Galway land database records about the Westbys:

> Nicholas Westby of Ennis, county Clare, Collector of Customs, was one member of a syndicate of three (Francis Burton, James MacDonnell) who purchased in 1698 the forfeited estates of Viscount Clare from the Earl of Albemarle. The Earl had bought the estates, situated in county Clare, in 1692. Westby's descendants through advantageous marriages acquired estates in counties Wicklow, Kildare and King's Co (county Offaly). Burke's Irish Family Records (1976) records Nicholas Westby of Kilballyowen, county Clare and of London, who held extensive estates in county Clare in the mid-nineteenth century, mainly located in the baronies of Moyarta (centred on the parish of Kilballyowen) and Islands (centred on the parish of Kilmaley) but also in at least five other baronies.

Bateman assigns him 67 acres in Dublin as well as the Clare acreage.

Lord Inchquin of Dromoland, Ennis, County Clare, had 20,321 acres in the county in 1876, with a valuation of £11,681 about £981,204 in modern money. The only acreage accorded to Lord Inchquin by Bateman is the Clare acreage. For those interested in the detailed vagaries of Irish history over ten centuries, few can beat the O'Brien record at Dromoland, much of it on the web. The family claim descent from the last High King of Ireland, Brian Boru, killed at the Battle of Clontarf in 1014. They claim residence in the area, and possession of the lands since the same period, or earlier. The title is in the peerage of Ireland created in 1543. The present holder, the 18th Baron, Conor Myles John O'Brien, lives in County Clare. The entry in Debrett's peerage runs to three and a half pages, longer than that of the Dukes of Westminster. The estate was broken up by the Land Commission, who did not buy the castle, which is now a luxury hotel owned by American interests.

Colonel Crofton Moore Vandeleur of Kilrush House, Kilrush, had 19,790 acres in the county in 1876, with a valuation of £11,216 about £942,144 in modern money. The name is corrected in Bateman to that of Hector Stewart Vandeleur at the same address. He was Eton educated and served in the Rifle Brigade. He also had 416 acres in Limerick, giving him a total acreage of 20,206 with a valuation of £11,596.

The Vandeleurs are an example of kind instincts being defeated by the inherent economic disaster of land monopoly. According to the NUI Galway Landed estates record:

> The Vandeleur family are descended from Maxmilian Van Der Leur, a Dutch merchant, who had settled in Ireland by the early seventeenth century. John Ormsby Vandeleur played a major role in the development of the town of Kilrush in the early nineteenth century and built Kilrush House in 1808. He died in 1828. His son Colonel Crofton Moore Vandeleur gave land for the building of the Catholic Church, convent, a fever hospital and the workhouse but he is principally associated with the large number of evictions that took place in the Kilrush Union during the Famine years. Hector Steward Vandeleur inherited the estate in 1881 but spent very little time in county Clare and large scale evictions again took place under his ownership in the late 1880s. Kilrush House was burned down accidentally in 1897 and the estate was taken over by the Land Commission in the 1910s.

The Hon. Charles William White of Cahercon House, Killadysart, County Clare, had 18,266 acres in 1876, with a valuation of £6,601 about £554,484 in modern money. We also encounter the White family in County Dublin and in Tipperary. They were descendants of Luke White, described by Ferres as an impecunious bookseller who started life on the streets of Belfast and then moved to Dublin in 1798, lending the Irish government £1 million to put down the rebellion of that year. The original Luke White was also a lottery operator, based on a government licence. The loan wasn't actually £1 million, but £650,000 discounted at £65 per share at an interest rate of 5 per cent.

Bateman's entry for the Clare estate of Luke White's descendant is interesting:

> The return gives him [The Hon. William White] 23,957 acres in County Clare and Tipperary. 'Truth' [a correspondent of Bateman's] in 1879 asserted that these estates are partly sold and partly on sale. The gross annual valuation was £9,548, Mr Phelps has, he informs the compiler, bought 7,141 acres of the Clare Estate.

Bateman's entry for John Vandeleur Phelps of the Lodge Bradford shows 7,291 acres at a valuation of £6,793.

Ferres tells us that:

> The Vandeleurs lived in Cahercon at the beginning of the twentieth century. In 1920, it was purchased by the Maynooth Mission to China, and they in turn sold it to the Salesians Sisters of St John Bosco in 1962. Until 2002, Cahercon House operated as a secondary school, boarding school and convent.

H.V. Macnamara of Doolin, Ennis, had £15,246 acres in Clare in 1876, with a valuation of £6,932 about £582,288 in modern money. Bateman corrects the entry and the address, giving Henry Valentine Macnamara as the holder of the estate.

The landed estates database at NUI Galway has some interesting items on this estate:

> This branch of the Macnamara family was established in the barony of Burren, north county Clare, at the beginning of the eighteenth century by Bartholomew Macnamara, born 1685 ... By the time of Griffith's Valuation Captain Francis Macnamara of Doolin had a large estate in the baronies of Burren and Corcomroe, mainly concentrated in the parishes of Carran (Burren) and Killilagh, Kilmacrehy and Kilmanaheen (Corcomroe), including the town of Ennistymon. In the 1870s the estate of his two sons, Henry Valentine and William James Macnamara, amounted to 15,246 acres and their great uncle, Admiral Sir Burton Macnamara of Tromra House, owned 732 acres in the county. This Macnamara family has now died out in the male line but the twentieth century female members included an author and Caitlín, the wife of Welsh poet, Dylan Thomas. The house at Doolin was burnt in the 1920s. Some lands owned by John McNamara close to Fanore were sold in the Encumbered Estates Court in 1856.

Sir Augustine Fitzgerald, of Carrigoran Ennis, County Clare, had 14,915 acres in 1876 with a valuation of £8,000 about £672,000 in modern money. This army officer, educated at Harrow, Eton's rival and sister school, served in the Bengal Horse Artillery and had 1,436 acres in Cornwall. With his Clare acreage this gave him 16,351 acres and a valuation of £9,600.

The Fitzgerald family have ancient roots in Clare but these ended when Sir Augustine died in 1908 and the title became extinct. The Cornish property was at Trevaylor. When the Baronet's widow died in 1922 the house was sold to the Sisters of Charity of the Incarnate Word but was demolished in the 1980s, according to Ferres.

The Butler heiresses, Anna, Sophia and Henrietta, of Castle Crine, Sixmilebridge, had 11,389 acres in 1876, with a valuation of £3,859 about £324,156 in modern money. There is little in the current public record to say what the three, quite rich, heiresses did with the estate, although Ferres adds a helpful note. The second daughter, Sophia Mary Butler, married the 5th Lord Clarina, though had no male issue, and on the marriage of her eldest daughter, the Hon. Sophia (Zoë) Butler-Massey, to the Hon. Eric Henderson, the Castle Crine estate was settled upon her, subject to the life interests of her mother and aunts. On the death, in 1938, of Miss Anna Frances Butler, the last survivor, Mrs Butler-Henderson (who with her husband assumed the surname of Butler in addition to that of Henderson) succeeded to the Castle Crine estate. Her daughter, Mrs Wordsworth, resided there until 1951, when the estate was sold.

The Estates data base at NUI Galway has a little of the prehistory and how the land was accumulated:

> The Butlers of Castlecrine, parish of Kilfinaghta, barony of Bunratty Lower, county Clare, descend from Thomas Butler, one of the trustees of the ['49 settlement] Officers and younger son of James Butler of Boytonrath, county Tipperary, who was hanged in 1653. William Butler of Rossroe Castle, county Clare, a lawyer by profession, acquired much of the estate through purchase from families such as the Burtons, Westbyus, McDonnells, O'Briens and Lysaghts. He had two sons, Henry of Rossroe and Thomas of Castlecrine. Thomas had a son, William of Castlecrine, who inherited the estate of his cousin Henry Butler of O'Brien's Castle in 1791. James Butler who died in 1857 was succeeded by his three daughters and heiresses, Anna, Sophia and Henrietta, who are recorded in the 1870s as owning 11,389 acres in county Clare.

Horace De Stafford O'Brien of Cratloe Woods, Cratloe, had 11,105 acres in Clare in 1876, with a valuation of £5,706 about £479,304 in modern money. De Stafford O'Brien of Blatherwycke Park, Wansford, had 562 acres in Rutland, 1,955 acres in Northampton, 5,263 acres in Limerick and 7,984 acres in Tipperary. The total with the Clare acres was 27,394 acres with a valuation of £17,472. There is a brief entry in the NUI Galway estates database but nothing that advances the considerable detail of Griffith's. O'Brien was a very large landowner and Bateman writes that he served in the 2nd Dragoons, an expensive cavalry regiment of the British Army.

List of owners over 2,000 acres

		Acreage	Valuation in 1876 (£)	Valuation Current (£)
1	Lord Leconfield of Petworth House, Sussex	37,292	15,699	1,318,716
2.	The Marquis of Conyngham of Slane Castle, Co. Meath	27,613	10,808	908,872
3	Westby, Edward P., Roebuck Castle, Dundrum, Co. Dublin	25,779	7,691	646,044
4	Inchiquin, Lord, Dromoland, Ennis	20,321	11,681	981,204
5	Vandeleur, Colonel Crofton Moore, Kilrush House, Kilrush	19,790	11,216	942,144
6	White, The Hon. Chas Wm, Cahercon House, Killadysart, Co. Clare	18,266	6,601	554,484
7	MacNamara, H.V. and MacNamara W.J. (minors), Ennistymon House, Co. Clare	15,246	6,932	582,288
8	Fitzgerald, Sir A. Bart, Carrigoran, New-Market-on-Fergus	14,915	6,455	542,220
9	Butler, Anna Sophia Henrietta (minors, co heiresses) Castlecrine, Co. Clare	11,389	3,859	324,156
10	De Stafford O'Brien, H., Cratloe Woods, Cratloe	11,105	5,706	479,304
11	Arthur, Francis, Dublin	10,534	3,550	298,200
12	Molony, Major W. Mills, Kiltanon, Tulla, Co. Clare	10,095	2,596	218,064
13	Burton, Francis N., Carnelly and Carrigaholt, Co. Clare	9,669	4,392	368,928
14	Fitzgerald, Wm H.W., Cliffe Hall, Darlington	9,164	3,473	291,732
15	Gore, Major Edward A., Derrymore, O'Callaghan's Mills, Co. Clare	8,561	4,722	396,648
16	Sampson, Donat, 3 Hampton Sq., London	8,501	940	78,960
17	O'Callaghan, Captain Charles George, Ballainahinch, Tulla, Co. Clare	8,270	3,590	301,560
18	Henn, Thomas Rice, Paradise House, Killadysert, Co. Clare	7,664	2,675	224,700

		Acreage	Valuation in 1876 (£)	Valuation Current (£)
19	Butler, Colonel Augustine, Ballyline, Crusheen, Co. Clare	7,460	2,390	200,760
20	Stackpoole, William, Ballyalla, Ennis	7,441	3,609	303,156
21	Stackpoole, Richard, Edenvale, Ennis	7,381	2,641	221,844
22	Wandesford, Hon. C.B., Mount Juliet, Thomastown, Co. Kilkenny	6,737	2,511	210,924
23	M'Donnell, Colonel Wm E.A., New Hall, Ennis	6,610	2,947	247,548
24	Scott, John C., Conservative Club, London	6,431	2,933	246,372
25	Purdon, George F., Tineranna, Killaloe	6,298	2,564	215,376
26	Crowe, Thomas, Dromore, Ruan, Co. Clare	6,121	2,509	210,756
27	Creagh, Cornelius, Dangan, Tulla, Co. Clare	6,004	2,724	228,816
28	Browne, Wyndham, Newgrove, Tulla, Co. Clare	5,960	2,885	242,340
29	Kenny, Captain Thomas Kelly, 2nd Queen's Royal Regiment	5,736	926	77,784
30	Molony, Henry G., Limerick	5,664	821	68,964
31	O'Brien, James, Ballymalackan Castle, Lisdoonvarna	5,575	1,653	138,852
32	Moreland, Wm J.H., Rabelus Manor, Tomgraney	5,118	1,652	138,768
33	Griffith, Richard, Cork	4,949	1,131	95,004
34	O'Callaghan, Colonel John, Maryfort, Tulla, Co. Clare	4,842	1,919	161,196
35	Keane, Marcus, Beechpark, Ennis	4,784	1,349	113,316
36	O'Connell, John Charles Wm Coppinger, Ballylean Lodge, Killadysart, Co. Clare	4,740	1,293	108,612
37	Hall, Major, Narrow Water, Co. Down	4,718	665	55,860
38	MacMahon, Sir William S. Bart, Windsor	4,671	1,747	146,748
39	Massy, Lady Mary Dillon, Doonass, Clonlara	4,625	3,173	266,532
40	Stewart, Jon Vandeleur, Rock Hill, Co. Donegal	4,551	1,055	88,620

		Acreage	Valuation in 1876 (£)	Valuation Current (£)
41	Blood, Baggott, Wellington Road, Dublin	4,460	1,636	137,424
42	Paterson, Colonel Marcus, Clifden House, Corrofin	4,347	1,097	92,148
43	Callaghan, Fredrick M., Cork	4,318	996	83,664
44	Westropp, John, Attyflinn, Patrick's Well, Co. Limerick	3,683	2,627	220,668
45	Sampson, George, Belmont, Castleconnell, Co. Limerick	3,596	1,029	86,436
46	Fitzgerald, Wm Foster Vesy, Derrybrick, Killmihill, Co. Clare	3,581	893	75,012
47	Keogh, Cornelius K., Birchfield, Liscannor, Co. Clare	3,351	935	78,540
48	D'Arcy, Hyacinth, New Forest, Ballinasloe, Co. Galway	3,129	733	61,572
49	Crowe, Wainwright Reps, Cahercalla, Ennis	3,126	2,022	169,848
50	Lynch, Major John W., Renmore Lodge, Galway	3,106	1,056	88,704
51	Gore, Francis William (a minor), Kilmore, Knock, Co. Clare	3,042	1,980	166,320
52	Hickman, Hugh P., Fenloe, Newmarket-on-Fergus	3,030	1,419	119,196
53	Arthur, Colonel Thomas, Manor House, Desborough, Market Harborough, Leicestershire	3,026	2,453	206,052
54	Pocklington, General E.H.T., Horse Guards, London	2,987	1,075	90,300
55	Synge, Lieutenant Colonel G.C., Mount Callan, Inagh, Co. Clare	2,940	204	17,136
56	Synge, Mrs Elizabeth Anne, Dysart, Corrofin	2,920	1,260	105,840
57	Quin, Lord George, 15 Belgrave Sq., London	2,850	2,018	169,512
58	D'Esterre, Henry V., Rosmanagher, Sixmile Bridge	2,833	1,625	136,500
59	Skerrett, Captain William Joseph, Finnavara, Burrin, Co. Clare	2,679	1,303	109,452
60	Reeves, Robert William C., Bessborough, Killimer, Kilrush	2,628	1,455	122,220

		Acreage	Valuation in 1876 (£)	Valuation Current (£)
61	Studdert, Major Richard, Fort House, Kilrush	2,572	616	51,744
62	Kane, Sir Robert, 51 Stephen's Green, Dublin	2,539	469	39,396
63	M'Grath, William H., 9 Upper Merrion St, Dublin and Toonagh, Ennis, Co. Clare	2,533	1,174	98,616
64	Whitelock, James, Amboise, France	2,529	427	35,868
65	Blood, Edmond M., Florence	2,502	1,241	104,244
66	De Boisi, Countess and Smythe, Lary John, 243 Boulevard St Germains, Paris, and 4 Rue D'Aboukir, Courbevoire, Paris	2,502	752	63,168
67	Bentley, William, Hurdleston, Broadford	2,497	888	74,592
68	Tymons, Rec Fredrick, Baskin Hill, Co. Dublin	2,470	839	70,476
69	Blood, W. Bindon, Hatch Street, Dublin	2,464	565	47,460
70	Norbury, Earl of, Valence, Westerham, Edenbridge, Kent	2,453	782	65,688
71	Westropp, Ralph, Athlacca, Bruree, Limerick	2,352	995	83,580
72	Butler, Wm Reps, 27 South Terrace, Cork	2,352	505	42,420
73	Finucane, Pierce, 19 Pembroke Road, Dublin	2,333	1,285	107,940
74	Mahon, Charles George, Bray	2,318	265	22,260
75	Studdert, Major Robert, Kilkishen House, Kilkishen, Co. Clare	2,317	1,464	122,976
76	Bouchier, John, Nenagh, Co. Tipperary	2,252	850	71,400
77	Fitzgerald, John Foster Vesy, 11 Chester Sq., London	2,224	636	53,424
78	Stratford, John W., Addington House, Kent	2,213	916	76,944
79	Martin, Nicholas H., Brook Lodge, Tulla, Co. Clare	2,213	351	29,484
80	Armstrong, Edward J., 44 Lower Leeson St, Dublin	2,190	1,333	111,972

		Acreage	**Valuation in 1876 (£)**	**Valuation Current (£)**
81	Studdert, Rev. George, Edwardstown Vicarage, Boxford, Colchester, Essex	2,187	815	68,460
82	Butler, Nicholas, Walterstown, Crusheen, Co. Clare	2,184	480	40,320
83	Burton, William W., Booterstown Avenue, Co. Dublin	2,133	612	51,408
84	MacMahon, Timothy, Trim, Co. Meath	2,060	282	23,688
85	Fitzgerald, George F., 24 Camden Row, Kensington, London	2,060	185	15,540
86	Cullinane, John F., Riverview, Ennis, Co. Clare	2,051	723	60,732
87	O'Connell, Daniel, Kilgory, O'Callaghan's Mills, Co. Clare	2,019	946	79,464
88	Martyn, John G., Gregan's Castle, Burrin	1,992	506	42,504
89	Finucan, Miss Anastasia, 9 Onslow Gardens, London	1,972	577	48,468
90	Comyn, Francis, Harcourt St, Dublin	1,961	494	41,496
91	Joly, Dr Jasper, Dublin	1,952	550	46,200
92	Singleton, John, Quinville Abbey, Quin, Co. Clare	1,927	1,205	101,220
93	Creagh, Simon Pierce, Mount Elva, Lisdoonvarna, Co. Clare	1,907	512	43,008
94	Morony, Ellen L., Milltown House, Co. Clare	1,904	1,875	157,500
95	Mahon, Thomas G.S., 18 Beaufort Gardens, London	1,887	1,178	98,952
96	Vandeleur, Mrs Mary, 2 Beauchamp Terrace, Lemington, England	1,887	1,035	86,940
97	Russel, Walter, 2 Drummond Place, Stirling, Scotland	1,847	260	21,840
98	Westropp, Ralph Jnr, St Catherin's, Co. Clare	1,784	925	77,700
99	O'Brien, John S., Park View, Tanderagee, Co. Armagh	1,769	480	40,320
100	M'Adam, Colonel Thomas, Blackwater House, Limerick	1,747	1,041	87,444
101	Delmege, John C., Castle Park, Limerick	1,641	512	43,008

Top 20 landowners in county Clare in 1876 ranked by valuation

		Acreage	Valuation 1876 (£)	Valuation Current (£)
1	Leaconfield, Lord, Petworth Hall, Sussex, England	37,292	15,699	1,318,716
2	Inchiquin, Lord, Dromoland, Ennis	20,321	11,681	981,204
3	Vandeleur, Colonel Crofton Moore, Kilrush House, Kilrush	19,790	11,216	942,144
4	Conyngham, Marquess of, Slane Castle, Co. Meath	27,613	10,808	907,872
5	Westby, Edward P., Roebuck Castle, Dundrum, Co. Dublin	25,779	7,691	646,044
6	MacNamara, H.V. and MacNamara W.J. (minors), Ennistymon House, Co. Clare	15,246	6,932	582,288
7	White, The Hon. Chas Wm, Cahercon House, Killadysart, Co. Clare	18,266	6,601	554,484
8	Fitzgerald, Sir A. Bart, Carrigoran, New-Market-on-Fergus	14,915	6,455	542,220
9	De Stafford O'Brien, H., Cratloe Woods, Cratloe	11,105	5,706	479,304
10	Gore, Major Edward A., Derrymore, O'Callaghan's Mills, Co. Clare	8,561	4,722	396,648
11	Burton, Francis N., Carnelly and Carrigaholt, Co. Clare	9,669	4,392	368,928
12	Butler, Anna Sophia Henrietta (minors, co heiresses), Castlecrine, Co. Clare	11,389	3,859	324,156
13	Stackpoole, William, Ballyalla, Ennis	7,441	3,609	303,156
14	O'Callaghan, Captain Charles George, Ballainahinch, Tulla, Co. Clare	8,270	3,590	301,560
15	Arthur, Francis, Dublin	10,534	3,550	298,200
16	Fitzgerald, Wm H.W., Cliffe Hall, Darlington	9,164	3,473	291,732
17	Massy, Lady Mary Dillon, Doonass, Clonlara	4,625	3,173	266,532
18	M'Donnell, Colonel Wm E.A., New Hall, Ennis	6,610	2,947	247,548
19	Scott, John C., Conservative Club, London	6,431	2,933	246,372
20	Browne, Wyndham, Newgrove, Tulla, Co. Clare	5,960	2,885	242,340

CORK

WITH THE CITY OF THE COUNTY

	1876	2020 Est
Population in County Cork	517,076	519,302
All owners of land	2,888	–
Percentage of the population	1.48	–
Owners of nothing at all	509,387	145,510
Percentage of the population	98.52	–
Size of County	1,822,739 acres (add 2,080 for the city)	1,841,920 acres
Number of dwellings (of which rented in 1876) Owned in 2020	84,789 (81,901)	187,555
Number of owned farm holdings	4,508	14,222

County comparisons

	Acreage in 1876	**Population in 1876**
Cork	1,822,729	517,076
Lincolnshire, England	1,606,543	436,599
Perthshire, Scotland	1,612,840	147,768

The Earl of Bantry of Macroom Castle, East Ferry, County Cork, had 69,500 acres in the county in 1876, with a valuation of £14,561 about £1,223,124 in modern money. The first title arrived in 1797 when the then Simon White led British forces against French troops at Bantry Bay. The French had arrived to assist the United Irishmen's rebellion of 1798.

This title became extinct in 1891 when the 4th and last Earl died. The castle survived the War of Independence and was sold in trust in 1924 by its last owner, Lady Ardilaun, for the benefit of the people of Macroom.

The Earl of Bandon had 40,941 acres in County Cork in 1876, with a valuation of £19,215 about £1,614,060 in modern money. Bateman reduces this Eton-educated titan of land by some significant acres with the following note: 'Exclusive of and rental from perpetually leased lands, returned in the names of the middlemen.' It would be a nice task for someone at some later date to go through the Cork returns and correlate them with Griffith's to see who were getting this financial curiosity called a perpetual lease.

Ferres traces the family back to a German knight who arrived in England in 1066 to do a little rape and profitable pillage alongside William the Bastard. They were successful and obtained large tracts of land in Westmorland, Yorkshire and Northamptonshire.

The first of the Bernards, Francis, arrived in Ireland during the reign of Elizabeth I and bought extensive estates. The following century those estates were confiscated by James I but restored by William and Mary. The beneficiary of the restored estates, Francis Bernard, was made Solicitor-General for Ireland and a judge. He became an MP and by 1793 the then Francis was made a peer, shortly afterwards a Viscount and in 1800 an Earl.

The family continue to live near the castle, having received the equivalent of £4.9 million in compensation from the Irish government for the burning down of Castle Barnard by the IRA in 1921.

The 5th Earl of Bandon, who also lived near the castle, died in 1979 and with him the title became extinct. He was an Air Vice Marshal of the Royal Air Force, maintaining the military tradition of the family to the end.

The Duke of Devonshire of Lismore Castle, County Waterford, had 32,550 acres in County Cork in 1876 with a valuation of £19,326 about £1,623,384 in modern money. The 7th Duke of Devonshire held land in fourteen counties, three of them in Ireland. His total holdings came to 198,572 acres with a valuation of £180,750. The family name is Cavendish and the Cavendish laboratories at Cambridge University arose from a donation from the 7th Duke, who was a Fellow of the Royal Society, one of the world's premier scientific bodies. The 7th Duke's contribution was to fund the Cavendish professorship of Experimental Physics in 1874. James Clerk Maxwell was the first holder. Successive fellows at the laboratory have won the Nobel Prize for physics, chemistry and related sciences on twenty-nine occasions. Few donations in history can have had such extraordinary results over the decades. The Cavendish family, who got the Dukedom in 1694, have been enormously influential in British politics both before and after that time. Money, and they had it in titanic quantities throughout the period, helped. It helped to buy votes throughout the country when you needed property to vote. The intertwining of palace, power and politics was fairly total in the pre-democratic period and the Cavendishs were at the nexus of these three strands for most of the last 500 years. The 60,000 acres in Ireland gave the Dukedom huge influence here. In a way, you could say that kings came and kings went but the Cavendishs went on forever, seemingly.

The Land Commission reduced the Irish acres but 8,000 acres remain around Lismore Castle, making it one of the biggest estates in the country. The 2017 *Sunday Times* Rich List values the present Dukes at £880 million, a serious underestimate given the 70,000 acres they still own in the north of England, and the Raphaels, Van Dycks and Rembrandts in the art collection.

Sir George St John Colthurst Bart of Ardrum, Inniscarra, and Ballyvourney, County Cork, had 31,260 in the county in 1836, with a valuation of £9,664 about £811,776 in modern money. Bateman alters the address to Blarney Castle, County Cork.

Ferres is nothing if not laconic when he notes that the founder of the family in Ireland, Colonel John Coldhurst, was murdered by native Irish rebels in 1607. Still, the family persevered, became MPs, acquired a baronetage and, of course, extensive lands, including Blarney Castle. The castle contains the Blarney Stone, which tourists queue to kiss.

The family still live on the estate, and the Eton-educated holder of the title, the 10th Baronet Charles St John Colthurst, practices as a solicitor in Cork.

Anna Countess of Kingston, of Mitchelstown Castle, County Cork, had 24,421 acres in the county in 1876, with a valuation of £17,845 about £1,498,980 in modern money. The Earl of Kingston had his big acreage in Roscommon, but the Countess had her acreage in Cork. And it was extensive, making her a millionairess and an heiress. There are three interlinked estates in Bateman and the public record does not explain in any detail why the Countess became the heiress to the Gothic castle and its estate.

Her second husband was William Downes Webber of Kellyville. He had 350 acres in Leitrim, 200 acres in Kildare, 504 acres in Queen's County and 2,756 acres in County Sligo. Added together with her acreage, the total came to 28,481 acres, with a valuation of £19,650.

The Earl of Kingston of Kilronan Castle, Carrick-on-Shannon, had 17,756 acres in Roscommon, 1,783 acres in Sligo, 1554 acres in Leitrim, 196 acres in County Dublin and 48 acres in Westmeath, a total of 21,307 acres with a valuation of £9,064.

In 1823 the estate was over 100,000 acres and the then Earl spent over £100,000 rebuilding Mitchelstown Castle. The scheme beggared the estate, 70,000 acres of which were sold through the Encumbered Estates Court soon after the Great Famine (1845–51). The loss of rents during the famine were followed by the Land War in the 1880s and then by the War of Independence, during which the castle was burned down by the IRA. Some compensation was paid but not enough to rebuild the castle.

The 11th Earl was the subject of child custody proceedings in both the Irish and UK courts. One of the claimants wanted him sent to prep school in England to prepare him for Eton, drawing the following comment about Eton from the eminent Irish Judge Mr Justice Kingsmill Moore. 'There does seem to persist in England a certain amount of the attitude towards Irish schools and surroundings that flavours of contemptuousness. There seems to be an attitude that we are not a completely civilised nation.'

The boy went to Winchester instead. He went to Sandhurst and joined the British Army as an officer but left while still a lieutenant. He married four times and died apparently penniless. The *Telegraph* obituary gives all the gory details.

The current 12th Earl, Robert Charles Henry King-Tenison, was educated at Repton and is a former international hurdler. He lives in New Zealand.

The 4th Earl of Kenmare of Killarney House, County Kerry, had 22,700 acres in Cork in 1876, with a valuation of £3,497 about £293,748 in modern money. Bateman adds to the Cork acres 91,080 acres in County Kerry and 4,826 acres in Limerick for a total of 118,606 acres with a valuation of £34,473. It appears that the Earl contacted Bateman and told him that the value of the land was 'much underestimated'. This is an interesting comment as the Earl was the thirty-second largest landowner in the Great Britain at the time.

He was also, as Bateman sets out, Comptroller of the Household, Vice Chamberlain, Lord in Waiting and eventually Lord Chamberlain. These were all positions in Buckingham Palace, home of the Queen Empress Victoria, and were unsalaried as such. You were meant to be able to support the dignities of the positions with the rents from your estates, hence the sensitivity. But he was hugely important in the Victorian era and wielded enormous influence in London. He was also the MP for Kerry.

The first Killarney House was commissioned in 1872 by the 4th Earl, encouraged by his wife, who was the granddaughter of the 2nd Marquis of Bath of Longleat House in Wiltshire. The cost was estimated at around £100,000, over £8 million in modern money.

In 1956 the niece of the 7th Earl and granddaughter of the Duke of Westminster, Mrs Beatrice Grosvenor, sold 25,000 acres of the estate to an American syndicate. She later donated other parts of the estate to the Irish nation as a national park. Eventually, the 25,000 acres sold to the Americans was sold back to the Irish state and is now part of the park.

The family name of the Earls of Kenmare was Browne. The title became extinct in 1952 when the 7th Earl died.

The Earl of Cork and Orrery of Marston Hall, Frome in Somerset, had 20,165 acres in Cork in 1876 with a valuation of £6,943 about £583,212 in modern money.

The 9th Earl of Cork and Orrery was everything the Irish people hated at the period. He was an absentee landlord and sat as MP for Frome in Somerset. He had a minor role at Buckingham Palace as Master of the Buckhounds, a government appointment. The holder had the royal duty of representing the Crown at Ascot races. Bateman notes that, as well as the Cork acres, the Earl had 3,398 acres in Somerset, 11,531 acres in Kerry and 3,189 acres in Limerick, giving a total of 38,313 acres, with a valuation of £17,343. He was educated at Eton.

The family name of the Earldom is Boyle and the ancestry is interesting. The first Boyle in Ireland arrived from Canterbury in 1588, later married an Irish heiress and bought large estates in Cork. He became Lord Treasurer of Ireland and had four of his sons made peers. But it was his remaining son, Roger Boyle, who made the family immortal. He discovered Boyle's Law.

In British history the family retained a link to science. In 1748 William Cavendish, Marquess of Hartington and later 4th Duke of Devonshire, married Charlotte Boyle, only surviving child of the 3rd Earl of Burlington and 4th Earl of Cork. Her estates were added to the Cavendish lands, which by 1876 were the eleventh largest estate in the whole of Great Britain, and helped to found the Cavendish laboratory in Cambridge.

The title still exists and is held by John (Jonathan) Richard Boyle, the 15th Earl, who lives in Sussex.

Sir Henry Wrixon Becher Bart of Ballygiblin, Mallow, held 18,933 acres of Cork in 1876, with a valuation of £10,528 about £884,352 in modern money. Sir Henry was an Eton-educated soldier who had served in the Rifle Brigade, an infantry unit in the British Army. Bateman corrects the address to Castle Hyde Fermoy and adds 358 acres in Tipperary, to give a total acreage of 19,291 with a valuation of £10,823.

The family arrived in Ireland during the reign of Elizabeth I and obtained 12,000 acres of land in Cork. The Baronetcy was granted in 1831. Somewhat laconically, the NUI Database records him marrying an actress, a Miss O'Neill, and having a number of children. By 1854 some Becher lands were in trouble and 2,000 acres were offered in the Encumbered Estates Court. Earlier in 1851 17,000 acres was offered for sale in the same court. The *Journal of the Cork Historical and Archaeological Society* has published an extensive account of the estate.

The title still exists and is held by Sir John Michael William Wrixon-Becher, the 6th Baronet, who was educated at Harrow. He had a career in the financial services sector.

The Earl of Egmont of Lohort Castle, Mallow, County Cork, had 16,766 acres in 1876, with a valuation of £13,594 about £1,141,896 in modern money. The Earl of Egmont, not to be confused with the Wyndham

Barons' Egremont, was an Irish title created in 1733, but now extinct in all its forms since 2011, confirmed in 2012. For those with an interest in such things, there was, back in the 1920s a claim from Canada for the title, which was dormant, but not extinct. The claimant, Joseph Trevelyan Perceval, died in 1932 without having proved his claim. In 1939 the House of Lords allowed the claim of his only son, Fredrick George Moore Perceval, who became the 11th Earl. Debrett's then records a 12th Earl in its 2010 edition. He gives as his address PO Box 218 Nanton, Alberta, Canada.

But what of the estates?

In 1876 the Earl of Egmont, with an address at Nork House, Epsom, had 14,021 acres in Sussex, 3,466 acres in Surrey, 585 acres in Bucks, 134 acres in Lincoln and 16,766 acres in County Cork. The total acreage was 34,972 with a valuation of £35,510. The then Earl had been educated at Radley. This was, even for its time, a huge and very valuable estate. Had it remained attached to the title, the Canadian cousins would have been well motivated to pursue the issue, but they didn't. In the late 1700s the title of Baroness was created for Catherine Perceval, Countess of Egmont, who was a daughter of a younger son of the Earl of Northampton, another of the core landowning dynasties of the UK. This British peerage reflected the fact that the Egmont peer was mainly active in the UK, as an MP and peer. A member of the Egmont family, Spencer Perceval, became Prime minister of the United Kingdom in 1809. He was assassinated inside Parliament on 11 May 1812 by a disgruntled businessman, John Bellingham. Spencer Perceval was found to have only £106 in his bank account when he died and Parliament voted £50,000, about £4.2 million in modern money, for the support of his thirteen children. The inquest was held on 12 May in the Cat & Bagpipes pub on the corner of Downing Street. A verdict of murder was returned. Bellingham was tried for murder, found guilty and hanged on 18 May 1812.

Earlier, in 1732, the then Lord Egmont obtained a charter to colonise the province of Georgia, in America, and was made president of that place. In the UK he was made an Earl the following year. The Georgia charter came with a vast land grant to the Egmont Percevals. As with the estates of 1876, little is recorded of what happened to the acreage.

Robert Hedges Eyre White of Glengariff, Bantry, Cork, held 16,175 acres in the county in 1836, with a valuation of £4,227 about £355,068 in modern money. The only thing Bateman tells us about Robert White is that he was educated at Rugby School and served in the Rifle Brigade. The acreage is as stated.

The NUI estates database fills in some detail about the estate prior to 1876 but nothing afterwards:

November 1853, over 33,000 acres of the Bantry estate in the baronies of East Carbery, Bantry and Bere, were offered for sale in the Encumbered Estates Court. A separate sale notice at the same time relates to the sale of Bere Island and includes a geological survey produced by Dr. Whitty. The Freeman's Journal reported details of the purchasers. The sale realised over £20,000. Lord Charles Pelham Clinton bought the Bere Island estate of 4,377 acres and over 5,700 acres around Berehaven. In December 1852, over 6,000 acres of fee farm and fee simple property belonging to members of the White family and others, were offered for sale in the Encumbered Estates Court.

Top 176 owners in Cork ranked by acreage in 1876

		Acreage	Valuation 1876 (£)	Valuation Current (£)
1	Bantry, Earl of, Bantry	69,500	14,561	1,223,124
2	Bandon, Earl of, Castle Bernard, Bandon	40,941	19,251	1,617,084
3	Devonshire, Duke of, Lismore Castle, Co. Waterford	32,550	19,326	1,623,384
4	Colthurst, Sir George C., Ardrum, Inniscarra, and Ballyvourney, Co. Cork	31,260	9,664	811,776
5	Kingston, Countess of, Mitchelstown Castle, Mitchelstown	24,421	17,845	1,498,980
6	Kenmare, Earl of, Killarney	22,700	3,497	293,748
7	Cork and Orrery, Earl of, Marston Hall, Frome	20,165	6,943	583,212
8	Becher, Sir Henry Wrixon, Ballygiblin, Mallow	18,933	10,528	884,352
9	Egmont, Earl of, Lohort Castle, Mallow	16,766	13,594	1,141,896
10	White, Robert H.E., Glengariff, Bantry	16,175	4,227	355,068
11	Fermoy, Lord, Trabolgan, Whitegate	15,543	6,572	552,048
12	Trustees of Lord Carbery, Agents Stewart and Kincaid, Leinster Street, Dublin	13,692	6,179	519,036
13	Massy, William H., Macroom	13,363	3,105	260,820
14	Shukdham, Major E.A., Coolkelure, Dunmanway	13,039	2,231	187,404

		Acreage	Valuation 1876 (£)	Valuation Current (£)
15	Barry, Arthur H. Smith, Foaty, Queenstown	12,890	15,680	1,317,120
16	Stawell, Colonel Wm St Leger Alcock, Kilbrittain Castle, Bandon	11,336	6,452	541,968
17	Shannon, Earl of, Castlemartyr, Cork	11,232	12,319	1,034,796
18	Longfield, M. Reps, Castlemary, Cloyne	10,813	7,883	662,172
19	Ponsonby, C.W.T., Park House, Youghal	10,367	6,768	568,512
20	Wise, Francis, Cork	9,912	8,921	749,364
21	Longfield, Robert, Longueville, Mallow	9,410	4,540	381,360
22	Puxley, Henry L., Dunboy Castle, Berehaven	9,158	2,716	228,144
23	Hyde, John, Cregg, Fermoy	8,919	3,524	296,016
24	Townsend, Rev. W.T. Reps, England	8,665	4,794	402,696
25	Doneraile, Viscount, Doneraile Court, Doneraile	8,374	8,112	681,408
26	Limerick, John, Union Hall, Leap, Co. Cork	8,181	2,260	189,840
27	Barry, Richard H.S., Ballyedmund, Midleton	8,137	5,460	458,640
28	Aldworth, Richard Oliver, Newmarket House, Newmarket	8,064	2,540	213,360
29	Hutchins, Emanuel, Ardnagashill, Bantry, Co. Cork	7,858	3,222	270,649
30	Warren, Sir A.R., Warren's Court, Lisardagh	7,787	3,738	313,992
31	Grehan, George, Clonmeen, Banteer, Kanturk	7,419	2,726	228,984
32	Oliver, Silver Charles, Inchera, Glounthane	6,738	2,150	180,600
33	Midleton, Viscount, Pepper, Harrow, Surrey	6,188	6,588	553,396
34	Newman, John A.R., Dromore House, Mallow	6,146	3,375	283,500
35	Townsend, John H., Myrosswood, Leap	6,083	2,139	179,676

		Acreage	Valuation 1876 (£)	Valuation Current (£)
36	Lismore, Viscount, Shanbally, Clogheen	6,067	2,555	214,620
37	Swanton, James H., 122 Pembroke Road, Dublin	6,049	1,635	137,340
38	Townsend, Richard, Clantoff House, Union Hall	5,977	1,322	111,048
39	Mountcashell, Earl of, Moore Park, Kilworth	5,961	3,606	302,904
40	O'Leary, M'Carthy John, Coomlegane, Millstreet	5,896	2,034	170,856
41	Crofton, Henry E., Dublin	5,809	2,475	207,900
42	Clarke, William, Farran, Ovens, Cork	5,679	2,588	217,392
43	Leader, N.P., Dromagh Castle, Kanturk	5,632	3,337	280,308
44	Leader, Mrs William, Rosnalee, Banteer	5,586	1,564	131,376
45	Listowel, Earl of, Convamore, Mallow	5,541	4,078	342,552
46	Lysaght, Hon. George, Queenstown	5,408	1,389	116,676
47	French, Sampson T.W., Cuskenny, Queenstown	5,310	2,807	235,788
48	Fitzgerald, Robert of Corkbeg, Whitegate	5,307	4,450	373,800
49	Collis, Rev. Dr Maurice Atkin Cooke, Queenstown	5,177	2,177	182,868
50	Hudson, Henry, Glenville, Co. Cork	5,086	1,126	94,584
51	Wallis (a minor), Drishane Castle, Mill Street	5,000	2,444	205,296
52	Browne, Rev. John, England (Agent J. Russell, Cork)	4,919	1,553	130,452
53	Leahy, Thomas J., Cork	4,874	661	55,524
54	Chatterton, General Sir James Reps,	4,660	1,480	124,320
55	M'Bride, James, Greenock, Scotland	4,629	2,602	218,568
56	Clinton, Lord C.P., England	4,563	3,063	257,292
57	Putland, Charles, Bray, Co. Wicklow	4,521	3,139	263,676
58	Coote, Charles Purdon, Ballyclough Castle, Mallow	4,510	2,894	243,096

		Acreage	Valuation 1876 (£)	Valuation Current (£)
59	Delacour, James, Mallow	4,507	1,944	163,296
60	Coltsmann, Daniel, Killarney	4,478	1,309	109,956
61	O'Sullivan, Daniel, of Sidney Place, Cork	4,274	559	46,956
62	Conner, Daniel, Manch House, Balineen	4,194	1,587	133,308
63	Harding, Henry Reps, Firville, Macroom	4,161	1,748	146,832
64	Levis, John S., Glenview	4,149	896	75,296
65	Welply, James, Upton House, Bandon	4,039	1,726	144,984
66	Townsend, Richard, Garrycloyne, Cork	3,932	1,255	105,420
67	Barry, Captain James, Ballyclogh, Fermoy	3,910	2,631	221,004
68	Cuthbert, Thomas, Garrettstown, Ballinspitle, Kinsale	3,906	2,865	240,660
69	Woodley, Francis W., Leeds House, Macroom	3,857	1,506	126,504
70	Beamish, Robert D., Castleview, Glanmire	3,852	1,355	113,820
71	M'Carthy, Alexander, Liscreagh	3,832	1,080	90,720
72	Jones, William Bence, Lisselane, Clonakilty	3,789	1,924	161,616
73	Cotter, Sir James L. Bart, Sunny Hill, Mallow	3,785	1,119	93,996
74	Leader, Captain Thomas, Ashgrove, Macroom	3,709	1,368	114,912
75	Young, Henry Lindsay, Leemount, Cork	3,625	2,026	170,184
76	O'Donovan, The, Lissarda, Skibereen	3,620	1,510	126,840
78	Chancery, Court of, Dublin	3,594	856	71,904
79	Hassett, John Reps, Forest, Killenardrish	3,583	1,152	96.768
80	Barter, John, Droumcarra, Macroom	3,566	637	53,508
81	Hungerford, Hen. Jones, Cahermore House, Roscarbery	3,532	1,512	127,008

		Acreage	Valuation 1876 (£)	Valuation Current (£)
82	Newman, Adam, Monkstown	3,527	1,253	105,252
83	Jackson, William O., Ahanesk, Fermoy	3,491	1,538	129,192
84	Westhead, Joshua Proctor B., Yorkshire	3,473	2,180	183,120
85	Downing, M'Carthy, Prospect House, Skibareen	3,466	1,375	115,500
86	Beamish, Thomas Reps, Kilmalooda, Clonakilty	3,446	1,657	139,188
87	M'Cartie, Justin, Carrignavar	3,435	1,025	86,100
88	Rye, Captain Richard Tonson, Rye Court, Crookstown	3,412	2,354	197,736
89	Wood, Andrew Jordaine, 10 Sydney Place, Cork	3,395	1,072	90,048
90	Herrick, Thomas B., Shippool, Innishannon	3,289	1,477	124,068
91	Sullivan, Thomas Kingston, Bandon	3,264	1,397	117,348
92	Fleming, Beecher Lionel, New Court, Skibereen	3,256	904	75,936
93	Stawell George, Crobeg, Doneraile	3,222	1,540	129,360
94	Collins, Caroline Maria, London	3,193	959	80,556
95	Baldwin, Jas Reps, Mount Pleasant, Bandon	3,188	1,425	119,700
96	Beamish, Sampson, Kilmalooda, Timoleague	3,180	1,473	123,732
97	Pine, Jasper Reps, Passage, Cork	3,178	436	36,624
98	Foot, Henry B., Carrigacunna Castle	3,171	676	56,784
99	Davis, John, Rathpeacon, Cork	3,167	2,059	172,956
100	Sweete, G.S., Greenville, Lissardagh	3,094	1,209	101,556
101	Murphy, Edward C., Streamhill, Doneraile	3,049	554	46,536
102	Evans, Admiral Geo and Evans, Captain John, England	2,962	1,663	139,692
103	Creagh, George Washington Brazier, Creagh Castle, Doneraile	2,873	1,356	113,904
104	Pratt, Robert, Gawsworth, Cork	2,870	623	52,332

		Acreage	Valuation 1876 (£)	Valuation Current (£)
105	Railway Company, Great Southern and Western, King's Bridge, Dublin	2,860	26,892	2,258,928
106	French, Pasco Savage, Cuskenny, Queenstown	2,849	1,746	146,664
107	Bennett, Francis E., Classes, Coachford	2,846	1,244	104,496
108	Nagle, Jos Chichester, Tiverton, England	2,838	1,828	153,552
109	Hoare, William Barry, Passage West Cork	2,815	730	61,320
110	Longfield, Henry Reps, Sea Court, Courtmacsherry	2,810	505	42,420
111	Newenham, Rev. Edw H., Coolmore, Carrigaline	2,740	3,643	306,012
112	Burns, Thomas, Butter Exchange, Cork	2,730	309	25,955
113	Frewen, Richard, -	2,722	1,961	164,724
114	Teulon, George Beamish, Bandon	2,714	2,029	170,436
115	Gillman, Thos R eps, In Chancery	2,698	827	69,468
116	Nason, Rev. Henry William, The Glebe, Rathcormac	2,679	1,629	136,836
117	Dunscombe, Nicholas, Kingwilliamstown	2,678	455	38,220
118	Hull, Richard Edward, Lemcon Manor, Skull	2,671	812	68,208
119	Boyce, Captain Thomas, Charles St, St James, London	2,669	1,188	99,792
120	Egan, Carbery Baldwin, Monkstown, Co. Cork	2,663	915	76,860
121	Hoare, William Jessie, Carrigrohane	2,641	1,004	84,336
122	Chesney, Louisa, Ballyardle Newry, Co. Down	2,630	584	49,056
123	Longfield, Major John P., Seafield, Queenstown	2,560	585	49,140
124	Burke, Edmund, Lota Park, Cork	2,543	930	78,120
125	Cleary, William Henry, Cork	2,534	815	68,460
126	Geale, Hamilton, Glenroe, Kilfrinan	2,521	120	10,080

		Acreage	Valuation 1876 (£)	Valuation Current (£)
127	Clarke, John W. and Mary E., Mortlake and Dublin	2,518	586	49,224
128	Boyle, Lady, Courtmasherry	2,515	284	23,856
129	Wood, George A., Lota House, Cork	2,502	2,054	172,536
130	Fitzpatrick, P.P., Aldershot, England	2,479	800	67,200
131	Powell, Henry C., Bawnlahan	2,475	778	65,352
132	Hartopp, Lieutenant Edward, 10th Hussars, England	2,467	1,293	108,612
133	Langford, Arthur, Rowls, Newmarket	2,439	392	32,928
134	Wood, Shaw Benjamin, Cork	2,435	1,391	32,844
135	Harrison, Henry, Castle Harrison Charleyville	2,431	1,931	162,204
136	Leader, Henry, Clonmoyle, Coachford	2,418	1,169	98,196
137	O'Sullivan, Herbert B., Carrigphooka, Macroom	2,410	534	44,856
138	Evans, John W., Carker House	2,392	626	52,584
139	Harnett, Mary Reps, Hanover Hall, Macroom	2,382	843	70,812
140	Baldwin, William B. Reps, Glandore	2,381	624	52,416
141	Deane, James, Cork	2,377	130	10,920
142	Blennerhasset, Rev. J., Ryme Rectory, Sherbourne, Dorset	2,374	630	52,920
143	Leahy, Daniel F., Shanakill, Cork	2,364	1,455	122,220
144	Gollock, Rev. James, Desertserges, Glebe, Bandon	2,346	587	49,308
145	Evanson, Rev. Richard, LLansory Rectory, Monmouthshire	2,272	367	30,828
146	Hamilton, James, Dublin	2,266	1,433	120,372
147	Perrott, John Walker, Monkstown, Cork	2,262	2,161	181,524
148	Davis, Roger Greene Reps, Cork	2,253	769	64,596
149	Lysaght, William, Hazlewood, Mallow	2,252	382	32,080
150	Beamish, Francis, Killinear, Enniskean	2,249	896	75,264

		Acreage	Valuation 1876 (£)	Valuation Current (£)
151	Daunt, Achilles Reps, Kinsale	2,248	1,241	104,244
152	Gray, Pope, Cork	2,245	732	61,488
153	Lambkin, Grace, Sunday's Well, Cork	2,244	329	27,636
154	Lambkin, Jas Reps, Patrick St, Cork	2,232	737	61,908
155	Ormanthwaite, Lord, Warfield Park, Bracknell, Berks	2,206	1,708	143,472
156	Open, Richard Ashe, Elm Park, Farran, Co. Cork	2,204	549	46,116
157	M'Carthy, Denis, Leeson Park, Co. Dublin	2,175	1,036	87,024
158	Carmichael, John md, Patrick Street, Cork	2,164	1,178	98,952
159	M'Namara, Thomas, Limerick	2,157	50	4,200
160	Wheatly, John H., Sligo	2,151	1,955	164,220
161	Evans, E. Eyre, Ashill Towers, Kilmallock	2,148	1,564	131,376
162	Brooke, Captain Sir William, Market Harborough, England	2,132	2,171	182,364
163	Hunt, James, Danesfort, Mallow	2,120	1,091	91,644
164	White, John Hamiliton, St Luke's, Cork	2,113	283	23,772
165	Becher, Michael Richard Alleyn, Ballyduvane, Clonakilty	2,101	888	74,592
166	Sealy, W.R., Barleyfield, Bandon	2,097	1,188	99,792
167	Johnson, Noble, Rockingham, Cork	2,076	1,250	105,000
168	Power, Maurice Reps, Queenstown	2,067	728	61.152
169	Morrogh, James, Oldcourt, Doneraile	2,057	1,035	86,940
170	Fitzgerald, Lady, England	2,054	872	73,248
171	Hill, James L., Rathkeale	2,053	990	83,160
172	Coppinger, Francis H., Monkstown, Dublin	2,047	413	34,692
173	Hawkes, John Devonsher, Kilcrea	2,029	1,526	128,184
174	Stubbs, H.C., Dublin	2,027	952	79,968
175	Moriarty, John, Mallow	2,020	484	40,656
176	Heard Robert, Pallastown Kinsale	2,005	1,783	149,772

Top 21 landowners in Cork ranked by valuation (income) in 1876

		Acreage	Valuation 1876 (£)	Valuation Current (£)
1	Railway Company, Great Southern and Western, King's Bridge, Dublin	2,860	26,892	2,258,928
2	Devonshire, Duke of, Lismore Castle, Co. Waterford	32,550	19,326	1,623,384
3	Bandon, Earl of, Castle Bernard, Bandon	40,941	19,251	1,617,084
4	Kingston, Countess of, Mitchelstown Castle, Mitchesltown	24,421	17,845	1,498,980
5	Barry, Arthur H. Smith, Foaty, Queenstown	12,890	15,680	1,317,120
6	Bantry, Earl of, Bantry	69,500	14,561	1,223,124
7	Egmont, Earl of, Lohort Castle, Mallow	16,766	13,594	1,141,896
8	Shannon, Earl of, Castlemartyr, Cork	11,232	12,319	1,034,796
9	Becher, Sir Henry Wrixon, Ballygiblin, Mallow	18,933	10,528	884,352
10	Colthurst, Sir George C., Ardrum Inniscarra and Ballyvourney, Co. Cork	31,260	9,664	811,776
11	Wise, Francis, Cork	9,912	8,921	749,364
12	Doneraile, Viscount, Doneraile Court, Doneraile	8,374	8,112	681,408
13	Longfield, M. Reps, Castlemary, Cloyne	10,813	7,883	662,172
14	Cork and Orrery, Earl of, Marston Hall, Frome	20,165	6,943	583,212
15	Ponsonby, C.W.T., Park House, Youghal	10,367	6,768	568,512
16	Midleton, Viscount, Pepper, Harrow, Surrey	6,188	6,588	553,396
17	Fermoy, Lord, Trabolgan, Whitegate	15,543	6,572	552,048
18	Stawell, Colonel Wm St Leger Alcock, Kilbrittain Castle, Bandon	11,336	6,452	541,968
19	Trustees of Lord Carbery, Agents Stewart and Kincaid, Leinster Street, Dublin	13,692	6,179	519,036
20	Barry, Richard H.S., Ballyedmund, Midleton	8,137	5,460	458,640
21	Townsend, Rev. W.T. Reps, England	8,665	4,794	402,696

DONEGAL

	1876	2020 Est
Population in County Donegal	217,992	161,137 (2011, est for 2016)
All owners of land	2,174	-
Percentage of the population	0.99	-
Owners of nothing at all	215,818	119,614
Percentage of the population	99.1	-
Size of County	1,172,586 acres	1,200,640 acres
Number of dwellings	40,800	157,721
Number of owned farm holdings	1,003 (over 1 acre)	9,240

County comparisons

	Acreage 1876	Population 1876
Donegal	1,172,586	217,992
Norfolk, England	1,234,884	438,656
Aberdeenshire, Scotland	1,255,138	264,603

The Marquis of Conyngham of Slane Castle, County Meath, had 122,300 acres in Donegal in 1876, with a valuation of £15,166.

See Page 65.

The Earl of Leitrim of Lough Rynn, Dromod Mohill, County Leitrim, had 54,352 acres in County Donegal in 1876, with a valuation of £9,406 about £790,104 in modern money. Bateman makes significant alterations to the Return. The Earl by 1883 was living at 44 Grosvenor Street, London, and his Leitrim acreage had fallen to just 2,500 acres, with a valuation of £1,600. In addition he had 54,352 acres in Donegal, with a valuation of £9,406. According to Bateman, the 3rd Earl served in the Royal Navy. Born in Dublin, he was educated at the Sandhurst and was commissioned as an ensign in the 43rd Foot in 1824. In 1831 he was promoted captain, having served in Portugal between 1826 and 1827, and that same year was appointed an aide-de-camp to the Lord Lieutenant of Ireland.

In 1835 he transferred to the 51st Foot. In 1839, on the death of his elder brother, he became known as Viscount Clements and also succeeded his brother as a Member of Parliament for County Leitrim, a seat he held until 1847. On his father's death in 1854, Clements succeeded as the 3rd Earl.

In 1855 he was promoted lieutenant-colonel and subsequently retired from the British Army. Over the next two decades, his overbearing behaviour as a landlord brought him 'much hatred from his tenants, both Catholic and Protestant alike, whom he evicted with equal enthusiasm'. Leitrim was deeply opposed to Gladstone's Irish Land Act of 1870 and was one of eight peers to protest against the legislation when it reached the House of Lords. Among those he also quarrelled with were the Presbyterian minister of Milford, County Donegal, and the Lord Lieutenant himself, the 7th Earl of Carlisle, who removed him from his appointments as a justice of the peace for Counties Leitrim, Donegal and Galway. In April 1878, after surviving various attempts on his life, Lord Leitrim was murdered along with his clerk and driver while on his way to his house at Milford.

He was buried in Dublin, amid scenes of great agitation, and despite the offer of a large reward his assassins were never apprehended. They were named as the brothers Thomas and Patrick McGranaghan, but some historians suggest they were Michael McElwee and Neil Sheils from Fanad. A monument with a cross was set up at Kindrum in 1960 honoring McElwee, Shiels, and Michael Heraghty as the men whose actions 'Ended the tyranny of landlordism'.

The NUI Database has some additional information:

> The Clements family in Ireland were descended from Daniel Clements, a Cromwellian officer, originally granted lands in county Cavan. McParlan records Lord Clements and Mr. Clements as the owners of large estates in Leitrim but not having a residence there in 1802. In the 1870s the 3rd Earl of Leitrim owned 22,038 acres in county Leitrim, [But *see* Bateman] 18,145 acres in county Galway, 54,352 acres in county Donegal and 471 acres in county Kildare. Henry Theophilus Clements, of Ashfield House, Cootehill, county Cavan, owned over 700 acres in Leitrim in the 1870s and his uncle John Marcus Clements of Monkstown, county Dublin, owned 6,773 acres in county Leitrim. These lands were advertised for sale in May 1858. Henry T. Clements inherited the Lough Rynn estate following the assassination of the 3rd Earl of Leitrim in 1878. The Clements family continued to own Lough Rynn until the 1970s although the bulk of the land had been sold off to former tenants by the Land Commission.

Horatio Granville Murray-Stewart of Cally, Gatehouse, had 50,818 acres in Donegal in 1876, with a valuation of £6,500 about £546,000 in modern money. This Harrow-educated landowner was the forty-eighth largest landowner in Great Britain in 1876. With his Donegal acres he had 45,867 acres in Kircudbright and 1,584 acres in Wigtown, a total of 98,269 acres with a valuation of £22,822. His father was an officer in the Rifle Brigade, but Horatio Granvill does not seem to have engaged in military pursuits. He was a justice of the peace in both Donegal and Kircudbright and was High Sheriff of Donegal in 1858, where he was also Deputy Lord Lieutenant. His home in Donegal was at Killybegs. Bateman suggests that he attended Christ Church College, Oxford University, but it has not been possible to ascertain whether he ever took a degree – a situation that is a regular occurrence in the Bateman entries. Donegal County Council holds some papers relating to the estate but nothing to show how it was disposed of, if it was.

William H.M. Style of Glenmore is recorded in the Return with 39,564 acres in Donegal in 1876, with a valuation of £3,806 about £319,704 in modern money. Bateman corrects this entry substantially, giving back the holder at the time his Baronetcy, so that the record now reads:

> Sir William Henry Marsham Style Bart, of Glenmore County Donegal. The knight was educated at Eton and the family had historic connections with the City of London and the Palace, an ancestor having been a gentleman in attendance upon Henry VIII.

Alexander John Robert Stewart of Ards, Cashlemore, had 39,306 acres in Donegal in 1876 with a valuation of £9,135 about £767,340 in modern money. Bateman gives very few biographical details about Alexander Stewart of Ards, but does add in 5,002 acres of County Down to give him a total acreage of 44,308 acres, with a valuation of £15,655.

This fairly obscure landowner was the grandnephew of the Marquis of Drogheda, who had 19,297 acres in 1876. His great uncle was the Marquis of Londonderry, who had 50,325 acres in 1876. His mother was the daughter of the Marquis of Camden, who had 17,399 acres in 1876. His father was MP for Londonderry and also High Sheriff of Donegal. The family papers are held in the Northern Ireland Record office.

John Leslie of Glasslough, County Monaghan, had 28,827 acres in Donegal in 1867, with a valuation of £3,473 about £291,732 in modern money. Bateman corrects this entry by restoring John Leslie's baronetage and he becomes Sir John Leslie Bart, of Glasslough, Co. Monaghan with, in addition to the Donegal acres, 13,674 acres in Monaghan, 1,103 in Tyrone and 877 in Fermanagh. He had a total of 44,481 acres, with a valuation of £16,579.

Sir John was educated at Harrow School, and was an officer in the 1st Life Guards. He sat as MP for Co. Monaghan. The family trace their recent ancestry to John Leslie Bishop of the Isles, who moved to the Church of Ireland diocese of Raphoe and Clogher, acquiring the Glasslough estate on the way. In the years leading up to the twentieth century the family became Catholic, with Ampleforth College swapped for Harrow School and the Irish Guards for the Life Guards.

The estate, though much smaller, remains in the hands of the family.

Robert Harvey of Fairfield House, Cheltenham, had 25,593 acres in Donegal in 1876, with a valuation of £3,398 about £285,432 in modern money. There is no easily accessible public reference to this man or his estate. An ancestor of his may have owned Malin House, Donegal, and a relative from Cheltenham may have become the Royal Philatelist after the First World War, but of the estate, nothing.

Lord George Hill of Augusta, Ballyvar, Ramelton, had 24,189 acres in Donegal in 1876, with a valuation of £1,308 about £109,872 in modern money. He died in 1879, when the estate passed to his son, Arthur Blundell Sandys Hill, another army officer. The family home was Ballyane House, Ramelton.

This entry is important because, although not in Bateman because the valuation was too low, and because Bateman has failed to notice Lord Hill's death in 1879, he was totally typical of aristocratic landowners.

The unamended incumbent was a Lord because he was the son of the 2nd Marquis of Downshire and wrote a book on landlords and tenants called *Facts from Gweedore*, which was not well received by the Parliamentary commission to which it was addressed.

Stephen Farrell, in his contribution to the *History of Parliament*, tells us that:

> His (Lord Hill's) *Facts from Gweedore*, which went through five editions between 1845 and 1887, played a large part in the bitter public debates about the effects of Irish landlordism. The Commons select committee on destitution in Gweedore and Cloughaneely, to which he gave evidence on the 23rd and 24th June 1858, was critical of his actions, and he was gradually borne down by the weight of local resistance to his well-meaning endeavours.

Spouting owners' rights and bad laws did nothing to save the lives of those dying in the ditches around the estate. And neither Lord Hill nor his son appeared any more able than any of their landowning colleagues to separate the system from its dire consequences.

His career, not dissimilar to that of his son who succeeded to the estate, though not the title in 1879, was almost entirely military. He was in the Duke of Wellington's Regiment and then the Royal Irish Hussars between 1817 and 1825. Farrell also notes that:

> He exchanged into the 47th Foot, 23 Mar. 1838, but sold his commission the following day. That year he was apparently provided by his family (that of the Marquis of Downshire, the richest man in Ireland at the time) with sufficient funds to buy an extensive estate at Gweedore in Donegal. There he devoted the rest of his life to agricultural improvements.

For a while he was the MP for Carrickfergus, though he never spoke in Parliament.

Messers Musgrave of Drumglass House, Belfast, had 23,673 acres of Donegal in 1876, with a valuation of £2,012 about £169,008 in modern money. Bateman gives Messers Musgrave, in practice the brothers James and John Musgrave, a below the line entry, and moves Drumglass, by mistake, to Donegal. The estate was at Carrick. He makes no change to the acreage or valuation.

The family at the time of the Returns were businessmen in Belfast. A Baronetcy was awarded to James in 1879 for a significant contribution to Belfast's development as a port and for numerous charitable donations. The family, Ferres tells us, came from Cumberland to Ireland in 1649, at the end of the Cromwellian period, and settled in County Down. The Donegal estate at Carrick seems to have been acquired in the mid 1800, as the family businesses prospered in Belfast. Some of the Musgrave land in the Malone road area became a children's playground, and was later incorporated into a girls' school.

Sir Samuel Hayes Bart, of Drumboe Castle, had 22,828 acres in Donegal in 1876, with a valuation of £6,536 about £549,024 in modern money. The father of the holder of the estate in 1883 was Sir Samuel Hercules Hayes, whose father had been an ardent Conservative, founder of the conservative Carlton Club in London and Grand Master of the Orange Lodge in Donegal. There is a record of his father's life in the *Parliamentary History Record* by Stephen Farrell because he was an MP.

Sir Samuel's grandfather had signed the anti-Catholic petition of the Irish noblemen and gentlemen earlier that year, inheriting the castle and estate in 1827. He was returned as a Conservative MP for Donegal in 1832 and held his seat until he died in 1860. The baronetage became extinct with the death of his second son in 1912.

100 owners of land in County Donegal in 1876 ranked by acreage

		Acreage	Valuation in 1876 (£)	Valuation in Current (£)
1	Conyngham, Marquess of, Slane Castle, Co. Meath	122,300	15,166	1,273,944
2	Leitrim, Earl of, Lough Rynn, Dromod, Mohill, Co. Leitrim	54,352	9,406	790,104
3	Stewart, H.G. Murray, Gullygate House, Scotland	50,818	6,500	546,000
4	Style, William H.M., Glenmore	39,564	3,806	319,704
5	Stewart, Alexander John Robert, Ards, Cashelmore	39,306	9,135	767,340
6	Leslie, John, Glasslough, Co. Monghan	28,827	3,473	291,732
7	Harvey, Robert. Fairfield House, Cheltenham	25,593	3,398	295,432
8	Hill, Lord George Augusta, Ballyvar, Ramelton	24,189	1,308	109,872
9	Musgrave, Messers, Drumglass House, Belfast	23,673	2,012	169,008
10	Hayes, Sir Samuel H. Bart, Drumboe Castle	22,828	6,536	549,024
11	Connolly, Thomas, Castletown, Co. Dublin	22,736	6,283	527,772
12	Church Temporalities, Commissioners of, Dublin	21,489	6,840	574,560
13	Olpherts, Wybrants, Ballyconnell House, Falcarragh	18,133	1,802	151,368
14	Adair, John George, Glenveagh, Lettererkenny	16,308	583	48,972
15	Abercorn, the Duke of, Baronscourt, Newtownstewart	15,942	10,382	872,080
16	Brooke, Thos Young, Lough Esk, Donegal	15,134	1,134	95,256
17	Irvine, Edward, Enniskillen, Co. Fermangh	14,352	263	22,092
18	Humphries, J.K. Reps, Cavancore, Lifford	13,314	567	47,628
19	Harvey, George Henry, Harold Hall, Bedford	11,308	2,244	188,496
20	Lifford, Viscount, Meenglass	11,210	825	69,300

		Acreage	Valuation in 1876 (£)	Valuation in Current (£)
21	M'Glead, Francis, Belfast	11,207	545	45,780
22	Templemore, Lord, -	10,856	7,055	592,620
23	Newton, Courtney, Kilkeel, Dungannon	10,486	2,151	180,684
24	Harvey, George Millar, Malin Hall, Malin	10,363	2,727	229,068
25	Bustard, Ebenezer, Bellville, Dunkineely	10,249	2,576	216,384
26	Hamilton, John, St Ernan's, Donegal	9,448	1,955	164,220
27	Key, Richard W., Dunlewy	9,229	204	17,136
28	Nixon, Rev. Alexander Brown, Knockballymore, Clones	9,084	553	46,452
29	Montgomery, Robert G., convoy House, Raphoe	8,861	3,640	305,760
30	Hamilton, James, Brown Hall, Ballintra	8,507	785	65,940
31	Barton, Baptist Johnson of Greenfort, Croaghross, Milford, Letterkenny	8,017	1,320	110,880
32	Young, George, Culdaff House, Culdaff	7,989	2,358	198,912
33	Commissioners of Endowed Schools, -	7,837	643	54,012
34	Stewart, Sir James Bart, Fortstewart, Ramelton	7,547	4,486	376,824
35	Forster, Arthur S.B., Roshin Lodge, Dunloe	7,281	354	29,736
36	Stewart, Mrs Anne, St James Terrace, Malahide	7,274	799	67,116
37	Arran, Earl of, Pavillion House, London	6,883	3,145	264,180
38	Harte, George V., Kilderry, Muff, Co. Donegal	6,598	2,306	193,704
39	Nicholson, James S., Falmore, Moville	6,531	1,622	136,248
40	Charley, John S., Fenaghy House, Belfast	6,498	564	47,376
41	Wicklow, Earl of, Shelton Abbey, Arklow	6,440	4,818	404,712

		Acreage	Valuation in 1876 (£)	Valuation in Current (£)
42	Doherty, Richard, Redcastle	6,363	2,040	171,360
43	Tredenick, Rev. G.N., Woodhill, Ardara	6,297	1,447	121,548
44	Stewart, William, The Elms, Rugby, England	6,163	725	60,900
45	Sinclair, William, Hollyhill, Strabane	5,947	988	82,992
46	Delap, Rev. Robert, Monellan, Killygordon	5,923	2,031	170,604
47	Dixon, George, Glenveagh, Church Hill	5,755	82	6,888
48	Dixon, John, Glenveagh, Church Hill	5,755	81	6,804
49	Lane, Michael B., Londonderry	5,556	278	23,352
50	Donegall, the Marquess, London★ *see* Antrim	5,521	1,438	120,792
51	Norman, Thomas, Glengollan, Fahan, Derry	5,411	2,333	195,972
52	Deazley, Charles, Pembroke, England	5,362	637	53,508
53	Watt, Mrs Mary Reps, care David Watt, Distiller, Derry	5,281	1,155	97,020
54	Dunbar, George, Woburn, Donghadee	5,247	1,522	127,848
55	Ryan, Valentine, Mountrath, Queen's Co.	5,162	406	34,104
56	Fenwick, William Reps, Greenhills, Raphoe	5,005	959	80,556
57	Boyd, John, Mallymacool, Letterkenny	5,001	2,036	171,024
58	Erne, the Earl of, Crom Castle, Newtownbutler	4,826	4,324	363,216
59	Alexander, Leslie, Buncrana	4,771	918	77,112
60	Lyle, Major, Moville	4,561	1,750	147,000
61	Maxwell, Rev. Robt, Birdstown, Derry	4,516	2,123	178,332
62	Richardson, J.G., Dungannon	4,512	288	24,192
63	Stewart, Chas Fredk, Horn Head, Dunfanaghy	4,458	651	54,684

		Acreage	Valuation in 1876 (£)	Valuation in Current (£)
64	Batt, Thomas, Rathmullen, Ramelton, Letterkenny	4,377	2,176	182,784
65	Rankin, Samuel, Tiernalegue, Carndonagh	4,277	1,437	120,708
66	Joule, Benj St John B., Manchester	4,168	224	18,816
67	Scott, Thomas and Trustees of Lord O'Neill, Shane's Castle, Co. Antrim	4,158	650	54,600
68	Stevenson, Robert, Ardkill, Co. Derry	4,037	588	49,392
69	Hamilton, Anna, Fintra, Killybegs	3,999	404	33,936
70	Gilliland, Samuel, Londonderry	3,940	1,248	104,832
71	Hamilton, Chichester, Kingstown, Co. Dublin	3,901	1,535	128,940
72	Mortimer, Rev. William, Ballinahinch, Co. Down	3,825	619	51,996
73	Ferguson, John, London	3,769	2,225	186,900
74	Knox, George, Prehen, Derry	3,641	1,916	160,944
75	Atkinson, Thomas J., Cavangraden	3,491	975	81,900
76	Byrne, Mrs Mary and Dillon, Miss Frances, Blackrock, Co. Dublin	3,379	96	8,064
77	Montgomery, Rev. Samuel Reps, -	3,373	1,892	158,928
78	Heygate, Sir Fredrick, Bellarena, Derry	3,338	1,702	142,968
79	Harvey, Miss Eliza, care of J. Cochrane, Lifford	3,288	1,241	104,244
80	Stewart, John, Loughreagh House, Church Hill	3,264	734	61,656
81	Hamilton, Rev. John, Manorhamilton	3,181	418	35,112
82	Faussett, Robert, County Inspector, Armagh	3,006	813	68,292
83	Brassy and Wagstaff, Messers, -	2,996	1,796	148,176
84	Carey, Tristram, Ballybrack, Moville	2,854	462	38,808

		Acreage	Valuation in 1876 (£)	Valuation in Current (£)
85	Tredenick, William, Fortwilliam, Ballyshannon	2,779	1,306	109,704
86 87	Irwin, Burton, Streamstown, Ballymote, Co. Sligo	2,750	797	66,946
88	Alexander, Rt Rev. Dr, The Palace, Derry	2,680	917	77,028
89	Crawford, Alex, Londonderry	2,660	114	9,576
90	Mackey, James Thompson, Belmount, Londonderry	2,647	1,502	126,168
91	Thompson, Samuel, Muckamore Abbey, Antrim	2,598	411	34,524
92	Foster, Arthur H., Bell Isle, Ballintra	2,594	913	76,692
93	Lyle, Thomas, Strabane	2,576	125	10,500
94	Johnston, Joseph, Woodlands, Sranorlar	2,564	946	79,464
95	Leslie, John, Ballyward, Co. Down	2,462	1,498	125,832
96	Haslett, Arthur K., Carrownaff, Moville	2,416	902	75,768
97	Hamilton, Alex Reps, Coxtown, Ballintra	2,383	753	63,252
98	Johnston, Chas Reps, Tullyhook, Laghy	2,378	863	72,492
99	Foster, William John, Londonderry	2,369	714	59,976
100	M'Sheffrey, James, Dromaville, Carndonagh	2,310	516	43,344
101	Sinclair, James Reps, Dundarg, Coleraine	2,276	1,344	112,896
102	Graham, Thomas, Glasgow	2,228	255	21,420
103	Doherty, John, Gravesend, England	2,203	572	48,048
104	Cary, Arthur L., Castlecary, Moville	2,182	374	31,416
105	Grove, James G., Castlegrove, Ballymaleel	2,140	863	72,492
106	Teevan, Stevenson, Raceview, Enniskillen	2,051	1,259	105,756

Donegal

		Acreage	Valuation in 1876 (£)	Valuation in Current (£)
107	Colquhoun, Thomas, Rockfort, Buncrana	2,051	1,221	102,564
108	M'Clleland, Rev. Thomas, Greencastle, Moville	2,050	965	81,060
109	M'Clintock, Robert, Dunmore, Carrigans, Derry	1,977	1,341	112,644
110	Column, John, Enniskillen	1,902	281	23,604
111	Orr, Moore, Londonderry	1,855	133	11,172
112	Loughrey, John, Burt, Derry	1,847	364	30,576
113	M'Clintock, Thompson, Germany	1,813	1,657	139,188
114	Young William, Mount Hall, Killygordon	1,791	727	61,068
115	Folliott, Lieutenant Colonel John, Holybrook, Boyle	1,783	845	70,980
116	Dixon, Thomas, Pettigo	1,702	89	7,476
117	Stewart, Arthur P., Dublin	1,679	354	29,736
118	Londonderry, Marquis of, -	1,673	1,185	99,540
119	Wray, William, Oak Park, Letterkenny	1,624	745	62,580
120	Hart, Thomas Bernard, Glenulla Ray, Ramelton	1,599	367	30,828
121	Kennedy, John, London	1,508	159	13,356
122	Woodhouse, Currey, of Omeath Park, Newry and Carrowkeel,	1,470	380	31,920
123	Lepper, Robert, Foyle View, Redcastle	1,352	231	19,404
124	Beresford, John B., Ashbrook	1,342	446	37,464
125	Doherty, Edward, Customs House, Dublin	1,294	140	11,760
126	Fawcett, Robert, Downpatrick	1,272	44	3,696
127	Layard, Henry St G., Hollymount, Carndonagh	1,248	260	21,840
128	Hamilton, Thomas, Moy	1,240	318	26,712
129	Craig, John, Killygordon	1,231	416	34,944
130	Mansfield, Francis, Ardrummon, Ballymaleel	1,225	928	77,952

		Acreage	Valuation in 1876 (£)	Valuation in Current (£)
131	Mitchell, George H., Riverton, Buncrana	1,209	131	11,004
132	Crawford, Rev., Wm, Cookstown	1,195	209	17,556
133	Loughrey, Anne, Binion, Clonmany	1,181	392	32,088
134	M'Devitt, Daniel, Glenties	1,176	81	6,804
135	Johnston, James, Summerhill, Stranorlar	1,168	762	64,008
136	Southwell, Viscount, Rathkeale, Co. Limerick	1,147	1,201	100,884
137	Kelly, Peter, Ballyshannon	1,131	427	35,868
138	Smith, Henry W., -	1,116	936	78,624
139	Darcus, Solomon, Gardenmore, Larne	1,116	411	34,524
140	Johnston, Sir William Reps, -	1,096	125	10,500
141	M'Neill, Hector S., Lanark Militia, Lanark	1,083	303	25,452
142	Ramsay, Robert, Lisnenaw, Letterkenny	1,082	607	50,988
143	M'Clure, Wm Reps, Londonderry	1,055	411	34,524
144	Knox, Wm Reps, Clonleigh	1,041	889	74,676
145	Saunderson, Mary Anne, Dublin	1,006	870	73,080

Top 20 landowners in Donegal in 1876 by valuation (income)

		Acreage	Valuation 1876 (£)	Valuation current (£)
1	Conyngham, Marquess of, Slane Castle, Co. Meath	122,300	15,166	1,273,944
2	Abercorn, the Duke of, Baronscourt, Newtownstewart	15,942	10,382	872,080
3	Leitrim, Earl of, Lough Rynn Dromod, Mohill, Co. Leitrim	54,352	9,406	790,104
4	Stewart, Alexander John Robert, Ards, Cashelmore	39,306	9,135	767,340
5	Templemore, Lord, -	10,856	7,055	592,620

		Acreage	Valuation 1876 (£)	Valuation current (£)
6	Church Temporalities, Commissioners of, Dublin	21,489	6,840	574,560
7	Hayes, Sir Samuel H. Bart, Drumboe Castle	22,828	6,536	549,024
8	Stewart, H.G. Murray, Gullygate House, Scotland	50,818	6,500	546,000
9	Connolly, Thomas, Castletown, Co. Dublin	22,736	6,283	527,772
10	Wicklow, Earl of, Shelton Abbey, Arklow	6,440	4,818	404,712
11	Stewart, Sir James Bart, Fortstewart, Ramelton	7,547	4,486	376,824
12	Erne, the Earl of, Crom Castle, Newtownbutler	4,826	4,324	363,216
13	Style, William H.M., Glenmore	39,564	3,806	319,704
14	Montgomery, Robert G., Convoy House, Raphoe	8,861	3,640	305,760
15	Harvey, George. Fairfield House, Cheltenham	25,593	3,398	295,432
16	Leslie, John, Glasslough, Co. Monghan	28,827	3,473	291,732
17	Arran, Earl of, Pavillion House, London	6,883	3,145	264,180
18	Harvey, George Millar, Malin Hall, Malin	10,363	2,727	229,068
19	Bustard, Ebenezer, Bellville, Dunkineely	10,249	2,576	216,384
20	Young, George, Culdaff House, Culdaff	7,989	2,358	198,912

DOWN

	1876	2020 est
Population in County Down	293,449	531,665 (2011, est for 2016-2020)
All owners of land	3,605	–
Percentage of the population	–	–
Owners of nothing at all	293,449	Figures not available
Percentage of the population	–	–
Size of County	608,214 acres	604,800 acres
Number of dwellings (of which rented)	58,343 (54,738)	–
Number of owned farm holdings	1,003	4,762

County Comparisons

	Acreage in 1876	Population in 1876
County Down	608,214	293,449
Cheshire, England	602,219	561,201
Kirkcudbrightshire, Scotland	571,950	41,859
Carmarthenshire, Wales	510,574	115,710

The Marquis of Downshire of Castle Hillsborough had 64,356 acres in County Down in 1876, with a valuation of £62,783 about £5,273,772 in modern money. The Eton-educated 7th Marquis of Downshire, Arthur Wills John Wellington Blundell Trumbull Hill, who held the estate in 1876, was what the media of that time called a true 'Don Magnifico'. His total acreage recorded in Bateman came to 120,189 acres, valued at £96,691. He was the 31st largest landowner in Great Britain in 1876, and the eighteenth in terms of wealth based on the valuation. Bateman corrects the County Down acreage, from 64,356, to 78,051 acres, and the valuation from £62,783 to £73,738.

He was the richest aristocrat living in Ireland at the time. He had 5,287 acres in Berks, 281 acres in Suffolk, 15,766 acres in Wicklow, 13,679 acres in King's County (Offaly) 5,787 acres in Antrim and 1,338 acres in Kildare, which with the Down acres came to a total an estate of 120,189 acres, with a valuation of £96,691. The castle, now the quarters of the Secretary of State for Northern

Ireland, was bought by the British Government in 1925 for £25,000 from the 8th Marquess. The castle is regularly seen on TV, especially during Royal visits to Northern Ireland. The family seat is now Clifden Castle in Yorkshire although the Marquis practices as an accountant and non-executive director of various companies, having worked at the accounting company of Touche Ross for a time.

A somewhat over-generous obituary of the 8th Marquis, who died in 2003, in the *Telegraph* newspaper states that the 8th Marquis successfully re-established his once great Ulster landholding family in North Yorkshire after the Irish Land Acts and Bracknell New Town had largely deprived them of their original estates – as set out above.

The value of 5,287 acres as the basis of a new town in England is not stated. Neither is the amount of money paid by the Land Commission to the estate before 1921 – the Land Commission did not much function in Northern Ireland after partition in 1921.

The dissolution of an estate once almost the size of a small English county (Middlesex, 143,014 acres) deserves at least a book, if only to explain how vast quantities of land change hands in Britain and Ireland, well hidden from the public gaze.

The trustees of the Kilmerley (Kilmorey) Estate of Woburn Park, Chertsey Surrey held 37,454 acres in County Down in 1876, with a valuation of £13,708 about £1,151,472 in modern money. This huge landholding was acquired by the owners of Woburn Park in Chertsey Surrey in the late nineteenth century. The estate was sold in 1814 to Charles Stirling, Vice Admiral of the White, part of the Royal Navy. In 1834 it passed to the Dowager Lady King. She in turn sold the estate to the Earl of Kilmorey, who held 40,000 acres of Down according to Bateman. That 40,000 acres is almost certainly this estate. The Earl was MP for Newry in County Down. The entry is almost certainly a spelling error in the Return. By 1884 the Surrey estate was back in the hands of the Petre family, who had been previous owners.

The Earldom of Kilmorey still exists and is held by the Rt Hon. Sir Richard Francis Needham. He was an MP in the UK House of Commons from 1979 to 1997. He did not use the title nor the hereditary Abbotship of the Exempt Jurisdiction of Newry and Mourne. He gives the family seat as Mourne Park, Kilkeel County Down but lives near Cirencester in Gloucestershire.

The house burnt down in 2013 but had been subject to a controversial family dispute in 2002. With a residual 147 acres it was recently advertised for sale.

The 5th Earl of Annesley of Castlewellan had 23,567 acres in the county in 1876, with a valuation of £18,886 about £1,586,424 in modern money.
See page 53.

Rt Hon. Colonel William Brownlow Forde MP, of Seaforde, County Down, had 19,882 acres in the county in 1876, with a valuation of £15,404 about £1,293,936 in modern money. Bateman corrects the acreage to 20,106 acres and the valuation to £15,990. Bateman records the colonel as an officer in the 67th Regiment of Foot of the British Army.

The estate originated at Coolgreaney in Wexford, which was granted to an ancestor of the Fordes in the early 1600s. In 1637 Matthew Ford, a Dublin MP, obtained lands then known as 'McCartan's County', in county Down, from the 1st Viscount Lecale. The Fords remained in control of the Wexford acreage.

By 1876 the estate was in the hands of The Rt Hon. William Brownlow Forde JP DL (1823–1902), of Seaforde, High Sheriff of County Down, 1853; Lieutenant-Colonel, the Royal South Down Militia; Colonel, 1854–81, 5th Battalion, Royal Irish Rifles; MP for County Down, 1857–74; Privy Counsellor. He had married, in 1855, Adelaide, daughter of General the Hon. Robert Meade, second son of the 1st Earl of Clanwilliam.

Two later marriages are of interest. Lieutenant-Colonel Desmond Charles Forde, a Deputy Lieutenant of the County and High Sheriff (1906–61), married, in 1938, the Hon. Margaret Bertha Meriel Ward, youngest daughter of the 6th Viscount Bangor OBE PC. His only son, Patrick Mathew Desmond Ford, justice of the peace and Deputy Lieutenant of the County (1940–2010), married Lady Anthea Lowry-Corry, eldest daughter of the 7th Earl of Belmore and the present 8th Earl's sister.

Ferres tells us that the estate is now about 1,000 acres.

The Earl of Dufferin, of Clandeboy, Bangor, had 18,000 acres in the county in 1876, with a valuation of £21,043 about £1,767,612 in modern money. This is possibly one of the longest biographical entries in Bateman, who was notably succinct. The then Earl of Dufferin was, by the standards of the time, enormously distinguished. He was educated at Eton and became Governor General of Canada, a commissioner in Syria, was the Ambassador to Russia and, in 1883, was the Ambassador to the Ottoman Empire at Constantinople. He had been the Under Secretary of State for India and for War and was Chancellor of the Duchy of Lancaster. In 1884, after Bateman appeared, Dufferin became Viceroy of India. In 1888 he was made Marquis of Dufferin, with the addition of Ava in Burma. He had been active in Burma, annexing it for the British Empire.

He sold large parts of the estate to pay his huge debts, about £300,000 in the 1870s.

The title became extinct in 1988. There is a peerage associated with the Marquisate, that of Baron Blackwood of Clandeboy. The claimant lives in Australia. Parts of the estate remain in the family.

Robert Narcissus Batt of Purdysburn, Belfast, had 12,010 acres in County Down in 1876, with a valuation of £6,535 about £548,940 in modern money. This family, like a number of others in Northern Ireland, came to Ireland in Cromwell's army and obtained land, first in Wexford at Ozier Hill. According to Ferres, they came from Cornwall originally.

The family prospered, married well and became bankers, founding what was originally known as the Belfast, later the Northern Bank.

The family developed much of what became Donegal Square and Donegal Place, the main shopping centres in modern Belfast.

The 5th Viscount Bangor of Castle Ward, Downpatrick, had 9,861 acres in the county in 1876, with a valuation of £13,156 about £1,105,104 in modern money. This landowner was educated at Rugby School and Sandhurst and served in the Kaffir War 1851–53, as an officer in the 43rd Regiment of Foot. His successor, the 6th Viscount, was an Irish representative peer in the House of Lords from 1886 to 1911. He was a member of the Senate of Northern Ireland and its speaker from 1930 to 1950.

The peerage is still extant and is held by William Maxwell David Ward, the 8th Viscount, who lives in London.

The family seat, Castle Ward, is a National Trust property.

The Trustees of the Marquis of Downshire, of Hillsborough Castle, had 9,246 acres in the county in 1876, with a valuation of £10,595 about £889,980 in modern money. (*see* Marquis of Downshire, above)

The Downshire estate was enormous, running to over 120,000 acres. It was also extremely complicated and it is not clear which part of the estate this was, or whether it was being held in trust for the estate of a deceased predecessor or for a relative.

The Earl of Roden of Tollymore Park, Bryansford, and of Hyde Hall, Sawbridgeworth, had 8,903 acres in the county in 1876, with a valuation of £3,264 about £274,176 in modern money. This Harrow-educated infantry officer served in the Scots Foot Guards in the Crimea, according to Bateman. The estate was an interesting mix of land in Great Britain and Ireland, with 4,151 acres in County Louth, 1,134 acres in Essex and 408 acres in Herts, which, together with the Co. Down estate came to 14,596 acres, with a valuation of £13,077.

The title still exists and is held by Robert John Jocelyn, the 10th Earl. He cites neither seat nor address.

The English element of this family have a recorded lineage that, even for England, is unusual. They fetched up at Sawbridgeworth in Herts sometime after the Norman Conquest and by the time of the Tudors were executors of the wills of

Henry VIII and Anne Boleyn. They were originally responsible for the foundation of a number of monastic institutions in the eleventh century but were commissioners for the dissolution of the monasteries under Henry VIII in the 1530s.

They moved to Ireland during the Williamite wars, perhaps earlier, and between 1739 and 1756 Robert Jocelyn, having been an MP, became Lord High Chancellor of Ireland, collecting the first Irish peerage in 1743, that of Baron Newport. The Earldom, in the peerage of Ireland, came in 1771. The 1st Earl married Anne Hamilton, who brought the Down estate at Tollymore to the Jocelyns. The estate was sold to the Ministry of Agriculture of Northern Ireland between 1930 and 1941.

Robert Perceval Maxwell of Finnebrogue, Downpatrick, and Groomsport House, Belfast, had 8,347 acres in the county in 1876, with a valuation of £8,801 about £739,284 in modern money. Bateman records little in the biography of Robert Perceval Maxwell, but, despite the absence of a title, the family were both aristocratic and related to a range of aristocratic families, including those of the Earls of Egmont, Farnham and of Usher. The estate, which consisted of land in four counties, including Co. Down, held 2,353 acres in Co. Tipperary, 911 acres in Co. Meath and 695 acres in Co Cork for a total estate of 12,428 acres with a valuation of £12,132.

As with so many of the families in this account, there are interlinked military and clerical strands, leading, inevitably, to large estates of land. Robert Maxwell's immediate ancestor, Robert Perceval, who died in 1839, was Physician-General to HM Forces in Ireland during Lord Talbot's viceroyalty, and professor of chemistry at Trinity College, Dublin.

A descendant of Robert Maxwell, Major John Robert Perceval-Maxwell of Finnebrogue, was an MP in the Northern Ireland House of Commons and a member of the Northern Ireland Senate. He was High Sheriff of County Down and a Deputy Lieutenant, and was a founder of the Northern Ireland Committee of the National Trust. He was Parliamentary Secretary of the Ministry of Commerce between 1945 and 1949. He died in 1963. The family papers and estate records are at the Northern Ireland Public Records Office.

Top 68 owners of land in County Down in 1876 ranked by acreage

		Acreage	Valuation 1876 (£)	Valuation current (£)
1	Downshire, The Marquis of, The Castle, Hillsborough	64,356	62,783	5,273,772
2	Trustees of the Kilmerly Estate, Woburn Park, Chertsey, Surrey	37,454	13,708	1,151,472

		Acreage	Valuation 1876 (£)	Valuation current (£)
3	Annesley, Earl of, Castlewellan	23,567	18,886	1,586,424
4	Forde, Colonel Wm B., Seaforde	19,882	15,404	1,293,936
5	Dufferin, Earl of, Clandeboy, Bangor	18,238	21,043	1,767,612
6	Batt, Robert N., Purdysburn, Belfast	12,010	6,535	548,940
7	Bangor, Viscount, Castleward, Strangford	9,861	13,156	1,105,104
8	Trustees of the Marquis of Downshire, Hillsborough	9,246	10,595	889,980
9	Roden, the Earl of, Tollymore Park, Bryansford	8,903	3,264	274,176
10	Maxwell, Robert P., Finnebrogue, Downpatrick, and Groomsport House, Belfast	8,347	8,801	739,284
11	Trustees of Hon. R. Mead, Dromore	8,099	8,116	681,744
12	Price, James C., Saintfield House, Saintfield	6,807	7,641	641,844
13	Mulholland, John, Ballywalter Park, Belfast	6,769	10,668	897,792
14	Bateson, Sir Thomas Bart, Belvoir Park, Belfast	6,348	9,330	783,720
15	Crawford, John S., Crawfordsburn, Belfast	5,748	5,943	499,212
16	Ward, Robert E., Bangor Castle, Bangor	5,735	8,517	715,428
17	Trustees of Hon. Robert Meade, Gill Hall, Dromore	5,393	5,603	470,652
18	Church Temporalities, Commissioners of, 24 Upper Merrion St, Dublin	5,354	6,501	546,084
19	Stewart, Alex J.R., Ards, Co. Donegal	5,002	6,520	547,680
20	Canning, Hon. H.S.G., Rostrevor	4,928	1,458	122,472
21	Gordon, Robert F., Florida Manor, Killinchy	4,768	5,507	424,788
22	Cleland, John, Stormont Castle, Dundonald	4,385	6,174	518,616
23	Boyd, William, Ballydugan, Downpatrick	4,191	5,238	439,992

		Acreage	Valuation 1876 (£)	Valuation current (£)
24	Montgomery, Hugh, Rosemount, Greyabbey	3,739	4,036	339,024
25	Harrison, Henry Reps, Holywood House, Belfast	3,653	3,921	329,364
26	Hall, Major William Thomas, Narrowwater Castle, Warrenpoint	3,648	4,358	366,072
27	Clanwilliam, Earl of, Deal Castle, Kent, England	3,584	4,305	361,620
28	Cleland, James, Tobarmhuire, Crossgar	3,544	4,230	355,320
29	Beauclerk, Aubrey De Vere, Ardglass	3,494	5,560	467,040
30	Mussenden, William, England	3,098	3,520	295,680
31	Meredyth, Henry Wm, Kilkenny	3,071	3,216	270,144
32	Montgomery, Captain Hugh, Tyrella	3,005	3,163	265,692
33	De Ros, Lord, Strangford	2,952	3,866	324,744
34	Douglas, Charles, Grace Hall, Lurgan	2,791	3,293	276,612
35	Whittle, Elizabeth, Dublin	2,711	3,615	303,660
36	Wallace, Sir Richard, Antrim Castle, Co. Antrim	2,693	6,244	524,496
37	Allan, George, Mount Panther, Dondrum	2,585	3,132	263,088
38	Waring, Thomas, Waringstown House, Co. Down	2,438	3,469	291,396
39	Thompson, Captain Wm, Rostrevor	2,259	2,429	204,036
40	Murland, Samuel, Castlewellan	2,237	3,220	270,480
41	Thompson, Eleanor, Newry	1,936	1,125	94,500
42	Maginnis, Colonel H., Cambridge	1,788	1,349	113,316
43	Whyte, John Jospeph, Loughbrickland	1,712	2,292	192,528
44	Gartlan, George H., Cabra House, Newry	1,637	1,300	109,200
45	Martin, Robert, Kilbroney, Rostrevor	1,531	786	66,024
46	M'Creight, Andrew William, Ardmore House, Armagh	1,526	239	20,076
47	Echlin, Rev. J.R., England	1,510	1,618	135,912

		Acreage	Valuation 1876 (£)	Valuation current (£)
48	Gore, William, Enniskillen	1,366	1,358	114,072
49	Delacherois, Daniel, Donaghadee	1,356	4,124	346,416
50	O'Donnell, Mrs Nicholas, Felix House, Hornsey, England	1,352	243	20,412
51	M'Donnell, Miss R.M., Glenariffe, Larne	1,311	1,035	86,940
52	Stuart, James C., Banbridge	1,287	1,635	137,340
53	Cowan, Andrew, Bangor	1,280	1,628	136,752
54	Mathew, Chas R eps, England	1,207	1,186	99,624
55	M'Cartan, Thomas, Baymount House, Rostervor	1,187	577	48,468
56	Garvagh, Lady, Garvagh	1,176	1,462	122,808
57	Clarke, George, Belfast	1,145	1,139	95,676
58	Cleland, John, Vianstown, Downpatrick	1,143	1,294	108,696
59	Fowler, Edward W., Sligo	1,141	985	82,740
60	M'Convill, Peter, North Street, Newry	1,110	654	54,936
61	Crommelin, Samuel D., Carrowdore Castle	1,082	1,676	140,784
62	Hamilton, Robert, Belfast	1,070	1,019	85,596
63	Dickinson, J.W., Dublin	1,057	1,059	88,956
64	Maguire, Captain Thomas, Brentwood, Essex	1,052	1,142	95,928
65	Hamilton, Mrs Cath, Killyleagh Castle	1,041	2,173	182,532
66	Hanna, Samuel, Cork	1,032	834	70,056
67	Calvert, Eliza, England	1,007	1,377	115,668
68	Blakeney, Robert, Dublin	986	872	73,248

The top 20 landowners in County Down in 1876 ranked by valuation (income)

		Acreage	Valuation 1876 (£)	Valuation current (£)
1	Downshire, The Marquis of, The Castle, Hillsborough	64,356	62,783	5,273,772

		Acreage	Valuation 1876 (£)	Valuation current (£)
2	Dufferin, Earl of, Clandeboy, Bangor	18,238	21,043	1,767,612
3	Annesley, Earl of, Castlewellan	23,567	18,886	1,586,424
4	Forde, Colonel Wm B., Seaforde	19,882	15,404	1,293936
5	Trustees of the Kilmerly Estate, Woburn Park, Chertsey, Surrey	37,454	13,708	1,151,472
6	Bangor, Viscount, Castleward, Strangford	9,861	13,156	1,105,104
7	Mulholland, John, Ballywalter Park, Belfast	6,769	10,668	897,792
8	Trustees of the Marquis of Downshire, Hillsborough	9,246	10,595	889,980
9	Bateson, Sir Thomas Bart, Belvoir Park, Belfast	6,348	9,330	783,720
10	Maxwell, Robert P., Finnebrogue, Downpatrick, and Groomsport, House Belfast	8,347	8,801	739,284
11	Ward, Robert E., Bangor Castle, Bangor	5,735	8,517	715,428
12	Trustees of Hon. R. Mead, Dromore	8,099	8,116	681,744
13	Price, James C., Saintfield House, Saintfield	6,807	7,641	641,844
14	Batt, Robert N., Purdysburn, Belfast	12,010	6,535	548,940
15	Stewart, Alex J.R., Ards, Co. Donegal	5,002	6,520	547,680
16	Church Temporalities, Commissioners of, 24 Upper Merrion St, Dublin	5,354	6,501	546,084
17	Wallace, Sir Richard, Antrim Castle, Co. Antrim	2,693	6,244	524,496
18	Cleland, John, Stormont Castle, Dundonald	4,385	6,174	518,616
19	Crawford, John S., Crawfordsburn, Belfast	5,748	5,943	499,212
20	Trustees of Hon. Robert Meade, Gill Hall, Dromore	5,393	5,603	470,652

DUBLIN CITY

	1876	2020 Est
Population in Dublin City	246,326 (1871)	527,612
All owners of land	7,290	223,637 (city and county)
Percentage of the population	2.95	–
Owners of nothing at all	239,036	145,492
Percentage of the population	97.05	–
Size of County	3,267 acres	–
Number of dwellings (of which rented in 1876, oqwned in 2020)	298	207,847
Number of owned farm holdings	1,003 (over 1 acre)	–

It is not possible to make a comparison between the Return of Owners of Land in Dublin and the Returns for the rest of the United Kingdom. London was not included in the English Returns and would not make a good basis for comparison anyhow. That said, the actual Dublin city returns should be treated as a guide and with a little caution, subject to further academic study. There are some significant owners, especially the Catholic teaching and nursing orders who had begun to buy land, buildings and consolidate their presence in the city, who do not appear. The Royal Dublin Society (RDS) and King's Inn acreage looks a little small, as indeed does the Trinity College Dublin (TCD) acreage. Had TCD followed the British universities it would have disclosed its out of town holdings in the counties. There is no mention of the Earl of Longford, despite the massive entry under his name for Dublin, in Bateman. His 450 acres of Dublin, with a valuation of £31,713, is unlikely to have been far outside the city, with an average valuation per acre of over £70 then. The best estates in rural Ireland were getting £1 an acre, the Longford estate was getting seventy times that. These acres do appear under Dublin County in the Returns, however.

There is another point, too. The publication of the Returns in mainland Great Britain, with Scotland in the lead in 1873 and all the English and Welsh counties arriving in print in 1874, caused a huge furore amongst the landowners. In England nothing like this had appeared since the Domesday Book in 1086, and in Ireland nothing like this had ever appeared before. The Griffith valuations might compare, but were too voluminous and did not highlight the ownership easily. The Return of Owners of Land was Ireland's first Domesday. Whatever record exists of the publication of the Returns was ignored by Bateman and has not been revisited by academics or other commentators since.

The fuss in Great Britain was concentrated in the so called 'Gentlemen's' London clubs, as Bateman records in *The Great Landowners of Great Britain and Ireland* (4th Edition, Harrison and Co., London, 1883):

> That the affairs of one's neighbours are of no little interest to men of every class of life has perhaps never been more strongly proved by the production of and great demand for 'The Modern Domesday Book'. Not only have Mr Fredrick Purdy and others analysed it, Mr Lyulph Stanley abused it, Mr John Bright moved its digestion in the House, and the 'Spectator' and other London journals scathingly criticised it, but the immense herd of country newspapers have actually reproduced it, as far as their own neighbourhoods are concerned, in their columns, much probably, to the satisfaction of the bulk of readers, to whom twenty six shillings is prohibitory. As an example of this, I may mention, that having a small party in my house during one of those dubious weeks which comes in 'twixt the close of the hunting and the beginning of the London season, I was saved all Marthean cares as to the amusement of my guests simply by leaving lying about on the table the two huge volumes of 'The Modern Domesday', over which I found bowed with the utmost constancy two or more heads.
>
> I heard from one of my guests that the copy of the work at the 'Ultratorioum' was reduced to rags and tatters within a fortnight of its arrival- a lesson which was not wasted on the library committee of my own club, which caused the book to be so bound as to defy anything short of a twelve year old schoolboy.

There are several curiosities here. The original Domesday was not a list of landowners, but a survey of taxable assets, ordered by William the Bastard in 1085, completed in 1086.

As such, it is a common occurrence in historic records as far back as the Pharaohs in Memphis, Egypt, in 3000 BC, and in China throughout Imperial times. What is unique, however, was the 1876 (1874) Domesday. It listed every holder of land over 1 acre, in four countries. So far, no similar record has turned up, anywhere. The second curiosity is that it was published while Karl Marx was still alive and writing *Das Kapital*, and it was available to him at the British Library. His figures for landownership in Russia are exceptionally poor, but here, right under his nose in the city in which he lived and worked, in the library he toiled in, were the most accurate figures ever produced on the landownership and population of four countries. As we show in the introduction, the Returns demonstrated with great precision the extent to which the primary economic good in Great Britain and Ireland at the time, land, was concentrated in the hands of fewer than 1.8 per cent of the population. This was monopoly capitalism, malfunctioning even on its own internal terms.

The market, because there was no real market, was pricing nothing efficiently and distributing nothing efficiently. This was reinforced by the possession of total power by the monopolists. They owned all the land; the public owned next to nothing. The landowners controlled the Parliamentary franchise through statute by imposing a land holder requirement until 1884. After that, control was exercised via rotten boroughs where votes were purchased. The landlords entirely dominated both houses of Parliament. The acuity of this hypercontrol is more clearly demonstrated, in numbers and in facts, in Ireland, in the Returns, than anywhere else on the planet.

This was all, even by the standards of the time, corruption, wrapped about itself and devouring, not only itself, but the entire potential market place, while the passing populace starved some of the time and were destitute most of the time.

However, corruption, once installed in the centres of power, reached other places. It reached the Church of Ireland, which was simply the landowners at prayer to a landlord god crafted in their own image and petitioned to keep them in the style and manner to which they had become accustomed. Their tenants do not seem to have been a frequent subject of their prayers. The history and economics departments of Trinity College seemed never to have heard of the Returns before their partial recovery in 2001. But then, a great many of Ireland's landlords were 'Trinity men'. It was unlikely they'd have had much time for studying the corruption that not merely propped up the system, but which was the system. The formation of additional universities in Ireland began in 1845. There is no sign that any department in any of the constituent bodies, Queen's Belfast, Galway, Cork or Dublin, ever allocated time or expertise to studying conceivably the most important demographic, history and economic study ever made in Ireland, of Ireland. If any of them did any work there are no research papers in the public domain to show for it.

In 1870 the slums of Dublin were described by F.X. Lyons in her book *The Great Hunger* as the worst in Europe. Here we meet the landlords.

The Crown owned 142 acres in Dublin in 1876, with a valuation of £26,813 about £2,252,292 in modern money. The Crown escapes Bateman's notice as it was not an individual but an institution, one with extensive acreage in the small area that was Dublin city in 1876. It held both the largest acreage and the highest valuation in the city.

Little serious work has been done to establish what property the Crown owned, but the key buildings and sites would have been military barracks and prisons. The main military establishments were: The Royal Hospital Kilmainham, home of the general officer commanding Eastern Command Ireland, built on a former priory of the order of St John of Jerusalem in 1679. Then there was the Royal Barracks between the City and the Phoenix Park. There was the Richmond Barracks near Golden Bridge on the Grand Canal and the Porto Bello Barracks, also on the Grand Canal; both were very large with extensive stables. The main recruitment centre for Ireland was at Beggars Bush Barracks and there was a large artillery barracks at Island Bridge. These sites alone would come close to 140 acres, if not more.

In 1876, the year of the Returns, an important initiative began when the Dublin Artisans Dwelling Corporation, backed by Baron Ardilaun (a Guinness) and others, started to build homes for rent around the city. The Guinness family had always been paternalistic employers and had already built dwellings for some of their workers. The railway and tram companies did the same. What was always missing was ownership. The rent-based system in rural areas was perpetuated in the cities' new housing structures.

The majority of these initiatives were rental based. Aversion to ownership was ingrained in the system. Renting was for the plebs, ownership for the upper class.

The Rt Hon. Viscount Monck GCMG, of Charleville, Bray, had 58 acres in Dublin in 1876, with a valuation of £1,604 about £134,736 in modern money. Bateman expands Monck's biography significantly. Monck was a Trinity man and a Commissioner of the Church Temporalities, Governor General of Canada, a Lord of the Treasury and Lord Privy Seal to the Prince of Wales. He was also the MP for Portsmouth. Aside from the Dublin city acres, which are not mentioned in Bateman, he had 5,544 acres in Kilkenny, 2,478 acres in Wicklow, 5,717 acres in Wexford, 193 acres in County Dublin and 212 acres in Co. Westmeath. The total acreage was 14,144 acres, with a valuation of £10,466. He was classed as poor in the political terms of the time, but as Governor General of Canada he beat off American attempts to invade and annex Canada, then known as British North America. After that he quite literally created the Canadian Federation, as a final bulwark against American aggression. He said he took the Canadian job 'for the money' as the estates he inherited were loaded with debt.

Between 1882 and 1884 he was a commissioner of the new Irish Lands Act, and between 1874 and 1892 he held the office of lord lieutenant and *custos rotulorum* of County Dublin. The title still exists, having been granted in 1801 in return for voting for the Union. The current Viscount, the 7th, does not use the title.

The Hon. W. Cowper-Temple, later Baron Mount-Temple, of 17 Curzon Street, London, is shown with 38 acres in Dublin City, with a valuation of £,1,426 about £119,784 in modern money. This Eton-educated aristocrat had over 10,000 acres in Sligo at Mullaghabawn, including the unfinished Classibawn Castle. These acres are not shown in Bateman, where he is recorded holding 6,153 acres in Hants, 1,249 acres in Yorkshire, 23 acres in Herts and 738 acres in Co. Dublin. The Dublin acres had a valuation of £6,788. His total acreage was 8,142 acres, with a valuation of £16,270. He was the nephew of one Prime Minister, Lord Melbourne, and then the stepson of another Prime Minister, Lord Palmerston, whose estates he inherited. He was MP for Hereford for thirty-three years but at the same time became a brevet major in the Royal Horse Guards. His stepfather, Lord Palmerston, gave him the Home Office in 1855. He died in 1888 at his Broadlands estate in Hampshire, later purchased by the Mountbatten family. His estates were inherited by his nephew, the Rt Hon. Evelyn Ashley, the second son of Anthony Ashley-Cooper, 7th Earl of Shaftesbury, who had 21,785 acres in 1876.

Sir Arthur Guinness, c/o A.E. Bart and Co., 18 Lower Leeson Street, Dublin, had 37 acres in 1876 with a valuation of £5,115 about £429,660 in modern money. Sir Arthur Guinness, who later became Baron Ardilaun, was probably the most famous man in Dublin in this period, and one of the richest. However, the family firm, of which his brother, Sir Edward, later the Earl of Iveagh, became chairman, originally had 4 acres, later 64 acres, at St James Gate, the site of their famous brewery. Portions of the freehold still belong to the family, who bought out the lease at various times, starting in the 1900s. Originally the lease was for 9,000 years at an annual rent of £45 from 1759, about £6,000 in modern money. It was held from Mark Rainsford, grandson of a previous brewer on the site, and originated with the Dublin City Corporation. A copy of the lease is still displayed at the brewery. The Returns treated leases over 999 years as de facto freeholds, which is a way of saying that the Dublin land record in the Returns is probably deficient. Sir Arthur sold out his interest in the company in 1876 for £600,000, about £50 million in modern money It says a lot about brewing profits that his brother was able to raise that kind of money to buy him out. Sir Arthur, by now Baron Ardilaun, then acquired a huge estate mainly in the west of Ireland, some by purchase, some by inheritance from his father. He had 27,111 acres in Co. Galway, 3,747 acres in Mayo and 484 acres in Dublin.

The valuation of the Dublin acres was £1,302, suggesting that the land was in the county, not the city. His total holding was 31,342 acres with a valuation of £6,573.

There is no record in Bateman of his brother's (Iveagh's) acreage and his brother's estate at Elveden in Suffolk is recorded by Bateman in the name of H.H. the Maharajah Duleep Singh, who had been 'relocated' to the UK after the British Empire and the East India Company 'acquired' his kingdom of the Punjab in India.

The scale and impact of Guinness philanthropy in Dublin, other parts of Ireland and in the UK is hard to underestimate. The Iveagh Trust built houses and flats for the working poor. Ardilaun helped, with other notable Dublin landowners including William La Touche and John Jamison to set up the Dublin Artisan Dwelling Corporation, which eventually built over 2,500 flats at a time when Dublin Corporation was doing little or nothing to house the city's poor, leaving most forms of housing in the city to private, often slum, landlords. Murray Fraser, in his history of public housing in Ireland, notes that from the outset the Dublin Artisans Corporation was run as an efficient business and paid a dividend of between 4 and 5 per cent to shareholders. It may have set out to build affordable houses for the working class of Dublin, but it *was* a business.

Both Guinness brothers, Ardilaun and Iveagh, were, however philanthropic, also staunch Conservatives and Unionists. They ran into direct difficulties with the rising tide of Irish nationalism and land agitation. Ardilaun was a resident landlord, not an absentee, and invested in his estates. Nonetheless, two of his agents were murdered and he suffered from a rent strike. During the 'great lockout' strike in Dublin in 1913, however, his brother, Iveagh, refused to lock out his workers.

Iveagh was Eton educated, although there is no record of Ardilaun's education, save that he was a Trinity man. Iveagh married a cousin from the banking side of the Guinness family and the title still exists with the 4th Earl, known as 'Ned Guinness', living at Elveden in Suffolk, now a 25,000-acre estate. Ardilaun had no children and the peerage died with him in 1915.

The Guinness family were the richest that Ireland has ever known. They made their fortune from trade, not land, the source of wealth of almost all of those around them. They bought land, Ardilaun in Ireland and Iveagh in England, after they became rich.

They sought to be like those they actually outshone in every way. Instead, they stand as an historic contradiction, exposing how capitalism malfunctions and at the same time how humans can be good, but limit that goodness because they cannot or won't fight the system to which they belong.

The Guinness brewery never had tied pubs. The family succeeded in the open market and never sought to abuse it in the way many brewing companies do by tying pubs to their product, but they avoided applying the same principle to the one thing they did not understand about wealth, land.

The Guinness family were titans of philanthropy and did it on a scale almost unknown amongst the aristocrats whose ranks they joined. In Dublin they built homes for their workers when few did, and for the poor when no one, not even the Corporation, did. But they could not see over the wall of privilege they created around themselves personally. They could not see that what the ordinary people needed, and what contradicted the very core of their commercial operation's principle was land. They could not see that the free market principle that made them wealthy, was, in relation to land in Ireland, non-operational. They epitomised the issue of personal wealth and collective poverty. They had great wealth, based on a unique product, sold in a relatively free market in which they did not attempt the monopoly of tied houses. They were genuine Christians within their personal limits, but they were unable to crack the conundrum identified in this book by just two numbers; the landed and the landless. They system they triumphed in beat them in the end.

The Earl of Pembroke of Wilton House, Salisbury, had 32 acres in the city of Dublin in 1876, with a valuation of £15,734 about £1,321,656

in modern money. The shadow of the Earls of Pembroke lies long across Irish history. Benevolence was never its hallmark and its last residue in modern Dublin, the ground rents from centuries of manipulated law, are still there.

There is a further problem. The current Earldom is that of the 10th creation, possibly the 11th if a suspected creation by William Rufus between 1087 and 1100 is considered. This means that the British monarchy, for different reasons, handed the title out to ten different people or families over the course of ten centuries. Each of the families involved were more than intimate with the English monarchs when monarchy was absolute, marrying, variously, the monarchs sisters, lovers and mistresses, and equally variously, losing heads and the title. There are workable accounts on Wikipedia, none of which are in the slightest analytical, but serve as a narrative, two-dimensional account of the relationship between this Earldom and Ireland. And a good early script for *Game of Thrones*.

In 1876 the lands in Dublin were held by the Eton-educated George Robert Charles Herbert, 13th Earl of Pembroke, 10th Earl of Montgomery, of the 10th Creation. The City of Dublin acres are not recorded separately in Bateman, who lists the Earl as having 42,244 acres in Wiltshire, 31 Acres in Westmorland, 2,301 acres in County Dublin and 230 acres in County Wicklow. The total acreage was 44,806 with a valuation of £77,720. Bateman notes that only the English acres are corrected, which may explain the lack of distinction between the Dublin city and county acres. The acreage listed for Co. Dublin, 2,301 had an enormous valuation at £35,586. Much of this came from slum dwellings. The Earl, as a peer, was the Secretary of State for War at a time when regular war was the real and true business of Empire. Like the Guinnesses, he attempted educational philanthropy, but on a marginal scale relative to his wealth. What he did not attempt was reform of land ownership, a matter too close to his heart to deal with.

The Earl of Meath of Kilruddery, Castle Bray, County Wicklow, held 28 acres in Dublin City in 1876, with a valuation of £1,785 about £149,940 in modern money. Bateman records the Earl as holding 36 acres in County Dublin, with the remainder of his Irish acreage, 14,717 acres in extent, in Wicklow. His total acreage was 15,448, with 695 acres in Hereford in England. The total valuation was £9,398.

This title still exists, although the holder, John Anthony Brabazon, the 15th Earl, does not sit in the UK House of Lords. It is also one of the few peerages of Ireland to appear in recent rich lists, based on the acreages still retained around Kilruddery in Bray. During the financial boom (2005–08) that acreage, on the edge of a rapidly expanding Dublin, was valued at many millions per acre. The title was first created in 1627, though based on earlier service to the British Crown in Ireland. The ancestor, Sir Edward Brabazon, was MP for Wicklow in 1585 and a member of the Privy Council. A peerage of the United Kingdom, that of Baron Chaworth of Eaton Hall, Hereford, was added in 1831, giving the then Earl the right to sit in the UK Parliament, there being no Irish House of Lords for him to sit in as Earl. In the Bateman record for 1876 there are 36 acres in Dublin valued at 1,934 and 695 acres in Hereford, a residue of the fifteenth-century estate in that county.

The Wikipedia entry sticks very closely to the Debrett's entry (which is acknowledged), that is to say it reads like the 'begat' section of the Old Testament, without a single reference to the acreage or money upon which the aristocrat's standing depended.

Part of the huge Wicklow estate at Ballinacor came to the Brabazon family via the Kemmis landowners of County Laois in 1876. In 2001, 4,152 acres of Ballincor were sold to Sir Robert Davis-Goff and his wife, Sheelagh, for a figure said to be around £10 million. The Davis-Goffs' ancestors were senior civil servants in the Government who came from Waterford, although the 1876 Return records no acreage in Waterford held by the family. The Goff-Davises have restored Ballincor House and run a shooting estate there. In 2001 the Earl started major renovations at Kilruddery, having retained the 800 acres there, according to the *Irish Times*. He appears in the *Sunday Times* Irish rich list on various occasion in the 2000s.

The overall estate raises links from the past that are very alive in the present. The Ballincor element of the estate goes back to the Mansergh family from Greenane in Tipperary, a descendent of which, Michael Masergh, was recently an Irish Senator and a critical player in the Northern Ireland peace talks. In the UK, a distant cousin of the Earl, Baron Brabazon of Tara, became an elected hereditary peer in 1999 and influential in internal committees of the House of Lords. The past is never quite as dead as it seems. It still shapes and lives in the present, in turn shaping the future.

Mrs Malton of 16 Great Cumberland Street, Hyde Park, London, had 18 acres in Dublin city in 1876, with a valuation of £667 about £56,028 in modern money. Mrs Isabella Malton makes it into Bateman, but not on her Dublin city acres. She owned 2,883 acres in County Meath and 847 acres in County Dublin, a total of 3,730 acres with a valuation of £5,793. Despite the expensive London address, there appears to be no further public record of this clearly quite wealthy lady. She does appear in the Failteromat listings of Dublin land/lease holders but without an address. This is an area where Griffith's should be able to provide both further pattern and detail to how a form of ownership was trickling into the population via leases. But there is not enough information yet, in a digestible form, to use easily.

Top 75 owners of land in Dublin City in 1876 ranked by acreage

Rank	Name and address	Acreage	GRV (£)	Equiv current (£)
1	Crown, The, -	142	26,813	2,252,292
2	Railway Company, Midland Gt Western, Broadstone, Dublin	82	3,570	299,880
3	Canal Company, James Street, Harbour, Dublin	62	1,787	150,108
4	Monck, Viscount, Charleville, Bray	58	1,604	134,736
5	Corporation of the City of Dublin, City Hall	55	19,483	1,636,572
6	Trustees of Richmond Lunatic Asylum, North Brunswick St	52	2,222	186,648
7	Dublin Port and Docks Board, Westmorland St	49	7,710	647,640
8	Cowper-Temple, The Hon. W., 17 Curzon St, London	38	1,426	119,784
9	Guinness, Sir Arthur, A.E. Bart and Co., 18 Lower Leeson St	37	5,115	429,660
10	Pembroke, Earl of, Wilton House	32	15,734	1,321,656
11	Railway Company, Dublin & Drogheda, Amiens St	31	1,693	142,212
12	Meath, Earl of, Kilruddery Castle, Bray, Co. Wicklow	28	1,785	149,940
13	Railway Company, Great Southern and Western, Kingsbridge	27	2,086	175,224
14	Trinity College, Dublin	21	6,882	578,080
15	Malton, Mrs, Great Cumberland St, Hyde Park, London	18	667	56,028
16	Local Government Board, Custom House	17	2,604	218,736
17	Railway Company, Dublin Wicklow & Wexford, Westland Row	16	4,845	406,980
18	Church Temporalities Commissioners, 24 Upper Merrion St	15	4,095	343,980
19	Church Representative Body, 52 St Stephen's Green East	14	6,008	504,672

Rank	Name and address	Acreage	GRV (£)	Equiv current (£)
20	Chancery Receivers in the Irish Court, -	11	4,278	359,352
21	Pim Brothers & Co, 75 to 80 St George's St	11	2,496	209,664
22	Kane, William J. & Son, 60 to 64 North Wall Quay	11	687	57,708
23	Courtenay, David C., 24 Fitzwilliam Place	10	634	53,256
24	Gas Company Alliance and Dublin Consumers, 114 Grafton St.	9	3,122	262,248
25	Society, Royal Dublin, Kildare St	8	2,500	210,000
26	Arnott, Sir John, 14 Henry Street, Dublin	8	2,030	170,520
27	Roe, George and Co., Thomas St	8	1,681	141,204
28	Trustees of Steven's Hospital, Steven's Lane	8	969	81,396
29	Guinness, Edward Cecil, 80 St Stephen's Green South	8	900	75,600
30	Bewley, Webb & Co., 15 East Wall	8	331	27,804
31	Jameson, Wm & Co., 43 Marrowbone Lane	7	947	79,548
32	Trustees of Swift's Hospital, Bow Lane	6	816	68,544
33	Bewley Moss & Co., 111 Great Brunswick St	6	600	50,400
34	Verschoyle, John James, Tapsaggard House	5	1,659	139,356
35	Governors of Rotunda Hospital, Rutland Square	5	1,525	128,100
36	Carroll, Sir William, 4 Upper Fitzwilliam St	5	1,231	103,404
37	Society Hon. King's Inns, Henrietta St	5	1,000	84,000
38	Railway Company, London and North Western, Euston Station, London	5	689	57,876
39	D'Arcy, John and Son, Anchor Brewery, 18 to 26 Bridgefoot Street	4	1,058	88,872

Rank	Name and address	Acreage	GRV (£)	Equiv current (£)
40	Trustees, Mater Misericordia Hospital, Berkeley Road	4	1,042	87,528
41	Curtin, Susan, Susan Villa, Crumlin	4	865	72,660
42	Manders, R. & Co., 114 James Street	4	696	58,464
42	Lemon, Graham, Yew Park, Clontarf, Co. Dublin	3	2,424	203,616
44	Munster, Bank Directors of, 9 Dame Street, Dublin	3	2,143	202,692
45	Corballis, John H., of Rosemount, Roebuck, Clonskea, Co. Dublin	3	1,419	119,196
46	Bowen, Charles H., Portarlington	3	1,240	104,160
47	Dombrain, Sir James Reps of, Woodstock, Sandford	3	1,092	91,728
48	Findlater, Alex, 30 and 31 Upper Sackville St	3	1,078	90,552
49	Brewery Company, Blackpits	3	546	45,864
50	Governors and Company of the Bank of Ireland, College Green	2	4,043	339,612
51	Williamson, Charles, 14 Upper Mount, St Dublin	2	1,657	139,188
52	Jervis-White-Jervis, Colonel H., 94 Piccadilly W	2	1,568	131,712
53	Clifden, Rt Hon. Viscount, Gowran Castle, Kilkenny	2	1,256	105,504
54	Jameson, John & Son, 49 & 50 Bow St	2	878	73,752
55	O'Connor, V. O'B Reps, Rockfield, Blackrock	2	809	67,956
56	Jameson, Pim & Co, North Anne St	2	760	63,840
57	Jebb, Robert, Killiney	2	733	61,572
58	Trustees of Simpsons's Hospital, Great Britain St	2	713	59,892
59	Lennon, William G., 81 Haddington Road, Dublin	2	662	55,608
60	Watkins, Joseph & Co., Ardee St, Dublin	2	662	55,608

Rank	Name and address	Acreage	GRV (£)	Equiv current (£)
61	Carysfort, Earl of, Glenart Castle, Arklow, Co. Wicklow	2	514	43,176
62	Tickell, George, 17 and 18 Mary St	1	1,326	113,904
63	Dawson, Colonel Robert Peel, Londonderry	1	1,319	110,796
64	Trumbull, Robert N., Beechwood, Malahide	1	1,004	84,336
65	Moses, Marcus, 5 Winton Road, Dublin	1	902	75,768
66	Lee, Robert, 2 Inns Quay	1	785	65,940
67	Lee, Rev. Sackville U.B., Bolton, Essex	1	744	62,496
68	Jackson, William H., 56 Mountjoy Square	1	715	60,060
69	Russell, William John, 66 Mountjoy Square	1	677	56,856
70	Cash, George R., 20 Waterloo Road	1	662	55,608
71	Walsh, Sir John Allen Johnston, Ballykilcavan, Queen's County	1	580	48,720
72	Clarke, Joshua, 13 Herbert St, Dublin	1	555	46,620
73	Burton, Rev. R.W., 52 Lansdown Road	1	535	44,940
74	Butler, Walter, 24 Rue de L'ermitage, Versailles, France	1	512	43,008
75	Barrington, Sir John, 202 Great Britain St	1	450	37,800

The 20 largest rental income streams in the City of Dublin in 1876

Rank	Name and Address	Acreage	GER (£)	Equiv current (£)
1	Crown, The, -	142	26,813	2,252,292
2	Corporation of the City of Dublin, City Hall	55	19,483	1,636,572
3	Pembroke, Earl of, Wilton House	32	15,734	1,321,656
4	Dublin Port and Docks Board, Westmorland St	49	7,710	647,640

Rank	Name and Address	Acreage	GER (£)	Equiv current (£)
5	Trinity College, Dublin	21	6,882	578,080
6	Church Representative Body, 52 St Stephen's Green East	14	6,008	504,672
7	Guinness, Sir Arthur, A.E. Bart and Co., 18 Lower Leeson St	37	5,115	429,660
8	Railway Company, Dublin Wicklow & Wexford, Westland Row	16	4,845	406,980
9	Chancery Receivers in the Irish Court, -	11	4,278	359,352
10	Church Temporalities Commissioners, 24 Upper Merrion St	15	4,095	343,980
11	Governors and Company of the Bank of Ireland, College Green	2	4,043	339,612
12	Railway Company, Midland Gt Western, Broadstone, Dublin	82	3,570	299,880
13	Gas Company alliance and Dublin Consumers, 114 Grafton St.	9	3,122	262,248
14	Local Government Board, Custom House	17	2,604	218,736
15	Society, Royal Dublin, Kildare St	8	2,500	210,000
16	Pim Brothers & Co., 75 to 80 St George's St	11	2,496	209,664
17	Lemon, Graham, Yew Park Clontarf Co., Dublin	3	2,424	203,616
18	Munster Bank, Directors of, 9 Dame Street, Dublin	3	2,143	202,692
19	Trustees of Richmond Lunatic Asylum, North Brunswick St	52	2,222	186,648
20	Railway Company, Great Southern and Western, Kingsbridge	27	2,086	175,224

COUNTY DUBLIN

	1876	2020 est
Population in County Dublin	156,936	745,457
All owners of land	1,574 (1871)	222,637
Percentage of the population	2.6	–
Owners of nothing at all	157,362	182,382
Percentage of the population	97.4	–
Size of County	217,457 acres (excl. city)	285,440 acres
Number of dwellings (of which rented in 1876 but owned in 2020)	28,858 (27,284) (1871)	259,406
Number of owned farm holdings	1.574 (1871)	798

County Comparisons

	Acreage 1876	Population 1876
Dublin County	217,457	156,936
Middlesex,★ England	143,014	253,197
Dunbartonshire, Scotland	153,736	58,857
Radnorshire, Wales	207,394	25,430

★ This county is chosen because it most closely resembles the relationship between the Irish capital Dublin, and the county it impinges on most closely, Dublin County. London has nowadays virtually swallowed up Middlesex.

Charles Cobbe of Newbridge House, Donabate, County Dublin, had 9,662 acres in County Dublin in 1876, with a valuation of £3,206 about £269,304 in modern money. The family start in Ireland was the commonplace one we have seen before, uniting clerical distinction, political connections, and the acquisition of large tracts of land. The first Cobbe was Thomas Cobbe, who became Archbishop of Dublin and Primate of All Ireland in 1743. He had previously been Lord Bishop of Killala, of Dromore and then of Kildare, getting his start as the chaplain to the then Lord Lieutenant of Ireland. As Archbishop of Dublin he was high in the Government of Ireland – no separation of Church and State then. He married a daughter of the Speaker of the Irish House of Commons, Sir Richard Levinge. Their son, Thomas, was a colonel in the militia, an MP, a justice of the peace and Deputy Lieutenant of the County. He married a daughter of

Marcus Beresford, 1st Earl of Tyrone, and sister of the Marquis of Waterford. Their son, Charles, became an MP and married a daughter of the 1st Earl of Clancarty. One of the sons became a general in the army, another a vicar, another a captain in the Royal Navy and one joined the East India Company.

The family were avid art collectors with a number of old masters and one of the only known portraits of William Shakespeare at Newbridge House. The Charles Cobbe in possession in 1876 was High Sheriff of County Dublin and County Louth. He had 9,948 acres in Co. Dublin and 1,419 acres in Co. Louth, a total of 11,367 acres with a valuation of £4,635.

Fingal Council bought the residue of the estate from the family in 1986, with rights of residence at Newbridge House granted to the family.

The Earl of Howth of Castle Howth had 7,377 acres in the county in 1876, with a valuation of £11,222 about £942,648 in modern money. This was one of the very ancient titles in the peerage of Ireland, created for the male head of the St Lawrence family around 1425. They were Catholics when it was unfashionable and even dangerous to be such. The Howth peers opposed Government taxation in the 1570s and, perhaps more importantly, opposed the penal laws designed to extinguish the Catholic faith in Ireland in the 1700s. The Irish Barony was elevated to an Earldom in 1767. The peer who held the estates in 1876 was MP for Galway and was made Baron Howth in 1881 in the peerage of the United Kingdom. He was educated at Eton and had, in addition to the Dublin acres, 2,061 acres in County Meath, a total of 9,438 acres with a valuation of £18,936. Many of the St Lawrence ancestors had been soldiers and he served in the 7th Hussars. All the titles became extinct when he died in 1909 but the estate passed to a female line of the family.

Sir Charles Compton Domville Bt, of Santry House, Santry, County Dublin had 6,262 acres in 1876, with a valuation of £10,177 about £854,868 in modern money. This is one of two Domville entries for Co. Dublin, the other being William C. Domville of Haywood Abbeyleix, in Queen's County. And Bateman finds another, 3rd Domville, with a Baronetcy, Sir Graham Domville Bart of Palermo with acreage in Kent, Herts and Lincoln.

The first Domville in Ireland of which there is a record was Gilbert Domville, who came over during the reign of James I (1603–25) and became Clerk of the Crown and Hanaper in the government of Ireland (a Hanaper was a clerk in the chancery court who looked after bills and writs from the public, and stored them in a wicker hamper – for a fee, often considerable). In a pattern that is now familiar, he married a daughter of the Lord Archbishop of Dublin Thomas Jones, who was also Lord Chancellor of Ireland and father of the 1st Viscount Ranelagh. Gilbert Domville's son became attorney general for Ireland in 1660, MP for

Dublin and a Privy Councillor. We now fast forward to the holder of the estate and the Baronetcy in 1876, the 2nd Baronet. He held, according to Bateman, 6,262 acres in the county with a valuation of £17,374. His cousin, William Compton Domville, of Thornhill, Co. Wicklow, held a further 9,066 acres, with a valuation of £4,876.

Santry House, a palatial construction, survived until 1947 when a fire damaged the structure beyond repair. The estate was still in the hands of the 4th and last Baronet when he died in 1935, and with him the title. The Irish state seems to have acquired the estate sometime after that, with parts of Ballymun as well.

Bateman makes a very important note on Sir Charles's estate. He says that: 'Sir C Domville's acreage is much larger as 11 of his biggest tenants are returned as owners of their holdings.' This is a pointer to potential 'inaccuracies' in the Returns themselves.

George Woods of Milverton Hall, Ballbriggan, County Dublin, held 4,141 acres in the county in 1876, with a valuation of £3,965 about £333,060 in modern money. Recalling that the Returns were drawn up for entries between 1872 and 1876 and that Bateman's 4th and final edition appeared in 1883, we have two major changes for this landowner. He was succeeded by his heir, Edward Hamilton Woods, of the same address, but the acreage had changed significantly. The acreage for Co. Dublin is down to 2,504 acres with a valuation of £3,269. There are 1,433 acres shown for Co. Meath, with a valuation of £1,860. The family were very active in local and Parliamentary politics from 1800 onwards. Some of the estate survived Irish independence and is still run by family descendants. Ferres gives an estimate of 467 acres for the modern estate, which was sited in one of the most heavily developed areas of Dublin during the so called 'Celtic Tiger Boom' (2003–08).

Sir Roger Palmer Bart of Kenure Park, Rush, had 3,991 acres in the county in 1876, with a valuation of £4,706 about £395,304 in modern money. This Eton-educated landowner, soldier and politician was one of the largest landowners in Ireland, with lesser holdings in English and Welsh counties. Bateman locates him at Keenagh, Crossmolina, Co. Mayo, in which county he had 80,990 acres, with a valuation of £14,625. In Sligo he had 9,570 acres, with a valuation of £1,229. In Dublin County he had 3,991 acres with a valuation of £4,706. He had 3,329 acres in Cambridge with a valuation of £4,338, in Denbigh he had 1,011 acres with a valuation of £1,357. In Flint he had 45 acres with a valuation of £114, in Dorest 11 acres with a valuation of £34 and in Berks 7 acres with a valuation of £258. His total acreage was 98,954 with a valuation of £26,661. He ranked as the forty-first largest landowner in the United Kingdom in 1876.

The Earl of Longford of Packenham Hall, Castlepollard, County Westmeath, had 420 acres in County Dublin in 1876 with a valuation of £31,713 about £2,663,892 in modern money. The valuation suggests Dublin City rather than Dublin County. It is inserted here, out of the acreage table sequence, because of the huge valuation, which made the Earl of Longford one of the richest landowners in Ireland in 1876. (*See* Westmeath entry)

Ion Trant Hamilton MP of Abbotstown House, Dublin, had 3,647 acres in Dublin in 1876, with a valuation of £6,788 about £570,192 in modern money. The Hamilton family, the Domville Family and the family of Luke White treated the Parliamentary seats in the locality as a form of alternative country sport to fox hunting, granting tenancies and buying votes over dinner, occasionally in pubs, in order to win seats. They were the earliest to feel the tide of nationalism rising around their ankles as far back as the early 1800s when the smallholders, many of them Catholics, started to agitate for better conditions, for both their religion and their livelihoods. But after Catholic emancipation in 1832, the tide abated a bit, though Daniel O'Connell's son appeared in the area to fight for a seat and was unsuccessful. Bateman sets out Hamilton's landholdings in full. Apart from the Dublin acreage, he had 2,245 acres in Queen's County, 751 acres in Co. Down and 246 acres in Co. Meath, totalling 6,889 acres with a valuation of £8,869.

Mrs White of Kilakee, Whitechurch, had 3,422 acres in County Dublin in 1876 with a valuation of £1,402 about £117,768 in modern money. There is no Bateman entry for this woman, but an inscription in the Whitchurch cemetery records probably lists her relatives:

> Sacred to the Memory of | Lieut. Colonel SAMUEL WHITE | of Killakee, County of Dublin | for many years | Member of Parliament for the County Leitrim | whoentered into glory, on the 29th of May 1854 | This Tablet is erected by his sorrowing widow | as a small token of affectionate remembrance of her | beloved and most excellent husband | to an amiable, endearing and affectionate disposition | he united the sterling characteristics of active benevolence, high principles and truly Christian piety | He was a most indulgent and considerate Landlord | His generosity was unbounded as it was noble | He was beloved and respected by all classes | and his loss is deeply mourned.

There is a Bateman 'below the main list' record for W.H. White of Kildera Leitrim, with 6,152 acres and a valuation of £2,292, enough to pay for a seat in Parliament in those days.

W.W. Hackett, of 36 Leeson Park, Dublin, had 3,198 acres in the county in 1876, with a valuation of £1,878 about £157,752 in modern money. There is no Bateman entry for this person. Bateman records a Colonel Hackett at Moor Park Tipperary and King's County with 3,700 acres and a valuation of £2,378.

The Coote Eyre representatives in the English Court of Chancery held 3,107 acres in trust in county Dublin in 1876, with a valuation of £2,830 about £237,720 in modern money. The huge Coote landholding was at Mountrath in Co. Laois (Queen's County) and these were almost certainly cousins of those Cootes.

They were based in County Limerick and employed a land agent based in Dublin to look after the estate. This short reference to an exchange in the House of Commons in 1880 is included here to illustrate the native Irish antipathy to both landlords in general and absentee landlords in particular.

Questions about the arrest of the Rev. Father Sheehy, and others in Kilmallock under the terms of the Peace Preservation Act, were raised in the House of Commons on 20 May 1881 and reported in Hansard. Comments about the land agent, William, are unfavourable; the:

> 'landlord had an agent named Townsend, and for the last 20 years his conduct had been most tyrannical to the tenantry on several properties round Kilmallock and Kilfinane. There was no opportunity that occurred, whether the death of a father or mother, or the marriage of a son, that he did not try to advance the rent, and the consequence was that the rents on the estates in many cases were double what they were 20 years ago. Another of his tenants had been served with notice to quit, so that between Mr. Coote and his agent, Townsend, the neighbourhood was unfortunately in a disturbed condition. The trouble had been brewing for many years, for there was no occasion that had not been taken advantage of to raise the rent, until at last the rents were beyond what the tenants could pay. Then they revolted against the agent'

This illustrates the nature of the land war occurring even as the Returns were being compiled built Parliament.

> There was in his neighbourhood, and in many other parts of County Limerick, a great many rack-rented tenants; but there was particularly, on one estate in that neighbourhood, the most rack-rented tenantry in any part of Ireland – that was on the estate of a man named Coote. It had been stated in that House that the purchasers in the Landed Estates Court were the greatest rack-renters; but this man was not a purchaser in the Landed Estates Court. He was one of the

real old Cromwellian settlers, and he was a man that rack-rented his tenantry more than any other landlord in the County Limerick. Writs were flying about on that estate for a half-year's and a year's rent. The tenants had paid their rents as long as they possibly could out of the little capital they bad; but in the bad years of 1878 and 1879 they were not able to pay these rack rents.

Robert Quin Alexander of Acton Poyntzpass, County Armagh, had 2,973 acres in County Dublin in 1876 with a valuation of £2,928 about £245,952 in modern money. There are no fewer than five Alexanders mentioned in Bateman, holding estates large enough to obtain an entry in his book of the great landowners. Robert Quin Alexander's acreage is given as 192 acres in Armagh, which, with the Dublin acreage gave him a total of 3,165 acres, with a valuation of £3,192. He was a magistrate on the Armagh bench. The current entry in the Armagh County Directory 1862 gives a very clear picture of how the entire public space, and all positions of authority, control and power, were held by landowners, but mainly by large estate owners. (www.libraryireland.com/Thom1862/Armagh.php)

Thom's *County Armagh Directory* for 1862 gives a description of the county and lists of office holders Messers *Alexander*, Acton and Armstrong.

The largest landowners of County Dublin by acreage in 1876

		Acreage	Valuation 1876 (£)3	Valuantion current (£)
1	Cobbe, Charles, Newbridge House, Donabate, Co. Dublin	9,662	3,206	269,304
2	Howth, Earl of, The Castle, Howth	7,377	11,222	942,648
3	Domville, Sir Charles Compton Bt, Santry House, Santry, Co. Dublin	6,262	10,177	854,868
4	Woods, George, Milverton Hall, Ballbriggan	4,141	3,965	333,060
5	Palmer, Sir Roger, Kenure Park, Rush	3,991	4,706	395,304
6	Hamilton, Ion Trant, Abbotstown, Castleknock, Co. Dublin	3,647	6,788	570,192
7	White, Mrs, Kilakee, Whitechurch	3,422	1,402	117,768
8	Hackett, W.W., 36 Leeson Park, Dublin	3,198	1,878	157,752

		Acreage	Valuation 1876 (£)3	Valuantion current (£)
9	Coote, Eyre Reps, English Court of Chancery	3,107	2,830	237,720
10	Alexander, R.Q., Poyntzpass, Acton, Co. Armagh	2,973	2,928	245,952
11	Pembroke, Earl of, Wilton House, Salisbury	2,269	19,852	1,667,568
12	Annally, Lord, Woodlands, Clonsilla	2,139	3,697	310,548
13	Lansdowne, Marquis of, Lansdown House, Berkeley Sq., London	2,132	3,182	267,288
14	Fitzsimon, Christopher O'Connell, Glencullen, Golden Ball	1,975	637	53,508
15	Governors of St Patrick's Hospital (Swifts), 24 Dame St, Dublin	1,953	1,963	164,892
16	Talbot de Malahide, The Castle, Malahide	1,893	3,908	328,272
17	Verner, Edward W., The Aske, Bray	1,752	661	55,524
18	De Robeck, Baron, Gowran Grange, Naas	1,660	2,098	176,232
19	Carysfort, Earl of, Glenart Castle, Arklow	1,586	13,110	1,101,240
20	Vesey, Charles C., Lucan House, Lucan	1,523	2,609	219,156
21	Domville, William C., Haywood, Abbyleix	1,513	1,819	152,796
22	Staples, Sir Nathaniel, Lissan, Cookstown, Co. Tyrone	1,457	1,416	118,944
23	Evans, George, Portrane House, Donabate	1,456	1,427	119,868
24	Kennedy, Sir Charles J., Johnstown, Rathcoole	1,447	1,183	99,372
25	Whitesed, Lady, Greystones, Delgany, Co. Wicklow	1,420	1,443	121,212
26	Gormanstown, Viscount, Gormanstown, Castle Balbriggan	1,327	1,337	112,308
27	Corporation of Dublin, City Hall, Dublin	1,265	3,338	280,392

County Dublin

		Acreage	Valuation 1876 (£)3	Valuantion current (£)
28	Trimleston, Lord 24 Park Lane, London	1,238	1,261	105,924
29	Caldbeck, Thomas Fulbeck, Eaton Brae, Loughlinstown	1,162	1,182	99,288
30	Connolly, Thomas, Castletown, Celbridge	1,152	2,982	250,488
31	Thompson, Captain Wm T., Hollywoodrath, Clogranhuddart	1,135	1,605	134,820
32	Hamilton v Hamilton In Chancery	1,107	2,796	234,864
33	Baker, Henry, Balheary, Swords	1,077	1,467	123,228
34	Hone, Nathaniel, St Dulough's Park	1,058	1,446	121,464
35	Pratt, Joseph Tynte, Tynte Park, Dunlavin	1,047	1,163	97,692
36	Shaw, Rt Hon. Sir Fredrick, Bushy Park, Ternure	996	2,974	249,816
37	Rochfort, Horace, Clogrennan, Carlow	972	1,397	117,348
38	Skerrott, Peter R., Athgoe Park, Rathcoole	969	1,179	99,036
39	Wills, John, Willsbrook, Lucan	949	1,476	123,984
40	Wakefield, Francis, Ashford, Co. Wicklow	929	815	68,460
41	Davies, Richard, Menai Bridge, Wales	921	620	52,080
42	Davies, Robert, Menai Bridge, Wales	921	620	52,080
43	Cloncurry, Lord, Lyons House, Hazelhatch	919	1,276	107,184
44	Digby, William R., Oldtown, Co. Dublin	919	779	65,436
45	Baker, Francis, Courtlough, Balbriggan	915	893	75,012
46	Verschoyle, John J., Tassaggart, Saggart	905	822	69,048
47	John, Bolton Massey, Kingstown	903	1,035	86,940
48	Guinness, Thomas, Tibradden	903	542	45,528
49	Kirkpatrick, Alexander, Coolmine, Castleknock	870	1,546	129,864

		Acreage	Valuation 1876 (£)3	Valuantion current (£)
50	Carrol, George, -	861	785	65,940
51	Malton, Mrs, England	827	2,911	244,524
52	Leathley, Forde, 3 Longford Tce, Kingstown, Co. Dublin	821	451	37,884
53	Clifden, Viscount, Gowarn Castle, Kilkenny	819	1,030	86,520
54	Taylor, Rt Hon. Thomas, Ardgillan, Castle Balbriggan	805	1,004	84,336
55	Leonard, John, 27 Rutland Sq., North Dublin	796	1,149	96,516
56	M'Donnell, Christopher, -	779	952	137,760
57	Sullivan, Rev. John, Leopardstown, Stillorgan	772	1,459	122,556
58	Radcliffee v Lee, In Chancery	765	727	61,068
59	Vernon, John E.V., Clontarf Castle, Clontarf	751	6,681	561,204
60	Grierson, Philip, Baldonnel, Saggart	740	980	82,320
61	Fitzsimon, Henry O'Connell, Mountseskin, Tallaght	715	261	21,924
62	La Touche, John, Harristown, Newbridge	706	849	71,316
63	Cowper-Temple, Rt Hon. Wm, 17 Curzon St, London	700	5,362	450,400
64	Knox, Colonel, -	698	651	54,684
65	Hutchinson, John Hely, Seafield House, Donabate	688	948	79,632
66	Lentaigne, John, 1 Great Denmark St, Dublin	636	1,112	93,408
67	Church Temporalities Commissioners, 24 Upper Merrion St, Dublin	615	1,494	125,495
68	Kennedy, Robert, Baronrath, Straffan	604	587	49,308
69	Baker, Henry Reps, Mallahon, Naul, Balbriggan	601	536	45,024
70	Hussey, Malachai S., Westown House, Naul, Balbriggan	600	661	55,524

		Acreage	Valuation 1876 (£)3	Valuantion current (£)
71	French-Brewster, R.A., 2 Merrion Sq., East Dublin (with William French)	599	741	62,244
72	Lewis, Henry O., Jenniskeen, Co. Monaghan	590	692	58,128
73	Dunne, General Fras Plunket, Brittas, Clonaslee, Queen's Co.	583	727	61,068
74	Robertson, John J., Gleedswood, Miltown	574	566	47,544
75	Segreve, O'Neill, Kyltymon, Newtownmountkennedy	570	1,536	129,024
76	Godley, John, Fonthill, Palmerston	562	854	71,736
77	Dwyer, Thomas, -	562	587	49,308
78	Molesworth, Rev. E., Rochdale, Lancashire	547	818	68,712
79	Jameson, James, Burrow, Malahide	514	321	26,964
80	O'Rourke, John, Jamestown	500	789	66,276
81	Kirk, Rev. J.E., Trelow Rectory, Wicksworth, Derbyshire England	494	435	36,540
82	Kennedy, Jas Marinus, 15 Lower Mount St	491	848	71,232
83	Aungier, Peter, Eccles Street, Dublin	491	542	45,528
84	Hyland, James K., 13 Rutland Sq., East Dublin	490	730	61,320
85	Gartlan, James, Mountjoy Sq., Dublin	489	529	44,436
86	Aungier, Charles, 17 Lower Dominick St, Dublin	484	446	37,464
87	Ely, Marquis of, Ely Castle, Enniskillen	460	281	23,604
88	Aungier, Robert, Kilshane, Finglass	450	548	46,032
89	Caulfield, Montgomery, Trafalgarter, Monkstown	437	718	60,312
90	Kelly, James, Castlebaggot, Rathcoole	433	605	50,820
91	Longford, Lord, Castlepollard, Co. Weestmeath	420	31,713	2,663,892

		Acreage	Valuation 1876 (£)3	Valuantion current (£)
92	Longford, Lord, Castlepollard, Co. Westmeath	420	31,713	2,663,892
93	Baker, Maria, Ballbriggan	381	521	43,764
94	Bagnal, George, 16 Suffolk St, Dublin	342	195	16,380
95	Railway Company, Dublin & Drogheda, Amiens St	304	13,941	1,171,044
96	Riall Phineas, Old Connaught, Bray	289	1,030	86,520
97	Bayly, Catherine, Tolka Lodge, Finglas	286	962	80,808
98	Abbot, John, Victoria Lodge, Roundwood	266	410	34,440
99	Railway Company, Midland Great Western, Broadstone	256	6,317	530,628
100	Railway Company, Dublin Wicklow and Wexford	223	22,606	1,898,904
101	M'Birney, David, 17 Astons Quay, Dublin.	219	1,640	137,760
102	Barrington, Mancliffe, Brennanstown, Cabintealy	200	348	29,232
103	Railway Company, Great Southern and Western, Kingsbridge	179	8,558	718,872
104	Railway Company, Dublin and Kingstown, Westland Row, Dublin	21	10,078	846,552
105	Gas Company and Alliance of Dublin Consumers, 114 Grafton St, Dublin	18	1,286	108,024
106	Murphy, Michael, Belvedere Place, Mountjoy Sq., Dublin	16	1,595	133,980
107	Ormsby Arthur, America	15	1,147	96,348
108	Railway Company, Dublin and Meath, Broadstone	9	53	4,452
109	Meade Michael, Aylesbury Rd, Merrion	6	1,018	85,512

Largest income from land in 1876 (30 to allow for the railways)

		Acreage	Valuation 1876 (£)	Valuation current (£)
1	Longford, Lord, Castlepollard, Co. Westmeath	420	31,713	2,663,892
2	Railway Company, Dublin, Wicklow and Wexford	223	22,606	1,898,904
3	Pembroke, Earl of, Wilton House, Salisbury	2,269	19,852	1,667,568
4	Railway Company, Dublin & Drogheda, Amiens St	304	13,941	1,171,044
5	Carysfort, Earl of, Glenart Castle, Arklow	1,586	13,110	1,101,240
6	Howth, Earl of, The Castle, Howth	7,377	11,222	942,648
7	Domville, Sir Charles Compton Bt, Santry House, Santry Co., Dublin	6,262	10,177	854,868
8	Railway Company, Dublin and Kingstown, Westland Row, Dublin	21	10,078	846,552
9	Railway Company, Great Southern and Western, Kingsbridge	179	8,558	718,872
10	Hamilton, Ion Trant, Abbotstown, Castleknock, Co. Dublin	3,647	6,788	570,192
11	Vernon, John E.V., Clontarf Castle, Clontarf	751	6,681	561,204
12	Railway Company, Midland Great Western, Broadstone	256	6,317	530,628
13	Cowper-Temple, Rt Hon. Wm, 17 Curzon St, London	700	5,362	450,400
14	Palmer, Sir Roger, Kenure Park, Rush	3,991	4,706	395,304
15	Woods, George, Milverton Hall, Ballbriggan	4,141	3,965	333,060
16	Talbot de Malahide, The Castle, Malahide	1,893	3,908	328,272
17	Annally, Lord, Woodlands, Clonsilla	2,139	3,697	310,548

		Acreage	Valuation 1876 (£)	Valuation current (£)
18	L(a)ongford, Lord, Summerhill, Co. Meath	3,659	3,472	291,648
19	Corporation of Dublin, City Hall, Dublin	1,265	3,338	280,392
20	Cobbe, Charles, Newbridge House, Donabate, Co, Dublin	9,662	3,206	269,304
21	Lansdowne, Marquis of, Lansdown House, Berkeley Sq., London	2,132	3,182	267,288
22	Connolly, Thomas, Castletown, Celbridge	1,152	2,982	250,488
23	Shaw, Rt Hon. Sir Fredrick, Bushy Park, Ternure	996	2,974	249,816
24	Alexander, R.Q., Poyntzpass, Acton, Co. Armagh	2,973	2,928	245,952
25	Malton, Mrs, England	827	2,911	244,524
26	Coote, Eyre Reps, English Court of Chancery	3,107	2,830	237,720
27	Hamilton v Hamilton In Chancery	1,107	2,796	234,864
28	Vesey, Charles C., Lucan House, Lucan	1,523	2,609	219,156
29	De Robeck, Baron, Gowran Grange, Naas	1,660	2,098	176,232
30	Governors of St Patrick's Hospital (Swifts), 24 Dame St, Dublin	1,953	1,963	164,892

FERMANAGH

	1876	2020 est
Population in County Fermanagh	92,688	61,805
All owners of land	697	-
Percentage of the population	0.75	-
Owners of nothing at all	91,991	Figures not available
Percentage of the population	99.25	-
Size of County	408,923 acres	414,080 acres
Number of dwellings (of which rented in 1876, owned in 2020)	17,516 (16,819)	-
Number of owned farm holdings	697	2,910

County comparison

	Acreage 1876	Population 1876
County Fermanagh	408,932	92,688
Worcestershire, England	441,061	338,837
Banffshire, Scotland	407,501	62,032
Cardiganshire, Wales	391,685	73,441

The Marquis of Ely, of Ely Lodge, Enniskillen, had 34,879 acres in 1876, with a valuation of £13,983 about £1,174,572 in modern money. The Marquis of Ely, a title that continues, was one of the behemoths of landowning in Ireland in 1876. His 15,000 acres in Wexford were well outclassed by the 34,000 acres at his seat, Ely Lodge, in Fermanagh. The *Ulster Historian* identifies the Wexford acres as part of a family nexus of landholdings involving mainly three families, those of Tottenham, Loftus and Ogle, all of whom are represented in the 1876 Return and are the result of the Elizabethan and Cromwellian settlements.

The current 9th Marquis of Ely, who lives in Canada, traces his ancestry in Debrett's back to an MP in New Ross in the 1770s called John Tottenham. The *Ulster Historian* more accurately traces the line back to the Elizabethan Archbishop of Dublin and Armagh, Adam Loftus. Among other things, Archbishop Loftus arranged the torture and execution of the Archbishop of Cashel, Dermot O'Hurley, against whom judges had found no case. He also accumulated land and benefits on a non-Christian scale and at the expense of Irish Catholic landowners.

What is clear from the *Ulster Historian*, is that, while this was about money, which is not much mentioned directly, it was more centrally about power:

> Their [the Loftus-Tottenham] power was concentrated in Co. Wexford, which returned 18 MPs, (to the Irish House of Commons) and they returned at least nine: six for the boroughs of Bannow, Clonmines and Fethard, one for Wexford town, one for New Ross and one for the county.

The title is an Irish peerage and the 8th Marquis sat in the House of Lords as Baron Loftus of Long Loftus in the county of York. It was a title his ancestor obtained in 1801, the year after the Act of Union, conveniently replacing the seat he lost in the Irish House of Lords with a seat in the British Parliament.

Meanwhile, here is what was happening to some of his tenants (from *Being Poor in Modern Europe* by Inga Brandes, published by Peter Lang in 2006).

> When some of Ely's tenants were evicted in 1886 and entered the Work House at New Ross they were given special treatment by the local board of Guardians. The Local Government Board objected to this but got the following reply from the Guardians. 'We have refused to treat persons who have been rendered homeless and destitute by the tyranny of a brainless agent as ordinary paupers.'

The administrative chain of irresponsibility was a lengthy one, starting with the lack of secure tenancies, a situation that Ely was responsible for on two counts, first as a particular landlord and then as a political one who failed to reform the laws that enabled him to legally dump his tenants 'at will'. And to do it second hand, via an agent. The inhumanity of bureaucracy, which should never be underestimated, then intervened to ensure that everyone in the workhouse was treated in the same inhumane way. 'It was,' they said, 'the law.' It usually is.

In 1948 the family were mainly living in Loftus Hall in Wexford. The Marquis sold Ely Lodge and some, if not all of the estate, to Lieutenant Colonel George Grosvenor, who later inherited the Westminster Dukedom as the 5th Duke. His son, Gerald, became the 6th Duke and he died in 2017. The 6th Duke's mother, the Lord Lieutenant of Fermanagh and a daughter of the Earl of Erne, was killed in a car crash in 1987. Ferres tells us that her agent, Charles Plunkett, inherited the estate and sold it privately in 1994.

The Earl of Erne, of Crom Castle, Newtownbutler, had 31,389 acres in Fermanagh in 1876, with a valuation of £17,039 about £1,431,276 in modern money. This title is still extant and the holder, John Henry Michael Ninian Crichton, the 7th Earl, gives his seat as Crom Castle but lives in London. His ancestor in 1876, the 3rd Earl, had, with the Fermanagh acreage, 4,826 acres in Donegal, 2,184 acres in County Mayo and 1,966 acres in Sligo to give a total acreage of 40,365, with a valuation of £23,850. He was the Lord Lieutenant of Fermanagh and he was created Baron Fermanagh in the peerage of the United Kingdom in 1872. The 1,900 acres residue of the estate was given to the National Trust in 1987 and the last master of Crom Castle, the 6th Earl, died in 2015. The estate records are held at the Public Record Office of Northern Ireland. By 1909 the various land acts had caught up with the estate and the 4th Earl, and he sold most of the Fermanagh acreage to the tenants, raising close to £250,000. The Sligo and Donegal estates were sold around 1905. During the Second World War the residual estate was in the hands of trustees and was rented to the armed forces, including those of the USA. The trustees are reported to have made a profit. More recently the castle was used as a film location for the BBC *Blandings* series.

The Earl of Enniskillen of Florence Court, Enniskillen, had 29,635 acres in the county in 1876, with a valuation of £18,795 about £1,578,780 in modern money. This title still exists and is held by Andrew John Galbraith Cole, the 7th Earl, who lives on a 40,000-acre estate at Lake Naivasha in Kenya. He has clearly improved on the ancestral acreage by a considerable amount. He was educated at Eton and was a captain in the Irish Guards. His ancestor in 1876, the 3rd Earl, was a noted palaeontologist and was elected a Fellow of the Royal Society. He also sat as Conservative MP for Fermanagh. The 3rd Earl had, with the Fermanagh acreage, 569 acres in Wiltshire, a total estate of 30,204 acres with a valuation of £19,290.

Florence Court is now a National Trust property. The 6th Earl and his wife lived there until 1972, when they moved to Scotland.

Sir Victor Alexander Brooke Bart of Colebrook, County Fermanagh, had 27,994 acres in the county in 1876, with a valuation of £13,288 about £1,116,192 in modern money. This estate is an ancient one, acquired by Sir Basil Brooke, described as a 'captain in the English army in Ireland who was Governor of County Donegal'. His dates are Elizabethan and it can be assumed he was there to enforce that plantation. His son, Sir Henry Brook, who was granted the lands at Colebrook, succeeded his father as governor of Donegal and became an MP in the Irish Parliament. Official recognition by way of honours was slow to come, with the Baronetcy only being created in 1822, despite members of the family having sat as MPs for both Dundalk and Fermanagh.

The holder of the estate in 1876 was the 3rd Baronet, Sir Victor. Bateman mentions only that he was educated at Harrow. The entire family holding was at Colebrook. The 5th Baronet, a prominent politician and Prime Minister of Northern Ireland from 1943 to 1963, was elevated to the peerage as Viscount Brookborough in 1952. That peerage is still extant and is held by Alan Henry

Brooke, the 3rd Viscount, who lives in London but does give the family seat as Colebrook.

In 1946 Winston Churchill's wartime Chief of the Imperial General Staff, Field Marshal Sir Alan Brooke, was created a Viscount. At the time of writing that peerage was still extant and was held by Alan Victor Harold Brooke. The 1st Viscount's statue looks across Whitehall towards No. 10 Downing St, alongside statues of the other wartime British military leaders, Field Marshal Viscount Montgomery and Field Marshal Viscount Slim, both with links to Ulster. It is a peculiarly Irish triumvirate of English military heros.

Mervyn Edward Archdale (Archdall) MP of Castle Archdale, Enniskillen, held 27,410 acres in Fermanagh in 1876, with a valuation of £13,517 about £1,135,428 in modern money. This cavalry officer, who served in the Inniskilling Dragoons, was MP for Fermanagh. He had, as well as the Fermanagh acres, 5,605 acres in Tyrone for a total estate of 33,015 acres, with a valuation of £16,991.

In the History of Parliament record he is referred to as Archdall. Stephen Farrell, in that history, records that: 'Five members of the family, over four generations, therefore provided representatives for the county in an unbroken run of 154 years, which is thought to be a unique record (at least, in relation to Ireland).'

At number sixteen in the list of Fermanagh landowners is Mervyn Edward's cousin, William Humphrey Archdale (Archdall). He had 5,627 acres in the county with a valuation of £3,182. Bateman records a correction from Archdall, that his acreage was stated: 'Exclusive of a large amount of land on perpetual leases, which appear in tenants' names.'

Put another way, these cousins held between 35,000 and 40,000 acres of Fermanagh in 1876. They had an estate in the county that was almost certainly larger than their aristocratic neighbour, the Marquis of Ely.

The estate included parts of Lough Erne and was used as a flying boat base by the RAF during the Battle of the Atlantic in the Second World War. The RAF held on to the site until 1957. Sometime after that the NI Government acquired the estate, which is now a country park. Some of the estate may have been sold off via the Land Commission in 1906 or thereabouts.

John Madden of Roslea, County Fermanagh, had 14,074 acres in the county in 1876, with a valuation of £7,323 about £615,132 in modern money. By the time of Bateman's 4th and final edition in 1883, Madden, who had been an infantry officer in the 41st Regiment of Foot in First Anglo-Afghan War, had corrected the estate downwards to 10,498 acres, with a valuation of £4,076. He also held 628 acres in Monaghan, giving him a total estate of 11,126 acres. He was educated at Harrow. He was High Sheriff of the County in 1848. The descendants moved to Hilton Park and now live there, according to Ferres.

His cousin, also John Madden, educated at Eton, had 4,644 acres in Monaghan at Hilton Park near Clones, and 3,549 acres in Leitrim, a total estate of 8,193 acres, with a valuation of £4,867. This cousinhood had over 20,000 acres in the Fermanagh–Monaghan–Leitrim area, a huge concentration of ownership.

The family emigrated to New Zealand, where the last male of the line died in 2009. The estate papers are at the Northern Ireland Public Records Office.

Colonel John Gerard Irvine of Killadeas, Enniskillen, had 11,388 acres in the county in 1876, with a valuation of £5,476 about £459,984 in modern money. This soldier's ancestor had fought in the American War of Independence against the rebels. By 1876 John Gerard Irvine was Colonel Commanding the 3rd Battalion, the Royal Inniskilling Fusiliers. He was a Deputy Lieutenant of the County and a justice of the peace. His eldest son married a daughter of Captain Mervyn Archdale (*see* below). The house was requisitioned during the Second World War as a base for American forces and is still a hotel overlooking lower Lough Erne.

In 1876 John Gerard Irvine had, along with the Fermanagh acres, 2,033 acres in Tyrone, 9 acres in Monaghan and 470 acres in County Louth, for a total of 14,114 acres with a valuation of £6,806.

The representatives of the Rev. John Grey Porter, of Belleisle, Enniskillen, held 11,880 acres in the county in 1876, with a valuation of £5,166 about £433,944 in modern money. In Bateman the owner is recorded as John Grey Vesey, of Belleisle, Enniskillen, the son of the Rev. John Porter. Here is Bateman's account: 'The bulk of these estates is given in the Return to Reps of Rev. J. G. Porter, his father. Mr Porter only shows his ownership of 5,160 acres in Fermanagh, and a half share in 28 small farms with his sister.'

That said, Bateman then records John Porter, along with the Fermanagh acres, holding 5,024 acres in Co. Longford and 4,756 acres in Tyrone for a total of 21,660 acres with a valuation of £10,512. No mean estate.

This estate was first acquired around 1797 by the Regius Professor of Hebrew at Cambridge, the Rev. John Porter DD, who, via a stint at the Vice Regal lodge, became Bishop of Clogher, via the Bishopric of Killala. Most of the records spell Belle Isle as two words. The Bishop's sons fared well, one becoming a general in the Army and another a captain in the Royal Navy. In 1991 the owner of the estate was Lavinia Baird, who sold it to the Duke of Abercorn. (*See* County Tyrone)

The Church Temporality Commissioners in Dublin held 10,357 acres in Fermanagh in 1876, with a valuation of £6,341 about £532,644 in

modern money. For the Church Temporality Commissioners, *see* County Dublin. The estate in Fermanagh was one of the larger in the commissioners' portfolio and no address is given.

Hugh De Fellenberg Montgomery of Blessingbourne, Fivemiletown, County Tyrone, had 7,996 acres in Fermanagh in 1876, with a valuation of £2,441 about £205,044 in modern money. This was another estate founded by military and uniformed clergy acquisitive for land in Ireland. The first lands were acquired by Hugh Montgomery, with assistance from his cousin, the Rt Rev. George Montgomery, the Bishop of Clogher. A son of the family was a captain in William of Orange's army.

The holder of the estate in 1876 was Captain, The Rt Hon. Hugh De Fellenberg Montgomery, of Blessingbourne, who was High Sheriff of Fermanagh and of Tyrone and a captain in the Fermanagh Militia. He was married to daughter of the Rector of Enniskillen, thus maintaining both the clerical and military tradition in the family.

He had, with the Fermanagh acres, 4,552 acres in Tyrone, for a total estate of 12,548 acres. The estate is still in the family, with self-catering apartments at Blessington House. The De Fellenberg element of the name comes from Switzerland, where the holder was a Landsman of the Republic of Berne and whose daughter married Hugh Montgomery in 1843.

The landowners of over 1,000 acres in 1876

Fermanagh, that land of small and well stocked lakes, Ireland's own little Finland, 'pivoted' around three enormous estates and their owners in 1876. These were the 34,879-acre estate of the Marquis of Ely at Ely Lodge near Enniskillen, producing £13,983 in rents.

Next came the 29,635-acre estate of the Earl of Enniskillen, at Florence Court, also near Enniskillen and producing £18,795 in rentals. Finally there is the estate of the Earl of Erne with 31,389 acres at Crom Castle, yielding £17,039 in rentals. This last estate, like the other two, was sited close to Enniskillen.

Thirty per cent of the land of Fermanagh is water covered, mostly in the form of lakes, the largest of which is Lough Erne.

The 20 largest landowners in County Fermanagh in 1876 by acreage

		Acreage	Valuation 1976 (£)	Valuation current (£)
1	Ely, Marquis of, Ely Lodge, Enniskillen	34,879	13,983	1,174,572
2	Erne, Earl of	31,389	17,039	1,431,276
3	Enniskillen, Earl of, Florence Court, Enniskillen	29,635	18,795	1,578,780
4	Brooke, Sir Victor, Colebrook Park, Brookboro	27,994	13,288	1,116,192
5	Archdall, Mervyn, Castle Archdall, Enniskillen	27,410	13,517	1,135,428
6	Madden, John, Roslea Manor, Roslea	14,074	7,323	615,132
7	Irvine, John Gerard, Killadeas, Enniskillen	11,388	5,476	459,984
8	Porter, Rev. John Grey Reps of, Dublin	11,015	5,166	433,944
9	Church Temporalities Commissioners, Dublin	10,357	6,341	532,644
10	Montgomery, Hugh De Fellenberg, Fivemiletown	7,996	2,441	205,044
11	Lanesboro, Earl of, Lanesborough Lodge, Belturbet	6,606	5,339	448,476
12	Hall, Richard, 9 Norfolk St, Park Lane, London	6,540	2,407	202,188
13	Irvine, H.M. D'Arcy, Castleirvine, Irvinestown	6,187	5,547	465,984
14	Collum, John, Belleview, Enniskillen	5,945	4,555	382,620
15	Commissioners of Education, Dublin	5,656	3,032	254,688
16	Archdall, William, Riversdale, Ballycastle	5,627	3,122	262,248
17	Bryan, John D., Castletown, Monea	5,085	1,894	159,096
18	Belmore, Earl of, Castlecoole	4,990	3,429	288,036
19	Johnston, Robert E., Maheramena, Belleek	4,891	1,845	154,980
20	Bloomfield, J.C., Castlecaldwell, Bellek	4,865	2,342	196,728

The 20 richest landowners in County Fermanagh in 1876 by rental valuation

		Acreage	Valuation 1876 (£)	Valuation 2017 (£)
1	Enniskillen, Earl of, Florence Court, Enniskillen	29,635	18,795	1,578,780
2	Erne, Earl of	31,389	17,039	1,431,276
3	Ely, Marquis of, Ely Lodge, Enniskillen	34,879	13,983	1,174,572
4	Archdall, Mervyn, Castle Archdall, Enniskillen	27,410	13,517	1,135,428
5	Brook, Sir Victor, Colebrook Park, Brookboro	27,994	13,288	1,116,192
6	Madden, John, Roslea Manor, Roslea	14,074	7,323	615,132
7	Church Temporalities Commissioners, Dublin	10,357	6,341	532,644
8	Irvine, H.M. D'Arcy, Castleirvine, Irvinestown	6,187	5,547	465,984
9	Irvine, John Gerard, Killadeas, Enniskillen	11,388	5,476	459,984
10	Lanesboro, Earl of, Lanesborough Lodge, Belturbet	6,606	5,339	448,476
11	Porter, Rev. John Grey Reps of, Dublin	11,015	5,166	433,944
12	Collum, John, Belleview, Enniskillen	5,945	4,555	382,620
13	Belmore, Earl of, Castlecoole	4,990	3,429	288,036
14	Archdall, William, Riversdale, Ballycastle	5,627	3,122	262,248
15	Commissioners of Education, Dublin	5,656	3,032	254,688
16	Rathdonell, Lord, Drumcar	3,751	2,683	225,372
17	Montgomery, Hugh De Fellenberg, Fivemiletown	7,996	2,441	205,044
18	Hall Richard, 9 Norfolk St, Park Lane, London	6,540	2,407	202,188
19	Bloomfield, J.C., Castlecaldwell, Bellek	4,865	2,342	196,728
20	Singleton, Thomas, Fortsingleton, Co. Monaghan	3,216	1,971	165,564

Master list by acreage. All owners of over 1,000 acres

		Acreage	Valuation 1876 (£)	Valuation current (£)
1	Ely, Marquis of, Ely Lodge, Enniskillen	34,879	13,983	1,174,572
2	Erne, Earl of	31,389	17,039	1,431,276
3	Enniskillen, Earl of, Florence Court, Enniskillen	29,635	18,795	1,578,780
4	Brook, Sir Victor, Colebrook Park, Brookboro	27,994	13,288	1,116,192
5	Archdall, Mervyn, Castle Archdall, Enniskillen	27,410	13,517	1,135,428
6	Madden, John, Roslea Manor, Roslea	14,074	7,323	615,132
7	Irvine, John Gerard, Killadeas, Enniskillen	11,388	5,476	459,984
8	Porter, Rev. John Grey Reps of, Dublin	11,015	5,166	433,944
9	Church Temporalities Commissioners, Dublin	10,357	6,341	532,644
10	Montgomery, Hugh De Fellenberg, Fivemiletown	7,996	2,441	205,044
11	Lanesboro, Earl of, Lanesborough Lodge, Belturbet	6,606	5,339	448,476
12	Hall, Richard, 9 Norfolk St, Park Lane, London	6,540	2,407	202,188
13	Irvine, H.M. D'Arcy, Castleirvine, Irvinestown	6,187	5,547	465,984
14	Collum, John, Belleview, Enniskillen	5,945	4,555	382,620
15	Commissioners of Education, Dublin	5,656	3,032	254,688
16	Archdall, William, Riversdale, Ballycastle	5,627	3,122	262,248
17	Bryan, John D., Castletown, Monea	5,085	1,894	159,096
18	Belmore, Earl of, Castlecoole	4,990	3,429	288,036
19	Johnston, Robert E., Maheramena, Belleek	4,891	1,845	154,980
20	Bloomfield, J.C., Castlecaldwell, Bellek	4,865	2,342	196,728

		Acreage	Valuation 1876 (£)	Valuation current (£)
21	Rathdonell, Lord, Drumcar	3,751	2,683	225,372
22	Hamilton, Jones Thomas M., Moneyglass House, Toome	3,690	1,428	119,952
23	Collins, Eleanor, Ardbracken, Co. Meath	3,670	1,263	106,092
24	Richards, John W., Belmullet	3,219	1,093	91,812
25	Singleton, Thomas, Fortsingleton, Co. Monaghan	3,216	1,971	165,564
26	Governors of Vaughan's Charity, Tubbrid School, Kesh	3,190	1,898	159,432
27	L'Estrange, Carleton, Dublin	2,886	842	70,728
28	Irvine, Edward, Reps of, Derrygore, Enniskillen	2,697	1,888	158,592
29	Barton, Edward, Clonelly	2,659	1,634	137,256
30	Dixon, Mrs and others, -	2,416	1,404	117,936
31	Tennant, Sir William Emerson, Tempo House	2,408	1,461	122,724
32	Denny, Sarah Jane, Cheltenham, England	2,353	1,732	145,488
33	Johnston, Robert E. reps of, Magheramena, Belleek	2,266	1,040	87,360
34	Richardson, Henry Mervyn, Rossfad, Ballycassidy	1,852	1,143	96,012
35	Graham, Francis J., Drumgoon, Maguires Bridge	1,845	1,087	91,308
36	Armstrong, Thomas, England	1,735	930	78,120
37	Hurst, George, Drumderg, Tempo	1,663	805	67,620
38	Brady, John, Johnstown	1,659	1,128	94,752
39	Ogle, Francis H. & Selina, Newry	1,617	178	14,952
40	Barton, C.R., Mount Prospect, Kinlough	1,591	664	55,756
41	Collum, Robert, London	1,543	1,160	97,440
42	Clarke, Rev. William Hall, Dublin	1,494	795	66,780
43	Erck, Wentworth, Dublin	1,403	768	64,512
44	Tredennick, John A., Camlin Castle, Ballshannon	1,375	467	39,228
45	Bracken, James, Toam, Blacklion	1,268	373	31,332
46	L'Estrange, Christopher, Sligo	1,252	58	4,872

		Acreage	Valuation 1876 (£)	Valuation current (£)
47	Richardson, John, Summerhill	1,154	908	76,272
48	D'Arcy, Francis, Castle Irvine, Irvinestown	1,108	538	45,192
49	Gledstanes, Mountray, Fardross, Clogher	1,107	890	74,760
50	Lendrum, James, Magheracross, Ballinamallard	1,067	613	51,492
51	Mayne Robert, Dublin	1,067	302	25,368
52	Blackley Captain, -	1,017	529	44,436

GALWAY

INCLUDING THE COUNTY OF THE TOWN

	1876	2020 est
Population in County Galway	248,458 (city 19,843, county 228,615)	250,653 (city and county CSO figures)
All owners of land	1,767	143,266
Percentage of the population	0.71	–
Owners of nothing at all	246,691	75,283
Percentage of the population	99.29	–
Size of County	1,483,367 acres	1,503,360 acres
Number of dwellings (of which rented in 1876, owned in 2020)	45,564 (43,797)	88,341
Number of owned farm holdings	1,767	13,445

County comparison

	Acreage 1876	Population 1836
County Galway	1,483,367	248,458
Devon, England	1,516,981	601,374
Perthshire, Scotland	1,612,840	147,768

Richard Berridge of Clifden Castle, Connemara, Galway, had 159,898 acres in the county in 1876, with a valuation of £6,321 about £530,964 in modern money. This is an unusual estate with an interesting history. Its owner in the late part of the eighteenth century was Richard 'Humanity' Martin MP, the founder of the SPCA, later the RSPCA. By 1800 it was the biggest estate in Ireland with Martin bragging to his pal, the Prince of Wales, later George IV, that he had 'an approach from my gatehouse to my hall of 30 miles length'. (Ferres)

Martin's wife was alleged to have had a child by the tutor hired to educate their son, Theobald Wolfe Tone. Richard Martin died in 1834 and left the vast estate to his granddaughter, Mary Martin. It was heavily mortgaged then, a result of his expenses keeping up his position as an MP. In 1831 Martin borrowed £42,000, about £3.5 million nowadays, and there were charges on the estate of over £94,000 in 1841. Those debts and the Great Famine finished off the estate, which was sold in the Encumbered Estate Court to Richard Berridge, a brewer from London, via the Law Life Assurance Society in 1872.

Bateman records Berridge as the largest landowner in Ireland, with, in addition to the Galway acres, 9,965 acres in Mayo, 321 acres in Middlesex and 79 acres in Kent, a total of 170,517 acres, with a valuation of £9,503. Richard Berridge was the sixteenth largest landowner in Great Britain in 1876.

The Galway estate was purchased for sporting purposes and the Berridges built a number of fishing lodges, including those at Inagh, Fermoyle and Screebe. The estate remained in the family's possession for only two generations. Over 70,000 acres was vested in the Congested Districts' Board on 31 March 1915. Some fishing rights were retained by the family until recently.

The Marquis of Clanricarde of Portumna Castle, Galway, had 49,025 acres in the county in 1876, with a valuation of £19,634 about £1,649,256 in modern money. In theory this should have been one of the greatest Irish titles of them all – an ancestry in the mists of time, going back to the Norman invasion of England in 1066 and then the Norman invasion of Ireland in 1169. Vast estates, high titles of all sorts, the only one missing; a Dukedom.

Nonetheless, the holder's son, the 2nd Marquis, was subject to one of the most unusual bills ever passed in the House of Commons. The bill was for the expropriation of Clanricarde's estates on the grounds of his misconduct towards his tenants. It was proposed by the Irish nationalist members of Parliament but had the support of Campbell Bannerman, the Prime Minister. Here is a brief account of the debate:

> Never had Clanricarde visited his estates, despite the many thousands of families that had been evicted from them during that time, resulting in mass destitution. So universal is the execration in which this particular nobleman is held by people of every political party that when the question of this bill was put to the vote by the speaker, liberals, liberal unionists and conservatives all voted with the Irish party, only three of the nearly 700 members of the house of Commons opposing the vote, which would otherwise have been unanimous.

The Marquis, a recluse living in London, fought efforts to evict him from his estates until 1915, when the Congested Districts Board finally obtained possession. The Marquis died the following year, and the Marquisate with him. The Earldom attached to the Marquisate passed to the Marquis of Sligo.

There is an excellent synopsis of the life of the 1st Marquis in the John Joseph Conwell book *A Galway Landlord during the Great Famine* available from the Irish Workhouse Centre in Galway.

It nicely illustrates the key theme in this book, that it is the system that needs investigation, not the good or bad individuals who used or abused the system. The 1st Marquis was married to the daughter of George Canning, the former Foreign Secretary and Prime Minister, and held a number of government posts. Many of the proposals he made were logical and reasonable. What was neither reasonable nor logical was his approach to his tenants, who were evicted, at times in the cruellest of circumstances. His son followed in his footsteps, clearly.

Lord Dunsandle and Clanconal of Dunsandle, Loughrea, had 33,543 acres in the county in 1836, with a valuation of £11,860 about £996,240 in modern money. Bateman credits Lord Dunsandle (Daly) with 3,514 acres in Tipperary, which, added to his Galway holdings, gave him a total acreage of 37,057 acres, with a valuation of £17,193. He was an officer in the 11th Light Dragoons.

The Daly family of Dunsandle derived from Daly of Carnakelly in the parish of Kiltullagh. They bought the Dunsandle estate from the Clanricarde family in 1708. By the 1870s they owned one of the largest estates in Co. Galway, amounting to over 33,000 acres, and wielded considerable political power throughout the eighteenth and nineteenth centuries. Denis Daly had married Henrietta Maxwell, heiress of the Earl of Farnham (*see* Cavan) in the late eighteenth century. They acquired an estate in Tipperary including much of the town of Thurles. The Rev. Robert Daly, son of Denis Daly, MP, served as Church of Ireland Bishop of Cashel and Waterford in 1843–72. Lord Dunsandle accepted an offer on over 1,500 acres of his estate from the Congested Districts Board after 1909. (From the NUI Galway Estates Database)

Allan Pollock of Lismany, Ballinasloe, had 29,366 acres in the county in 1876, with a valuation of £12,727 about £1,069,068 in modern money. By the time we get to Bateman in 1883 this estate is in the hands of John Broom Pollock, Allan Pollock's son, a Scottish businessman who had 211 acres in Dublin, 3,761 acres in Renfrew, 5,046 acres in Argyll, 702 acres in Ayr and 50 acres in Lanark, a total estate, with the Galway lands, of 39,136 acres. The valuation was £18,536.

There is a good deal about the intervention of Allan Pollock in East Galway in *The Parish of Clontuskert: Glimpses into its Past* by the Clontuskert Heritage Group (available on their website).

Between 1853 and 1858 Allan Pollock, using wealth accumulated in the shipping, timber and mining business, bought over 25,000 acres in Galway and Roscommon, paying £212,460 for the land. His plans, while theoretically sensible, backfired from the beginning.

Pollock failed to understand either the rapidly developing political situation in Ireland, in which tenants were demanding ownership of their land, or his plans, which were to convert tenants into labourers on his ranch-style estate and to evict those who wouldn't accept his terms. It was a classic clearance operation, based on the implicit theory that the famine had removed or killed off enough people to make ranch farming such as Pollock's viable. The irony is that this was a collision between two forms of capitalism; the monopoly, abusive reductionist kind imposed by Pollock because he had the money to do it, and the small-scale private capitalism of the sitting tenants, who wanted to own their own land, as any good capitalist would. Pollock found himself abused publicly in Parliament over the way he treated his tenants, namely because he was evicting so many of them. He didn't understand. He just thought he was being a good businessman. His actual technical operation of the farms themselves, on the other hand, drew much public praise.

Eventually the estate was taken over in 1911 under the Wyndham Act of 1903 and sold to the tenants, as were most other estates in the west of Ireland. There is an excellent paper by Tom Tonge on the subject titled *The Impact of the Wyndham Land Act 1903 on County Galway* at eprints.maynoothuniversity.ie/5077/1/Tom_Tonge_20140620152731.pdf

Lord Clonbrock of Clonbrock, Ahascragh, County Galway, had 28,246 acres in the county in 1876, with a valuation of £11,442 about £961,128 in modern money. The NUI Galway Estates Database tells us that:

> The Dillons (the family name of the Clonbrock peerage) were a Norman family who initially received grants of land in Westmeath and who later acquired properties in neighbouring counties including Roscommon and Galway. Some land was offered for sale in the Encumbered Estates court in July 1854. In 1906 Lord Clonbrock held over 2000 acres of untenanted land and the mansion house at Clonbrock.

Sir Thomas J. Burke of Marble Hill, Loughrea, had 25,258 acres in the county in 1876, with a valuation of £7,564 about £635,376 in modern money. The family were soldiers and the holder in 1876, Sir Thomas, was the son of the MP for Galway County for many years.

They were a keen horse racing family and their cup is still raced for at the Curragh. The title is extant and the holder, Sir James Stanley Gilbert Burke, the 9th Baronet, lives in Switzerland. Sir Henry Burke of Marble Hill, near Loughrea, sold his estate in 1908. The estate, by then smaller by over 10,000 acres, at 14,716 acres, was distributed among 615 tenants.

The Earl of Clancarty of Garbally, Ballinasloe, had 23,896 acres in the county in 1876, with a valuation of £11,724 about £984,816 in modern money. This title still exists and is held by Nicholas Power Richard Le Poer Trench, the 9th Earl, who is also the Marquis of Heusden in the Netherlands. He sits in the House of Lords as an elected hereditary peer under his UK title of Viscount Clancarty. He is a film-maker and lives in Kingston-upon-Thames. Between the years 1911 and 1914, the Earl of Clancarty's lands, near Ballinasloe, comprising 7,700 acres, were shared by 308 tenants. Some land leased from the estate had appeared in the Encumbered Estates Court in the early 1850s. The family had a long record as MPs in the area and came to Ireland in the early 1630s.

Sir Arthur Edward Guinness Bart, of Dublin, had 19,944 acres in County Galway in 1876, with a valuation of £3,266 about £274,344 in modern money. By the time we get to Bateman in 1883, Sir Arthur is Baron Ardilaun and has 27,111 acres in Galway, 3,747 in Mayo and 494 acres in Dublin, a total of 31,342 acres with a valuation of £6,573. (*See* Dublin City)

Sir Arthur Guinness, c/o A.E. Bart and Co., 18 Lower Leeson Street, Dublin, had 37 acres in 1876 with a valuation of £5,115 about £429,660 in modern money.

See page 118.

Patrick Blake of Gortnamona had 17,355 acres in Galway in 1876, with a valuation of £1,815 about £152,460 in modern money. Bateman records four Blakes with land in Galway, none of which are Patrick Blake:

Maurice Charles Joseph Blake of Towerhill, Ballyglass, Co. Mayo, had 7,690 acres in Galway, with 4,198 acres in Mayo, a total of 11,888 acres with a valuation of £4,096.

Walter Martin Blake of Ballyglunin Park, Athenry, had 10,452 acres in Galway, with a valuation of £3,968.

T.M. Blake of Frenchfort had 5,103 acres in Galway with a valuation of £2,006.

John Blake of Abbert, Galway, had 7,504 acres with a valuation of £2,579.

Henry Hodgson of Merlin Park, Galway, had 17,064 acres in the county in 1876, with a valuation of £1,121 about £94,164 in modern money. The NUI Database provides an interesting note on this family who seemed to have been mainly interested in mining, despite the acreage they acquired:

> The Hodgson family came to Ireland from Whitehaven in Cumberland, England, and were mine owners in Avoca, Co. Wicklow before they moved

west in the mid-nineteenth century. Pádraig Lane writes that they spent over £22,000 buying 2,800 acres in the Galway area from George F. O'Flahertie, Robert H. Eyre, William H. Gregory, Charles Blake, the Reverend T. Kelly and Christopher St George. They mined copper and lead on their estate in the west of Ireland. In 1852 Henry Hodgson bought Merlin Park from the sale of the estate of Charles Blake in the Encumbered Estates' Court. The Merlin Park estate of 1,109 acres, including the marble quarries at Dohiskey, and some land at Castle Waller (321 acres) in Co. Tipperary, were advertised for sale in the Landed Estates' Court in 1868 but it was not until 1876 that the Waithmans bought the Merlin Park estate, too late for Bateman. Henry Hodgson still owned over 17,000 acres in Co. Galway in the early 1870s.
(See also Bateman and the Return)

The largest landowners of County Galway by acreage in 1876

		Acreage	Valuation 1876 (£)	Valuation current (£)
1	Berridge, Richard, London	159,898	6,321	530,964
2	Clanricarde, Marquis of, Portumna, Castle	49,025	19,634	1,649,256
3	Dunsandle, Lord, Dunsandle, Loughrea	33,543	11,860	996,240
4	Pollok, Allan, Lismany, Ballinasloe	29,366	12,727	1,069,068
5	Clonbrock, Lord, Clonbrock, Ahascrag, Co. Galway	28,246	11,442	961,128
6	Burke, Sir Thomas J., Marble Hill, Loughrea	25,258	7,564	635,376
7	Clancarty, Earl of, Garbally, Ballinasloe	23,896	11,724	984,816
8	Guinness, Sir Arthur Edward, Bart, Dublin	19,944	3,266	274,344
9	Blake, Patrick, Gortnamona	17,355	1,815	152,460
10	Hodgson, Henry, Merlin Park, Galway	17,064	1,121	94,164
11	St George, Christopher, Tyrone House	15,777	4,453	374,052
12	Westmeath, Earl of, Pallas, Tynagh	14,604	4,377	367,668
13	Bagot, Christopher N., Aghrane, Castle Ballygar	12,396	4,400	369,600
14	Persse, Dudley, Roxboro, Loughrea	12,394	4,998	419,832

		Acreage	Valuation 1876 (£)	Valuation current (£)
15	Daly, John A.B., Raford, Kiltulla, Athenry	11,709	3,621	304,164
16	Deering, George, Dunmore House, Dunmore	11,206	4,502	378,168
17	Lahiff, Daniel, Cloon, Gort	10,779	3,853	323,652
18	Bellew, Sir Henry B. Bart (a minor), Mount Bellew	10,516	5,355	449,820
19	Blake, Walter M., Ballyglunin	10,336	3,330	279,720
20	French, Robert, Monivea Castle, Monivea	10,121	3,703	311,052
21	Smyth, John, Masonbrook, Loughrea	9,670	5,049	424,116
22	Redington, Christopher T., Kilcornan Castle, Oranmore, Co. Galway	9,626	4,393	369,012
23	Henry, Mitchell, Kylemore Castle, Recess	9,252	639	53,676
24	M'Donnell, Martin, Dunmore, Co. Galway	9,114	2,065	173,460
25	Graham, Francis J., Letterfrack	8,641	354	29,736
26	Mahon, Rev. Sir Wm O.R. Bart, Castlegar, Ahascragh, and Rotherham, Yorkshire	8,619	3,788	318,192
27	Kirwan, Mrs, Castlehackett	8,374	2,924	245,616
28	Ashtown, Lord, Woodlawn, Galway	8,310	3,570	299,880
29	Eyre, John Joseph, Clifden Castle, Clifden	8,204	1,526	128,184
30	Thompson, Colin H., Lalruck	8,111	519	43,596
31	Hancock, John S. Reps, Carrintrila, Dunmore	7,865	3,459	290,556
32	Churcher, Emmanuel, Gosport, England	7,823	2,427	203,868
33	Blake, Val O'Connor, Bunowen Castle, Clifden	7,690	2,191	184,044
34	Taylor, Walter Shaw, Castle Taylor, Ardrahan	7,605	3,016	253,344
35	Blakeney, John, Abbert, Ballyglunin	7,504	2,579	216,636
36	St George, Richd J.U., Headford Castle	7,495	4,460	374,640

		Acreage	Valuation 1876 (£)	Valuation current (£)
37	Lynch, Richard, Peteresburgh, Cloonbur	7,260	638	53,597
38	Kirwan, Thomas, Blindwell, Tuam	6,954	1,590	133,560
39	Bagot, J.L., Ballytevin	6,907	2,667	224,028
40	Nolan, John P., Ballinderry, Tuam	6,866	1,560	131,040
41	Lewis, John M.A. Reps, Ballinagar, Loughrea	6,683	1,339	112,476
42	Gough, Lord, Lough Cutra Castle	6,628	3,812	320,208
43	Bodkin, Robert, Annagh, Ballyglunin	6,481	2,448	205,632
44	Persse, Burton R.P., Moyode Castle, Athenry	6,468	2,920	245,280
45	Henry, Hugh, Firmont, Co. Kildare	6,247	2,077	174,468
46	Comyn, Francis L., Woodstock, Galway	6,198	657	55,188
47	Cheevers, Michael J., Killynn, Ballymore	6,116	2,336	196,224
48	Vesey, George, Longdillan, Surrey, England	6,061	1,932	162,288
49	Joyce, Martin B., Rusheen, Cloonbur	6,059	200	16,800
50	Stanus, Walter Trevor, Manor House, Lisburn, Co. Antrim	5,935	1,711	143,724
51	Whitaker, Rev. Chas, North Wales, England	5,826	36	3,024
52	Martin, Robert, Ross, Oughterard	5,767	1,326	111,384
53	Blake, James, Annaghdown, Drumgriffin	5,615	1,723	144,732
54	Barfoot, Henriett A., Landestown, Naas	5,596	801	67,284
55	Digby, Elizabet F., Lauderstown, Naas	5,596	801	67,284
56	Trench, Chas O'Hara, Clonfert, Eyrecourt	5,409	2,141	179,844
57	Lynch, John Wilson, Renmore, Galway	5,408	1,567	131,628
58	Joyce, John, Clifden	5,365	76	6,384
59	Clanmorris, Lord, Cregeclare, Ardrahan	5,295	1,899	159,516

		Acreage	Valuation 1876 (£)	Valuation current (£)
60	O' Ferrall, Charles, Dalyston, Loughrea	5,131	2,493	209,412
61	Blake, Theobold, 31 Raglan Road, Dublin	5,103	2,006	168,504
62	Stratheden, Lord, Hartrigge House, Jedburgh	5,060	1,074	90,216
63	Cannon, William J., Castlegrove, Foxhall	4,979	2,194	184,296
64	Martyn, Edward, Tullyra Castle	4,932	2,424	203,616
65	Digby, William J., Moate, Mylough	4,930	1,178	98,952
66	Gregory, Wm Henry, Governor of Ceylon	4,893	2,378	199,752
67	Reade, Philip, The Wood Parks, Scariff	4,882	953	80,052
68	Blake, Mrs Anne, Cloughballymore	4,847	1,394	117,096
69	Lambert, Thomas, Castle Lambert, Athenry	4,686	808	67,872
70	Blake, Caroline J., Renvyle, Letterfrack	4,682	1,011	84,924
71	Galbraith, James, Cappard	4,636	944	79,296
72	Caulfield, St George, Dunamon Castle, Roscommon	4,604	2,170	182,280
73	D'Arcy, Hyacinth, New Forrest, Ballinasloe	4,434	1,057	88,788
74	Wilberforce, H.W., London	4,378	715	60,060
75	Kirwan, Richard, Baunmore, Drumgriffin	4,308	1,323	111,132
76	Kelly, General Sir Richard D., 8 Clyde Road, Dublin	4,168	786	66,024
77	Hall, Anne, Merrion, Co. Dublin	4,139	1,061	89,124
78	Maxwell, Annie, St Cieran's, Craughwell	4,120	2,240	188,160
79	Lynch, Marcus, Barna, Galway	4,100	205	17,220
80	O'Reilly, Myles W.P., Knockabbey Castle, Dundalk, Co. Louth	4,088	1,380	115,920
81	Richardson, Charles, Newry	3,862	100	8,400
82	Lambert, Walter, Castle Ellen, Athenry	3,829	1,442	121,128

		Acreage	Valuation 1876 (£)	Valuation current (£)
83	Ffrench, Martin C., Ballinamore Park, Ballinamore Bridge	3,818	1,655	139,020
84	Joyce, Pierce, Merview, Galway	3,743	1,357	113,988
85	Skerritt, Peter R., Athgal Park, Rathgoole	3,733	1,050	88,200
86	Butson, Ven Archdeacon, St Brendon's, Eyre Court	3,719	1,394	117,096
87	Fitzgerald, James V., Glantragee, Cloonbur	3,715	169	14,196
88	Huntingdon, Earl of, Clashmore, Waterford	3,694	880	73,920
89	Ussher, Christopher, Eastwell, KIlconnel	3,666	1,781	149,604
90	Reilly, Michael, Glenamaddy, Co. Galway	3,631	1,077	90,468
91	M'Dermott, James, Ramore, Killimore	3,626	1,963	164,892
92	Clanricarde, Marquess of, Portumna	3,576	1,202	100,968
93	Forster, Captain B., Galway	3,543	1,505	126,420
94	Kenny, James C.F., Clogher House, Ballyglass, Co. Mayo	3,540	1,090	91,560
95	Daly, James, Castle Daly	3,495	584	49,056
96	Perth. Earl and Countess of, Brussels	3,439	1,138	95,562
97	Lambert, John W.H., Aggard, Croughwell	3,410	1,611	135,324
98	Haugh, Rev. John F. Reps, Graystown, Kinnegad	3,358	131	11,004
100	Browne, James, Glenamaddy. Co. Galway	3,352	1,026	86,184
101	Longworth, John, Glynwood, Athlone	3,271	1,971	165,564
102	Foreman, William, Wigan, England	3,236	306	25,704
103	Roche, Thomas Redington, Ryehill, Monivea	3,217	1,178	98,952
104	O'Kelly, Michael, Cooloo, Dangan, Barnaderg	3,152	716	60,144
105	Jameson, Harry W., Windfield, Moylough	3,123	1,288	108,192

		Acreage	Valuation 1876 (£)	Valuation current (£)
106	Kilkelly, Charles md, India	3,107	294	24,696
107	Stratheden, Lord, Hurtrigge House, Jedburgh	3,060	712	59,808
108	D'Arcy, Martin, Welfort, Kilkerrin, Galway	2,974	721	60,564
109	Smith, B., Leigh, -	2,943	12	1,008
110	Church Temporalities Commissioners, Dublin	2,931	1,663	139,692
111	Meldon, John D., Dublin	2,897	901	75,684
112	Kendall, John, Lincoln's Inn, London	2,892	273	22,932
113	O'Hara, James, Lenaboy, Galway	2,887	1,176	98,784
114	Seymour, Thomas, Ballymore Castle, Laurencetown	2,879	1,245	104,580
115	Wallscourt, Lord, Ardfry, Oranmore	2,827	1,970	165,480
116	Ruttledge, Thomas, Cornfield, Mayo	2,799	123	10,332
117	Murphy, Mrs, Northampton House	2,747	1,084	91,056
118	O'Malley, Mary Jane, Galway	2,743	38	3,192
119	Frewwn, Moreton, Oxford, England	2,709	177	14,868
120	Bradstreet, Sir John Bart, Castilla, Clontarf	2,696	804	67,536
121	Lambert, Captain Thomas C., near Galway	2,621	1,017	85,428
122	Lynch, Michael, Tynagh, Loughrea	2,616	939	78,876
123	Fallon, John, Netterville Lodge, Mount Bellew	2,594	879	73,836
124	Gore, Sir St George Bt, Solicitor's office, 17 Merrion Sq., Dublin	2,592	724	60,816
125	M'Dermott, Mrs, Springfield, Ballymoe, Co. Galway	2,571	948	79,632
126	Barrett, John S., Ballintava, Dunmore, Co. Galway	2,563	1,061	89,124
127	Richardson, Thomas A., Tyaquin, Moineva	2,561	659	55,356
128	Kilkelly, Charles, Dublin	2,550	157	13,188
129	Richards, Solomon Reps, Rent Office, Church View, Tuam	2,544	1,121	94,164

		Acreage	Valuation 1876 (£)	Valuation current (£)
130	Magee, Rev. Anthony, Boolard, Clifden	2,543	381	32,004
131	Burke, George E., Danesfield, Moycullen	2,480	515	43,260
132	Smythe, William B., Co. Westmeath	2,449	298	25,032
133	King, Peter, Killery Lodge, Leenane	2,401	110	9,240
134	Newton, Philip, Carlow	2,399	15	1,260
135	Cowan, Patrick, Prospect, Eyrecourt	2,373	1,008	84,672
136	Daly, Hon. Skefington, Dunsandle, Loughrea	2,352	622	52,248
137	O'Flahertie, Theobald O., Lemonfield, Oughterard	2,340	604	50,736
138	Crooke. James, Gosport, England	2,325	675	56,700
139	Bodkin, John, Kilclooney, Miltown	2,312	1,267	106,428
140	Goodbody, Marcus, Clara	2,309	929	78,036
141	Gunning, John J., Kilroe, Headford	2,284	742	62,328
142	Canal Company, Grand, Dublin	2,281	111	9,324
143	Browne, Thomas Reps, Brownsgrove, Tuam	2,259	1,013	85,092
144	Guilfoyle, Edward, Galway	2,176	290	24,360
145	Kilmaine, Lord, Neal, Co. Mayo	2,151	166	13,944
146	Kelly, Charles, Newtown, Ballyglunin	2,129	913	76,692
147	O'Flaherty, Martin, Lisdona, Headford	2,128	788	66,192
148	O'Flaherty, Edmond, Gurtreeragh, Oughterard	2,091	514	43,176
149	Trustees of Kircaldys, Edinburgh, Scotland	2,090	1,051	88,298
150	Wade, Francis, Ballinsaloe	2,066	593	49,812
151	Ruttledge, David, Barbersfort, Tuam	2,059	827	69,468
152	Langan, Fredrick H., Hill of Down	2,051	469	39,396
153	Woodstock, Mary and Geo Stanford Reps, -	2,049	300	25,200
154	MacHale, His Grace the Most Rev. Dr R., Tuam	2,048	691	58,044

		Acreage	Valuation 1876 (£)	Valuation current (£)
155	Blake, Sir Valentine, Menlo Castle, Galway	2,030	350	29,400
156	Livesay, Charles E., Caslough, Ballinrobe	1,970	206	17,304
157	Carter, Willoughby H., -	1,963	703	59,052
158	Blair, William, Cappagha, Kilrush	1,942	418	35,112
159	Browne, Colonel Andrew, Mount Hazel, Glentane	1,939	1,076	90,384
160	Burke, William, Leigh, Belgrum	1,931	856	71,904
161	Donnellan, Thomas O'C. Reps, Sylain Belclare	1,917	625	52,500
162	O'Kelly, Cornelius, Gallagh, Tuam	1,916	780	65,520
163	Young, William, Stradbally, Queen's County	1,888	203	17,052
164	Burke, Walter, Rahasane	1,856	914	76,776
165	Nolan, Walter M., Army and Navy Club, London	1,852	787	66,108
166	Lynch, James Reps, Salt Hill, Galway	1,812	669	56,196
167	Fetherstonehaugh, Wm, Derryhirney, Ballinasloe	1,803	1,087	91,308
168	Trustees of Robert Martin Junior, -	1,789	257	21,588
169	Seagriff, Henry, Wolverhampton	1,788	864	72,576
170	Mahon, Henry B., Belleville, Athenry	1,786	425	35,700
171	Joyce, Walter, Corgary House, Castleblakeney	1,776	892	74,928
172	Meldon, James D., 14 Upper Ormond Quay, Dublin	1,753	694	58,296
173	Eyre, Thomas J., Eyreville, Kiltormer	1,752	890	74,760
174	Netterville, Viscount, Cruicerath, Co. Meath	1,713	765	64,260
175	Lynch, Marcus, Barna	1,711	800	67,200
176	Blake, Peter, Hollypark, Athenry	1,710	976	81,984
177	Harter, James C., Hartivell Hall, England	1,699	713	59,892
178	Sweeney, Bernard, Caher, Castlerea	1,673	23	1,932

		Acreage	Valuation 1876 (£)	Valuation current (£)
179	Turbett, Jas Reps, Oaklawn, Co. Tipperary	1,669	319	26,796
180	French, Danl O'Connell, Deeds Office, Dublin	1,640	468	39,312
181	Browne, James, Dublin	1,612	289	24,276
182	Kelly, James, Cahercon	1,610	264	22,176
183	West, Very Rev. A.W., Edgeworthstown	1,600	527	44,268
184	Graham, Henry Torrens, Dublin	1,595	709	59,556
185	D'Arcy, Francis, Woodvile	1,590	1,079	90,636
186	Armstrong, Andrew, Dublin	1,588	47	3,948
187	Trustees of Erasmus Smith, Dublin	1,585	1,753	147,252
188	Burke, Rev. Michael, Ballydoogan, Loughrea	1,574	705	59,220
189	M'Donagh, James W., Lowville, Ahascragh	1,562	1,295	108,780
190	Trench, Henry, Cangort Park, Roscrea	1,561	798	67,032
191	Close, Allan P., Derrymacloghney, Athenry	1,558	425	35,700
192	Waithman, Robert W., Moyne	1,540	799	67,116
193	Geoghegan, John, Dartfield, Loughrea	1,530	746	62,664
194	De Nesbett, Countess Lucia & Mary Anne, Lexlip, Co. Kildare	1,529	692	58,128
195	Fitzpatrick, Joseph, Knockbane, Moycullen	1,522	303	25,452
196	Armstrong, John, Clooncunney, Creggs, Co. Galway	1,520	541	45,444
197	Browne, Gillman, Rossleague, Letterfrack	1,507	232	19,488
198	Vandeleur, Crofton Thos, Wardenstown, Killucan	1,505	439	36,876
199	Leonard, Dominick B., The Mall, Tuam	1,496	370	31,080
200	D'Arcy, Lionel M.A. (a minor), Rockhill, Oranmore	1,490	488	40,992
201	Kirwan, James, Monkstown, Co. Dublin	1,485	403	33,852

		Acreage	Valuation 1876 (£)	Valuation current (£)
202	Roe Thomas J, Carlton House Dunmore Co Galway	1,470	385	32,340
203	Martins (Lunatics –in– Chancery), -	1,462	746	62,664
204	Sampson, Francis C., Williamstadt, Whitegate	1,462	643	54,012
205	Fitzgerald & Vesey, Very Rev. Lord Reps, -	1,437	461	38,724
206	Knox, Captain, -	1,423	292	24,528
207	Athy, Randal E.L. Reps, Renville, Oranmore	1,415	943	79,212
208	De Clifford, Lady, London	1,406	535	44,940
209	Blake, Peter, Crumlin, Ballyglunin, Co. Galway	1,405	333	27,972
210	Kirwan, Henry J., Gardenfield	1,403	645	54,180
211	Higgins, Michael, Rusheen, Clonbur	1,399	49	4,116
212	Butler, William, Bunmahon House	1,396	541	45,444
213	Staunton, George L., Clydagh, Headford	1,395	518	43,512
214	Dolphin, Peter U., Danesfort, Loughrea	1,389	530	44,520
215	Lynch, Catherine, -	1,386	670	56,280
216	Blake, Sir Valentine, Menlo Castle, Galway	1,373	413	34,692
217	Redington, Mrs Elinor, Dangan, Galway	1,372	64	5,376
218	Lynch, Isidore, Arrandale, Spiddal	1,366	670	56,280
219	Lopdell, Captain, Athenry	1,365	331	27,804
220	Green, Thomas, Stephen's Green, Dublin	1,341	719	60,369
221	Knox, Fras B. Reps, Dublin	1,337	547	45,948
222	Taffe, Philip, Kilkelly, Co. Mayo	1,313	370	31,080
223	Cooper, Isabella, Bermingham, Tuam	1,312	481	40,404
224	Blake, Mrs Maria L., Bradford, Yorkshire	1,304	634	53,256
225	Mahon, John D., Ballydonnellan, Kilreckle	1,299	837	70,308

		Acreage	Valuation 1876 (£)	Valuation current (£)
226	Morris, Rt Hon., Chief Justice, 22 Lower Fitzwilliam St, Dublin	1,274	386	32,424
227	Ireland, Mrs, Woodlawn	1,267	328	27,552
228	Lewen, Fredrickn T., Cloughan, Foxhall, Tuam	1,266	529	44,436
229	Clark, Courtney K., Larchill, Dublin	1,256	500	42,000
230	Thompson, Alexander, Dublin	1,244	112	9,408
231	Murphy, William, -	1,236	704	59,136
232	Butler, Joseph S., Winterfield, Drumgriffin	1,234	321	26,964
233	Cowan, Stephen J., Gortnamona, Ballinasloe	1,222	720	60,480
234	Keating, Michael D., Woodgift, Kilkenny	1,211	481	40,404
235	Wade, Rochford R., Fairfield, Aughrim	1,189	791	66,444
236	Nolan, Michl Reps, Ballybanagher, Cummer	1,186	455	38,220
237	Jennings, George, Ironpool, Foxhall	1,183	349	29,316
238	Matthews, Edward P., Derryounlan	1,183	294	24,696
239	Dolphin, Oliver, Turoe, Loughrea	1,171	630	52,920
240	Collingham, George, Annakeelane	1,140	46	3,864
241	Johnston, St George R., Rathcline House, Co. Longford	1,139	406	34,104
242	Donnellan, Stephen J., Killagh, Kilconnell	1,138	665	55,608
243	Kenny, Mathew, Ennis	1,133	249	20,916
244	Synge, Catherine, Rathmines, Co. Dublin	1,131	331	27,804
245	Maunsell, John W., Springlawn, Mount Bellew	1,124	250	21,000
246	Lambert, Alexander C., Derrylesnagane	1,121	306	25,704
247	Waithman Robert W., Moyne House, Ballyglunin	1,109	619	51,996
248	Johnston, James, Fohaney, Ahascragh	1,092	486	40,824
249	Prior, Thomas Young of Ballinakill	1,084	311	26,124

		Acreage	Valuation 1876 (£)	Valuation current (£)
250	Hallam, C.M., Murvey Lodge, Roundstone	1,073	150	12,600
251	Comyn, Francis L., Woodstock, Galway	1,069	282	23,688
252	Jackson, James, Killaguile, Oughterard	1,062	91	7,644
253	O'Rorke, Charles, Cloonburne, Moylough	1,061	280	23,520
254	Trench, Hon. Charles J., Merrion Sq., Dublin	1,051	690	57,960
255	Henry, Fredrick H., Lodge Park, Straffan	1,044	289	24,276
256	Trench, Emily M., Newlands, Clondalkin	1,042	292	24,528
257	Evans, Mary, Cross House, Menlough	1,038	480	40,320
258	Blake, Richard, Annaghdown, Drumgriffin	1,037	242	20,328
259	Donnellan, Mrs, Galway	1,034	387	32,508
260	Tighe, Thomas, Ballinrobe, Co. Mayo	1,025	566	47,544
261	Kilkelly, John, Mossfort. Caherlistrane	1,009	527	44,268
262	Leitrim, Earl of, Lough Rynn, Mohill	1,845	870	73,080
263	Clarke, James, Graig Abbey, Athenry	1,870	701	58,884

The top 20 landowners in Galway by income (valuation)

		Acreage	Valuation 1876 (£)	Valuation current (£)
1	Clanricarde, Marquis of, Portumna Castle	49,025	19,634	1,649,256
2	Pollok, Allan, Lismany, Ballinasloe	29,366	12,727	1,069,068
3	Dunsandle, Lord, Dunsandle, Loughrea	33,543	11,860	996,240
4	Clancarty, Earl of, Garbally, Ballinasloe	23,896	11,724	984,816

		Acreage	Valuation 1876 (£)	Valuation current (£)
5	Clonbrock, Lord, Clonbrock, Ahascrag, Co. Galway	28,246	11,442	961,128
6	Burke, Sir Thomas J., Marble Hill, Loughrea	25,258	7,564	635,376
7	Berridge, Richard, London	159,898	6,321	530,964
8	Bellew, Sir Henry B. Bart (a minor), Mount Bellew	10,516	5,355	449,820
9	Smyth, John, Masonbrook, Loughrea	9,670	5,049	424,116
10	Persse, Dudley, Roxboro, Loughrea	12,394	4,998	419,832
11	Deering, George, Dunmore House, Dunmore	11,206	4,502	378,168
12	St George, Richd J.U., Headford Castle	7,495	4,460	374,640
13	St George, Christopher, Tyrone House	15,777	4,453	374,052
14	Bagot, Christopher N., Aghrane Castle, Ballygar	12,396	4,400	369,600
15	Redington, Christopher T., Kilcornan Castle, Oranmore, Co. Galway	9,626	4,393	369,012
16	Westmeath, Earl of, Pallas, Tynagh	14,604	4,377	367,668
17	Lahiff, Daniel, Cloon, Gort	10,779	3,853	323,652
18	Gough, Lord, Lough Cutra Castle	6,628	3,812	320,208
19	Mahon, Rev. Sir Wm O.R. Bart, Castlegar, Ahascragh and Rotherham, Yorkshire	8,619	3,788	318,192
20	French, Robert, Monivea Castle, Monivea	10,121	3,703	311,052

KERRY

	1876	2016
Population in County Kerry	196,586	145,502
All owners of land	1,166	94,624
Percentage of the population	0.59	–
Owners of nothing at all	195,420	45,573
Percentage of the population	99.41	–
Size of County	1,153,373 acres	1,161,600 acres
Number of dwellings (of which rented)	32,240 (31,603)	53,088
Number of owned farm holdings	1,166	8,412

Top ten landowners in Kerry in 1876 by acreage

		Acreage 1876	Valuation 1876	Equivalent current £
1	Lansdowne, Marquis of, Lansdowne House, London ★	94,953	£9,553	£802,452
2	Ventry, Rt Hon. Lord, Burnham House, Dingle ★	93,629	£17.067	£1,433,628
3	Kenmare, Earl of, Killarney House, Killarney	91,080	£25,252	£2,121,168
4	Herbert, Henry A., Muckross, Killarney ★	47,238	£10,547	£885,948
5	Drummond, Robert, Charing Cross, London	29,780	£3,065	£257,460
6	Mahony, Richard, Dromore Castle, Kenmare	26,173	£2,636	£221,424
7	Listowel, Earl of, Convamore, Mallow ★★	25,964	£12,073	£1,014,132
8	Bland, Francis, Derryquin Castle, Sneem	25,576	£1,862	£156,408
9	Hartopp, Edward Bouchier, Dalby House, Leicester	24,222	£2,408	£202,072
10	Denny, Sir Edward, London ★	21,479	£9,685	£813,540

★ Title still extant ★★Holder sits in the House of Lords

Top 10 Landowners in Kerry in 1876 ranked by estimated gross rental value in Kerry

		Acreage	Valuation 1876 (£)	Current equivalent (£)
1	Kenmare, Earl of, Killarney House, Killarney	91,080	25,252	2,121,168
2	Ventry, Rt Hon. Lord, Burnham House, Dingle ★	93,629	17,067	1,433,628
3	Listowel, Earl of, Convamore, Mallow★★	25,964	12,073	1,014,132
4	Herbert, Henry A., Muckross, Killarney ★	47,238	10,547	885,948
5	Denny, Sir Edward, London★	21,479	9,685	813,540
6	Lansdowne, Marquis of, Lansdowne House, London★	94,953	9,553	802,452
7	Crosbie, William Talbot, Ardfert Abbey, Ardfert, Tralee	9,913	4,638	389,592
8	Blennerhasset, Arthur (a minor), Ballyseedy, Tralee	12,621	4,157	346,668
9	Gun Wilson, Rattoo, Causeway	11,819	3,951	331,884
10	Crosbie, Major James, Ballyheigue Castle, Ballyheigue	13,422	3,793	318,612

★ Title still extant ★★ Holder sits in the House of Lords

The Marquis of Lansdowne. 94,953 acres. Wealth ranking in 1876 was sixth, with an income of £9,553, about £802,452 in modern money just, from from his Kerry acreage. The landowner in 1876 was the 5th Marquis of Lansdowne, whose seat was at Bowood Park in Wiltshire and who was a British landowner of vast acreage, 142,916 in total, with an income of £69,025. He was an Old Etonian and was a leading politician in Britain, serving in the Cabinet between 1895 and 1905, and again in 1915. He was Governor General of Canada from 1883 to 1888, and Viceroy of India from 1888 to 1894. He was Minister for War from 1895 to 1900 and Foreign Secretary from 1900 to 1905. He married a daughter of James Hamilton, the 1st Duke of Abercorn (acreage in 1876, 78,662), herself a granddaughter of the 6th Duke of Bedford (acreage in 1876, 86,335) He was also the Earl of Shelbourne and the Earl of Kerry. The family name lives on in Dublin via the Shelbourne Hotel and Lansdowne Road, home of Irish rugby.

It is worth setting out his full set of landholdings because, even in the Britain of his time, they were huge and ranked him the twenty-second largest landowner in the UK as a whole.

County	Acreage	Rental value 1876 (£)	Equivalent Current £
Wilts (England)	11,145	20,824	1,749,216
Hants (England)	4	45	3,780
Kerry (Ireland)	94,983	9,553	802,452
Meath (Ireland)	12,995	10,790	906,360
Queen's Co. (Ireland)	8,980	5,310	446,040
Dublin (Ireland)	2,132	3,182	267,288
Limerick (Ireland)	1,642	2,965	249,060
King's Co. (Offaly)(Ireland)	617	542	45,528
Perth (Scotland)	9,070	8,025	674,100
Kinross (Scotland)	1,348	789	66,276
Total	142,916	62,025	5,210,100

Lansdowne was the great grandson of Prime Minister William Petty, 1st Marquess of Lansdowne (better known as the Earl of Shelburne) via his second marriage to Lady Louisa, daughter of John FitzPatrick, 1st Earl of Upper Ossory. He was educated at Westminster School, the University of Edinburgh, and Trinity College, Cambridge. The family still live at Bowood House and the Marquis, like his ancestor, is an Old Etonian.

Lord Ventry, 93,629 acres. The second wealthiest landowner in Kerry with a gross estimated income of £17,067 about £1,433,628 in modern money. The title still exists and is held by Andrew Wesley Daubeney de Moleyns as the 8th Baron, who lives in France. The family are descendants of a Colonel Fredrick Mullins of Burnham in Norfolk, who arrived in Ireland around 1666. A Baronetcy was first granted in 1797 and that was upgraded to that of Baron Ventry in 1800, in the peerage of Ireland. This was somewhat politically suicidal as the peerage was granted for Mullins' assistance to Castlereigh's uniting Ireland with the Crown and thereby abolishing the Irish House of Lords. On 18 June 1793, over 4,000 people marched in Dingle to protest against high rents and the establishment of a local militia. Mullins, who assumed responsibility for the town on behalf of the Crown, brought in seventy soldiers from Limerick to break up the demonstration. The riot was quelled when soldiers were ordered to shoot at the crowd, and fourteen farmers were killed with many others being injured.

From the NUI Galway Estates Database:

His uncle, the second Baron, had bought the Trants' county Kerry estate in 1813. The Ordnance Survey Name Books mention David P. Thompson of Tralee as Lord Ventry's agent. Lands in Killorgan had been offered for sale in the Encumbered Estates Court in 1851. A manuscript note on the sale notice indicates the purchasers were Hunt, Stokes and Booker. Part of Lord Ventry's estate, was offered for sale in July 1852 and the Cork land again in December 1852. On the latter occasion Mr. Creagh, solicitor, was declared the purchaser in trust. In the 1870s the de Moleyns estate amounted to over 91,000 acres in county Kerry. An offer was made by the Congested Districts Board on over 80,000 acres of Lord Ventry's estate in 1913.

The 4th Earl of Kenmare of Killarney House, County Kerry, had 22,700 acres in Cork in 1876, with a valuation of £3,497 about £293,748 in modern money.

See page 80.

Henry Albert Herbert of Muckross Abbey, Killarney, had 47,238 acres in the county in 1876, with a valuation of £10,547 about £885,948 in modern money. The Herberts were granted land in Kerry during the reign of Elizabeth I. The Irish BLG (Herbert) indicates that two members of the family received lands in Kerry after the Desmond rebellion, Sir William Herbert received over 13,000 acres while Charles Herbert received over 3,000 acres. The Herbert who eventually settled there was Thomas, descended from a family in Montgomery, Powys, in Wales.

Henry Albert Herbert was the great grandson of Thomas Herbert, who made his millions by mining copper on the Muckross Peninsula and Ross Island. Prior to that the Herbert family had inherited the estates of the Clan MacCarthy in 1770. According to Bateman, he was an MP for Kerry and was an officer in the Coldstream Guards. From 1857 to 1858 he was Chief Secretary for Ireland and hosted Queen Victoria when she visited the country in 1861. The centre of this large estate was at Muckross, close to Killarney, much of it now included in the Killarney National Park. The family fortunes declined systematically in the late nineteenth century and most of the estate was sold in the 1890s. An offer was made by the Congested Districts Board on over 400 acres of the Herbert estate in 1914.

NUI Estates Records (McCoole) states that the Herberts had a house on the Muckross peninsula since at least the early eighteenth century, on lands leased from the MacCarthaigh Mor family. A new house was constructed in the 1770s. In 1837 Lewis described Muckross as 'situated in a demesne of enchanting beauty'. The present Muckross House, was built in 1839–43. It continued to be owned by the Herbert family until the 1890s, when, the family fortunes having declined, it was sold by the Standard Life Assurance Company, and purchased by Lord Ardilaun. He was the owner in 1906 when it was valued at £130. In 1910 it was sold to an American family, Bowers Bourn, who in turn gave it to their daughter and son-in-law, Maud and Arthur Vincent. It was presented to the nation in 1932 and now forms the centre of the Killarney National Park.

Robert Drummond of Charing Cross, London, had 29,780 acres in Kerry in 1876, with a valuation of £3,065 about £257,640 in modern money. Bateman moves Robert Drummond from Charing Cross to Palace Gate in Kensington and notes that, like so many Irish landowners, he was educated at Eton College. An offer was made by the Congested Districts Board on over 1,500 acres of the Drummond estate in 1903 and 1909.

Richard Mahony of Dromore, Castle Kenmare, had 26,173 acres in Kerry in 1876, with a valuation of £2,636 about £221,424 in modern money. According to the NUI Galway Estates database, this branch of the ancient Gaelic family of O'Mahony is descended from the county Cork family of Kinalmeaky, mostly through marriages into the O'Connell and O'Sullivan families in the early modern period. In 1860 over 5,600 acres of John Mahony's estate was offered for sale in the Landed Estates Court. The tenure details indicate the Mahonys had leased this property from the Sullivan family in 1697. Of Dromore Castle, the NUI Database states the following:

> The reps of Rev. D. Mahony were occupying a property valued at £66, at the time of Griffith's Valuation. Lewis mentions 'a noble edifice in the Gothic castellated style' as the seat of Rev. Denis Mahony in 1837. In 1906 it was owned by H.S. Mahony and valued at £66 15s. Barry states that it was built by Sir Thomas Deane for Rev. Denis Mahony in the 1830s. It remained in the Mahony family until the early years of the twentieth century. It then passed by marriage to the Hood family. The Irish Tourist Association survey in 1943 indicates it was the property of Colonel E. Hood whose wife was 'the last of the O'Mahonys, a family associated with the area for over 300 years'. It later pass from them to the Wallers, cousins of the Hoods. Dromore Castle is still extant and the National Inventory of Architectural Heritage states that it was renovated in 1998.

The Earl of Listowel of Convamore, Mallow, County Cork, had 25,964 acres in Kerry with a valuation of £12,073 about £1,014,132. Francis Michael Hare, the 6th Earl, is an elected hereditary peer in the House of Lords in London. He sits under his UK title of Baron Hare, created in 1869. His predecessor in 1876, the 3rd Earl, was a Lord in waiting to Queen Victoria and was an officer in the Scots Fusilier Guards. Bateman corrects the acreage, from 25,964 acres to 30,000 acres, and increases the valuation to £16,000. With the Cork acreage the Earl had a total of 35,541 acres with a valuation of £19,500. The present Earl was educated at Westminster School, his predecessor in 1876 having been educated at Eton.

The NUI Database tells us that the Hare family had come to Ireland after the Cromwellian settlement and acquired property initially in Dublin and later in Cork. Their influence extended to Kerry at the end of the eighteenth century when Richard Hare purchased 20,000 acres of the Knight of Kerry's estate around Listowel. In 1854 the estate was petitioner to the sale of 150 acres of the estate of Edward Church, at Kilmolane. This estate (Tipperary portion) was advertised for sale in March 1861. The *Irish Times* reported that the purchasers included Messers. John Dwyer, Francis Trent, William Bolton and Peter Ryan. In the 1870s the Honourable Richard Hare of Devonport, England, owned 3,687 acres in Co. Limerick. He was a brother of the 2nd Earl of Listowel. His nephew, Robert Dillon Hare of Ballymore, owned 944 acres in Co. Cork.

Francis Bland of Derryquin Castle, Sneem, County Kerry, held 25,576 acres in Kerry in 1876, with a valuation of £1,862 about £156,408 in modern money. Francis Bland makes it below the line in Bateman, confirming the above basic facts. The NUI Database adds the following additional facts:

> The Blands were originally a Yorkshire family who settled in Kerry in the early eighteenth century. In 1865, lands at Laharan were offered for sale in the Landed Estates Court in the name of John Kelly. This had been part of the Bland estate at the time of Griffith's Valuation. The property was purchased in trust by Mr. Sullivan, for Maurice J. O'Connell. In the 1830s, the Ordnance Survey Name Books record that James Hewson was acting as agent for the estate of the late Nathaniel Bland, in the parish of Caher, where some of the lands were let to John Primrose. In the 1870s the estate of Francis C. Bland amounted to over 32,500 acres in county Kerry.

Edward Bouchier Hartopp MP of Dalby Hall, Melton Mowbray, Leicester, held 24,222 acres in Kerry in 1876, with a valuation of £2,408 about £202,272 in modern money. This Eton-educated politician had 5,423 acres in Leicester, where he sat as MP, and 4,545 acres in Limerick together with the Kerry land totalling 34,190 acres with a valuation of £13,845.

The NUI Database adds the following information:

> Edward Bourchier Hartopp of Dalby House, Melton Mowbray, Leicestershire, was the grandson of Edward Hartopp who married Juliana Evans, daughter of

George, 3rd Lord Carbery, in 1782. Anthony Malcomson writes in his introduction to the Bisbrooke Papers that following the death of her brother, 4th Baron Carbery, in 1804 Mrs Hartopp inherited the unentailed part of the Irish property of her father. David Roche was his agent circa 1840. In the 1870s his address is given as Leicester. Bateman notes it as Dalby Hall, Melton Mowbray. He owned over 24,000 acres in county Kerry at that time, together with 4,545 acres in county Limerick and 2,467 acres in county Cork. [Cork acres not recorded in Bateman] In 1906 terms had been arranged by the Congested Districts Board for the purchase of over 15,000 acres of the Burns-Hartopp estate in county Kerry. This land was acquired by the Board in 1908.

Sir Edward Denny, Bart of Tralee, resident at 31, The Grove, West Brompton, London, had 21,479 acres in Kerry in 1876, with a valuation of £9,685 about £813,540 in modern money. This Baronetcy still exists and is shown in a recent edition of Debrett's as held by Sir Anthony Conyngham de Waltham Denny, the 8th Baronet, who lives in London.

Smith indicates that the first Sir Edward Denny was granted over 6,000 acres in Co. Kerry after the Desmond Rebellion. Sir Arthur Denny was granted an estate in 1666 following the Acts of Settlement. Land leased by Richard Jeffcott from the Denny estate, were offered for sale in the Landed Estates Court. The *Irish Times* reports that they were purchased by Christopher Jeffcott and Mr Hurley. In 1867, property which had been leased by Rev. Robert Day Denny to Michael Lynch was offered for sale in the Landed Estates Court. In the 1870s the Denny estate in Co. Kerry amounted to over 21,000 acres. A junior branch of this family held land in Co. Tipperary and in counties Fermanagh and Monaghan. Anthony Denny married Sarah Jane, daughter of the Reverend G.P. Lockwood, and their son was the Reverend Edward Denny (born 1853) of Moorestown, Co. Tipperary. In the 1870s the trustees of the late Anthony Denny held 1,988 acres in Tipperary and estates in Fermanagh and Monaghan.

Prior to their arrival in Ireland, members of this family had been high officers in both Henry VIII's court and that of Elizabeth I. An ancestor is said to have been the only courtier brave enough to approach Henry VIII on his deathbed and tell him he was about to die, for which Denny was given a gift of pearl embroidered gloves that the family still have. At one stage the family were the Earls of Norwich. They were also Governors of Kerry and Desmond in Ireland.

All landowners of over 1,000 acres in Kerry in 1876

		Acreage	Valuation 1876 (£)	Valuation current (£)
1	Lansdowne, Marquis of, Lansdowne House, London	94,953	9,553	802,452
2	Ventry, Rt Hon. Lord, Burnham House, Dingle	93,629	17,067	1,433,628
3	Kenmare, Earl of, Killarney House, Killarney	91,080	25,252	2,121,168
4	Herbert, Henry A., Muckross, Killarney	47,238	10,547	885,948
5	Drummond, Robert, Charing Cross, London	29,780	3,065	257,460
6	Mahony, Richard, Dromore Castle, Kenmare	26,173	2,636	221,424
7	Listowel, Earl of, Convamore, Mallow	25,964	12,073	1,014,132
8	Bland, Francis, Derryquin Castle, Sneem	25,576	1,862	156,408
9	Hartopp, Edward Bouchier, Dalby House, Leicester	24,222	2,408	202,072
10	Denny, Sir Edward, London	21,479	9,685	813,540
11	O'Connell, Sir Maurice James, Lakeview House, Killarney	18,752	3,050	256,200
12	O'Connell, Daniel, Derrynane Abbey, Cahirciveen	17,394	1,626	136,584
13	M'Gilcuddy, Reps of, Whitefield, Killarney	15,518	2,175	182,700
14	Winn, Hon. Roland, Rossbehy, Glanbeigh	13,913	1,382	116,088
15	Hickson, Robert C., Fermoyle, Castlegregory	13,443	2,533	212,772
16	Crosbie, Major James, Ballyheigue Castle, Ballyheigue	13,422	3,793	318,612
17	Orpen, Sir Richard, 41 North Gt George's St, Dublin	12,873	1,197	100,548
18	Headley, Rt Hon. Lord, Aghadoe House, Killarney	12,769	3,297	276,948
19	Blennerhasset, Arthur (a minor), Ballyseedy, Tralee	12,621	4,157	346,668
20	Gun, Wilson, Rattoo, Causeway	11,819	3,951	331,884

		Acreage	Valuation 1876 (£)	Valuation current (£)
21	Stoughton, Thomas Anthony, Ballyhorgan, Ballyduff, Tralee	11,710	2,398	201,432
22	Mahony, Edward, Lunatic Asylum, Dublin	11,688	1,338	112,392
23	Cork, Earl of, Marston Frome, Somerset	11,531	2,447	205,548
24	Sandes, Maurice F., Oakpark, Tralee	11,172	3,297	276,948
25	Trinity, College, Dublin	10,341	3,223	270,732
26	Chute, Francis B., Chute Hall, Tralee	10,328	2,627	224,864
27	Coltsmann, Daniel, Glenflesk Castle, Killarney	10,316	786	66,024
28	Crosbie, William Talbot, Ardfert Abbey, Ardfert, Tralee	9,913	4,638	389,592
29	O'Connell, Chas J., Bantry	9,807	890	74,760
30	Hurley, John, Fenit House, Spa, Tralee	9,675	1,800	151,200
31	Wise, Francis, North Mall, Cork	9,636	443	37,212
32	The O'Donoghue, Summerhill, Killarney	9,463	868	72,912
33	Ormanthwaite, Lord, Warfield Park, Berks	8,907	2,619	219,996
34	Blennerhasset, Sir Rowland, Churchtown House, Beaufort Killarney	8,390	2,145	180,180
35	Mahony, John, Dunloe Castle, Killarney	8,229	949	79,716
36	Blacker, St John Thomas, Killea, Armagh	8,159	2,298	193,032
37	Mahony, Thomas McDonagh, Cullinagh, Killarney	7,322	425	35,700
38	Sandes, Thomas, Sallowglin, Tarbert	7,147	2,783	233,772
39	Bernard, Edward M., Shehehroe, Killarney	7,136	1,194	100,296
40	Corkery, Daniel O'Brien, Kenmare	6,439	730	61,320
41	Eagar, Eusebius McGillycuddy, Lake Cara Castle, Killorglin	6,404	298	25,032

		Acreage	Valuation 1876 (£)	Valuation current (£)
42	Blennerhasset, Rowland, Kells Lodge, Cahirciveen	6,234	504	42,336
43	Blennerhasset, Thomas, Shanavalley, Tralee	5,995	1,689	141,876
44	Godfrey, Sir John, Kilcoleman Abbey, Milltown	5,986	3,218	270,312
45	Marshall, Richard J., Callinafercy, Milltown	5,955	2,403	201,852
46	Mundy, Major General and Vernon, the Rt Hon., London	5,892	1,711	143,724
47	Harenc, Henry R., Lowndes Sq., London	5,879	2,121	178,164
48	Rae, Langford, Keel House, Castlemanin	5,870	981	82,404
49	Leahy, John White, South Hill, Killarney	5,511	1,425	119,700
50	Fitzgerald, Peter The Knight of Kerry, Glanleam, Valencia	5,372	2,207	185,338
51	Chute, Rev. George, Market Drayton, Shropshire	5,094	891	82,404
52	Mahony George P. Gun, Kilmorna, Listowel	5,020	1,748	146,832
53	Oliver, Richard, London	4,804	2,270	190,680
54	Sugrue, Chas Reps of, Sidney Place, Cork	4,622	658	55,272
55	Simpson, Stephen, Fitzwilliam Sq., Dublin	4,609	582	48,888
56	Orpen, Richard H., Killaha Castle, Killarney	4,348	578	48,552
57	Hussey, Edward, The Grove, Dingle	3,954	651	54,684
58	Williams, Fras Edward, Cappanagroun Lodge, Waterville	3,804	124	10,416
59	Julian, Samuel, Jersey Villa, Cheltenham	3,711	651	54,684
60	Collis, Stephen Edward, Tierdclea, Tarbert	3,598	1,207	101,388
61	Dennis, Meade C., Fort Granite, Baltinglass	3,550	1,103	92,652
62	Hussey, Samuel M., Edenburn, Tralee	3,526	1,283	107,772

		Acreage	Valuation 1876 (£)	Valuation current (£)
63	Cuthbert, Thomas (a minor), England	3,407	685	57,540
64	Hickie, William C., Kilelton, Ballylongford	3,368	1,220	£102,480
65	Mayberry, George M.D., Riverdale, Killarney	3,160	346	29,064
66	Mahony, Kean, Cullina, Beaufort	3,104	234	19,656
67	Herbert, Henry, Cahirnane, Killarney	3,016	1,995	167,580
68	M'Carthy, Alexander, Cork	2,979	438	36,792
69	Bland, Ven Archdeacon, Knockane Rectory, Beaufort	2,960	651	54,684
70	Stokes, George D., Day Place, Tralee	2,747	875	73,500
71	Goff, Joseph, Hales Park, Salisbury, Wilts	2,625	393	33,012
72	Usburne, Thomas M., Cork	2,560	1,248	104,832
73	Hurley, Conway (a minor), Bridge House, Tralee	2,559	1,230	103,320
74	Stoughton, William, Grosvenor Place, London	2,495	891	74,844
75	Wren, Leslie, Tralee	2,466	1,088	91,392
76	Taylor, Adrian M.D., Clontoo, Kilgarvan	2,409	244	20,496
77	Bateman, John, in Chancery, Lunatic Asylum, Dublin	2,406	1,469	123,396
78	Fitzgerald, W.N.F., Derrybrick, Clare	2,400	914	76,776
79	Monteagle, Lord, Limerick	2,310	1,091	91,644
80	Sullivan, Thomas Kingston, The Retreat, Bandon	2,303	378	31,752
81	Day, Rev. John F., Beaufort, Killarney	2,264	1,348	113,232
82	Saunders, J.L. Reps, Cloughjordan, Tipperary	2,221	775	65,100
83	Brennan, Daniel, Dromhall, Killarney	2,220	340	28,560
84	M'Carthy, Daniel, Headfort, Killarney	2,203	467	39,228
85	Fitzmaurice, O. Reps, Dublin	2,170	794	66,696

		Acreage	**Valuation 1876 (£)**	**Valuation current (£)**
86	O'Sullivan, Daniel Reps, Dooaghs, Killorglin	2,160	66	5,544
87	Palmer, Robert, Trafalgar Sq., London	2,104	277	23,268
88	Browne, John P., Crotta, Kilflynn	2,065	770	64,680
89	Coltsmann, Catherine, Dublin	2,016	738	61,992
90	Hickson, Robert A., London	2,000	929	78,036
91	Barry, John, Villa Nova, Caherciveen	1,964	256	21,504
92	Blackwood, Sir Henry, London	1,940	534	44,856
93	Meredith, Richard, Dicksgrove, Farranfore	1,839	320	26,880
94	Downing, Francis Henry, New Street, Killarney	1,803	355	29,820
95	Hewson, Rev. Francis, Rectory, Killarney	1,772	79	6,636
96	Raymond, George, Dublin	1,756	304	25,536
97	Deane, James, Cork	1,753	300	25,200
98	Leslie, Robert, Tarbert House, Tarbert	1,747	1,738	145,992
99	Mahony, John H., Tubrid, Kenmare	1,723	380	31,920
100	Day, Francis, Milltown, Kerry	1,704	890	74,760
101	Busteed, Mary, Dublin	1,685	644	54,096
102	Harte, Mahony Reps of, Tralee	1,682	667	56,028
103	Orkney, Earl of, England	1,642	125	10,500
104	Magill, Captain James, Churchtown House, Killarney	1,628	234	19,656
105	Chute, Algernon, Dublin	1,606	296	24,864
106	Foley, Edward, Ballyard, Tralee	1,604	555	46,620
107	Foley, James Snr Reps, Killorglin	1,603	160	13,440
108	Dennehy, Mary, Killarney	1,574	145	12,180
109	Galway, Edward, Queen's County	1,571	116	9,744
110	Rowan, Major William, Belmont, Tralee	1,550	815	68,460
111	Nash, Charles F., Ballycarachy, Tralee	1,531	469	39,396
112	Church Temporalities Commisioners of, Dublin	1,500	694	58,296
113	Harnett, William, England	1,489	203	17,052

		Acreage	Valuation 1876 (£)	Valuation current (£)
114	Browne, Rev. George, Nottingham	1,477	524	44,016
115	Fosberry, Mr, Curragh Bridge, Limerick	1,437	413	34,692
116	Palmer, John, Fortwilliam, Tralee	1,427	259	21,756
117	Butler, James, Waterville, Caherciveen	1,417	639	53,676
118	Strange, Miss Barbara, Parkgariffe, Kenmare	1,387	115	9,660
119	Lawlor, Denis Shine, Grenagh, Killarney	1,374	607	50,988
120	Mahony, David, Wiltslane	1,370	381	32,004
121	Oliver, Major Reps of, Co. Cork	1,369	581	48,084
122	Blennerhasset, John, Shanavalley, Ballymacelligot	1,352	572	48,048
123	Fitzgerald, Rev. Richard, Ballydonehoe, Tarbert	1,349	363	30,492
124	Driscoll, John, Knightstown, Valencia	1,346	248	20,832
125	Donovan, Nichols, Denny Street, Tralee	1,295	814	68,376
126	Bateman, Rowland, Tralee	1,259	397	33,348
127	Roche, Redmond, Castleisland	1,255	355	29,820
128	Rice, Justice D., Bushmount, Causeway	1,233	398	33,432
129	Leonard, Rev. S.B., Banteer, Cork	1,212	228	19,152
130	Hewson, George. Ennismore, Listowel	1,208	455	38,220
131	Stack, Major General N.M. Reps, Lake Caraigh, Killarney	1,205	397	33,248
132	Hickson, Robert James, Asylum, Killarney	1,183	230	26,880
133	Curtayne, James, Bellville, Killarney	1,165	53	4,452
134	Tuohill, Richard M.D., Merrion Sq., Dublin	1,164	106	8,904
135	Chute, Charles, Stoughton's Row, Tralee	1,141	283	23,772
136	Neligan, William J., Denny Street, Tralee	1,087	635	53,340
137	Fitzgerald, Robert M., Dublin	1,086	220	18,480

		Acreage	Valuation 1876 (£)	Valuation current (£)
138	Lawlor, Martin Reps of, Killarney	1,075	183	15,372
139	Leahy, Colonel Arthur, Flesk Lodge, Killarney	1,068	300	25,200
140	King, Nicholas M.D., Dublin	1,058	262	22,008
141	Butterly, Laurence Reps of, Listowel	1,052	244	20,496
142	O'Rorke, Charles Denis, Clonbrum, Moloch, Galway	1,047	282	23,688
143	Kitson, George L., Waterloo Road, Dublin	1,040	£267	22,428
144	M'Carthy, Daniel, Srugreana, Cahirciveen	1,033	106	8,904
145	Mahony, Kean, Glasnevin, Dublin	1,024	27	2,268
147	Roche, Stephen, Stephen's Green, Dublin	1,007	287	24,108
146	Roche, Catherine, Knights Lodge, Charleville	1,007	287	24,108
148	Dunraven, Earl of, Adare Manor, Limerick	1,005	123	10,332
149	Dodd, William Henry, Killorglin	1,000	55	4,620

Landowners of over 1,000 acres in Kerry in 1876 ranked by value then and now

		Acreage 1876	Gross estimated rental Valuation 1876 (£)	Valuation 2016 (£)
1	Kenmare, Earl of, Killarney House, Killarney	91,080	25,252	2,121,168
2	Ventry, Rt Hon. Lord, Burnham House, Dingle	93,629	17,067	1,433,628
3	Listowel, Earl of, Convamore, Mallow	25,964	12,073	1,014,132
4	Herbert, Henry A., Muckross, Killarney	47,238	10,547	885,948
5	Denny, Sir Edward, London	21,479	9,685	813,540
6	Lansdowne, Marquis of, Lansdowne House, London	94,953	9,553	802,452

		Acreage 1876	Gross estimated rental Valuation 1876 (£)	Valuation 2016 (£)
7	Crosbie, William Talbot, Ardfert Abbey, Ardfert, Tralee	9,913	4,638	389,592
8	Blennerhasset, Arthur (a minor), Ballyseedy, Tralee	12,621	4,157	346,668
9	Gun, Wilson, Rattoo, Causeway	11,819	3,951	331,884
10	Crosbie, Major James, Ballyheigue Castle, Ballyheigue	13,422	3,793	318,612
11	Headley, Rt Hon. Lord, Aghadoe House, Killarney	12,769	3,297	276,948
12	Sandes, Maurice F., Oakpark, Tralee	11,172	3,297	276,948
13	Trinity College, Dublin	10,341	3,223	270,732
14	Godfrey, Sir John, Kilcoleman Abbey, Milltown	5,986	3,218	270,312
15	Drummond, Robert, Charing Cross, London	29,780	3,065	257,460
16	O'Connell, Sir Maurice James, Lakeview House, Killarney	18,752	3,050	256,200
17	Sandes, Thomas, Sallowglin, Tarbert	7,147	2,783	233,772
18	Chute, Francis B., Chute Hall, Tralee	10,328	2,627	224,864
19	Mahony, Richard, Dromore Castle, Kenmare	26,173	2,636	221,424
20	Ormanthwaite, Lord, Warfield Park, Berks	8,907	2,619	219,996
21	Hickson, Robert C., Fermoyle, Castlegregory	13,443	2,533	212,772
22	Cork, Earl of, Marston, Frome, Somerset	11,531	2,447	205,548
23	Hartopp, Edward Bouchier, Dalby House, Leicester	24,222	2,408	202,072
24	Marshall, Richard J., Callinafercy, Milltown	5,955	2,403	201,852
25	Stoughton, Thomas Anthony, Ballyhorgan, Ballyduff, Tralee	11,710	2,398	201,432
26	Blacker, St John Thomas, Killea, Armagh	8,159	2,298	193,032

		Acreage 1876	Gross estimated rental Valuation 1876 (£)	Valuation 2016 (£)
27	Oliver, Richard, London	4,804	2,270	190,680
28	Fitzgerald, Peter The Knight of Kerry, Glanleam, Valencia	5,372	2,207	185,338
29	M'Gilcuddy, Reps of, Whitefield, Killarney	15,518	2,175	182,700
30	Blennerhasset, Sir Rowland, Churchtown House, Beaufort Killarney	8,390	2,145	180,180
31	Harenc, Henry R., Lowndes Sq., London	5,879	2,121	178,164
32	Herbert, Henry, Cahirnane, Killarney	3,016	1,995	167,580
33	Bland, Francis, Derryquin Castle, Sneem	25,576	1,862	156,408
34	Hurley, John, Fenit House, Spa, Tralee	9,675	1,800	151,200
35	Mahony, George P. Gun, Kilmorna, Listowel	5,020	1,748	146,832
36	Leslie, Robert, Tarbert House, Tarbert	1,747	1,738	145,992
37	Mundy, Major General, and Vernon, the Rt Hon., London	5,892	1,711	143,724
38	Blennerhasset, Thomas, Shanavalley, Tralee	5,995	1,689	141,876
39	O'Connell, Daniel, Derrynane Abbey, Cahirciveen	17,394	1,626	136,584
40	Bateman, John, in Chancery, Lunatic Asylum, Dublin	2,406	1,469	123,396
41	Leahy, John White, South Hill, Killarney	5,511	1,425	119,700
42	Winn, Hon. Roland, Rossbehy, Glanbeigh	13,913	1,382	116,088
43	Day, Rev. John F., Beaufort, Killarney	2,264	1,348	113,232
44	Mahony, Edward, Lunatic Asylum, Dublin	11,688	1,338	112,392
45	Hussey, Samuel M., Edenburn, Tralee	3,526	1,283	107,772
46	Usburne, Thomas M., Cork	2,560	1,248	104,832

		Acreage 1876	Gross estimated rental Valuation 1876 (£)	Valuation 2016 (£)
47	Hurley, Conway (a minor), Bridge House, Tralee	2,559	1,230	103,320
48	Hickie, William C., Kilelton, Ballylongford	3,368	1,220	102,480
49	Collis, Stephen Edward, Tierdclea, Tarbert	3,598	1,207	101,388
50	Orpen, Sir Richard, 41 North Gt George's St, Dublin	12,873	1,197	100,548
51	Bernard, Edward M., Shehehroe, Killarney	7,136	1,194	100,296
52	Dennis, Meade C., Fort Granite, Baltinglass	3,550	1,103	92,652
53	Monteagle, Lord, Limerick	2,310	1,091	91,644
54	Wren, Leslie, Tralee	2,466	1,088	91,392
55	Rae, Langford, Keel House, Castlemanin	5,870	981	82,404
56	Chute, Rev. George, Market Drayton, Shropshire	5,094	891	82,404
57	Mahony, John, Dunloe Castle, Killarney	8,229	949	79,716
58	Hickson, Robert A., London	2,000	929	78,036
59	Fitzgerald, W.N.F., Derrybrick, Clare	2,400	914	76,776
60	Stoughton, William, Grosvenor Place, London	2,495	891	74,844
61	O'Connell, Chas J., Bantry	9,807	890	74,760
62	Day, Francis, Milltown, Kerry	1,704	890	74,760
63	Stokes, George D., Day Place, Tralee	2,747	875	73,500
64	The O'Donoghue, Summerhill, Killarney	9,463	868	72,912
65	Rowan, Major William, Belmont, Tralee	1,550	815	68,460
66	Donovan, Nichols, Denny Street, Tralee	1,295	814	68,376
67	Fitzmaurice, O. Reps, Dublin	2,170	794	66,696

		Acreage 1876	Gross estimated rental Valuation 1876 (£)	Valuation 2016 (£)
68	Coltsmann, Daniel, Glenflesk Castle, Killarney	10,316	786	66,024
69	Saunders, J.L. Reps, Cloughjordan, Tipperary	2,221	775	65,100
70	Browne, John P., Crotta, Kilflynn	2,065	770	64,680
71	Coltsmann, Catherine, Dublin	2,016	738	61,992
72	Corkery, Daniel O'Brien, Kenmare	6,439	730	61,320
73	Church Temporalities Commisisoners of, Dublin	1,500	694	58,296
74	Cuthbert, Thomas (a minor), England	3,407	685	57,540
75	Harte, Mahony Reps of, Tralee	1,682	667	56,028
76	Sugrue, Chas Reps of, Sidney Place, Cork	4,622	658	55,272
77	Hussey, Edward, The Grove, Dingle	3,954	651	54,684
78	Julian, Samuel, Jersey Villa, Cheltenham	3,711	651	54,684
79	Bland, Ven Archdeacon, Knockane Rectory, Beaufort	2,960	651	54,684
80	Busteed, Mary, Dublin	1,685	644	54,096
81	Butler, James, Waterville, Caherciveen	1,417	639	53,676
82	Neligan, William J., Denny Street, Tralee	1,087	635	53,340
83	Lawlor, Denis Shine, Grenagh, Killarney	1,374	607	50,988
84	Simpson, Stephen, Fitzwilliam Sq., Dublin	4,609	582	48,888
85	Orpen, Richard H., Killaha Castle, Killarney	4,348	578	48,552
86	Oliver, Major Reps of, Co. Cork	1,369	581	48,084
87	Blennerhasset, John, Shanavalley, Ballymacelligot	1,352	572	48,048
88	Foley, Edward, Ballyard, Tralee	1,604	555	46,620
89	Blackwood, Sir Henry, London	1,940	534	44,856
90	Browne, Rev. George, Nottingham	1,477	524	44,016

		Acreage 1876	Gross estimated rental Valuation 1876 (£)	Valuation 2016 (£)
91	Blennerhasset, Rowland, Kells Lodge, Cahirciveen	6,234	504	42,336
92	Nash, Charles F., Ballycarachy, Tralee	1,531	469	39,396
93	M'Carthy, Daniel, Headfort, Killarney	2,203	467	39,228
94	Hewson, George. Ennismore, Listowel	1,208	455	38,220
95	Wise, Francis, North Mall, Cork	9,636	443	37,212
96	M'Carthy, Alexander, Cork	2,979	438	36,792
97	Mahony, Thomas McDonagh, Cullinagh, Killarney	7,322	425	35,700
98	Fosberry, Mr, Curragh Bridge, Limerick	1,437	413	34,692
99	Rice, Justice D., Bushmount, Causeway	1,233	398	33,432
100	Bateman, Rowland, Tralee	1,259	397	33,348
101	Stack, Major General N.M. Reps, Lake Caraigh, Killarney	1,205	397	33,248
102	Goff, Joseph, Hales Park, Salisbury, Wilts	2,625	393	33,012
103	Mahony, David, Wiltslane	1,370	381	32,004
104	Mahony, John H., Tubrid, Kenmare	1,723	380	31,920
105	Sullivan, Thomas Kingston, The Retreat, Bandon	2,303	378	31,752
106	Fitzgerald, Rev. Richard, Ballydonehoe, Tarbert	1,349	363	30,492
107	Downing, Francis Henry, New Street, Killarney	1,803	355	29,820
108	Roche, Redmond, Castleisland	1,255	355	29,820
109	Mayberry, George M.D., Riverdale, Killarney	3,160	346	29,064
110	Brennan, Daniel, Dromhall, Killarney	2,220	340	28,560
111	Meredith, Richard, Dicksgrove, Farranfore	1,839	320	26,880
112	Raymond, George, Dublin	1,756	304	25,536

		Acreage 1876	Gross estimated rental Valuation 1876 (£)	Valuation 2016 (£)
113	Deane, James, Cork	1,753	300	25,200
114	Leahy, Colonel Arthur, Flesk Lodge, Killarney	1,068	300	25,200
115	Eagar, Eusebius McGillycuddy, Lake Cara Castle Killorglin	6,404	298	25,032
116	Chute, Algernon, Dublin	1,606	296	24,864
117	Roche, Catherine, Knights Lodge, Charleville	1,007	287	24,108
118	Roche, Stephen, Stephen's Green, Dublin	1,007	287	24,108
119	Chute, Charles, Stoughton's Row, Tralee	1,141	283	23,772
120	O'Rorke, Charles Denis, Clonbrum, Moloch, Galway	1,047	282	23,688
121	Palmer, Robert, Trafalgar Sq., London	2,104	277	23,268
122	Kitson, George L., Waterloo Road, Dublin	1,040	267	22,428
123	King, Nicholas M.D., Dublin	1,058	262	22,008
124	Palmer, John, Fortwilliam, Tralee	1,427	259	21,756
125	Barry, John, Villa Nova, Caherciveen	1,964	256	21,504
126	Driscoll, John, Knightstown, Valencia	1,346	248	20,832
127	Taylor, Adrian M.D., Clontoo, Kilgarvan	2,409	244	20,496
128	Butterly, Laurence Reps of, Listowel	1,052	244	20,496
129	Mahony, Kean, Cullina, Beaufort	3,104	234	19,656
130	Magill, Captain James, Churchtown House, Killarney	1,628	234	19,656
131	Hickson, Robert James, Asylum, Killarney	1,183	230	26,880
132	Leonard, Rev. S.B., Banteer, Cork	1,212	228	19,152
133	Fitzgerald, Robert M., Dublin	1,086	220	18,480
134	Harnett, William, England	1,489	203	17,052
135	Lawlor, Martin Reps of, Killarney	1,075	183	15,372

		Acreage 1876	Gross estimated rental Valuation 1876 (£)	Valuation 2016 (£)
136	Foley, James Snr Reps, Killorglin	1,603	160	13,440
137	Dennehy, Mary, Killarney	1,574	145	12,180
138	Orkney, Earl of, England	1,642	125	10,500
139	Williams, Fras Edward, Cappanagroun Lodge, Waterville	3,804	124	10,416
140	Dunraven, Earl of, Adare Manor, Limerick	1,005	123	10,332
141	Galway, Edward, Queen's County	1,571	116	9,744
142	Strange, Miss Barbara, Parkgariffe, Kenmare	1,387	115	9,660
143	Tuohill, Richard M.D., Merrion Sq., Dublin	1,164	106	8,904
144	M'Carthy, Daniel, Srugreana, Cahirciveen	1,033	106	8,904
145	Hewson, Rev. Francis, Rectory, Killarney	1,772	79	6,636
147	O'Sullivan, Daniel Reps, Dooaghs, Killorglin	2,160	66	5,544
146	Dodd, William Henry, Killorglin	1,000	55	4,620
148	Curtayne, James, Bellville, Killarney	1,165	53	4,452
149	Mahony, Kean, Glasnevin, Dublin	1,024	27	2,268

KILDARE

	1876	2020 Est
Population in County Kildare	83,614	210,312
All owners of land	1,766	76,500
Percentage of the population	2.11	-
Owners of nothing at all	81,848	51,930
Percentage of the population	97.89	-
Size of County	412,490 acres	418,560 acres
Number of dwellings (of which 1876 rented, owned in 2020)	14,166 (12,400) (1871)	70,504
Number of owned farm holdings	846 (1871)	2,578

County comparisons

	Acreage in 1876	Population in 1876
County Kildare	412,490	83,614
Surrey, England	398,746	342,113
Banffshire, Scotland	407,501	62,032
Montgomeryshire, Wales	380,384	67,263

Viscount Harberton, whose residence is given as 60 Rutland Gate, London, and in Bateman as Lyston Court, Ross, Herefordshire, has 5,167 acres in County Kildare in 1876 with a valuation of £3,658 about £307,272 in modern money. The title and that of Baron Harberton, created in 1783, are still extant and the family live in the UK, in Somerset. Prior to his elevation to the peerage, Arthur Pomeroy was MP for Kildare in the Irish House of Commons. An ancestor with the same name had arrived in Ireland in the late seventeenth century and acquired the Deanery of Cork. By 1764 his descendant was High Sheriff of Kildare and then MP. Being Irish titles, the Harbertons did not sit in the House of Lords. His son, the 2nd Viscount, was a barrister and MP before he succeeded to his father's titles in 1798. The Galway Estates register merely notes the arrival in Ireland of the first Pomeroy, and the later purchase of land from the Earl of Shannon. Bateman makes an adjustment of £141 to the valuation, suggesting that Harberton was in touch with him.

William Wilson of Coolcarrigan, Donadea, had 5,432 acres in Kildare in 1876, valued at £1,883 about £158,172 in modern money. The valuation was well below the threshold set by Bateman (£3,000) and Wilson does not appear in the Bateman's book, the *Great Landowners of Great Britain and Ireland* (See Bibliography). The clue here is the name of the house, still lived in by descendants of William Wilson. The family are descended from a Cromwellian soldier, Captain James Wright, who landed in Dublin in 1649. He was granted lands in Monaghan at Golagh. By 1688 James II had stripped him of the estates. This did not prevent a descendant becoming High Sheriff of Monaghan, another becoming a barrister in Dublin and yet another becoming Professor of Botany at Trinity College Dublin. Yet another, the Rev. Charles Henry Hamilton Wright, married a daughter of Nils Almroth, daughter of the director of the Swedish royal mint. Their son, a leading physician, worked with Alexander Fleming and was knighted and married Georgina, daughter of Robert Mackay Wilson of Coolcarrigan, which she inherited. A lot of the estate was bought by the Irish Government when it was setting up the Bord na Mona turf corporation. There is still a farm with the house, and the garden is open to visitors. Sir Almroth Edward's brother became the High Sheriff of Kildare in 1921, the last before the Free State was created.

William Murphy of Lullymore, Kildare. William Murphy owned 5,522 acres in Kildare in 1876 with a valuation of £705 about £59,220 in modern money. William Murphy's acreage was enough to get him into Bateman, but the valuation was well short of Bateman's criteria (£3,000). The acreage was large and Lullymore is close to the bog of Allen. The valuation would suggest that it was bogland or otherwise not very fertile. He is not recounted in Debrett's *Landed Gentry of Ireland*.

Major Robert Higginson Borrowes of Gilltown, Newbridge, County Kildare, had 6,089 acres in 1876 with a valuation of £4,013 about £337,092 in modern money. The Eton-educated major was an officer in the 13th Light Dragoons and, according to Bateman, owned house property in Dublin. Major Borrowes was serving at a time when commissions in the British Army were purchased. This practice was abolished in 1871 but Major Borrowes was likely to have paid about £4,575 for his commission as a major, about £320,000 in current values.

The Borrowes were Baronets (Sir) in the Gilltown area from about 1661. The title became extinct in 1939 with the death of the 11th Baronet.

There is no record of what happened to the estate.

The 4th Lord Cloncurry of Lyons, Hazlehatch, Kildare, had 6,121 acres in the county in 1876 with a valuation of £6,202 about £520,968 in

modern money. This Eton-educated peer, whose family name was Lawless, came from a family of bankers and wool merchants first made Baronets in 1776 and raised to the Irish peerage in 1789.

The Cloncurry estate reached well beyond Kildare and Bateman records 5,137 acres in Limerick, 923 acres in Dublin and 306 acres in Meath, totalling 12,487 acres with a valuation of £10,443. The estate was where Daniel O'Connel killed John D'Esterre in a duel, but the acres would never have supported the purchase of art made in Italy by the 2nd Baron Cloncurry, or the £200,000 he spent on renovating the house in 1804. This peer had spent time in the Tower of London on suspicion of being involved with the United Irishmen in the rebellion of 1798, and again with Robert Emmet in the rebellion of 1803. He survived and became a close advisor to the Viceroy of Ireland, the Marquis of Anglesea in 1828 and 1829.

Despite this rebellious past, the Baron was made a British peer in 1831, a few days after the coronation of William IV. The estate itself has been much in the news in recent years. In 1963 the University of Dublin (UCD) bought the house and 1,200 acres of land, price undisclosed. In the late 1990s, Tony Ryan, the founder of Ryanair, bought the house and about 600 acres for £3.5 million. He is then rumoured to have spent £80 million renovating the house and estate. He left it to his wife when he died in 2009. It was put on the market in the early 2000s with an asking price of £65 million, later reduced to £25 million. It is in the heart of Irish racing country, surrounded by some of the most important studs and stables in the world.

Conway Richard Dobbs MP of Castle Dobbs, Carrickfergus, County Antrim, owned 7,971 acres in Kildare in 1876 with a valuation of £2,424 about £203,616 in modern money. The Dobbs family, from their lair in Antrim, were huge owners of land in Ireland. Conway Dobbs' acres included, as well as the Kildare acres, 5,060 acres in Antrim valued at £5,065. His total acreage was 13,031 with a valuation of £7,489. A relative named as Conway Edward Dobbs of Leeson Street, Dublin, is recorded in the Returns as holding 5,348 acres in Co. Antrim with a valuation of £539. Bateman also notes a C.E. Dobbs of Glenariff in Kildare with an estate of 7,648 acres and valuation of £2,446.

The family arrived in Ireland in 1596 in the person of John Dobbs, son of a Lord Mayor of London who became deputy treasurer of Ulster. His descendant, Arthur Dobbs, was one of those who welcomed William of Orange when he landed at Carrickfergus in June 1690 to make preparations for the Battle of the Boyne. Successors were regularly High Sheriffs and MPs for Antrim. In 1753 another descendant was Governor of North Carolina and he had an estate of 400,000 acres there. A female descendant married into the Borrowes family (*see* Borrowes). The holder of the estate in 1876 was Conway Richard Dobbs, a

Justice of the Peace, Deputy Lieutenant of the County and MP for Carrickfergus. Ferres remarks on the fact that the Dobbs never received a peerage or baronetage despite their enduring service to the Crown in Northern Ireland. But neither did the Dobbs' estate in the north suffer the fate of their relatives in the Republic, at the hands of the Land Commission. A large estate still surrounds Castle Dobbs.

John La Touche of Harristown, Newbridge, County Kildare, had 11,282 acres in the county in 1876 valued at £7,951 about £667,884 in modern money. Bateman records La Touche holding a further 3,323 acres in Leitrim and 700 acres in Dublin with a total of 15,311 acres and a valuation of £10,160. It is worth mentioning his cousin, William La Touche in Leitrim, who lived at Bellvue in Delgany, Co. Wicklow, but whose major acreage was in Leitrim. This means that he escaped notice in the Leitrim Biogs, ranking only number 13 in that county. He had 8,234 acres in Leitrim, 1,798 acres in Wicklow and £1,347 acres in Tipperary, a total of 11,379 acres valued at £7,557. The La Touche family were important bankers in Dublin who arrived with William of Orange in 1690 as Huguenot refugees fleeing religious persecution in France.

Essentially, they were frugal and hardworking, and most of all they married well. They settled in Dublin after James I fled Ireland and William became King in England. Descendants of the 1st La Touche in Dublin, David Digues De La Touche married into the Uniake family of Cork, who had about 3,000 acres around Killeagh, in turn a relative of the Fitzgerald Dukes of Leinster who had 67,000 acres (*see* Duke of Leinster). A later descendant married a daughter of the Earl of Clancarty. Others married into the aristocratic families of Bangor, 9,864 acres, Dysart, 27,190 acres and Clonmell, 27,646 acres. They were also MPs. Turtle Bunbury, the travel writer, notes other landowning marriages including to the Earl of Lanesborough, who had 16,397 acres in 1876 with two large homes at Bellvue and Harristown. Harristown, still lived in by La Touch relatives as late as 1921, was bought by Major Michael Beaumont and the family still live there, according to Ferres. There were five La Touch MPs in the last session of the Irish House of Commons, only one of whom voted for the Union. The family were noted by Dean Swift for their charitable works.

The land commission acquired most of the land around Harristown and the Forestry Commission the land around Bellvue.

Sir Gerald George Aylmer, Bart of The Castle, Donadea, County Kildare, had 15,396 acres in Kildare in 1876 with a valuation of £6,890 about £578,760 in modern money. Bateman has Sir George with an unknown number of acres in Cumberland, with a valuation of £500. Presumably they were insufficient for Sir George to have corrected the earlier Bateman editions. In a rare pre-1600s reference in Debrett's, the family state that they were established in Ireland in the thirteenth century, in Dublin and at the manor of Lyons in Kildare. That house is mentioned in the Cloncurry biography, below. This mention is in the Debrett's entry for the baronetage of Sir Richard John Aylmer, a baronetage that is still extant and where there is also mention of perhaps the most famous of the many military men in the Aylmer family; Lieutenant General Sir Fenton John Aylmer, who was awarded the Victoria Cross in India in 1891.

There are two lines in the Aylmer family, both still extant. Rear Admiral Matthew Aylmer, a commander of the British fleet, was elevated to the peerage of Ireland in 1718 as Baron Aylmer of Balrath. That peerage is still extant, with the 14th Baron a solicitor who practices in London.

The 16th Baronet, Sir Richard John Aylmer of Donadea in Kildare, is a writer and lives in Canada where the Aylmers served, as in England and Ireland, in the army and navy.

Bateman notes another Aylmer estate in Kildare in 1876, that of Michael Aylmer of Courtown, Kilcock, who had 3,871 acres in Kildare, 732 acres in King's County and 9 acres in Dublin; a total of 4,612 acres with a valuation of £4,089. During the United Irishmen rebellion of 1798 the Aylmers fought on both sides.

Caroline Maria Aylmer, who was the daughter of Sir Gerald George Aylmer, 9th Baronet, was the last Aylmer to live at Donadea. She died in 1935, leaving the estate to the Church of Ireland who, in turn, passed it on to the Irish state.

The 3rd and last Marquis of Drogheda, Henry Francis Seymour Moore, of Moore Abbey, Monastrevan, County Kildare, held 16,609 acres in Kildare with a valuation of £8,951 about £751,884 in modern money. This marquisate was fairly short lived. Created in 1791 for the 6th Earl of Drogheda, who eventually became a Field Marshal in the British Army, it ended when the above holder of the estates died in 1892. In 1801 the 1st Marquis was also made a British Baron, meaning that he could sit in the House of Lords, the Irish House of Lords having shut with the act of Union the year before. He had been both an MP and the Grand Master of the Freemasons in Ireland. Bateman records the 3rd Marquis with 2,688 acres in Queen's County, to give him a total acreage of 19,297 acres with a valuation of £10,466.

The Current Earl of Drogheda, the 12th, is Henry 'Derry' Moore. Like his ancestor, he was educated at Eton, was a second lieutenant in the Life Guards and is a photographer. He lives in London.

Moore Abbey and 300 acres were put up for sale in 1937 after the then Earl recovered the lease from the family of Count John McCormack, the famous Irish tenor. The house was bought by the Sisters of Charity, who became infamous when details of the Magdalene laundries that they ran became public. The

10th Earl was a minister in Churchill's government during the Second World War. The 11th Earl became Chairman of the *Financial Times* and of the Royal Opera House. In an article on the Moore family written by Turtle Bunbury, the following quotes about the 11th Earl are made. 'As to his character, *The Spectator's* Clement Crisp regarded him as 'a brilliant and great man', Norman Lebrecht as an 'insufferable snob' and Richard Witts as 'one of the dimmest men ever to dither with the arts'.

The Duke of Leinster MP, of Carton Maynooth, County Kildare, held, according to the Return, 67,227 acres in Kildare with a valuation of £46,571 about £3,911,964 in modern money. Bateman makes a substantial correction, presumably on the advice of the Duke's agent. The acreage goes up to 71,977 acres and the valuation to £54,714, a somewhat poor Duke compared with some of his fellow Dukes in the UK. Bateman adds in 1,123 acres in Meath to bring the total acreage to 73,100 and the valuation to £55,877. The Duke of Leinster was the only Duke in Ireland at the time.

In relation to the antiquity of the title, which still exists, the Debrett's entry opens boldly: 'Gerald Fitzgerald baron of Offaly in county Kildare in right of his wife before 1203, died about 1203; succeeded by his son Sir Maurice, 2nd Baron and Lord Chief Justice of Ireland.'

The function, that of Lord Chief Justice, was one they were to hold again and again. As with a saga that began 814 years ago, this one had an immensity of event and incident and only a few can be mentioned. The Fitzgeralds were Norman Catholics, creating monasteries and introducing the great monastic orders of the early Middle Ages, Dominicans and Franciscans, into Ireland. Maurice, the 3rd Baron, became Chief Governor of Ireland during the reign of Henry III. The Fitzgeralds stayed at the top but, having become integrated, rebelled against the English monarchy fairly regularly. Henry VIII executed five Fitzgerald brothers at Tyburn in London in one batch, having persuaded a nephew who was also included to take his word that he would be pardoned. Henry VIII was as dangerous to his higher subjects as he was to his wives. The Fitzgeralds got the titles and lands back from Queen Mary, Elizabeth I's half-sister, until she too got the chop on Elizabeth's orders.

In relation to this huge estate, however, there are extraordinary issues. Some accounts suggest other Fitzgerald estates around the country, but they do not appear in Bateman or in the Returns. In Terence Dooley's book on the family, *The Fitzgeralds of Carton House*, he points out that no records exist as to how the estate was disposed of.

Carton remained in the control of the Fitzgeralds until the early 1920s, when the 7th Duke sold his birthright to a moneylender, Sir Harry Mallaby Deeley, in order to pay off gambling debts of £67,500.

He was third in line to succeed and so did not think he would ever inherit, but one of his brothers died in the war and another of a brain tumour, and so Carton, via the 7th Duke, was lost to the Fitzgeralds.

In 1923 a local unit of the IRA went to Carton with the intention of burning it down. However, they were stopped when a member of the Fitzgerald family brought a large painting of Lord Edward Fitzgerald to the door and pointed out that they would be burning the house of a revered Irish patriot.

Landowners of over 1,000 acres or close in 1876 Kildare

		Acreage	Valuation 1876 (£)	Valuation current (£)
1	Leinster, Duke of, Carton Maynooth	67,227	46,571	3,911,964
2	Drogheda, Marquis, Moore Abbey, Monasterevan	16,609	8,951	752,724
3	Aylmer, Sir G.G. Bart, Donadea Castle, Donadea	15,396	6,890	578,760
4	La Touche, John, Harristown, Brannoxtown	11,282	7,951	667,884
5	Dobbs, Conway, Castle Dobbs, Co. Antrim	7,971	2,424	203,616
6	Cloncurry, Lord, Lyons, Hazelhatch	6,121	6,202	520,968
7	Borrowes, Major R.H., Gilltown, Newbridge	6,089	4,013	337,092
8	Murphy, William, Lullymore	5,522	705	59,220
9	Wilson, William, Coolcarrigan, Donadea	5,432	1,883	158,172
10	Harberton, Viscount, 60 Rutland Gate, London	5,167	3,658	307,272
11	Barton, Hugh L., Straffan House, Straffan	5,044	5,096	428,064
12	Mayo, Earl of, Palmerstown, Naas	4,915	5,247	440,748
13	Fitzgerald, F.L., 9 Boscable Place, Regents Park, London	4,381	2,774	233,016
14	Colley, Hon. George F., Jerney, Stillorgin	4,216	2,637	221,508
15	Mansfield, G.P.L., Morristown, Lattin, Naas	4,057	3,313	278,292
16	Verschoyle, Lieutenant Col, Army & Navy Club, London	3,998	1,475	123,900

		Acreage	Valuation 1876 (£)	Valuation current (£)
17	Aylmer, Michael, Courtown, Kilcock	3,871	3,645	306,180
18	O'Ferrall, Rt Hon. M., Ballina Moyvalley, Enfield	3,213	2,305	193,620
19	O'Kelly, P. de Penthony, Barretstown, Newbridge	3,152	2,117	177,828
20	Hendrick, Thomas, Naas	3,088	2,535	212,940
21	Archbold, Robert, Davidstown, Catledermot	3,075	2,022	169,848
22	Wilson, George Orr, Dunardagh, Blackrock, Co. Dublin	2,990	2,035	170,940
23	Kelly, J., Castlebaggot, Rathcoole	2,826	1,367	114,828
24	Vesey, Charles C., Lucan House, Lucan	2,778	1,529	127,932
25	Bunbury, Kane Reps, Moyle Park, Carlow	2,695	1,784	149,856
26	Valentia, Viscount, Bletchington, Oxford	2,695	1,215	102,060
27	Connolly, Thomas, Castletown, Celbridge	2,605	3,346	282,576
28	Dalyell, Robert A., Scotland	2,450	517	43,428
29	Molyneux, Sir Capel, Castledillon, Co. Armagh	2,426	1,530	128,520
30	Magan, Eliza, Killyon, Mearn, Hill of Downs	2,374	1,086	91,224
31	Borrowes, Sir E.D. Bart, Barretstown, Castle Ballymore, Eustace	2,351	1,340	112,560
32	Digby, K.H., London	2,345	1,536	129,024
33	Palmer, Charles C., Rahin, Edenderry	2,342	2,048	172,032
34	Tickell, Captain Thos (RN)	2,240	2,037	171,108
35	Annesley, R. Joynt Reps, Mount Anthony, Rathmines	2,226	1,410	118,440
36	Canal Company, Grand, James Street Harbour, Dublin	2,182	4,195	352,380
37	Browne, Thomas W., 7 Ashbrook Terrace, South Circular Road, Dublin	2,178	1,755	147,420
38	Roberts, C.T.C., Sallymount, Newbridge	2,135	1,606	134,904

		Acreage	Valuation 1876 (£)	Valuation current (£)
39	Cogan, Rt Hon. W.H.F., Tinode, Blessington	2,087	1,560	131,040
40	Rice, S.R., Carrickfergus	2,037	936	78,624
41	Sweetman, Patrick, Longtown, Clane, Co. Kildare	1,994	1,701	142,884
42	Coates, William Reps, Knockinally, Kilcock	1,962	2'005	168,420
43	Fleming, Beecher P., Rush House, Co. Dublin	1,958	454	38,136
44	Clonmel, The Earl of, Bishopscourt, Straffan	1,906	1,917	161,028
45	Hort, Sir Josiah Wm Bt, 1 Merrion Sq., East Dublin	1,847	1,143	96,012
46	De Robeck, Baron, Gowran Grange, Naas	1,838	1,358	114,072
47	Cockburne, P.C., Shangangh Castle, Bray	1,816	1,255	105,420
48	Nicholls, George A., Garrisker, Moyvalley, Enfield	1,632	1,165	97,860
49	Bryan, George, Jenkinstown, Co. Kilkenny	1,627	1,223	102,732
50	Steel, Robert B., Donegal	1,594	1,128	94,752
51	Drake, John D., New Ross	1,568	1,112	93,408
52	Fitzwilliam, Earl, Coolattin Park	1,539	1,255	105,420
53	Fitzpatrick, Rev. Fred, Cloon, Ardagh	1,518	934	78,456
54	Browne, Robert, Riverstown, Monasterevan	1,495	572	48,048
55	Medlicott, James E., Dunmurry, Kildare	1,490	941	79,044
56	Seaton, Lord, Bert House, Athy	1,429	794	66,696
57	Eustace, Charles S., England	1,406	927	77,868
58	Wolfe, Richard, Forenaught, Naas	1,397	1,208	101,304
59	Geary, Francis, 10 Cadogan Place, London	1,382	1,149	96,156
60	Rich, George W., -	1,361	894	75,096
61	O'Farrell, Edward Reps, Kildangan, Monasterevan	1,354	715	60,060

		Acreage	Valuation 1876 (£)	Valuation current (£)
62	Downshire, Marquis of, Willsboro, Co. Down	1,338	940	78,960
63	Vesey, John T., 15 South Fredrick St, Dublin	1,332	803	67,452
64	Thompson, C.W., Hollywood Rath, Cloghran, Huddart, Co. Dublin	1,329	491	41,244
65	Maunsell, John, Oakley Park, Celbridge	1,308	1,277	107,268
66	De Burgh, T.J., Oldtown, Naas	1,281	2,318	194,712
67	Tylden, Sir John, -	1,242	781	65,604
68	Powell, Charlotte, 5 Brighton Terrace, Monkstown	1,234	2,767	232,428
69	Coates, Denis, Stapelstown, Donadea	1,209	896	75,264
70	Carysfort, Earl of, Glenart Castle, Arklow	1,206	955	80,220
71	Sherlock, Rev. William, Bray	1,201	1,397	117,348
72	Bury, Charles Michael, Downings, Prosperous	1,199	724	60,816
73	Laurenson, L., Nurney House, Kildare	1,177	590	49,560
74	Grattan, Richard, Drummond, Carbury	1,174	565	47,460
75	Mills, Samuel, Turnings, Straffan	1,142	1,077	90,468
76	M'Donnell, F.E.J., Rathangan, Co. Kildare	1,126	807	67,788
77	Finlay, Rev. J.W., Corkagh, Clondalkin	1,119	1,048	88,032
78	Henchy, D. O'Connor, Stonebrook, Ballymore, Eustace	1,090	1,002	84,168
79	Dunne, Denis, Newtown or Merginstown, Dunlavin	1,065	840	70,560
80	Errington, Michael, -	1,064	225	18,900
81	Hartley, Barthw, Colagan House, Carbury	1,057	794	66,696
82	Rorke, L.R., Knockmittenm Clondalkin	1,033	627	52,668
83	Ryndm Christopher, Mount Armstrong, Donadea	1,008	1,124	94,416
84	Dames, Francis L., -	990	284	23,856

		Acreage	Valuation 1876 (£)	Valuation current (£)
85	Reid, Philip, -	989	659	55,356
86	Wakefield, Thomas C., Bentown, Ballintore	987	676	56,784
87	Aldborough, Earl of, Belan Hall, Co. Kildare	964	764	66,696
88	Blackers (minors), Castlemartin, Kilcullen	948	909	76,356
89	Spencer, Thomas C., Waterford	927	509	42,756
90	Bookey, Wm Thomas, Derrybane, Rathdrum	895	830	69,720
91	Bolton, Chichester, -	882	487	40,908
92	Coote, Sir Charles Bt, Ballyfinn, Queen's County	878	601	50,484
93	Bor, William Loftus, Ballindolin, Edenderry	875	748	62,832
94	Paine, Wentworth, Ballinscarrig	872	527	44,268
95	Bonham, Rev. John, 5 Ounslow Crescent, South Kensington, London	868	699	58,716
96	Bulwer, Walter R., Barrowford, Athy	852	688	57,792
97	Jones, Rev. James, Kilmore, Co. Armagh	829	575	48,300
98	Kennedy, Elias, Ballyshannon	828	572	48,048
99	Cockburne, Miss, -	800	617	51,828
100	Myle, Mrs, Moone	786	610	51,240
101	Smith, Rev. Thomas, Co. Westmeath	785	318	26,712
102	Baggot, Christopher, Kildone, Kildare	595	317	26,628

Top 20 by income in 1876

		Acreage	Valuation 1876 (£)	Valuation current (£)
1	Leinster, Duke of, Carton, Maynooth	67,227	46,571	3,911,964
2	Drogheda, Marquis, Moore Abbey, Monasterevan	16,609	8,951	752,724

		Acreage	Valuation 1876 (£)	Valuation current (£)
4	La Touche, John, Harristown, Brannoxtown	11,282	7,951	667,884
5	Aylmer, Sir G.G. Bart, Donadea Castle, Donadea	15,396	6,890	578,760
6	Cloncurry, Lord, Lyons, Hazelhatch	6,121	6,202	520,968
7	Mayo, Earl of, Palmerstown, Naas	4,915	5,247	440,748
8	Barton, Hugh L., Straffan House, Straffan	5,044	5,096	428,064
9	Canal Company, Grand, James Street Harbour, Dublin	2,182	4,195	352,380
10	Borrowes, Major R.H., Gilltown, Newbridge	6,089	4,013	337,092
11	Harberton, Viscount, 60 Rutland Gate, London	5,167	3,658	307,272
12	Aylmer, Michael, Courtown, Kilcock	3,871	3,645	306,180
13	Connolly, Thomas, Castletown, Celbridge	2,605	3,346	282,576
14	Mansfield, G.P.L., Morristown, Lattin, Naas	4,057	3,313	278,292
15	Fitzgerald, F.L., 9 Boscable Place, Regents Park, London	4,381	2,774	233,016
16	Powell, Charlotte, 5 Brighton Terrace, Monkstown	1,234	2,767	232,428
17	Colley, Hon. George F., Jerney, Stillorgin	4,216	2,637	221,508
18	Hendrick, Thomas, Naas	3,088	2,535	212,940
19	Dobbs, Conway, Castle Dobbs, Co. Antrim	7,971	2,424	203,616
20	De Burgh, T.J., Oldtown, Naas	1,281	2,318	194,712

KILKENNY

	1876	2020 est
Population in County Kilkenny	103,379 (1871)	95,419
All owners of land	1,906	49,457
Percentage of the population	1.74	-
Owners of nothing at all	107,473	27,245
Percentage of the population	98.26	-
Size of County	505,309 acres	509,440 acres
Number of dwellings (of which rented)	20,577 (8,671) (1871)	33,583
Number of owned farm holdings	903 (1871)	3,737

County comparisons

	Acreage in 1876	Population in 1876
County Kilkenny	505,309	103,379
Warwickshire, England	541,022	634,189
Kirkcudbrightshire, Scotland	571,950	41,859
Carmarthenshire, Wales	510,574	115,710

The 6th Viscount Ashbrook of The Castle, Durrow, Kilkenny, held 7,190 acres in the county with a valuation of £3,455. The Viscount was, like so many entrants in our list, Eton educated and a military man in the 52nd of Foot, an infantry regiment. His corrections to Bateman's early edition had his Kilkenny acres increased to 9,292 acres and the valuation upped to £4,709. His other acreage included 7,746 acres in King's County, 4,643 acres in Queen's exists and the present holder is the 11th Viscount, Michael Llowarch Warburton Flower, a solicitor who lives in Cheshire, where he is Vice Lord Lieutenant of the County. Like the county, 860 acres in Limerick and 509 acres in Dublin, totalling 23,050 acres with a valuation of £13,911. The title still 10th Viscount, he was educated at Eton and was an officer in the infantry, this time the Grenadier Guards. The line began in the usual way, with a member of the family an MP in the Irish House of Commons, then being promoted a Baron and moving up to the Irish House of Lords as Baron Castle Durrow of County Kilkenny in 1733. His son was promoted to the rank of Viscount in 1751, all titles in the peerage of Ireland.

Ferres tells us that the family originated as Flore, or Flower, formerly seated at Oakham, Rutland, and represented that county in Parliament during the reign of Richard II who died in 1399, and in the person of Roger Flore, speaker of the House of Commons, during the time of Henry VI, who died in 1427. The Irish branch was founded by Sir George Flower, a Knight, who, in the reign of Elizabeth I, was a very active and brave officer against the rebels in Ireland, having command of 100 foot soldiers in the old army.

The Flower family sold the castle in 1922. The Forestry Commission and a private individual later took over the woods and the Land Commission the land. The castle is now an hotel.

Arthur MacMurrough Kavanagh of Borris House, Carlow, had 7,314 acres in Kilkenny in 1876, with a valuation of £5,032. There is a fuller biography of Arthur MacMurrough Kavanagh in the Carlow chapter. Here are the basics. By 1876 they had managed to hold on to a grand total of 29,025 acres, with a valuation of £15,608. Arthur had 16,051 acres in Carlow, 7,341 acres in Kilkenny, 5,013 acres in Wexford and 620 acres in Meath.

Arthur was, by any reckoning, an extraordinary man. He was almost limbless but learned to ride at 3, spent time in a harem, and sat in Parliament with his manservant propping him up. He was a protestant and a conservative but was widely respected by his tenants. He died in 1880.

The Earl of Desart of Desart Court, Kilkenny, had 8,000 acres in the county in 1876 with a valuation of £5,778. William Ulick O'Connor Cuffe, the 4th Earl who held the estate in 1876, had, in addition to the Kilkenny acres, 932 acres in Tipperary, giving him a total of 8,932 acres with a valuation of £6,278. He was educated at Eton and was an officer in the Grenadier Guards. His second marriage was to Odette Bischoffscheim, daughter of a banker in London. When he died, Ellen, Countess of Desart, became a senator in the Free State Senate from 1922 to 1933 and was the first Jewish person to sit in the Free State Parliament. She funded many charitable projects in Kilkenny and succeeded her brother-in-law as President of the Kilkenny Gaelic League, the first and probably only Jewish countess ever to hold such a post.

The family originated in Somerset and came with the Earl of Essex, getting 6,000 acres in Cork. A later member of the family, Joseph Cuffe, served in Cromwell's army in 1649 and was granted more land. The title became extinct when the 5th Earl died in 1934. The house was burnt down in 1923, presumably by enemies of the Free State, one of whose senators occupied it. It was rebuilt by the daughter of the 4th Earl, Lady Kathleen Milborne-Swinnerton-Pilkington, but was finally demolished in 1957.

The Hon. Leopold George Bryan of Jenkinstown, Kilkenny, had 8,209 acres in the county in 1876 with a valuation of £5,721. This family first appear as landowners in Kilkenny on a grant from the Earl of Ormonde in 1568. In the late 1600s a member of the family, Aylmer Bryan, was a brigadier in the French Army. A later descendant married the Countess of Rutaut from Lorraine in France. A later daughter married the 2nd Baron Bellew, who had 4,314 acres (*see* Co. Louth). That title still exists and the 4th Earl lived at Jenkinstown. The house became dilapidated but is believed to have been bought by the singer-songwriter Jimmy McCarthy, who is renovating it.

The holder of the estate in 1876 was the Hon. George Leopold Bryan, who was MP for County Kilkenny and High Sheriff in 1852. In 1849 he married Lady Elizabeth Georgina Conyngham, daughter of Francis Nathaniel, 2nd Marquess Conyngham, a landowner from Kent with over 166,710 acres, 123,000 of them in Donegal.

Viscount Mountgarret of South Audley St, London, and Ballyconra, Kilkenny, had 11,919 acres in the county in 1876 with a valuation of £7,226. Bateman upgrades the Viscount's holdings in Kilkenny considerably, to 14,073 acres, and the valuation to £8,503. Mountgarret had 505 acres in Wexford and 120 acres in Yorkshire, giving him a total acreage of 14,698 and a valuation of £9,606.

No school is recorded but the current Viscount, the 18th, Piers James Richard Butler was educated at Eton. He is the senior known heir to the Earldoms of Ormonde and Ossory. The Viscountancy was created in the Irish peerage in 1550, and there is also a UK Baronetcy dating from 1911. He gives an address in Yorkshire.

The Marquis of Ormonde had 11,960 acres in this county in 1876 with a valuation of £8,191. This essentially English aristocrat was educated at Harrow, Eton's great rival and sister school, and like so many of the big Irish landowners, he served in the Life Guards, clinging closely to the Royals. The Ormondes' title is of Gaelic Irish origin. Ormonde was a kingdom north of the Decies, as part of Waterford was known. Once the Norman settlement had taken hold in Ireland, Ormonde became the fiefdom of the Butler family and it stayed in that family for the better part of eight centuries. The biggest break was in 1528 when Thomas Boleyn, father of Henry VIII's mistress Anne Boleyn and grandfather of Elizabeth I, was granted the title. There were beheadings, a poisoning and much treason to follow, but by the Restoration of the monarchy in 1660, the then Butler Earl was made a Duke in both the Irish and English peerages. The 2nd Duke prospered under the new order but lost everything in 1715, two years after the House of Hanover took the British throne. The Marquissate, though restored by 1825, became extinct in 1997 and the Earldom dormant. Two daughters of the 7th and last Marquis, Lady Constance Anne and Lady Violet Cynthia, were married and living in the United States in the 1980s.

The combined Tipperary and Kilkenny holdings came to 27,725 acres in 1876, with a valuation of £15,431. The family home, Kilkenny Castle, is a possession of the Irish state and a major tourist attraction. Parts of the estate were sold off as early as the 1850s and the Land Commission later distributed land from what was left of the estate.

Colonel the Rt Hon. Fredrick Edwards Bunbury Tighe of Woodstock, Kilkenny, and the Priory, Christchurch, Hants, had 11,970 acres in Kilkenny in 1876, with a valuation of £5,332. The Eton-educated colonel had, in addition to the Kilkenny acres, 5,211 acres in Westmeath, 2,185 acres in Carlow, 1,803 acres in Tipperary, 591 acres in Wexford and 3 acres in Dublin. The total acreage was 21,763 with a valuation of £11,889. Bateman has him serving with the 53rd and 82nd of Foot, both infantry regiments.

Ferres, working from Debrett's *Landed Gentry of Ireland*, locates the original Tighe family in Rutland with a first settler arriving in Ireland pre-1641. By 1649 Richard Tighe was Sheriff of Dublin, a colonel in the militia and Mayor of Dublin in 1651–55. He sat for Dublin in Cromwell's Union Parliament in 1656.

In relation to the holder of the estate in 1876, there is an issue. Bateman cites Colonel Fredrick Edward Bunbury as the holder. He was the nephew of the Rt Hon. William Fredrick Fownes Tighe, who is given no military title and who was married to Lady Lennox, the fifth daughter of the 4th Duke of Richmond, a landholder in England with 286,411 acres. He died in 1878 but it looks as if he may have passed on the estate earlier. Fredrick Edward Bunbury married Louisa Ponsonby, a daughter of the 4th Earl of Bessborough, an Irish peer with 35,440 acres, 23,967 of them in Kilkenny.

There is no public record of what happened to the estate. Kilkenny County Council tend to the gardens, which are open to the public. The house is a ruin.

Charles B.C. Wandesforde of Castlecomer in County Kilkenny had 22,232 acres with a valuation of £11,745. The Wandesforde landed record is complex, made more so by a misleading item in the NUI estates database. This states that:

> The Wandesforde family acquired land in counties Limerick and Clare following the marriage in 1750 of Agnes Elizabeth, daughter of John Southwell of Enniscouch Co Limerick, and John Wandesforde, 5th Viscount Castlecomer and 1st Earl Wandesforde.

Whatever lands were in Limerick and Clare, and they can be assumed to be those recorded below, they were nothing like the estate that Agnes Elizabeth married into, which was at least 22,232 acres in extent.

The Castlecomer estate, which had working anthracite coal mines, is not formally confirmed by Bateman, who records that Henry Butler-Clarke-Southwell-Wandesforde, of Ulcomber Place, Staplehurst, Kent, had 4,137 acres in Co. Limerick and 6,737 acres in Clare, together with 1,207 acres in Derby and 8,50 acres in Kent valued at £8,141.

The Returns, but not Bateman, record that The Hon. C.B. Wandesforde of Mount Juliet in County Kilkenny had 6,737 acres in County Clare, valued at £2,511, and that Henry Thomas Butler Wandesforde of Palmerstown, County Dublin, had 4,137 acres in Limerick, with a valuation of £2,190.

The NUI mention, taken as a reference point, fails to point out the 5th Viscount and the 1st Earl, who were the same person, were also the last of both peerages, which became extinct, with a Yorkshire Baronetage, when the 1st Earl died in 1784.

This begs the fate of the estate, which actually came into the Wandesforde family in 1636 by way of confiscation and grant. Christopher Wandesforde, who got the estate via Wentworth, to whom he was secretary, played an interesting role in the dispute between King Charles I and Parliament concerning his demands for £1 million.

The final owner of the estate, according to Ferres, was Captain Henry Henry Prior Wandesforde, who set up local industries around the mines and founded a co-operative bank and a co-operative shop. The house fell into ruin and there is no mention of what became of this estate, with mines and thousands of acres of woodland. That is a task for local historians in Castlecomer.

The 5th Earl of Bessborough of Bessborough House, Piltown, in County Kilkenny, had 23,967 acres with a valuation of £15,484. The Harrow-educated 5th Earl of Bessborough, who held the estate in 1876, had a series of critical government appointments in that period. He was Steward of the Household and Master of Her Majesty's Staghounds, Her Majesty being the Queen Empress Victoria. Bateman records the Earl holding, in addition to the Kilkenny acreage, 10,578 acres in Carlow, 200 acres in Tipperary, an acre of Waterford and 694 acres in Leicestershire, a total of 35,440 acres with a valuation of £22,384.

The family name is Ponsonby, derived from a manor in Cumberland. Their ancestor, a knight, is said by Debrett's to have landed in England with William the Bastard. Sir John Ponsonby came to Ireland as a colonel in Cromwell's army and had various functions in the administration, winding up as an MP in the Restoration Parliament after 1660. They are the hereditary barbers to the King;

hairdressers to the Queen though no one has noted this change. During the eighteenth century the family had cemented their position at the very heart of the British Imperial establishment via a series of strategic marriages to aristocratic landowners. William Ponsonby, the 2nd Earl, married Lady Caroline Cavendish, the eldest daughter of the Duke of Devonshire, who later held 198,572 acres with a valuation of £180,750. Catherine Ponsonby, a daughter of the 3rd Earl, married the 5th Duke of St Albans, who held 8,998 acres. Another daughter, Charlotte, married the 4th Earl, Fitzwilliam, who had 115,743 acres with a valuation of £138,801. The current Earl, the 12th, is Miles Fitzhugh Longfield Ponsonby, who is a chartered accountant and lives in Hampshire.

The house was burnt in 1923 and rebuilt in 1929. It was sold to the Oblate fathers, who eventually sold it to the Irish Department of Agriculture. Finding the fate of the lands would require a detailed search of the Land Commission records.

Viscount Clifden of Gowran, Castle Kilkenny, had 35,288 acres with a valuation of £20,793. The Viscount held land in five English counties and four Irish counties, making him one of the great landowners of the time. Aside from the Kilkenny acreage he had 4,774 acres in Northampton, 2,976 acres in Bucks, 2,537 acres in Somerset, 1,107 acres in Oxford, 821 acres in Dublin, 978 acres in Kildare and 500 acres in Meath, totalling 49,017 acres with a valuation of £38,915.

The original family name Robartes is Cornish. The Irish peerages of Clifden and the British title of Robartes became extinct in 1974. Members of the family were courtiers to Queen Victoria. John Robartes of Lanhydrock in Cornwall was created Viscount Bodmin and Earl of Radnor between 1634 and 1679. He vacillated between monarchy and Parliament but fought for Parliament and Cromwell during the English Civil War, when he came to Ireland. He returned to England and towards the end of his life was Lord President of the Council. In 1876 Lord Robartes of Lanhydrock in Cornwall had 22,234 acres in that county with a valuation of £30,730. There is no mention of the Robartes family in the predecessors of the current Earl of Radnor.

Gowran was a place with local kings as early as the fifth century, and local place names indicate prehistoric habitation. The area was occupied by the Normans soon after the invasion of 1171. The first castle built there was in 1385. After Irish independence the Land Commission became involved. There were obscure questions in the Dail in the 1950s that got equally obscure and unhelpful answers. For an estate as huge as this there should be a huge volume of records, somewhere. The castle has been restored and there is a large stud farm in the area.

Kilkenny's County by largest acreage 1876

		Acreage	Valuation 1876 (£)	Valuation current (£)
1	Clifden, Viscount, Gowran Castle, Gowran, Kilkenny	35,288	20,793	1,746,612
2	Bessborough, Earl of, Bessborough, Piltown	23,967	15,484	1,300,656
3	Wandesforde, Charles B.C., Castlecomer, Co. Kilkenny	22,232	11,745	986,580
4	Tighe, The Rt Hon. Col W.F. Inistiogue, Co. Kilkenny	11,970	5,332	447,888
5	Ormonde, Marquess of, The Castle, Kilkenny	11,960	8,191	688,044
6	Mountgarret, Viscount, South Audley St, London	11,919	7,226	606,984
7	Bryan, George Leopold, Jenkinstown, Kilkenny	8,209	5,721	480,564
8	Desart, Earl of, Kilkenny	8,000	5,778	485,352
9	Kavanagh, Arthur MacMorrough, Borris House, Carlow	7,341	5,032	422,699
10	Ashbrook, Viscount, Durrow, Queen's County	7,190	3,455	290,220
11	Healy, Captain George, Foulkscourt Castle, Johnstown	6,461	4,010	336,840
12	De Montmorency, Rev. Waller, Castle Morreas, Knoctopher	4,808	2,630	220,920
13	Flood, William H., Farmley, Kilkenny	4,687	4,155	349,020
14	Frankfort, Viscount, Office of Stewart and Kincaid, 6 Leinster Street, Dublin	4,604	2,088	175,392
15	Coghill, Sir Joclyn, Belvedere, Drumcondra, Co. Dublin	4,564	2,622	223,608
16	Flood, William, Paulstown Castle, Kilkenny	3,852	2,345	196,980
17	Power, J.O.N., Snowhill, Waterford	3,788	2,857	239,988
18	Sullivan, Michael, Lacken Hall, Kilkenny	3,770	2,062	173,208
19	Aylward, James K., Shankill Castle, Whitehall, Co. Kilkenny	3,376	2,420	203,280

		Acreage	Valuation 1876 (£)	Valuation current (£)
20	Normanton, Earl of, Rochecourt, Salisbury	3,285	2,421	203,364
21	Barker, William Ponsonby, Kilcooley Abbey, Co. Tipperary	3,260	1,910	160,440
22	Putland, George Reps, Bray	3,229	949	79,716
23	Meredyth, Henry W., Norelands, Stoneyford	3,217	3,152	264,768
24	Clayton, Richard C.B., Carrickbyrne, New Ross	3,063	2,122	178,248
25	St George, Howard J., Kilrush House, Freshford	2,873	1,710	143,640
26	Stuart, Catherine Villiers, Castletown, Carrick-on-Suir	2,790	2,241	188,244
27	Power, Sir Richard Bt, Kilfane, Thomastown	2,650	1,888	158,592
28	Langrishe, Sir James, Knocktopher Abbey, Knocktopher	2,615	1,877	157,660
29	Marsh, Francis, Springmount, Mountrath	2,605	1,510	126,840
30	Nixon, James A., Ballyragget, Co. Kilkenny	2,493	1,565	131,460
31	Waring, John, Pottlerath House, Kilmanagh	2,488	1,297	108,948
32	Stephenson, Patrick Reps, Kiltorkan, Knocktopher	2,457	1,269	106,596
33	O'Shea, Nicholas P., Gardenmorris, Kilmacthomas	2,417	1,975	165,900
34	Boyse, Captain H.S.H., Bannow, Wexford	2,372	1,595	133,980
35	Congreve, Ambrose, Mount Congreve, Waterford	2,295	1,868	156,912
36	Trustees of Joseph Evans, Kilkenny	2,289	1,472	123,648
37	Johnston, Frances M., Ballytobin, Kilkenny	2,258	1,753	147,252
38	Cahill, Michael, Ballyconra, Ballyragget	2,249	1,480	124,320
39	Cliffe, Anthony, Bellvue, Enniscorthy	2,236	936	78,624
40	Clonmel, Earl of, Bishop's Court, Straffan, Co. Kildare	2,135	1,434	120,456

		Acreage	Valuation 1876 (£)	Valuation current (£)
41	Connellan, Peter, Coolmore, Thomastown	2,135	891	74,844
42	Kearney, J.C., Blanchfieldtown, Gowran	2,107	1,692	142,128
43	Church Temporalities Commissioner, Dublin	2,104	1,763	148,092
44	Granard, Earl of, and Morgan, Ho.n Mrs Deane, Johnstown Castle, Wexford, Enniscorthy	2,069	638	53,592
45	Humphries, Hugh, Ballyhaise, Cavan	2,061	865	72,660
46	Davis, Sydenham Wm, Mount Michael, Templeogue	2,049	1,518	127,512
47	Thomas, Francis A., Army	1,968	606	50,904
48	Smithwick, Edmond, Kilcreene House, Kilkenny	1,957	1,839	154,476
49	Keatinge, Michael D., Woodgift House, Urlingford	1,912	1,136	95,424
50	Power, Nicholas A., Belview, Waterford	1,911	2,141	179,844
51	Eyre, Thomas, Uppercourt, Freshford, Co. Kilkenny	1,909	2,165	181,860
52	Wemys, Major Otway, Danesfort, Kilkenny	1,870	1,423	119,532
53	Blunden, Sir John Bt, Castle Blunden, Kilkenny	1,846	1,385	116,340
54	Murphy, John, Mount Loftus, Goresbridge	1,793	1,283	107,772
55	Hughes, Right Rev. Joshua and Mrs, St Asaph's, North Wales	1,771	1,123	94,332
56	Bush, Gervaise P., Glencairne Abbey, Lismore	1,746	1,444	121,296
57	Cuffe, Sir Charles F.W. Bart, Lyrath, Kilkenny	1,738	1,388	116,592
58	Greene, Hugh, Rockview, Inistiogue	1,717	831	69,804
59	Anderson, T.W., Gracedieu, Waterford	1,704	1,131	95,004
60	Trustees of John Flood, Flood Hall, Stonyford	1,683	1,278	107,352

		Acreage	Valuation 1876 (£)	Valuation current (£)
61	Izod, Lorenzo Z., Chapleizod House, Thomastown	1,661	1,420	119,280
62	Warren, Edward Lewis, Lodge Park, Freshford	1,661	1,246	104,664
63	Jeffares, Joseph Rep, New Ross	1,607	1,095	91,980
64	Scully, William, Castlepark, Co. Tipperary	1,607	742	62,328
65	Roche, T.R., Ryehill, Co. Galway	1,572	1,943	163,212
66	Bowers, Maunsell (minors) E. Roberts, Waterford Receivers	1,568	950	79,800
67	Gaussen, Charles, Dublin	1,559	965	81,060
68	Davis, John, Summerhill, Thomastown	1,538	1,272	106,848
69	Dunsany, Lord, Dunsany Castle, Dunshaughlin	1,530	483	40,572
70	Pope, Elizabeth, Dublin	1,524	537	45,108
71	Morris, George Wall, Gracedieu Lodge, Waterford	1,520	1,109	93,156
72	Caulfield, St George, Tyndhurst, Hants	1,514	738	61,992
73	Tighe, Daniel, Ashford, Co. Wicklow	1,514	737	61,908
74	Cuffe, Harriett, Norfolk Street, Park Lane, London	1,513	738	61,992
75	Reade, Fredrick R.M., Rossenara, Kilmoganny	1,506	1,034	86,856
76	Chancery, Court of, Dublin	1,488	813	68,292
77	Stannard, Robert, The Grange, Ballyragget, Co. Kilkenny	1,395	894	75,096
78	Greene, W.H., Dublin	1,395	694	58,296
79	Carrick, Earl of, Mount Juliet, Thomas Town	1,368	1,182	99,288
80	Mosse, Arthur Wellesley, Ballyconra, Ballyragget	1,350	1,024	86,016
81	Tighe, Very Rev. H.U., Londonderry	1,347	616	51,744

		Acreage	Valuation 1876 (£)	Valuation current (£)
82	Strangeways, James and Loughnan, Connell Reps, Agents Jas M. Loughman, Crow Hill, Freshford, Co. Kilkenny	1,331	801	67,284
83	Butler, Henry, Kilmurry, Thomastown	1,304	1,006	84,504
84	Dobbyn, Margaret, Waterford	1,301	671	56,364
85	Cooke, John, Ballyneal, New Ross	1,290	714	59,976
86	Stannard, Rev. Henry, Kilkenny	1,241	1,012	85,008
87	Moore, Ponsonby Arthur, Whitehall Gardens, London	1,240	966	81,144
88	Tucker, Francis, London	1,191	1,088	91,392
89	Persse, Burton R., Moyode Castle, Athenry	1,182	605	50,820
90	Vaux of Harrowden Lord, Rosmead, Delvin, Co. Westmeath	1,182	375	31,500
91	Poe, Arthur, Harley Park, Callan	1,170	889	74,676
92	Jone,s John H., Mullinabro, Waterford	1,168	1,073	90,132
93	Sullivan, Francis, Castle Bamford, Kilkenny	1,158	375	31,500
94	Flood, Henry, Viewmount, Gowran, Co. Kilkenny	1,137	831	69,804
95	Parnell, H.D.D., -	1,107	737	61,908
96	Sheppard, William, Inistioge	1,106	631	53,004
97	Trustees of Judge Compton, Hampshire	1,100	559	46,956
98	Mackessy, G.L., Agent H.V. Mackessy, Waterford	1,097	832	69,888
99	Villiers, M.C., Beechill, Co. Galway	1,097	715	60,060
100	Webb, George Oliver, Webbsborough, Castlecomer	1,089	621	52,164
101	Maher, Matthias Aidan, Ballinkeel, Enniscorthy	1,081	740	62,160
102	Rossal, Thomas H., Jamaica	1,068	603	50,652
103	Brady, Miss L.G.B., Weston, Duleek	1,065	736	61,824
104	Cuffe, Susan, Waterford	1,059	288	24,192

		Acreage	Valuation 1876 (£)	Valuation current (£)
105	Lymbery, Rev. J., Fethard, Co. Wexford	1,046	590	49,560
106	Tyndall, Robert, Oaklands, New Ross	1,015	1,080	90,720
107	Greene, John, Inistiogue	1,014	424	35,616
108	Andrews, John Reps, Comber, Co. Down	993	794	66,696
109	Boyd, Thomas, New Ross	984	670	56,280
110	Conn, J.L., Mount Ida, Waterford	971	681	57,204
111	Butler, William, Urlingford	906	559	46,956
112	Andrews, Anne Jane, 88 Lower Baggot St, Dublin	840	827	69,468
113	Andrews, William D., 2 Gardiner's Place, Dublin	840	427	35,868
114	Ayres, Rev. George, Leixlip, Co. Dublin	832	478	40,152
115	Buggy, Eliza, Cantwell's Court, Kilkenny	826	352	29,568
116	Barnes, Thomas, Stephen's Green, Dublin	809	317	26,628
117	M'Carthy, Justin, 13 Charlotte Quay, Cork	800	567	47,628
118	Bolger, W.H., Rower, New Ross	798	493	41,412
119	Ball, Hannah S., Three Castles, Co. Kilkenny	756	734	61,656
120	Meredyth, Sir Edward N., office of Guiness & Mahon, 17 College Green, Dublin	730	407	34,188

Top 20 in Kilkenny by gross estimated rental income, 1876

		Acreage	Valuation 1876 (£)	Valuation current (£)
1	Clifden, Viscount, Gowran Castle, Gowran, Kilkenny	35,288	20,793	1,746,612
2	Bessborough, Earl of, Bessborough, Piltown	23,967	15,484	1,300,656

		Acreage	Valuation 1876 (£)	Valuation current (£)
3	Wandesforde, Charles B.C., Castlecomer, Co. Kilkenny	22,232	11,745	986,580
4	Ormonde, Marquess of, The Castle, Kilkenny	11,960	8,191	688,044
5	Mountgarret, Viscount, South Audley St, London	11,919	7,226	606,984
6	Desart, Earl of, Kilkenny	8,000	5,778	485,352
7	Bryan, George Leopold, Jenkinstown, Kilkenny	8,209	5,721	480,564
8	Tighe, The Rt Hon. Col W.F., Inistiogue, Co. Kilkenny	11,970	5,332	447,888
9	Kavanagh, Arthur MacMorrough, Borris House, Carlow	7,341	5,032	422,699
10	Flood, William H., Farmley, Kilkenny	4,687	4,155	349,020
11	Healy, Captain George, Foulkscourt Castle, Johnstown	6,461	4,010	336,840
12	Ashbrook, Viscount, Durrow, Queen's County	7,190	3,455	290,220
13	Meredyth, Henry W., Norelands, Stoneyford	3,217	3,152	264,768
14	Power, J.O.N., Snowhill, Waterford	3,788	2,857	239,988
15	De Montmorency, Rev. Waller, Castle Morres, Knoctopher	4,808	2,630	220,920
16	Coghill, Sir Joclyn, Belvedere, Drumcondra, Co. Dublin	4,564	2,622	223,608
17	Normanton, Earl of, Rochecourt, Salisbury	3,285	2,421	203,364
18	Aylward, James K., Shankill Castle, Whitehall, Co. Kilkenny	3,376	2,420	203,280
19	Flood, William, Paulstown Castle, Kilkenny	3,852	2,345	196,980
20	Stuart, Catherine Villiers, Castletown, Carrick-on-Suir	2,790	2,241	188,244

OFFALY (KING'S COUNTY)

	1876	2020 Est
Population in King's County	75,900	76,687 (2017)
All owners of land	1,138	40,124
Percentage of the population	1.49	-
Owners of nothing at all	95,518	22,040
Percentage of the population	98.51	
Size of County	491,629 acres	493,440 acres
Number of dwellings (of which rented)	14,799 (13,661)	26,543
Number of owned farm holdings	1,138 (1871)	3,460

County comparisons

	Acreage 1876	Population 1876
King's County	491,629	75,900
Buckinghamshire, England	456,210	175,879
Caithness, Scotland	471,763	39,992
Carmarthenshire, Wales	510,574	115,710

Thomas L. Dames of Greenhill, Edenderry, had 6,798 acres in King's County in 1876, with a valuation of £1,917 about £161,028. Dames' low valuation keeps him out of Bateman. The name occurs twice in the Return:

Dames, Francis T. L.	21 Herbert Street, Dublin	owned 285 acres
Dames, Thomas L.	Greenhill, Edenderry	owned 6,798 acres

A short description of the workhouse in Edenderry will help to illustrate living conditions for the poor and landless at the time, who were looked after by local landowners who paid the rates for the upkeep of the place. Edenderry Poor Law Union was formally declared on 7 May 1839 and covered an area of 290 square miles. Its operation was overseen by an elected Board of Guardians, twenty-two in number, representing its seventeen electoral divisions as listed below (all of them landowners):

King's County: Ballinakill, Ballyburly, Ballymacwilliam, Clonmore, Clonsast (2), Croghan, Edenderry (3).

Co. Kildare: Ardkill, Ballynadrimna, Cadamstown, Carbury, Cloncurry, Mylerstown, Rathangan (2).
Co. Meath: Ballyboggan, Castlejordan, Clonard (2). The Board also included 7 *ex-officio* Guardians, making a total of 29.

The Guardians met each week on Saturday. The population falling within the Union at the 1831 census had been 35,536, with divisions ranging in size from Ballinakill (population 1,081) to Edenderry itself (4,535). (There was no public transport. You walked to the workhouse.)

The new Edenderry Union workhouse was erected on a 6-acre site half a mile to the south-west of Edenderry. Designed by the Poor Law Commissioners' architect George Wilkinson, the building was based on one of his standard plans to accommodate 600 inmates. Its construction cost £5,300 plus £1,110 for fittings, etc.

The workhouse was declared fit for the reception of paupers on 21 December 1841, and received its first admissions on 19 March 1842.

Edward Williams of Herrington, Dorchester, had 6,884 acres in King's County in 1876, with a valuation of £1,568 about £131,712 in modern money. Mr Williams presents us with the same problem as the Dames, below. His valuation is too small to get him into Bateman. There is no other public record available on him.

Viscount Ashbrook of Durrow Castle, Durrow, Queen's County, had 7,476 acres in King's County with a valuation of £2,593 about £217,812 in modern money.

See page 201.

The Church Temporalities Commissioners of 24 Upper Merrion St Dublin had 7,647 acres in King's County in 1876, with a valuation of £4,000 about £336,000 in modern money.

See page 25.

John Gilbert King of Ballylin Ferbane, King's County, had 8,741 acres with a valuation of £4,073 about £342,132 in modern money. John Gilbert King was the MP for King's County and, based on his correction to the early Bateman editions, had 10,242 acres in the county with a valuation of £4,673. He also had 954 acres in Roscommon, giving him a total acreage of £11,196 with a valuation of £5,517. The first record of this family in Ireland is dated 1593 when the Rt Rev. Edward King from Stukeley in Huntingdon was elected a Fellow of Trinity College Dublin. He later became Lord Bishop of Elphin. The clerical element of the family reoccurred regularly, with descendants marrying the clergy or becoming clergymen themselves. The first John King at Ballylin was succeeded by his son, the Rev. Henry King. He married a sister of the Countess of Rosse. Their son became the local MP and was High Sheriff. A daughter married Viscount Bangor. The family left Ballylin and the house was destroyed in the 1940s.

Colonel Thomas Bernard of Castle Bernard, Kinnetty, had 13,153 acres in the county with a valuation of £6,032 about £506,688. This military family – Bateman had the owner in 1876 a colonel in the 12th Lancers, a cavalry regiment in the British Army – first appear at Kinnetty 1769. The family were High Sheriffs in King's County and the MP for the county. Thomas's ancestors at Castle Bernard, or Castle Kinnitty as it was later known, were officers in the local militia, justices of the peace and married well, including to the family of Lord Dunally (21,081 acres in Tipperary) and the MP Francis Healy Hutchinson. Thomas Bernard, who was Lord Lieutenant of King's County, died unmarried in 1882. The castle was burnt down by the IRA in 1922, and rebuilt in 1928 at the expense of the new taxpayers of the Irish Free State. The castle was sold to Lord Decies by the Bernard family in 1946. He sold it to the Irish Government in 1951. It was later converted into an hotel by the Ryan family.

The Marquis of Downshire of Hillsborough Castle, County Down, had 13,679 acres in 1876 with a valuation of £7,261.

See page 105.

The Earl of Charleville of Charleville Forest, Tullamore, held 20,032 acres in the county in 1876, with a valuation of £10,052 about £844,368 in modern money. Bateman shows the Charleville Forest estate as the sole possession of the Countess of Charleville. The Wiki entry says that the Countess of Charleville died in 1851. In fact, the estates went to the sister of the 3rd Earl, who was not, because she was the sister of an Earl, a Countess. She was a Lady, as daughter of an Earl. There are a number of mentions in Burke's that illustrate some of the problems of being a landowner in Ireland from time to time. The Charleville peerage, whose name was Bury, were part of the Moore family associated with Drogheda. The first two Moores, Sir Thomas and Sir Edward, came to Ireland as soldiers of fortune in the reign of Elizabeth I.

What soldiers of fortune did was steal land and murder people. It is unlikely these two were any different from their professional colleagues. Debrett's then tells us that: 'Thomas Moore obtained by grant from the Crown, in 1577, the castle of Castletown, with 758 acres of land thereunto adjoining, in the King's County, being styled in the said grant, *'Thomas Moore of Croghan.'*

Mr Moore received, subsequently, the honour of knighthood for his services against the Irish, by whom he was eventually put to death in his castle.

A later descendant became Earl of Charleville and here is how *Country Life*, 27 September 1962, cited by Ferres, describes how you got promoted to Earl at the time:

> Charles William Bury (1764–1835) [was] a landowner of considerable wealth, derived partly from [Shannongrove], the Bury estate in Co. Limerick (where the family had settled in 1666), and partly from property in [and around] Tullamore, King's County, inherited through his father's mother, the only sister and heiress of Charles Moore (1712–1764), Earl of Charleville and Baron Moore of Tullamoore [as the Moores liked to call it]. He himself was created Lord Tullamoore in 1797, Viscount Charleville in 1800 and Earl of Charleville in 1806.

This was mainly because in 1795 he had purchased political control of the borough of Carlow, which continued to be represented in the Parliament of the UK after the Union, and used his nomination of members for Carlow to bargain for his advancement in the peerage.

The titles descended from father to son until the early death of his grandson, the 4th Earl, in 1874, who was succeeded by his uncle, the 5th Earl.

The 5th Earl was childless and, on his decease in 1875, the titles expired. The castle, substantially restored, is perhaps the most famous haunted castle in the world and is visited by ghost hunters, who claim to regularly encounter ghosts of all sorts within its walls. Druids even.

The Earl of Rosse of Birr Castle, Parsonstown, held 22,513 acres in the county in 1876 with a valuation of £8,964 about £752,976 in modern money. Bateman credits the Earl of Rosse with 22,513 acres in King's County in 1876, with a valuation of £8,964. The Earl also held 2,633 acres in Tipperary and 1,340 acres in Yorkshire, a total acreage of 26,486 with a valuation of £15,549.

The story of the Parson Earls of Rosse is a hugely positive story of how one Anglo–Irish family made itself part of the new Republic and made a significant contribution to that state and to Birr. The peerage is still intact and the family still live at Birr Castle, first occupied by them in 1620. The family in fact made substantial contributions to science and engineering in both the UK and Ireland.

The 3rd Earl built the largest telescope in the world there in the early 1840s and there is now a museum and park. C.A. Parsons, a member of the family created C.A. Parsons, later Reyrolle Parsons, an engineering company that was once the largest employer on Tyneside.

Birr Castle was built in 1620 by Sir Laurence Parsons, who had obtained lands in Ireland in the 1600s. Aengus Fanning makes an interesting comment about Brendan Parsons, the current Earl:

> The seventh Earl of Rosse of Birr Castle, known to some as Brendan Parsons, occupies a somewhat ambiguous place in Irish society. We don't know whether to consider him an Irishman or a British aristocrat, though Lord Rosse himself, at 73, is in no doubt as to his credentials as an Irishman.

The current Earl, the 7th, did an interesting interview with Rosita Boland of the *Irish Times* in which he told a little about being an Irish landowner at Eton College in 1970.

> I went to Eton at 12. I was put into a house where I was the only person from outside Britain. I was seen as the Paddy and certainly not accepted on the same basis as everyone else. One was referred to as the Paddy.
>
> The whole emphasis at Eton was to get one to conform; to be good at sports, which I hated, and not to be doing anything seen to be sissy, such as going off for music lessons, which I loved.

He left Eton for a period due to illness but when he returned he was expelled.

> I went back to Eton for one term. Then I was sacked. Expelled. I was expelled for quite badly cutting up the face of someone who had been [making my life a misery], one of many … 114
> Being expelled] was a huge relief.

In fairness he says his father had a very different experience at Eton:

> My father didn't understand it, because he had had a very different experience at Eton in a different era, and my mother couldn't understand it, as she had never been to school; she was brought up by governesses and tutors.
>
> After school I went into military training. I was lucky enough to be in the Irish Guards for three years, joining the regiment that my father had served in during the Second World War and in which my grandfather had fought and been killed in the First World War.
>
> The estate now is about 881 hectares (2,178 acres), which is literally 9 per cent of the estate my father inherited. He inherited 9,000 hectares (21,780 acres) although most of that was bog. Most of the great estates were broken up when the tenancies were redistributed under the Land Acts. There was no incentive for either party to improve the land, and I bear no grudge at all.

Lord Digby of 1 Elm Court, Temple, London, held 29,722 acres in King's County in 1876, with a valuation of £12,745 about £1,070,580 in modern money. The most famous Digby of modern times gets no mention in Debrett's, the Bible of the peerage. This is Pamela Digby Churchill Harriman. She was a daughter of the 11th Baron Digby, whose grandfather, the 9th holder of the title, was the owner of the acreage in 1876. Pamela married Sir Winston Churchill's only son in 1939. She eventually married Avrill Harriman, one of America's super rich, assisted Bill Clinton to the US Presidency and died in office as the US Ambassador in Paris in 1997.

The title is originally Irish, from 1620, but there is also a British peerage from 1765. The title still exists, held by the 12th Baron, Edward Henry Kenelm Digby, who was educated at Eton and served in the Coldstream Guards. He still lives at the ancestral home in Dorset.

The title was first created in 1620 for Robert Digby Governor of King's County. By 1876 the family had land in five counties; in Dorset the family seat, 1,886 acres, 124 acres in Warwick, 938 acres in Queen's County and 6,835 acres in Mayo. The total acreage, together with the King's County acres, was 39,505 with a valuation of £39,505.

The title, in the manner of the peerage, became a Viscountcy and then an Earldom. Both titles became extinct in 1856.

The family were linked by marriage and decent to some of the great landowners of the United Kingdom, including that of the Earl of Ilchester who, in 1876, had 32,849 acres with a valuation of £43,452.

King's County by largest acreage 1876

		Acreage	Valuation 1876 (£)	Valuation Current (£)
1	Digby, Lord, 1 Elm Court, Temple, London	29,722	12,745	1,070,580
2	Rosse, Earl of, Birr Castle Parsonstown	22,513	8,965	753,060
3	Charleville, Earl of, Charleville Forest, Tullamore	20,032	10,052	844,368
4	Downshire, Marquis of, -	13,679	7,261	609,924
5	Bernard, Colonel Thomas, Castlebernard, Kinnetty	13,153	6,032	506,688
6	King, John Gilbert, Ballylinn, Ferbane	8,741	4,073	342,132
7	Church Temporarilities Commissioner, 24 Upper Merrion St, Dublin	7,647	4,000	336,000

		Acreage	Valuation 1876 (£)	Valuation Current (£)
8	Ashbrook, Lord, Durrow Castle, Durrow, Queen's County	7,476	2,593	217,812
9	Williams, Edward W., Herrington, Dorchester	6,884	1,568	131,172
10	Dames, Thomas L., Greenhill, Edenderry	6,798	1,917	161,028
11	Malone, Rev. Saville L'E., Armagh	5,678	1,656	139,104
12	Bennett, Francis J., Thomastown House, Frankford	5,480	2,707	227,388
13	Warburton, Richard, Garryhinch, Portarlington	5,336	1,564	131,376
14	Lloyd, John, Gloster, Roscrea	4,536	1,474	123,816
15	Toler, Hon. Otway J.G., Albermarle St, London	4,524	2,526	212,184
16	Thompson, P.H., Cornamona, Bangher	4,485	1,442	121,128
17	Coote, Rev. Algernon, Tunbridge Wells, Kent	4,436	2,491	209,244
18	Darby, William H., Leap Castle, Roscrea	4,367	2,780	233,520
19	Mooney, Robert J.E., The Doone, Athlone	4,344	1,582	132,888
20	Mullock, Thomas, Kilnagarna, Ferbane	4,300	972	81,648
21	Armstrong, Rev. Sir E.F., Castlefleming, Errill, Templemore	4,231	953	80,052
22	Kemmis, Arthur H.M., Upper Norwood, Surrey	4,159	1,620	136,080
23	Lauder, John D., Moyclare, Ferbane	4,018	1,115	93,660
24	Banon, E.J. Reps, Broughall Castle, Frankford	3,896	1,211	101,724
25	Vaughan, William P.H.L., Goldengrove, Roscrea	3,748	1,883	158,172
26	O'Brien, Reps of, -	3,688	1,687	141,708
27	Armstrong, William B. Bel Iver, Banagher	3,650	1,306	109,704
28	Drought, John H., Lettybrook, Kinnetty	3,594	2,014	169,176
29	Cassidy, John V., Monasterevan	3,470	1,566	131,544
30	Hastings, Viscount, Sharavogue, Roscrea	3,379	1,919	161,196

Offaly (King's County)

		Acreage	Valuation 1876 (£)	Valuation Current (£)
31	Grogan, Sir Edward Bt, 10 Harcourt St, Dublin	3,207	1,853	155,652
32	Seaton, Lord, Bert House, Athy, Co. Kildare	3,101	413	34,692
33	Fox, Captain Maxwell, Annaghmore, Tullamore	2,864	819	68,796
34	Briscoe, Edward T., Riversdale, Killucan	2,836	1,084	91,056
35	Alexander, Samuel, Killester Abbey, Artane, Co. Dublin	2,815	818	68,712
36	Atkinson, Guy N., Cangort, Shinrone	2,787	1,298	109,032
37	Ashtown, Lord, -	2,780	1,385	116,340
38	Burdett, Arthur, Coolfin, Banagher	2,732	1,331	111,804
39	Purdon, Hon. Louisa Reps, Telerana, Co. Clare	2,504	1,817	152,628
40	Trimleston, Lord, -	2,496	1,983	166,572
41	Longworth, John, Glynwood, Athlone	2,422	459	38,556
42	Biddulph, Mrs Lucy, Rathrobin, Tullamore	2,237	1,102	92,568
43	Goodbody, Jonathan, Charlestown House, Clara	2,128	1,009	84,756
44	Trench, Henry, Cangort Park, Roscrea	2,113	1,758	147,672
45	Gamble, Richard W., 51 Fitzwilliam Sq., London	2,064	779	65,436
46	Champagne, Arthur H., Old Broad Street, London	2,045	431	36,204
47	Manley, Joshua, Monasteroris, Edenderry	1,995	1,328	111,552
48	Hart, Charles, -	1,961	314	26,376
49	Tollemache, A.L. Reps, per W.T. Trench, Cangort Park	1,922	906	76,104
50	Armstrong, John P., Claremount, Banagher	1,913	722	60,648
51	Guise, Mrs Isabella, St Walleran, Gorey	1,879	943	79,212
52	Palmer, Sandford R., Ballinlough	1,856	1,006	84,504
53	Chinevex, Sophia, Hyde Park, London	1,808	794	66,696

		Acreage	Valuation 1876 (£)	Valuation Current (£)
54	Lucas, John Reps, -	1,804	544	45,696
55	Taffe, John, Smarmoe Castle, Ardee	1,769	777	65,268
56	Jackson, Henry Vincent, Inane	1,765	829	69,636
57	Morris, Wm O'Connor, 23 Rutland Sq., Dublin	1,734	834	70,056
58	Wakely, John, Ballyburley, Rhode, Edenderry	1,722	1,462	122,808
59	Coslett, Mrs O., 7 Clarinda Park W, Kingstown	1,715	450	37,800
60	Canal Company, Grand, James's Street, Dublin	1,706	2,216	186,144
61	Casey, George, St Leonards-on-Sea, East Sussex	1,703	588	49,392
62	Pierce, Captain Thomas Acres, Tullamore	1,694	231	19,404
63	Ridgeway, John, Ballydermot, Clanbullogue	1,684	956	80,304
64	Daly, Bernard, Tullamore	1,660	983	82,572
65	Biddulph, Nicholas, Congur House, Borrisokane	1,611	866	72,744
66	Goodbody, Marcus, Inchmore House, Clara	1,608	1,224	102,816
67	Lusi, Countess, -	1,599	1,006	84,504
68	Towsend, Richard, Nice	1,594	767	64,428
69	Bride, Mrs M.H.H., of Ballymahon, Co. Longford	1,579	705	59,220
70	Nesbitt, C.T.D., Toberdaly, Rhode, Edenderry	1,526	880	73,920
71	Rolleston, James Frank, Frankford, Roscrea	1,517	913	76,692
72	Nesbitt, John A., -	1,508	304	25,536
73	Graves, Major William Grogan, Cloghan Castle, Banagher	1,503	772	64,848
74	Nesbitt, Alexander, -	1,482	276	23,184
75	Doorley, Ter, Cloghan	1,456	760	63,840
76	Hackett, Major Simpson, Moorpark, Parsonstown	1,441	833	69,972
77	Fletcher, Fredrick W.H., -	1,427	716	60,144

		Acreage	Valuation 1876 (£)	Valuation Current (£)
78	White, Henry, Charleville	1,406	573	48,132
79	Burriss, Richard, Groffin, Cloughjordan	1,406	561	47,124
80	Hoare, Rev. Edward, -	1,384	342	28,728
81	L'Estrange, Edmund, Kilcummin, Bangher	1,365	380	31,920
82	Fox, Patrick H. Reps, Kilmore, Ferbane	1,340	397	33,348
83	M'Neale, Mrs Margaret, Cheltenham	1,319	392	32,928
84	Goodwin, Simon, Cloncrane, Clonbullouge	1,305	225	18,900
85	Fuller, Abraham, Rockfield, Moate	1,292	625	52,500
86	Johnston, Edward G. jnr, United Services Club, London	1,277	520	43,680
87	Bailey, Daniel Reps, Morrock House, Clara	1,277	446	37,464
88	Persse, Burton, Moyode Castle, Athenry	1,273	435	36,540
89	Telford, Thomas, M.D., 23 Clarinda Park, Kingstown	1,234	461	38,724
90	Fottrell, George D., 46 Fleet St, Dublin	1,211	301	25,284
91	Baldwin, Miss F.E.G., Stratton, Torquay, Devonshire	1,208	644	54,096
92	Hamilton, Rev. Hans F., The Rectory, Coombe St Nicholas, Chard, England	1,208	643	54,012
93	Spunner, Thomas, Spunner White, Miltown	1,207	686	57,624
94	Spunner, Charles Rolleston QC, Glanhouse	1,177	700	58,800
95	Stacpoole, Stephen, Frenchchurch St, Portarlington	1,152	578	48,552
96	Berry Thomas, 4 Hume St, Dublin	1,136	494	41,496
97	Portarlington the Earl of, Emo Park, Portarlington	1,126	364	30,576
98	Drought, J.W., Whigsborough, Fivealley	1,125	481	40,404

		Acreage	Valuation 1876 (£)	Valuation Current (£)
99	Spunner, Eliza, Clyduff, Roscrea	1,111	575	48,300
100	Parsons, Hon. L., 15 Lowndes Sq., London	1,108	590	49,560
101	Cox, Captain A.C., Clara House, Clara	1,096	985	82,740
102	Holmes, Rev. Edward, Marsh Gibbon Rectory, Bicester, England	1,091	755	63,420
103	Tuthill, Charles E., Sloperton Lodge, Kingstown	1,086	233	19,572
104	Marshall, Mrs S.J., Baronne Court, Parsonstown	1,079	532	44,688
105	Mulock, Thomas H., Bellair, Ballycumber	1,071	422	35,448
106	Champ, Issac, Coolgeggan, Rathangan	1,068	177	14,868
107	Molloy, Laurence Bomford, Clonbela, Parsonstown	1,061	390	32,760
108	Reynolds, Michael, Guildford, Tyrrelspass	1,041	175	14,700
109	Radcliffe, Joseph, Union Club, Trafalgar Square, London	1,039	592	49,728
110	Nesbitt, Miss Downing, -	1,029	762	64,008
111	Magan, Eliza G., Hill of Down, Westmeath	1,023	652	54,768
112	Drought, Robert S., Ridgemont, Frankford	1,016	458	38,472
113	Dooley, Samuel, Mountbriscoe, Phillipstown	1,002	274	23,016
114	Adamson, GAG, per J.J. Walker, Belfield, Shinrone	975	474	39,816

Top 20 by estimated rental income in 1876

		Acreage	Valuation 1876 (£)	Valuation current (£)
1	Digby, Lord, 1 Elm Court, Temple, London	29,722	12,745	1,070,580
2	Charleville, Earl of, Charleville Forest, Tullamore	20,032	10,052	844,368

Offaly (King's County)

		Acreage	Valuation 1876 (£)	Valuation current (£)
3	Rosse, Earl of, Birr Castle, Parsonstown	22,513	8,965	753,060
4	Downshire, Marquis of, -	13,679	7,261	609,924
5	Bernard, Colonel Thomas, Castlebernard, Kinnetty	13,153	6,032	506,688
6	King, John Gilbert, Ballylinn, Ferbane	8,741	4,073	342,132
7	Church, Temporarilities Commissioner, 24 Upper Merrion St, Dublin	7,647	4,000	336,000
8	Darby, William H., Leap Castle, Roscrea	4,367	2,780	233,520
9	Bennett, Francis J., Thomastown House, Frankford	5,480	2,707	227,388
10	Ashbrook, Lord, Durrow Castle, Durrow, Queen's County	7,476	2,593	217,812
11	Toler, Hon. Otway J.G., Albermarle St, London	4,524	2,526	212,184
12	Coote, Rev. Algernon, Tunbridge Wells, Kent	4,436	2,491	209,244
13	Canal Company, Grand, Jame's Street, Dublin	1,706	2,216	186,144
14	Drought, John H., Lettybrook, Kinnetty	3,594	2,014	169,176
15	Trimleston, Lord, -	2,496	1,983	166,572
16	Hastings, Viscount, Sharavogue, Roscrea	3,379	1,919	161,196
17	Dames, Thomas L., Greenhill, Edenderry	6,798	1,917	161,028
18	Vaughan, William P.H.L., Goldengrove, Roscrea	3,748	1,883	158,172
19	Grogan, Sir Edward Bt, 10 Harcourt St, Dublin	3,207	1,853	155,652
20	Purdon, Hon. Louisa Reps, Telerana, Co. Clare	2,504	1,817	152,628

LAOIS (QUEEN'S COUNTY)

KNOWN AS QUEEN'S COUNTY IN 1876

	1876	2020 est
Population in County Laois/Queen's County	79,771	80,155
All owners of land	1,049	43,835
Percentage of the population	–	–
Owners of nothing at all	78,722	22,951
Percentage of the population	–	–
Size of County	423,825 acres	424,960 acres
Number of dwellings	15,519 (14,470 rented)	28,057 (27,916 privately owned)
Number of owned farm holdings	1,049	3,312

This county was compiled with the help of Ivo Cahill, assisted by Arlo Cahill

County comparisons

	Acreage 1876
County Laois	423,825
Berkshire, England	430,849
Roxburghshire, Scotland	423,463
Glamorganshire, Wales	428,386

Laois, or Queen's County as it was known in 1876, is a county of shining, silver streams, stuffed with the chubbiest of trout. I would remember, I would know. I lived there long ago. The land between the low-lying Slieve Bloom Mountains in the west and the lower reaches of the huge Bog of Allan in the east, is fertile but tough. Long fields yield good grain and better grazing, but it all has to be worked for. Nature gives no freebies in County Laois. It is densely underpopulated, meaning there are houses everywhere, but set well apart, sometimes miles apart. The towns, too, are well spread out. But what also sets Laois apart is its very low population. In 1876, at the time of the second English Domesday, but the first Irish Domesday, the county was home to just under 80,000 souls, a population that it is only reaching again after 140 years.

In a comparably sized county in England, Berkshire, the population in 1876 was 196,000, and is now 796,000. The Irish, especially the Laois, figures, are the long shadow of the famine years of 1845–50, a famine that reduced a population of 8 million in Ireland in 1841 to 4 million by the mid 1850s.

The population of Laois had probably doubled between 1800 and 1841, the time of the previous, now lost, census. But between 1845 and 1876 it had almost certainly fallen by half or more.

Elsewhere in Europe, not even war has done this devastation to a population, in such a short period of time, with the exception maybe of the German invasion of Russian in 1941 and the subsequent fighting until 1945. There is no accounting for the 27 million who died in those four cataclysmic years, that we might live. And like Irelands' famine dead, most of them have no names and no graves.

The memory of the famine was a pervasive theme in the lives of even small children in Laois in the late 1940s and '50s. You'd be shuffling an overboiled cabbage leaf around your dinner plate – we called lunch dinner in those days – and you'd not hear the granny arrive till your ear took a belt and her voice would rasp at you that, 'Your cousins died for want of a cabbage leaf like that in the famine. Eat that.'

And we believed her because we thought she'd grown up during the famine and endured its horrors. But she hadn't. Granny Cahill was born in 1868. She had little formal education, just the local primary school. She wasn't unlettered but there had been no books for the poor in that cruel part of history she'd come from.

Perhaps it was she who first thought me, however subliminally, that history is real and, as James Joyce called it 'a nightmare'. Her own childhood had clearly been shaped much more closely than ours by the famine.

She wasn't teaching us a history lesson though, but transmitting a trauma, a trauma that hung over the county more than 100 years after it happened. Her famine tales were always used pragmatically, to get us wee ones to clean our plates and be glad that we had food on them. Nor did she dwell on the subject. But one day I saw, by accident, what the famine was. Laois in the 1950s was a lonely place, far away from Dublin, but with the loneliness came safety. Kids, even very young ones, could wander for miles away from home, in that largely empty landscape. One day, aged about 8, I was on a wander and came across something unusual. A ruined house. Not a big one, but two storeyed. The roof was long gone. The walls had leaned away out in the winds and rain, and fallen. What was unusual was it had no name, but wasn't that far from Rathdowney and it should have had a name. Every other old ruin about the place had a name.

Coming through the bushes towards the house, I suddenly realised it was surrounded by small mounds, body-sized mounds, irregularly placed. These were those who'd died where they fell down, maybe having sought food and refuge at the house, during the famine. It was too far to walk to any coast and the coffin ships. They died where they lay. From that moment I understood my fierce, tiny granny. I ate all my cabbage, always. Still do.

But after the famine and in the decades that followed something extraordinary happened, something that was certainly never explained to us at school, then or later, and this book, the *Return of Owners of Land*, holds the key. It's all in the numbers, really, and only two matter very much.

The first is the population as a whole in 1876 – 79,771 – and the second figure, the one such histories that do exist about land always leave out, the number of people who owned nothing at all, which was 78,722. That figure will include children, whereas the figure for owners of land is predominantly adult male, although about 10 per cent of land over 1 acre was owned by women, much the same figure as in England. Contrast that with the figures for landowners in Laois in 2016 and what happened becomes clear.

There are 43,000 owners of land in Laois, slightly over half the population. That figure will include owners of homes, dwellings in the Returns. But the inhabited houses in the Returns also tell us how extraordinary the transformation actually was. Nominally, the figures for owners of under an acre should include home owners. On the basis that it does, a maximum of only 426 were owned by those who lived in them in Laois in 1876. The rest, 15,093, were rented.

The later growth in 'land' ownership in Laois was much the same as in the rest of Ireland and in England; it was ultimately driven by home ownership. But in rural Laois, which is to say most of the county, the rise in landownership was driven, first by the Wyndham Acts, and then by the Land Commission. From a figure of 623 people owning virtually all rural land in Laois, the numbers rose to over 20,000. It took 150 years, but it happened and it happened nowhere else in any developing country between those two dates, 1876 and 2020. In theory, the landless population of 1876 have descendants, most of whom either owned or have a stake in some land. And with rare exception hardly one of the descendants of the owners of most of the county in 1876 owns anything at all in modern Ireland. There are no 'great' estates in Laois, at all.

In 1876 Laois's largest landowner, based at Ballyfin just outside Mountrath, was Sir Charles Henry Coote, Bart. He owned 47,471 acres, with a valuation of £18,007 about £1,512,588 in modern money. He owned more than 10 per cent of all land in the county. In addition he had 1,017 acres in Roscommon, 878 acres in Kildare and 340 acres in Limerick. His holdings made him one of the largest landowners in the four countries of the UK at the time and his estimated rental income of £19,255 would be worth close to £2 million in modern money. Like so many other landowners then and in England now, he was educated at Eton College and afterwards went to Trinity College, Dublin. Sir Charles' great, great, great granddaughter is Lady Clinton, wife of the largest landowner in modern Devon, the 22nd Baron Clinton, who has 25,000 acres.

In 2001 the school founded by the Patrician Brothers, a Catholic religious order, moved into Mountrath and the buildings and estate were sold to an American couple, Fred and Kay Krehbiel, who having restored it, now running it as a five-star hotel. In October 2016 Condé Nast Best Hotels of the World awards, Ballyfin Demesne in Co. Laois took the acclaimed top spot. The annual awards ranks the best hotels, resorts, cities, islands, airlines and cruise lines in the world. The results were compiled from more than 300,000 readers' votes.

Lord Castletown was the 2nd largest landowner in Laois in 1876 with 22,510 acres and a valuation of £15,006 about £1,260,504 in modern money. This was a short-lived peerage, but one with a long lineage. The family name is Fitzpatrick, which is essentially Norman in origin. He was educated at Eton College and inherited the Irish estates in 1842. Earlier he had been High Sheriff of Queen's County and sat for the county as MP between 1837 and 1841. His son, Bernard, was educated at Eton and married a daughter of another Old Etonian, Viscount Doneraile, who had 28,700 acres in Cork and Waterford. Bernard Castletown started out as a professional soldier and fought in the Boer War. Later he set up the Celtic Association, and helped finance other Anglo–Irish attempts to foster what the aristocracy deemed to be Irish culture. He died in 1937. He was one of the few Irish aristocrats who spoke some Irish.

The next major Landowner in Laois in 1876, the 4th Viscount De Vesci of Abbeyleix, had 15,069 acres and a valuation of £9,410 about £790,440 in modern money. He too was an Old Etonian, as is his descendant in 2016, the 7th Viscount. In 1876 Viscount De Vesci owned 15,069 acres in Laois, 420 acres in Dublin, 818 acres in Cork and 375 acres in Kent. Unlike many of the large acre owners, he had a huge income, most of it coming from the 420 acres in Dublin. According to the records, his Dublin acres had an annual rental valuation of £31,713, about £2.6 million in modern values. After the bishop with his Baronetcy, there then came the peerage, that of Knapton in 1750. That title was upgraded in 1776 to a Viscountcy. In the 1800s the Viscounts de Vesci were MPs, peers sitting in the House of Lords and on the way, in 1884, picked up an English peerage, that of Baron de Vesci. This was important later when Ireland became independent and only English peers could sit in the House of Lords, a situation that is now almost ended. The title still exists and the holder, Thomas Eustace Vesey, the 7th Viscount and 9th Baron, lives in a quiet street in London.

The 3rd Earl of Portarlington, whose family name is Dawson Damer, had 11,149 acres in Laois, 4,756 acres in Tyrone, 2,897 acres in Tipperary and 1,126 acres in King's County (Offaly) in 1876. The Laois acres had a valuation of £6,050 about £508,200 in modern money. His school is not listed but all recent holders of the title were Etonians. The title arose from a combination of two titles, that of Viscount Carlow, family name Dawson, to which the name Damer was later added.

With a nominal rent roll of £10,797, the title was well funded but valuable landed wealth in England arrived when the Earl inherited the Dorchester estates of his aunt, Lady Caroline Damer. These lands did not appear in the Returns. The title still exists but most of the family, including the Earl, live in Australia. There is an English estate and he was page of honour to Queen Elizabeth II for the coronation in 1953.

On the face of it Mrs Grattan Bellow of Galway breaks the run of Etonians and aristocrats, but not quite. They had 10,593 acres in Laois, with a valuation of £5,923, about £497,532 in modern money. The head of the family was her son, Sir Henry Grattan-Bellew Bt, who owned the other half of the estate of 23,004 acres, with 10,516 acres in Galway and 1,985 acres in Roscommon. The title was created in 1838, relatively recent in terms of the landowners. It is still extant and the family live in Dublin with a claim upon the smaller of the Saltee Islands in Wexford. The current holder of the title was well known in journalistic and broadcasting circles. He was educated at Ampleforth, the Catholic equivalent of Eton College.

Lt Col Robert Ashworth Godolphin Cosby, Stradbally, was an MP with a daughter married into the Trench family. He had 10,110 acres in Laois, with a valuation of £7,077 about £594,468 in modern money. There were also linked to Lord Ashtown of Moate. With 10,110 acres, he was a seriously significant landowner in 1876. An Old Etonian, the Godolphin in his name links him to the one-time owners of large parts of Cornwall, the Godolphin family. He was a professional soldier, as were both his sons. He had five daughters and the estates had been in the family for several generations.

John 'Jack' Adair of Ballybrittas was a businessman who had 9,655 acres and later owned a Texas ranch of over 1.2 million acres. His Laois acres had a valuation of £3,719 about £312,396 in modern money. He was immensely rich but had no heirs. He became notorious for the eviction of forty-seven families in Donegal, where he had land at Glenveigh Castle. Adair represents a break in both the Etonian connection and high aristocratic Anglo–Irish links. His family claimed descent from one of William of Orange's soldiers who was knighted at the Boyne in 1690.

The estate in Donegall was given to the Irish state by Henry McIlhenny, along with the restored castle. The Laois house was burned down in 1887 and is a ruin. One of his wife's descendants became a member of the US Congress.

The Misses Dunne of Brittas, 9,215 acres. The Dunne family had a long history in the area. There are frequent mentions of their ancestors in the Annals of the Four Masters, compiled between 1632 and 1636. Their acreage is recorded in Bateman 1881 as 9,215 acres in Laois, 1,544 acres in Roscommon and 583 acres in County Dublin. In 1901 the estate at Brittas, Clonaslie, and Dunsogley Castle in Dublin, with its small estate, were back in the hands of the Dunne daughters. Brittas House or Castle burned down in 1942 and has not been restored. The Dunnes were part of the Plunkett family, who are a constant in much of Irish history, with a Lord Plunket being the Bishop of Meath and holding 3,567 acres in 1876 and Robert Pigott at Rosenallis in Laois almost certainly a cousin and holding 4,932 acres in the county.

The 5th Marquis of Lansdowne, whose seat was at Bowood Park in Wiltshire, was a British landowner of vast acreage, 142,916 in total, with an income of £69,025. Of this total, 8,980 acres were in Queen's County.

See page 170.

Robert Stubber of Moyne, Durrow had 7,388 acres in Laois valued at £4,601 about £386,484 in modern money. This is one of the few estates where the family mansion from the 1730s, Moyne House, is still occupied by the Hamilton Stubber family. Originally descended from a Scot who came to Ireland in the 1600s, the family married into local clergy and gentry, winding up with the Durrow estate of 7,388 acres. The estimated rental value in 1876 was £4,061, the modern equivalent of about £400,000 a year. A great granddaughter married into the Grosvenor family of the Duke of Westminster in 1920. A midsummer ball and one-day polo tournament is held in June; a two-day tournament on the penultimate weekend in July; and a tournament in August with the emphasis on junior polo.

Richard Warburton of Portarlington had 6,285 acres in Laois at a valuation of £5,273 about £442,932 in modern money. This family are English in origin and first appear in Dublin in 1622. A brief history is worth recounting as the family were both influential and at the same time typical of those a rank below the aristocracy, who held no formal title. The first mention of the seat at Garryhinch occurs in 1662, which is post the Restoration of the monarchy in England when Richard Warburton was a junior clerk of the Council in Ireland in 1654, and afterwards clerk-assistant to the Irish House of Commons.

The 100 largest landowners of Queen's County/Laois in 1876 ranked by acreage

		Acreage	Valuation 1876 (£)	Valuation current (£)
1	Coote, Sir Charles, Ballyfin, Mountrath★+	47,451	18,007	1,512,588
2	Castletown, Lord Rt Hon., Lisduff, Erril	22,241	14,151	1,188,684
3	De Vesci, Viscount, Abbeyleix★+	15,069	9,410	790,440
4	Portarlington, the Earl of, Emo★	11,149	6,050	506,200
5	Bellew, Mrs Grattan, Mount Bellew, Galway	10,593	5.923	497,532
6	Cosby, Lt Col Robert, MP, Stradbally	10,110	6,738	565,992
7	Adair, John, Monasterevan	9,655	3,719	312,396
8	Dunne, (Edward) Misses, Brittas, Clonaslee	9,215	2,833	237,972
9	Lansdowne, Marquis of, Kenmare★	8,980	5,310	446,040
10	Stubber, Robert, Durrow	7,388	4,061	341,124
11	Kemmis, Thomas, Maryborough	5,800	3,325	279,300
12	Molyneux, Sir Caple, Armagh	5,463	952	79,968
13	Pigot, Robert, Rosenallis	4,932	1,073	90,132
14	McNeil, Mrs, Cheltenham	4,716	2,417	203,028
15	Kemmis, William, Rathdrum	4,706	2,483	208,572
16	Ashbrook, Viscount, The Castle, Durrow★	4,515	3,412	286,608
17	Congleton, Lord, Marble Arch, London★	4,247	2,365	198,660
18	Kirk, William, Gorey, Wexford	4,052	2,733	229,572
19	Verschoyle, James, Dublin	3,980	589	49,476
20	Church Commissioners, Dublin	3,738	2,524	212,016
21	Close, Maxwell, Dunbanagher, Loughbrickland	3,678	2,576	216,384
22	Edge, Samuel, Ballacolla	3,627	1,587	133,308
23	Fitzgerald, Gerald, Benfield, England	3,516	2,074	174,216
24	Warburton, Richard, Portarlington	3,490	2,400	201,600
25	Crosdaile, Captain, Rossenallis	3,185	1,316	110,544
26	Allen, Walsh Sir, Stradbally	3,131	2,101	176,484

		Acreage	Valuation 1876 (£)	Valuation current (£)
27	Toler, Hon., Otway, -	3,076	1,881	158,004
28	Carbery, Lord, The Castle, Cork ★	2,919	1,344	112,896
29	Drogheda, Marquis, Monasteravan★	2,688	1,515	127,260
30	Cooper, William, Ballickmoyler	2,644	2,170	182,280
31	Smyth, Edward, Ballybrittas	2,589	1,583	132,972
32	Weldon, Sir A.C., Athy★	2,498	2,008	168,672
33	Annesley, Earl of, Castlewellan, Co. Down ★	2,489	1,606	134,904
34	Borrowes, Sir Erasmus, Ballymore-Eustace	2,467	1,254	105,336
35	Hutchinson, John, Roscrea	2,442	412	34,608
36	Pattison, Henry, Dublin	2,381	333	27,972
37	Morton, Captain Matthew, Clonmel	2,307	992	93,328
38	Hamilton, Ion Tront, Castleknock	2,245	1,025	86,100
39	Carden, Major, Knightstown, Portarlington	2,225	1,015	65,260
40	Bowen, Captain, Portarlington	2,120	1,324	111,218
41	Grace, J.D., Ballylinan	2,111	1,058	88,872
42	Duckett, F., Carlow	2,075	1,526	128,184
43	Cassan, Matthew, Maryborough	1,979	1,131	95,004
44	Milltown, Earl of, Blessington	1,898	877	73,668
45	FitzMaurice, James, Old Derry	1,894	511	42,924
46	Stanhope, Earl of, Mayfair, London ★+	1,863	1,992	167,328
47	Commissioner of Education, Dublin	1,771	1,491	125,244
48	Sandes, William, Dublin	1,760	635	53,340
49	Scott, James, Mountrath	1,754	1,108	93,072
50	Grace, Sir William, Mayfair, London	1,740	1,145	96,180
51	Kemmis, Thomas (Reps), Portartlington	1,710	1,086	91,224
52	Moore, Rev., Arthur, Ballymote	1,700	764	64,176
53	Doyne, Mrs C., Carlow	1,655	904	75,936
54	Edge, John H., -	1,576	826	69,384
55	Edge, Benjamin, Carlow	1,575	851	71,484
56	Dawson, Damer, - see Earl of Portarlington	1,548	1,015	85,260

		Acreage	Valuation 1876 (£)	Valuation current (£)
57	Coote, Eyre, Mountrath	1,524	1,423	119,532
58	Domville, William, Ballinakill	1,512	999	83,916
59	Lyster, John, Borris-in-Ossary and Abbyleix	1,506	1,081	90,804
60	Brown, Francis Stafford, of Slaney, Co. Wicklow	1,493	440	36,960
61	Orkney, Earl of, Scotland ★	1,438	932	78,288
62	Staples, Robert, Durrow	1,424	931	78,204
63	Warnford, Rev. John, Wilts, England	1,410	838	70,392
64	Chetwode, Knighgtley, Portarlington	1,389	603	50,652
65	Edge, William, Tolerton	1,339	808	67,872
66	Dooner, John, Dublin	1,336	845	70,980
67	Trinity College, Dublin	1,265	593	49,812
68	Booth, Juliana, Bath, Somerset	1,252	693	58,212
69	Lecky, J. reps of, Portarlington	1,236	668	56,112
70	Sandford, William, Somerset	1,210	743	62,412
71	Despard, Richard, Rathymolyn	1,202	689	57,876
72	Sweetman, Mrs, Maryborough	1,198	1,189	99,876
73	Ryan, Val, Mountrath	1,179	376	31,584
74	Putland, Charles, Dublin	1,174	890	74,760
75	Evans, George, Rush	1,163	326	27,384
76	Meredith, Rice, Clonaslee	1,152	138	11,592
77	Collis, Abraham, Ballyfallin, Co. Meath	1,137	655	55,020
78	White, Robert, Dublin	1,104	730	61,320
79	Carew, Lord, Enniscorthy★+	1,098	662	55,608
80	Brooks, Richard, Castle Howard, Co. Wicklow	1,096	566	47,544
81	Butler, Edward, -	1,077	532	44,688
82	Gough, Viscount, Dublin ★	1,045	783	65,688
83	Pim, Joshua, Dublin	1,045	290	24,360
84	Des Voeux, Major, Portarlington	1,037	926	52,564
85	King-Harman, The Hon of Boyle Co Roscommon	1,024	786	66,024
87	Trench, Rev. F.F., -	1,006	487	40,908
86	Irwin, Mrs, Portumna, Galway	1,006	292	24,528

		Acreage	Valuation 1876 (£)	Valuation current (£)
88	Preston, John, Dublin	984	518	43,512
89	Bland, John, Abbeyleix	978	634	53,256
90	Owen, William, Blessington	973	811	68,124
91	Digby, Lord, Gease Hill Castle, Tullamore ★	938	542	45,528
92	Warburton, William, Dublin	922	259	21,756
93	Bailey, Thomas, Castledermot	893	499	41,916
94	Harrick, John, -	884	390	32,760
95	Wakefield, Thomas, Dublin	869	445	37,380
96	Whitty, Thomas, -	862	220	18,480
97	Vernon Charles, Dublin	860	273	22,932
98	Hort, Sir J., Dublin	851	396	33,264
99	O'Brien, Sir Patrick, Dublin ★	824	796	66,864
100	Pilkington, George, Rathdowney	823	576	48,384

★ Title still exists. + An Irish link still exists.

Top 20 by estimated rental income in 1876

		Acres 1876	Valuation 1876 (£)	Valuation 2017 (£)
1	Coote, Sir Charles, Ballyfin, Mountrath ★+	47,451	18,007	1,512,588
2	Castletown, Lord Rt Hon., Lisduff, Erril	22,241	14,151	1,188,684
3	De Vesci, Viscount, Abbeyleix ★+	15,069	9,410	790,440
4	Cosby, Lt Col Robert, MP, Stradbally	10,110	6,738	565,992
5	Portarlington, the Earl of, Emo ★	11,149	6,050	506,200
6	Bellew, Mrs Grattan, Mount Bellew, Galway	10,593	5,923	497,532
7	Lansdowne, Marquis of, Kenmare ★	8,980	5,310	446,040
8	Stubber, Robert, Durrow	7,388	4,061	341,124
9	Adair, John, Monasterevan	9,655	3,719	312,396
10	Ashbrook, Viscount, The Castle Durrow ★	4,515	3,412	286,608
11	Kemmis, Thomas, Maryborough	5,800	3,325	279,300

		Acres 1876	Valuation 1876 (£)	Valuation 2017 (£)
12	Dunne, (Edward) Misses, Brittas, Clonaslee	9,215	2,833	237,972
13	Kirk, William, Gorey, Wexford	4,052	2,733	229,572
14	Church Commissioners, Dublin	3,738	2,524	212,016
15	Kemmis, William, Rathdrum	4,706	2,483	208,572
16	McNeil, Mrs, Cheltenham	4,716	2,417	203,028
17	Congleton, Lord, Marble Arch, London ★	4,247	2,365	198,660
18	Pigot, Robert, Rosenallis	4,932	1,073	90,132
19	Molyneux, Sir Caple, Armagh	5,463	952	79,968
20	Verschoyle, James, Dublin	3,980	589	49,476

★ Title still exists. + An Irish link still exists.

LEITRIM

	1876	2020 est
Population in County Leitrim	95,324	31,798
All owners of land	327	31,957
Percentage of the population	0.34	-
Owners of nothing at all	94,873	15,856
Percentage of the population	99.66	-
Size of County	371,371 acres	392,960 acres
Number of dwellings(rented in 1876, mostly owned in 2020	17,405 (rented)	n/a
Number of owned farm holdings	451	3,673

County comparisons

	Acreage 1876	Population 1876
County Leitrim	371,371	95,324
Hertfordshire, England	384,809	192,226
Banffshire, Scotland	407,501	62,032
Cardiganshire, Wales	391,685	73,441

Lord Massy of the Hermitage Castle, Connell, County Limerick, had 24,571 acres in Leitrim in 1876 with a valuation of £6,220 about £522,480 in modern money. Bateman corrects both the acreage and the valuation, to 24,571 and £6,660 respectively. Lord Massey had 8,423 acres in Co. Limerick with a total acreage of 33,003 and a valuation of £12,101. (also *see* County Limerick)

In the 1870s Lord Massy owned 8,568 acres in Co. Limerick and 1,120 acres in Tipperary (not noted in Bateman); however, his largest estate was in Leitrim. The Massy family had property in north Leitrim with the bequest of the White estate at Lareen to John Massy, afterwards 6th Lord Massy. In the 1830s the Massy estate also owned property in Co. Galway (not noted in Bateman), where the agent was George Falkner of Tipperary. This property seems to have been leased by Richard Rathbourne of Ballymore. It was offered for sale in the Encumbered Estates Court in May 1852. Most of the Massy lands were sold in the last two decades of the nineteenth century and the family residences in the early years of the twentieth century.

The title is still extant and is held by David Hamon Somerset Massy, the 10th Baron, who lives in Leicester.

The 3rd Earl of Leitrim of Lough Rynn, Drumod, had 22,038 acres in Leitrim in the Return of 1876, with a valuation of £9,160 about £769,440 in modern money. Bateman makes significant alterations to the Return. The Earl by 1883 was living at 44 Grosvenor Street, London and his Leitrim acreage had fallen to just 2,500 acres, with a valuation of £1,600. In addition he had 54,352 acres in Donegal, with a valuation of £9,406. According to Bateman, the 3rd Earl served in the Royal Navy. Born in Dublin, he was educated at the Sandhurst and was commissioned as an ensign in the 43rd Foot in 1824. In 1831 he was promoted captain, having served in Portugal between 1826 and 1827, and that same year was appointed an aide-de-camp to the Lord Lieutenant of Ireland.

In 1835 he transferred to the 51st Foot in the army. In 1839, on the death of his elder brother, he became known as Viscount Clements and also succeeded his brother as a Member of Parliament for County Leitrim, a seat he held until 1847. On his father's death in 1854, Clements succeeded as the 3rd Earl.

In 1855 he was promoted lieutenant-colonel and subsequently retired from the British Army. Over the next two decades, his overbearing behaviour as a landlord brought him 'much hatred from his tenants, both Catholic and Protestant alike, whom he evicted with equal enthusiasm'. Leitrim was deeply opposed to Gladstone's Irish Land Act of 1870 and was one of eight peers to protest against the legislation when it reached the House of Lords. Among those he also quarrelled with were the Presbyterian minister of Milford, County Donegal, and the Lord Lieutenant himself, the 7th Earl of Carlisle, who removed him from his appointments as a justice of the peace for Counties Leitrim, Donegal and Galway. In April 1878, after surviving various attempts on his life, Lord Leitrim was murdered along with his clerk and driver while on his way to his house at Milford.

He was buried in Dublin, amid scenes of great agitation, and despite the offer of a large reward, his assassins were never apprehended. They were named as the brothers Thomas and Patrick McGranaghan, but some historians suggest they were Michael McElwee and Neil Sheils from Fanad. A monument with a cross was set up at Kindrum in 1960 honouring McElwee, Shiels, and Michael Heraghty as the men whose actions 'Ended the tyranny of landlordism'.

The NUI Database has some additional information:

> The Clements family in Ireland were descended from Daniel Clements, a Cromwellian officer, originally granted lands in county Cavan. McParlan records Lord Clements and Mr. Clements as the owners of large estates in

Leitrim but not having a residence there in 1802. In the 1870s the 3rd Earl of Leitrim owned 22,038 acres in county Leitrim, [But *see* Bateman] 18,145 acres in county Galway, 54,352 acres in county Donegal and 471 acres in county Kildare. Henry Theophilus Clements, of Ashfield House, Cootehill, county Cavan, owned over 700 acres in Leitrim in the 1870s and his uncle John Marcus Clements of Monkstown, county Dublin, owned 6,773 acres in county Leitrim. These lands were advertised for sale in May 1858. Henry T. Clements inherited the Lough Rynn estate following the assassination of the 3rd Earl of Leitrim in 1878. The Clements family continued to own Lough Rynn until the 1970s although the bulk of the land had been sold off to former tenants by the Land Commission.

George Lane Fox MP, of Bramham Park, Tadcaster, England, held 18,850 acres in County Leitrim in 1876, with a valuation of £7,524 about £632,016 in modern money. There is some confusion in the accounts of this estate and its holder in 1876. The estate had landholdings in Yorkshire of 15,000 acres, in Leitrim of 18,850 acres and in Waterford of 5,219 acres, a total of 39,069 acres with a valuation of £26,000. According to the Wiki account George Land Fox was succeeded by his brother Sackville Lane Fox in 1840. His son, also named George Lane Fox, who died in 1896 was High Sheriff of Leitrim and Yorkshire. A descendant became Lord Bingley, a peerage that no longer exists.

Owen Wynne of Hazlewood, Sligo, had 15,436 acres in Leitrim in 1876, with a valuation of £4,380 about £367,920 in modern money.
This Harrow-educated infantry officer had, in addition to the Leitrim acreage, 12,982 acres in Sligo with a total of 28,418 acres with a valuation of £14,091.

According to the NUI Database, the Wynne family 'established themselves in Sligo in the later seventeenth century. They went on to become one of the dominant forces in political and economic life for the next two centuries.' It is not clear how. Owen Wynne served as High Sheriff of Leitrim in 1724 and went on to become High Sheriff of Sligo later. John Wynne, a descendant, also served as High Sheriff of Leitrim, in 1834. The Wynnes' Tireragh lands were held under fee farm grant from John ffolliott and Edward Nicholson.

In 1876 Owen Wynne offered for sale some of his estate. The *Irish Times* reported that many of the lots were sold out of court, while it also gave a detailed breakdown of the purchasers' of the other lots. Properties that Owen Wynne offered for sale in the Land Judges' Court in 1881 in and around the town of Sligo included lands leased from the Wood Martin estate. In 1906 Owen Wynne is recorded as the occupier of Hazelwood Demesne, including a mansion house. The NUI Database records the sale of the estate and the house to the Land Commission in the 1920s.

Arthur Loftus Tottenham, of Glenfarne Hall, Enniskillen, had 14,561 acres in Leitrim in 1876, with a valuation of £3,656 about £307,104 in modern money. This infantry soldier who was educated at Eton and was MP for Leitrim, had 257 acres in County Clare, giving him a total of 14,818 acres with a valuation of £4,431.

The NUI Database tells us that: 'the Tottenham family's main properties were based in Leinster, especially in the counties of Wicklow and Wexford. However, they also held property in Leitrim, Roscommon, Sligo and Waterford.'

The authors might also have added that the two families, those of Loftus and Tottenham, were unusual in history as land grabbers. Effectively, they shanghaied about 5 per cent of the island of Ireland between the Elizabethan and Cromwellian periods. The names have become obscured by the titles they acquired, including that of Marquis of Ely, as part of the process of using Parliament to consolidate their grip on power and wealth.

Almost 6,000 acres of the Leitrim estate was offered for sale in the Land Judges' Court (Encumbered Estates Court) in 1878 and 1883.

The Church Temporalities Commissioners of 24 Merrion St, Dublin, held 11,950 acres in County Leitrim with a valuation of £4,539 about £381,276 in modern money. The Church (of Ireland) Temporalities Commissioners are dealt with under Dublin City.

William Johnston of Kinlough House, Kinlough, held 10,633 acres in Leitrim in 1876, with a valuation of £4,027 about £338,268 in modern money. The Johnston family, who came from Fermanagh, bought this land in Leitrim in the early eighteenth century, according to the NUI Database, which also notes that Weir and Elizabeth Johnston offered for sale almost 400 acres in January 1869. This appears to have been leased from the Earl of Leitrim's estate through the Armstrong and Cullen estates. This complex system of inter-estate leasing needs to be further examined as to whether it was the predecessor to a more open system of land transactions, or a means of consolidating overall control within the families who already had possession of land. An offer from the Congested Districts Board on over 250 acres of Forbes Johnston's estate was accepted in 1913.

Hugh Lyons Montgomery of Belavel held 10,179 acres in Leitrim in 1876, with a valuation of £2,791 about £234,444 in modern money. This estate does not get a main mention in Bateman. Hugh Lyons Montgomery was the MP for Leitrim between 1852 and 1857 and was also High Sheriff. The family went bankrupt in 1880. In 1900 Belavel was demolished by the Land Commission. There is no mention of the estate but the assumption is that the Land Commission took it over and redistributed it. The family seem to have arrived in Ireland during the Williamite wars and obtained land, possibly in Louth. They married into all the right families and had the correct links to the clergy to become, as they were in 1876, country gentry.

Miss Catherine P. Jones of Hayle Place, Maidstone, Kent, had 9,839 acres in Leitrim in 1876, with a valuation of £4,213 about £253,892 in modern money. Catherine Jones gets awful short shift in Bateman. She was born in 1811 and had 65 acres in Kent as well as her Leitrim acreage, giving her 9,904 acres in all, with a valuation of £4,702.

The NUI Database offers a few facts about the family and property:

> Property in and near the town of Ballinamore, leased by the Jones Estate, was offered for sale in the Landed Estates' Court by Mary Anne Heran and others, in April 1870. Two sisters of Catherine Penelope Jones of Headford married members of the Marsham family, Earls of Romney, and she was succeeded by her nephew George Marsham. Thomas H. Jones and Theophilus B. Jones, both of Drumard, served as High Sheriffs of Leitrim in 1822 and 1835 while members of the Jones of Headford family served as High Sheriffs over ten times in the seventeenth and eighteenth centuries.

Sir Morgan George Crofton Bart, of Mohill Castle, County Leitrim, had 9,590 acres in the county in 1876, with a valuation of £5,387 about £452,508 in modern momey. There are three branches of this family, all with lands in Ireland at the time of the Return. All had titles. The incumbent at Mohill Castle in 1876 was Eton educated and though not mentioned in Bateman appears to have been a soldier:

> This family arrived in Ireland during the English Civil War, in about 1643 on a Patent or licence from Charles 1st who lost the war in England to Cromwell, and his head. The first title in the family was that of a baronetcy (hereditary knight) granted to Morgan Crofton in 1801. Like so many of the landowners the male head of the family was a serious soldier during most of this period. The 6th Baronet was a colonel in the Life Guards and was wounded at the battle of Ladysmith during the 2nd Boer war. A cousin was a lieutenant general in the army. The 6th Baronets diaries from World War 1 are unusual for a soldier and are critical of the military leadership. *Massacre of the Innocents: The Crofton Diaries, Ypres 1914–1915.*

The NUI Database tells us that 'members of the family served as High Sheriffs and MPs for Leitrim from the seventeenth to the twentieth centuries. McParlan includes Duke Crofton of Mohill on a list of 'resident gentlemen of property' in 1802. (There is no record of Duke Crofton, but there is a still extant peerage of Crofton held by Edward Harry Piers Crofton, the 8th Baron, who lives in Somerset.

A Morgan Crofton is recorded as the agent to Lord Lorton in the Barony of Boyle, Co. Roscommon, at the time of the first Ordnance Survey. It is probably the same Morgan Crofton who is recorded as a member of the Grand Panel of Co. Roscommon in 1828. According to Bateman, Sir Morgan Crofton of Mohill owned 9,590 acres in Co. Leitrim, 1,608 acres in Co. Longford and 271 acres in Co. Roscommon with a total acreage of 11,469 and a valuation of £6,222.

Landowners of over 1,000 acres in 1876

		Acreage	Valuation 1876 (£)	Valuation current (£)
1	Massy, Lord, Hermitage, Co. Limerick	24,751	6,220	522,480
2	Leitrim, Earl of, Lough Rynn, Drumod	22,038	9,416	790,944
3	Fox, George Lane, Braham Park, York, England	18,850	7,524	632,016
4	Wynn, Owen, Hazlewood, Co. Sligo	15,436	4,380	367,920
5	Tottenham, Arthur Loftus, Glenfarne Hall, Enniskillen	14,561	3,656	307,104
6	Church Temporalities Commissioners, 24 Merrion St, Dublin	11,950	4,539	381,276
7	Johnston, William, Kinlough House, Kinlough	10,633	4,027	338,268
8	Montgomery, Hugh Lyons of Bellhaven	10,179	2,791	234,444
9	Jones, Miss Catherine P., Hayle Place, Maidstone, Kent	9,839	4,213	353,892
10	Crofton, Sir Morgan G., Sunnyside Box, Wiltshire	9,590	5,387	452,508
11	Whyte, Col John James, Newtown Manor	9,326	2,397	201,348
12	La Touche, Wm Robert, Belle Vue, Delgany	8,234	3,981	334,404
13	O'Beirne, Hugh, Jamestown House, Drumsna	7,662	3,329	279,636

		Acreage	Valuation 1876 (£)	Valuation current (£)
14	Gore, W.R. Ormsby, Derrycarne, Drumod	7,480	3,124	262,416
15	Clements, John Marcus, Queenspark, Monkstown	6,773	1,702	142,968
16	White, Captain George, Kilmore, Artane, Co. Dublin	6,152	2,292	192,528
17	Granard, Earl of, Castleforbes, Newtownforbes, Co. Longford	4,266	1,576	132,384
18	Maguire, Edward, Gortoral, Swanlinbar	4,138	741	62,244
19	Southwell, Lord, Victoria Castle, Kingstown	4,017	1,491	125,244
20	Peyton, William, Castlecarrow, Carrick-on-Shannon	3,920	1,124	94,416
21	Lawder, William, Lawderdale, Finagh	3,748	1,440	120,960
22	Madden, John, Hilton Park	3,549	1,400	117,600
23	La Touche, John, Harristown	3,323	1,360	114,240
24	Ellis, Arthur, 7 Great Denmark St, Dublin	3,047	264	22,176
25	Johnston, Robert St George, Port Nassau, Ballyshannon	2,957	414	34,776
26	Butler, Miss, Belturbet	2,877	848	71,232
27	Kiernan, Thomas, 55 Middle Abbey St, Dublin	2,842	869	72,996
28	Crofton, Morgan Reps, Shanganagh, Kingstown, Co. Dublin	2,792	444	37,296
29	Kane, John, The Castle, Mohill	2,564	862	72,408
30	Dickson, John R., Tullaghan House, Tulaghan	2,558	875	73,500
31	Peyton, Richard Reynolds Reps, Loughscar, Keshcarrigan	2,514	1,207	101,388
32	M'Ternan, Hugh, Listowel, Co. Kerry	2,514	477	40,068
33	Albermarle, Earl of Quiddenham Hall, Attleborough, Norfolk England	2,506	1,064	89,376
34	King, John, Rospay Indre, France	2,496	888	74,592
35	Brady, John, 21 Chesham St, London	2,444	810	68,040

		Acreage	Valuation 1876 (£)	Valuation current (£)
36	Slack, Rev. William R, Newcastle, Co. Down	2,390	751	63,084
37	Rowley, Josias rn, Mount Campbell, Drumsna	2,374	1,295	108,780
38	Godley, Archibald, Killegar, Belturbet	2,310	1,074	90,216
39	King, James, Enniskillen	2,223	846	71,064
40	Cullen, Cairncross T., Glenade House, Manorhamilton	2,210	298	25,032
41	Gore, John R Ormsby, of Parkington Hall, England	2,154	625	52,500
42	Parke, Roger Charles, Doonally, Co. Sligo	2,105	550	46,200
43	Jones, Michael Reps, Carney, Co. Sligo	1,928	150	12,600
44	Brien, The Misses Harriett and Isabella, John Reville and Fredrick Beatty, Newcastle House, Greystairs	1,843	270	22,680
45	Blackall, Robert, Coolamber	1,805	620	52,080
46	Armstrong, John M.D., -	1,742	495	41,580
47	Lefroy, Thomas, Ardmore, Bray, Dublin	1,699	952	79,968
48	St George, Mrs Ingri Christini Reps, Hatley Manor, Carrick-on-Shannon	1,663	1,990	167,160
49	Acton, William, 16 Fleet St, Dublin	1,652	882	74,088
50	Simpson, Pierce, Cloncorrick Castle, Carrigallen	1,652	762	64,008
51	Palmer, Thomas Robert, Friarstown	1,616	601	50,484
52	Kiernan, James, Enniskillen	1,587	227	19,068
53	Forbes, Colonel the Hon. William Francis, -	1,584	784	65,856
54	Tenison, Edward King, Kilronan Castle, Keadue	1,554	141	11,844
55	O' Brien, William A., Drumsilla	1,489	746	62,664
56	Story, Joseph, Bingfield	1,479	733	61,572
57	Folliot, Lt Colonel John, Hollybrook, Boyle	1,473	349	29,316
58	Birchall, Arthur J.V.L., Blackrock, Drumshambo	1,402	463	38,892

		Acreage	Valuation 1876 (£)	Valuation current (£)
59	Cullen, William Parke, Clonkeen, Co. Galway	1,369	55	4,620
60	Palmer, Isabella, Drumkeel, Belhavel	1,331	632	53,088
61	Le Nauze, Elinor, 19 Clarinda Park, Kingstown	1,325	238	19,992
62	Godley, Denis, 24 Upper Merrion St, Dublin	1,306	709	59,556
63	Lawder, Mrs W.A. Reps, Flanker House, Drumsna	1,293	688	57,792
64	Barton, Chas W.R., Waterfoot, Pettigo	1,277	369	30,996
65	Lloyde, Guy, Croghan	1,262	738	61,992
66	Peyton, Rev. Walter C., Billis Virginia, Co. Cavan	1,210	258	21,672
67	Ensor, Charles, Rostrevor	1,153	533	44,772
68	White, Adam, White Hall	1,139	353	29,652
69	Phibbs, Margaret Reps, 38 Gloucester Street, Dublin	1,129	427	35,868
70	Newton, Andrew, Dungannon	1,126	397	33,348
71	Roberts, Robert L., America	1,102	204	17,136
72	Brady, John, Johnstown, Clones	1,036	527	44,268
73	Browne, Eliza M., Kilbracken, Carrigallen	1,026	382	32,088
74	Johnston, Forbes, Brookhill, Kinlough	1,024	398	33,432
75	Martin, Rev. Henry, Sadlers Wells, England	1,020	347	29,148

Landowners of over 1,000 acres in 1876 ranked by gross estimated income

		Acreage	Valuation 1876 (£)	Valuation current (£)
1	Leitrim, Earl of, Lough Rynn, Drumod	22,038	9,416	790,944
2	Fox, George Lane, Braham Park, York, England	18,850	7,524	632,016

		Acreage	Valuation 1876 (£)	Valuationcurrent (£)
3	Massy, Lord, Hermitage, Co. Limerick	24,751	6,220	522,480
4	Crofton, Sir Morgan G., Sunnyside, Box, Wiltshire	9,590	5,387	452,508
5	Church Temporalities Commissioners, 24 Merrion St, Dublin	11,950	4,539	381,276
6	Wynn, Owen, Hazlewood, Co. Sligo	15,436	4,380	367,920
7	Jones, Miss Catherine P., Hayle Place, Maidstone, Kent	9,839	4,213	353,892
8	Johnston, William, Kinlough House, Kinlough	10,633	4,027	338,268
9	La Touche, Wm Robert, Belle Vue, Delgany	8,234	3,981	334,404
10	Tottenham, Arthur Loftus, Glenfarne Hall, Enniskillen	14,561	3,656	307,104
11	O'Beirne, Hugh, Jamestown House, Drumsna	7,662	3,329	279,636
12	Gore, W.R. Ormsby, Derrycarne, Drumod	7,480	3,124	262,416
13	Montgomery, Hugh Lyons, of Bellhaven	10,179	2,791	234,444
14	Whyte, Col John James, Newtown Manor	9,326	2,397	201,348
15	White, Captain George, Kilmore, Artane, Co. Dublin	6,152	2,292	192,528
16	St George, Mrs Ingri Christini Reps, Hatley Manor, Carrick-on-Shannon	1,663	1,990	167,160
17	Clements, John Marcus, Queenspark, Monkstown	6,773	1,702	142,968
18	Granard, Earl of, Castleforbes, Newtownforbes. Co. Longford	4,266	1,576	132,384
19	Southwell, Lord, Victoria Castle, Kingstown	4,017	1,491	125,244
20	Lawder, William, Lawderdale, Finagh	3,748	1,440	120,960

LIMERICK

TOGETHER WITH THE COUNTY OF THE TOWN

	1876	2020 est
Population in County Limerick	191,936 (County 152,583, city 39,353)	191,809
All owners of land	2,333	43,835
Percentage of the population	1.21	-
Owners of nothing at all	190,260	54,585
Percentage of the population	98.8	-
Size of County	662,457 acres (County 660,386, city 2,071)	680,960 acres
Number of dwellings(Rented in 1876, owned in 2020	31,863 (City 5,518) (29,320 rented)	69,421
Number of owned farm holdings	1,767	5,991

County comparisons

	Acreage 1876	Population 1876
County Limerick (not inc. city)	660,386	152,583
Staffordshire, England	638,084	858,326
Dumfriesshire, Scotland	676,971	74,808
Carmarthenshire, Wales	510,574	115,710

The Earl of Devon of Powderham Castle, Exeter, had 33,026 acres in the county in 1876, with a valuation of £14,525 about £1,220,100 in modern money. The Earl of Devon, whose family name is Courtenay and who lives in Devon, should not be confused with the Duke of Devonshire, whose family name is Cavendish and who lives in Derbyshire. Both, however, had vast estates in Ireland. This 1876 Devon Earl, the 11th, was an MP for South Devon and had a number of important posts during the worst of the famine years. He was a poor law inspector, Secretary of the Poor Law board, Chancellor of the Duchy of Lancaster, President of the Poor Law Board and, unlike most of his landowning contemporaries, was educated at Westminster School in London.

He had 20,049 acres in Devon and 33,026 acres in County Limerick, with a total acreage of 53,075 acres and a valuation of £45,520, about £3,823,680 in modern money. He was the eighty-fourth richest landowner in Great Britain by valuation in 1876. From an Irish perspective he was an absentee landlord, running his huge estate through agents and middlemen (gombeen men).

There are references to the estate in the NUI Galway Estates Database. The Limerick estate was acquired by Sir William Courtenay of Powerham, Devon, in 1591, part of the Elizabethan plantation confiscations. The estate eventually reached 85,000 acres in extent. The estate was finally sold in 1908 but prior to that parts of the holding had been sold off, indicating serious decline. Alfred Furlong of Newcastle was the agent in the early 1840s and he is recorded as resident at Courtenay Castle. The Curling family took over in 1848 and Edward Curling, his son, Charles Edward Napier Curling, and grandson, Richbell Curling, were successively land agents to the Devon estate, The castle at Newcastle West was eventually bought by the Curlings in the early twentieth century.

The Earl of Dunraven, of Adare Manor, Limerick, had 14,298 acres in the county in 1876, with a valuation of £10,814 about £908,376 in modern money. This peerage, whose family name is Wyndham Quin and which is ancient Irish in origin, played a decisive role in the fate of land in Ireland in the late nineteenth and early twentieth century. In 1903 the Wyndham Act was passed, increasing the power of tenants to buy their lands from landlords.

This was one of five land sale acts passed by the British Parliament in various attempts to resolve the post-famine crisis in Ireland. It was also the most effective, setting the scene for the rural Ireland that emerged during the twentieth century far more than the Rebellion of 1916 did. The economic crisis in Ireland following the Great Famine is, however, wrongly characterised as primarily a nationalist and political problem exacerbated by crop failure. It was in reality a crisis generated within the governance system itself and stemming from it. The system of governance in Ireland, from a Parliament in London after the act of Union in 1800, had failed to win the support of the Irish population, who were both landless and disenfranchised. In this respect the population did not count, at all. 'Ireland' was, given the nature of the Parliament in London, the sum of its mainly aristocratic owners and their interests, which were land and rents. The actual population were no more than a necessary economic inconvenience, to be ignored in place of their betters, who, in a situation of utter surreality, claimed to represent them. How someone, educated at Eton, sitting on Parliament's green and red benches, in tails and a top hat, could represent a destitute peasant in the wilds of west Mayo is a bottom line too often left unconsidered by the commentators of the time. But the economic and legal infrastructure underpinning the real interests of these comic representatives was failing under the weight of its own inconsistencies. All the famine did was bring it to the surface. Unlike the evolution of law and civil society in England, the bedrock of the Irish system, tenants paying rent without security of tenure, had failed. The public measure of failure was the Encumbered Estates Court, set up in 1848 and 1849, to provide a financial exit route for financially failed landlords. Many Irish estates were already subject to this court, long before the first Land Act of 1870 got on the statute books. To use a cliché, the writing was on the wall, but those who needed to read what was written on the stones of history were suffering moral and economic myopia of an extreme kind. This kind of blindness leads to extinction, as it did.

The last holder of the title, Thady Windham Thomas Wyndham Quin, the 7th Earl, died in 2011, much mourned in the new Ireland his predecessors did so much to shape. Afflicted with polio as a child, he was chairperson of the Irish Wheelchair Association for twenty-five years and did an enormous amount to get better help and support for the disabled in Ireland. He was an active and enthusiastic horse breeder and managed the family estates himself, from his wheelchair. He was educated in Switzerland at Le Rosy, the international school for the super rich. His sister, Caroline, married the 8th Marquis of Waterford, another large landowner.

The 4th Earl, who held the estates in 1876, had 23,751 acres in Glamorgan, 537 acres in Gloucester, 1,005 acres in Kerry and 164 acres in Clare, which, together with the Limerick acres, came to a total of 39,755 acres with a valuation of £35,478. The 4th Earl was an officer in the 1st Life Guards, the most expensive cavalry regiment in the British Army. The NUI Estates database merely repeats Bateman. There is an implication that the Dunraven estates have stayed largely intact and the Irish company that owns some of the current assets is an unlimited company, which usually means that it is sufficiently asset rich to do without the ministrations of bank borrowing.

Lord Ashtown of Clonodfoy, Kilfinane, had 11,273 acres in Limerick in 1876, with a valuation of £4,214 about £353,976 in modern money. Eton-educated Lord Ashtown had land in nine counties, eight in Ireland. He had 6,386 acres in Yorkshire, 11,273 acres in Limericak, 8,310 acres in Galway, 2,780 acres in King's County, 4,526 acres in Tipperary, 841 acres in Roscommon, 50 acres in Dublin and 42 acres in Westmeath. His total acreage, with the Waterford holdings, were 43,643 acres with a valuation of £34,689. He inherited this huge estate and, it was rumoured, £1 million, at the age of 12. The family seat was Woodlawn House, near Ballinasloe, County Galway. Woodlawn House was sold by the 4th Baron in 1947 and is still extant, although semi-derelict. It is currently in the process of being gradually restored. The 8th and current Baron Ashtown, Rodrick Nigel Godolphin Trench, was educated at Eton and lives in East Sussex.

The Venerable Archdeacon Goold of Athea, County Limerick, had 10,966 acres in the county in 1876, with a valuation of £3,090 about £259,560 in modern money. By the time Bateman printed his fourth and final edition this estate was in the hands of Mrs Goold of Dromadda, Glin, County Limerick. The NUI Estates Database provides some useful detail but no account of the ultimate fate of the estate:

> Maurice Roach was agent to Thomas Goold, Master in Chancery, Dublin, in the early 1840s. The Dunraven genealogy traces the lineage of Thomas Goold, who was a great grandson of John Quin of Rosbrien, near Limerick city, born in 1692. Thomas Goold bought the Athea estate from Lord Courtenay in 1817, His son Wyndham Goold, Member of Parliament for county Limerick (died 1854), was the proprietor by the early 1850s. In the 1870s Wyndham's brother Archdeacon Goold of Athea, county Limerick, owned 10,966 acres in the county. In 1873 the Archdeacon's daughter and co heiress, Frances Goold, married Reverend Hamilton Stuart Verschoyle of county Donegal and their son, Hamilton Frederick Stuart Goold Verschoyle, assumed the additional name of Goold. The Archdeacon's sister, Augusta Charlotte, married her cousin, the 3rd Earl of Dunraven. In 1906 the representatives of the Venerable F.F. Goold held about 400 acres of untenanted land at Athea Upper.

Lady Louisa Fitzgibbon of Mount Shannon, County Limerick, held 10,316 acres in the county in 1876 with a valuation of £6,694 about £562,296 in modern money. Lady Louisa was the daughter of the 3rd and last Earl of Clare (of the 3rd creation). The 1st Earl had been the Lord Chancellor of Ireland and had accumulated large estates in Limerick and Tipperary.

Ferres gives a somewhat romantic, if melodramatic, account of Lady Louisa's life, omitting her first marriage to a son of Viscount Dillion (*see* Galway). She lived an extravagant lifestyle without the income to sustain it. In an effort to repair her fortunes, she married the Sicilian Marquis de Rochella, who married her hoping her apparent fortune would repair his equally depleted one. The bailiffs arrived during the engagement party at Mountshannon House. They married but inevitably the house and estate were sold, the house being burnt down by the IRA in 1920. No member of the Fitzgibbon clan was in residence, Lady Fitzgibbon having retired to a convent in the Isle of Wight in 1887, where she eventually died.

The Irish Land Commission eventually acquired and redistributed what was left of the lands of the estate.

Sir Croker Barrington Bart, (4th) of Glenstal, Murroe, had 9,453 acres in the county in 1876, with a valuation of £4,999 about £419,916 in modern money. This baronetage still exists and the holder, Sir Benjamin Barrington (8th Baronet), lives in Calgary, in Canada. The estate was not an old one and came into the Barrington family in 1831, centred around a Gothic revival castle built on the site of a former abbey. The family had been active in Limerick city and the 5th Baronet was a colonel in the Limerick City Royal Field reserve artillery and High Sheriff of the county.

The family left Ireland in 1925 after the only daughter of the 5th Baronet was earlier shot dead by the IRA when she was travelling with a Black and Tan officer who was the actual target of the ambush. By then the estate had been reduced to about 1,000 acres. The family offered Glenstal Abbey to the Free State but it could not afford the upkeep. In 1927 monks of the Order of St Benedict (Benedictines) acquired the castle and opened a boys' boarding school in 1932, modelled on its public schools in England (Downside and Ampleforth). The school has been hugely successful.

Lord Massy of the Hermitage Castle, Connell, had 8,568 acres in Limerick in 1876, with a valuation of £4,751 about £399,084 in modern money. This peerage is still extant and the holder of the title, Hugh Somerset Massy, the 10th Baron, lives in Leicester in the UK.

There are three people with the name Massy, and significant landholdings, recorded in Bateman. John Bolton-Massy of Clareville, Blackrock, Dublin, had 2,259 acres in Limerick and 908 acres in Dublin, a total of 3,167 acres with a valuation of £3,274.

Lady Massy of Doonas House, Cloonlara, Co. Clare, had 4,623 acres in that county with a valuation of £3,173.

William Hugh Massy Hutchinson Massy of Mount Massy, Macroom, Co. Cork, had 13,363 acres in the county in 1876 with a valuation of £3,105.

The NUI Galway estates database tells us that the Massy family are descended from a Cromwellian soldier, Captain Hugh Massy, who was granted 3,055 acres in the Barony of Coshlea, Co. Limerick, for his military services. Two of his great grandsons became the 1st Baron Massy of Duntrileague and the 1st Baron Clarina of Elm Park. During the eighteenth century, Duntrileague was the family seat but in the nineteenth century their main residence was Hermitage, close to Limerick city. The Massy estate was offered for sale in the Encumbered Estates Court in May 1852.

Most of the Massy lands were sold in the last two decades of the nineteenth century and the family residences in the early years of the twentieth century.

Colonel William Dickson of 26 Portman Square, London, had 8,559 acres in the county in 1876 with a valuation of £2,924 about £245,616 in modern money. By the time we get to Bateman, the colonel has become a major general in the army, with 1,294 acres in Berkshire and 513 acres in Tipperary, giving him, with the Limerick acres, a total of 10,366 acres and a valuation of £4,985. His address is given as Croom Castle, Limerick.

The NUI Galway database notes the following:

In the mid nineteenth century Major General William Dickson of Berkshire, fifth son of Samuel Dickson and Mary Norris and younger brother of Stephen Dickson and the Reverend Richard Dickson, held lands in Limerick, while the representatives of Samuel Dickson held land in various parishes. His agent was Samuel Dickson Power of Catherine Street, Limerick. Major General Dickson married Harriet Dallas and had two sons, Samuel Auchmuty Dickson of Croom Castle, county Limerick and Major General Willliam Thomas Dickson, 16th Lancers, neither of whom had children. In 1847 Fanny Charlotte, daughter of Major General Dickson, married Baron Sackville of Knole, Kent. Croom Castle and its 107-acre demesne were advertised for sale in February 1864. Samuel A. Dickson died in 1870.

The following also appears in the NUI data base:

Croom Castle. Originally a Fitzgerald Castle, subsequently granted to the Duke of Richmond who sold it to John Croker in 1721. Reverend Fitzgerald writes that Croker was agent to the Duke. A residence was built with some of the stone from the old castle. Situated on the outskirts of the town of Croom this house was occupied by Samuel A. Dickson in the mid nineteenth century who held it from the Crokers. The buildings were valued at £30. Sold in the late 1880s to the Lyons family and bought by Michael Corry in 1936. Now functions as self catering accommodation.

The Hon. Fredrick Charles Trench Gascoigne of Parlingford Park, Aberford, Yorkshire, had 7,766 acres in Limerick in 1876, with a valuation of £5,548 about £466,032 in modern money. The colonel's immediate relatives do much to explain his appearance among the landowners in Bateman. He was the only son of the brother of the first Lord Ashtown (*see* above) and of Anna, the eldest daughter of Luke White (*see* County Dublin).

Bateman records the colonel having 5,685 acres in Yorkshire, 5,591 acres in Argyll and 313 acres in Westmeath; with the Limerick acres a total of 19,355 acres, with a valuation of £16,399.

He was a professional soldier who served for sixteen years in the 66th of Foot, making the rank of captain. He was a colonel in the local volunteers. Colonel Gascoigne was a JP and DL for the County of York, JP for the County of Limerick and the County of Argyle, and High Sheriff for the County of Limerick in 1854 and the County of York in 1864. Upon the death of his wife in 1891 he entered a life tenure of Parlington and survived her nearly fifteen years. He died at Parlington after a short illness in June 1905, aged 91, and was buried at Aberford on 15 June 1905. There is no mention in the records of any children.

Nathaniel Buckley MP of Ryecroft, Ashton-under-Lyme, had 7,563 acres in Limerick in 1876, with a valuation of £1,208 about £101,472 in modern money. Bateman has Nathaniel Buckley with just 62 acres in Lancashire, where he sat as MP for Stalybridge. His other acres were 13,260 in Tipperary, 2 in Cheshire and 11 in Darby. Clearly, with the House of Commons in mind, he was covering his angles. His total acreage was 20,898 with a valuation of £6,826.

Ferres gives a good account of the family. Here are some of the salient points:

> By the 1870s, Buckley was a millionaire Lancashire cotton mill owner and, in 1873, he purchased the Galtee estate, near Mitchelstown in County Cork, from the Earl of Kingston.
>
> Following a revaluation, he issued rent demands to his new tenants showing increases of between 50 and 500 per cent. This led to a great deal of agrarian unrest, evictions and an attempted assassination of Buckley's land agent. His actions also demonstrated weaknesses in the Irish Land Acts, which were consequently amended.
>
> The estate had been purchased by his uncle, Nathaniel Buckley DL, MP, in 1873.
>
> Galtee Castle, County Tipperary, was situated at the foothills of the Galtee Mountains, not far from Mitchelstown. The original structure was built as a hunting lodge for the 2nd Earl of Kingston, c.1780. The 3rd Earl remodelled it c.1825. In the 1850s, the Kingstons were forced to sell off vast amounts of their landed estate due to debts, including the lodge and approximately 20,000 acres surrounding it. The building was remodelled and expanded c.1892, when its new owner, Abel Buckley, inherited the estate from his brother Nathaniel, who had previously purchased sole ownership in 1873.

The Irish Land Commission, a government agency, acquired the demesne and house in the late 1930s, after allocating the land between afforestation and farmers.

Top 100 owners in Limerick ranked by acreage in 1876

		Acreage	Valuation 1876 (£)	Valuation current (£)
1	Devon, Earl of, Powderham Castle, Exeter	33,026	14,525	1,220,100
2	Dunraven, Earl of, Adare Manor, Adare	14,298	10,814	908,376
3	Ashtown, Lord, Clonodfoy, Kilfinane	11,273	4,214	353,976
4	Goold, Ven Archdeacon, Athea, Co. Limerick	10,966	3,090	259,560
5	Fitzgibbon, Lady Louisa, Mount Shannon, Co. Limerick	10,316	6,694	562,296
6	Barrington, Sir Croker Bart, Glenstal, Murroe	9,453	4,999	419,916
7	Massy, Lord, Hermitage, Castleconnell	8,568	4,751	399,084
8	Dickson, Wm Colonel, 26 Portman Square London	8,559	2,924	245,616
9	Gascoigne the Hon. F.C.T., Partinghton, Yorkshire	7,766	5,548	466,032
10	Buckley, Nathaniel, Manchester	7,563	1,208	101,472
11	Walter, Rev. Thomas John, Castletown, Pallaskenry	6,636	4,289	360,276
12	Monteagle, Lord, Mt Trenchard, Foynes	6,445	5,046	423,864
13	Leconfield, Lord, Petworth, Sussex	6,269	4,820	404,880
14	Annaly, Lord, Woodlands, Clonsilla, Co. Dublin	5,428	3,101	260,484
15	Fitzgerald, Desmond J.E. (Knight of Glin), Glin Castle	5,268	3,187	267,708
16	De Stafford, O'Brien Henry, Cratloe Woods, Cratloe	5,263	1,277	107,268
17	Cloncurry, Lord, Lyons, Hazlehatch, Co. Kildare	5,137	2,563	215,292
18	Maunsell, John, Edenmore Raheany, Co. Dublin	5,011	2,559	214,956
19	O'Brien, Edward W., Carmoyle, Co. Limerick	4,990	3,630	304,920
20	O'Grady, Hon. Cecelia, Rockbarton, Bruff	4,977	4,070	341,880

Limerick

		Acreage	Valuation 1876 (£)	Valuation current (£)
21	Kenmare, Earl of, Kenmare Castle, Killarney	4,826	5,724	480,816
22	Massy, Edward Taylor, Cottermore, Haverfordwest, South Wales	4,620	1,493	125,412
23	Hartopp, Edward B., Dalby Hall, Melton Mowbray, Leicestershire	4,545	3,251	273,084
24	Harkness, William H., Cragbeg, Clarina	4,323	1,432	120,288
25	Governors of Erasmus Smith Schools, Dublin	4,279	3,400	285,600
26	Maunsell, Daniel M., Ballywilliam, Rathkeale	4,231	1,351	113,484
27	Staveley, James B., Croydon Park, Fairview Avenue, Dublin	4,169	2,070	173,880
28	De Vere, Sir Vere Edmond Bart, Curra Chase, Adare, Co. Limerick	4,163	2,108	177,072
29	Wandesforde, Henry Thomas Butler, Palmerstown, Co. Dublin	4,137	2,190	183,960
30	Limerick, the Earl of, Dromore Castle, Pallaskenry	4,035	5,055	424,620
31	Southwell, Viscount, Merrion Sq., Dublin	4,032	3,190	267,960
32	De Salis, Count, Tandragee, Armagh	4,026	3,349	281,316
33	Roche, Sir D.V. Bart, Carass, Croom	3,951	3,457	290,388
34	Langford, Lord, Summerville House, Co. Meath	3,855	3,634	137,256
35	Sandwich, Earl of, Grosvenor Sq., London	3,844	3,082	258,888
36	De Burgho, Lady, Castleconnell	3,844	2,290	192,360
37	Guillamore, Viscount, Caherguillmore, Bruff, Co. Limerick	3,750	2,028	170,352
38	Hare, Hon. Richard, St Michael's Lodge, Devonport, England	3,687	2,524	212,016
39	Gabbett, Rev. Joseph, Ardvullen, Kilmallock	3,518	3,040	255,360
40	Pigott, H.A. Robert, Capard, Rosenallis, Queen's County	3,477	2,590	217,560
41	Barker, William P., Kilcooley Abbey, Co. Tipperary	3,426	2,614	219,576

		Acreage	Valuation 1876 (£)	Valuation current (£)
42	Caulfield, Annie R., Copswood, Pallaskenry	3,350	2,513	211,092
43	Croker, John Monck, Ballinagarde, Limerick	3,328	3,647	306,348
44	O'Grady, Waller, Castlegarde, Pallasgreen	3,279	1,038	87,192
45	Lowe, John, Sunville, Kilfinane	3,204	2,109	177,156
46	Franks, John, Ballyscadane, Knocklong	3,196	1,643	138,012
47	Cork and Orrery, Earl of, Grafton Street, London	3,189	2,859	240,156
48	Muskerry, Lord, Springfield Castle, Drumcolloher, Co. Limerick	3,161	1,976	165,984
49	Delmege, John C., Castle Park, Limerick	3,066	1,172	98,448
50	Bateson, Sir Thomas, Belvoir Park, Belfast	2,927	991	83,244
51	St Leger, Colonel John, 6 Park Hill, Rotherham, Yorkshire	2,900	1,920	161,280
52	Synan, Edward J., Ashbourne, Limerick	2,792	2,272	190,848
53	Rose, Robert de Ros, Ahabeg, Co. Limerick	2,747	1,006	84,504
54	Trustees of Lord Carbery, Castlefreke, Roscarbery	2,724	2,992	251,328
55	Royce, the Misses, Ballinvyrick, Askeaton	2,689	1,140	95,760
56	Coote, C. John A., Mount Coote, Kilmallock	2,688	2,888	242,592
57	Atkinson, Edward, Glenwilliam Castle, Ballingarry	2,655	1,573	132,132
58	Taylor, William, Holly Park, Pallaskenry	2,570	2,782	233,688
59	Dickson, Samuel F., Creaves, Askeaton	2,540	2,076	174,384
60	Stratford, John Wingfield, Addington Place, Maidstone, Kent	2,502	1,855	155,820
61	Cantillon, John Heffernan, Mannister House, Croom	2,465	1,602	134,568

		Acreage	Valuation 1876 (£)	Valuation current (£)
62	White, John P., Nantenan House, Rathkeele	2,447	1,808	151,872
63	Conyers, Charles, Castletownconyers	2,425	1,386	116,424
64	Gough, George, Birdhill, Clonmel	2,398	2,539	213,276
65	Massy, Hugh, Ballinacurry House, Limerick	2,309	1,249	104,916
66	Massy, John Bolton, Ballywire, Tipperary	2,259	2,150	180,600
67	Emly, Lord, Tervoe, Clarina	2,246	1,937	162,708
68	Church Temporalities Commissioners, Dublin	2,202	2,811	236,124
69	Kelly, James Reps, Castle Bagot, Rathcoole, Co. Dublin	2,177	2,110	177,240
70	Oliver, Silver C., Dunkettle, Co. Cork	2,156	1,824	153,216
71	Duncan, James, 8 Upper Merrion St, Dublin	2,149	1,167	98,028
72	Croker, Captain Edward, The Grange, Limerick	2,121	1,952	163,968
73	Buckinghamshire Eral of, Richmond Lodge, Sidmouth, Devonshire	2,082	2,200	184,800
74	Hayes, Patrick Reps, In Chancery	2,057	430	36,120
75	Ellis, Richard, Glensharone Abbey, Fuerty	2,055	1,138	95,592
76	Clarina, Lord, Elm Park, Clarina	2,012	2,497	209,748
77	O'Grady, The, Kilballyowen, Bruff	1,943	2,232	187,488
78	Carroll, Thomas, Mitchelstown	1,942	1,822	153,048
79	M'Murray, John, Roxborough House, Limerick	1,931	1,166	97,944
80	Trench, Henry, Cangort Park, Roscrea	1,926	821	68,964
81	Lloyd Eyre, Prospect, Castleconnell	1,912	1,695	142,380
82	Clonmel, Earl of, Bishop's Court, Straffan, Co. Kildare	1,904	748	62,832
83	Hunt, Robert, George St, Limerick	1,903	1,406	118,104
84	Longfield, Richard, Longueville, Co. Cork	1,881	1,514	127,176

		Acreage	Valuation 1876 (£)	Valuation current (£)
85	Blennerhasset, John B., Rockfiled, Kilpecon	1,829	807	67,788
86	Webber, Captain Robert F., India	1,814	546	45,864
87	Bateson, Colonel Richard, First Life Guards, Knightsbridge Barracks, London	1,808	1,169	98,196
88	Harnett, John C., Abbeyfeale	1,796	292	24,528
89	Plummer, Brudenal of Killoory Glebe, Causeway, Co. Kerry	1,773	669	56,196
90	Farnell, George, Caherelly, Limerick	1,741	1,759	147,756
91	Palmer, Robert S, 4 Trafalgar Sq., London	1,681	1,192	100,128
92	Piele, W.T., St John's Wood Park, Hampstead	1,669	347	29,148
93	Wise, Francis E., Cork	1,666	1,850	155,400
94	Lyons, Henry E., Croom House, Croom	1,665	1,646	138,264
95	Greene, Francis, Greenmount, Patrickswell	1,606	1,258	105,672
96	Newenham, William H., Monkstown, Co. Dublin	1,591	1,104	92,736
97	Smith, Charles Wilmot, Ballynanty House, Bruss	1,549	1,007	84,588
98	Lansdowne, Marquess of, Derreen, Co. Kerry	1,526	2,701	226,884
99	Fosbery, Thomas, Kilgobbin, Patrick's Well	1,488	1,141	92,844
100	O'Grady Edward, Stephen's Green Dublin	1,438	519	43,596
101	Hewson, John B., Castle Hewson, Askeaton	1,435	1,061	89,124

Top Twenty owners in Limerick ranked by acreage in 1876

		Acreage	Valuation 1876 (£)	Valuation current (£)
1	Devon, Earl of, Powderham Castle, Exeter	33,026	14,525	1,220,100

		Acreage	Valuation 1876 (£)	Valuation current (£)
2	Dunraven, Earl of, Adare Manor, Adare	14,298	10,814	908,376
3	Fitzgibbon, Lady Louisa, Mount Shannon, Co. Limerick	10,316	6,694	562,296
4	Kenmare, Earl of, Kenmare Castle, Killarney	4,826	5,724	480,816
5	Gascoigne, the Hon. F.C.T., Partinghton, Yorkshire	7,766	5,548	466,032
6	Limerick, the Earl of, Dromore Castle, Pallaskenry	4,035	5,055	424,620
7	Monteagle, Lord, Mt Trenchard, Foynes	6,445	5,046	423,864
8	Barrington, Sir Croker Bart, Glenstal, Murroe	9,453	4,999	419,916
9	Leconfield, Lord, Petworth, Sussex	6,269	4,820	404,880
10	Massy, Lord, Hermitage, Castleconnell	8,568	4,751	399,084
11	Walter, Rev. Thomas John, Castletown, Pallaskenry	6,636	4,289	360,276
12	Ashtown, Lord, Clonodfoy, Kilfinane	11,273	4,214	353,976
13	O'Grady, Hon. Cecelia, Rockbarton, Bruff	4,977	4,070	341,880
14	Croker, John Monck, Ballinagarde, Limerick	3,328	3,647	306,348
15	Langford, Lord, Summerville House, Co. Meath	3,855	3,634	137,256
16	O'Brien, Edward W., Carmoyle, Co. Limerick	4,990	3,630	304,920
17	Roche, Sir D.V. Bart, Carass, Croom	3,951	3,457	290,388
18	Governors of Erasmus Smith Schools, Dublin	4,279	3,400	285,600
19	De Salis, Count, Tandragee, Armagh	4,026	3,349	281,316
20	Hartopp, Edward B., Dalby Hall, Melton Mowbray, Leicestershire	4,545	3,251	273,084

LONDONDERRY OR DERRY

	1876	2016
Population in County Londonderry	173,932	247,132
All owners of land	2,178	43,835
Percentage of the population	1.25	–
Owners of nothing at all	171,754	Figures not available
Percentage of the population	98.75	–
Size of County	511,838 acres	512,640 acres
Number of dwellings	32,601 (30,423 rented)	–
Number of owned farm holdings	1,380	3,309

County Comparisons

	Acreage in 1876	Population in 1876
County Londonderry	511,838	173,932
Cambridgeshire, England	522,208	186,903
Angus, Scotland	555,994	257,567
Carmarthenshire, Wales	510,574	115,710

The 'League' of London Livery companies – the largest owners of the county in 1876

In the year of the Return it emerged that seven London Livery companies still owned 153,369 acres of Londonderry. That was just under 30 per cent. It is the only county in Ireland where aristocrats do not head the lists of landowners in 1876, and the only one dominated by corporate interests.

To explain the Livery companies and their power in London it is worth noting that the City has a permanent representative in Parliament, called the Remembrancer. His job is to ensure that the interests of the City of London, the financial district, are looked after; and to remind the House if they are not being looked after. Historically it was to the city that the monarchs, governments and Parliaments of the UK turned when they wanted money. From time immemorial those three interests have always wanted money, all the time and lots of it. The Liveries became powerful because they accumulated huge assets, especially cash, over the ages. They were rather like corporate Warren Buffetts (the American investor) who had sat on their accumulating investments for hundreds of years rather than one lifetime. And, physically, the three, Crown, Parliament and Government, were a quick hour's stroll down the Thames embankment from Parliament, a tad further from the Palace, but not much.

The Livery companies started out as tradesmen's guilds in the eleventh century or earlier, there to protect specific trades from competition and to regulate affairs between the guilds. But gradually the guilds became de facto bankers to the state and others. There are total of about 110 Livery companies in the modern city of London, of which the twelve Great Livery companies are the most important. Membership of the Liveries is made up of people, most of whom work in the City, who are granted the freedom of the City of London; women are included and are masters of a number of modern liveries. The companies dominate the official life of the City, even now. They donate over £44 million a year to charity and run a significant number of schools and educational institutions. The City Mayor is chosen from among the Liveries and the City Council – the Corporation of the City of London – is heavily populated with Liverymen and women. But back to the past.

In 1610, James I decided to end rebellion in Ulster by planting the province with Protestant English settlers. To do this he coerced the Livery companies of the City of London to provide finance and support, on a huge scale, even for the period. The Liveries did not queue up to assist the King but by 1613 he had got his way. According to Professor James Curl:

> It was only when several respectable citizens had been gaoled, fined, and further threatened that the City knew it had no chance of avoiding the will of the Crown, and the City of London was obliged to commit its resources and ingenuity to carrying out colonisation of part of the territory.

A delegation from the City visited Ulster on what we would nowadays call a PR trip. The delegation of four were only shown the fertile parts of Ulster, and were taken nowhere near the parts inhabited by the dispossessed Irish, mainly the Sperrin Mountains. The visitors were given hospitality, but only in already established English manors, castles and forts.

The four worthies taken over to Ulster were in the care of Sir Arthur Chichester, an ambitious landowner and knight from Raleigh in Devon. His descendants were later created the Marquises of Donegal – the prizes for the managers and participants in the plantation were extraordinarily high, in both titles and money – and, once the right level of duress had been applied the Liveries soon set about doing what they had been told to do by James I.

The Liveries then and now do much charitable work, but they were never merely charities. They were ancient capitalism, red in tooth and claw. They made investments and expected dividends. To go ahead with the plantation of Ulster, they demanded huge grants of land and the Crown handed over what we can see in the Londonderry land grants, and much else besides. These were mainly the estates of the Irish landlords who had left in what is described as the 'Flight of the Earls' in 1607. Those estates fell forfeit to the Crown because of the rebellion of the Earls, which under the laws of the time was treason.

The 'great' or most senior, twelve Livery companies
In 1516 the Livery companies were given an order of precedence by the Lord Mayor of the time. The precedence list was basically organised around wealth but did include, among other considerations, the date of foundation as well as the Royal Charter date. Some of the companies were incredibly wealthy and consequently very powerful. At that time there were only forty-eight companies but the ranks have now grown to over 110. Out of the original forty-eight, a 'Great Twelve' were created.

These were the twelve most powerful and influential companies in the City of London, controlling all sorts of aspects of daily life and trade, not merely in the City but throughout the country and the Empire as it was created and grew. In a very significant way, the City of London financed the creation of the British Empire and drew appropriate benefits is cash and kind as a result.

By themselves, the Great Twelve did not have the resources to carry out the plantation, so they arranged consortia of other Livery companies, which would chip in and support the endeavour. It is extremely difficult to get a proper comparative estimate of the cost of the plantation. What the Liveries were doing was paying King James, or granting him loans, for the estates he'd stolen or confiscated from the native Irish landlords after they had fled. Put simply, the King was charging money, one way or another, for land he'd acquired for nothing. One way of arriving at an estimate of what the land might have cost, in modern money, at about £3,000 an acre, would be £890 million; and that's before all the other costs surrounding forts, castles, cannon, troops and agricultural equipment. The total allocation or grant made by the King in 1613 was 296,960 acres.

Who joined the Great Twelve for the plantation of Ulster and the acreage they originally got, together with the acreage in 1876?

The Worshipful Company of Mercers of London, with R.H. Dolling as agent, had 21,241 acres in the county in 1876, with a valuation of £11,740. The word 'Mercer' comes from the Latin term for merchandise and the Mercers were generally traders. The 'Mercery' was a market area that existed around the church of St Mary le Bow in the City of London. The first recorded charter is 1394. The Mercers brought the Masons, the Innholders, the Cooks and the Broderers into their group for the plantation. The Mercers' grant in 1613 (with its centre or capital at Movanagher and later at Kilrea) consisted of some 21,440 acres.

The Worshipful Company of Grocers of London had 11,639 acres in the county in 1876, with a valuation of £6,457. Originally known as the Ancient Guild of Pepperers, the name was changed in 1376 to the Company of Grocers. Its first royal charter was granted in 1428 by Henry VI. The original Pepperers were responsible for 'garbling', which was the prevention of the impairment of spices and drugs. The Grocers took on no co-investors for the plantation; they raised the full levy themselves. The Grocers' grant in 1613 (with its centre or capital at Muff, later renamed Eglinton) was 15,936 acres.

The Drapers Company of London had 27,025 acres in the county in 1876, with a valuation of £14,859. The Drapers traded in wool and cloth and had powers to regulate the woollen cloth trade in the City. It controlled the sale of cloth at cloth fairs and determined the unit of measurement by which wool and cloth was sold. The company itself had its first Royal Charter issued in 1364. The Drapers joined with the Tallow-Chandlers to plant Ulster but bought them out soon after it became clear that the plantation might work. The Drapers estate centred on Moneymore, later extended to Drapertown, had a grant in 1613 of 38,784 acres.

The Worshipful Company of Fishmongers of London had 20,509 acres in the county in 1876, with a valuation of £9,159. The Fishmongers were granted their first Royal Charter by Edward I in 1272. At one time they enjoyed a monopoly in the trade in fish in the city. The Fishmongers, who stood to gain a great deal from the fisheries of the Bann, Foyle and Lough Neagh, took on board for the plantation the Leathersellers, Plaisterers, Musicians, Basket Makers and Glaziers. The Fishmongers were centred at 'New Walworth', now Ballykelly, and the grant in 1613 was 24,128 acres.

The Goldsmiths Company is not recorded as a holder of land in County Londonderry in 1876. The Goldsmiths were responsible for testing the quality and gold and silver and regulated the trade of the goldsmith. The word 'trademark' comes from the time when craftsmen were required to bring their goods to the hall for 'assaying and marking'. It was also responsible (and still is) for checking the quality of the coins produced by the Royal Mint in a process called 'The Trial of the Pyx'. The name 'Pyx' refers to the chests in which the coins were transported. The Goldsmith's Royal Charter dates from 1327. For the plantation the Goldsmiths took in the Armourers, the Cordwainers and the Painter-Stainers, perhaps anticipating plenty of war and some church building. The Goldsmiths were centred at New Buildings and obtained a grant of 11,040 acres in 1613.

The Merchant Taylors Company is not recorded as holding any land in the county in 1876. The Merchant Taylors were given their first Royal Charter by Edward III in 1327. Initially an association of citizens who worked as tailors and linen armourers, the company grew to such an extent that it controlled the tailoring trade. Linen armourers made the padded tunics worn underneath suits of armour. The Merchant Taylors, perhaps foreseeing the linen trade, went in on their own. The Merchant Taylors settled around Macosquin and had an 18,720-acre grant.

In 1876 the Worshipful Company of Skinners of London had 34,772 acres in the county, with a valuation of £9,511. The Skinners Company developed from the medieval trade guild of furriers and was incorporated by Royal Charter in 1327. Today it is a major not-for-profit organisation involved in running schools, sheltered housing and grant programmes for individuals, educational institutions, and a wide range of small organisations throughout the UK. In the reign of Henry II (1154–89) workers skilled in dressing skins were described as 'pelliparii', 'peleters', or skinners, which will explain the name given to the portion of Ulster awarded to the Skinners.

In 1610 James I ordered the Great Twelve of the Livery companies to undertake the settlement, or plantation, of the Ulster counties of Derry and Tyrone. The lands to be settled were divided into lots. The Skinners Company drew lot number 12. Its lands came to be known as the Manor of Pellipar. The formal conveyance was made after the King had granted the Charter that created the city and county of Londonderry in 1613. The deed, dated 22 March 1617, granted the Manor of Pellipar, and all profits arising out of it, to the Skinners Company, to hold 'to the only use and behoof of the said maister, wardens, and comunaltie of the misterie of the Skinners of London, their successors and assigns for ever'. The Company finally sold its lands in Ireland in 1912 (alternating with position 6 every year with the Merchant Taylors).

The Skinners had their origin in the fur trade which back in medieval times was a luxury item. Expensive as it was to import, it was a status item and its use was strictly controlled. Different types of fur were restricted to different classes, Ermine and Sable for example was only for Royalty, and the common folk had to make do with less exotic furs from rabbit or cat. The Company was granted its first Royal Charter in 1327 by Edward III. The Skinners took in for the Plantation as associate investors The Whitebakers, The Girdlers, and The Stationers. The Skinners started their estate at the Priory church near Dungiven, then at Fort Dungiven, itself another manor or castle at Crosalt (possibly Brackfield) and got the largest estate of all, of 48,960 acres.

The Haberdashers Company of London had no recorded landholdings in the county in 1876. Haberdashers sold things such as ribbons, gloves, pins and caps and hats. The company first received its Royal Charter in 1448 and were joined by the Hatmakers Fraternity in 1502. For the plantation the Haberdashers took the Wax-Chandlers, the Founders, and the Turners with them. The Haberdashers staked their claim around Ballycastle with a second centre at Artikelly, on an estate of 23,104 acres.

The Worshipful Company of Salters of London had 19,445 acres in the county in 1876, with a valuation of £17,263. Salt was an important commodity in medieval times as it was used extensively to preserve meat and fish. The importance of salt as a commodity goes back centuries and the word 'Sal' is the origin of the word 'salary' as Roman soldiers were given salt rations. The company received its first licence from Richard II in 1394. The Salters took in the Dyers, Cutlers, Saddlers, Joiners and Woolmen. The Salters had their estate around Magherafelt. There was a castle and settlement at Salterstown, near Lough Neagh. They had an estate of 23,296 acres.

The Worshipful Company of Ironmongers of London had 12,714 acres in the county in 1876, with a valuation of £8,032. Originally known as the Ferroners, the Ironmongers Company regulated the quality of iron, which would have been used extensively in the wheels of carts used to transport goods and cannon. They were given their Royal Charter in 1463 by Edward IV. The Ironmongers formed a consortium with the Brewers, Pewterers, Barber-Surgeons, Carpenters, Coopers, Scriveners and other City investors. The Ironmongers settled at Agivey with an estate of 25,536 acres.

The Vintners Company had no recorded landholdings in the county in 1876. Vintners controlled the important wine trade in medieval England and its first charter of 1363 gave it a monopoly for trade with Gascony. Today the Vintners Company still retains the right to sell wine without licence in the City of London but a lot of its other purposes have changed to more charitable works. The Vintners had financial back-up for the plantation from the Grocers, which had been oversubscribed, but also obtained money from the Curriers, Plumbers, Poulters, Tylers and Bricklayers, Blacksmiths, Weavers, Woodmongers and Fruiterers. The Vintners took up residence around Bellaghy and renamed it Vintnerstown but it eventually reverted to Bellaghy. They had a grant of 32,576 acres.

The Clothworkers Company had no recorded landholdings in the county in 1876. The Clothworkers were formed following the amalgamation of the Fullers and the Shearmen in 1528. The Clothworkers, like the Vintners, had overflow investors from the Merchant Taylors but linked up with the Butchers, Bowyers, Fletchers, Brownbakers and Upholsterers.

The Clothworkers set up at Killowen, close to Coleraine, after Londonderry the second most important urban development in the plantation. They had another centre at Articlave. The Clothworkers sponsored the development of Castlerock as a seaside resort in the nineteenth century, making use of the railway between Belfast and Londonderry. They had an estate of 13,440 acres.

Thanks to Professor James Curl's *The City of London and the Plantation of Ulster* on BBC History which was a useful guide when compiling this information.

The Honourable the Irish Society of London had 6,075 acres in the county in 1876, with a valuation of £11,336 about £952,224 in modern money. This body is described in its foundation document as 'The Society of the Governor and Assistants, London, of the New Plantation in Ulster, within the Realm of Ireland, commonly called the Irish Society or The Honourable The Irish Society'.

The Honourable The Irish Society was the manager of the consortium of livery companies of the City of London set up in 1613 to colonise the newly created County Londonderry during the Plantation of Ulster. It was incorporated by royal charter of James I and consists of 'six and twenty honest and discreet citizens of London' nominated by the livery companies. In its first decades it rebuilt the city of Derry and town of Coleraine, and for centuries it owned property and fishing rights near both towns. Some of the society's profits were used to develop the economy and infrastructure of the area, while some was returned to the London investors, and some used for charitable work.

The society remains in existence as a 'relatively small grant-giving charitable body', with an office close to the City's Guildhall.

Other owners of land in County Londonderry in 1876.

Sir Henry Harvey Bruce MP of Downhill, Coleraine, had 20,801 acres in the county in 1876, with a valuation of £11,397 about £957,348 in modern money. This landowner served in the Life Guards and was the MP for Coleraine. He had, in addition to the Londonderry acres, 713 acres in Montgomery, for a total estate of 21,514 acres, with a valuation of £12,409. The estate arose from the legacy of the 4th Earl of Bristol, who was Lord Bishop of Derry and built what was Downhill Castle. The castle had a flush toilet installed in the late 1770s, well in advance of the two in the Robing room of the House of Lords installed during the reign of Queen Victoria, for her convenience, it is said The title is still extant and is held by Sir Hervey Hamish Peter Bruce-Clifton, the 8th Baronet, who lives in London.

Thomas Richardson (Representatives of) of Somerset, Coleraine, had 18,159 acres in the county in 1876, with a valuation of £7,424 about £623,616 in modern money. Bateman mentions Thomas Richardson as 'the late' but gives no details at all of the owner of what was, even by the standards of the time, a very large and rich estate. Ferres helps us out, writing that the estate passed to Thomas's four aunts. He also mentions that the estate arose from the purchase of land from the Merchant Taylors company (*see* above). The final holder of the estate was John Arthur Wellesley O'Neill Torrens, who was a justice of the peace, Vice Lord Lieutenant of County Londonderry and High Sheriff of the County. He was a major in the Scots Greys, the senior cavalary regiment in the British Army. There is mention of a property in Co. Antrim, but there are no details.

Stewart C. Bruce of the Cedars, Putney, London, had 13,651 with a valuation of £1,504 about £126,336 in modern money. Based on acreage this was the eighth largest estate in the county in 1876. Because of the low valuation, Stewart Bruce does not make it into Bateman. It is highly likely that he was a Scottish descendant or settler.

The Church Temporalities Commissioners of Upper Merrion St, Dublin, had 13,413 acres in the county in 1876, with a valuation of £9,642 about £809,928 in modern money. This is one of the larger estates held by the Church of Ireland Temporalities Commissioners and is likely to have been disposed of through the Land Commission.

Connolly Thomas M'Causland of Drenagh, Limavady, had 12,886 acres in the county in 1876, with a valuation of £6,257 about £525,588 in modern money. This Eton-educated landowner was in the diplomatic service, usually a very expensive occupation in those days. In addition to the Londonderry acreage he also had 4,799 acres in Roscommon, for a total estate of 17,685 acres with a valuation of £9,168. In 1902 about 75 per cent of the estate was acquired by the Land Commission but the house survived and is now a luxury hotel. The family history, which is romantic, is summarised on the hotel website. The Roscommon estate was sold through the Landed Estates Court in 1859.

Top 69 owners of land in County Londonderry in 1876 ranked by acreage

		Acreage	Valuation 1876 (£)	Valuation current (£)
1	The Worshipful Company of Skinners, London	34,772	9,511	798,924
2	Drapers Company, London	27,025	14,859	1,248,156
3	The Worshipful Company of Mercers of London, R.H. Dolling, Agent	21,241	11,740	986,160
4	Bruce, Sir Henry Hervey Bart, Downhill, Coleraine	20,801	11,397	957,348
5	Fishmongers, Worshipful Company of, London	20,509	9,159	769,356
6	The Worshipful Company of Salters, London	19,445	17,263	1,450,092
7	Richardson, Thomas R. Reps, Somerset, Coleraine	18,159	7,424	623,616
8	Bruce, Stewart C., The Cedars, Putney, London	13,651	1,504	126,336
9	Church Temporalities, Commissioners of, Upper Merrion St, Dublin	13,413	9,642	809,928
10	M'Causland, C.T., Dreenagh, Newtownlimavady	12,886	6,257	525,588
11	Ironmongers, Worshipful Company of, London	12,714	8,032	674,688
12	Grocers, Worshipful Company of, London	11,638	6,457	542,388
13	Beresford, John B., Ashbrook, Londonderry	10,420	3,889	326,676
14	Ogilby, R.L. Reps, Ardnargle, Newtownlimavady	9,735	3,805	319,620
15	Stevenson, James, Fort William, Tobermore	8,454	1,124	94,416
16	Beresford, Lord Charles, Waterford	7,946	3,484	292,656
17	Stafford, Earl of, London	7,647	2,738	229,992
18	Garvagh, Lady, Garvagh House, Garvagh	7,388	3,815	350,460
19	The Honourable the Irish Society, London	6,075	11,336	952,224

		Acreage	Valuation 1876 (£)	Valuation current (£)
20	Nesbitt, Catherine T. Downing, Leixlip, Dublin	5,638	2,221	186,564
21	Heygate, Sir F.W. Bart, Balarena	5,507	2,584	217,056
22	Alexander, Samuel Maxwell, Roe Park, Newtownlimavady	5,229	3,843	322,812
23	Brown, George, Cumber House, Claudy, Co. Londonderry	4,958	1,856	155,904
24	O'Neill, Hon. Robert Thomas, Derrynoid Lodge, Draperstown	4,844	1,542	129,528
25	Staples, Robert, Dromore, Durrow, Queen's County	4,003	1,739	146,076
26	Dolling, Robert H., Manor House, Kilrea, Ballymena	3,609	1,833	153,972
27	Maxwell, Rev. R.W., Birdstown, Londonderry	3,570	1,451	121,884
28	Clarke, James J., Largantoher House, Maghera	3,555	2,069	173,796
29	Miller, Rev. Alexander, Muff, Glebe, Moneymore	3,456	586	49,224
30	Cromee, John, Cromore, Coleraine	3,315	4,306	361,704
31	Henry, E.C.C. (a minor), Castle Townsend, Essex	3,171	2,058	172,872
32	Lyle, Rev. John, Knocklerna, Coleraine	3,071	2,772	232,848
33	Bruce, Captain H.S.B., Talbot House, Cloughton, Cheshire, England	2,991	1,683	141,372
34	Orr, James Reps, Flowerfield, Portstewart	2,972	1,643	138,012
35	Alexander, Nathaniel, Portglenone	2,866	1,518	127,512
36	Lyle, James Acheson, of The Oaks, Derry	2,711	1,259	105,756
37	Dawson, Colonel Robert Peel, Moyola, Castledawson	2,618	1,835	155,652
38	Scott, Thomas Reps, Willsboro	2,515	2,115	177,660
39	Tillie, William, Londonderry	2,506	1,493	125,412
40	Lyle, Hugh Reps, Oaks, Derry	2,413	951	79,884
41	Hunter, John C.F., Straid, Feeney	2,265	1,117	93,828

		Acreage	Valuation 1876 (£)	Valuation current (£)
42	Londonderry, Marquis of, Wynard Park, Durham	2,189	1,542	129,528
43	Martin, Sir Samuel, Newtownlimavady	2,166	2,422	203,448
44	Rankin, Robert and William, Lisboy, Garvagh	2,162	745	62,580
45	Alexander, George, Portglernone	2,135	1,224	102,816
46	Ogilby, James, Pellipar, Dungiven	2,087	604	50,736
47	Stephenson, Jos, Ardkiln	1,986	1,050	88,200
48	Adams, John, Ballydevitt, Ballemoney	1,960	1,214	101,976
49	Templemore, Lord, Carlton Club, London	1,890	979	82,236
50	Kyle, Henry, Laurel Hill, Coleraine	1,876	1,186	99,624
51	Bennett, Thoma, Castleroe, Coleraine	1,655	1,581	132,804
52	Stirling, J.B. Reps, Moneycarrie, Gravagh and Portrush	1,576	1,337	112,308
53	Babington, Hume, Creevagh, Derry	1,540	273	22,932
54	Olpehrts, Captain Richard, Red House, Ardee, Co. Louth	1,522	1,908	160,672
55	King, Michael, Strangemore, Dungiven	1,473	896	75,264
56	Bogle, The Messers, Glasgow	1,431	1,333	111,972
57	Courtney, James, Glenburne, Portglenone	1,415	839	70,478
58	Mauleverer, Bellingham Reps, -	1,262	1,256	105,504
59	Campbell, Mrs Colin, Lurgan Brae, Brookborough, Co. Fermanagh	1,248	391	32,844
60	Stephenson, Robert, Ardkiln	1,245	539	45,276
61	Lane, Benjamin, Ballycarton, Bellarena	1,213	109	9,156
62	Skipton, Kennedy, Beech Hill	1,169	1,142	95,928
63	Tyrell, Fredrick, Eglinton	1,155	1,144	96,096
64	Church, James, Oatlands, Newtownlimavady	1,107	909	76,356
65	Cathcart, John Steele, Belfast	1,104	386	32,424

		Acreage	Valuation 1876 (£)	Valuation current (£)
66	Patterson, Alexander, Carnamony, Draperstown	1,078	681	57,204
67	Garvagh, Lord Garvagh House, Garvagh	1,039	644	54,096
68	Rankin, Miss, Garvagh	1,017	136	11,424
69	M'Intyre, William, Warwick Lodge, Ballymaguigan, Castledawson	982	732	61,488

The top 20 landowners in Londonderry in 1876 ranked by valuation (income)

		Acreage	Valuation 1876 (£)	Valuation current (£)
1	The Worshipful Company of Salters, London	19,445	17,263	1,450,092
2	Drapers Company, London	27,025	14,859	1,248,156
3	The Worshipful Company of Mercers of London, R.H. Dolling, Agent	21,241	11,740	986,160
4	Bruce, Sir Henry Hervey Bart, Downhill, Coleraine	20,801	11,397	957,348
5	The Honourable the Irish Society, London	6,075	11,336	952,224
6	Church Temporalities, Commissioners of, Upper Merrion St, Dublin	13,413	9,642	809,928
7	The Worshipful Company of Skinners, London	34,772	9,511	798,924
8	Fishmongers, Worshipful Company of, London	20,509	9,159	769,356
9	Ironmongers, Worshipful Company of, London	12,714	8,032	674,688
10	Richardson, Thomas R Reps, Somerset, Coleraine	18,159	7,424	623,616
11	Grocers, Worshipful Company of, London	11,638	6,457	542,388
12	M'Causland, C.T., Dreenagh, Newtownlimavady	12,886	6,257	525,588
13	Cromee, John, Cromore, Coleraine	3,315	4,306	361,704

		Acreage	Valuation 1876 (£)	Valuation current (£)
14	Beresford, John B., Ashbrook, Londonderry	10,420	3,889	326,676
15	Alexander, Samuel Maxwell, Roe Park, Newtownlimavady	5,229	3,843	322,812
16	Garvagh, Lady, Garvagh House, Garvagh	7,388	3,815	350,460
17	Ogilby, R.L. Reps, Ardnargle, Newtownlimavady	9,735	3,805	319,620
18	Beresford, Lord Charles, Waterford	7,946	3,484	292,656
19	Lyle, Rev. John, Knocklerna, Coleraine	3,071	2,772	232,848
20	Stafford Earl of, London	7,647	2,738	229,992

LONGFORD

	1876	2020 est
Population in County Longford	64,501	39,000
All owners of land	436 (372 in 1871)	26,037
Percentage of the population	0.6	-
Owners of nothing at all	64,065	12,688
Percentage of the population	99.4	-
Size of County	256,668 acres	257,920 acres
Number of dwellings	12,002 (11,566 rented)	14,410
Number of owned farm holdings	372	2,601

County Comparisons

	Acres in 1876	Population in 1876
County Longford	256,668	64,501
Huntingdonshire, England	225,613	63,708
Kincardinshire, Scotland	244,585	34,630
Radnorshire, Wales	207,394	25,430

Robert Blackall of Coolamber, Lisryan, County Longford, had 4,643 acres in County Longford in 1876 with a valuation of £2,759 about £231,756 in modern money. Robert Blackall was promoted major in the 30th Foot in Bateman and, with his 1,805 acres in Leitrim made an entry with 6,448 acres at a valuation of £3,379.

According to one of Ferres' respondents, the family were based at Lisryan at least as far back as 1641, but had their lands confiscated by James I, presumably for siding with the rebel Parliamentarians. The lands were restored by Charles II after the restoration in 1660. The family produced two Lord Mayors of Dublin, one in 1694 and another in 1769. Major Blackall's grandfather, a High Sheriff and MP for Longford, left the Irish 'colony' to govern other colonial subjects, becoming the Lieutenant Governor of Dominica, High Sheriff of County Tyrone, Governor of Sierra Leone, Governor of the West Africa settlements and finally Governor of Queensland between 1868 and 1871, when he died.

Coolamber House has been restored and refurbished, and is surrounded by an estate of 157 acres.

Thomas A. Cusack of 61 St Stephen's Green, Dublin, had 4,980 acres in Longford in 1876, with a valuation of £2,812 about £236,208 in modern money. Thomas Cusack gets a brief mention in Bateman, a line below the main entries, mainly because his valuation fell below Bateman's level of £3,000. He does give us an address in Longford, however, at Carraboola. There are no other references in public documents to what is a sizable holding, with a potentially reasonable income.

George Maconchy of Cadwell, Torquay, England, had 10,319 acres in Longford in 1876 with a valuation of £3,137 about £263,508 in modern money. The only modern reference to this family and estate arises because a thirteenth son of either the holder of the estate in 1876, or an immediate descendant, became a brigadier general in the British Army and was one of the senior officers in Dublin when the 1916 rebellions broke out. He presided over at least three of the courts martial that sentenced rebel leaders to death. However, he protested his role on the grounds he was Irish himself and was relieved of his duties. His biography revealed that the early orders to put the convicted Sinn Feiners before the firing squads had arrived 'full of detail' but unsigned. Bateman corrects the UK address to Corrinagh, Torquay.

Willoughby Bond of Farra Longford had 5,977 acres with a valuation of £3,375 about £283,500 in modern money. Bateman corrects the address to Farragh and fills out the full acreage held by Willoughby. He had, apart from his Longford acres, 1,525 acres in County Meath and 1,057 acres in County Westmeath, totalling 9,156 acres with a valuation of £5,696.

Ferres writes that the Bonds started out in Ireland as merchants in Londonderry, arriving from Yorkshire around 1650 at the end of the English Civil War.

This family appear unusual. One of their number is recorded as a Presbyterian minister, in short a dissenter who was, with the Catholic majority, subject to the Penal laws and would have found it difficult to own land. The Bonds did well, becoming High Sheriffs on several occasion, however, and married well but never into the aristocracy. The house was sold in the 1960s and later levelled.

The Rev. Sir George Ralph Fetherston Bart, of Ardagh House, Longford, had 7,420 acres in Longford in 1876 with a valuation of £4,905 about £412,020 in modern money. Bateman makes several corrections to this entry from the Return. The acreage is increased to 8,711 and the valuation to £5,606. Bateman also notes that the titled vicar lives in Chapmanslade, Westbury, Wiltshire, an absentee, as were a considerable number of vicars after the disestablishment of the Church of Ireland in 1869–71. The disappearance of so many landowning

Irish vicars to parishes on the British mainland has never really been investigated but this looks like a classic example.

The family had something of a rough period in England before coming to Ireland. The then Sir Thomas Fetherstonehough, an alternative spelling of the family name, fought for King Charles II at the final battle of the English Civil War at Worcester on 3 September 1651. Both Cromwell and the King led their forces but Cromwell emerged victorious. Cromwell's forces captured many royalists and executed some, including the Earl of Derby and Sir Thomas, who was beheaded.

Most of the surviving royalist soldiers were pressganged into the New Model Army and sent to Ireland. Somewhere among them was Cuthbert Fetherston. His son, also Cuthbert, settled at Ardagh.

The final holder of the title and the estates was the 6th Baronet, Rev. Sir George Ralph Fetherston. The estate was sold to about 300 of the tenants by Sir George, outside the normal land commission arrangements, although the commission did make the loans so the purchases could be made. Sir George died in 1923 and the title became extinct. The Sisters of Mercy, an order of Catholic nuns, bought Ardagh House.

General the Rt Hon. the Earl of Longford, Packenham Hall, Castlepollard, County Westmeath, had 4,555 acres in County Longford in 1876, with a valuation of £6,101 about £512,484 in modern money. The real secret of the Longford peerage is revealed in Bateman. While the Westmeath acreage, together with 4,555 acres in Longford, were enough to keep any nobleman of the period in the style to which they were accustomed, it was 420 acres in Dublin, valued at £31,713 about £2.6 million in modern money, which made them really important. The Earl who held this huge estate in 1876 was Secretary of State for War, Adjutant General for India and the Crimea and a general in the army. The expression 'military family' fairly well covers the Pakenhams, one of whom commanded the Life Guards, and another of whom was killed in the Dardanelles in the First World War.

The 7th Earl was once one of the best-known peers in Modern Britain, attending the House of Lords into his 90s, diligently assisted by the doorkeepers there. He supported Labour and was First Lord of the Admiralty, Secretary of State for the Colonies and Minister of Civil Aviation. The family are Catholic, still live at the family home and are engaged in many activities in the Republic. The present peer, the 8th, does not use his title.

The estate, now down to 1,500 acres, went from the 6th Earl to the 8th and present Earl, together with 62 per cent death duties that took fifteen years to pay off.

The Rt Hon. the Earl of Granard, of Castleforbes, Newtown Forbes, Longford, had 14,978 acres in the county in 1876, with a valuation of £6,636 about £557,424 in modern money. This title still exists and is held by the 10th Earl, Peter Andrew Edward Hasting Forbes, who lives on the Isle of Man. The family motto is unusual: 'The incitement to glory is the firebrand of the mind'.

The 7th Earl, the holder of the title and estate in 1876, had 4,266 acres in Leitrim and 2,050 acres in Wexford; a total of 21,294 acres with a valuation of £9,840. The 7th Earl married twice, firstly to a daughter of the Grogan family of Johnston Castle, Co. Wexford – holders of over 15,000 acres there – then to a daughter of Baron Petre, who had 19,085 acres in Essex. (Debrett's did not enable me to unravel the connection between the Lady Forbes who held the Johnston Castle estate and the family of the Earl of Granard.) The 7th Earl was educated at Eton and was Lord Lieutenant of Leitrim. He was a member of the Privy Council, probably of Ireland.

Lord Annaly of Woodlawn, Clonsilla, Dublin, had 12,160 acres in Longford in 1876 with a valuation of £6,954 about £584,136 in modern money. This is an unusual title, estate and family. The total acreage in 1876 was 12,560 acres in Longford, which, with the Dublin land, came to 16,514 acres with a valuation of £14,761. The family originated with a one-time 'impecunious' Dublin bookseller called Luke White. Here is how Ferres writes about him:

> Luke White changed its (Luttrelstown Castle) name to Woodlands, but his great-grandson, the 3rd Lord Annaly, reverted to Luttrellstown Castle. In 1778, Luke White started as an impecunious book dealer, buying in Dublin and reselling around the country. By 1798, during the rebellion, he helped the Irish government with a loan of £1 million (at £65 per £100 share at 5 per cent). He became MP for Leitrim, and died in 1824 leaving properties worth £175,000 per annum.

Very few private individuals had money like that in 1798 and those who did were usually dukes or bankers. By 1786 there was no estate in Ireland worth even a fraction of that by way of income.

The title, which is in the peerage of the United Kingdom, is still extant and the holder, Luke Richard White, lives in Oxfordshire. He was educated at Eton and the Royal Military Academy Sandhurst. Luttrellstwon Castle has been owned successively by the Guinnesses, the Primwest Group, and, since 2006, by J.P. McManus, John Magnier and Aidan Brooks.

The castle is a super resort with an estate of about 550 acres.

Algernon Greville of Granard, resident at 45 Sussex Gardens, London, had 8,821 acres in Longford in 1876 with a valuation of £7,896 about £658,224 in modern money. This Eton-educated infantry officer in the army had his address amended by Bateman, the acreage amended from 8,811 to 8,821 and the valuation to £7,896. Beyond that there is nothing in the public record about the man or his estate. His full name was Algernon William Bellingham, so he may be a relative of the Bellingham family in County Louth. And there is a possibility he is a relative of Lord Greville of Clonyn Castle, Co. Westmeath.

The Rt Hon. L.H. King-Harman, reps of Rockingham, Boyle, County Roscommon, had 28,779 acres in Longford in 1876, with a valuation of £14,683 about £1,233,372 in modern money. Bateman amends this record to include the heir to the estate, Edward Robert King-Harman, who had inherited by the time the 1883 and fourth edition of Bateman had appeared. Edward Robert was, like so many entrants in this book, an Old Etonian, and an infantry officer in the 60th Rifles, later a colonel in the Connaught Rangers. He was also an MP, in his case, for Sligo, then for Dublin and finally for the Isle of Thanet in the UK. He was Lord Lieutenant of Roscommon.

The full inheritance was colossal, a total of 72,913 acres in five Irish counties, with a valuation of £40,105 about £3.3 milllion in modern money. Along with the Longford acres, there were 29,242 acres in Roscommon, 12,629 acres in Sligo, 1,239 acres in Westmeath and 1,024 acres in Queen's County.

The Harman family appeared in Ireland during the reign of James I (reigned 1603–25) in Carlow. By 1664 the head of the family had a knighthood, was an officer in the army and got the Longford estate under the original 1607 Act of Settlement. A descendant was a captain in the Battle-Axe Guards in the 1680s. Later, another descendant, Lawrence Parsons Harman, married a daughter of the 1st Earl of Kingston, who had 24,671 acres in 1876. The same Lawrence Harman was made Lord Oxmantown in 1792, and in 1806 became the Earl of Rosse. The Rosse family (*see* King's County) had 26,486 acres in 1876. There is a link by marriage to the Annaly family (*see* below). This is just one illustration of how a family, already hugely endowed with land, increased its acreage through marriage. The transactions occurred inside a system of multi-abusive political, judicial and economic monopoly, the true extent of which is shown in the figures for the landed and the landless.

Longford over 1,000 acres in 1876

		Acreage	Valuation 1876 (£)	Valuation current (£)
1	King-Harman, the Hon. L.H. Reps of, Rockingham, Boyle	28,779	14,683	1,233,372
2	Greville, Algernon W.B., 45 Sussex Gardens, London	8,811	7,897	663,348
3	Annally, Lord, Woodlands, Clonsilla	12,160	6,954	584,136
4	Granard, The Rt Hon. the Earl of, Castleforbes, Newtown Forbes	14,978	6,636	557,424
5	Longford, Rt Hon. the Earl of, Packenham Hall, Castlepollard	4,555	6,101	512,484
6	Fetherston, Sir George R., Ardagh House, Ardagh	7,420	4,905	412,020
7	Bond, Willoughby, Farra, Longford	5,977	3,375	283,500
8	Machonchy, George, Cadwell, Torquay, England	10,319	3,137	263,508
9	Cusack, Thomas A., 61 Stephen's Green, Dublin	4,980	2,812	236,208
10	Blackall, Robert, Coolamber, Lisryan	4,643	2,759	231,756
11	Shuldham, John, Gortmore, Ballybrocke	2,571	2,681	225,204
12	Porter, Rev. John Grey Reps, Lisnaskea, Co. Fermanagh	5,024	2,581	216,804
13	Edgeworth, Antonie E., Edgeworthstown	3,255	2,536	213,024
14	Lefroy, Anthony, Carriglass, Longford	4,229	2,470	207,480
15	Douglas, Henry S., Beechfield, Millbank, Southampton	4,152	2,141	179,844
16	Fox, Richard E., Foxhall, Lennamore	3,085	1,675	140,700
17	White, Henry W., United Services Club, Dublin	3,197	1,627	136,668
18	Bond, William, Newtownbond, Edgeworthstown	3,152	1,597	134,148
19	Tuite, Joseph, Sonna, Mullingar	2,307	1,424	119,616
20	Church Temporalities Commissioner, Dublin	1,736	1,366	114,744

		Acreage	Valuation 1876 (£)	Valuation current (£)
21	O'Reilly, Joseph Richard, Booterstown	2,464	1,276	107,184
22	Edgeworth, Michael Packenham, Mostrim House, Anerly, London	1,659	1,264	106,176
23	Collum, William M.D. Reps, 14 St James Square, London	2,741	1,261	105,924
24	Dopping-Hempenstall, Major R.A., Derrycassin, Dring, Granard	1,701	1,109	93,156
25	O'Ferrall, John L., Granite Hall, Kingstown, and Lissard and Edgeworthstown	1,689	1,108	93,072
26	Ball, Arthur William, Navan, Co. Meath	1,667	1,046	87,864
27	Thompson, John E., Cloonfin, Granard	1,662	1,036	87,024
28	Gunning, Rev. Sir Henry, Horton, Northampton, England	2,033	1,035	86,940
29	Greville, Lord, Clonyn, Delvin	1,236	955	80,220
30	Masters, Henry, Bryanstown, Longford	1,827	935	78,540
31	Wilson-Slator, G.W., Carton, Edgeworthstown	1,300	934	78,456
32	Ledwith, Captain Jas, Isle of Man	1,984	933	78,372
33	Maude, Captain Francis, Onslow Sq., London	1,235	932	78,288
34	M'Evoy, Edward, Tobertinan, Trim, Co. Meath	2,508	930	78,120
35	Bond, John, Castlecon, Ballymahon	1,179	855	71,820
36	Hutton, Albert & Stanford, Killashandra, Co. Cavan, and Putney Park, London	1,608	853	71,652
37	Edgeworth, Rev. Essex, Kilshrewley, Ballinalee	1,565	853	71,652
38	White, Luke, Eversham, Blackrock	1,394	850	71,400
39	Wilson, William, of Street, Rathewen, Co. Westmeath	2,432	839	70,476
40	Wilson, James, Currygrane, Edgeworthstown	1,158	835	70,140
41	Conroy, Thomas Reps, Not Known	1,211	743	62,412

		Acreage	Valuation 1876 (£)	Valuation current (£)
42	Jessop, John H., 31 Mount St, Dublin	1,544	730	61,320
43	Slator, Bevan, Clinan, Colehill	1,016	710	59,640
44	Fetherston, Sir Thomas, Wilton Castle, Co. Wexford	1,291	701	58,884
45	Galbraith, John S., Clonabogan, Omagh	2,254	686	57,624
46	Fetherston, Francis Reps, Wicklow	1,343	653	54,852
47	Murphy, George James, The Grange, Trim, Co. Meath	1,102	629	52,836
48	Crofton, Sir Morgan G., Mohill, Co. Leitrim	1,608	606	50,904
49	Synge, Francis H., -	1,664	600	50,400
50	Quinn, Catherine, 98 Lower Gardiner Street, Dublin	1,623	590	49,560
51	Cruikshank, Rev. A., Brighton, England	1,214	590	49,560
52	Armstrong, Henry B. Reps, Killylea House, Co, Armagh	2,017	555	46,620
53	Woodward, Very Rev. Thomas, Downpatrick	1,222	489	41,076
54	Tyrrell, James, 2 Kildare St, Dublin	1,145	477	40,086
55	O'Brien, Robert, Mgt and H. Dundas, of Gorthill, Mohill.	1,014	357	29,988
56	Dudgeon, Charles S., Clogher and Rynn, Cloondra	1,055	353	29,652

Top 20 by estimated gross rental income

		Acreage	Valuation 1876 (£)3	Valuation current (£)
1	King-Harman, the Hon. L.H. Reps of, Rockingham, Boyle	28,779	14,683	1,233,372
2	Greville, Algernon W.B., 45 Sussex Gardens, London	8,811	7,897	663,348
3	Annally, Lord, Woodlands, Clonsilla	12,160	6,954	584,136
4	Granard, The Rt Hon. the Earl of, Castleforbes, Newtown Forbes	14,978	6,636	557,424

		Acreage	Valuation 1876 (£)3	Valuation current (£)
5	Longford, Rt Hon. the Earl of, Packenham Hall, Castlepollard	4,555	6,101	512,484
6	Fetherston, Sir George R., Ardagh House, Ardagh	7,420	4,905	412,020
7	Bond, Willoughby, Farra, Longford	5,977	3,375	283,500
8	Machonchy, George, Cadwell, Torquay, England	10,319	3,137	263,508
9	Cusack, Thomas A., 61 Stephen's Green, Dublin	4,980	2,812	236,208
10	Blackall, Robert, Coolamber, Lisryan	4,643	2,759	231,756
11	Shuldham, John, Gortmore, Ballybrocke	2,571	2,681	225,204
12	Porter, Rev. John Grey Reps, Lisnaskea, Co. Fermanagh	5,024	2,581	216,804
13	Edgeworth, Antonie E., Edgeworthstown	3,255	2,536	213,024
14	Lefroy, Anthony, Carriglass, Longford	4,229	2,470	207,480
15	Douglas, Henry S., Beechfield, Millbank, Southampton	4,152	2,141	179,844
16	Fox, Richard E., Foxhall, Lennamore	3,085	1,675	140,700
17	White, Henry W., United Services Club, Dublin	3,197	1,627	136,668
18	Bond, William, Newtownbond, Edgeworthstown	3,152	1,597	134,148
19	Tuite, Joseph, Sonna, Mullingar	2,307	1,424	119,616
20	Church Temporalities Commissioner, Dublin	1,736	1,366	114,744

LOUTH

	1876	2016
Population in County Louth	70,511 (1871)	84,051
All owners of land	1,279 (1871)	47,252
Percentage of the population	1.9	–
Owners of nothing at all	62,232	32,403
Percentage of the population	98.1	–
Size of County	200,287 acres	203,520 acres
Number of dwellings (of which rented in 1876 but owned in 2020)	16,885 (15,606)	43,897
Number of owned farm holdings	772	1,676

County comparisons

	Acreage 1876	Population 1876
County Louth	200,287	70,511
Huntingdonshire, England	225,613	63,708
Orkney, Scotland	220,873	31,274
Radnorshire, Wales	207,394	25,430

Lord Rathdonnell of Drumcar, Dunleer, County Louth, had 3,188 acres in Louth in 1876 with a valuation of £3,251 about £273,084 in modern money. This Eton-educated peer and soldier amended his Louth holding downwards for Bateman, so 3,188 acres becomes 3,000 acres, with a valuation of 2,500. Not that this left him short of acreage in seven other counties. He had 8,058 acres in Carlow, 2,600 acres in Fermanagh, 1,006 acres in Monaghan, 2,886 acres in Tyrone 1,215 acres in Meath, 600 acres in Dublin and 558 acres in Kildare, a total of 19,923 acres with a valuation of £15,400.

The first estate purchased in Ireland by this family from Argyllshire was in 1597, at Trinta in Donegal. There is no record of any acreage in Donegal in 1876. By the late 1700s the heir was MP for Enniskillen, then for Belturbet, thus taking the first steps on the road to the peerage granted to John McClintock MP for Louth in 1868, long after the Irish House of Lords had closed its doors. In 1874 he married a daughter of the Rt Hon. Henry Bruen, who had 16,477 acres in Carlow.

The peerage is still extant and the family live at the family seat at Lisnaveagh in Carlow. Some of the estate still surrounds the house and is cultivated and managed.

Lord Louth of Louth Hall, Ardee, had 3,578 acres in the county in 1876 with a valuation of £3,983 about £334,572 in modern money. Bateman records that Lady Louth owned the Meath Estate. This is one of the five Plunkett peerages mentioned in the Meath biographies (Earl of Fingall). The grandfather of the present holder, Otway Michael James Oliver Plunkett, the 16th Baron, lived in Jersey and was educated at Downside, indicating that this was of Catholic Plunkett descent. Back in 1876 the Eton-educated then peer, the 13th, did not himself own the Louth acreage but did own 161 acres in Meath, 178 acres in Monaghan, 4 acres in Galway and 178 acres in Somerset. The total acreage with his wife's holding was 4,099 acres with a valuation of £4,604.

The title was first created in 1541 for Sir Oliver Plunkett Kt but there was an earlier creation in 1458, for Sir Thomas Bathe, Chief Baron of the Irish Exchequer. During the Cromwellian wars Baron Plunkett sided with the royalists and was outlawed in 1642. The outlawry was reversed in 1798, in favour of the 11th Baron, who just had time to take his seat before the Irish House of Lords was prorogued for good in 1800. Jonathan Oliver Plunkett succeeded to the title as the 17th Baron following his father's death in 2013.

The 5th Earl of Roden of Tullymore Park, Castlewellan and, in Bateman, of Hyde Hall Sawbridgeworth, had 4,151 acres in County Louth in 1876, with a valuation of £7,944 about £667,296 in modern money. This Harrow-educated soldier and peer had 8,903 acres in County Down, 1,134 acres in Essex and 408 acres in Hertfordshire, a total acreages of 14,596 in 1876, with a valuation of £13,077. The family are recorded in England at the time of Edward the Confessor, but reappear with William the Bastard when he invaded England in 1066. The origin of the Irish estates is not clearly recorded in Debrett's or Burke's *Peerages* but during the reigns of George I and George II the Rt Hon. Robert Jocelyn was Solicitor-General and Attorney-General. His ancestor in the 1400s had twice been Lord Mayor of London, in 1464 and 1476, and a livery man of the city and its MP. This implied great wealth. In 1739 the Rt Hon. Robert was appointed Lord Chancellor of Ireland. In 1743 he was made Baron Newport and in 1755 promoted to Viscount Jocelyn. His son was further promoted to the rank of Earl in 1771. Prior to succeeding to the title the 1st Earl's son sat in the Irish House of Commons for Dundalk, and, after the Act of Union and the permanent prorogue of the Irish House of Lords, served as an Irish Representative peer in the British House of Lords between 1800 and 1820. The 2nd Earl was a professional soldier who helped suppress the United Irish rebellion of 1798. He was infamous for his cruelty, which tainted the Earldom permanently.

The title still exists and is held by the 10th Earl, Robert John Jocelyn. Various components of the estate in Ireland were dispersed via the Land Commission.

Sir Alan Edward Bellingham Bart of Castle Bellingham, County Louth, held 4,186 acres in the county in 1876 with a valuation of £4,291 about £360,440 in modern money. In 1876 Sir Alan had, in addition to his Louth acreage, 11,810 acres in Mayo with a valuation of £295. His total acreage was 15,996 acres with a valuation of £4,586. Debrett's starts this family out in Northumberland in 1279 but they do not appear in Ireland until sometime during the English Civil War. Prior to that the head of the family had become a livery man of the Goldsmiths Guild in London, which would imply significant wealth at that time.

When William of Orange arrived in Ireland in 1690 the then Thomas Bellingham was a colonel in the Williamite army. He guided the King to the Boyne battlesite but had Castle Bellingham burnt to the ground in 1689 by Jacobite troops. In 1796 a Baronetcy was conferred on William Bellingham, which is still extant and is held by Sir Anthony Edward Norman Bellingham, the 8th Baronet of the 2nd creation. Although the seat is identified as Castle Bellingham, his residence is given as Bangkok.

The castle was sold via the Land Commission in 1958 and is now an hotel.

Rev. Henry Stobart of Warkton Rectory in England held 4,249 acres of the county in 1876 with a valuation of £2,018 about £169,512 in modern money. Henry Stobart's estate in Louth failed to make Bateman as the valuation was too low. But it is typical of a recurrent situation among the Irish estates where the holder is a clergyman, absent in England. The Church of Ireland had been disestablished in 1869 by the Gladstone administration, with significant opposition from the Lords and intervention by Queen Victoria to make sure that those clergymen made redundant got adequate compensation. The church had a tiny following among the Irish population, well below 5 per cent, but all had to pay tithes to support the church, whether they adhered to it or not. Without the Louth address it has been impossible to trace this estate.

Lord Bellew of Barmeath Castle, Dunleer, County Louth, held 5,109 acres in the county in 1876 with a valuation of £5,092 about £427,728 in modern money. The older Burke's trace this family to William the Bastard's arrival in England in 1066 and then arriving in Ireland with Strongbow (*see* McMurrough-Kavanagh, Carlow) There are extant English records of the Bellews that portray them as perpetually fighting as knights and obtaining and losing a series of titles over the centuries. The current title was created in the peerage of Ireland in 1848. This title still exists and the holders modestly commence the Debrett's lineage with a Baronetcy in 1688.

The estate in 1876 was not huge. It carries Bateman's Gothic 'S', indicating that the land had been held in unbroken male succession since the time of Henry VII

(1485–1509). There were 4,110 acres in Louth, and 204 acres in Meath. The total acreage was 4,314 with a valuation of £5,092. The current holder of the title, the 8th Baron, Bryan Edward Bellew, gives his address as Barmeath Castle. He was educated at Eton and Sandhurst before he joined the Irish Guards.

Colonel John Charles William Fortescue of Stephenstown, Dundalk, had 5,262 acres in the county in 1876, with a valuation of £5,070 about £425,880 in modern money. The largest landowner in Co. Louth in 1876 was Lord Cleremont of Newry and the Fortescues were his cousins. The Fortescues were professional soldiers, justices of the peace and High Sheriffs, and held no land outside the county.

The house, according to Ferres, was sold in 1974 by a descendant of Colonel Fortescue and had become a ruin by the 1980s.

A.H. Smith-Barry of Foaty (Fota), Queenstown, County Cork, held 6,239 acres in County Louth in 1876, with a valuation of £4,620 about £388,080 in modern money. This family and its three estates occur separately in Bateman and are best recorded in that way. The families were closely related. The senior member of the Smith Barry family in 1876 was Arthur Hugh, who is recorded in Bateman at his main address on Fota Island, Queenstown (Cobh), Co. Cork. He was an Old Etonian who sat as MP for Cork. His holdings were 12,969 acres in Cork, 8,620 acres in Tipperary, 3,124 acres in Cheshire and 2,079 acres in Huntingdon, a total of 26,792 acres with a valuation of £37,279. He was an MP, justice of the peace and a Deputy Lieutenant for Cork.

The Louth acres are assigned to James Hugh and no address is given. Like his cousins in Cork, he was an Old Etonian who served in the Grenadier Guards. He had 6,273 acres with a valuation of £6,050. He was a justice of the peace and a Deputy Lieutenant for Cork.

The third Smith-Barry is Richard Hugh of Ballyedmond, Middleton, Co. Cork. Like his cousins, he was an Old Etonian and a soldier, serving in the 12th Lancers. He had 8,137 acres in Cork and 269 acres in Limerick, a total of 8,406 acres with a valuation of £8,225. He was a soldier, a justice of the peace and a Deputy Lieutenant for Cork.

The total acreage of the three Smith-Barrys was 41,471 acres and the total valuation was £51,554.

This family microcosm illustrates both the scale and the nature of the overall problem in Ireland in the period after the famine. The government was in the hands of a tiny oligarchy, all with a common interest, land, and none willing to expose that monopoly to market forces or, more specifically, to the needs of the population. There were three pillars to the governance structure at the time: government, military and justice (or law). The first was Parliament, composed almost entirely of landowners in both houses, Commons and Lords – and you had to have land to vote. Over 98 per cent of the population had no land. The landlords in Ireland were almost uniformly men, most of whom were soldiers, if not professionally, then in the local militia. The population had neither arms nor access to arms. The local justice system was composed entirely of landowners, most having nothing in common with the population at large. Into this mix came religion. Most of the landowners were Protestant; perhaps 90–95 per cent of the population, on the other hand, were Catholic, paying tithes to support both the minority religion and paying rents to sustain the landlords. The Church of Ireland was, in turn, a major landowner, at one with the 1.8 per cent of the population who were also landowners and deeply entrenched within the government structure.

The structure was identical to the slave-based so called democracy of ancient Athens. Ireland was governed by de facto guardians, there because they owned the place. They held all offices of state and voted among themselves, for themselves. The 'people' were serfs by definition of that word, and de facto they were slaves, their safety and lives at the whim of the rulers. But then, 90 per cent of the Irish guardians, the landowners, went to the same school, Eton, where classics and the false Athenian version of democracy were taught.

Lord Massereene of Oriel Temple, Collon, County Louth, had 7,193 acres in the county in 1876 with a valuation of £5,234 about £439,656 in modern money. Lord Masserene is more properly described in Bateman as Viscount Massereene and Ferrard, Oriel Temple, Co. Louth.

Bateman records the then Viscount having 11,777 acres in Antrim, 2,045 acres in Meath and 9 acres in Monaghan, together with the Louth land a total of 21,024 acres with a valuation of £15,031. The address given in Debrett's is Antrim Castle, which was burnt down by the IRA in 1922. There is no mention in Debrett's of the non-Irish acreage, which is unusual. The Massereenes had an estate in Kent in Yorkshire at the time of the Returns.

The title and confirmation of the estates in Ireland were a gift from Charles II when the Restoration occurred in England in 1660. The children of the 3rd Viscount then made the classic Irish landowner moves. The eldest daughter, Jane, married a landowner, Sir Hans Hamiliton Bart, of Mount Hamilton in Armagh. The next daughter, Rachel, married the 4th Earl of Antrim, whose descendants had over 34,000 acres in 1876, and the third daughter, Mary, married the Bishop of Down and Connor. The 4th Viscount married Lady Catherine Chichester, the eldest daughter of the 4th Earl of Donegall, who had almost 23,000 acres in 1876. In 1756 the then Viscount was made the Earl of Massareene, although this title became extinct in 1816. The other titles were inherited by his daughter, Harriett Viscountess Massereene. She married the Viscount Ferrard, which is where the merged titles come from.

Ferres tells us that:

> in 1668, the Massereenes owned about 45,000 acres in Ireland; however, by 1701, the land appears to have shrunk to 10,000 acres; and, by 1713, the County Antrim estates comprised 8,178 acres. Land acquisition through marriage etc meant that the land-holdings amounted to 11,778 acres in 1887. In the 1600s the Massereenes possessed the lucrative fishing rights to Lough Neagh by means of a ninety-nine-year lease and they were also accorded the honour, *Captains of Lough Neagh,* for a period.

The current peer, the 14th, John David Clotworthy Whyte Melville Foster, is one of the hereditaries dispossessed from the House of Lord in 1999. He lives in Yorkshire, served in the Grenadier Guards and has been a stockbroker. He further describes himself as a landowner.

Lord Cleremont MP of Ravensdale Park, Newry, had 20,369 acres in Louth in 1876, with a valuation of £15,262 about £1,282,008 in modern money. This family became prominent in England after the Norman invasion, having arrived with the army of William the Bastard. They appear in Ireland during the Williamite wars, obtaining land in County Louth and a knighthood sometime in the late 1600s. According to Debrett's, the Rt Hon. William Henry Fortescue, who had been an MP, was made Baron Cleremont in 1770, and promoted to Viscount and then Earl in 1777. The Earldom expired when he died in 1806, but the other titles were revived by inheritance and re-creation. Apart from sitting as an MP, prior to the peerage Bateman notes nothing of interest about the Lord. Ravensdale was burnt down in the 1920s. Lord Cleremont was the largest landowner in County Louth in 1876, with 758 acres in Armagh. His total acreage was 21,127 acres, with a valuation of £15,784.

There is nothing in the public domain about the disposal of the estate. The titles are all extinct.

Owners of over 1,000 acres in 1876

		Acreage	Valuation 1876 (£)3	Valuation 2017 (£)
1	Clermont Lord, Ravensdale Park, Newry	20,369	15,262	1,282,008
2	Massereene, Lord, Oriel Temple, Collon	7,193	5,234	439,656

		Acreage	Valuation 1876 (£)3	Valuation 2017 (£)
3	Smith-Barry, A.H., Foaty (Fota), Queeenstown, Co. Cork	6,239	4,620	388,080
4	Fortescue, Colonel J.C.W., Stephenstown House, Dundalk	5,262	5,070	425,880
5	Bellew, Lord, Barmeath, Dunleer	5,109	4,943	415,212
6	Stobart, Rev. Henry, Warkton Rectory, England	4,249	2,018	169,512
7	Bellingham, Sir A.E., Castlebellingham	4,186	4,291	360,444
8	Roden, Earl of, Tullymore Park, Castlewellan	4,151	7,944	667,296
9	Louth, Lord, Louth Hall, Ardee	3,578	3,983	334,572
10	Rathdonnell, Lord, Drumcar, Dunleer	3,188	3,251	273,084
11	Balfour, Blaney T., Townley Hall, Drogheda	3,137	2,856	239,904
12	Clive, Rev. Archer, Whitfield, Hereford	3,103	3,016	253,344
13	Marley, Charles B., St Catherine's Lodge, London	3,067	3,126	262,584
14	Foster, Fredrick J., Ballymascanlon, Dundalk	3,005	2,830	237,720
15	Robinson, Sir John S., Rokeby Hall, Dunleer	2,941	2,733	229,572
16	Murphy, John, Castletown, Dundalk	2,799	2,715	228,060
17	Foster, Rev. Sir Cavendish, England	2,769	2,685	225,540
18	Dobbs, Conway E., 41 Lr Leeson St, Dublin	2,270	1,467	123,228
19	Ruxton, William, Ardee House	2,262	2,279	191,436
20	Filgate, T.P.H.M., Lother Lodge, Balbriggan	2,250	1,876	157,584
21	Chester, Henrietta, Cartown, Drogheda	1,978	1,600	134,400
22	Fitzgerald, Percy, 37 St George's Road, Pimlico, London	1,938	2,008	168,672
23	O'Reilly-Dease M., Dee Farm, Dunleer	1,894	1,902	159,768
24	Woodhouse, John O., 82 Pembroke Road, Dublin	1,861	573	48,132

		Acreage	Valuation 1876 (£)3	Valuation 2017 (£)
25	Upton, Lewis, Stansteadbury, Ware, Herts, England	1,829	1,786	150,024
26	Moore, Colonel T.A., Dublin	1,614	1,419	119,196
27	Cremorne, Lord, Dartry Castle, Monaghan	1,578	1,576	132,384
28	Trinity College Dublin Provost and Fellows	1,521	1,399	117,516
29	Singleton, Edward A.H., Collon	1,513	837	70,308
30	Singleton, H.S., London	1,463	2,168	182,112
31	Carlingford, Lord, Red House, Ardee	1,452	1,719	144,396
32	Montgomery, Richard T., Beaulieu, Drogheda	1,364	1,500	126,000
33	Taffe, John, Smarmore Castle, Ardee	1,277	1,415	118,860
34	Macann, Richard, Drumcashel, Castlebellingham	1,245	1,384	116,256
35	Tipping, Edward, Bellurgan, Ballymascanlon	1,245	1,055	88,620
36	Dunlop, Robert Foster, Monasterboice House, Collon	1,214	1,076	90,384
37	Caraher, Michael, Cardistown, Ardee	1,211	1,298	109,032
38	Brabazon, Eliza C., Bennet's Court, Queenstown	1,185	1,264	106,176
39	Normon, Thomas Lee, Corballis, Ardee	1,182	1,308	109,872
40	Garstin, Edward Reps, Bragganstown	1,168	912	76,608
41	O'Callaghan, Fredrick, Clonsilla, Dublin	1,166	540	45,360
42	Brabazon, Rev. Wm, Dardisrath, Thermonfeckin	1,155	1,159	97,356
43	O'Byrne, Count, Corville, Roscrea	1,152	1,031	86,604
44	Bredan, Alexander M., Portadown	1,115	443	37,212
45	Chester, Finlay, Williamstown House, Castlebellingham	1,081	1,185	99.540
46	Russell, Earl, Chesham Place, London	1,017	764	64,176

Owners of over 1,000 acres in 1876 ranked by gross estimated rentals

		Acreage	Valuation 1876 (£)3	Valuation current (£)
1	Clermont, Lord, Ravensdale Park, Newry	20,369	15,262	1,282,008
2	Roden, Earl of, Tullymore Park, Castlewellan	4,151	7,944	667,296
3	Masserene, Lord, Oriel Temple, Collon	7,193	5,234	439,656
4	Fortescue, Colonel J.C.W., Stephenstown House, Dundalk	5,262	5,070	425,880
5	Bellew, Lord, Barmeath, Dunleer	5,109	4,943	415,212
6	Smith-Barry, A.H., Foaty (Fota), Queeenstown, Co. Cork	6,239	4,620	388,080
7	Bellingham, Sir A.E., Castlebellingham	4,186	4,291	360,444
8	Louth, Lord, Louth Hall, Ardee	3,578	3,983	334,572
9	Rathdonnell, Lord, Drumcar, Dunleer	3,188	3,251	273,084
10	Marley, Charles B., St Catherine's Lodge, London	3,067	3,126	262,584
11	Clive, Rev. Archer, Whitfield, Hereford	3,103	3,016	253,344
12	Balfour, Blaney T., Townley Hall, Drogheda	3,137	2,856	239,904
13	Foster, Fredrick J., Ballymascanlon, Dundalk	3,005	2,830	237,720
14	Robinson, Sir John S., Rokeby Hall, Dunleer	2,941	2,733	229,572
15	Murphy, John, Castletown, Dundalk	2,799	2,715	228,060
16	Foster, Rev. Sir Cavendish, England	2,769	2,685	225,540
17	Ruxton, William, Ardee House	2,262	2,279	191,436
18	Singleton, H.S., London	1,463	2,168	182,112
19	Stobart, Rev. Henry, Warkton Rectory, England	4,249	2,018	169,512
20	Fitzgerald, Percy, 37 St George's Road, Pimlico, London	1,938	2,008	168,672

MAYO

	1876	2020 est
Population in County Mayo	245,855	130,638
All owners of land	1,483	102,963
Percentage of the population	0.63	-
Owners of nothing at all	244,372	46,014
Percentage of the population	99.37	-
Size of County	1,308,366 acres	1,381,760 acres
Number of dwellings (of which rented in 1876 mostly owned in 2020)	44,091 (42,608)	47,932
Number of owned farm holdings	608	12,458

County comparisons

	Acreage 1876	Population 1876	Population 2016
County Mayo	1,308,366	245,855	130,638
Devon, England	1,234,884	438,656	800,000
Aberdeen, Scotland	1,255,136	264,603	228,610

This beautiful county sits, wave and wind washed, by that great shining, turbulent crucible, the Atlantic Ocean. Mayo's land, as the agricultural figures show, is often poor and unworkable, but what land is workable is good and fertile. It is enough to comfortably support its people nowadays but that wasn't always so.

Mayo is but a step away from New York – well a long step, the width of the Atlantic if you really want to push the analogy – but one that hundreds of thousands of its inhabitants had to take over centuries. Along with their mostly rag-wrapped possessions, they often took with them bitter resentment of landlords (and of Britain) to the New World, which many of them then helped to shape. But they left behind them a burning desire on the part of those trapped in Mayo to get out of the futility into which they were born, and whose outcome had too often proved fatal. This was the life of tenants. When the tenants of Mayo rebelled, propelled into action by the devastation of the Great Famine of 1845 to 1849, they were not starting an original revolution and they were not alone, historically.

Over the centuries and millennia the peasants of China alone rebelled over 2,700 times, forty-seven of them successfully. Many uprisings were against rapacious landlords rather than the imperial government.

And long before Mahmata Gandhi rediscovered passive resistance in the twentieth century, the poor of Mayo did passive resistance in the nineteenth century, because without arms there was noting else they could do. And like Gandhi, they won out, in the end. Indeed they achieved what India has still not achieved, land reform.

But first, a look at the population of the county. The population census of Mayo before 1845, mainly the census of 1841, was lost when the Irish records were burnt in 1921. The figure for 1876 is tentative because of the way it was collected, but it will be a portion of the pre-famine total, minus those who died and those who left, some to the UK some to the US and other places such as Canada and Australia. If we assume that the pre-famine figure was one third greater than the 'remain' figure of 1876, then Mayo lost about 80,000 people between 1845 and 1876. And it has gone on losing them ever since. In 2016 we wind up with just over half the 1876 figure – and one-third of the estimated 1841 figure. This is extremely unusual in Europe, and in most of the world. A largely fertile land apparently abandoned by its people.

So why was the Great Famine what it was? At one level it was simply nature red in tooth and claw and random in its actions. In 1845 a disease struck the potato, the staple diet of the peasant tenantry of Mayo and the rest of Ireland, about 98 per cent of the population then. The vulnerability of mass dependence on a single food source, however, was the outcome of man-made structures, not nature. Those we will consider briefly, but first the immediate consequences. These are demonstrated in the two key figures for Mayo from 1876; the population of 245,855, then the owners of all land in Mayo in 1876, who numbered 1,483 in total, and finally, those who owned nothing at all in 1876, 244,372. This mass of humanity, the landless, had, prior to 1845, enough soil to grow food on, mainly potatoes, but mostly at the whim of their masters, their landlords. Many tenants in Mayo, even as late as 1876, had never seen a coin or any form of currency. The landlords took the crops the peasants tilled and sold them. The tenants subsisted on what was left, and back in 1845 all that was left was mainly the humble potato. The Mayo landlords were made of the same humanity as the rest of us, and reacted in much the same way many of us would to this disaster. They tried to hang on to what they had, land, and shoved the problem, the starving, away from their estates, onto what public charity there was; mostly workhouses and emigration. Many landlords paid the passage for their tenants to emigrate. Others paid for some food distribution, as did the imperial government. But other landlords simply turned the people out on the side of the laneways, to chance their lives on food in the fields they could not touch because of the laws of the time; laws enforced by an armed soldiery and a judiciary that was almost entirely made up of local Mayo landowners. The turnip in the field that might save your life could cost you ten years in jail if you were caught stealing it.

In summary then, the tenantry of Mayo, about 98.4 per cent of the population in 1845, had no security of tenure and, consequently, no security of food. Those who survived the famine saw security of tenure, ultimately ownership, as the only road to security of life itself. There was nothing nationalistic about this. It was an issue of survival.

It was this drive, without arms or open insurrection, that exposed the other fatal flaw in the system, the one the landlords depended on; rents.

The landlords of Mayo and the rest of Ireland depended on a fatally flawed version of capitalism to survive. Their business model was that of substantial rents perpetually coming in from their landed assets, propping up what was often extreme extravagance in the imperial capital, London. The palaces and great houses of the metropolis were paid for by peasants who'd often never seen the coin of the realm, who mostly could not read or write and who clung to life in physical situations akin to and not unlike a few very remote parts of the world today. But even capitalism itself implies that assets have to be maintained, invested in. The landlords of Ireland in the main did not invest in their estates, which were theoretically cash cows to be milked and, where the milk of rents failed, to be borrowed against.

At the bottom of the chain were the tenants, mostly paid nothing at all, living on barter, in a form of serfdom or neo-slavery akin to that of the feudal serfs of Russia of the same period. The scene was set for armed revolution, but that's not what happened. The peasantry of Mayo set about the last link to reality that kept their landlords in the opulence they had come to expect, rents. Rents were denied to oppressive landlords, and refusnick tenants were supported in court by the Mayo Tenants Defence League. This was founded at a meeting in Castlebar on 26 Oct 1878 with a demand that the land of Ireland should be for the people of Ireland. It had mass appeal; 98 per cent of the population of Ireland were landless. This event led to a gathering of 20,000 people near Claremorris in April 1879. Such gatherings had not been seen in Ireland since the time of Daniel O'Connell MP and his demands for Catholic emancipation in the 1830s and '40s. These two meetings led to the founding of the Irish National Land League at the Imperial Hotel in Castlebar on 21 October 1879.

This in turn led to the real revolution, whose outcome is demonstrated in another figure for Mayo, the one for ownership in 2016. But the oddity of this revolution was that it was made and enforced by the very antithesis of revolution, the imperial government in London. A series of Land Acts were passed in the British Parliament between 1870 and 1903, enabling Irish tenants to buy their holdings. The acts were not passed out of kindness to Irish peasants, but in order to bale out that portion of the British ruling class, mostly aristocratic, who were in possession of bankrupt Irish estates. The Irish were not given their holdings, they were sold them with Government-sourced sixty-year mortgages, from which the former landlords eventually got the proceeds.

An Ireland of huge bankrupt capitalist landed estates became an Ireland of small capitalist farmers, owning, for the first time in history, an asset, their land. This is what shaped the real Ireland of today. This is Mayo's message from history.

The 20 largest landowners in County Mayo in 1876 by acreage

		Acreage	Value 1876 (£)	Value current (£)
1	Sligo, the Marquis of, Westport House, Westport	114,881	16,157	1,357,388
2	Dillon, Viscount, Loughglynn House, Castlerea	83,749	19,937	1,674,708
3	Palmer, Colonel Sir Roger William H., Cefn Park, Wrexham, Kenure Park, Dublin & Carlton Club, London	80,890	14,625	1,228,500
4	Lucan, Earl of, Castlebar House, Co. Mayo	60,570	12,940	1,086,960
5	Carter, Thomas Shaen, Watlington, Oxfordshire	37,773	2,644	222,096
6	Clive, George, Claggan, Ballycroy	35,229	837	70,308
7	Earl of Arran, Castlegore Mayo, and Hans Place, London	29,644	6,967	585,228
8	Knox, Captain Charles Howe, Cranmore, Ballinrobe	24,374	8,550	718,200
9	Trustees of Achill Mission, Doogort	19,155	1,011	84,924
10	Pratt, Mervyn, Enniscoe, Crossmolina, Mayo and Cabra Castle, Kingscourt, Co. Cavan	17,955	3,393	285,012
11	Gore, Sir Charles A. Knox, Belleek Manor, Ballina	17,608	6,332	531,999
12	Blosse, Sir Robert Lynch, Athaville House, Balla, Mayo	17,555	7,383	620,172
13	Mitchell, Abraham and Joseph, Tourmakeady, Ballinrobe	14,179	1,164	97,776
14	Bingham, Letitia, Dalkey	12,525	157	13,188
15	Moore, George A., Moore Hall, Ballyglass	12,371	3,524	296,016
16	Clanmorris, Lord, Creg Clare, Ardrahan, Co. Galway	12,337	6,210	521,640
17	Bellingham, Sir Allan, Knockmoyleean, Ballycroy	11,810	295	24,780

		Acreage	Value 1876 (£)	Value current (£)
18	De Clifford, Lord, 3 Carlton House Tce, London	11,594	5,156	433,104
19	Kilmaine, Lord Gaulston Park Killucan, Co. Westmeath	11,564	5,363	450,492
20	Orme, William, Owenmore, Crossmolina	11,230	1,730	145,320

The 20 wealthiest landowners in Mayo in 1876 based on rental valuation

		Acreage	Rental valuation 1876 (£)	Equivalent (£)
1	Dillon, Viscount, Loughglynn House, Castlerea	83,749	19,937	1,674,708
2	Sligo, the Marquis of, Westport House, Westport	114,881	16,157	1,357,188
3	Palmer, Colonel Sir Roger William H., Cefn Park, Wrexham, Kenure Park, Dublin, and Carlton Club, London	80,890	14,625	1,228,500
4	Lucan, Earl of, Castlebar House, Co. Mayo	60,570	12,940	1,086,960
5	Knox, Captain Charles Howe, Cranmore, Ballinrobe	24,374	8,550	718,200
6	Blosse, Sir Robert Lynch, Athaville House, Balla, Mayo	17,555	7,383	620,172
7	Earl of Arran, Castlegore, Mayo, and Hans Place, London	29,644	6,967	585,228
8	Gore, Sir Charles A. Knox, Belleek Manor, Ballina	17,608	6,332	531,888
9	Clanmorris, Lord, Creg Clare, Ardrahan, Co. Galway	12,337	6,210	521,640
10	Kilmain, Lord. The Neal Park, Ballinrobe, Co. Mayo, and Gallstone House, Co. Westmeath	11,564	5,363	450,492
11	De Clifford, Lord, 3 Carlton House Tce, London	11,594	5,156	433,104
12	Lindsay, Miss Mary, Hollymount House, Hollymount	5,194	3,856	322,904

		Acreage	Rental valuation 1876 (£)	Equivalent (£)
13	Fitzgerald, Chas Lionel, Turlough Park, Castlebar	8,339	3,779	317,436
14	Moore, George A., Moore Hall, Ballyglass	12,371	3,524	296,016
15	Pratt, Mervyn, Enniscoe, Crossmolina, Mayo and Cabra Castle, Kingscourt, Co. Cavan	17,955	3,393	285,012
16	Farrell, John Nolan, Logboy House, Ballyhaunis, Co. Mayo	9,731	3,072	258,048
17	Taaffe, James, Woodfield, Kilkelly	9,030	2,721	228,564
18	Carter, Thomas, Shaen, Watlington, Oxfordshire	37,773	2,644	220,096
19	Oranmore, Lord, Castlemacgarrett, Balandine	4,243	2,321	194,464
20	O'Donnell, Sir Richard A., Kingstown	7,488	2,232	187,488

In 1876 Theobold Dominick Geoffrey Dillon, The 15th Viscount Dillon, Count of France, of Loughglynn House, Castlerea, and Ditchley Park, Oxford, held 83,000 acres in Mayo, 5,444 acres in Oxford, 5,435 acres in Roscommon and 136 acres in Westmeath. He was the wealthiest man in Mayo in his time. The Mayo acres were valued at £19,231 about £1,615,404 in modern money.

This title still exists and is held by Henry (Harry) Benedict Charles Dillon, the 22nd Viscount, who lives in London. The Dillons claim Norman Irish ancestry and date their arrival on the island to around 1185. At the time of the Returns the present Viscount's ancestor, the 15th Viscount, held the second largest estate in Mayo but with the highest valuation in the county, the modern equivalent of over £1.6 million a year. The peer's total income from his several estates was £28,762. The 15th Viscount owned Ditchley Park in Oxford in 1876, one of the most beautiful country estates in England, but never sat in the British House of Lords as the original title, created in 1622, was an Irish one. There is a second title, an unusual one, that of Count of France. The 4th Viscount had the Irish title revoked, with prejudice, for life, by Cromwell in 1652, following his defence of Connought against the Parliamentary forces in Ireland, while civil war raged in England. The title and lands were restored in 1660. But in 1690 the 7th Viscount joined the wrong side, again, against William of Orange and the title was again revoked and he was outlawed. This outlawry was revoked in favour of his son, the 8th Viscount.

Come the 10th Viscount, things were on the up on the Continent, where the Dillons now lived and practised the profession of arms as mercenary soldiers. The 10th Viscount was created a Count by Louis XIV in 1711, made an Earl by the Old Pretender (James III) in 1721 and made a Knight by the same displaced monarch in 1722. His son, the 11th Viscount, was a colonel in the French army but by 1788 his son, the 12th Viscount, had rebuilt his bridges with the British establishment, converted to the Church of England, had his title confirmed to sit in the Irish House of Lords, but not the English one, and got his lands back.

In 1800 the Irish House of Lords closed for good, as Castlereagh elbowed through the act of Union, making Ireland a part of the United Kingdom, governed from Westminster. After that the family built a large residence at Loughglynn in Mayo, but they almost never lived there, preferring the English seat of Ditchley Park in Oxford. The Irish estate was run by agents and the Dillons became absentee landlords marrying into the British aristocracy, including the family of the Earl of Lichfield, from whom they inherited Ditchley Park. They were popular in Royal circles and the 20th Viscount, Michael 'Paddy' Dillon, became a colonel in the Royal Horse Guards, the most elite of elite British army regiments. But while he was earlier soldiering in the Middle East and acquiring a DSO and other awards, the estate in Ireland had been broken up and Loughglynn had become a convent.

In 1933 Ditchley Park was sold to an Anglo–American millionaire and MP, Ronald Tree. Between 1940 and 1942 Winston Churchill, the wartime leader of Britain, used Ditchley Park as a country retreat to avoid German bombers targeting his country home at Chartwell on their way to and from bombing London.

Tree sold the estate and house to Sir David Wills, an heir to the Wills tobacco fortune. The house and estate now belong to a charitable trust that encourages and facilitates Anglo–American relations; it is often a gathering place for the Intelligence communities from all over. An aunt of the current peer, The Hon. Madeleine Marie Louludis, is a lady in waiting to HRH the Princess Royal.

Hubert Browne was the 2nd Marquis of Sligo and held the largest estate in the county in 1876, with 114,881 acres valued at £19,000 about £1,956,000 in modern money. He was educated at Eton College. Like the Dillons, the name is of Norman origin and is associated with a huge cousinhood, even now.

The title survives with the 12th Marquess, Sebastian Browne, who inherited the peerage from the 11th Marquis, Jeremy Ulick Browne, in 2014 and lives in Australia. The 11th Marquis had no male heirs but his five daughters inherited Westport House and the 800-acre residue of the once huge estate around it. Politically the Brownes were of great historic importance, having been Governors of Connaught in the time of Elizabeth I and then risen to the Lord Lieutenancy of Ireland via a link to the Earldom of Ulster. The family describe themselves as the feudal lords of Clanrickarde, also in Mayo. This was the base from which they projected themselves, again and again, into the fractious politics of England and Ireland at the time the British Empire was being formed. One holder of the Clanricarde estate, Ulrick MacRichard Burke, led the Irish forces against Cromwell but lost, being a better diplomat than soldier. He was the son of Frances Walshingham, the 1st Secretary of State and the first of England's formal spymasters, giving the family a significant position at the very pinnacle of English power that they were to retain for decades.

An avid collector of titles, Ulrick was the 2nd Earl of St Albans and the 1st Marquis of Clanricarde. He forfeited his lands to Cromwell in 1652 but the family got them back in 1662, after the Restoration. Like the Dillons, the holder of the title in 1691 sided with James against William of Orange, and lost both titles and lands. They were restored in 1702 by act of Parliament. The family remained at the pinnacle of power. Ulrick John, the 14th Earl of Clanricarde, married the Hon. Harriet, daughter of the Rt Hon. George Canning, a hugely important British Secretary of State, Prime Minister and Earl.

Which is all fine and well but what of the peasants of Westport and Clanricarde all this time? The answer is, 'not much'. Their lives went on as they always had, on the edge of survival and without comfort. Their situation poses a very important question, given that the same aristocratic family had been defining the meaning of their existence in Mayo for over 400 years, depending which genealogy you read – the PR for Westport House describes the Brownes as a family originally from Sussex in the sixteenth century, and not the Norman *fado fado* of Irish history. The hard question, however, is this; does history matter and the short answer is that, if you're at the bottom of the heap, it limits your life totally, and very often ends it prematurely. The only way out is up, and the way up for the peasantry had been effectively blocked for centuries by the political structures of the time.

Those structures only finally begun to unravel after the founding of the Irish National Land league at the Imperial Hotel in Castlebar in October 1879. The Brownes had been among the 'good' famine landlords, importing food for the starving, supporting the workhouses and trying to care for their tenants. But good people cannot usually defeat a bad system and a system that kept tenants in virtual serfdom finally had to fall. That fall began in the Imperial Hotel in Castlebar, not many miles from the Sligo estates of the Browne family.

The 11th Marquis held many titles and survived the virtual elimination of the hereditary peers from the UK House of lords in 1999, continuing to have a potential right to sit there as the Baron Monteagle if a vacancy occurred and he could get himself elected by his fellow peers. There is no sign of the 12th Marquis attempting to exercise that option from Australia, however.

Colonel Sir Roger Palmer Bart, of Keenagh, Crossmolina Co Mayo, had 80,990 acres in Mayo valued at £14,625 about £1,228,500 in modern money The Palmer title, a hereditary knighthood (Bt) is long gone, as is the estate, which the family acquired as early as 1684 during attempts to plant Connaught with settlers from England and Scotland. The Galway estates database describes the estate as being over 80,000 acres in Mayo, 9,570 acres in Sligo and 4,202 acres in Dublin. Bateman confirms this, although giving only 3,991 acres for Dublin while adding in Sir Roger's English and Welsh acres, with 3,329 acres in Cambridge, 1,011 acres in Denbigh, 45 in Flint, 11 in Dorset and 7 in Berks. The trivial acres at the tail end of the list would have given Sir Roger votes in each of those places and were probably held for that reason.

Palmer's overall holdings made him the forty-sixth largest landowner in Victoria's Britain and one of the richest men in the realm with an income of £26,661 about £2,239,524 in modern money. Like so many others in our list, he was educated at Eton College, was an officer in the Life Guards cavalry regiment, with direct responsibility for the safety of the 'blood royal', and had fought in the Crimean War. He wound up a lieutenant general in the British Army and sat as an MP for Mayo in the House of Commons. The estate had been added to in the late 1850s but had been sold down to its 1876 acreage by the late 1860s. Most of the time the estate was handled by agents, was wildly unpopular as result of famine evictions and was poorly organised to defend itself against the twin pincers of rent refusals and lengthy litigation against tenants supported by their league. Most of the Mayo estate was sold to the Congested District Board in 1916. Almost all the Sligo acreage went to the same body in 1909.

The Palmer estate, run as it was by agents for an absentee proprietor most of the time, epitomised the failing nature of the underlying business model itself. Investment was seldom if ever made and the gap between the proprietor's income of over £2 million a year, and the pay of an agricultural day labourer on his estates at £25 a year, was vast. This differential, however, is now being approached or exceeded by many chief executives and the people they employ in their companies. The landed estates depended hugely on the law, which was written largely in favour of landlords, in a Parliament that they dominated, and enforced by a local judiciary made up almost entirely of landlords.

Behind that was the military and the militia in which landowners constituted most of the officer class. It was not a model for the building of social and political cohesion, even on the relatively limited basis that did work in mainland UK. The surprising thing was that the political explosion did not come for another thirty-six years, in 1916. It was about sixty-six years late and the real work of transferring Irish land to Irish people was unstoppable by then – and substantially accomplished, starting in Mayo.

The 3rd Earl of Lucan, George Charles Bingham of Laleham House, Chertsey owned 60,000 acres of Mayo in 1876. He was, eventually, a field marshal in the British Army. His Mayo acres had a valuation of £12,940 about £1,108,696 in modern money. He also had 32 acres in Dublin, 159 acres in Surrey, 984 acres in Middlesex and 1,191 acres in Cheshire. This title still exists and the holder, the 8th Earl, is George Charles Bingham, a banker, who lives in London. He succeeded his father, the 7th Earl, who went missing on 8 November 1974, the night the family's nanny was murdered. The 7th Earl was assumed dead by the courts on 3 February 2016 and the titles formally passed to George Charles, who does not believe his father had anything to do with the death of the nanny, Sandra Rivett. Both father and son went to Eton College and ground rents are still collected in Mayo, on behalf of the estate.

The title itself is an interesting one. The original 1st Earl of Lucan, Patrick Sarsfield, was the Jacobite army commander at the battle of the Boyne in 1690. He was created the Earl of Lucan by the defeated King James while in exile in France. That title became extinct and the current Earldom of Lucan was in 1795 conferred on Sir Charles Bingham, the MP for Co. Mayo who had earlier been created Baron Lucan in the Irish peerage in 1776. Sir Charles was, however, the great grandson of Patrick Sarsfield.

But in 1876 the 3rd Earl held the estate. Unusually, he was educated at Westminster School, not Eton, not that he stayed long at Westminster. He left at 16 to become an (ensign) junior officer in the British infantry. He was an absolutely typical aristocrat of the high imperial period. And he was rich. His rent roll gave him an income of £17,423 a year. In those days you bought your officers commission and by the age of 26 Lucan had bought his way to the rank of lieutenant colonel of the 17th Lancers, a very exclusive cavalry regiment. In those days, too, officers bought their own uniforms and horses as well as their commissions. Lucan, or Lord Bingham as he was known until he inherited the Eardom on the death of his father in 1839, made sure his officers had the best uniforms and the best horses by helping to pay for both, while back in Mayo his tenants lived on the edge of starvation. The rents they paid led to Lucan's regiment becoming known as 'Bingham's Dandies'. When the famine struck, Lucan treated his tenants with the brutality with which he later treated his soldiers in the Crimea. He instigated mass evictions, sending starving people, men women and children, into the harsh Irish winters, in many cases to die on the side of the road. His nickname was the Exterminator and he is reviled still in Mayo, over 170 years later. He sat as MP for Mayo between 1826 and 1830. By the start of the Famine in 1845, as well as being a brigadier in the army, he was Lord Lieutenant of Mayo, a county that did not have a good famine. During the disaster Lucan sat in the House of Lords as a representative Irish peer but made no contribution to the pathetic efforts of the Government to try and relieve the catastrophe in Ireland.

Indeed, had the mechanics of administrative incompetence been understood, it might have been possible to foresee the incompetence with which Lucan would handle the army in Russia in 1854. He gave the order for the charge of the Light Brigade, a suicidal advance at the gallop straight into Russian artillery guns that resulted in many of the brigade being killed. He was refused a 'courts martial of honour', but exonerated himself with a speech in the Lords where he laid the blame on his subordinates.

He was subsequently made a Knight Commander of the Bath and later still he was made commanding officer of the 1st Regiment of the Life Guards, quite the poshest appointment in the British army. He died a field marshal, having obtained this final promotion by lobbying for it in the House of Lords, not for commanding an army. Thus he can be said to have helped to start that very modern trend of being promoted because of the disasters you inflict, not the success you achieve or the good that you do.

The fifth largest landowner in Mayo in 1876 was Thomas Shaen Carter, of Watlington Park, Oxfordshire, who held 37,000 acres in Mayo (corrected to 40,698 acres in Bateman), with 1,137 acres in County Westmeath, 166 acres in County Meath and 537 acres in Oxford. He was a justice of the peace and a magistrate. He died in 1875 and was succeeded by his son, Henry Tilson Shaen Carter. His Mayo acres were valued at £2,764 about £232,176 in modern money.

Carter was in every way a typical imperial landowner in Ireland. He lived in Oxford in England, was educated at Eton College and went to the Military Academy at Sandhurst. He served in the 17th Lancers, a very exclusive cavalry regiment. They had a total of eleven children, two of whom died young and only one of whom, George, survived into the nineteenth century.

The family started in Ireland with land grants after the Battle of the Boyne. Ferres tells us that Thomas Carter (1650–1726), of Robertstown, Co. Meath, a Sergeant-at-Arms, was a gentleman whose services at the Revolution were very considerable, for he not only served William III at the Battle of the Boyne, but secured useful books and writings belonging to King James II and his secretaries when they were fleeing from the scene of the battle. His successor, the Rt Hon Thomas Carter, was Master of the Rolls, a Privy Councillor and Secretary of State in Ireland.

The NUI Galway database tells us that the Carter family of Castlemartin, Co. Kildare, inherited half the Shaen lands in the Barony of Erris, Co. Mayo, through marriage with a Shaen heiress in 1750. In the mid 1820s they founded the town of Belmullet and developed it with the assistance of John Crampton, their agent, and the engineer, Patrick Knight. Land in Athlone and elsewhere were offered for sale with other estates in counties Meath, Kildare and King's County (County

Offaly) in May 1855. Lands, the property of Adelaide Shaen-Carter, were sold in the Land Judges' Court in June 1885. The purchaser was John Conway.

George Clive of Claggan, Ballycroy, had 35,229 acres in Mayo in 1876, with a valuation of £837 about £70,308 in modern money.

The low valuation kept Clive out of Bateman. The NUI Database has the following notes on the estate:

> George Clive, Member of Parliament and barrister, of Perrystone Court, Herefordshire, built up an extensive estate of 35,229 acres (1876) in the barony of Erris by purchasing land from the O'Donels, Marquess of Sligo and the Birch family. The final offer by the Congested Districts' Board for the purchase of almost 33,000 acres of the estate had been accepted by March 1916. George Clive of Ballycroy also owned 4,869 acres in county Tipperary [bought by the Clives from the Minchins in the 1770s. The Clive family were related to the Boltons of Knock, county Louth and to Dr Bolton, Archbishop of Cashel.

The Earl of Arran of Castlegore, County Mayo, and Hans Place, London, had 29,644 acres in Mayo in 1876, with a valuation of £6,967 about £585,228 in modern money.

The Earl was a diplomat who served as Charge d'Affaires in Buenos Aires. He had 6,883 acres in Donegal, which, with the Mayo acres, gave him a total acreage of 36,527 with a valuation of £10,112.

The NUI Galway database tells us that in 1666 the Gores were granted extensive estates, over 14,700 acres, in the Barony of Tirawley, Co. Mayo, and in Co. Sligo under the Acts of Settlement. In 1686 the Manor of Castle-Gore was created from these estates and other lands bought by the Gores. They also acquired the Manor of Belleek from the O'Haras, Barons Tyrawley, and owned estates in Donegal. In the nineteenth century much of their estate was let to middlemen or administered by agents and the Gores were largely absentee, as they had inherited the Saunders estate in Co. Wexford. John Perkins of Ballybroony, near Ballina, was their main agent in the 1830s.

This peerage is still extant and is the Earldom of the Arran Islands created in the peerage of Ireland in 1762. This peerage has been created several times in the peerage of Ireland and is held by Arthur Desmond Colquhoun Gore, the 9th Earl, who lives in Devon. Having no male heirs, his heir presumptive is his very distant cousin, William Henry Gore (born 1950), who lives in Australia, descended from the youngest brother of the 4th Earl.

Captain Charles Howe Cuff Knox of Creagh, Ballinrobe, had 24,374 acres in Mayo in 1876, with a valuation of £8,550 about £718,200 in modern

money. This cavalry officer, who served in the 8th Hussars, was educated at Harrow School and had 446 acres in Donegal, giving him a total acreage of 24,820 acres, with a valuation of £9,572.

The Knox family were originally from Co. Donegal and in 1778 William Knox married Elizabeth Nesbitt of Scurmore, Sligo. Their son, Charles Nesbitt Knox, married Jane Cuff, eventual heiress to the settled estates of her father, James Cuff, Lord Tyrawley. Alexander Clendining Lambert was agent to the Knoxes. Colonel C.H.C. Knox sold his estate to the Congested Districts' Board in July and December 1913 and February 1914.

The Achill Mission of Dogort in Mayo held 19,155 acres in 1876, with a valuation of £1,011 about £84,924 in modern money.

The mission was a doomed, if well-intentioned, attempt to develop the Protestant religion on the Catholic Irish-speaking island in Mayo. The mission was led by the Rev. Edward Nangle, a clergyman from Morehampton Road in Dublin. It started in 1834 and did give assistance to the poor and destitute during the Great Famine. But there was intense public antipathy from both Catholic and Protestants to the whole idea, even though a working village was erected. Much has been written about the episode and can be found on the web. The NUI Database has the following notes:

> The O'Donel estate on the island of Achill was bought by Trustees of the Achill Mission in association with Thomas Brassey, William Pike and Samuel Holme, who each paid £2,333 6s 8d for small estates on the island in the early 1850s. The Mission's share was 23,452 acres for which they paid £10,500. By March 1916 the Achill Mission had accepted an offer from the Congested Districts' Board for the purchase of their estate, which the Board took over in 1921.

Mervyn Pratt of Cabra, Castle Kingscourt, County Cavan, and Enniscoe Crossmolina, County Mayo, had 17,955 acres in Mayo, with a valuation of £3,393 about £285,012 in modern money.

Bateman records Mervyn Pratt holding 8,095 acres in Cavan and 1,014 acres in Meath, which together with the Mayo acreage gave him a total of 27,064 acres and a valuation of £9,471. Ferrres tells us that Mervyn Pratt was a JP, Deputy Lieutenant of Cavan, High Sheriff of Co. Cavan, 1841, Co. Mayo, 1843, and Co. Meath, 1875. His grandson, Major Mervyn Pratt DSO and justice of the peace, was badly wounded in the Boer War and never married.

His younger brother, Colonel Audley Pratt, was killed in the First World War. He had never married. Major Pratt died at Enniscoe and bequeathed Cabra to his nearest male relative, Mervyn Sheppard, a Malayan civil servant. In 1964 the castle was sold.

In 1916 the Congested Districts' Board made a final offer of just under £50,000 for the Pratts Mayo estate. Enniscoe was inherited by the Nicholson family in the twentieth century and the nucleus of the property has remained in the ownership of descendants of the Jacksons for over 300 years.

Owners of 1,000 acres or more in Mayo in 1876

		Acreage	Valuation 1876	Valuation current £
1	Sligo, the Marquis of, Westport House, Westport	114,881	16,157	1,357,188
2	Dillon, Viscount, Loughglynn House, Castlerea	83,749	19,937	1,674,708
3	Palmer, Colonel Sir Roger William H., Cefn Park, Wrexham, Kenure Park, Dublin and Carlton Club, London	80,890	14,625	1,228,500
4	Lucan, Earl of, Castlebar House, Co. Mayo	60,570	12,940	1,086,960
5	Carter, Thomas Shaen, Watlington, Oxfordshire	37,773	2,644	222,096
6	Clive, George, Claggan, Ballycroy	35,229	837	70,308
7	Earl of Arran, Castlegore, Mayo, and Hans Place, London	29,644	6,967	585,288
8	Knox, Captain Charles Howe, Cranmore, Ballinrobe	24,374	8,550	718,200
9	Trustees of Achill Mission, Doogort	19,155	1,011	84,924
10	Pratt, Mervyn, Enniscoe, Crossmolina, Mayo and Cabra Castle, Kingscourt, Co. Cavan	17,955	3,393	285,012
11	Gore, Sir Charles A. Knox, Belleek Manor, Ballina	17,608	6,332	531,888
12	Blosse, Sir Robert Lynch, Athaville House, Balla, Mayo	17,555	7,383	620,172
13	Mitchell, Abraham & Joseph, Tourmakeady, Ballinrobe	14,179	1,164	97,776
14	Bingham, Letitia, Dalkey	12,525	157	13,188
15	Moore, George A., Moore Hall, Ballyglass	12,371	3,524	296,016
16	Clanmorris, Lord, Creg Clare, Ardrahan, Co. Galway	12,337	6,210	521,640

		Acreage	Valuation 1876	Valuation current £
17	Bellingham, Sir Allan, Knockmoyleean, Ballycroy	11,810	295	24,780
18	De Clifford, Lord, 3 Carlton House Tce, London	11,594	5,156	433,104
19	Kilmain, Lord. The Neal Park, Ballinrobe, Co. Mayo and Gallstone House, Co. Westmeath	11,564	5,363	450,492
20	Orme, William, Owenmore, Crossmolina	11,230	1,730	145,320
21	Pike, William, Glendarery, Achill	10,697	673	56,532
22	Beridge, Richard, 18 Gt Russell St, London	9,965	2,222	186,648
23	Farrell, John Nolan, Logboy House, Ballyhaunis, Co. Mayo	9,731	3,072	258,048
24	Bingham, Henry, Annagh House, Belmullet	9,471	536	45,024
25	Featherstone, H. Godfrey	9,361	1,669	140,196
26	Taaffe, James, Woodfield, Kilkelly	9,030	2,721	228,564
27	Forde, John Ross, Rochester	9,008	145	12,180
28	Laprimandaye, Captain, Treenlaur, Newport	8,937	349	29,316
29	Kirkwood, John Townsend, 34 Imperial Sq., Cheltenham	8,345	1,590	133,560
30	Fitzgerald, Chas Lionel, Turlough Park, Castlebar	8,339	3,779	317,436
31	Simes, R.P., Roigh	8,162	493	41,412
32	Coyne, Charles M., 17 Waterloo Road, Dublin	8,012	495	41,580
33	Dickens, Charles S.S., England	7,888	327	27,468
34	Costello, Edward, Edmonstown	7,513	1,567	131,268
35	O'Donnell, Sir Richard A., Kingstown	7,488	2,232	187,488
36	Thompson, David Reps of, Clonskeagh Castle, Dublin	7,390	692	58,128
37	Jackson, John, Dublin	7,012	106	8,904
38	Knox, John Henry Reps of, Greenwood Park, Ballina	6,909	637	53,508
39	Brabazon, Captain, Guards Club, Pall Mall and Swinford, Co. Mayo	6,857	2,081	174,804
40	Digby, Captain the Hon. E.H.T., Geashill, King's County	6,835	162	13,608

		Acreage	Valuation 1876	Valuation current £
41	O'Connor, Mrs Margaret, Mount Druid	6,817	1,051	88,284
42	Stoney, Robert Vesey, Newport	6,757	831	69,804
43	John, Cormack Walsh, Castlehill, Crossmolina, Mayo	6,472	1,242	104,328
44	O'Reilly, Thomas F., Carne House, Belmullet	6,472	517	43,428
45	Kennedy, Victor C., Curraunboy	6,198	767	64,428
46	Trustees of H.J. Grant, Logduff, Ballycroy	6,152	229	19,236
47	Domville, William C., Heywood, Ballinakill	6,040	2,056	172,704
48	Blacker, M.M., Virginia, USA	5,665	346	29,064
49	Rashleigh, Jonathan, St James Sq., London	5,475	833	69,972
50	Atkinson, Elizabeth, Armagh Glencastle, Belmullet	5,317	583	48,972
51	Lindsay, Miss Mary, Hollymount House, Hollymount	5,194	3,856	323,904
52	National Building & Land Investment Company of Ireland Ltd, 27 Dame St, Dublin	5,179	841	70,644
53	Perry, Edmund H., Beleek Castle, Ballina	5,108	2,082	174,888
54	Bingham, Denis, Bingham Castle, Bellmullet	4,827	818	68,712
55	Knox, Harry Blake, Ulverton Place, Dalkey	4,662	1,146	96,262
56	Downing, Charles, Oatlands, Ballina & Kingstown	4,500	538	45,192
57	Ormsby, Anthony, Ballinamore House, Kiltinagh	4,492	1,685	141,540
58	Bournes, George S., Beechmount, Clara	4,435	228	19,152
59	Gore, Sir A. Francis, Belleek Castle, Ballina	4,415	1,962	164,808
60	Joynt, Henry, Ballina, Co. Mayo	4,331	1,617	135,828
61	Rutledge, David, Barbersford, Tuam	4,329	1,664	139,776
62	Oranmore, Lord, Castlemacgarrett, Balandine	4,243	2,321	194,964
63	Blake, Valentine O'C., Tower Hill House, Ballyglass, Mayo	4,198	1,905	160,020
64	Bourke, Captain Joe, Cunaleagh, Claremorris	4,141	1,505	126,420
65	Gibbings, Rev. Richard, Rossbeg	4,096	462	38,808

		Acreage	Valuation 1876	Valuation current £
66	O'Farrell, Edward More, Kildangan Castle, Monsterevan	4,086	1,337	112,308
67	Gardiner, Harriett, Farmhill, Killala	4,073	1,501	126,804
68	Madden, Joseph William of Ballycastle	4,039	591	49,644
69	D'Arcy, Hyacinth, New Forrest, Co. Galway	3,871	990	83,160
70	Guinness, Sir A.E., of Ashford, Cong	3,747	1,707	143,388
71	Comyn, Francis L., Woodstock, Co. Galway	3,653	741	62,244
72	Mudge, Arthur, Sidney House, Plympton, Devon	3,634	80	6,720
73	Browne, J.D.H., 39 Rutland Gate, London	3,629	1,316	110,544
74	Clive, Rev. Archer, Hereford, England	3,457	364	30,576
75	M'Carrick, Roger, Killglass, Enniscrone	3,453	685	57,540
76	M'Callum, Captain Arthur, Glenturk, Bangor, Erris	3,370	71	5,964
77	Bingham, Anne, Dalkey	3,346	229	19,236
78	Garvey, James William, Tully House, Louisburg	3,270	128	10,752
79	Cuff, Colonel St George, Deel Castle, Ballina, Mayo	3,205	1,299	109,116
80	Ormsby, John, Gortneraabbey, Cros,s Molin, and Middle Temple	3,186	659	55,356
81	Knox, Annesley, Rappa Castle, Ballina	3,143	2,043	171,612
82	Knox, Elizabeth, Rappa Castle, Ballina	3,143	257	21,588
83	Smyth, William F., Green St, St Helier, Jersey	3,138	105	8,820
84	Jackson, Oliver Vaughan, Carrowmore, Ballina	3,134	1,313	110,292
85	Orme, Robert, The Priory, Monkstown Road	3,094	895	75,180
86	Rutledge, Robert, Bloomfield, Hollymount	2,949	1,582	132,888
87	Browne, Andrew, Mount Hazel, Galway	2,935	336	28,224
88	Carter, Henry T. Shaen, Rathmines Rd, Co. Dublin	2,925	129	10,836
89	Meade, Joseph F., Eastwood, Newtownmountkennedy	2,872	111	9,324

		Acreage	Valuation 1876	Valuation current £
90	Jones, Anne Elizabeth, 16 Park Road Upper, Sydenham, London	2,837	709	59,556
91	Browne, George, 33 Palace Gardens Tce, London, and Brownestown, Ballinrobe	2,809	1,121	94,164
92	Bourke, Walter, Curranebay, Belmullet	2,755	95	7,980
93	Gibbons, Mrs Sarah, The Vicarage, High Harrowgate	2,749	117	9,828
94	Knox, Mrs Mina, Netley Park, Ballina	2,744	514	43,176
95	Avonmore, Viscount, Ballyisle, Tipperary	2,697	673	56,532
96	Jackson, George H., Fortland, Crossmolina	2,695	438	36,792
97	Chapman, William, Southill, Delvin	2,664	88	7,392
98	M'Cormack, John, Dublin	2,629	143	12,012
99	Nicholson, Charlotte, 11 Oxford Road, Kilburn, London	2,477	302	25,368
100	Scott, H. Hope Reps of, QC in London	2,462	474	39,816
101	Irwin, John, Greyford, Ballina	2,370	432	36,288
102	O'Reilly-Dease, Maria, Bray	2,366	53	4,452
103	Stratford, J. Wingfield, Maidstone, Kent, England	2,361	238	19,992
104	Lynch, Major Patrick C., Cloher House, Ballyglass	2,337	944	79,296
105	Browne, Hans S.H., Brownehall, Balla, Co. Mayo	2,320	845	70,980
106	Bingham, Colonel Henry, London	2,311	170	14,280
107	Blake, Mark, Ballinafad House, Ballyglass, Mayo	2,234	1,276	102,080
108	Richards, John W.O., Barnagh House, Belmullet	2,228	231	19,404
109	Vesey, George Long, Dilton, Surrey, England	2,227	969	81,396
110	Livingstone, William, Westport	2,223	1,827	153,468
111	Armstrong, Henry, Chaffpool, Sligo	2,222	683	57,372
112	Erne, Earl of, Crom Castle, Newtownbutler, Fermanagh	2,184	1,012	85,008
113	Foley, William M.D., Kilrush, Co. Clare	2,159	60	5,040
114	Baxter, Edward, Dundee, Scotland	2,151	629	52,836
115	White, Lady Mary, 31 Montague Sq., Hyde Park, London	2,128	458	38,472

		Acreage	Valuation 1876	Valuation current £
116	Noughton, Rev. Michael, Sligo	2,107	39	3,276
117	Knox, Utred H., Mount Falcon, Ballina	2,065	1,071	89,964
118	Handy, Samuel, Springfield House, Philipstown	2,030	200	16,800
119	Chapman, Sir Benjamin, Killna Castle Clonmellon Westmeath	2,024	36	3,024
120	Blake, Charles, 9 Merrion Sq., South Dublin	1,981	916	76,944
121	Kirkwood, William Rutledge, Crosspatrick, Killala	1,948	257	21,588
122	Gibbons, Stephen, The Mall, Westport	1,939	693	58,212
123	Cavan, the Earl of, Doogurt, Achill	1,900	126	10,564
124	Garvey, Francis Christopher, Murrisk Abbey, Westport	1,890	450	37,800
125	M'Donnell, Thomas D. Reps of, Cloona Lodge, Westport	1,878	554	46,536
126	Blake, Isidore P, Inver Lodge, Belmullet	1,844	217	18,226
127	Jameson, Rev. William, -	1,831	774	65,016
128	Coyne, Bernard, Lahardane, Crossmolina, Co. Mayo	1,816	343	28,812
129	Irwin, Christopher Thomas P., Rosse's Point, Sligo	1,803	728	61,152
130	Jordan, Myles, Castlebar	1,801	531	44,604
131	Plunket, the Hon. Mr, Montebello, Co. Dublin	1,777	705	59,220
132	Fair, Robert Reps of, Bushfield, Hollymount	1,765	989	83,076
133	Crotty, Charles, Kinneury House, Westport, Co. Mayo	1,739	266	22,344
134	Tighe, Thomas, The Heath, Ballindine	1,720	999	83,916
135	Jennings, Charles B., Mount Jennings, Hollymount	1,702	908	76,272
136	Kelly, James, Limerick	1,701	75	6,300
137	Paget, Thomas, Eastwood, Bagnalstown	1,682	740	62,160
138	Bourke, Rev. William, Heathfield, Ballycastle	1,663	572	48,048
139	Bingham, Arthur Shaen, Doolough Lodge, Belmullet	1,662	222	18,648

		Acreage	Valuation 1876	Valuation current £
140	Jackson, Very Rev Dean, Killanley, Glebe, Enniscrone	1,643	454	38,136
141	Bell, E.G. Reps of, Castleconnell, Co. Limerick	1,636	531	44,604
142	Gildea, Anthony Knox, Clooncormack, Hollymount	1,635	678	56,952
143	Churcher, Emanuel, Gosport, England	1,633	804	67,536
144	M'Cormack, William O., Kingstown, Co. Dublin	1,609	679	57,036
145	O'Malley, Owen, Newcastle, Swinford, Co. Mayo	1,589	855	71,820
146	Browne, Dominick A., Breaghwy House, Castlebar, Co. Mayo	1,577	748	62,832
147	Cooper, Richard Augustus, Hillmartin, Paddon, Warwickshire	1,549	687	57,708
148	Higgins, Mrs Margaret, Ursuline Convent, Cork	1,537	621	52,164
149	Orme, William R., 8th Regiment, Manchester	1,521	644	54,096
150	O'Donel, Dominick, Kilcommon Lodge, Belmullet	1,461	125	10,500
151	Mostyn, Hon. Montague, Rosmead, Delvin, Westmeath	1,460	159	13,356
152	Kennedy, Chas Preston, Inisherkin, Newport	1,450	84	7,056
153	Martyn, Alexander, Curraghmore, Ballinrobe	1,443	821	68,964
154	Gallagher, Matt, Attymachue	1,440	218	18,312
155	Lynch, Charles, Ballycurren Castle, Headford	1,436	662	55,608
156	Bingham, Anne, 3 Martello Tower, Kingstown	1,422	21	1,764
157	Lynch, Anthony, Salerno, Salthill, Co. Galway	1,410	322	27,048
158	Lambert, Alexander C., Brookhil,l Claremorris	1,409	1,105	92,820
159	Miller, Crossdaile C.B., Milford, Foxhall, Tuam	1,404	866	72,744
160	Bourke, Surgeon Major Jos, Fareham, Hants, England	1,394	529	44,436

		Acreage	Valuation 1876	Valuation current £
161	Staples, Robert, Dunmore, Durrow, Queen's County	1,385	865	72,660
162	Gore, Mrs Mary J. Ormsby, Tetworth, Sunninghill	1,372	286	24,024
163	Carey, Martin, Newport	1,368	551	46,284
164	Knox, Lt Colonel Wm, Brittas Castle, Thurles	1,352	487	40,908
165	Tuohy, Malachy, Oxford, Kiltanagh	1,347	529	44,436
166	Bournes, William, Carrowtyne, Clara	1,325	95	7,980
167	Brett, Henry C.E., Rosemount, Booterstown	1,322	380	31,920
168	Peyton, Bernard, Creagh's Villa, Castlebar, Mayo	1,307	351	29,484
169	Stock, St George H., Jersey	1,299	472	39,648
170	M'Chale, His Grace the Most Rev. Dr, St Jarleth's, Tuam	1,284	128	10,752
171	O'Rourke, Hugh, New Row, Dublin	1,260	480	40,320
172	Daly, Thomas, Boghadoon	1,254	38	3,192
173	Lynch, Major General Edward P., Partry House, Ballinrobe	1,237	335	28,140
174	O'Grady, Richard J., Tavrane, Kilkelly	1,236	555	45,620
175	Walsh. Rev. William, -	1,229	14	1,176
176	Blake, Mrs Margaret Louisa, Ballinafad House, Ballyglass, Mayo	1,209	521	43,764
177	Seymour, Rev. D.B., Athlone	1,190	466	39,144
178	Blake, Edward, -	1,187	665	55,860
179	Knox, Granville H., Ballinbroney, Ballina	1,182	539	45,276
180	Gore, Major William Ormsby, Derrycarne, Drumod	1,174	320	26,880
181	Morell, Fredrick J., England	1,170	124	10,416
182	Carey, Mrs John, Pickle Point, Belmullet	1,155	94	7,896
183	Hazard, Robert, Parkmore, County Antrim	1,146	58	4,872
184	Higgins, Michael, Claremorris	1,118	562	47,208
185	Logan, Lt Colonel Abraham, Barracks, Kinsale	1,118	77	6,468
186	Ormsby, Rev. Horatio, Mallow, Co. Cork	1,114	513	43,092
187	M'Cormack, James C., Dublin	1,110	94	7,896

		Acreage	Valuation 1876	Valuation current £
188	D'Arcy, Dominick, Doo Castle, Ballymoat	1,091	430	36,120
189	Carey, Mrs Michael, Liverpool	1,080	66	5,544
190	M'Gloin, John, Foxford	1,078	322	27,048
191	Treston, Michael F., Cloontreston, Claremorris	1,074	309	25,956
192	Phibbs, Colonel Bernard, 13 Rutland Gate, London	1,071	408	34,272
193	Busby J., Inner Temple, London	1,058	11	924
194	Norbury, Lord Reps, Valence, Edinbridge, Wederham, Kent, England	1,024	264	22,176
195	De Montmorency, Fredrick, Broughillstown House, Baltinglass	1,022	343	28,812
196	Waller, Sir Edward, The Wilderness, Kingston upon Thames, England	1,011	460	38,640
197	Bingham, Mrs Sarah, -	1,010	65	5,460
198	Crooks, James, Gosport, England	1,001	477	40,068
199	Rutledge, Thomas, Cornfield, Hollymount	1,000	622	52,248

MEATH

	1876	2020 est
Population in County Meath	95,558	130,638
All owners of land	1,324 (1871)	86,217
Percentage of the population	1.38%	–
Owners of nothing at all	92,234	47,914
Percentage of the population	98.62%	–
Size of County	577,893	572,200 acres
Number of dwellings (of which rented in 1876, owned in 2020)	18,814 (17,490) (1871)	61,922
Number of owned farm holdings	1,324 (1871)	4,569

County comparisons

	Acreage 1876	Population 1876
County Meath	577,893	215,855
Northamptonshire, England	592,771	243,891
Lanarkshire, Scotland	557,919 acres	785,339
Carmarthenshire, Wales	510,574 acres	115,710

John Joseph Preston of Ballinter, Navan, held 7,415 acres in 1876 with a valuation of £6,839 about £574,476 in modern money. Bateman tells us little about J.J. Preston save that he was a Trinity man. The family acquired the lands soon after the Cromwellian settlement by buying them from Cromwellian soldiers who did not want to come to Ireland, which many, quite correctly, believed was hostile.

The house changed hands several times after 1876, with the Dublin family of Briscoe having it at one time, the Holdsworth family occupying it in the late 1950s and later the Sisters of Mount Sion ran it as a conference centre. About 1,737 acres was placed in trust in the 1700s for the support of two schools, one at Navan and the other at Ballyroan in Queen's County. This is thought to have been a device to protect the land from any of the soldiers who changed their minds and wanted the land back. Breaking charitable trusts is very difficult and expensive.

A Royal Commission later considered the school as 'one of the most remarkable instances of an abused trust'. The school survived until 1969, when it was amalgamated with Wilson's Hospital School. The Navan Shopping centre was built on the site of the school.

The 3rd Marquis of Headfort of Headfort House, Kells, had 7,443 acres in County Meath in 1876, with a valuation of £7,433 about £624,372 in modern money.

See page 54.

Christopher Armytage Nicholson of Balrath, Burry Kells, had 7,693 acres in County Meath in 1876 with a valuation of £6,277 about £527,268 in modern money. The family, originally from Yorkshire, then Lancashire, came to Ireland before the Cromwellian wars and then joined the wars on the wrong, Royalist, side. They didn't get their military wages until after the Restoration of Charles II in 1660, together with grants of land. The original grants in Monaghan were sold and in 1669 Gilbert Nicholson bought Balrath. This family, though playing significant roles in the Crown administration, picked up no formal titles.

Gilbert's successors were regularly High Sheriffs and justices of the peace in the county. There were regular marriages between the Nicholson heirs and senior figures in the Church of Ireland. One descendant married a daughter of the Lord Archbishop of Armagh and another, John Armytage Nicholson, High Sheriff, Deputy Lieutenant of Meath and a justice of the peace, married a daughter of the lord Bishop of Meath, who in turn was a nephew of the Earl of Caledon, who held 34,060 acres in Tyrone in 1876.

Balrath House passed to a descendant in the 1960s but was later sold.

Robert Fowler, a Trinity (Dublin) man, of Rahinston, Enfield, County Meath, had 8,026 acres in the county with a valuation of £6,884 about £578,256 in modern money. This estate is an interesting example of the relationship between the Church of Ireland and estates in Ireland. It is first recorded in the hands of the Fowler family when the head of the family was Lord Archbishop of Dublin, having been appointed by the Crown in person, George II. Robert Fowler had been Prebendary at Westminster. He was first appointed Lord Bishop of Killaloe and Kilfenora in 1771, before being translated to Dublin in 1773. He was appointed (sworn of) the Privy Council and became the 1st Chancellor of the Most Illustrious Order of St Patrick, the equivalent in Ireland of Knights of the Bath. His daughter, Mildred, married the Earl of Kilkenny. His son, the Rt Rev. Robert Fowler, was, successively Dean of St Patrick's Cathedral, Archdeacon of Dublin and Lord Bishop of Ossory and Ferns. He married the eldest daughter of Viscount Mountjoy, a landowner, and sister of the Earl of Blessington, another landowner. His son married a sister of the 3rd Earl of Erne whose family had 40,365 acres in 1876. When she died he married a daughter of the Marquis of Ormonde whose family had 27,725 acres in 1876. Later members of the family engaged in the Irish racing industry and there is still a stud farm at Rahinston.

The 14th Viscount Gormanston, of Gormanston, Castle Ballbriggan, County Meath, had 9,468 acres in Meath in 1876 with a valuation of £9,468 about £795,312 in modern money. The 14th Viscount also held 1,300 acres in County Dublin with a total acreage of 10,957 valued at £9,364. He was an officer in the 60th Regiment of foot and served during the Mutiny in India in 1857-58. He was later a Commissioner for Education in Ireland.

The peerage and the estate are both very ancient and intertwined with a great deal of Irish history, especially during the rebellion in 1641 and subsequently.

The family name of this peerage is Preston from the Lancashire manor and later city of that name. The first Baron Preston, an Irish peerage created between 1365 and 1370, obtained land at Gormanston, Co. Meath, and became Lord Chancellor of Ireland in 1388. The Prestons first came to Ireland before 1320 and by 1331 Roger De Preston was a justice of the Common pleas. In 1361 Sir Robert Preston was knighted on the field of battle by Lionel, Duke of Clarence and Earl of Ulster, who made the Gormanston holding a holding 'in perpetuity'. The Viscountcy came in 1478. In the wars between 1641 and 1649, the then Viscount, the 7th, was on the losing side, losing both Waterford and Galway, the latter the last Irish city to hold out against Cromwellian force, to sieges. He was outlawed for high treason and the title was cancelled.

In 1800 the 12th Viscount had the outlawry revoked and got the title back, just as the Irish House of Lords closed and with it went his seat. In 1868 the absence of a place to sit was remedied with a United Kingdom peerage, that of Baron Gormanston. There is a local legend that says when the head of the household is about to die, foxes gather around Gormanston Castle. The family crest has two foxes on it.

The castle was acquired by the Order of St Francis of Assisi, the Franciscans, in 1947 and has become a thriving secondary school. The peerage is still extant and the current holder, the 17th Viscount, lives in London.

The 10th Earl of Fingall of Kileen Castle, Dunshaughlin, County Meath, had 9,589 acres in the county in 1876 with a valuation of £8,680 about £729,120 in modern money. This title, now extinct, and estate, belonged to the Plunkett family, who were from time to time and among other things, Protestant Archbishops of Dublin but with a saint and martyr of the Catholic Church among their number. They were also, as a family, among the largest landowners in Ireland with a pedigree that really is lost in the mists of long ago, *'fado fado'* as they say in Ireland. Burke's *Landed Gentry* sets the tone:

> This noble family was of Danish origin, but its settlement in Ireland is so remote that nothing certain can be ascertained as to the precise period. So early as the 11th century, we find JOHN PLUNKETT, of Beaulieu, County Meath, the constant residence of the elder branch of his descendants. The successor at Beaulieu at the beginning of the 13th century, JOHN PLUNKETT, living at the time of HENRY III, had two sons, John, *ancestor of the* BARONS LOUTH; RICHARD, *of whom hereafter*. RICHARD PLUNKETT, of Rathregan, County Meath, who, with his son and heir, RICHARD PLUNKETT, by royal writs of parliamentary summons, was summoned to, and sat in, the parliaments and council of 1374; the one as a baron, and the other *'de consilio regis'*. (Councillor to the King)

In summary, subsequently, Christopher Plunkett who became Baron Plunkett in 1426, had seven sons, five of whom set up five separate branches of the Plunkett family. They had estates at Dunsany, Dunsoghly, Rathmore and two other places. The Earldom was bought in 1628 by the then Baron Kileen for a sum of £2,700, between half a million and a million in modern money, which is still the secret going rate for a peerage in these times.

The castle suffered an arson attack in 1981 but has been rebuilt and there is a stud farm nearby, run by the 12th Earl for many years. All the titles became extinct when he died in 1984.

Lord Athlumney of Somerville House, Navan, County Meath, had 10,213 acres in 1876 with a valuation of £9,131 about £767,004 in modern money. Bateman records this estate under the Irish title, Lord Athlumney, who was made Baron Meredyth in the peerage of the United Kingdom in 1866. The family name is Somerville and Sir William Meredyth Somerville was the MP for Drogheda and the Chief Secretary of Ireland between 1847 and 1852, the worst years of the Great Famine. Incompetent administration from London, together with a structure of grotesque laws, even for the period, made the famine hugely worse than it needed to be, had food been retained in the country and not exported. Athlumney lost his seat in Drogheda and the peerage became extinct in 1929 when the 2nd Baron Meredyth died. The Baronetcy is dormant but there are descendants recorded in Debrett's Peerage and Baronage of 2011.

The 5th Marquis of Lansdowne had 12,995 acres in County Meath in 1876 with a valuation of £10,790 about £906,360 in modern money.

See page 170.

James Lennox Naper held 18,863 acres in County Meath in 1876, with a valuation of £15,581 about £1,308,804 in modern money. This Eton-educated landowner also had 176 acres in Co. Westmeath, which together with his Meath acreage, came to a total of 19,039 acres with a valuation of £15,658.

Burke's *Landed Gentry* claims, in a claim repeated by Ferres, that the Naper estates eventually rose to 180,000 acres in counties Meath, Westmeath and Cavan, helped by the colonel's marriage to the sister of Sir William Petty, a senior Dublin Castle official. This official was the ancestor of the Marquis of Lansdowne.

Burke's sets the family much further back in Irish history and has the first Baron sitting for Kerry in the Irish Parliament in 1295.

The 180,000 acres would have put the estate into the top fifteen landowners of the whole UK in 1872 (See *Who Owns Britain and Ireland*) It would be interesting to see how this claim was composed. The actual Naper estate in 1876 is as set out above. It would not take much addition to the Marquis of Lansdowne's estates to get to the figure of 180,000 acres, however, but he was not a close relative, if a part of the Petty cousinhood.

Predecessors of James Naper regularly held posts in the county, mainly as High Sheriffs. None appear to have been MPs, and although intermarrying with the aristocracy, no peerage ever seems to have come their way. Burke's has this quotation about him: 'A busy landlord and writer, he served as chairman of the Poor Law Guardians during the Famine years and subsidised the emigration of tenants to Canada in the 1830s.'

Emigration had always been a safety valve for the Irish population, especially as that population exploded after the early 1800s. Landlords had often helped their tenants to get away by paying their passage to North America. But during the famine many died on the side of the road, especially in the winter of 1847. Administration of the poor law and the workhouses was inadequate, incompetent and lethally inefficient. Not many landlords were able to rise to the situation, nor the system with them.

The estate was damaged by a dissolute marriage in the 1940s and seems to have been down to less than 1,000 acres by the 1960s. The house burned down in 1964. In 1967 the Land Commission acquired 600 acres from the estate. Members of the family were still farming land nearby until recently.

The 6th Earl of Darnley of Cobham Hall Gravesend had 21,858 acres in Meath in 1876 with a valuation of £18,186 about £1,527,624 in modern money. Bateman, acting on the Earl's update, considerably increases the Meath acreage, to 25,463 acres, and adds 9,309 acres in Kent. The total acreage comes to 34,772 acres with a valuation of £37,350.

To those who remember their history, the Earl of Darnley, who actually had lots of other titles, a vile temper and a drink problem, was the husband of Mary

Queen of Scots. That Earl of Darnley was murdered, a murder in which his wife was implicated and for which, along with a treason charge, she was eventually executed. The title Earl of Darnley was created twice in the peerage of Scotland and once in the peerage of Ireland. Dynastically, the Scottish titles were important as they potentially conveyed claims to the Crown of Scotland – the 4th (Irish) Earl of Darnley applied for the Scottish Dukedom of Lennox in 1829.

The first member of this family was John Blight, a city of London adventurer who came to Ireland in 1641 to try and acquire estates confiscated by Cromwell. He did. He became an MP in the first Parliament after the Restoration in 1660. His eldest son and successor was made a peer in Ireland as Baron Clifton in 1721. In 1725 he became Earl of Darnley. A later descendant, the 4th Earl, applied to the House of Lords to be treated as the successor to the 6th Duke of Lennox and the 4th Duke of Richmond. He was able to do this because the royal line of Stuart ran out of male heirs when Cardinal the Duke of York died in 1807. Darnley had links through the female line to the Scottish title holders. The House of Lords never reached a decision on the application, which is now timed out for good, since 1999 and the expulsion of most of the hereditary peers from the House of Lords.

In 1909 the 8th Earl sold the town of Atboy in Co. Meath, part of the estate. The Darnley Estate Office closed in 1948 and the family now live in Hereford, where the Countess was made Lord Lieutenant in 2008.

List of owners of over 1,000 acres with top 20 ranked by acreage in 1876

		Acreage	Valuation 1876 (£)	Valuation current(£)
1	Darnley, Earl of, Clifton Lodge, Athboy	21,858	18,186	1,527,624
2	Naper, James Lennox, Lougherew, Oldcastle	18,863	15,581	1,308,804
3	Lansdowne, Marquis of, Berkeley Sq., London	12,995	10,790	906,360
4	Athlumney, Lord, Somerville, Co. Meath	10,213	9,131	767,004
5	Fingall, Earl of, Kileen Castle, Dunshaughlin	9,589	8,680	729,120
6	Gormanston, Viscount, Gormanston Castle, Co. Meath	9,468	7,875	661,500
7	Fowler, Robert, Robinstown, Enfield	8,026	6,884	578,256

		Acreage	Valuation 1876 (£)	Valuation current(£)
8	Nicholson, Christopher A., Balrath Burry, Kells	7,693	6,277	527,268
9	Headfort, Marquis of, Headfort House, Kells	7,443	10,188	855,792
10	Preston, John Joseph, Ballinter, Navan	7,415	6,839	574,476
11	Taylor, Rt Hon. Thomas E., Ardgillan Castle, Balbriggan	7,135	6,227	523,068
12	Conyngham, The Marquis, Slane Castle, Slane, Co. Meath	7,060	6,670	560,280
13	Trustees of Edward, Bligh Hamilton, Charles, William and Hamilton, Arthur, 40 Lower Dominick Street, Dublin	5,289	3,739	314,076
14	Rotheram, Edward, Crossdrum, Oldcastle	5,046	4,672	392,448
15	Corbally, Hon. Mrs, Corbalton Hall. Tara. Navan. Co. Meath	5,035	5,220	438,480
16	Singleton. H.C., Aclare, Drumconrath	4,877	4,352	365,568
17	Gerrard, Thomas, Boyne Hill, Navan	4,748	5,034	422,856
18	Magan, Mrs E.G., Killyon Hill of Down, Co. Westmeath	4,418	3,086	259,224
19	Wade, Robert C., Clonbraney, Crosskeel	4,160	4,578	384,552
20	Hussey, Malachi S., Weston, Naul, Balbriggan	4,100	2,659	223,356
21	Jameson, John J., St Marnock. Malahide. Co. Dublin	4,092	3,741	314,224
22	Farrell, John Arthur, Moynalty	4,084	3,810	320,040
23	Dunsany, Lord, Dunsany Castle, Dunsany, Co. Meath	3,988	3,883	326,172
24	Bolton, Francis G., Bective, Navan	3,516	3,034	254,856
25	Dillon, Sir John Bart, Lismullen, Navan	3,209	3,106	260,904
26	Russell, Earl, 37 Chesham Place, London	3,167	3,763	316,092
27	Rothwell, Thomas, Rockfield Kells, Co. Meath	3,161	3,407	286,188

		Acreage	Valuation 1876 (£)	Valuation current(£)
28	Bryan, George, Jenkinstown Castle, Co. Kilkenny	3,055	1,953	164,052
29	Trimleston, Lord, 24 Park Lane, London	3,025	2,971	249,564
30	Garnett, William Stawell, Williamstown House, Kells	3,014	3,184	267,456
31	Church Temporalities Commissioners, Dublin	2,919	3,874	325,416
32	Hussey, Edward, Rathkenny, Slane, Co. Meath	2,917	2,604	218,736
33	Boylan, Thomas, Hilltown House, Drogheda	2,914	2,970	249,480
34	Malton, Isabella, 16 Great Cumberland St, Hyde Park, London	2,883	2,215	186,060
35	Barnwall, Thomas, Bloomsbury, Kells	2,782	2,754	231,336
36	Boyne, Lord, Burwarton, Shropshire, England	2,739	2,972	249,648
37	Waller, James Noble, Allenstown, Navan	2,687	2,642	221,928
38	Murphy, William, Mount Merrion, Stillorgan, Co. Dublin	2,660	2,665	223,860
39	Tisdall, John, Charesfort, Kells, Co. Meath	2,653	2,896	243,264
40	Coddington, Henry B., Oldbridge, Drogheda	2,604	2,678	224,952
41	O'Ferrall, Edward More Reps, Monasterevan	2,598	2,881	242,004
42	Woods, Hans H., Milverton, Balbriggan	2,572	2,371	199,164
43	Whitshed, Miss E., Collon House, Co. Louth	2,470	1,593	133,812
44	Bomford, George, Oakley Park, Kells	2,436	2,405	202,020
45	M'Evoy, Edward, Tobertynan, Rathmolyon	2,411	1,877	157,668
46	Kearney, Patrick J., Milton House, Clonmellon, Co. Westmeath	2,374	2,297	192,948
47	Mayo, Earl of, Hayes, Navan	2,360	2,192	184,128

		Acreage	Valuation 1876 (£)	Valuation current(£)
48	Leslie, John, Glasslough, Co. Monahan	2,344	1,746	146,664
49	Everard, Nugent T., Randalstown, Navan	2,311	2,188	183,792
50	M'Veigh, Ferdinand, Drewstown, Athboy, Co. Meath	2,270	2,135	180,852
51	Langford Lord, Summer Hill Castle, Summer Hill, Co. Meath	2,231	2,175	182,700
52	Montgomery, Alex S., Kilmor House, Balliver, Kells	2,199	1,839	154,476
53	Westenra, Captain J.J., United Services Club, Dublin	2,164	1,302	109,368
54	Trustees of Thomas Bligh, 40 Lower Dominick Street, Dublin	2,154	2,229	187,236
55	Thompson, William, Rathnally, Trim	2,154	2,225	186,900
56	Chaloner, Richard, Kingscourt, Moynalty	2,100	1,726	144,984
57	Howth, Earl of, Howth Castle, Co Dublin	2,061	2,088	175,392
58	Masserene, Lord, Oriel Temple, Collon	2,045	1,122	94,248
59	Fitzherbert, Thomas, Blackcastle, Navan	2,011	2,694	226,296
60	Pepper, Thomas St George, Ballygarth Castle, Co. Meath	1,884	2,070	173,880
61	Thomond, Marchioness reps of, England	1,779	1,894	159,096
62	Hodgens, Henry, Beaufort House, Rathfarnham	1,729	1,325	111,300
63	Rotheram, George, Fairy Hill, Blackrock	1,701	1,048	88,032
64	Farrell, James, 30 Merrion Sq., Dublin	1,673	1,574	132,216
65	Shaw, William J.A., Travellers Club, London	1,673	1,496	125,664
66	Caldwell, Charles B., England	1,661	1,778	149,352
67	Winter, James S., Agher, Enfield	1,640	1,648	138,432
68	Hone, Nathaniel, Malahide, Dublin	1,618	936	78,624

		Acreage	Valuation 1876 (£)	Valuation current(£)
69	Woods, George, Milverton House, Balbriggan	1,585	1,504	126,336
70	Ennis, John, Athlone	1,573	1,817	152,628
71	O'Reilly, Anthony Reps, Baltrasna, Oldcastle	1,536	738	61,992
72	Hamilton, Rev. James, Ballymacoll, Dunboyne, Co. Meath	1,535	1,637	137,508
73	Bond, Willoughby, Farragh, Longford	1,525	1,372	115,248
74	Reynell, Samuel A., Archerstown, Killucan	1,519	1,431	120,204
75	Johnston, Eliza M., Wanestown, Dunsany, Navan	1,503	1,792	150,526
76	Rowley, Hon. H.L., Carlton Club, London	1,492	1,545	129,780
77	Balfour, Blaney T., Townley Hall, Drogheda	1,453	1,201	100,884
78	Rynd, R.F. Reps, Ryndville, Enfield	1,426	1,449	121,716
79	De Bath, Sir Henry P. Bart, London	1,407	1,231	103,404
80	Scott, Rev. Charles B., Deansyard, Westminster	1,390	1,408	118,272
81	Chapman, William, Southill, Delvin	1,386	1,217	102,228
82	Blackwood, Hon. and Rev. W.S., -	1,374	1,080	90,720
83	Caddell, Robert, Harbourstown, Balbriggan	1,372	1,365	114,660
84	Joly, Jasper R., 38 Rathmines Road, Co. Dublin	1,346	1,032	86,688
85	Garnett, Samuel, Arch Hall, Navan	1,336	1,306	109,704
86	Trustees of G. Hamilton, Chester Place, Chester Sq., London	1,333	1,210	101,640
87	Donaldson, Richard, Hartstown, Clonmellon	1,321	1,207	101,388
88	Taylor, General Richard C.H., Ardgillan Castle, Balbriggan	1,304	1,218	102,312
89	Essex, Earl of, London	1,303	2,443	205,212
90	Hartley, Richard W., Beechpark, Clonsilla, Co. Dublin	1,298	1,328	111,552
91	Rich, George W., -	1,284	759	63,756
92	Devine, Anne Reps, St Helens, England	1,271	1,148	96,432

		Acreage	Valuation 1876 (£)	Valuation current(£)
93	Coghill, Sir John J., Castletownsend, Co. Cork	1,269	1,108	93,072
94	Gardiner, Rev. William, -	1,253	800	67,200
95	Goslin, Mrs, Vesy Place, Kingstown	1,250	1,231	103,404
96	Burrowes, T.A. Reps, -	1,248	992	83,328
97	Dyas, Nathaniel H., Athboy Lodge, Athboy	1,237	1,331	111,804
98	Preston, Nathaniel F., Swainstown, Dunsany, Navan	1,234	1,072	90,048
99	Cusack, Sir Ralph S., 24 Rutland Sq., Dublin	1,229	1,062	89,208
100	Smyth, Richard A., Lara, Portarlington	1,220	960	80,640
101	Purcell, Rev. Francis, Tradley, Litchfield, England	1,217	1,226	102,984
102	Murphy, J.S., Cork	1,196	907	76,188
103	Garnett, Richard, Somerset, Clonee	1,195	1,467	123,228
104	Corballis, John R., Rathoath	1,182	866	72,744
105	Cairnes, Thomas, Stameen House, Drogheda	1,175	740	62,160
106	Pollock, Maria, Mountainstown, Navan	1,174	905	76,020
107	Murland, William J., Fitzwilliam Sq., Dublin	1,167	771	64,764
108	Kingston, Mrs Jane, -	1,166	945	79,380
109	Rowley, Standish G., Sylvan Park, Crosskeel	1,165	826	69,384
110	Rowley, Hon. Richard, -	1,144	869	72,996
111	Forbes, A.K., Alfred H. Wynne Agent, Collon	1,140	895	75,180
112	Verschoyle, Mrs, Eden Sq., London	1,137	1,133	95,172
113	M'Dermott, Thos Reps, Wicklow	1,125	745	62,580
114	Governors of Steven's Hospital, Dublin	1,120	1,228	103,152
115	Barlow, John, Sybil Hill, Co. Dublin	1,118	1,048	88,032
116	Cullen, His Eminence Paul Cardinal (In trust), 59 Eccles St, Dublin	1,101	1,011	84,924
117	Carty, Thomas Reps, Drogheda	1,094	946	79,464

		Acreage	Valuation 1876 (£)	Valuation current(£)
118	Sheffield, Earl of, England	1,085	1,031	86,604
119	Grote, Joseph, Newcastle-upon-Tyne, England	1,080	1,042	87,528
120	Macann, James Reps, Drogheda	1,072	1,063	89,292
121	Thunder, Michael, Lagore, Dunshauglin	1,065	1,072	90,048
122	Chambers, E.C. Reps, -	1,048	1,230	103,320
123	Leinster, Duke of, Carton, Maynooth	1,044	1,075	90,300
124	Browne, Anthony, Elm Grove, Balincor	1,017	855	71,820
125	Pratt, Mervyn, Cabra Castle, Kingscourt	1,014	793	66,612
126	Nugent, George, -	1,013	691	58,044
127	Gannon, Edward J., Stephen's Green Club, Dublin	1,007	970	81,480

The 20 largest landowners in County Meath by valuation in 1876

		Acreage	Valuation 1876 (£)	Valuation current (£)
1	Darnley, Earl of, Clifton Lodge, Athboy	21,858	18,186	1,527,624
2	Naper, James Lennox, Lougherew, Oldcastle	18,863	15,581	1,308,804
3	Lansdowne, Marquis of, Berkeley Sq., London	12,995	10,790	906,360
4	Headfort, Marquis of, Headfort House, Kells	7,443	10,188	855,792
5	Athlumney, Lord, Somerville, Co. Meath	10,213	9,131	767,004
6	Fingall, Earl of, Kileen Castle, Dunshaughlin	9,589	8,680	729,120
7	Gormanstown, Vicount, Gormanstown Castle, Co. Meath	9,468	7,875	661,500
8	Fowler, Robert, Robinstown, Enfield	8,026	6,884	578,256
9	Preston, John Joseph, Ballinter, Navan	7,415	6,839	574,476

		Acreage	Valuation 1876 (£)	Valuation current (£)
10	Conyngham, The Marquis, Slane Castle, Slane, Co. Meath	7,060	6,670	560,280
11	Nicholson, Christopher A., Balrath, Burry, Kells	7,693	6,277	527,268
12	Taylor, Rt Hon. Thomas E., Ardgillan Castle, Balbriggan	7,135	6,227	523,068
13	Corbally, Hon. Mrs, Corbalton Hall, Tara, Navan, Co. Meath	5,035	5,220	438,480
14	Gerrard, Thomas, Boyne Hill, Navan	4,748	5,034	422,856
15	Rotheram, Edward, Crossdrum, Oldcastle	5,046	4,672	392,448
16	Wade, Robert C., Clonbraney, Crosskeel	4,160	4,578	384,552
17	Singleton H.C., Aclare, Drumconrath	4,877	4,352	365,568
18	Dunsany, Lord, Dunsany Castle, Dunsany, Co. Meath	3,988	3,883	326,172
19	Church Temporalities Commissioners, Dublin	2,919	3,874	325,416
20	Farrell, John Arthur, Moynalty	4,084	3,810	320,040

MONAGHAN

	1876	2020 est
Population in County Monaghan	112,785	60,483
All owners of land	1,471	86,217
Percentage of the population	1.3	-
Owners of nothing at all	111,315	19,188
Percentage of the population	98.7	-
Size of County	311,439	320,439 acres
Number of dwellings (of which rented)	21,821 (20,351)	21,176
Number of owned farm holdings	637	4,365

County comparisons

	Acreage 1876	Population 1876
County Monaghan	311,439	112,785
Westmorland, England	335,160	65,010
Fife, Scotland	304,363	160,735
Brecknock, Wales	302,237	59,901

Evelyn Philip Shirley MP of Loughgea, Carrickmacross, had 26,386 acres in the county in 1876, with a valuation of £20,744 about £1,742,496 in modern money. Bateman corrects the address of this Eton-educated MP to Ettington Park, Stratford-on-Avon, a place the Shirley family had occupied since the time of Henry VII (reigned 1485 to 1509) in an unbroken male line.

Evelyn Shirley had, in addition to the Monaghan acres at Lough Fea, 1,769 acres in Warwick and 605 acres in Worcester; a total of 28,760 acres with a valuation of £23,744. The Shirley estate was the scene of serious and extended violence even before the Great Famine began, as Shirley, an absentee landlord operating through agents, tried to evict tenants in arrears with their rents. At one stage his agent, with armed troops and the bailiffs from Carrickmacross, faced a crowd of over 20,000 people. The troops panicked and fired on the crowd outside a Catholic church, killing a 12-year-old child. Local legend has it that the only reason the troops and bailiffs weren't overwhelmed and massacred on the spot was due to the intervention of the parish priest. The lack of any weapons carried by the tenantry may also have had something to do with it. During this period

Shirley was MP for Monaghan and also High Sheriff. His agent, Sandy Mitchell, was described as the most tyrannical estate agent the tenants had ever known. His replacement, Trench, wasn't much better. He had called out the troops who shot the child, having said that he would collect the rents at the point of a bayonet if he had to.

The child's parents, having no money to pay for the funeral and in arrears with rent, were later evicted by Trench. Their hut was torn down, they were forced onto the road and lost sight of to history, possibly via the workhouse.

Most of the estate was sold off through the Land Commission before the First World War, although the family continued to reside on a residual 1,000 acres until well into the twentieth century.

Whatever the Irish landlords did try to do to relieve distress, they faced a civil servant, Charles Trevelyan, head of administration for famine relief in Ireland, who summarised the religious, racial and economic philosophy of the British Empire towards the Irish when he said, 'The judgement of God sent the calamity to teach the Irish a lesson, that calamity must not be too much mitigated... The real evil with which we have to contend is not the physical evil of the Famine, but the moral evil of the selfish, perverse and turbulent character of the people.'

The Government's chief economist, Nassau Senior, went even further: '[existing policies] will not kill more than one million Irish in 1848 and that will scarcely be enough to do much good.'

The Most Honourable the Marquis of Bath, of 48 Berkeley Square, London, had 22,762 acres in Monaghan in 1876, with a valuation of £19,651 about £1,650684 in modern money. Bateman, in no small way a minor eccentric, did not give this Eton-educated landowner his honorific prefix 'The most Hon.'. He's just the Marquis of Bath, of Longleat, Warminster, Wilts, who, like his neighbour, Shirley, had held the lands at Longleat since the time of Henry VII, in unbroken male succession. In 1876, in addition to the Monaghan acres at Farney, Bath had 19,984 acres in Wiltshire, 8,212 acres in Somerset, 699 acres in Hereford, 3,508 acres in Shropshire and 409 acres in Sussex, for a total of 55,574 acres with a valuation of £68,015. Bath was about 103 in the ranks of landlords by acreage and by valuation the thirty-eighth richest landowner in Great Britain and Ireland.

The Bath estate in Monaghan was administered, like Shirley's, by agents. It suffered, pre-famine, from the rising tide of land agitation and rent resistance, with frequent encounters between hostile crowds and the militia and bailiffs. The growing resistance to landlords and the lack of security of tenure failed to penetrate an obdurate bureaucracy in Whitehall, who chose, Canute-like, to ignore the tide of history flowing towards them.

The Shirley estate records are kept at the Public Records Office of Northern Ireland and state that while Shirley visited his estates at least twice a year, Bath almost never did, making him a true absentee. The two families had a common ancestor in Walter Devereux, the 1st Earl of Essex, who got the Monaghan acres via the Elizabethan plantations.

The Earl of Dartrey, of Dartrey, Castle Rockcorry, had 17,345 acres in the county in 1876, with a valuation of £12,883 about £1,802,172 in modern money. The Eton-educated Earl of Dartrey had land in three other Irish counties: 17,732 acres in Monaghan, 1,665 acres in Armagh and 1,792 acres in Louth, with 5 acres in Devon. The total acreage was 30,112 with a valuation of £21,669.

This family came to Ireland at the end of the Elizabethan era but advanced their position when a son joined Cromwell in 1641 as a cavalry officer. As with so many others, they were MPs in both the pre-Union Parliament of Ireland and in the British Parliament afterwards. The Earldom was created in 1866, for the then Baron Dartrey, a government whip in the Palmerston and Russell administrations. Members of the family made senior ranks in both the Royal Navy and in the British Army. The 3rd Earl died in 1933 without male heirs and the title became extinct. The contents of the family home, Dartry House, a vast rambling building, were sold off in 1937, much going to the Hammond Lane foundry in Dublin for £3,000 as scrap. The house itself was demolished in 1946.

The 5th Lord Rossmore of Rossmore Park, County Monaghan, had 14,839 acres in the county in 1876, with a valuation of £13,427 about £1,127,868 in modern money. This title still exists and is held by the Eton-educated William Warner Westenra, the 7th Baron. He lives in England. His ancestor in 1876 was educated at Rugby School, a rare change from the Irish landlord preference for Eton. But he reverted to type when it came to the army, where he served in the 1st Life Guards and the 9th Lancers. He was Lord Lieutenant of Monaghan until 1921.

The estate partly survived into the twentieth century and with it the house. This was abandoned in the mid 1970s due to dry rot. At one stage the family owned half the island of Jura, the possession of an illegitimate daughter of the 6th Duke of Hamilton who married a Rossmore.

The family are of Dutch origin and were widely employed in Europe as mercenaries in the sixteenth and seventeenth centuries. Ferres tells us that the Westenras are descended from the family of Van Wassenaer of Wassenburg. They settled in Ireland during the reign of Charles II and became citizens of Ireland by act of the Irish Parliament.

Sir John Leslie of Glasslough County Monaghan had 13,621 acres in the county in 1876, with a valuation of £11,486 about £964,824 in modern money. Bateman corrects this entry by restoring John Leslie's Baronetage and he becomes Sir John Leslie Bart, of Glasslough, Co. Monaghan with, in addition to the Donegal acres, 13,674 acres in Monaghan, 1,103 in Tyrone and 877 in Fermanagh. He had a total of 44,481 acres, with a valuation of £16,579.

Sir John was educated at Harrow School, and was an officer in the 1st Life Guards. He sat as MP for Co. Monaghan. The family trace their recent ancestry to John Leslie, Bishop of the Isles, who moved to the Church of Ireland diocese of Raphoe and Clogher, acquiring the Glasslough estate on the way. In the years leading up to the twentieth century the family became Catholic, with Ampleforth College swapped for Harrow School and the Irish Guards for the Life Guards.

The estate, though much smaller, remains in the hands of the family.

General the Viscount Templetown of Templepatrick, County Antrim, had 12,845 acres in Monaghan in 1876, with a valuation of £8,649 about £726,516 in modern money. He also had 11,924 acres in Co. Antrim, to give him a total estate of 24,769 acres, with a valuation of £19,217. He was educated at Eton, commanded the Coldstream Guards in the Crimea and was wounded at the Battle of Inkerman. Afterwards he commanded the 60th Rifles and the 2nd Life Guards, and he finished his military career as a general in command of Western and Southern districts. He sat as MP for County Antrim before he succeeded to the Viscountcy. The peerage became extinct in 1981 with the death of the 5th Viscount.

Anne Adile Hope of Castleblaney had 11,700 acres in County Monaghan in 1876, with a valuation of £10,333 about £867,972 in modern money. By the time we get to Bateman in 1883 Anne Adile has become Mrs Hope of Deepdene, Dorking, in Surrey, and is both a very considerable and very wealthy landholder. She has, with the Monaghan acreage, 3,931 acres in Surrey, 4,893 acres in Gloucester and 1,249 acres in Warwick for a total of 21,773 acres, with a valuation of £22,138. She was the wife of Henry Thomas Hope of Deepdene, who was brother of Sir Alexander Beresford Hope (their mother was a Beresford). Anne Adile's maiden name was Bichat. The Monaghan acres were almost certainly part of the Beresford family estates.

Edward Scudamore Lucas (his representatives) of Castle Shane had 9,955 acres in the county in 1876 with a valuation of £7,934 about £666,456 in modern money By 1883 and his final edition Bateman has amended this entry to show Edward Scudamore Lucas as the holder of the Monaghan acres, with his mother holding 5,706 acres in Hereford and 804 acres in Monmouth. This gave the family a total estate of 16,465 acres with a valuation of £13,283. Bateman notes that he was educated at Eton.

The English ancestor of this family, Thomas Lucas of Saxham in Suffolk, had an interesting job. He was solicitor to Henry VIII, so presumably he was a specialist in matters of divorce.

The first Lucas at Castle Shane was an officer in the army and had obtained the lands there before 1657, when his will was probated. By 1876 the estate had passed to a nephew of the previous holder, the Rt Hon. Edward Lucas, who adopted the additional name Scudamore and was an honorary colonel in the 4th Battalion of the King's Shropshire Light Infantry. He was also a justice of the peace and a Deputy Lieutenant of the County. He had an additional estate and residence at Kentchurch Court in Hereford, where the family still live.

Sir T.B. Lennard of England had 7,920 acres in Monaghan in 1876, with a valuation of £10,908 about £916,272 in modern money. Bateman corrects this entry to Sir Thomas Barrett-Lennard Bart, of Belhus, Romford, who in addition to the Monaghan acreage, had 3,961 acres in Essex, 2,124 acres in Norfolk, 570 acres in Suffolk and 107 acres in Fermanagh for a total of 14,412 acres with a valuation of £18,779. The estate papers are held in the Public Records Office in Northern Ireland but only go as far as 1866. There is an extensive record of the 1st Baronet's Parliamentary activity in the History of Parliament series (See Bibliography) – he voted for Catholic emancipation in 1832.

William Ancketill, of Ancketill's Grove, Emyvale, had 7,504 acres in Monaghan in 1876, with a valuation of £4,304 about £361,536 in modern money. According to Ferres, citing Burke's *Landed Gentry* (see Bibliography), this family are mentioned in the first Domesday of 1086 and lived in Dorset.

They appear in Ireland in in the 1600s, with Captain Oliver Ancketill as a JP and High Sheriff of Monaghan in 1662. The estate was confirmed to the family by Charles II in the person of Matthew Anctkill.

The holder in 1876 was a lieutenant in the Royal Tyrone Fusiliers and a Deputy Lieutenant of the County. The estate was mortgaged by him in 1884 to the Scottish Provident Insurance Association. Scottish Provident began evictions almost at once: the estate was put up for sale in the Encumbered Estates Court in 1886 and the Scottish Provident became absolute owners of the land, with the exception of Ancketill Grove House, demesne and three townlands, according to Ferres.

In 1899, Scottish Provident received £4,800 in advances from the Government for sales to sixty-two tenants. In 1901, William Anketell received £3,820 for sales to thirty-three tenants (*Dublin Gazette*, 26 July 1901, pp. 1045–

1046). Sometime thereafter the Ancketills removed to Killyfaddy, near Clogher, Co. Tyrone. Ancketill Grove was purchased from the Irish Land Commission in 1922 by a local farmer. Ferres acknowledges the assistance of Henry Skeath in compiling the article.

Top 50 owners in Monaghan ranked by acreage in 1876

		Acreage	Valuation 1876 (£)	Valuation current (£)
1	Shirley, Evelyn Philip, Loughgea, Carrickmacross	26,386	20,744	1,742,496
2	Bath, Most Hon. the Marquess of, 48 Berkeley Sq., London, W	22,762	19,651	1,650,684
3	Dartrey, the Earl of, Datrey Castle, Rockcorry	17,345	12,883	1,082,172
4	Rossmore, the Lord, Rossmore, Monaghan	14,839	13,427	1,127,868
5	Leslie, John, Glasslough, Co. Monaghan	13,621	11,486	964,824
6	Templetown, Viscount, Templepatrick	12,845	8,649	726,516
7	HHope, Anne, Adile, Castleblaney	11,700	10,333	867,972
8	Lucas, Edward Scudamore. Reps, Castleshane. Monaghan	9,955	7,934	666,456
9	Lennard, Sir T.B., England	7,920	10,908	916,272
10	Ancketell, Wm, Ancketell Grove, Emmyvale	7,504	4,304	361,536
11	Hamilton, James, Cornacassa, Monaghan	7,315	4,168	351,624
12	Leslie, Emily, Ballybay	5,463	5,073	426,132
13	Madden, John, Hilton Park, Clones	4,644	3,467	291,228
14	Singleton, Thomas Crawford, Fortislington, Emyvale	4,489	1,378	115,752
15	Westenra, Henrietta, Queen's County	4,483	2,091	175,644
16	Shirley, Horatio, Portman Sq., London	4,197	2,829	237,636
17	Rose, Gertrude, Mullaghmore, Tedavnet	3,942	2,187	183,708

		Acreage	Valuation 1876 (£)	Valuation current (£)
18	Ker, Andre Allen Murray, Newbliss House, Newbliss	3,605	3,265	27,300
19	Woodright, William, Gola House, Scotstown.	3,264	1,048	88,032
20	Plunket, The Rt Hon. Lord, Old Connought, Bray	3,166	2,385	200,340
21	Brownlow, William Abbeyleix, Queen's County	2,959	2,394	201,096
22	Tennison, William, Shantoney, Castleblaney	2,696	2,013	169,092
23	Verner, Sir Wm Bart, Church Hill, Verner's Bridge, Moy	2,526	2,021	169,764
24	Lewis, Henry Owen, 43 Fitzwilliam Sq., Dublin	2,488	1,608	135,072
25	Fitzherbert, Thomas, Navan	2,387	1,877	157,668
26	Forster, Wm Reps, Ballymure, Clones	2,093	2,024	170,016
27	Forster, Sir Geo Bart, Coolderry, Carrickmacross	2,062	1,210	101,640
28	Clonmel, Lord, Naas	1,952	1,463	122,892
29	Coote, Captain Thomas, Raconnel House, Monaghan	1,905	1,746	146,664
30	Kenny, Plunkett, Rocksavage, Inniskreen, Dundalk	1,867	1,595	133,980
31	Mayne, Rev. Charles Reps, Killaloe, Co. Clare	1,810	1,240	104,160
32	Kane, William Francis De Visme, Drumreaske House, Monaghan	1,770	1,042	87,528
33	Mayne, Colburn, London	1,640	1,114	93,576
34	Church Temporalities Commissioners, 24 Upper Merrion St, Dublin	1,519	1,972	165,648
35	Quinn, Rev. John C., Rathfrieland, Newry	1,471	1,152	96,768
36	Langdale, Charles, The Abbey, Celbridge	1,390	1,090	91,560
37	Hamilton, William, Dublin	1,265	907	76,188
38	Evatt, Samuel Robert B., Mount Louis, Smithboro	1,241	999	83,916

		Acreage	Valuation 1876 (£)	Valuation current (£)
39	Bunbury, Kane, Wicklow	1,226	991	83,244
40	Fitzgerald, John Reps, Castleblaney	1,215	788	66,192
41	Montgomery, Alexander Nixon, Delgany, Co. Wicklow	1,186	751	63,084
42	Crofton, Charles, Dublin	1,136	528	44,352
43	Bolton, Richard Reps, Castlering, Knockbridge	1,134	1,035	86,940
44	Rowley, Henry Reps, Rockmullen, Ballybay	1,133	876	73,584
45	Johnston, Rev. Walter, The Rectory, Ballymena	1,110	1,049	88,116
46	Stanley, William Stone, Paulton, Southampton, England	1,050	747	62,748
47	Leslie, Captain John, Kiltybegs, Carrickmacross	1,027	835	70,140
48	Lloyd, Lieutenant Colonel, Ballyleck House, Monghan	999	899	75,516
49	Lentaigne, John, Tallaght House, Co. Dublin	976	971	81,564
50	Denny Anthony Reps, In Chancery	939	733	61,572

Top 20 owners by valuation/income in Monaghan in 1876

		Acreage	Valuation 1876 (£)	Valuation current (£)
1	Shirley, Evelyn Phillip, Loughgea, Carrickmacross	26,386	20,744	1,742,496
2	Bath, Most Hon. the Marquess of, 48 Berkeley Sq., London	22,762	19,651	1,650,684
3	Rossmore, the Lord, Rossmore, Monaghan	14,839	13,427	1,127,868
4	Dartrey, the Earl of, Datrey Castle, Rockcorry	17,345	12,883	1,082,172
5	Leslie, John, Glasslough, Co. Monaghan	13,621	11,486	964,824
6	Lennard, Sir T.B., England	7,920	10,908	916,272
7	HHope, Anne Adile, Castleblaney	11,700	10,333	867,972
8	Templetown, Viscount, Templepatrick	`12,845	8,649	726,516

		Acreage	Valuation 1876 (£)	Valuation current (£)
9	Lucas, Edward William, Lucas Edward L, Reps, Castleshane	9,955	7,934	666,456
10	Leslie, Emily, Ballybay	5,463	5,073	426,132
11	Ancketell, Wm, Ancketell Grove, Emmyvale	7,504	4,304	361,536
12	Hamilton, James, Cornacassa, Monaghan	7,315	4,168	351,624
13	Madden, John, Hilton Park, Clones	4,644	3,467	291,228
14	Ker, Andre Allen Murray, Newbliss House, Newbliss	3,605	3,265	27,300
15	Shirley, Horatio, Portman Sq., London	4,197	2,829	237,636
16	Brownlow, William Abbeyleix, Queen's County	2,959	2,394	201,096
17	Plunket, The Rt Hon. Lord, Old Connought, Bray	3,166	2,385	200,340
18	Rose, Gertrude, Mullaghmore, Tedavnet	3,942	2,187	183,708
19	Westenra, Henrietta, Queen's County	4,483	2,091	175,644
20	Forster, Wm Reps, Ballymure, Clones	2,093	2,024	170,016

ROSCOMMON

	1876	2020 Est
Population in County Roscommon	141,246	64,065
All owners of land	707	59,292
Percentage of the population	0.5	–
Owners of nothing at all	140,539	21,833
Percentage of the population	99.5	–
Size of County	577,998	629,760 acres
Number of dwellings (of which rented in 1876, owned in 2020)	25,792 (25,085)	23,601
Number of owned farm holdings	856	5,313

County comparisons

	Acreage 1876	Population 1876
County Roscommon	577,998	141,246
Cheshire, England	602,219	561,201
Angus, Scotland	555,994	257,567
Carmarthen, Wales	510,574	115,710

The Hon. L.H. King-Harman reps of, Rockingham, Boyle, had 29,242 acres in the county in 1876 with a valuation of £18,441.

See page 277.

Henry Sandford Pakenham-Mahon of Strokestown House, County Roscommon, had 28,980 acres in the county in 1876, with a valuation of £14,116 about £1,185,744 in modern money. The estate started with a captain from Cromwell's army sometime around 1660. (This was the year of the restoration of the Monarchy in England, so this does not quite reconcile.)

Bateman gives no school for this cavalry officer in the 8th Hussars but gives him 1,143 acres in Westmeath, which, with the the Roscommon acreage adds up to 28,123 acres, with a valuation of £15,080.

The house is now the official National Irish Famine Museum. The estate was the scene of one of the Famine tragedies. The first was the famine itself, which killed thousands. The then owner, Major Denis Mahon, tried to clear the estate by shipping evicted tenants to Quebec in Canada. On one ship about one-third of the passengers died and in 1847 Major Mahon was shot dead, largely because of the deaths on what became known as 'coffin ships'. Not long afterwards, a young Protestant clergyman was also killed in the area. The estate was heavily in debt, about £30,000. It was the marriage of Mahon's daughter, Grace Catherine, to the heir to the Pakenham and Sandford estates in Longford Westmeath and Roscommon that saved the day, although she never returned to Stroketown House. Under her husband, the estate continued the policy of shipping evicted tenants to Canada and the USA.

Over 8,600 acres of the Mahon estate was vested in the Congested Districts' Board in March 1911 and July 1912. The Strokestown House archive is now located at the OPW-NUI Maynooth Archive and Research Centre at Castletown, Co. Kildare.

Lord De Freyne of French Park had 25,436 acres in the county in 1876, with a valuation of £10,924 about £917,616 in modern money. Bateman gives Lord De Freyne's school as Downside, a Catholic Benedictine establishment that is approximately the Catholic equivalent of Harrow.

The title continues to exist and is held by Fulke Charles Arthur John French, the 8th Baron. who like his predecessor went to Downside School. He lives in London.

Ferres gives the family a fine kick-off from the old Debrett's:

The family of FRENCH, originally DE FREIGNE, or *De Fraxinis*, is of great antiquity; and claims descent from Rollo, 1st Duke of Normandy, who married Gisela, daughter of Charles the Simple, King of France. It was established in England by one of the companions of WILLIAM THE CONQUEROR, and was subsequently distinguished in English history.

In 1254, Will de Fraxinis was sent ambassador from HENRY III to Pope INNOCENT IV, who was then engaged in a project for the conquest of Naples; and undertook, for the assistance afforded to him by that king, to bestow the crown of that kingdom upon his second son, Edmond.

In 1302, Gerard de Freyne was sent ambassador by EDWARD I to the Count of Holland. The family started obtaining lands in the west of Ireland.

The 4th Baron De Freyne had 4,059 acres in Co. Sligo, 328 acres in Galway and 1 acre in May which, according to the peer, did not even raise £1 in rent. The total acreage was 38,788 with a valuation of £15,231.

The NUI Database tells us that the Cloonshanville estate, forming part of the French Park house demesne, was offered for sale in the Landed Estates' Court in February 1870. The *Irish Times* reported that the lots were purchased in trust for Baroness de Freyne. Over 36,000 acres of the French Park estate was vested in the Congested Districts' Board in July 1906.

Thomas G. Sandford of Castlerea House, Castlerea, had 24,410 acres in Roscommon in 1876, with a valuation of £10,194 about £856,296 in modern money. The NUI Database gives Sandford 949 acres in County Dublin, which do not appear in Bateman. Here is the NUI account of the estate. Sandford was educated at Harrow School:

> The descendants of Captain Theophilus Sandford of Moyglare, county Meath, settled at Castlerea, county Roscommon, in the late seventeenth century and represented the county in Parliament. Henry Moore Sandford (1751–1814) was created Baron Mount Sandford of Castlerea in July 1800. The title became extinct in 1846 following the death of George Sandford, 3rd Baron and the Sandford estates, passed to the families of his sisters of Willsgrove, Pakenham and Newenham. In the 1870s Thomas G. Wills Sandford owned 24,410 acres in county Roscommon and 949 acres in county Dublin. Over 1,200 acres of the Wills Sandford estate was vested in the Congested Districts' Board on 5 Nov 1911.

Edward Tenison of Kilronan Castle, Keadue, had 16,915 acres in Roscommon in 1876, with a valuation of £7,093 about £595,812 in modern money. This estate does not appear in Bateman but was at one time a property of Edward King Tenison, who was High Sheriff of Leitrim in 1845. Some of the estate in Dublin was sold in the Encumbered Estates Court in 1861.

The representatives of Colonel French of Errit Lodge, Castlerea, held 12,270 acres in 1876, with a valuation of £3,472 about £291,648 in modern money. Bateman records this estate as the property of Mrs French of Lough Errit, Frenchpark, Co. Roscommon in 1876. She had, as well as the Roscommon acres, 1,224 acres in Sligo and 79 acres in County Cork, a total of 13,573 acres with a valuation of £3,938.

In 1878, 3,817 acres of the estate were offered for sale in the Encumbered Estates Court. Prior to that over 7,000 acres were offered for sale in the same court in 1874.

Lord Crofton of Mote Park, Ballymurry, held 10,509 acres in Roscommon in 1876, with a valuation of £6,386 about £536,424 in modern money. Bateman amends the acreage slightly, from 10,509 acres to 11,053 acres, and the valuation to £7,332. Bateman then provides a longer record for the Lord's cousin, Sir Morgan George Crofton Bart, of Mohill Castle, Leitrim. See next entry.

Sir Morgan George Crofton Bart, of Mohill Castle, County Leitrim, had 9,590 acres in the county in 1876, with a valuation of £5,387 about £452,508 in modern money. There are three braches of this family, all with lands in Ireland at the time of the Return. All had titles. The incumbent at Mohill Castle in 1876 was Eton educated and though not mentioned in Bateman appears to have been a soldier. The family were certainly military, as the Wikipedia record shows:

> The Croftons of Mohill Castle settled in Ireland in 1643 following a patent from Charles I. Although this branch of the family was of some distinction, they remained untitled until 1801. The Crofton Baronetcy, of Mohill in the County of Leitrim, was created in the baronetage of the United Kingdom on 10 August 1801 for Morgan Crofton. The sixth Baronet was a Lieutenant-Colonel in the 2nd Life Guards and fought in the Second Boer War, where he was severely wounded at the Relief of Ladysmith, and in the two world wars. His diaries from the First World War are published as *Massacre of the Innocents: The Crofton Diaries, Ypres 1914–1915*, 2004. Another member of the family, James Crofton, grandson of Morgan Crofton, third son of the first Baronet, was a lieutenant general in the Army.

The NUI Database tells us that 'members of the family served as High Sheriffs and MPs for Leitrim from the seventeenth to the twentieth centuries. McParlan includes Duke Crofton of Mohill on a list of 'resident gentlemen of property' in 1802. (There is no record of Duke Crofton, but there is a still extant peerage of Crofton held by Edward Harry Piers Crofton, the 8th Baron, who lives in Somerset.)

A Morgan Crofton is recorded as the agent to Lord Lorton in the Barony of Boyle, Co. Roscommon, at the time of the first Ordnance Survey. It is probably the same Morgan Crofton who is recorded as a member of the Grand Panel of Co. Roscommon in 1828. According to Bateman, Sir Morgan Crofton of Mohill owned 9,590 acres in Co. Leitrim, 1,608 acres in Co. Longford and 271 acres in Co. Roscommon with a total acreage of 11,469 and a valuation of £6,222.

The O'Conor Don, of Cloonallis, Castlerea, held 10,467 acres in the county in 1876, with a valuation of £4,345 about £364,980 in modern money. The O'Conor Don is a title lost in the mists of Irish history in a way that no other is. Burke's *Landed Gentry of Great Britain* of 1871 begins the O'Conor Don lineage thus: 'Eochoid Morghmeodhin, son of Murdach Tireach, King of Ireland, died in AD 366'. There are good obituaries in the *Irish Times* of some of the recent holders of the title and some further details in *Who Owns Britain*, page 348. The family still own land in the area, which they have done for 1,654 years.

John Chidley Coote of Farmleigh, Castleknock, County Dublin had 10,318 acres in Roscommon 1876, with a valuation of £5,638 about £364,980 in modern money. Bateman has little to say about this landowner or his estate, save that he was an officer in the 43rd of Foot, an infantry regiment. His school is not listed and he has no other land of record. As we record in Laois (Queen's County), the principal seat of the Coote family was in that county. John Chidle Coote was the brother of Sir Charles Henry Coote of Ballyfin Mountrath in Laois. At some stage the Farmleigh estate passed to the Guinness family, who eventually sold it to the Government of the Irish Republic.

The Representatives of William Lloyd of Rockville, Drumsna, held 7,394 acres in the county in 1876, with a valuation of £4,438 about £372,792 in modern money. Bateman records William Lloyd of Rockville Drumsna with 300 acres in Galway, which, with the Roscommon acres, comes to a total of 7,694 acres with a valuation of £4,843. The NUI Database has some useful information but it appears to have been a very complicated estate. The database tells us that in the 1850s William Lloyd held land in the many parishes but that most of his estate was in the hands of the Court of Chancery at this time. The database later notes that over 2,200 acres of land were in the hands of the Congested Districts Board in 1915.

Long list of owners of over 1,000 acres in Roscommon 1876 ranked by acreage

		Acreage	Valuation 1876 (£)	Valuation current (£)
1	King-Harman, The Hon. L.H. Reps, Rockingham, Boyle	29,242	18,441	1,549,044
2	Mahon, H.S. Pakenham, Strokestown House, Strokestown	26,980	14,116	1,185,744
3	De Frayne, Lord, Frenchpark	25,436	10,924	917,616
4	Wills, Sandford Thos G., Castlerea House, Castlerea	24,410	10,194	856,296
5	Tenison, Edward, Kilronan Castle, Keadue	16,915	7,093	595,812
6	French, Colonel Reps, Erritt Lodge, Castlerea	12,270	3,472	291,648
7	Crofton, Lord, Mote Park, Ballymurray	10,509	6,386	536,424

		Acreage	Valuation 1876 (£)	Valuation current (£)
8	O'Conor, Don, Cloonallis, Castlerea	10,467	4,345	364,980
9	Coote, John Chidley, Farmleigh, Castleknock, Dublin	10,318	5,628	472,752
10	Lloyd, Wm Reps, Rockville, Drumsna	7,394	4,438	372,792
11	Lloyd, Guy, Croghan House, Boyle	7,302	4,238	355,992
12	O'Conor, Arthur Reps, Elphin	6,927	2,915	244,860
13	Balfe, Patrick, Southpark, Castlerea	6,024	3,961	332,724
14	Potts, William T., Coreen Castle, Ballinasloe	5,813	1,542	129,528
15	Kyle, William C., Clare Street, Dublin	5,589	1,182	99,288
16	Dillon, John T., Killashandra, Co. Cavan	5,538	1,500	126,000
17	Goff, Captain Thomas William, 4 Ovington Gardens, London	5,439	3,738	313,992
18	Dillon, Viscount, England	5,435	2,477	208,068
19	Murphy, John, Dublin	5,362	2,039	171,276
20	Ferrall, H. Taffe, Moylurg, Boyle	5,140	3,453	290,052
21	Naghten, Thomas Mahon, Thomastown Park, Athlone	4,829	1,853	155,652
22	M'Causland, Connolly Thomas, Drinagh, Newtownlimavady	4,799	2,573	216,132
23	Waltham, Robert Wm, Moyne, Ballyglunin, Co. Galway	4,631	1,911	160,524
24	Tredennick, William, Fortwilliam, Ballyshannon	4,546	1,152	96,768
25	Murphy, William, Mount Merrion, Dublin	4,522	3,779	317,436
26	Johnston, Lady, Belfast	4,332	2,155	181,020
27	Crichton, Alexander, Dirk Lodge, Dromard	4,021	1,961	164,724
28	Greville, Lord, Clonyn, Delvin	3,990	1,992	167,328
29	French, Christopher, Cloonyquin, Tulsk	3,701	2,933	246,372
30	Nesbitt, Catherine Downing, Leixlip House, Leixlip	3,641	1,627	136,668

Roscommon

		Acreage	Valuation 1876 (£)	Valuation current (£)
31	Caulfield, St George, Dunamon, Castle Dunamon, Roscommon	3,632	3,487	292,908
32	Irwin, Captain Richard, Rathmoyle, Ballinagare, Frenchpark	3,628	2,300	193,200
33	Talbot, William J. (a minor), Mount Talbot	3,500	1,564	131,376
34	Cadell, Robert O'F., Harbourstown House, Balbriggan	3,341	1,652	138,768
35	Grace, John D. Fitzgerald, Mantua, Elphin	3,276	1,255	105,420
36	Arres, John and James, Hall Rule, Scotland	3,264	1,309	109,956
37	William, Colonel Thomas M., Middlesex, England	3,062	963	80,892
38	Goff, Captain Robert, 34 Duke St, St James, London	3,029	1,725	147,168
39	Burke, John, Carrowroe Park, Roscommon	2,941	1,656	139,104
40	M'Donnell, Martin, Dunmore	2,940	994	83,496
41	Essex, Earl of, Cashionbury Park, Watford	2,906	2,672	224,448
42	Walsh, Walter H., Kilduff, Phillipstown	2,826	1,054	88,536
43	Mulloy, Fanny L., Oakport Cottage, Coote Hill	2,801	628	52,752
44	Hynes, W.J., Ballinasloe	2,690	1,050	88,200
45	Tabuteau, B.M., 123 Abbey Street, Dublin	2,619	626	52,584
46	Bayley, R.P., Rookwood, Athleague	2,590	1,757	147,588
47	Worthington, R.P., Dublin	2,572	405	34,020
48	MacDermot-Roe, Thomas C., Alderford, Ballyfarnan	2,505	1,113	93,492
49	Longfield, Robert, Dublin	2,448	1,043	87,612
50	O'Conor Patrick Hugh, Dundermott, Ballmoe	2,435	1,163	97,692
51	Talbot, John, Mount Talbot	2,416	1,125	94,500
52	Society Incorporated, 73 Harcourt St, Dublin	2,371	1,220	102,480
53	Newcome, George (a minor), Ward of Chancery	2,310	743	62,412

		Acreage	Valuation 1876 (£)	Valuation current (£)
54	Chichester, Colonel C. Raleigh, Runnamoat, Roscommon	2,306	1,915	160,860
55	Magan, Percy, Marlfield Gorey, Co. Wexford	2,253	890	74,760
56	Newcome, George, Co. Meath	2,245	670	56,280
57	Kelly, James, Johnstown, Athlone	2,233	501	42,084
58	Burke, Sir Thomas, Marble Hill, Loughrea	2,230	775	65,100
59	O'Conor, Charles, Mount Druid, Ballinagar	2,186	1,307	109,788
60	Caulfield, Colonel Robert, Ballyheelan, Co. Cavan	2,070	1,201	100,884
61	Lefroy, Thomas L., Cashel House, Cloondra, Longford	2,043	296	24,862
62	O'Conor, Denis M., Cloonallis, Castlerea	2,016	1,583	132,972
63	D'Arcy, Major John T., Castlepark, Ballinasloe	1,961	735	61,740
64	Glancy, James, Enfield, Ballintubber	1,959	1,428	119,952
65	Bellew, Sir Henry Grattan, Mount Bellew, Co. Galway	1,895	696	58,464
66	King, Sir Gilbert Bart, Charlestown House, Drumsna	1,858	1,280	107,520
67	Irwin, James Nolan, Beechwood, Roscommon	1,849	732	61,488
68	Mapother, Thomas A.J., Kilteevan House, Roscommon	1,777	902	75,768
69	St George, Kate, Hatley, Cheltenham	1,759	452	37,968
70	Blake, Edward, Brussels, Belgium	1,698	706	59,304
71	Goodall, George, South Africa and Junior Carlton Club	1,681	885	74,340
72	O'Rorke, Rev. John, Moylough	1,619	543	45,612
73	Clancarty, Earl of, Garbally, Ballinasloe	1,614	1,093	91,812
74	Rynardoon, Mrs, Littlecote, Hungerford, England	1,595	1,168	98,112
75	French, Arthur, Johnstown, Naas	1,570	722	60,648

		Acreage	Valuation 1876 (£)	Valuation current (£)
76	Flanagan, Hon. Stephen W., Fitzwilliam Place, Dublin	1,556	826	69,384
77	Dunne, Edward M., Mountrath	1,544	777	65,268
78	Pelly, Louise, 5 Charlemont Terrace, Kingstown	1,510	930	78,120
79	Johnston, Captain John, Roselawn Celbridge	1,489	402	33,768
80	O'Sullivan, John, Mount Florence, Athlone	1,489	354	29,736
81	Hyne, S.J., of Ballinasloe	1,479	674	56,616
82	M'Donnell, Patrick, Lackan House, Lecarrow	1,445	790	66,360
83	Biron, Rev. E., England	1,435	495	41,580
84	Jameson, William, 68 Harcourt St, Dublin	1,434	892	74,928
85	French-Brewster, R.A., Lieutenant, 1st Dragoon Guards	1,415	949	79,716
86	Stronge, J.C., Mount Temple, Clontarf	1,406	700	58,800
87	Churcher, Emanuel, Bridgemany House, Hants	1,400	562	47,208
88	Cruise, D.J., Killarney	1,386	449	37,716
89	Digby, Mrs, Drumdoff House, Kilrooskey, Roscommon	1,312	678	56,952
90	Sampey, Alex W., Willsboro, Ballinalough	1,302	358	30,072
91	St George, Ingri Christina Reps, Hatley Manor, Carrick-on-Shannon	1,293	934	78,456
92	King, John Gilbert, Ballylinn, Ferbane	1,274	634	53,256
93	Stevens, T.H., Kiltoom	1,258	495	41,580
94	M'Donagh, W.J., Ballinasloe	1,248	963	80,892
95	O'Kelly, William, Loughrea	1,246	323	27,132
96	Simpson, Pierce, Clooncorrick Castle, Carrigallen	1,243	676	56,784
97	Campbell, John Alderman, 27 Mountjoy Sq., East Dublin	1,226	622	52,248
98	Dickson, Harriett, Dublin	1,221	454	38,136

		Acreage	Valuation 1876 (£)	Valuation current (£)
99	French, William J., Blackall, Navan	1,214	925	77,700
100	O'Conor, Rodrick, Dublin	1,203	732	61,488
101	Brabazon, H.S., Ballina	1,203	172	14,448
102	Longworth, John, Glynwood, Athlone	1,192	593	49,812
103	Fawcett, John R., Prince of Wales Terrace, Bray	1,191	504	42,336
104	Carroll, J.W., 50 Leeson St, Dublin	1,180	401	33,684
105	Morton, Susan, Strokestown	1,130	531	44,604
106	Gannon, Thomas, Lissygrehan	1,118	126	10,584
107	Young, James, Harristown, Castlerea	1,103	734	61,656
108	O'Grady, Richard J., Favrane House, Kilkelly	1,099	310	26,040
109	Fosbery, W.F., Mosstown, Streamstown	1,094	511	42,924
110	Westmeath, Earl of, Pallas, Portumna	1,091	1,109	93,156
111	Dillon, John, Johnstone, Athlone	1,083	216	18,144
112	Knox, Edward Earnest, 5 Crosthwaite Park, Kingstown	1,074	654	54,936
113	Molloy, Rev. C.C., Edgeworthstown	1,064	465	39,060
114	Costello, A.R., Edmondstown	1,038	212	17,808
115	French, Richard, Dublin	1,037	661	55,524
116	M'Donnell, Farrell, Roscommon	1,034	695	58,360
117	Trant, H.D., Athlone	1,027	611	51,324
118	Coote, Sir Charles, Mountrath, Queen's County	1,017	286	24,024
119	French, William, Dublin	1,012	1,006	84,504
120	Davis, William, Cloonshanville, Frenchpark	1,010	304	25,536
121	St George, A., Camma, Athlone	1,008	428	35,952
122	M'Ivor, Rev. James, Moyle, Newtownstewart	1,007	482	40,488
123	Davies, John Thomas, Conreen, Lanesborough	1,007	331	27,804
124	Murtagh, James, Newpark, Athlone	1,004	483	40,572
125	O'Beirne, Connell Reps, Drumsna	1,000	185	7,140

List of top 20 owners of over 1,000 acres in Roscommon 1876 ranked by valuation

		Acreage	Valuation 1876 (£)	Valuation current (£)
1	King-Harman, The Hon. L.H. Reps, Rockingham, Boyle	29,242	18,441	1,549,044
2	Mahon, H.S. Pakenham, Strokestown House, Strokestown	26,980	14,116	1,185744
3	De Frayne, Lord, Frenchpark	25,436	10,924	917,616
4	Wills, Sandford Thos G., Castlerea House, Castlerea	24,410	10,194	856,296
5	Tenison, Edward, Kilronan Castle, Keadue	16,915	7,093	595,812
6	Crofton, Lord, Mote Park, Ballymurray	10,509	6,386	536,424
7	Coote, John Chidley, Farmleigh, Castleknock, Dublin	10,318	5,628	472,752
8	Lloyd, Wm Reps, Rockville, Drumsna	7,394	4,438	372,792
9	O'Conor, Don, Cloonallis, Castlerea	10,467	4,345	364,980
10	Lloyd, Guy, Croghan House, Boyle	7,302	4,238	355,992
11	Balfe, Patrick, Southpark, Castlerea	6,024	3,961	332,724
12	Murphy, William, Mount Merrion, Dublin	4,522	3,779	317,436
13	Goff, Captain Thomas William, 4 Ovington Gardens, London	5,439	3,738	313,992
14	Caulfield, St George, Dunamon Castle, Dunamon, Roscommon	3,632	3,487	292,908
15	French, Colonel Reps, Erritt Lodge, Castlerea	12,270	3,472	291,648
16	Ferrall, H. Taffe, Moylurg, Boyle	5,140	3,453	290,052
17	French, Christopher, Cloonyquin, Tulsk	3,701	2,933	246,372
18	O'Conor, Arthur Reps, Elphin	6,927	2,915	244,860
19	Essex, Earl of, Cashionbury Park, Watford	2,906	2,672	224,448
20	M'Causland, Connolly Thomas, Drinagh, Newtownlimavady	4,799	2,573	216,132

SLIGO

	1876	2016
Population in County Sligo	115,311	65,393
All owners of land	856	43,437
Percentage of the population	0.74	–
Owners of nothing at all	114,455	21,494
Percentage of the population	99.26	–
Size of County	447,527	453,760 acres
Number of dwellings (of which rented)	20,955 (20,099)	24,428
Number of owned farm holdings	405	4,395

County comparisons

	Acreage 1876	Population 1876
County Sligo	447,527	115,311
Berkshire, England	430,849	196,475
Caithness, Scotland	471,763	39,992
Glamorganshire, Wales	428,386	397,859

Colonel Edward Henry Cooper MP of Markree Castle, Collooney, had 34,120 acres in Sligo in 1876, with a valuation of £11,548 about £970,032 in modern money. Bateman tells us that this Eton-educated army officer served in both the infantry, the Grenadier Guards, and the cavalry, the 7th Hussars. He was also the MP for the county and had 1,118 acres in Limerick, which together with his Sligo acres gave him a total estate of 35,238 acres with a valuation of £12,735.

Working from the NUI Galway Database, the following can be written about the Coopers and their estate. Edward 'the Coronet' Cooper, was a soldier in the regiment of Edward Coote an officer in the Cromwellian wars who got huge grants of land in Laois. Colonel Cooper's ancestor was granted land in the Collooney area of Co. Sligo and in counties Limerick and Kerry in the Cromwellian settlement. Financial records exist from 1665. While not quite Birr Castle, weather observations have been taken at Markree Castle, the family seat, since 1828. In 1867 oyster beds and houses in the city of Dublin, associated with the estate of Edward Joshua Cooper, were offered for sale in the Landed Estates Court. In November of that year the *Irish Times* reported on the sale of Cooper property in the county of Sligo, to William Middleton. In 1906 Col Cooper's estate included almost 2000 acres of untenanted land. By March 1916 Richard E.S. Cooper had accepted an offer of £11,000 from the Congested Districts' Board for his 1,639 acres in county Mayo. The Board also acquired over 500 acres of the Sligo estate.

Sir Robert Gore Booth Bart, of Lissadell, Sligo, had 31,774 acres in the county in 1876, with a valuation of £16,774 about £1,409,016 in modern money. Bateman tells us that Sir Robert had become Sir Henry William Gore Booth Bart, by the time of his final edition in 1883. Eton-educated Sir Henry had a small estate in Lancashire, no acreage given, which upped his valuation to £17,346. Although made famous by the careers of his two daughters, Sir Robert was himself a noted Arctic explorer and writer.

The Gore Booth family came to Ireland in Cromwell's time and prospered in the west. The Famine proved a turning point for the estate. No landlord in Ireland, were there even saints amongst them, which there weren't, will ever escape criticism for what happened between 1845 and 1850 – *An Gorta Mór* – and a later famine in 1879–80. However, any close reading of what Sir Robert Gore Booth tried to do for his starving tenantry shows someone with humanity, who stuck by his post and was no absentee. He did what he could to relieve distress. But the famine overwhelmed everything in Ireland, the crisis hugely exacerbated by the passivity of the House of Commons and the perversity of the key UK civil servant involved, Charles Trevelyan. There is an excellent and balanced account in Famine, Lissadell House Online, and his landed estate in *County Sligo, 1814–1876, Land, Famine, Emigration & Politics* (2006, Four Courts Press) by Dr Gerard Moran.

What has lodged this family high in the annals of modern Irish history, however, are the two daughters of Sir Henry, Constance and Eva. Both became social and political revolutionaries, Constance in Ireland and Eva in Great Britain. Constance, known as the Countess Markievicz, took part in the rebellion in 1916, was sentenced to death but reprieved. She was the first woman ever elected to the House of Commons, in the election of 1918. She did not take her seat. She was a minister in the first government of the Irish Free State from 1919 to 1922, and was the first woman minister in any government in Europe. One of the family friends was W.B. Yeats, the poet, who was awarded the Nobel Prize for Literature in 1923.

After 1909 and again in 1915 offers were accepted from the Congested Districts Board on over 2,500 acres of the estate.

The Baronetcy still exists and is held by Sir Josslyn Henry Robert Gore Booth, the 9th Baronet. He was educated at Eton like his ancestors and lives in Yorkshire.

Charles O'Hara of Annaghamore, Collooney, had 21,070 acres in Sligo in 1876 with a valuation of £8,324 about £699,216 in modern money.

Bateman changes the address of this landowner to Cooper's Hill, Ballymote, and notes that he was MP for County Sligo. The O'Hara papers at the National Library are one of the key primary sources for the activities of the estate owners in the country between 1870 and 1920. The O'Haras were active in many areas of public life during this period.

Charles' son, Major Charles Kean O'Hara, was the last Lord Lieutenant of County Sligo. Descendants of the family still live at Annaghmore, a house built on a site in O'Hara possession since medieval times. There is no readily available account of the fate of the estate itself.

William R. Ormsby Gore of Derrynane, Drumod, County Leitrim, had 21,019 acres in Sligo in 1876, with a valuation of £5,933 about £498,372 in modern money. By the time we get to Bateman in 1883. Ormsby Gore had become Baron Harlech, a peerage of the United Kingdom, created in 1876. This Eton-educated landowner had all the standard qualifications for preferment in the UK. He was a former cavalry officer in the 13th Light Dragoons, a groom in waiting to Queen Victoria and had been MP for both North Shropshire and Carnarvonshire. In 1876 he was the ninety-third largest landowner in the United Kingdom, with a total of 58,358 acres in eleven counties in Wales, England and Ireland. These were Carnarvon 8,570 acres, Merioneth 6,354 acres, Salop (Shropshire) 3,600 acres, Montgomery 2,934 acres, Denbigh 711 acres, Berks 24 acres, Sligo 21,019 acres, Leitrim 9,634 acres, Westmeath 2,794 acres, Mayo 2,546 acres and Roscommon 172 acres with a valuation of £26,400.

The title still exists and is held by Francis David Ormsby Gore, the 6th Baron, who lives in Harlech in Wales. The NUI Database tells us that Lord Harlech sold 1,367 acres in Sligo to the Congested District Board in 1906 and a further 1,172 acres in 1912.

Owen Wynn of Hazlewood, Sligo, owned 12,982 acres in the county in 1876, with a valuation of £9,711 about £815,724 in modern money. This Harrow-educated infantry officer, who served in the 61st of Foot, had along with his Sligo acres 15,436 acres in Leitrim. This was a total of 28,418 acres, with a valuation of £14,091.

The Wynn family settled in Sligo and Leitrim at the end of the Williamite wars. With the other families at the top of our lists they controlled a good deal of economic and political life in the two counties between 1700 and 1900. The NUI Database tells us that some of the estate was sold, beginning in 1855, with more sold in 1876. There were further sales in the Encumbered Estates Court in 1881. A final note says that the estate, or what remained of it, was sold to the Land Commission in the 1920s.

The Hon. L.H. King-Harman, of Rockingham Castle, Boyle, County Roscommon, had 12,629 acres in Sligo in 1876, with a valuation of £5,344 about £448,896 in modern money.

See page 277.

The Hon. W.F. Cowper-Temple of Broadlands, Hampshire, had 12,426 acres in Sligo in 1876, with a valuation of £5,801 about £487,284 in modern money

See page 117.

William Phibbs of Seafield, Sligo, had 10,507 acres in the county in 1876, with a valuation of £5,133 about £431,172 in modern money. Bateman records this Trinity College man, who served as an officer in the 11th Light Dragoon cavalry regiment, having 834 acres in Roscommon, which, added to his Sligo acres, gave him a total acreage of 11,341, with a valuation of £6,055. Most of the other Phibbs estates in the long list are held by absentee owners, based in London and Australia. The NUI data base records three Phibbs estates, starting with Seafield.

Phibbs Seafield. The estate, which was held under fee farm grant from the Merediths, was offered for sale in the Landed Estates Court in January 1877. Earlier, in June 1852, William Phibbs had offered for sale over 300 acres of his Roscommon estate as well as over 2,000 acres of an estate in Co. Westmeath (not shown in Bateman) in the Encumbered Estates Court. In 1867 oyster beds and houses in the city of Dublin, associated with the estate of Edward Joshua Cooper, a relative, were offered for sale in the Landed Estates Court. The Congested Districts Board acquired almost 1,400 acres of the estate of Owen Phibbs in the early twentieth century.

Phibbs Tirerrill. William and Thomas Phibbs offered the estate at Heathfield for sale in May 1854. Harloe Phibbs was leasing extensive property in the town of Ballysadare to Robert Culbertson at the time of Griffith's Valuation. Harloe Phibbs owned over 700 acres in the 1870s, while Major Richard Phibbs was the owner of over 550. In 1906 Thomas Randle Phibbs is recorded as the owner of over 300 acres of untenanted land.

Phibbs Doobeg. The Phibbs family held estates in different parts of Sligo, this branch settled at Doobeg in the nineteenth century. There was significant land agitation on this estate in the early twentieth century.

Sir Roger William Henry Palmer Bart, of Keenagh, Crossmolina, County Mayo (and of Kenure Park, Rush, County Dublin) held 9,570 acres in

Sligo in 1876, with a valuation of £1,229 about £103,326 in modern money. This Eton-educated landowner soldier and politician was one of the largest landowners in Ireland, with lesser holdings in English and Welsh counties. Bateman locates him at Keenagh, Crossmolina, Co. Mayo, in which county he had 80,990 acres, with a valuation of £14,625. In Sligo he had 9,570 acres, with a valuation of £1,229. In Dublin County he had 3,991 acres with a valuation of £4,706. He had 3,329 acres in Cambridge with a valuation of £4,338, in Denbigh he had 1,011 acres with a valuation of £1,357. In Flint he had 45 acres with a valuation of £114, in Dorset 11 acres with a valuation of £34 and in Berks 7 acres with a valuation of £258. His total acreage was 98,954 with a valuation of £26,661. He ranked as the forty-fist largest landowner in the United Kingdom in 1876. He had served in the Life Guards and the 11th Hussars in the Crimea, later becoming a lieutenant general in the British Army. He sat as MP for Mayo.

Sir Charles Gore of Beleek Manor, Ballina, had 8,569 acres in the county with a valuation of £2,788 about £234,192 in modern money. This landowner does not appear in Bateman. The acreage was large enough but the valuation fell below Bateman's rule of a £3,000 valuation. A note in the DUI Galway database may help to explain this:

> Francis Annesley Knox Gore was created a baronet in 1868 and when the male line died out in 1891 the family became Saunders Knox Gore. The Knox Gore estate was centred around the town of Ballina. In 1876 the estate amounted to 22,023 acres in county Mayo and 8,569 acres in county Sligo. In 1906 Matilda and Sarah Knox Gore held over 1,500 acres of untenanted land in Sligo. Offers from the Congested Districts' Board to various members of the Knox Gore family had been accepted for the purchase of most of the county Mayo and Sligo estates by March 1916.

Long list of owners of over 1,000 acres in 1876 ranked by acreage

		Acreage	Valuation 1876 (£)	Valuation Current(£)
1	Cooper, Colonel E.H., Markree Castle, Collooney	34,120	11,548	970,032
2	Booth, Sir Robert Gore Bart, Lissadell, Sligo	31,774	16,774	1,409,016
3	O'Hara, Charles W., Annaghmore, Collooney	21,070	8,324	699,216
4	Gore, William R. Ormsby, Derrynane, Drumod	21,019	5,933	498,372

		Acreage	Valuation 1876 (£)	Valuation Current(£)
5	Wynn, Owen, Hazlewood, Sligo	12,982	9,711	815,724
6	King-Harman, the Hon. L.H. Reps, Rockingham Castle, Boyle	12,629	5,344	448,896
7	Cowper-Temple, the Hon. W.F., Broadlands, Hampshire	12,426	5,801	487,284
8	Phibbs, William, Seafield, Sligo	10,507	5,113	429,492
9	Palmer, Colonel Sir R.W.H. Bart, of Keenagh, Crossmolina Co Mayo	9,570	1,229	103,236
10	Gore, Sir Charles, Belleek Manor, Ballina	8,569	2,788	234,192
11	Hillas, Robert W., Sea View House, Dromore West	7,444	2,351	197,484
12	Percival, Alexander, Temple House, Ballymote	7,034	4,198	352,632
13	Brinkley, Richard G., Fortland, Dromore West	6,730	3,006	252,504
14	Stratford, John Wingfield, Maidstone, Co. Kent, England	6,555	3,085	259,140
15	Taffe, John, Ballybrach, Dublin	5,751	432	36,288
16	Martin, Captain Abraham, Claveragh, Sligo	5,430	3,456	290,304
17	O'Connor, Peter, Carmsfoot, Sligo	4,849	2,563	215,292
18	King, Sir Gilbert Bart, Charlestown, Drumsna	4,398	2,133	179,172
19	Young, Rev. John, Daraghmore, Dungannon	4,291	438	36,792
20	Armstrong, James W., Cliffpool, Tobercurry	4,182	1,974	165,816
21	Ffolliott, Colonel John, Hollybrook, Ballinafad	4,168	1,948	163,632
22	Keogh, John, Glencourt, Bray	4,056	1,247	104,748
23	De Frayne, Lord, Frenchpark	4,052	1,488	124,992
24	Sullivan, Rev. H.W., at Messrs Stewarts and Kincaids. 6 Leinster St, Dublin	3,708	1,420	119,280
25	Knox, Utred A., Mountfalcon, Ballina	3,524	1,175	98,700
26	Caulfield, Hon. E.M., Hockley, Armagh	3,478	554	46,536
27	Caddell, Richard O.F., Balbriggan, Co. Dublin	3,464	1,153	96,852

		Acreage	**Valuation 1876 (£)**	**Valuation Current(£)**
28	Crofton, Sir Malby (a minor), Longford House, Ballisadare	3,422	1,440	120,960
29	Duke, Jemmett, Newpark, Ballymote	3,285	1,734	145,656
30	Irwin, Burton, Fitzwilliam Place, Dublin	2,988	1,817	99,708
31	Hale, James, Templeview, Dromore West	2,952	1,695	142,380
32	Crichton, Alexander, Dirk Lodge, Drumod	2,826	1,749	146,916
33	Webber, William D., Killyville, Athty	2,756	1,019	85,596
34	Gethin, John, Ballindoon, Riverstown	2,530	1,440	120,960
35	Howley, John, Portsmouth, England	2,521	435	36,540
36	Guilfoyle, James F., Carrowcallen, Skreen	2,441	685	57,540
37	Jones, Captain James, 46 Grosvenor Sq., Rathmines	2,396	583	48,972
38	Dunne, George, Kinsale, Co. Cork	2,324	847	71,148
39	Phibbs, Harlow, Sligo	2,271	825	71,568
40	Verschoyle, Tanrago, Ballisodare	2,265	990	83,160
41	Nedden, Grace, Comcail, Dromore West	2,172	245	20,580
42	Keogh, Cornelius A., Oakport, Boyle	2,023	583	48,972
43	Flanagan, Hon. S.W., 20 Fitzwilliam Place, Dublin	2,017	1,009	84,756
44	Campbell, Harper, Hermitage, Sligo	2,014	869	75,264
45	Ormsby, John R., Castledargan, Collooney	1,999	602	50,568
46	Griffith, William J., Killery, Drumahare	1,999	491	41,244
47	Erne, Earl of, (near) Enniskillen	1,966	1,428	119,952
48	Phibbs, George, Melbourne, Australia	1,880	446	37,464
49	Tennison, Colonel E.K., Killoran Castle, Keadue	1,783	1,075	90,300
50	French, Arthur, Naas, Co. Kildare	1,706	404	33,936

Sligo

		Acreage	Valuation 1876 (£)	Valuation Current (£)
51	King, Henry Edward, Brisbane, Australia	1,670	776	65,184
52	Knox, John F., Hollywood, Ballina	1,667	348	29,232
53	Middleton, William, Wine Street, Sligo	1,658	2,231	187,404
54	Brett, Henry, Harrington Street, Dublin	1,654	551	46,284
55	Tottenham, Charles, Ballycurry, Ashford, Co. Wicklow	1,631	912	76,608
56	Newbury, Lady, At Mr Cogans, Lisconney	1,614	1,077	90,468
57	Phibbs, Colonel Richard, 12 Rutland Gate, London	1,598	534	44,856
58	Dodwell, James C. Shankill House, Bray	1,573	279	23,436
59	Webber, Charles P., Carrowcullen, Skreen	1,568	1,160	97,440
60	Eden, Alice Julia, Merton, Enniscorthy	1,548	533	44,772
61	Jones, Thomas Reps of, Dublin	1,522	1,270	106,680
62	Parke, Johnston, Clonmeehan, Ballymote	1,482	741	62,244
63	Lyons, Henry Reps, Market Street, Sligo	1,460	1,279	107,436
64	Boyd, John, Castle Corbally	1,444	833	69,972
65	Orme, Robert, Enniscrone, Ballina	1,405	1,291	108,444
66	Hewitson, Amelia Sarah, Merton, Enniscorthy	1,394	408	34,272
67	Thompson, Captain Meredith, Knockadoo, Collooney	1,389	666	55,944
68	Nicholson, Mary Agnes, Belfast	1,373	215	18,060
69	O'Reilly, Myles G., 6 Denmark Terrace, Brighton	1,365	711	59,724
70	Gethin, Captain Richard, Earlesfield, Ballmote	1,333	1,116	93,744
71	Costello, Charles Reps, Killfree, Gurteen	1,330	412	34,608
72	Meredith, Master, Cloonamahon, Coolaney	1,325	447	37,548

		Acreage	Valuation 1876 (£)	Valuation Current(£)
73	Wingfield, Thomas S., Maidstone, Kent, England	1,321	356	29,904
74	Walker, Roger Reps, Rathcarrick, Sligo	1,304	780	65,520
75	Farrell, Edward, 20 Caple St, Dublin	1,287	481	40,404
76	Carroll, Jane, London	1,282	211	17,724
77	Irwin, John, Raheen, Elphin	1,254	310	26,040
78	Weir, Minor, Castlebaldwin, Riverstown	1,248	830	69,720
79	French, Colonel Fitzspephen, Lough Erret, Frenchpark	1,224	427	35,860
80	Nolan, John, St Winifred's Road, Surrey, England	1,186	280	23,520
81	O'Connor, Don, Clonalis, Castlerea	1,184	487	40,908
82	Verschoyle, John James, Tassagart, Co. Dublin	1,168	707	59,388
83	Ormsby, James, Farrell, Mt Farrell, Dromore West	1,160	684	57,456
84	Collum, Mrs Eliza, Enniskillen	1,157	181	15,204
85	Holmes, Joseph A., Clogher, Ballymote	1,136	649	54,516
86	Knox, John, Broadlands, Killala	1,128	409	34,356
87	Knox, Francis of Lowvalley, Killala	1,128	408	34,272
88	Knox, Granvill, Netley Park, Ballina	1,128	408	34,272
89	Knox, Henry, Palmerstown, Killala	1,128	408	34,272
90	Knox, Richard, Woolwich, England	1,128	408	34,272
91	Reilly, Thomas, Butlersbridge, Co. Cavan	1,126	654	54,936
92	Wood, Rev. E.B. and Arthur, Easkey	1,085	480	40,320
93	Cogan, James, Sligo	1,079	280	23,520
94	Powell, Edward, Finglas, Co. Dublin	1,048	362	30,408
95	Duke, Alexander, Proby Square, Blackrock and Newpark, Ballymote	1,031	661	55,524
96	Rashleigh, Jonathan, Menabilly, Cornwall, England	1,023	658	55,272
97	Norbury, Lord Reps, Valence, Westhaven, Kent, London	1,006	313	26,292
98	William Thomas H, Sligo	1,136	158	13,272

Sligo's richest landowners in 1876 based on valuation

		Acreage	Valuation 1876 (£)	Valuation Current (£)
1	Booth, Sir Robert, Gore, Bart, Lissadil, Sligo	31,774	16,774	1,409,016
2	Cooper, Colonel E.H., Markree Castle, Collooney	34,120	11,548	970,032
3	Wynn, Owen, Hazlewood, Sligo	12,982	9,711	815,724
4	O'Hara, Charles W., Annaghmore, Collooney	21,070	8,324	699,216
5	Gore, William R., Ormsby, Derrynane, Drumod	21,019	5,933	498,372
6	Cowper-Temple, the Hon. W.F., Broadlands, Hampshire	12,426	5,801	487,284
7	King-Harman, the Hon. L.H. Reps, Rockingham Castle, Boyle	12,629	5,344	448,896
8	Phibbs, William, Seafield, Sligo	10,507	5,113	429,492
9	Percival, Alexander, Temple House, Ballymote	7,034	4,198	352,632
10	Martin, Captain Abraham, Claveragh, Sligo	5,430	3,456	290,304
11	Stratford, John Wingfield, Maidstone, Kent, England	6,555	3,085	259,140
12	Brinkley, Richard G., Fortland, Dromore West	6,730	3,006	252,504
13	Gore, Sir Charles, Belleek Manor, Ballina	8,569	2,788	234,192
14	O'Connor, Peter, Carmsfoot, Sligo	4,849	2,563	215,292
15	Hillas, Robert W., Sea View House, Dromore West	7,444	2,351	197,484
16	Middleton, William, Wine Street, Sligo	1,658	2,231	187,404
17	King, Sir Gilbert Bart, Charlestown, Drumsna	4,398	2,133	179,172
18	Armstrong, James W., Cliffpool, Tobercurry	4,182	1,974	165,816
19	Ffolliott, Colonel John, Hollybrook, Ballinafad	4,168	1,948	163,632
20	Irwin, Burton, Fitzwilliam Place, Dublin	2,988	1,817	99,708

TIPPERARY

	1876	2020 est
Population in County Tipperary	216,713	158,754
All owners of land	2,372	–
Percentage of the population	1.09	48,531
Owners of nothing at all	214,341	–
Percentage of the population	98.91	–
Size of County	1,042,457	1,054,080 acres
Number of dwellings	38,544	58,275
Number of owned farm holdings	1,767	7,739

County comparisons

	Acreage	Population 1876
County Tipperary	1,042,457	216,713
Lancashire, England	947,464	2,819,415
Aberdeen, Scotland	1,255,138	264,603
Carmarthen, Wales★	510,574	115,710

★ No easily comparable county as all Welsh counties are under 510,000 acres

Lord Bloomfield of Ciamalta, Newport, had 9,912 acres with a valuation of £1,240 about £104,160 in modern money. Only the British honours system could create the following confusion. There were two Baron Bloomfields, father and son. Both were landowners in Ireland. Each was enobled separately, and for different reasons. The elder of the two Baron Bloomfields was a British Army general, of Irish extraction with an estate in Galway, who fought the rebels at Vinegar Hill in Wexford in 1798. He was later made private secretary to the Prince of Wales and then King George IV in 1820 when the Prince succeeded to the throne. Bloomfield's mission was to cut the King's expenses, including diamonds for the Royal mistress or illegal wife – the King had both. Bloomfield was undermined politically by the King and his courtiers but eventually became an MP, Lieutenant General, and commandant of the Royal Artillery. In 1825 he was made baron in the peerage of Ireland.

His son, John, a diplomat, while posted in Stockholm had an illegitimate daughter by the leading Swedish soprano of the day, Emilie Hogquist. Despite this he later became Ambassador to Russia and Vienna. He succeeded to his father's

Irish title 1846, in the peerage of Ireland. When he retired from the diplomatic service in 1871, he was made a peer of the United Kingdom with a seat in the House of Lords. He died in 1879 without an heir and both titles became extinct. He is buried in Offaly. The acreage qualified him for an entry in Bateman but the valuation was too low.

Count Arthur John Moore MP KSG of Mooresfort, County Tipperary, had 10,199 aces with a valuation of £4,506 about £376,504 in modern money. Arthur John Moore was a prominent Catholic and nationalist MP for the constituency of Clonmel. His father, also an MP, bought the Tipperary estate from the Crosbie Moores in the mid 1850s, from his own holding in Antrim. In the Commons, Arthur Moore supported Home Rule but was also an ardent land reformer. He added Aherlow Castle, now a ruin, to the estate. He was created a Papal Count in 1879 and was a Chamberlain of Honour to the Pope, who also made him a Knight Commander of St Gregory and a Knight of the Equestrian Order of the Holy Sepulchre. A noted philanthropist, he set up a reform school and funded the creation of the Cistercian monastery of Mount St Joseph Roscrea. His son was an officer in the Irish Guards and was awarded a Military Cross in the First World War.

The Earl of Clonmell, Bishopscourt, Straffan, County Kildare, had 11,098 acres in Tipperary with a valuation of £6,946 about £583,464 in modern money. The 4th Earl, John Henry Reginald Scott, who held the estates in 1876, was the grandson of John Scott, the 1st Earl, who both obtained the title and first amassed the estates. By the time of the Return, the Earl had land in seven Irish counties and in England as well, though this is not recorded by Bateman. His Irish acreage, apart from Tipperary, was as follows: in Kildare 1,958 acres, in Kilkenny 2,226 acres, in Carlow 3,300 acres, in Monaghan 2,022 acres, in Limerick 1,902 acres and in Dublin a mere 51 acres, probably in Harcourt St and nearby, which were valued at £704. The total acreage was 27,646 acres with a valuation of £17,140.

The 1st Earl was Lord Chief Justice of the King's Bench for Ireland. He is described in a biography by Barrington as:

> courageous, vulgar, humorous, artificial; he knew the world well, and he profited by that knowledge. He cultivated the powerful; he bullied the timid; he fought the brave; he flattered the vain; he duped the credulous; and he amused the convivial. Half liked, half reprobated, he was too high to be despised, and too low to be respected. His language was coarse, and his principles arbitrary; but his passions were his slaves, and his cunning was his instrument.

Sheil, another Irish historian, writes of 'the matchless imperturbability of front to which the late Lord Clonmel was indebted for his brazen coronet'.

His mansion in Harcourt Street, Dublin, now divided into two houses, has given his name to a street opposite. The peerage became extinct in 1935.

Nathaniel Buckley MP, Galtee, Mitchelstown, had 13,260 acres in Tipperary with a valuation of £3,585 about £301,140 in modern money. Nathaniel Buckley was a Lancashire mill owner who used his millions to create a vast estate in Ireland based on the purchase of land, mainly that of the Earl of Kingston, which was heavily encumbered with debt. In theory a Liberal politician – he was elected to Parliament in 1871 on the Liberal ticket – his approach to his new Irish tenants was any anything but liberal. He increased the rents by up to 500 per cent. Riots ensued and his agent received death threats. The Irish Land Acts had to be amended to close the loopholes exploited by Buckley. He was a typical bandit capitalist of the period, and is much replicated in the modern financial industry. He had a posh address in Lancashire but Bateman only credits him with 62 acres in Lancashire, 2 acres in Cheshire and 11 acres in Derby. In Ireland he had, besides the Tipperary acreage, 7,563 acres in Limerick. His total acreage was 11,286 with a valuation of £6,826. More than a sixth of the valuation rested on the 11 Derbyshire acres, which had a valuation of £1,299.

The land commission broke up the estate in the 1930s and the stones and roof tiles of the castle were used to build a church in Cork in the 1940s.

The 4th Viscount Hawarden, Dondrum, Cashel, had 15,272 acres with a valuation of £8,781 about £737,604 in modern money. This Eton-educated aristocrat had little to connect him with Ireland save the land he owned there. His life, like that of so many of the other landowners, was focused in England and on politics in London. He sat in the House of Lords from 1862 to 1886 and was a Lord in Waiting in the administrations of the Earl of Derby and of Disraeli. In 1886 he was made a peer of the United Kingdom as Earl de Montalt, of Dundrum in County Tipperary, meaning he had a seat of his own in the House of Lords. Earlier, he was an officer in the Life Guards, the regiment dedicated to protecting the 'blood royal'.

The de Montalt name is a reference back to the supposed origin of the family as followers of Hugh Lupus, William the Bastard's nephew and Earl of Chester after the Norman occupation of England. It is said he gave land at Hawarden in Flintshire to Eustae de Mont Alto. That reference was used to give the 4th Viscount Hawarden the British Earldom that became extinct in 1905. The present Viscount Hawarden, the 9th, lives and farms at Canterbury in Kent. Hawarden Castle in

Flint became the home of the Victorian Prime Minister William Gladstone and is now a study centre and library.

The Marquis of Ormonde of Kilkenny Castle had 12,428 acres in Tipperary, with a valuation of £7,420 about £623,280 in modern money.
See page 315.

The Lady Margaret Charteris of the Lodge Caher (Cahir) had 16,616 acres in 1876, with a valuation of £11,635 about £977,340 in modern money. In the overall Returns for England, Wales, Scotland and Ireland about 10 per cent of the owners of land are shown as women. This was at a time when women's possessions were still generally held via their husbands. However, the overall conclusion of Sir John Habbacuk in his huge volume on English Land ownership, *Marriage Debt and the Estates System 1650–1950*, showed that the most common form of transmission of estate in England was via an heiress and marriage. (Sir John seemed unaware of the Returns and scarcely mentions them.)

Lady Margaret Butler, daughter of the 2nd Earl of Glengall, who was created Viscount Cahir and Earl of Glengall in 1815, married Lieutenant Colonel the Hon. Richard Charteris in 1858, the year her father died and the Earldom became extinct. Her husband was the son of the 9th Earl of Weymss, whose family still owned over 62,000 acres in Scotland and England in 1876, with a princely valuation of £54,968.

She built Cahir Park as the family home, which remained in her son's possession until 1961, when it was sold after his death at the age of 94. Ferres mentions that the family had a London residence at 54 Grosvenor St in Mayfair.

George Staunton King Massey-Dawson, of Ballynacourty, Tipperary, had 19,093 acres in the county in 1876, valued at £6,331 about £531,804 in modern money. This is another case of the long lineage of landowners first encouraged by Hugh Lupus, William the Bastard's nephew when he became Earl of Chester after the Norman Conquest of England. Prior to that the family claim to have been lords in the French area of Massey from about 876. More immediately, the Dawson acreage was first granted in 1666, after the restoration of the Monarchy in England, following on from the end of Cromwell's Commonwealth Republic. John Dawson had arrived in Ireland in 1641 to fight the Irish rebels but had remained a staunch royalist, getting his reward in 1666 by way of some land forfeited by King James in Tipperary. George Staunton was a cavalry officer in the 14th Light Dragoons.

Following a series of childless marriages, the estates were sold off and the castle became a ruin. Parts of it were restored as a restaurant and guest house more recently.

The 4th Lord Dunally of Kilboy House, Nenagh, had 21,081 acres at a valuation in 1876 of £7,162 about £601,608 in modern money. The current holder of this Irish title, the 7th Baron Dunalley, Henry Francis Cornelius Prittie, lives in the Shetlands, where he practiced as a probation officer. The Bateman entry is brief, giving no details of the 4th Baron, Henry Cornelius O'Callaghan Prittie, who was the last Lord Lieutenant of Tipperary from 1905 to 1922. The house was burnt down by the IRA in 1922, but rebuilt, most recently by Shane Ryan, the son of Tony Ryan, a founder of Guinness Peat Aviation and of Ryanair.

The 4th Baron's aunt was the wife of the 1st Viscount Lismore, whose successor was the largest landowner in Tipperary in 1876 (*see* below).

Viscount Lismore of Shanbally, Clogheen, Tipperary, has 34,945 acres in 1876 with a valuation of £13,089 about £1,099,476 in modern money. This is one of the very few Catholic Gaelic families to retain lands from the period before 1600. By 1785 however, the O'Callaghan family had become part of the establishment, obtaining a peerage, that of Baron Lismore, in 1785.

How this was done is illustrated by the marriages made by that Baron. He married Frances, a daughter of Speaker Ponsonby of the Irish House of Commons. She was the niece of Earl of Bessborough and also of one of the most powerful men in England, the Duke of Devonshire. Their second son was Sir Robert William O'Callaghan GCB, a general in the army. The Baron was raised to the rank of Viscount in 1806.

He married a daughter of the Earl of Ormonde and sister of the Marquis of Ormonde. By 1835 he was a Privy Councillor, Lord Lieutenant of Tipperary and keeper of the deeds, the Custos Rutulorum. The 1st Viscount was succeeded by his son, George Ponsonby, an officer in the 17th Lancers, High Sheriff of County Tipperary, 1853, and Lord Lieutenant of County Tipperary from 1857 to 1885. When the 2nd Viscount died in 1898 he had no surviving male heirs and the title became extinct. He left the castle and estate to two cousins, Lady Beatrice Pole Carew and Lady Constance Butler, daughters of the 3rd Marquis of Ormonde.

In 1954 the Land Commission bought the estate from Major Patrick Pole-Carew. Lord Sackville-West tried to buy and preserve the castle but it was demolished by the Irish Government in 1957. Ferres quotes the following remarks by Bill Power of the Mitchelstown Heritage Society about the demolition. 'Few acts of official vandalism rival the decision by the Irish Government in 1957 to proceed with plans to demolish Shanbally Castle.'

This particular biography illustrates, fairly clearly, the structural issues facing the landlords of Ireland, apart from the basic one of their position leaving no place in the country for 98 per cent of its people. The aristocracy, even after the Act of Union, monopolised all the Irish seats in the UK Parliament, Commons and Lords. They were representative peers and MPs but who did they represent? Only themselves. They reinforced the land monopoly conferred on them by law and inheritance, by marrying each other and almost never stepping outside the gilded realms of their great estates to seek partners. When marriages failed to produce heirs, the land went to the all-encompassing cousinhood, excluding the possibility of any form of economic rationality entering the equation. They were 'nice' people, mainly according to themselves. No peasants published books but the establishment did, mainly about themselves; how nice they all were and how educated and civilised they were. It is quite easy to be 'nice' on a million a year. This blinded them to the need to bring in a larger and wider gene pool, to strengthen a breed who may have looked good, but who were often thoroughly thick with it.

Long list of the top 110 landowners in Tipperary in 1876 by acreage

		Acreage	Valuation 1876 (£)	Valuation current (£)
1	Lismore, Viscount, Shanbally, Clogheen, Co Tipperary	34,945	13,089	1,099,476
2	Dunally, Lord, Kilboy House, Nenagh	21,081	7,162	601,608
3	Dawson, G.K.S.M., Ballinacourty, Tipperary	19,093	6,331	531,804
4	Charteris, Lady Margaret, The Lodge, Caher	16,616	11,635	977,340
5	Ormonde, Marquess of, Kilkenny Castle	15,765	7,420	623,280
6	Hawarden, Viscount, Dondrum, Cashel	15,272	8,781	737,604
7	Buckley, Nathaniel, Galtee Castle, Mitchelstown	13,260	3,585	301,140
8	Clonmel, Earl of, Bishopscourt, Straffan, Co. Kildare	11,098	6,946	583,464
9	Moore, Arthur, Moorsfort, Tipperary	10,199	4,506	378,504
10	Bloomfield, Lord, Ciamaltha, Newport	9,912	1,240	104,160
11	Heard, Robert, Kinsale, Co. Cork	8,846	1,001	84,084
12	Toler, Hon. O.F.G., Albermarle St, London	8,789	5,317	446,628

		Acreage	Valuation 1876 (£)	Valuation current (£)
13	Barry, A.H. Smith, Queenstown, Co. Cork	8,620	12,131	1,019,004
14	Farrar, William Dent, Gortalougha, Borrisokane	8,297	2,962	248,808
15	Barker, Wm Ponsonby, Kilcooley Abbey, Kilcooley	8,184	5,286	444,024
16	De Stafford-O'Brien, Henry, Blatherwick Park, England	7,984	6,532	548,688
17	Orkney, Earl of, Ennismore Place, Knightsbridge, London	7,877	4,113	345,492
18	Norbury, Earl of Reps, Westerham, Kent, England	7,798	3,050	256,200
19	Normanton, Earl of, Somerly, Ringwood, Hants, England	7,653	6,933	582,372
20	Purefoy, Colonel B. Edward, Greenfields, Cappawhite	7,607	3,069	257,796
21	Lalor, Edmond James Power Reps, Long Orchard, Templemore	7,311	2,841	238,644
22	Carden, Sir John C. Bart, Templemore Abbey, Templemore	6,680	8,344	700,896
23	Going, William, Ballyphillip, Kilennaule	6,398	3,434	288,456
24	O'Connor, William, 8 Merrion Sq., North	6,178	6,213	521,892
25	Armstrong, Edward M., Mealiffe, Thurles	6,006	1,920	161,280
26	White, Colonel the Hon. Charles, Clonsilla, Co. Dublin	5,731	2,947	247,548
27	Scully, Vincent, Castle Park, Cashel	5,599	3,820	320,880
28	Perry, William, Newcastle, Clonmel	5,583	1,534	128,856
29	Clarke, David, Macclesfield and Bushy Park, Borrisokane	5,362	3,060	257,040
30	Gibson, Captain, Rockforest, Roscrea	5,214	2,245	188,580
31	Barton, Samuel H., Grove Fethard, Tipperary	5,119	4,607	386,988
32	Murdoch, Robert, 36 Leeson St Lower, Dublin	5,084	1,360	114,240
33	Bowen, Robert Cole, Bowen's Court, Castletownroche	5,060	2,574	216,216

		Acreage	**Valuation 1876 (£)**	**Valuation current (£)**
34	Roe, Robert, Loran Park, Roscrea	4,972	2,440	204,960
35	Lowe, Francis W., Kilshane, Tipperary	4,949	4,121	346,164
36	Clive, George J., Ballycroy, Co. Mayo	4,869	2,135	179,340
37	Donoughmore, Earl of, Knocklofty, Clonmel	4,711	4,763	400,092
38	Trench, Henry, Cangort Park, Roscrea	4,707	1,996	167,664
39	Spaight, William, Derrycastle, Killaloe	4,597	1,949	163,716
40	Smith, John L., France	4,534	2,120	178,080
41	Ashtown, Lord, Woodlawn, Ballinsaloe	4,526	1,795	150,780
42	Maher, N.V. Reps, Turtulla, Thurles	4,452	2,993	251,412
43	Otway, Captain R.J., Castle Otway, Templemore	4,362	1,830	153,720
44	Bolton, George, Nenagh	4,301	2,452	205,968
45	Waldron, Laur Reps, Rutland Sq., Dublin	4,060	3,426	287,784
46	Hare, John Pennefather, Durrow, Queen's County	3,922	2,672	224,448
47	Hankey, Lady Emily, 7 Hyde Park Place, London	3,899	2,846	239,064
48	Henry, Charles J., Cheltenham, England	3,870	2,052	172,368
49	Parker, Anthony, Castlelough, Portroe	3,806	2,368	198,912
50	Hopkinson, Jonathan, Egypt	3,799	668	56,112
51	Commissioner of Town, Cashel	3,623	2,362	198,408
52	Palliser, John, Comragh House, Co. Waterford	3,561	2,588	217,392
53	Bagwell, John, Marlfield, Clonmel	3,519	8,480	712,320
54	Dunsandle, Lord, Dunsandle, Killtolla, Co. Galway	3,514	5,533	464,772
55	Waterpark, Lord, Doveridge Hall, Derby	3,465	3,017	253,428
56	Molony, William and Joseph, Thurles	3,366	1,586	133,224

		Acreage	Valuation 1876 (£)	Valuation current (£)
57	Langley, Henry, 31 Queen's Gate Terrace, South Kensington, London	3,321	809	67,956
58	Fitzgibbon, Lady Louisa, Mount Shannon, Lisnagry	3,178	1,426	119,784
59	Quinn, Lord George, 15 Belgrave Sq., London	3,078	753	63,252
60	De Boisi, Count and Countess, Paris	3,017	1,539	129,276
61	Trant, John, Doves House, Thurles	2,970	2,128	178,752
62	Hamilton, Fredrick, Douglas, Cork	2,966	633	53,172
63	Waller, Sir Edward Bart, Landsdown Villa, St Leonard's-on-Sea	2,962	1,573	132,132
64	Maude, Hon. Mrs, 75 Onslow Sq., London	2,957	1,341	112,644
65	Trustees of Erasmus Smith Schools, Dublin	2,903	1,641	137,844
66	Portarlington, Earl of, Emo Park, Portarlington	2,897	2,214	185,976
67	Lalor, Thomas, Cregg, Carrick-on-Suir	2,873	2,398	201,432
68	Power, Sir Richard C. Bart, Kilfane, Thomastown	2,850	1,406	118,104
69	Fawcett, Rev. John, St John's Park, Blackheath, London	2,808	1,333	111,972
70	Langley, Henry, Archerstown, Thurles	2,808	1,068	89,712
71	Hunt, George Reps, Carrolbridge, Adare	2,790	391	32,844
72	Stoney, Thomas B., Portland Park, Roscrea	2,778	1,704	143,136
73	Perry, Samuel, Woodroofe, Clonmel	2,768	2,873	241,332
74	O'Byrne, Count John, Corville, Roscrea	2,753	1,721	144,564
75	Clarke Charles, Graiguenoe Park, Holy Cross	2,740	1,795	150,780
76	Carden, Captain Andrew, Barnane, Templemore	2,709	2,001	168,084
77	Twiss, George, Birdhill	2,706	1,747	146,748

		Acreage	Valuation 1876 (£)	Valuation current (£)
78	Scully, Rodolph, 9 Fitzgibbon St, Dublin	2,695	1,962	164,808
79	Scully, James, 30 Elgin Road, Dublin	2,662	2,763	232,092
80	Malcomson, Robert, Kilcommon, Caher	2,644	2,600	218,400
81	Rosse, Earl of, Birr Castle, Parsonstown	2,633	1,496	125,664
82	Going, Caleb, Traverstown, Nenagh	2,590	1,287	108,108
83	Quinn, William, Loughloher, Caher	2,581	2,295	192,780
84	Hutchinson, John D., Timony Park	2,576	1,092	91,728
85	Marshall, Sophia J., Baronne Court, Parsonstown	2,543	1,263	106,092
86	Going, Samuel M., Liskeveen House, Littleton, Thurles	2,522	1,395	117,180
87	Jones, William R., Tudor House, Monkstown, Co. Dublin	2,493	1,508	126,672
88	O'Brien, Denis, Carlow	2,448	1,218	102,312
89	Wall, Rev. Garrett, Ballingarry	2,437	2,042	171,528
90	Maxwell, Robert, Groomsford House, Belfast	2,353	1,491	125,244
91	Butler, Thomas, Ballycarron, Golden	2,335	1,897	159,348
92	Levinge, William H., Kildare St Club, Dublin	2,333	1,071	89,964
93	Head, William Henry, Derrylahan Park, Parsonstown	2,330	790	66,360
94	Armstrong, William, Ballydavid Passage East, Waterford	2,260	636	53,424
95	Hunt, F. Robert, Julian's Hall, Monkstown	2,245	463	38,892
96	Church Temporalities Commissioners, Dublin	2,240	2,582	216,888
97	Griffith, Joseph, Aghsmear, Roscrea	2,218	1,354	128,856
98	Bianconi, Chas Reps, Longfield, Cashel	2,215	2,306	193,704
99	Philips, Richard, Gaile House, Cashel	2,133	1,074	90,216

		Acreage	Valuation 1876 (£)	Valuation current (£)
100	Tollemache, Arthur F.C., Ham House, Petersham	2,124	1,255	105,420
101	Atkinson, James N., Ashley Park, Nenagh	2,108	1,180	99,120
102	Manserg, M.R., Grenane, Tipperary	2,086	2,406	202,104
103	Ward, C.T. Reps, England	2,076	839	70,476
104	Stannix, Jeremiah Reps, In Chancery	2,054	767	64,428
105	Maberly, Colonel W., Manchester Sq., London, and 1 Albert Rd, Sandycove, Kingsdown	2,051	1,011	84,924
106	Nugent, Lady, Ballinboro' Castle, Co. Westmeath	2,033	685	57,540
107	Bunbury, Ralph H., Normount, Kilkenny	2,032	1,309	109,956
108	Armitage, Dr, of Noan, Ballinure, Thurles	2,019	1,166	97,944
109	Clarke, Jeremiah Reps, Ballyglasheen	2,011	1,281	107,604
110	Barnes, John, Ballyglasheen, Clonmel	2,002	1,054	88,536

The top 20 landowners in Tipperary in 1876 by rateable valuation (income)

		Acreage	Valuation 1876 (£)	Valuation current (£)
1	Lismore, Viscount, Shanbally, Clogheen, Co. Tipperary	34,945	13,089	1,099,476
2	Smith-Barry, A.H., of Fota Island Queenstown, Co. Cork	8,620	12,131	1,019,004
3	Charteris, Lady Margaret, The Lodge, Caher	16,616	11,635	977,340
4	Hawarden, Viscount, Dondrum, Cashel	15,272	8,781	737,604
5	Bagwell, John, Marlfield, Clonmel	3,519	8,480	712,320
6	Carden, Sir John C. Bart, Templemore Abbey, Templemore	6,680	8,344	700,896

		Acreage	Valuation 1876 (£)	Valuation current (£)
7	Ormonde, Marquess of, Kilkenny Castle	15,765	7,420	623,280
8	Dunally, Lord, Kilboy House, Nenagh	21,081	7,162	601,608
9	Clonmel, Earl of, Bishopscourt, Straffan, Co. Kildare	11,098	6,946	583,464
10	Normanton, Earl of, Somerly, Ringwood, Hants, England	7,653	6,933	582,372
11	De Stafford-O'Brien, Henry, Blatherwick Park, England	7,984	6,532	548,688
12	Dawson, G.K.S.M., Ballinacourty, Tipperary	19,093	6,331	531,804
13	O'Connor, William, 8 Merrion Sq., North	6,178	6,213	521,892
14	Dunsandle, Lord, Dunsandle, Killtolla, Co. Galway	3,514	5,533	464,772
15	Toler, Hon. O.F.G., Albermarle St, London	8,789	5,317	446,628
16	Barker, Wm Ponsonby, Kilcooley Abbey, Kilcooley	8,184	5,286	444,024
17	Donoughmore, Earl of, Knocklofty, Clonmel	4,711	4,763	400,092
18	Barton, Samuel H., Grove Fethard, Tipperary	5,119	4,607	386,988
19	Moore, Arthur, Moorsfort, Tipperary	10,199	4,506	378,504
20	Lowe, Francis W., Kilshane, Tipperary	4,949	4,121	346,164

TYRONE

	1876	2020 Est
Population in County Tyrone	215,668	179,886
All owners of land	2,787	86,217
Percentage of the population	1.6	–
Owners of nothing at all	212,881	Figures not available
Percentage of the population	98.4	–
Size of County	775,285	775,040 acres
Number of dwellings (of which rented)	41,263 (38,476)	–
Number of owned farm holdings	1,717	5,906

County comparisons

	Acreage in 2017	Population in 1876
County Tyrone	775,285	215,668
Cornwall, England	758,961	362,343
Ayrshire, Scotland	721,947	220,908
Carmarthenshire, Wales	510,574	115,710

The 1st Duke of Abercorn of Baronscourt, Newtownstewart, County Tyrone, had 47,615 acres in the county in 1876, with a valuation of £25,420 about £2,135,280 in modern money. This Harrow-educated Duke was the sixtieth largest landowner in the United Kingdom of Great Britain, Scotland, Ireland and Wales in 1876. He had a grand total of 78,662 acres in Ireland and Scotland. By the time Bateman was updating the records, the Duke's holdings in Tyrone had risen to 60,000 acres, with 16,500 acres in Donegal, 1,500 acres in Edinburgh and 662 acres in Renfrew, for a total of 78,662 acres, with a valuation of £53,400. Bateman merely notes that the Duke was twice Lord Lieutenant of Ireland. Three of his sons sat as MPs in the UK House of Commons, all for English constituencies. Ferres mentions estates in England but they do not appear in Bateman and the estate was undergoing an extensive acquisition programme under the management of the 1st Duke.

The title is recent; the Dukedom in the peerage of Ireland being a promotion from that of Marquis granted in 1868. The family history is, however, extremely complex with Ferres tracing the line back to France prior to the invasion of England in 1066. The family name is Hamilton and there is another Dukedom in the family, that of Hamilton and Brandon, the thirty-second largest landowner in Great Britain in 1876, with 157,368 acres. The estate in Ireland arose from grants made by James I to the then Earl of Abercorn in 1611. The family home remains lived in by the family and the estate is managed. The family also own the Belle Isle estate in County Fermanagh (*see* Porter).

The title is extant and the current Eton-educated Duke is James Hamilton, who sat as MP for Fermanagh and South Tyrone as an Ulster Unionist.

The Earl of Castle Stewart, Stuart Hall, Stewartstown, County Tyrone, had 32,615 acres in the county in 1876, with a valuation of £11,768 about £988,512 in modern money. This Earldom is still extant and is held, at the time of writing, by Arthur Patrick Avondale Stuart, the 8th Earl. He was educated at Eton and was a Lieutenant in the Scots Guards. He styles himself a retired farmer. The family still live on the estate, although the castle was destroyed by the IRA in 1972. They also have a town house in London's Barbican. His ancestor in 1876 had, with the Tyrone acres, 2,260 acres in Cavan for a total estate of 34,875 acres, with a valuation of £13,113.

As with the Duke of Abercorn, the Stuarts obtained their first land grant of 3,000 acres in Tyrone in 1611 and a peerage in 1619, from James I as part of the plantation of Ulster. The Stuarts are a royal line, tracing their lineage back to King Robert II of Scotland.

There is no public record of the estate itself, although records relating to it may exist at the Northern Ireland Public Records Office.

The 4th Earl of Caledon of Caledon had 29,236 acres in the county in 1876, with a valuation of £16,518 about £1,387,512 in modern money. This title is still extant and is held by Nicholas James Alexander, the 7th Earl. He was the Lord Lieutenant of Armagh in 1989. He gives his seat as Caledon Castle, County Tyrone.

The holder of the estates in 1876, the 4th Earl, who was educated at Harrow, had, with the Tyrone acreage, 2,877 acres in Armagh and 1,947 acres in Herts, England, for a total of 34,060 acres with a valuation of £ 22,321.

The current Earl opened the castle to the public for the first time in twenty years in 2015. The *Belfast Telegraph* variously reported the estate as being one of 3,000 acres, and then of 5,000 acres, with a further 3,000 acres in Herts. It also says that the family are intensely private.

The Caledon Village website has a note on the estate that says it was bought from the 7th Earl of Cork for £94,400 in 1776 by James Alexander, later the 1st Earl of Caledon. The Earls of Cork and Orrery had acquired the estate from the Hamilton family in 1738 (*see* Duke of Abercorn, above). The 1st Earl was a director of the East India Company who was said to have accumulated a fortune of over £250,000 by 1776. The Caledon Estate Company that runs the estate was formed in 1929.

The most famous 'son of the house' was Harold Alexander, later Earl of Tunis, who was supreme Allied commander in the Mediterranean during the Second World War. He was the son of the 4th Earl of Caledon and was the third of the three extraordinary Ulster generals who helped the Allies to success against the Nazis. (The other two were Field Marshal the Viscount Alan Brooke [*see* Fermanagh], and Field Marshal the Viscount Bernard Montgomery.)

The Church Temporalities Commisisoners of Dublin held 28,002 acres in County Tyrone in 1876, with a valuation of £13,462 about £1,130,808 in modern money. *See* County Dublin and Wicklow.

Sir John Marcus Stewart Bart of Balleygawley, County Tyrone, had 27,902 acres in the county in 1876, with a valuation of £6,409 about £538,536 in modern money. In 1876 this Rugby School-educated Baronet had, with the Tyrone acres, 629 acres in Galway for a total estate of 28,534 acres, with a valuation of £6,752. The estate was originally a Hamilton-Georges property, which the incumbent's grandfather bought in 1811. The grandfather was married to Mary, a daughter of Mervyn Archdale of Castle Archdale (*see* Fermanagh). He was also unusual in once being elected to Parliament for four different constituencies at the same election. He chose to sit for Bangor.

By 1922 the estate had been bought by Hugh McLaurin, owner of a fruit merchants in Belfast. That year the IRA attacked and burnt the castle. McLaurin then sold the estate.

Major Arthur Willoughby Cole-Hamilton of Beltrim, Gortin, NewtownStewart, had 16,682 acres in the county in 1876, with a valuation of £4,506 about £378,504 in modern money. Hamilton clearly amended the Returns when he contacted Bateman, adding his military title and changing the acreage to 16,811 acres and the valuation to £4,890.

The estate originated with the Rt Hon. Sir Claude Hamilton of Bodoney, County Tyrone, at the end of the Elizabethan plantations around 1600. He was the second son of the 1st Baron Paisley and brother of the 1st Earl of Abercorn. The marriages of the immediate family are of interest in the way they demonstrate the almost incestuous closeness with which landowners cling to landowners, land clearly coming before love or any other such trivialities. Major Hamilton Cole married Emilia daughter of Rev. Charles Cobbe Beresford and granddaughter of the Hon. John Beresford, second son of Marcus, 1st Earl of Tyrone and brother of George 1st Marquis of Waterford. His heir, William Claude, married Caroline daughter of the Hon. Andrew Godfrey Stewart and granddaughter of the 1st Earl of Castle Stewart.

The estate is now part of the Blakiston-Huston estate, whose owner, Richard Patrick Blakiston-Houston OBE, is a justice of the peace and a Deputy Lieutenant of the County. He was educated at Eton. He was High Sheriff of County Down in 1989. His wife is a relative of the Fitzalan-Howard branch of the Duke of Norfolk's family and a Deputy Lieutenant of the County. Some things continue as before.

Captain Sir William McMahon Bart (the reps of) of Fecarry House, Omagh, had 16,326 acres of the county in 1876, with a valuation of £3,375 about £283,500 in modern money. Information on this Baronet in Bateman is sketchy, despite the acreage, which in 1876 totalled, with the Tyrone acreage, 21,029 acres including 4,671 acres in Clare at Kilfenora, and 32 acres in County Dublin. The valuation was £5,302. Ferres simply quotes Bateman. McMahon was a captain in the Life Guards, a cavalry soldiers who guarded the 'blood royal'. He then went on to become an attaché at Imperial British embassies in Stuttgart, Florence, Munich and Constantinople, the latter an important post and known as the Legation to the 'Sublime Porte', the diplomatic name for the Ottoman Empire's diplomatic headquarters. Sir William died unmarried and the title went to his brother, Lionel, who was an infantry officer, High Sheriff and Deputy Lieutenant of the County, who died unmarried and upon whose death the title became extinct. There is some information on the Clare estate in the NUI Galway estate database.

Sir William Edward Hercules Verner Bart, of Church Hill, Moy, County Armagh, had 16,012 acres in County Tyrone in 1876, with a valuation of £6,622 about £556,248 in modern money. This very substantial landowner had, with the Tyrone acreage, 5,436 acres in Armagh, 2,526 acres in Monaghan, 140 acres in County Wicklow and 113 acres in county Dublin, for a total estate of 24,257 acres with a valuation of £13,138.

The 3rd Baronet, who held the estate in 1876 was the son of Sir William Verner, whose wife was Harriett Wingfield, a daughter of a son of the 3rd Viscount Powerscourt (*see* Wicklow). He was an MP and died in 1873. The 3rd Baronet, Sir William Edward, died of cirrhosis of the liver in London in 1886 and was succeeded by his cousin, Sir Edward Wingfield Verner, who became High Sheriff of County Dublin, MP for Lisburn and MP for County Armagh.

With the death of the 6th Baronet in 1975 the title became extinct. According to Ferres, the house at Church Hill was put up for sale for £12,000 in 1898, but did not sell. Parts of the estate were later sold to the Irish Peat Development company and by 1927 the entire estate had been sold.

The Earl of Belmore of Castle Coole, Enniskillen, had 14,388 acres in County Tyrone in 1876, with a valuation of £7,541 about £633,444 in modern money. This title is still extant and is held by John Armar Lowry-Corry, the 8th Earl. He is married to a daughter of the Earl of Clanwilliam.

The 4th Earl, who held the estates in 1876, had, with the Tyrone acres, 5,041 acres in Fermanagh, for a total acreage of 19,429 with a valuation of £11,015. He was an active politician in London, where he started out in the Home Office. He then went to Australia, where he was Governor of New South Wales. He came back to Ireland, where he was Commissioner for Education. His wife was a relative of Prime Minister William Gladstone. He came back to Ireland in 1872 and was one of the Lord Justices of Ireland during the absence of the Lord Lieutenant.

His ancestor, in his memoirs of Fermanagh and Tyrone, makes a very interesting comment, relative to the comments in the introduction about the exclusiveness of the political and power structure in 1876 and the period leading up to it. It should be recalled that the electorate was, like landownership, tiny relative to the population. You could only vote if you held property and only the landlords could grant you an adequate amount of land to vote. But what Belmore is saying is much simpler. The landlords did not sit on behalf of the people. They sat in their own interests, which had no connection with the interests of the population generally, and was in fact opposed it. There was no democracy in the UK at the time, just some form of derived Athenian elite oligarchy, with the population in general enduring a form of slavery or serfdom:

> It will be seen that as regards the county, (Tyrone) the members have been always chosen from amongst the landlords or their immediate relatives. Most of those who were actually landowners have been residents; whilst the great majority of the principal resident families have had at least one turn in the representation. I have taken the list of members as they are given in the Parliamentary Return of 1877. From this it appears that the Cole family has had seven members who nave represented the county, the Archdall family five, the Corry family three, the Brooke family three, the Crichton family two, the Hume family (now succeeded in the county by the Loftus family) two, and the Maguire, Davies, Blennerhasset, and Irvine families, one each. Of these families, the circumstances attending that of Archdall are, as far as I know, unique in Parliamentary history – five members of this family, belonging to only four successive generations, have continuously held one of the county seats for a period of upwards of one hundred and fifty-three years without interruption to the present day.
>
> The Earl of Belmore, 1886, Castle Coole

Thomas Arthur Hope, of Wavertree, Lancashire, and of Stanton, Bebington, Birkenhead, had 13,995 acres in Tyrone in 1876, with a valuation of £1,900 about £159,600 in modern money. The Bateman entry for this quite considerable landowner has no biographical details. To the Tyrone acres, which are corrected to 14,006 acres, and the valuation to £2,385, Bateman adds 2,220 acres in Cheshire, 447 acres in Flint, and 18 acres in Lancashire, for a total estate of 16,691 acres, with a valuation of £8,864.

There are no further records of this estate in the public domain.

Top 98 owners of land in County Tyrone in 1876 ranked by acreage

		Acreage	Valuation 1876 (£)	Valuation current (£)
1	Abercorn, Duke of, Baronscourt, Newtownstewart	47,615	25,420	2,135,280
2	Castlestuawart Earl of, Stuart Hal, lStewartstown	32,615	11,768	988,512
3	Caledon, Earl of, Caledon, Co. Tyrone	29,236	16,518	1,387,512
4	Church Temporalities, Commissioners of, Upper Merrion St, Dublin.	28,002	13,462	1,130,808
5	Stewart, Sir John M. Bart, Ballygawley House, Ballygawley	27,905	6,409	538,356
6	Hamilton, Arthur W. Cole, Beltrim, Gortin, Newtownstewart	16,682	4,506	378,504
7	McMahon, Sir William Bart Reps, Fecarry House, Omagh	16,326	3,375	283,500
8	Verner, Sir William, Church Hill, Moy	16,012	6,622	556,248
9	Belmore, Earl of, Castlecoole, Enniskillen	14,359	7,541	633,444
10	Hope, Thomas Arthur, Wavertree, Lancashire, England	13,995	1,900	159,600
11	Dorchester, Lord, Greywell Hall, Hants, England	12,607	727	61,068
12	Smith, Michael, Glasgow	10,967	1,476	123,984
13	De Bille, Louisa Eliz, Slaughtfreedan, Cookstown	10,452	1,842	154,728

		Acreage	Valuation 1876 (£)	Valuation current (£)
14	Browne, Thomas R., Aughintane Castle, Fivemiletown	10,125	3,973	333,732
15	Ranfurly, Earl of, Dungannon	9,467	10,958	950,472
16	Powerscourt, Viscount, Enniskerry, Co. Wicklow	9,230	8,322	699,048
17	Eccles, John S., Ecclesville, Fintona	9,227	5,074	426,216
18	Stronge, Sir James M. Bart, Tynan Abbey, Armagh	8,426	3,854	323,736
19	Lowry, Robert William, Pomeroy House, Dungannon	8,158	3,848	323,232
20	Gordon, Robert Francis, -	7,873	1,243	104,412
21	Gervais, Francis John of Cecil, Augher Co Tyrone	7,727	5,034	422,856
22	Ogilby, Claude, Altnachree Castle, Donemana	7,050	3,511	294,924
23	Greer, James, Omagh	6,905	3,113	261,492
24	Mountray, Rev. J.J of Favour Royal, Aughnacloy	6,545	4,762	400,008
25	Gunning, James, Laymount, Cookstown	5,950	4,283	359,772
26	Charlemont, Earl of, Roxboro Castle, Moy	5,903	7,043	591,612
27	Archdale, Mervyn, Castle Archdale, Lisnanick	5,605	3,474	291,816
28	Gardiner, Charles Reps, Court of Chancery, Dublin	5,506	1,745	146,580
29	Goff, Joseph, Dungannon	5,433	3,965	333,060
30	Maturin, Daniel Baird	4,900	2,471	207,564
31	M'Alpine, Colonel James Reps, Dublin	4,727	719	60,396
32	MClintock, Major G.P., Seskinore House, Omagh	4,563	3,209	269,556
33	Montgomery, H.D.F., Fivemiletown	4,452	2,484	208,656
34	Henry, Robert J., Castledawson, Co. Derry	4,361	995	83,580
35	M'Causland, Alexander, Drumnakilly, Omagh	4,295	1,574	132,216
36	Commissioners of Endowed Schools, Dublin	3,961	2,152	180,768

		Acreage	Valuation 1876 (£)	Valuation current (£)
37	Galbraith, John S., Clanabogan, Omagh	3,826	2,173	182,532
38	Porter, Rev. John G. Reps	3,468	1,796	150,864
39	Sinclair, James, Dundarg, Coleraine	3,247	449	37,716
40	Humphreys, John Reps, Miltown House, Strabane	3,193	563	47,292
41	Lowry, James Corry Jones, Rockdale House, Dungannon	3,141	2,348	197,232
42	Stack, George Hall, Mullaghmore, Omagh	3,134	835	70,140
43	Black, William F., Lislap, Omagh	3,082	842	70,728
44	Staples, Sir Nathaniel Alexander Bart, Lisson, Cookstown	3,078	2,036	171,024
45	Gledstanes, Mountray, Fardross House, Clogher	2,982	956	80,304
46	Lowry, John F.H., Pomeroy House, Dungannon	2,929	250	21,000
47	Lendrum, James, Magheracross, Ballinamallard	2,922	1,969	165,396
48	Mansfield, George A., Kilmore Lodge, Drumquin	2,839	410	34,440
49	Lindsay, Fredk Sandys, Loughry, Cookstown	2,821	2,645	222,180
50	Percival, John, M., -	2,805	1,283	107,772
51	Moore, Alexander M., -	2,686	2,110	177,240
52	Brackenridge, G.C., Ashfield Park, Clogher	2,649	843	70,812
53	Auchinleck, Captain Thomas, Creevenagh House, Omagh	2,616	1,316	110,544
54	Knox, William Reps, Clonleigh, Strabane	2,541	1,079	90,636
55	Cochrane, Wm Reps, -	2,523	738	61,992
56	Burges, John Ynyr, Parkanour, Dungannon	2,485	1,956	164,304
57	Clarke, James J., Lurgantogher House, Maghera	2,439	542	45,528
58	Martin, John, Shrigley Killyleagh, Co. Down	2,436	1,656	139,104

		Acreage	Valuation 1876 (£)	Valuation current (£)
59	Lindsay, John of Burlyns, Dastwoodhay, Hampshire	2,430	1,716	144,144
60	Jones, Mrs, Dublin	2,305	119	9,996
61	Hines, Mrs Rebecca, Warwick Terrace, Leeson Park, Dublin	2,278	515	43,260
62	Edie, Alexander Reps, 8 Alma Terrace, Monkstown, Co. Dublin	2,248	548	46,032
63	Maxwell, Isabella, Kilfaddy, Clogher	2,218	1,128	94,752
64	Chayne, Captain William, Portrush, Co. Antrim	2,180	871	73,164
65	Sinclair, William, Holly Hill, Artigarvin, Strabane	2,152	633	53,172
66	Kennedy, Chas George Belgrave, Mullantain, Stewardstown	2,108	1,693	142,212
67	Stewart, Alexander G., Union Club, Trafalgar Sq., London	2,097	1,535	128,940
68	Story, Rev. William, Corick, Clogher	2,065	293	24,612
69	West, Rev. W.J. Reps, -	2,061	316	26,544
70	Graham, Christopher Reps, Irvinestown	2,035	247	20,748
71	Johnston, S.Y., Snowhill, Brookboro'	1,981	1,327	111,468
72	Vesey, Samuel, Derrybard House, Seskinore	1,953	1,306	109,704
73	M'Crossan, Henry, Dublin	1,901	635	53,340
74	Todd, William, Orwell Road, Rathgar, Co. Dublin	1,824	1,080	90,720
75	Bailie, The Misses, Phoenix Lodge, Cookstown	1,798	1,266	106,344
76	Irvine, Lieutenant Colonel John G., Killadeas, Ballycasidy	1,795	662	55,608
77	Alexander, Robert J., Portglenone, Co. Antrim	1,769	1,178	98,952
78	M'Farland, John, Gortmore-ter, Omagh	1,732	436	36,624
79	Edwards, John, Kilcroagh, Castlederg	1,727	459	38,556
80	Gresson, Rev. W.R., Dublin	1,705	715	60,060

		Acreage	Valuation 1876 (£)	Valuation current (£)
81	D'Arcy, Francis, Castle Irvine, Irvinestown	1,689	1,008	84,672
82	King, Robert, Annesley Lodge, Coalisland	1,683	979	82,236
83	Buchanan, William, -	1,658	205	17,220
84	Ogilby, James, Dungiven	1,657	377	31,668
85	M'Farland, Henry, -	1,628	206	17,304
86	Gore, Hugh E., Clogher	1,627	935	78,540
87	Porter, Mrs Margaret Anne, Crosh House, Newtownstewart	1,625	622	52,248
88	Mountray, Henry Reps, -	1,620	1,111	93,324
89	Scott, John, Dromore, Co. Tyrone	1,604	930	78,120
90	Ellis, Robert Hawkes, Rash, Omagh	1,596	1,923	161,532
91	Conyngham, Wm F.L., Springhill, Moneymore	1,583	1,602	134,568
92	Patterson, Alexander, Carnamoney, Draperstown	1,580	333	27,972
93	Dunbar, George Reps, Woburn, Donaghadee	1,513	1,391	116,844
94	Irvine, Henry, Gutalowry House, Cookstown	1,474	490	41,160
95	Spottiswoode, Andrew, Manor House, Bellaghy, Co. Derry	1,412	721	60,564
96	Dawson, The Hon. Captain, Dartry, Co. Monaghan	1,387	1,042	87,528
97	Ashe, George Reps, Lisburn	1,216	126	10,584
98	Caulfield, James Alfred, -	1,190	1,133	95,172

Top 20 owners of land in Tyrone in 1876 by valuation (income)

		Acreage	Valuation 1876 (£)	Valuation current (£)
1	Abercorn, Duke of, Baronscourt, Newtownstewart	47,615	25,420	2,135,280
2	Caledon, Earl of, Caledon House, Caledon	29,236	16,518	1,387512

		Acreage	Valuation 1876 (£)	Valuation current (£)
3	Church Temporalities, Commissioners of, Upper Merrion St, Dublin	28,002	13,462	1,130,808
4	Castlestuart, Earl of, Stuartstown	32,615	11,768	988,512
5	Ranfurly, Earl of, Dungannon	9,467	10,958	950,472
6	Powerscourt, Viscount, Enniskerry, Co. Wicklow	9,230	8,322	699,048
7	Belmore, Earl of, Castlecoole, Enniskillen	14,359	7,541	633,444
8	Charlemont, Earl of, Roxboro Castle, Moy	5,903	7,043	591,612
9	Verner, Sir William, Church Hill, Moy	16,012	6,622	556,248
10	Stewart, Sir John M. Bart, Ballygawley House, Ballygawley	27,905	6,409	538,356
11	Eccles, John S., Ecclesville, Fintona	9,227	5,074	426,216
12	Gervais, Francis J., Cecil, Augher	7,727	5,034	422,856
13	Mountray, Rev J.J., of Favour Royal, Aughnacloy	6,545	4,762	400,008
14	Hamilton, Arthur W. Cole, Beltrim, Gortin, Newtownstewart	16,682	4,506	378,504
15	Gunning, James, Laymount, Cookstown	5,950	4,283	359,772
16	Browne, Thomas R., Aughintane Castle, Fivemiletown	10,125	3,973	333,732
17	Goff, Joseph, Dungannon	5,433	3,965	333,060
18	Stronge, Sir James M. Bart, Tynan Abbey, Armagh	8,426	3,854	323,736
19	Lowry, Robert William, Pomeroy House, Dungannon	8,158	3,848	323,232
20	Ogilby, Claude, Altnachree Castle, Donemana	7,050	3,511	294,924

WATERFORD

Population in County Waterford	248,458	113,795
All owners of land	1,767	48,185
Percentage of the population	0.96	42.3
Owners of nothing at all	246,691	32,328
Percentage of the population	99.04	–
Size of County	455,435 acres	456,320 acres
Number of dwellings (of which rented)	21,252 (20,099)	42,239
Number of owned farm holdings over one acre	1,767	2,761

County Comparisons

	Acreage 1876	Population 1876
County Waterford, Ireland	455,435 acres	248,458
Buckinghamshire, England	465,237	175,879
Caithness, Scotland	438,943	39,992
Cardiganshire, Wales (Ceredigion)	443,554	70,125

More than 800 years ago, in May 1169, on the edge of this county at Bannow Strand (or Bay) in Wexford, the initiating pattern for all subsequent Irish landed estates began. It happened when the dethroned King of Leinster, Dermot McMurrough, summoned some descendants of the Norman invaders of England to Ireland, to help him get his Leinster throne back. The words of St Agustin, quoted in Carlow County, describe the bunch who landed at Bannow Strand (now in the modern county of Wexford, but cited here because the invasion swiftly moved to Waterford) in 1169 fairly accurately as, 'ragamuffins'. And there were less than 500 of them. But it was the legal principle that the sovereign owned all land that distinguished Strongbow's rabble from those that Henry II brought with him, landing at Waterford on 17 October 1171. Henry brought that principle with him, installed it in Ireland and it is with us still, even if few of the estates are.

The county is rich in ancient ruins and the city itself is a rare Viking settlement. There are a huge number of prehistoric sites in Waterford, now set out on the Prehistoric Waterford web site. Beginning in the 5th century AD, when Ireland converted to Christianity, there was a flourishing of monastic foundations. There are the remains of many individual saints churches and cells. What is less well recorded was whether the Norman's, who always brought their own clergy along to bless the thievery and share in the spoils, granted the huge tracts of land to the monasteries that their confreres did in England. Unfortunately, wars do away with records as well as people. As with Carlow, there are a significant number of ruins with cited connections to the Knights Templar at Ballyvooney Preceptory, Bewley Preceptory, Cappagh Preceptory, Crooke Preceptory, Kilbarry Preceptory, Killongford Preceptory and Rivercrew Abbey. The Templars were immensely rich, and mobile. The Waterford coast and the rich and generally peaceful country behind the dunes would have made it a very attractive haven for these religious warriors. The haven would have been even more attractive if there were large monastic estates in it, as there were. Those institutions created stability and were often themselves the local bankers, interacting with the Templar's European operations and obtaining large cash and other assets from the settling Norman landowners.

Even today there is still a residue of the monastic tradition, with the austere Cistercian foundation and farm at Mount Melleray, in the Knockmealdown mountains, conducting services and retreats.

East of the city the rivers Barrow and the Suir meet, creating a wide estuary.

The major landowners

The Marquis of Waterford, KP, MP, Curraghmore, Portlaw. Acres in Waterford 39,883. Valuation £27,705. Modern equivalent approximately £2,237,220. The Beresford marquisate is not very old as such things go, having been created in 1789, a promotion from a previous Barony in 1786. No small cause of the promotion was the vast acreage the family had obtained, not just in Waterford, but all over Ireland. In the 1876 Returns the family name occurs many times, in many counties, including being missed several times as with the 1876 holder of the title, who had land in Kilkenny 406 acres, Cavan 305 acres, Kildare 55 acres. The Wicklow acreage at 26,055 acres is included. His combined holdings of 66,684 acres had a valuation of £32,752, the equivalent of about £2,751, 168 in 2020/21. Because this is one of the surviving great estates, with the current 9th Marquis Henry Nicholas de la Poer Beresford in residence at Curraghmore, there are a number of points to note. The 9th Marquis, unlike the incumbent in 1976, the 5th Marquis, was educated at Harrow but, like the 5th Marquis, his father the 8th Marquis, served in the poshest and most expensive regiment in the British army, the Life Guards. Service in that particular regiment also provided close proximity to the Crown, as the function of the officers of the regiment is to protect the blood royal, with their own lives if necessary. When his first wife died in 1873 the 5th Marquis married in 1874, a daughter of the Duke of Beaufort, whose own estate ran to over 51,000 acres in the west of England. The 5th Marquis also sat as an MP, was Lord Lieutenant of the County, and was Master of the Buckhounds, a ministerial appointment in Government. The web site for Curraghmore claims that the Beresford's arrived in England with William the Bastard, a claim the Beresford Family Society is unable to substantiate as yet (but they are working on it). However, look at the fifth entry for this county, Count Edmund de la Poer, and this is where there does appear to be a link to the Norman occupation of England.

The current estate is stated at 2,500 acres on the Curraghmore web site.

Lord Stuart de Decies, Drumana, Cappoquin. Acres in Waterford 30,822. Valuation £11,463, about £962,892 in current values. Lord Decies does not appear in Bateman as a landowner in Ireland, living instead at Morpeth in Northumberland. The actual title is confusing and is that of Lord Stuart de Decies, a member of the Villiers-Stuart family. That family were in fact the family of the Marquess of Bute, a Scottish aristocratic family who converted to Catholicism in 1868. The omission from Bateman may have arisen from the refusal of the Crown to recognise his father's marriage and disavowal the title in 1874. It is not clear what happened to the estate afterwards but the house at Dromana is still lived in by members of the family and the house is open to visitors. There is a family history with the Dromana House web site which gives further details of the family history in Ireland, which is fascinating, linking them to the Fitzgeralds and with Daniel O'Connell, whose own great, great, great, great grandson was the Rt Hon Lord Paddy Ashdown of Norton Sub Hamden and leader of the Liberal Democratic Party in the 1990s.

The Duke of Devonshire. Chatsworth, Bakewell, Derbyshire. Acres in Waterford 27,483. Valuation £15,000. The current equivalent would be about £1,260,000 in current values. The 7th Duke of Devonshire held land in fourteen counties, three of them in Ireland. His total holdings came to 198,572 acres with a valuation of £180,750, about £15,183,000 in current cash. The family name is Cavendish and the Cavendish laboratories at Cambridge University arose from a donation from the 7th Duke, who was a Fellow of the Royal Society, one of the world's premier scientific bodies. The 7th Duke's contribution was to fund the Cavendish professorship of Experimental Physics in 1874. James Clerk Maxwell was the first holder. Successive Fellows at the Laboratory have won the Noble Prize for physics, chemistry and related sciences on twenty-nine occasions. Few donations in history can have had such extraordinary results over the decades. The Cavendish family, who got the Dukedom in 1694, have been enormously influential in British politics both before and after that time. Money, and they had it in titanic quantities throughout the period, helped. It helped to buy votes throughout the country when you needed property to vote. The intertwining of Palace, power and politics was fairly total in the pre-democratic period and the Cavendishe's were at the nexus of these three strands for most of the last 500 years. The 60,000 acres in Ireland gave the Dukedom huge influence. In a way, you could say that kings came and king's went but the Cavendishe's went on forever, seemingly. The Land Commission reduced the Irish acres but 8,000 acres remain around Lismore Castle, making it one of the biggest estates in the country. The 2020 *Sunday Times* Rich List values the present Duke at £895 million, a serious underestimate given the 70,000 acres they still own in the North of England, and the Raphaels, Van Dyck's, and Rembrant's in the art collection.

Richard Chearnley (Henry Philip in Bateman) held 18,548 acres at Salterbridge in 1876 with a valuation of £5,408, about £454,272 in current values. The valuation indicates that, sizable though the acreage was, it was mostly poor, raising less than 30 pence an acre at a time when good acreage made a £1 per acre in Ireland and £2 in England. According to Bateman Chearnley was educated at Eton. He succeeded his brother to the estate in 1879. Henry Philip was High Sheriff of Waterford in 1882 and a major in the Waterford Artillery Militia. The estate stayed in the family until 1947 and according to Ferrers the current owners of the house are Philip and Susie Wingfield. It is occasionally open to the public.

Count Edmond de la Poer MP of Gurteen la Poer, Kilshheelan had 13,448 acres in Waterford valued at £4,920, about £413,280 in current values. This is an unusual estate, held by a Catholic peer, who was both an MP and private chamberlain to Pope Pious X. The peerage was the 18th Lord de la Poer and a subsidiary one of Baron Curraghmore, the site of the Marquis of Waterford's family home. Count Edmond was also a Knight of Malta and HM Lord Lieutenant of Waterford in 1909. The family name of the Beresford Marquesses of Waterford is De la Poer Beresford and the link goes back a long way. The papal peerage was created in 1864 just before the Count started work on Castle Gurteen. It has subsequently been the home to the artist Gottfried Helnwein and his family since 1998, originally sold by the 20th Baron de la Poer in 1979. The Wikipedia entry credits the de la Poer family with decent from Sir Robert De Poer, who came to Ireland with Strongbow, and were granted the City of Waterford, as well as being made Marshalls of Ireland by Henry II in 1172.

John Palliser CMG, of Comragh, Kilmacthomas had 9,825 acres in Waterford valued at £3,146 about the equivalent of £264,264 in modern money (2020). John Palliser was a commander of the order of St Michael and

St George, essentially a high British honour for diplomacy. Bateman credits him with serving on the (North American) Boundary Commission and helping draw the line between Lake Superior and the Pacific in the 1ate 1850's. Palliser later found a new pass through the Rocky Mountains, suitable for railroads. Palliser's Bateman entry shows 3,561 acres in Tipperary and 460 acres in Kilkenny, to give him a total acreage of 13,846 with a valuation of £6,800, about £571,200 in 2017 money. He led several other expeditions, including one to Nassau which has never been explained. For his expedition to Noya Zemlya in Russia he was rumoured to be a spy, not helped by the CMG in 1877. For his Canadian work he was awarded the Royal Geographical Society's medal in 1859. He poured his own money into the expeditions and the estates were in dire straits when he died in 1881.

The 3rd Lord Ashtown (Fredrick Trench) of Woodlawn, Co Galway had 9,435 acres in Waterford in 1876, with a valuation of £7,397, about £621,348 in current money. Eton educated Lord Ashtown had land in nine counties, eight in Ireland. He had 6,386 acres in Yorkshire, 11,273 acres in Limerick, 8,310 acres in Galway, 2,780 acres in King's County, 4,526 acres in Tipperary, 841 acres in Roscommon, 50 acres in Dublin and 42 acres in Westmeath. His total acreage, with then Waterford holdings were 43,643 acres with a valuation of £34,689, about £2,913,876 in 2017 money. He inherited this huge estate and, it was rumoured, £1m (about £84 million in 2017) at the age of 12. In 1894, he married Violet Grace Cosby, the youngest daughter of Col. Robert Ashworth Godolphin Cosby of Stradbally Hall, Queen's County (*see* Laois). He was a hard-line Unionist; in 1906–10 he edited a monthly publication, *Grievances from Ireland*, which denounced all political expressions of Irish nationalism as treasonable. He was elected a representative peer in 1908. He died in 1946. The family seat was Woodlawn House, near Ballinasloe, County Galway. Woodlawn House was sold by the 4th Baron in 1947 and is still extant, although semi-derelict. It is currently in the process of being gradually restored. The 8th and current Baron Ashtown Rodrick Nigel Godolphin Trench was educated at Eton and lives in East Sussex.

Sir John Henry Keane Bart, of Cappoquin House, Waterford had 8,909 acres in Waterford valued at £3,237, about £279,108 in current money. The baronetage was created in 1801 for a family active in politics, the 1st Baronet having sat for Bangor and then Youghal. The title still exists, held by the 6th Baronet Sir Richard Michael Keane who gives his residence as Cappoquin House in Waterford. The 5th Baronet embraced the fledgling state and became both a Senator and a member of the Council of State and finally a Governor of the Bank of Ireland. The 6th Baronet was a soldier and journalist who died aged 101, having restored both the house and the estate, although its size is unknown. The current baronet is Sir Charles Keane.

Sir Richard John Musgrave Bt of Tourin, Cappoquin has 8,282 acres in Waterford with a valuation of £5,245, about £440,580 in current money. The baronatege was created in 1782. The title is still extant and the present holder, the 8th Baronet Sir Christopher John Shane Keane Musgrave gives an address in Greece. The estates passed to the eldest daughter of the 5th Baronet, Joan Moira Maude Jameson, nee Musgrave, the baronet having no sons. Her descendants still live at Tourin. Their cousin, the 6th baronet Sir Christopher OBE of Norwood Tower, Strandtown, Belfast, was a Lieutenant-Colonel and Chief Commissioner of Scouts, Northern Ireland.

The Earl of Dartrey, Dartrey House, Coothill Co Monaghan had 7,985 acres in Waterford, with a valuation of £3,450, about £289,800 in current money. The Eton-educated Earl of Dartry had land in three other Irish counties, 17,732 acres in Monaghan, 1,665 acres in Armagh, 1,792 acres in Louth, with 5 acres in Devon. The total acreage was 30,112 with a valuation of £21,669, about £1,820,196 in current money. This family came to Ireland at the end of the Elizabethan era but advanced their position when a son joined Cromwell in 1641 as a cavalry officer. As with so many others, they were MP's in both the pre-Union Parliament of Ireland and in the British Parliament afterwards. The Earldom was created in 1866, for the then Baron Dartrey, a government whip in the Palmerston and Russell Imperial administrations. Members of the family made senior ranks in both the Royal Navy and in the British Army. The 3rd Earl died in 1933 without male heirs and the title became extinct. The contents of the family home, Dartry House, a vast rambling building, were sold off in 1937, much going to the Hammond Lane foundry in Dublin for £3,000 as scrap. The house itself was demolished in 1946.

	Name of landowner 1876	Acreage	GAV £	Approx. modern equivalent value £
1	Waterford Marquess of, Curraghmore Portlaw	39,883	27,705	2,327,220
2	Stuart de Decies Lord, Drumana, Cappoquin	30,822	11,463	962,892
3	Devonshire Duke of, Chatsworth Derbyshire	27,483	15,000	1,260,000
4	Chearnley Richard A, Salterbridge Cappoquin Co Waterford	18,165	5,408	454,272
5	De La Poer Edmond, Gurteen Killsheelin	13,448	4,920	413,280
6	Palliser John, Comragh Kilmacthomas	9,825	3,146	264,264
7	Ashtown Lord, Woodlawn Co Galway	9,435	4,379	367,836
8	Keane Sir John Henry Bart, Cappoquin	8,909	3,237	271,908
9	Musgrave Sir Richard John Bart, Tourin Cappoquin	8,282	5,245	440,580
10	Dartrey Earl of, Dartery House, Coothill Co Monaghan	7,985	3,450	289,800
11	Smyth Hon CWM, Ballinatray Youghal	7,124	3,610	303,240
12	Barry Captain James, Mocollop Castle Lismore	6,955	2,251	189,084
13	Kennedy Sir Chas EB, Johnstown Rathcoole Co Dublin	6,680	2,596	218,064
14	Doneraile Viscount, Doneraile Co Cork	6,584	5,626	472,584
15	Huntingdon Earl of, Gaultier Cottage Waterford	6,450	3,966	333,144
16	Humble Sir John Nugent, Cloncosckoran Castle, Dungarvan	6,435	3,918	329,112
17	Trustees of Mrs CJ Osborne, Newtown Anner, Clonmel	6,410	1,823	153,132
18	Barron Sir Henry BT, Barroncourt Waterford	6,281	3,625	304,500

	Name of landowner 1876	Acreage	GAV £	Approx. modern equivalent value £
19	Osborne Cath Isabella, Newtown Anner Clonmel	5,832	3,160	265,440
20	Quinn Mary H, Shanakill Carrick-on-Suir	5,686	1,203	101,052
21	Fox GL, Surrey England	5,219	4,350	365,400
22	O'Shea NP, Gardenmorris Co Waterford	4,995	2,941	247,044
23	O'Keefe John, Ballylemon Dungarvan	4,837	2,483	208,572
24	Power Patrick Joseph, Woodlands Waterford	4,699	3,268	274,512
25	Power Joseph O'N, Snowhill Waterford	4,524	4,007	336,588
26	Woodroof W Morton, Ballysaggartmore Lismore	4,435	954	80,136
27	Christmas Octavia, Cheltenham England	4,025	2,966	249,144
28	Fortescue Earl, Belgrave Sq London	3,958	2,985	250,740
29	College of King's and Queen's Physicians, Dublin	3,418	2,229	187,236
30	Smyth Percy, Headboro' Tallow	3,218	2,543	213,612
31	Power Pierse, Carrickbeg Carrick-on-Suir	3,193	876	73,584
32	Odell EGH, Carriglea Dungarvan	3,192	3,227	271,068
33	Bagge JH, Ardmore House Youghal	3,016	2,370	199,080
34	Wood Geo Abraham, Fota House Cork	2,910	706	59,304
35	Donoughmore Earl of, Knocklofty Clonmel	2,878	2,176	182,784
36	Corporation of Waterford, Waterford	2,475	4,170	350,280
37	Fitzgerald Thomas, Ballinaparka Cappoquin Co Waterford	2,372	1,307	109,788
38	Beresford Robert H, Woodhouse Stradbally	2,352	1,907	160,188

	Name of landowner 1876	Acreage	GAV £	Approx. modern equivalent value £
39	Carew RT, Ballinamona Waterford	2,315	1,578	132,552
40	Young Henry L, Leemount Cork	2,308	252	21,168
41	Fitzgerald John, Manchester England	2,276	2,081	174,804
42	Orpen Basil, Marston Ballyduff Lismore	2,188	690	57,960
43	Trench Rt Hon and Most Rev Dr, The Palace Dublin	2,092	996	83,664
44	Palliser WB, Annestown Tramore Co Waterford	2,024	1,491	125,244
45	Congreve Ambrose, Mount Congreve Waterford	1,972	1,935	162,540
46	Carew Lord, Castleboro' Co Wexford	1,953	1,834	154,056
47	Sherlock Thomas P, Carrigmoorna Kilmacthomas	1,953	1,157	97,188
48	Hearne John Bagge, Ardmore Co Waterford	1,937	543	45,612
49	Griffith D, Podworth House, Reading England	1,873	467	39,228
50	Ussher Richard J, Cappagh Cappoquin	1,869	1,262	106,008
51	Gumbleton RJ Maxwell, Glenatore Tallow	1,768	896	75,264
52	Bolton Jane, Bath England	1,623	847	71,148
53	Maxwell W Percival, Moore Hill Tallow	1,617	1,320	110,880
54	Jameson Henry, Dublin	1,578	66	5,544
55	Drew Barry, Flower Hill Lismore	1,555	331	27,804
56	Ussher John, 11 Grosvenor Gardens London	1,543	1,033	86,772
57	Power James, Tramore	1,537	1,083	90,972
58	Malcolmson Fredrick, Portlaw	1,481	835	70,140
59	Hargrave John, Silivoore Park Sunning Hill Berkshire	1,436	933	78,372

	Name of landowner 1876	Acreage	GAV £	Approx. modern equivalent value £
60	Ussher Christopher M, Camphire Cappoquin	1,414	998	83,832
61	Keily John, Clarebeg Laughlinstown Co Dublin	1,405	935	78,540
62	Watson Thomas W, London	1,339	549	46,116
63	Trustees of Waterford College, Waterford	1,292	920	77,280
64	Barron Catherine, Faha Kilmacthomas	1,274	626	52,584
65	Mansfield Captain Walter, Glenlodge Carrick	1,230	735	61,740
66	Grant Thomas St John, Kilmurry Kilworth Co Cork	1,217	653	54,852
67	Parker Rev John F, Kilmacthomas	1,201	629	52,836
68	Power Patrick W, Tramore Co Waterford	1,184	5,623	472,332
69	Perry Robert D, Clyda Mallow	1,167	423	35,532
70	Barron John M, Georgestown Kilmacthomas	1,148	504	42,336
71	Lloyd George Whitelock, Strancally Castle Cappoquin	1,106	695	58,380
72	Poer Samuel Reps, Bellville Cappoquin	1,058	756	63,504
73	Jackson William Oliver, Ahanesk Midleton Co Cork	1,052	529	44,436
74	Ardagh Wm Michael, Stradbally Kilmacthomas	1,043	695	58,380
75	Reade Joseph, Hillfield Hampstead Heath London	1,012	574	48,216
76	Baker Godfrey T, Fortwilliam Cork	1,008	620	52,080
77	St George Evge Christina Reps, Carrick-on–Shannon Co Leitrim	1,003	730	61,320

Top 20 landowners in Waterford in 1876 by rateable valuation

		Acreage	Valuation 1876 (£)	Valuation current (£)
1	Waterford Marquess of, Curraghmore Portlaw	39,883	27,705	2,327,220
2	Devonshire Duke of, Chatsworth Derbyshire	27,483	15,000	1,260,000
3	Stuart de Decies Lord, Drumana, Cappoquin	30,822	11,463	962,892
4	Doneraile Viscount, Doneraile Co Cork	6,584	5,626	472,584
5	Power Patrick W, Tramore Co Waterford	1,184	5,623	472,332
6	Chearnley Richard A, Salterbridge Cappoquin Co Waterford	18,165	5,408	454,272
7	Musgrave Sir Richard John Bart, Tourin Cappoquin	8,282	5,245	440,580
8	De La Poer Edmond, Gurteen Killsheelin	13,448	4,920	413,280
9	Ashtown Lord, Woodlawn Co Galway	9,435	4,379	367,836
10	Fox GL, Surrey England	5,219	4,350	365,400
11	Corporation of Waterford, Waterford	2,475	4,170	350,280
12	Power Joseph O'N, Snowhill Waterford	4,524	4,007	336,588
13	Huntingdon Earl of, Gaultier Cottage Waterford	6,450	3,966	333,144
14	Humble Sir John Nugent, Cloncosckoran Dungarvan	6,435	3,918	329,112
15	Barron Sir Henry BT, Barroncourt Waterford	6,281	3,625	304,500
16	Smyth Hon CWM, Ballinatray Youghal	7,124	3,610	303,240
17	Dartrey Earl of, Dartry House, Coothill Co Monaghan	7,985	3,450	289,800
18	Power Patrick Joseph, Woodlands Waterford	4,699	3,268	274,512
19	Keane Sir John Henry Bart, Cappoquin	8,909	3,237	271,908
20	Odell EGH, Carriglea Dungarvan	3,192	3,227	271,068

WESTMEATH

	1876	2016
Population in County Westmeath	78,432 (1871)	86,164
All owners of land	668 (1871)	46,275
Percentage of the population	0.85	–
Owners of nothing at all	77,764	24,985
Percentage of the population	99.15	–
Size of County	430,003	442,880 acres
Number of dwellings (of which rented)	15,152 (14,484) (1871)	30,624
Number of owned farm holdings	1,151	3,459

County comparisons

	Acreage in 1876	Population in 1876
County Westmeath	430,003	86,164
Berkshire, England	430,849	196,475
Roxboroughshire, Scotland	423,463	53,974
Glamorganshire, Wales	428,386	397,859

Sir John Ennis Bart MP of Ballnahown, Athlone, had 8,774 acres in Westmeath in 1876 valued at £4,912 about £412,618 in modern money. This very considerable estate was built up after about 1800 by Dublin merchant Andrew Ennis, whose family came originally from Down. During the early 1800s he bought land from the Malones and Rochforts, two families still in the top ten of Westmeath landowners in 1876. His key purchase was Ballinahowen Court, the seat of the Malones.

His additional acreage comprised 1,573 acres in Meath, 326 acres in Dublin and 262 acres in Roscommon. The total acreage was 10,935 acres, with a valuation of £7,403.

His son, John, the owner at the time of the Returns, was successively High Sheriff of the County and of Dublin, a director of the Bank of Ireland and MP for Athlone. In 1866 he was made a Baronet. His son repeated the family pattern by becoming High Sheriff and MP for Athlone. He died in 1884, when the Baronetcy became extinct.

Ferres notes that Ballinahown Court was subsequently inherited by the family of the O'Donoghue of the Glens, by whom it was sold *c.*1965 to Mr Basil Crofts-Greene, who resold the house *c.*1976.

Charles Brinsley Marlay of Belvedere, Mullingar, County Westmeath, owned 9,059 acres with a valuation of £5,766 about £484,344 in modern money. This Eton-educated landowner was described in the *Westmeath Independent* as the best landlord in Westmeath. He arrived at Belvedere in 1850 as the worst of the famine ended. Under his predecessor, the Rochfort son of the Countess of Belvedere, the tenants suffered terribly or were evicted, many dying on the side of the road. The estate has vanished and Marlay never married, committing most of his considerable fortune to endowing the Fitzwilliam Museum in Cambridge, his alma mater. The Countess built in the early 1800s what is now Belvedere College in Dublin. When Marlay died the house, but not the estate, passed to Charles Kenneth Hanbury-Bury, a soldier, who led the 1921 Expedition to Everest. He sold the house to Westmeath County Council in 1982. It is now a visitor centre and museum.

George Augustus Rochfort-Boyd of Middleton Park, Castletown, County Westmeath, had 16,397 acres in the county in 1876, at a valuation of £10,249 about £916,860 in modern money. This is a considerable increase in both the acreage and valuation in the Returns, but Bateman had checked both.

This landowner has left no records that appear to have caught the eye of posterity. Most recent local historical interest has focused on a notorious Earl of Belvedere (*see* Marlay) who imprisoned his wife for life for almost certainly imagined infidelity. That title became extinct in the 1800s. The family name of the Belvedere Earldom was Rochfort.

Sir Benjamin James Chapman, the 4th Bart MP of Killua Castle, Clonmellon, County Westmeath, had 9,516 acres in the county in 1876 with a valuation of £6,532 about £548,688 in modern money. This Baronet, unlike his inlaws (the Rochfort-Boyds) has come in for passing mention as his successor, Sir Thomas Robert Tighe Chapman, 7th Baronet, did many unconventional things, not least of which was falling in love with the family's Scottish maid and going to live with her. Her name was Lawrence, a name he took. And his second son with the maid was one Colonel Thomas Edward Lawrence, otherwise known as Lawrence of Arabia, one of the most romantic figures of the early twentieth century. Given his father's life style, it could be said that T.E., however indirectly, took after him.

The origins of the estate are described in the old Debrett's as follows:

John Chapman, and his brother William, through the influence of Sir Walter Raleigh, their cousin-german, received large grants of land in Ireland, and settled in that country. Benjamin, the son of William Chapman, was an officer of cavalry in Cromwell's army, and for his services received the castle and estates of Killua, sometime the seat of the family. The 3rd baronet sat as M.P. for Westmeath … Sir Benjamin James, 4th baronet, sat as M.P. for Westmeath … 1841–7 and was Lord Lieutenant of that county. The 5th baronet, Sir Montagu Richard, was High Sheriff of County Westmeath.

The residue of the estate came to a mere 1,249 acres and was sold in 1949.

Patrick Edward Murphy of Ballinacloon, Mullingar, County Westmeath, owned 9,693 acres of Westmeath in 1876, valued at £6,020 about £505,608 in modern money. This landowner does not occur in Burke's *Landed Gentry of Ireland* (pre-1900 editions). He is mentioned as both an esquire and a captain in a General Assizes Grand Jury list in the early 1840s. There is a reference to him in the Upton papers at the Royal Irish Academy. In the list of protected structures for County Westmeath there is mention of a brewery at Ballin(a)cloon. There is a final mention of a Murphy dying without children in 1914. For an estate of this size the lack of information is unusual.

Captain Thomas Smyth of Ballynagall, Mullingar, had 9,778 acres with a valuation of £6,884 about £578,256 in modern money. This Trinity College Dublin-educated landowner gets a substantial update in Bateman, with the rest of his acreage added; 150 acres in County Meath, 343 acres in King's County (Offaly) and 785 acres in Kildare. This gives him a total of 11,056 acres with a valuation of £7,768.

Thomas Smyth was archetypal Anglo–Irish county gentry. His father was a vicar in the Church of Ireland who married the daughter of an East India Company director, whose family had land in the area. The Ballynagall estate came by way of marriage in 1855. Three of his brothers were majors in the army and he was a captain in the Westmeath Rifles, the local militia. He was High Sheriff, a justice of the peace and a Deputy Lieutenant of the County. His only son Thomas married the daughter of another local landowner, Harry Corbyn Levinge of Knockdrin Castle Mullingar. The house, said to have cost £30,000 to build was abandoned in the 1960s according to Ferres.

Lord Fulke Greville MP of Clonyn, Castle Delvin, County Westmeath, had 9,783 acres in Westmeath in 1876, valued at £11,575 about £972,300 in modern money. Bateman updates this peer with the rest of his acreage in Ireland and England. This includes 3,990 acres in Roscommon, 1,970 acres in

Cavan, 1,236 acres in Longford, 451 acres in Cork and 1,178 acres in Kent. The total is 18,608 acres with a valuation of £18,194.

Although Greville sat as an MP for Longford, his clubs were strictly London. He married Rose, only daughter of the 1st and last Marquess of Westmeath, and through her he acquired Clonyn Castle. The Westmeath Marquissate became extinct in 1871 but occurs in Bateman as the Earldom of Westmeath, with acreage in Galway and Roscommon. That Earldom still exists, though there is no evidence of a landed estate. Greville himself is mentioned by Ferres as a part of the family of the Grevilles Earls of Warwick, who were owners of 10,102 acres in England in 1876. Greville's son followed his father into politics and was private secretary to William Gladstone in the 1870s, later a Lord of the Treasury.

The peerage became extinct in 1987 with the death of the 4th Baron Greville. The castle was sold in 1922. After the Second World War the castle, endowed by a Manchester businessman Yankel Levy, became a home for ninety-seven Jewish orphans, survivors of the Holocaust.

The castle still stands and was in the possession of Mrs Dillon, according to Ferres.

The 4th Lord Castlemaine of Moydrum Castle, Athlone, owned 11,444 acres in the county, valued at £7,053 about £592,452 in modern money. The family name of this peer was Handcock, with many interconnections in the landowning elite in Ireland. The following lineage is set out here to demonstrate the linkage between landowning, politics and the Church of Ireland. The proportion of Irish landowners who combined landowning with that of clergymen appears to be a good deal higher than in the rest of Great Britain at the time.

The Irish family originated with a William Handcock from Lancashire. who became an MP in the first post-Restoration Parliament under Charles II. He upgraded Twyford in Westmeath, where he was based and had acquired confiscated lands, to a manor and got a post on the Council of Connaught. He married Abigail, sister of Sir Thomas Stanley. His children became successively:

Thomas, his heir; who ran the estate and was an MP;
William (Sir), Knight; Recorder of Dublin;
Stephen (Very Rev.), Dean of Clonmacnoise;
Matthew (Ven), Archdeacon of Kilmore;
One son drowned and there were three daughters.
The eldest son,
Thomas Handcock MP, of Twyford, was succeeded by his eldest son,
William Handcock, who married Miss Warburton, and was succeeded by his eldest son,

William Handcock, who married Elizabeth Vesey, second daughter of the Rt Rev. Sir Thomas Vesey Bt, Lord Bishop of Ossory. They had no children and William was succeeded by his brother,

The Very Rev. Richard Handcock, Dean of Achonry, who had a numerous family and was succeeded by his eldest son,

The Rt Hon. and Very Rev. William Handcock MP (1761–1839), Dean of Achonry, Privy Counsellor, governor and constable of Athlone.

Dean Handcock married Sarah, only daughter and heiress of Richard Toler, of Ballintore, County Kildare, by whom he had,

William, 1st Baron Castlemaine;

Richard; Sarah; Susanna; Dorothy; Mary; Elizabeth; Anne.

Dean Handcock was succeeded by his eldest son.

The Rt Hon. William Handcock MP was elevated to the peerage in 1812 as Baron Castlemaine; and advanced to a Viscountcy, as Viscount Castlemaine, in 1822.

On Viscount Handcock's death the Viscountcy expired, though the Barony passed to his brother.

- William Handcock, 1st Viscount Castlemaine, 1st Baron Castlemaine (1761–1839)
- Richard Handcock, 2nd Baron (1767–1840)
- Richard Handcock, 3rd Baron (1791–1869)
- Richard Handcock, 4th Baron (1826–92)
- Albert Edward Handcock, 5th Baron (1863–1937) last Lord Lieutenant of Co. Westmeath.
- Robert Arthur Handcock, 6th Baron (1864–1954)
- John Michael Schomberg Staveley Handcock, 7th Baron (1904–73)
- Roland Thomas John Handcock MBE, a former major in the Army Air Corps and 8th Baron. He lives in Salisbury.

The house was burned down by the IRA in 1921 in reprisal for the burning of houses in the county by units of the British Army. The estate was broken up and sold by the Land Commission.

John Malone of Baronstown, Ballinacargy, Mullingar, had 12,715 acres in the county in 1876, valued at £9,303 about £781,452 in modern money. The Malone name is Gaelic Irish and probably pre-Norman in its origins. John Malone does not crop up in the records, probably because he was neither an MP, clergyman nor Anglo–Irish. Bateman upgrades the acreage to 13,715 and the valuation to £10,203.

General the Rt Hon. the 4th Earl of Longford of Packenham Hall, Castle Pollard, County Westmeath, owned 15,014 acres in the county in 1876

valued at £9,384 about £788,256 in modern money. It was the 420 acres in Dublin, valued at £31,713, about £2,663,892 in modern money that made the Longfords hugely influential in both Dublin and London.

See page 275 for more information.

There is an excellent interview with the 8th Earl that can be found by Googling independent.ie and entering his name

Long list of over 1,000 acres landowners in Westmeath in 1876

		Acreage	Valuation 1876 (£)	Valuation Current (£)
1	Longford, Rt Hon. the Earl of, Pakenham Hall, Castle Pollard	15,014	9,384	788,256
2	Malone, John, Ballynacargy	12,554	9,303	781,452
3	Castlemaine, Lord, Moydrum, Athlone	11,444	7,053	592,452
4	Greville, Lord, Clonyn, Castle Delvin, Co. Westmeath	9,783	11,575	972,300
5	Smyth, Captain Thomas, Ballynagall, Mullingar	9,778	6,884	578,256
6	Murphy, Patrick Edward, Ballinacloon, Multyfarnham	9,693	6,020	505,680
7	Chapman, Sir Benjamin Bart, Killua Castle, Clonmellon, Co. Westmeath	9,516	6,532	548,688
8	Rochfort-Boyd, Geo A., Middleton Park, Castletown-Geoghan	9,431	5,690	477,960
9	Marley, Chas Brinsley, Belvedere, Mullingar	9,059	5,766	484,344
10	Ennis, Sir John Bart, Ballynahown, Athlone	8,774	4,912	412,608
11	Tuite, Joseph, Sonna, Mullingar	7,391	5,817	488,628
12	Nugent, Sir Walter, Donore, Multyfarnham	7,218	4,637	389,508
13	Longworth, John, Glenwood, Athlone	6,547	3,665	307,860
14	Smyth, Robert, Gaybrook, Mullingar	6,287	4,711	395,724

		Acreage	Valuation 1876 (£)	Valuation Current (£)
15	Magan, Mrs Georgina, Killyon, Hill of Down	5,604	3,525	296,100
16	Urquhart, D.W. Pollard, Kinturk, Castlepollard	5,363	3,995	335,580
17	Tighe, Rt Hon. W.F.F., Woodstock, Kilkenny	5,211	3,327	279,468
18	Temple, Hon. R.T.H., Waterstown, Glasson	4,863	3,327	279,468
19	Fetherston, Cecil H. (a minor), Bracklyn Castle, Killucan	4,711	2,583	216,972
20	Chapman, William, Southhill, Delvin	4,707	3,156	265,104
21	Nugent, Lady, Ballinlough, Delvin	4,692	3,720	312,480
22	Cooke, Adolphus, Cooksboro, Mullingar	4,557	2,882	242,088
23	Trustees of Wilson's Hospital, Agent Chas Hamilton Esquire, 40 Dominick Street, Dublin	4,495	2,960	248,640
24	Smyth the Hon. Leicester CB of Drumcree, Killucan	4,431	3,188	267,792
25	Wilson, John of Street, Rathowen	3,720	1,445	121,380
26	Gradwell, Richard, Dowth Hall, Drogheda	3,169	1,428	119,952
27	Humphreys, William, Ballyhaise House, Cavan	3,164	1,719	144,396
28	Wilson, William, Salthill, Dublin	3,145	1,314	110,376
29	Nugent, Lieutenant Colonel John J., Clonlost, Killucan	3,140	2,308	193,872
30	Parnell, Hon. Henry W., Anneville, Mullingar	2,900	2,070	173,880
31	Gore, William, Ormsby, Derrycarney, Drumod	2,794	1,434	120,456
32	Fetherston, H. Richard, Rockview, Killucan	2,709	2,452	205,968
33	Kelly. John, Lunestown, Mullingar	2,596	1,943	163,212
34	Tottenham. Mrs Anna Maria, Rochfort, Mullingar	2,588	1,739	146,076
35	Whitney. Edmond W.F., Newpass, Rathowen	2,538	1,735	145,740

		Acreage	Valuation 1876 (£)	Valuation Current (£)
36	Vaux of Harrowden, Lord, Rosmead, Delvin	2,464	1,771	148,764
37	Meares, John Devenish, Mearscourt, Moyvore, Jersey	2,398	1,766	148,344
38	Kelly, Francis Hume, Glencarra, Mullingar	2,381	1,250	105,000
39	Dease, James A. Reps, Turbotston, Coole	2,315	1,698	142,632
40	Bond, William Perry, Ardglass, Rathowen	2,292	1,676	140,784
41	Paget, -, -	2,241	1,266	106,344
42	Sproule, Moses, Ballykildevan, Street	2,236	1,138	95,592
43	Fetherston, Rev. John Reps, Griffinstown, Kinnegad	2,234	1,628	136,752
44	Nugent, Colonel Andrew, Portaferry, Co. Down	2,137	1,670	140,280
45	Kilmaine, Lord, Galston Rochefort, Bridge	2,122	1,560	131,040
46	Smythe, Barlow, Barbaravilla, Collinstown	2,106	1,653	138,852
47	Grogan, Sir Edward Bt, Harcourt St, Dublin	1,950	1,318	110,712
48	Clibborn, Thomas, Moate	1,883	777	65,268
49	Talbot, Reginald, Lyme Regis, Dorchester	1,839	1,274	107,016
50	Oranmore, Lord, Castlemargaret, Claremorris, Co. Mayo	1,818	1,239	104,076
51	Tighe, R.M. Reps, -	1,809	1,242	104,328
52	Cooper, Colonel Joshua Henry, Dunboden Park, Mullingar	1,785	1,563	131,292
53	Somers, John R., Tyrrelspass	1,736	951	79,884
54	Montgomery, Alexander, Kilmer, Meath	1,697	583	48,972
55	Pilkington, Henry M., Tore, Tyrrellspass	1,683	735	61,740
56	Balfour, Blaney T., Townley Hall, Drogheda	1,623	1,246	104,664
57	Reynell, Samuel A., Archerstown. Killucan	1,566	530	44,520

		Acreage	Valuation 1876 (£)	Valuation Current (£)
58	Daniel, Robert George, Newforrest, Tyrellspass	1,559	551	46,284
59	Burton, R. Reps of, -	1,542	1,135	95,340
60	Tuite, Henry (a minor), Sonna, Mullingar	1,490	891	74,844
61	Rochfort, Captain Charles Guftavus, Ballytore, Co. Kildare	1,434	937	78,708
62	Gray, William H., Dorrington, Drumrancy	1,421	931	78,204
63	Molloy, Laurence B., Parsonstown	1,421	819	68,792
64	Busby, Alphonso, 4 Burlington Road, Dublin	1,408	1,043	87,612
65	Murray, Henry, Mount Murray, Mullingar	1,377	831	69,804
66	Lyons, John Charles (a minor), Ladistown, Mullingar	1,357	1,045	87,780
67	Carter, Thomas L., Hattington Park, Telsworth, Staffordshire	1,335	760	63,840
68	Grace, John D.F., Gracefield, Athy	1,329	846	71,064
69	Lowry, John F.H., Ballymore	1,328	1,162	97,608
70	Carey, H. Reps, -	1,316	1,131	95,004
71	Holmes, Robert, Kildare Club, Dublin	1,298	767	64,428
72	Purdon, Wellington, Joristown, Killucan	1,275	1,241	104,244
73	Wilson, William, Street Rathowen & Rathmines, Dublin	1,264	794	66,696
74	Smyth, Wm Edward, Glananea, Drumcree	1,256	1,003	84,252
75	King, Harman Hon. L.H. Reps, Newcastle, Ballymahon	1,239	851	71,484
76	Levinge, Sir Rich Bt, Knockdrin Castle, Mullingar	1,239	851	71,484
77	Batty, Rev. Edward, Ballyhealy, Delvin	1,215	748	62,832
78	M'Laughlin, Cornelius, Farmer's Club, Dublin	1,175	1,016	85,344
79	Dopping, William, Australia	1,171	784	65,856
80	Ellis, F, -	1,167	761	63,924

		Acreage	Valuation 1876 (£)	Valuation Current (£)
81	Connolly, Harriet and Frances, Collure, Castlepollard	1,146	816	68,544
82	Grogan, Captain William, Baltinglass, Co. Wicklow	1,141	726	60,984
83	Maunsell, George Woods, Merrion Sq., Dublin	1,140	833	69,972
84	Carter, William Henry, Castlemartyr, Co. Cork	1,137	669	56,196
85	Church Temporalities Commissioners, Upper Merrion St, Dublin	1,116	1,395	117,180
86	Goodbody, Marcus and Jonathan, Clara King's County	1,087	856	71,904
87	Fetherston, H. Wm, Grouse Lodge, Moate	1,075	687	57,708
88	Tuthill, Charles, Newstead Abbey, Milltown, Co. Dublin	1,065	608	51,072
89	Purdon, George Nugent, Lisnabin. Killucan	1,063	890	74,760
90	Bond, Willoughby, Farra, Longford	1,057	541	45,444
91	Chaigneau, Miss, Bunown	1,050	715	60,060
92	Eustance, Captain Charles, London	1,036	453	38,052
93	Hamilton, Charles, Dominick St, Dublin	1,031	643	54,012
94	Fetherston, H., Godfrey, Dublin	1,016	712	59,808
95	Evans, Nicholas, Lough Park, Killucan	1,011	605	50,820

Top 20 over 1,000 acres landowners by gross estimated income in Westmeath in 1876

		Acreage	Valuation 1876 (£)	Valuation Current (£)
1	Greville, Lord, Cloyne, Delvin	9,783	11,575	972,300
2	Longford, Rt Hon. the Earl of, Pakenham Hall, Castle Pollard	15,014	9,384	788,256
3	Malone, John, Ballynacargy	12,554	9,303	781,452

		Acreage	Valuation 1876 (£)	Valuation Current (£)
4	Castlemaine, Lord, Moydrum, Athlone	11,444	7,053	592,452
5	Smyth, Captain Thomas, Ballynagall, Mullingar	9,778	6,884	578,256
6	Chapman, Sir Benjamin Bart, Killua Castle, Clonmellon, Co. Westmeath	9,516	6,532	548,688
7	Murphy, Patrick Edward, Ballymacloon, Multyfarnham	9,693	6,020	505,680
8	Tuite, Joseph, Sonna, Mullingar	7,391	5,817	488,628
9	Marley, Chas Brinsley, Belvedere, Mullingar	9,059	5,766	484,344
10	Rochfort-Boyd Geo A., Middleton Park, Castletown Geoghegan	9,431	5,690	477,960
11	Ennis, Sir John Bart, Ballynahown, Athlone	8,774	4,912	412,608
12	Smyth, Robert, Gaybrook, Mullingar	6,287	4,711	395,724
13	Nugent, Sir Walter, Donore, Multyfarnham	7,218	4,637	389,508
14	Urquhart, D.W. Pollard, Kinturk, Castlepollard	5,363	3,995	335,580
15	Nugent, Lady, Ballinlough, Delvin	4,692	3,720	312,480
16	Longworth, John, Glenwood, Athlone	6,547	3,665	307,860
17	Magan, Mrs Georgina, Killyon, Hill of Down	5,604	3,525	296,100
18	Tighe, Rt Hon. W.F.F., Woodstock, Kilkenny	5,211	3,327	279,468
19	Temple, Hon. R.T.H., Waterstown, Glasson	4,863	3,327	279,468
20	Smyth, Hon. Leinster, Curzon, Drumcree	4,431	3,188	267,792

WEXFORD

	1876	2016
Population in County Wexford	132,666 (1871)	145,320
All owners of land	1,757 (1871)	75,684,891
Percentage of the population	1.32	–
Owners of nothing at all	130,929	41,067
Percentage of the population	98.68	–
Size of County	573,051	581,760 acres
Number of dwellings (of which rented)	24,982 (23,245) (1871)	52,345
Number of owned farm holdings	1,176	4,426 (2010)

County comparisons

	Acreage 1876	Population 1876
County Wexford	573,051	132,666
Cambridgeshire, England	522,208	186,903
Kircudbrightshire, Scotland	571,950	41,859
Carmarthenshire, Wales	510,574	115,710

The Rt Hon. the 1st Baron Carew of Castleborough, Enniscorthy, had 17,830 acres in 1876 with a valuation of £9,070 about £761,880 in modern money. Bateman qualifies Lord Carew with a Gothic 'S', a sign that Lord Carew held the land at the time of Henry VII and since then in unbroken male line. Henry VII reigned from 1485 to 1509 and was the father of Henry VIII. Ferres notes that the Carews were landowners in the west of England as far back as as Anglo–Saxon times but this peer is one of only four entries by Bateman for the Carew family.

The Wikipedia entry is, like most of the entries on both the titled landowners and the British and Irish aristocracy, long on subliminal praise and seriously short on facts. There is no mention of what Baron Carew did for his tenants in the famine, for instance. Nor is there anywhere mention of the percentage of the local population who lived at his whim, or shipped out to America to escape economic and political stagnation and serfdom in Ireland. In 1834 he was elevated to the Irish peerage, a gesture as there was no Irish House of Lords in which to sit. In 1838 this became a UK peerage, with a seat in the House of Lords. He was succeeded by his son, Robert Shapland Carew, the land holder in 1876. The house, Castleboro, was a fine piece of architecture. It was burnt down in 1923, at the expense of the Free State, whose taxpayers had to foot the bill for this piece of arson by parties unknown. The local paper, the *People*, was scathing:

> Castleboro, the ancestral home of the Right Hon. Lord Carew was burned to the ground on Monday night ... The reason for the destruction of one of the finest residences in Leinster remains a mystery to all but those who were responsible for the destructive work which will only add more thousands to the bill that the Co Wexford will have to foot when the time of reckoning comes.

The paper estimated that, based on the building costs of £200,000, the compensation would be heavy. The Irish Free State, in the manner of its predecessor institutions, did not reveal what was paid.

The 3rd Lord Carew died soon after his home was torched. The family left Ireland but the current heir, the 7th Baron, educated at Harrow and the Royal Military Academy Sandhurst, was a captain in the Royal Horse Guards, returned to Ireland and headed the Irish Equestrian Federation, and was chair of the International Equestrian Federation. He lives in County Kildare.

Another former seat cited by Bateman was Woodstown, County Waterford; former town residence 28 Belgrave Square, London.

Lady Adelaide Forbes of Johnstown Castle, Wexford, had 15,216 acres in 1876, valued at £15,216 about £1,026,144 in modern money. Lady Forbes does not rate a mention in Bateman, although she qualified on both acreage and valuation. By the time Bateman recorded his entries her name was Lady Maurice Fitzgerald, who had married the 2nd Son of the 4th Duke of Leinster (*see* Kildare) and brought with her a huge dowry to a family already well endowed with land.

The origins of the estate go far back into the post-Norman settlement and it was owned by the Esmondes. Cromwell confiscated it but it eventually came into the hands of a wealthy Protestant Wexford carpenter, John Grogan. It was confiscated again when his descendant, Cornelius Grogan, appointed the head of the Wexford Republic by the 1798 rebels, was executed for treason. The estate was restored to Cornelius' son in 1810.

When Adelaide Fitzgerald died in 1942 the estate and castle went to her grandson, Captain M.V. Lakin, who donated the estate and the castle to the Irish nation in 1945.

The Marquis of Ely of Loftus Hall, Fetherd, had 14,023 acres in 1876 valued at £9,168.
See page 140.

Viscount Powerscourt of Enniskerry in County Wicklow had 11,729 acres in Wexford with a valuation of £4,453 about £374,052 in modern money. This title continues to exist and the 11th Viscount, Mervyn Anthony Wingfield, is a regular visitor to the estate, which was sold by his father to his future wife's family in 1961. The building was destroyed by fire in 1974 and was rebuilt at huge cost. The estate now employs over 350 people and is one of the Republic's leading tourist attractions. The head gardener is a Slazanger and a cousin of the Viscount who lives in Bristol.

The title was first created in 1618 for Richard Wingfield, Elizabeth I's Governor in Ireland. He was made Marshal of Ireland by Elizabeth in 1600, was granted an estate of 45,000 acres at Powerscourt with other lands in Tyrone and Wexford in 1609 and got the title in 1618.

The Debrett's entry begins much later, with the MP for Boyle being made a Baron in 1743. In fact, the title was created three times, this being the third for the Wingfields, who kept running out of sons to carry it on directly.

The current gardens are about 47 acres and much of the 1876 estate seems to have been gone by 1923, when the Land Commission estimated that Lord Powerscourt had already sold many of the tenants their farms. The remainder, about 2,000 acres, was sold in 1932. The 7th Viscount, who held the land in 1876 was educated at Eton and was an officer in the Life Guards.

The 3rd Lord Templemore of Dunbrody Park Arthurstown held 11,327 acres in Wexford in 1876, valued at £7,046 about £591,864 in modern money. This Irish peerage is now incorporated with that of the 8th Marquis of Donegal, Arthur Patrick Chichester, who was recently still living at the family home of Dunbrody Park.

At the time of the Return the then Lord Templemore owned 2,543 acres in Hants, where he lived at the time. He also had 10,856 acres in Donegal, 1,890 acres in Londonderry and 26 acres in Down. This latter 26 acres had a valuation of £1,405. His total acreage was 26,642 with a valuation of £18,973. Like his fellow landowner in Wexford, Viscount Powerscourt, he was educated at Eton and was an officer in the Life Guards. At the same time, the Marquis of Donegal (*see* Donegal) held a total of 22,996 acres with a valuation of £41,649. The Donegal title hides the name of Chichester, soldier landowners from Devon who owned huge tracts of Belfast.

William Orme Foster, of Apley Park, Bridgenorth, owned 9,724 acres in Wexford in 1876, with a valuation of £4,686 about £393,624 in modern money. William Orme Foster came late to land, via a vast inheritance from his uncle, of the John Bradley Company, worth £700,000 in 1853. Foster sat as the Liberal MP for South Staffordshire from 1857 until 1868. In 1868 he bought the Apley Park estate of 8,547 acres from William Whitmore in 1867 for over £300,000. In 1876 he was High Sheriff of Wexford. He died in 1899 and his estate was probated at £2,888,000. He left everything to his son, William Henry Foster. In 1867 Foster's eldest daughter, Charlotte, married an Old Etonian, Hector Stewart Vandeleur, a Clare landowner (19,700 acres valuation £11,216).

The Vandaleur estate evicted many of its tenants in the late 1800s and eventually sold most of the farms to the remaining tenants by the 1920s.

The Hon. Mrs Deane Morgan of Ardcandarisk, Wexford, owned 9,412 acres in 1876 with a valuation of £7,007 about £588,588 in modern money. Hamilton Knox Grogan-Morgan was among the principal lessors in the parish of Desertserges, Barony of Kinalmeaky, Co. Cork, in 1851. He resided at Johnston Castle, Co. Wexford, and was an MP for that county. His daughter, Elizabeth, married R.F. Deane-Morgan, eldest son of Baron Muskerry. In the 1870s she was the owner of over 500 acres in county Cork. H.K. Grogan-Morgan was also among the principal lessors in the parish of Kilmacomb, Barony of Gaultiere, Waterford in 1848.

Mrs Deane-Morgan gets no personal mention in Bateman. This might be an error but that is unlikely as the house did exist.

Anne Colclough of Tintern Abbey, Kinnagh, owned 9,328 acres in 1876 valued at £5,479 about £460,236 in modern money. Bateman corrects this entry in the Return to Rossborough-Colclough Mrs, of Tintern Abbey New Ross, and ups her acreage to 13,329 acres and her valuation to £7,124. She came by the estate as an heiress-at-law and second cousin to the MP for Wexford, Caesar Colclough, when he died in 1842. Her full name was Mary Gray Wentworth Rossborough-Colclough and she was the heiress to the estate at Duffrey Hall. She married in 1848 John Thomas Rossborough JP, DL of Mullinagood, Co. Longford, eldest son of John Rossborough, of Nicholson's Court and Clancaulfield House, Longford, and grandson of Hugh Rossborough, of Mullingoan, Co. Fermanagh. By 1876 there were no lands in the name of Rossborough in Fermanagh or Longford.

Her eldest daughter, Louise Maria Susanna Coleclough-Biddulph-Coleclough, of Tintern Abbey, succeeding her mother in 1884, married, a year later, Captain Franc Digby Biddulph of the 3rd Middlesex Militia (who assumed the surname and arms of Colclough, 1886), youngest son of Francis Wellesley Marsh Biddulph, of Rathrobin. She died in 1912, having had two children. Caesar Franc Thomas Bickerstaff Plantagenet died in 1888. The insertion of Plantagent is unusual but at this time both Burke's and Debrett's *Peerage* gave two Royal lines for the UK; that of Plantagenet and then of Tudor. She was succeeded by her daughter, Lucy

Wilmot Maria Susanna Biddulph, born 1890. Lucy donated Tintern Abbey to the Irish state in 1958, but without including the land.

The Abbey has been part restored and is one of the most important monastic ruins in Ireland.

Sir John Talbot Power Bart MP of Edermine House, Enniscorthy, owned 8,598 acres valued at £6,220 about £522,480 in modern money. Bateman corrects Sir John's acreage, upping it to 10,205 acres and the valuation to £7,479. He also adds that he was a local MP. This estate is interesting because it is the estate of the Power whiskey family and the lineage opens thus, as set out in Ferres:

JAMES POWER, Innkeeper, of Thomas Street, Dublin, established a distillery for the production of whiskey at his premises in 1791.

The site selected by Mr Power was in the suburbs of Dublin, just outside the city walls, upon a plot of ground formerly known as the Friary Gardens of St John, adjacent to Wormwood (Ormond) Gate, the principal western entrance to the city, and was the property of the Countess of Charleville, by whom it was leased to James Power, by indenture bearing date 29th September, 1785. James Power continued to extend the distillery until his death, in 1817. Mr Power was succeeded by his son,

SIR JOHN POWER, 1st Baronet, JP, DL (1771–1855), of Roebuck House, County Dublin, and Sampton, County Wexford, who married, in 1799, Mary, eldest daughter of Thomas Brenann. The 1st Sir John was succeeded by his son James.

SIR JAMES POWER, 2nd Baronet, JP, DL (1800–77), MP for County Wexford, 1835–37, 1841–47, and 1865–68, who married, in 1843, Jane Anne Eliza, daughter and co-heiress of John Hyacinth Talbot DL MP, of Castle Talbot, County Wexford (1,300 acres in Wexford).

Sir James devoted himself to the further development of the business, and was Governor of the Bank of Ireland, Chairman of the Dublin, Wicklow & Wexford Railway; and, for many years, Commissioner for Charitable Bequests in Ireland. He was succeeded by his eldest son,

SIR JOHN TALBOT POWER JP DL (1845–1901), 3rd Baronet, of Edermine, County Wexford, MP for County Wexford, 1868–74, High Sheriff, 1880.

The title is now extinct.

Francis Augustine Leigh JP DL of Rosegarland, County Wexford, owned 8,280 acres in 1876 valued at £4,052 about £340,368 in modern money. This landowner was educated at Eton and served as an officer in the 10th Hussars. Mr Leigh's grandfather had two interesting posts; the Collector of Wexford and Sovereign of New Ross He was succeeded by John Robert, father of Francis Augustine. John Leigh, who was MP for Wexford, was succeded by his grandson, Francis.

The Rosegarland estate today is renowned for its equestrian and shooting activities and extends to approximately 650 acres.

Long list of owners of 1,000 or over acres in Wexford in 1876

		Acreage	Valuation 1876 (£)	Valuation Current (£)
1	Carew, Rt Hon. Lord, Castleboro, Enniscorthy	17,830	9,070	761,880
2	Forbes, Lady Adelaide, Johnstown Castle, Wexford	15,216	8,840	742,560
3	Ely, the Marquis of, Loftus Hall, Fethard	14,023	9,168	770,112
4	Powerscourt Viscount, Enniskerry	11,729	4,453	374,052
5	Templemore, Lord, Dunbrodypark, Arthurstown	11,327	7,046	591,864
6	Foster, William Orme, Apley Park	9,724	4,686	393,624
7	Morgan, Hon. Mrs Deane, Ardcandrisk, Wexford	9,412	7,007	588,588
8	Colclough, Anne, Tintern, Kinnagh	9,328	5,479	460,236
9	Power, Sir James, Edermine House, Enniscorthy	8,598	6,220	522,480
10	Leigh, F.A., Rosegarland, Fooksmills	8,280	4,052	340,368
11	Rowe, John H.R. Reps, Ballycross, Wexford	8,002	5,245	440,580
12	Doyne, Charles M., Wells, Oulart	7,134	4,692	394,128
13	Tottenham, Charles, Ballycurry, Ashford, Co. Wicklow	7,066	9,963	836,892
14	Bruen, Henry, Oakpark, Carlow, and Coolbawn, Enniscorthy	6,932	3,288	276,192
15	Bryan, Loftus A., In Chancery, Bormount, Enniscorthy	6,135	3,938	330,792

		Acreage	Valuation 1876 (£)	Valuation Current (£)
16	Brooks, George F., Gardiner's Row, Dublin	5,796	2,676	224,784
17	Monck, Viscount, Charleville, Bray, Co. Wicklow	5,663	2,896	243,264
18	Blacker, Rev. R.S.C., Woodbrook, Kilann	5,624	2,489	209,076
19	Alcock, Colonel Harry, Wilton Castle, Enniscorthy	5,571	2,930	246,120
20	Hall-Dare, R.W., Newtown, Barry	5,239	2,894	243,096
21	Kavanagh, Arthur Macmurrough, Borris House, Borris	5,013	2,201	184,884
22	Irvine, Captain Edward T., St Aidan's, Ferns	5,000	3,453	290,0052
23	Maher, Mathias A., Ballinkeel, Enniscorthy	4,950	3,392	284,928
24	Bridges, Rev. Thomas T., Danbury, Essex, England	4,769	1,797	150,948
25	Boyce, Captain, Bannow House, Bannow	4,589	3,960	332,640
26	Nunn, Edward Westly, Isle of Wight	4,249	3,948	331,632
27	Donovan, Richard, Ballymore, Ferns	3,971	2,345	196,980
28	Esmond, Sir John Bart, Ballynestragh, Gorey	3,533	2,780	233,520
29	Cookman, N.N., Monait House, Enniscorthy	3,408	1,583	132,972
30	Hatton, Villiers La Touche, London	3,252	1,953	164,052
31	Clayton, R.R., Carrigbyrne, Ballinaboola	3,191	1,441	121,044
32	Murphy, John, Richfield, Duncormick	3,069	1,816	152,544
33	Richards, Edward M.G.H., Grange, Killann	3,050	1,220	102,480
34	Richards, Solomon A. Reps, Ardamine	2,995	2,357	197,988
35	Quin, Henry, Borleigh	2,961	1,361	114,324
36	Redington, Chris N., Kilcornan, Co. Galway	2,954	1,487	124,908
37	Colclough, J.T.R. Reps, Tintern Abbey, Wexford	2,926	1,203	101,052

		Acreage	Valuation 1876 (£)	Valuation Current (£)
38	Glascott, W.M., Alderton, Priesthaggard	2,821	1,701	142,884
39	Stannard, James, Wilkinstown, Taghmon	2,722	1,105	92,820
40	Wolseley, Sir Clement, Mount Wolseley, Tullow, Co. Carlow	2,643	1,045	87,780
41	Goff, Strangman D., Horetown, Foulksmill	2,576	1,487	124,908
42	Beauman, Harriett, Hyde Park	2,537	1,896	159,264
43	Deveroux, John Daly, Ballyrankin House, Ferns	2,312	1,130	94,920
44	Walker, Thomas A., Tykillen, Kyle	2,272	1,626	136,584
45	Haughton, George Reps, Agent Mr Adair, 24 Fitzwilliam Sq., Dublin	2,230	1,342	112,728
46	Grogan, Rev. C.J., Dunclinchey, Bagnalstown	2,187	1,003	84,252
47	Trustees, of St Patrick's Hospital, -	2,181	960	80,640
48	King, Rev. Richard, Killurin, Wexford	2,136	1,463	122,892
49	D'Arcy, M.P., Merrion Sq., East Dublin	2,124	1,234	103,656
50	Bolton, William, The Island, Oulart	2,101	1,554	130,536
51	Dundas, Lorenzo, Clobernon Hall, Ferns	2,091	1,108	93,072
52	Redmond, John P., Raglan Road, Dublin	2,026	1,313	110,292
53	George, John D'Olier, Cahore	2,012	1,384	116,256
54	Kennedy, William Geganstown, Co. Kildare	2,006	916	76,944
55	Boxwell, Francis md, Butlerstown Castle, Wexford	1,955	1,238	103,992
56	Kilmaine, Rt Hon. Lord, The Neale, Ballinrobe, Co. Mayo	1,949	1,241	104,244
57	Close, Henry L., 3 Henry St, Dublin	1,922	929	78,036
58	Webb, R.W. Reps, Agent, -	1,907	805	67,620
59	Howlin, James, Ballycronigan, Broadway	1,899	1,244	104,496

		Acreage	Valuation 1876 (£)	Valuation Current (£)
60	Gifford, Nicholas, Ballysap, Priesthaggard	1,891	1,123	94,332
61	Leslie, C.J., Agent W., Breen, Slade, Fethard	1,861	885	74,340
62	Ram, Rev. Abel J., Rolleston	1,813	1,580	132,720
63	Boyde, James, Courtown, Gorey	1,790	1,015	85,260
64	Alcock, Margt Reps, Wilton Castle, Enniscorthy	1,775	871	73,164
65	Tottenham, C.J., Woodstock, Wicklow	1,774	1,140	95,760
66	Williamson, Richard, 8 Fitzwilliam Sq., Dublin	1,746	1,000	84,000
67	Thornton, Rev. Francis, -	1,715	645	54,180
68	Thunder, Andrew Reps, -	1,713	1,262	106,008
69	Richards, Rev. E., -	1,710	706	59,304
70	Keane, Hon. John M.A., Castletown, Tagoat	1,693	1,329	111,636
71	Phayre, William, -	1,662	819	68,796
72	Power, Nicholas, Faithlegg, Waterford	1,658	1,284	107,856
73	Moore, Rev. Charles, Agent T. Budgeon, Ballywillian, N. Ross	1,654	781	65,604
74	Flood, Fredrick, Slaney Lodge, Kyle	1,622	1,191	100,044
75	Richards, John, Mackmine, Enniscorthy	1,612	982	82,488
76	Power, John Talbot, Edermine House, Enniscorthy	1,607	1,027	86,268
77	Harvey, Percy L., Lonsdale, Kyle, Wexford	1,549	1,188	99,796
78	Swan, Joseph, Leamington, England	1,530	1,064	89,376
79	Harvey, William, -	1,527	523	43,932
80	Kirk, William M., Ramsfort	1,519	1,446	121,464
81	Richards, Solomon, Solsborough, Enniscorthy	1,486	992	83,328
82	Redmond, P.W., Ballytrent, Wexford	1,483	710	59,640

		Acreage	Valuation 1876 (£)	Valuation Current (£)
83	Wallace, Thomas W.J., Ballycoursey, Enniscorthy	1,475	604	50,736
84	Sheppard, Thomas, Waterford	1,466	923	77,532
85	Hobson, S. Le Hunt, Saville Row, London	1,464	810	68,040
86	Sankey, John, Agent Mr, Harman, Palace, New Ross	1,456	518	43,512
87	Hore, Hon. H. Walter, Harperstown House	1,453	1,085	91,140
88	Courtown, Earl of, Courtown House, Gorey	1,426	8,605	722,820
89	Day, Rev. A.B., Bristol	1,406	860	72,240
90	Guinness, Miss, -	1,405	860	72,240
91	Humphreys, John W., Craighill, Co. Carlow	1,398	517	43,428
92	Foote, Mat, -	1,398	307	25,788
93	Wilson, George O., Blackrock	1,356	837	70,308
94	Hobson, Mrs, Truro	1,356	586	49,224
95	Gibbon, William M., Shaleen, Adamstown	1,346	672	56,448
96	Hervey, C.V.J., Paris	1,345	1,816	152,544
97	Talbot, George, Dublin	1,341	953	80,052
98	Beatty, David V., Borodale, Enniscorthy	1,338	813	68,292
99	James. Rev. John Reps, -	1,335	657	55,188
100	Beatty, Mrs David, Kingstown, Dublin	1,333	841	70,644
101	Grogan, Sir Edward, 10 Harcourt St, Dublin	1,333	255	21,420
102	Harvey, John, Bargy Castle, Ballycoogan	1,323	1,109	93,156
103	Cormick, Issac, Cromwell's Fort, Wexford	1,312	927	77,868
104	Donoughmore, Earl of, Knocklofty, Clonmel	1,307	1,163	97,692
105	Vero, Christopher, Ballybrennan, Bree, Enniscorthy	1,291	520	43,680
106	Hatchell, John, Terenure, Co. Dublin	1,282	644	54,096

		Acreage	Valuation 1876 (£)	Valuation Current (£)
107	Le Hunte, George, Atramount, Castlebridge, Wexford	1,258	973	81,732
108	Daniel, E.M. and others, Cheltenham, England	1,252	708	59,472
109	Morrogh, Leonard and others, Sleedagh, Murrinstown, and Great Denmark St, Dublin	1,230	773	64,932
110	Jervis, Sir H.C.J.W. Bart, -	1,216	711	59,724
111	Boyce, John, Carnew Castle	1,212	512	43,008
112	Stanforth, John W., Killinnick	1,204	90	7,560
113	Rogers, Congreve, Tramore	1,180	700	58,800
114	Budgen, Thomas, Ballindoney, Enniscorthy	1,156	476	39,984
115	Barden, John, Coolcliffe, Fooksmills	1,145	712	59,808
116	Portsmouth, Earl of, Whitechurch, Hants, England	1,089	9,820	824,880
117	Edwards, Cadwalder, Lemington, England	1,086	925	77,700
118	Conlan, William, -	1,080	571	47,964
119	Hore, Walter, Linfield	1,039	570	47,880
120	Ireland, R.S. Reps, Stephen's Green, Dublin	1,034	419	35,196
121	Pigott, Edward C., Slevoy Castle, Taghmon	1,031	606	50,904
122	Whitney, Thomas A., Merton, Enniscorthy	1,023	488	40,992
123	Dawson, Montifort W., Charlesfort, Ferns	1,017	473	39,732
124	Doyle. Laurence Reps, Ballynabarna, Enniscorthy	1,016	555	46,620
125	Cliffe, Anthony, Belleview, Wexford	1,000	801	67,284
126	Deveroux, John T., George's St, Wexford	396	1,235	103,740

Top 20 landowners in Wexford in 1876 ranked by gross estimated rental income

		Acreage	Valuation 1876 (£)	Valuation Current (£)
1	Tottenham, Charles, Ballycurry, Ashford, Co. Wicklow	7,066	9,963	836,892
2	Portsmouth, Earl of, Whitechurch, Hants, England	1,089	9,820	824,880
3	Ely, the Marquis of, Loftus Hall, Fethard	14,023	9,168	770,112
4	Carew, Rt Hon. Lord, Castleboro, Enniscorthy	17,830	9,070	761,880
5	Forbes, Lady Adelaide, Johnstown Castle, Wexford	15,216	8,840	742,560
6	Courtown, Earl of, Courtown House, Gorey	1,426	8,605	722,820
7	Templemore, Lord, Dunbrodypark, Arthurstown	11,327	7,046	591,864
8	Morgan, Hon. Mrs Deane, Ardcandrisk, Wexford	9,412	7,007	588,588
9	Power, Sir James, Edermine House, Enniscorthy	8,598	6,220	522,480
10	Colclough, Anne, Tintern, Kinnagh	9,328	5,479	460,236
11	Rowe, John H.R. Reps, Ballycross, Wexford	8,002	5,245	440,580
12	Doyne, Charles M, Wells Oulart	7,134	4,692	394,128
13	Foster, William Orme, Apley Park	9,724	4,686	393,624
14	Powerscourt, Viscount, Enniskerry	11,729	4,453	374,052
15	Leigh, F.A., Rosegarland, Fooksmills	8,280	4,052	340,368
16	Boyce, Captain, Bannow House, Bannow	4,589	3,960	332,640
17	Nunn, Edward Westly, Isle of Wight	4,249	3,948	331,632
18	Bryan, Loftus A., In Chancery, Bormount, Enniscorthy	6,135	3,938	330,792
19	Irvine, Captain Edward T., St Aidan's, Ferns	5,000	3,453	290,0052
20	Maher, Mathias A., Ballinkeel, Enniscorthy	4,950	3,392	284,928

WICKLOW

	1876	2016
Population in County Wicklow	78,697 (1871)	142,332
All owners of land	1,041 (1871)	47,429
Percentage of the population	1.32	-
Owners of nothing at all	77,656	35,693
Percentage of the population	98.68	-
Size of County	497,656	500,480 acres
Number of dwellings (of which rented)	14,111 (13,070) (1871)	47,570
Number of owned farm holdings	507 (1871)	2,394 (2010)

County comparisons

	Acreage 1876	Population 1876
County Wicklow	497,656	78,697
Nottinghamshire, England	507,337	319,758
Caithness, Scotland	471,763	39,992
Carmarthenshire, Wales	510,574	115,710

Joseph Scott Moore of Kilbride Manor, Blessington, had 8,730 acres with a valuation of £1,595 about £133,980 in modern money. His valuation was too low to get him and entry in Bateman. Without a title he does not get into Debrett's either. But the Wiki local history record illustrates interesting issues about clerical incomes, debts and social life amongst the gentry. The story is that of Kilbride Manor.

In 1824 the Kilbride estate was purchased from George Ponsonby's widow by George Ogle Moore, barrister, MP for Dublin from 1826 to 1831 and Registrar of Deeds until 1846. Moore, described by James Ambercromby, a contemporary writer, as 'an orange lawyer of doubtful fame' and by Richard Lalor Sheil, a journalist as 'Sir Forcible Feeble', was an aggressive defender of the Protestant interest in Parliament, mocked by his opponents for his intemperate opposition to Catholic emancipation. George Moore was living in Kilbride Manor in 1844, when James Frazer, a writer at the time noted 'a new mansion and other improvements are in progress'. After Moore's death in 1847 his property passed to his son, the Reverend William Ogle Moore, the curate of Blessington and Kilbride parishes, whose financial difficulties are described in the diaries of Elizabeth Smith. In March 1853 she noted:

> Ogle Moore has completed the preliminaries of his sale. A few weeks now will see him an independent man. All debts paid, his little income clear, and twenty thousand pounds to leave among his six daughters. He will educate and start his sons and they must make their own way.

Moore's Estate Act of 1853 allowed Elizabeth Brown and her husband, Joseph Scott Moore, to purchase the Kilbride estate. In 1876, Joseph Scott Moore held 8,730 acres in Wicklow. Upon his death in 1884 he was succeeded by his son, Joseph Fletcher Moore, whose son, Colonel Joseph Scott Moore, died at Kilbride in 1950. All three served as justices of the peace and High Sheriffs of Wicklow.

Cornwallis Robert Ducarel Gun-Cunninghame of Mount Kennedy, County Wicklow, had 10,479 acres with a valuation of £5,809 about £487,596 in modern money. Cornwalls Robert was the son of Robert George Archibald Hamilton Gun-Cunninghame DL (1818–80), of Mount Kennedy and Coolawinna, County Wicklow. He was a colonel in the Wicklow Artillery, who married in 1844 Isabella, only daughter of the Rt Rev. Lord Robert Ponsonby Tottenham, Lord Bishop of Clogher (2nd son of the 1st Marquess of Ely), by the Hon. Alicia Maude, his wife, daughter of Cornwallis, 1st Viscount Hawarden.

Cornwallis Robert Ducarel Gun-Cunninghame JP DL (1857–1928), of Mount Kennedy, was High Sheriff of County Wicklow, 1886, and a captain and honorary major in the 7th Brigade, N Irish Division, Royal Artillery. He married firstly, in 1886, Isabella, youngest daughter of Richard Wingfield, and had issue. Gun-Cuninghame was succeeded by his elder son, Robert George Arthur Gun-Cuninghame (1896–1970), who married, in 1927, Emily Frances Grace, daughter of Cornelius Richard O'Callaghan.

The Earl of Meath MP of Kilruddery, Bray, County Wicklow, had 14,717 acres in Wicklow in 1876 with a valuation of £6,011 about £504,924 in modern money.

See page 120.

The Marquis of Downshire of Hillsborough Castle, County Down, had 15,766 acres in Wicklow in 1876, valued at £5,018 about £421,512 in modern money.

See page 105.

The 5th Earl of Carysfort of Glenart Castle, Arklow, owned 16,291 acres in 1876, valued at £11,856 about £995,904 in modern money. The Eton-educated 5th Earl, William Proby, held the title in the peerage of Ireland that has been extinct since 1909 and was a considerable landowner in both England and Ireland in 1876. He had, apart from his Wicklow acres, 3,972 acres in Huntingdonshire, 2,270 acres in Northampton, 1,250 acres in Dublin and 1,748 acres in Kildare, valued at £31,075. The Dublin acres were beginning to reflect the future values of acreage there, having a valuation of £8,123.

Despite the Irish title, the family were essentially London-based British politicians and soldiers in the imperial forces. The 5th Earl was the fourth son of Admiral Granville Proby, the 3rd Earl Carysfort. The 2nd Earl was a general in the British Army. The 4th Earl was a Liberal politician and had served as Comptroller of the Household from 1859 to 1866. It was only in the person of the 5th and final Earl that they returned to Ireland. He served as High Sheriff of Wicklow in 1866 and as Lord Lieutenant of County Wicklow from 1890 to 1909. The link between landowners was strong, a daughter of the 3rd Earl marrying a son of the Marquis of Hamilton, later Duke of Hamilton (*see* Londonderry).

Hugo John Mandevill of Landscape held 17,937 acres of Wicklow in 1876, valued at £1,246 about £104,664 in modern money. The inadequate valuation places Mandeville beneath Bateman's radar and he is not mentioned, despite the massive acreage. He is not picked up by Ferres either. He is definitely in the Return, but no house, village or parish called Landscape is mentioned. But how do you lose an estate of 17,000 acres? Perhaps someone will unravel this tiny mystery and let the author know the outcome.

The 5th Earl of Wicklow (Charles Francis Howard) owned 22,103 acres in Wicklow in 1876 valued at £10,762 about £904,008 in modern money. This title, which became extinct with the death of the 9th Earl in 1983, was, by the standards of the time, a very wealthy one. As well as the Wicklow acres, there were 6,440 acres of reasonable land in Donegal and 170 acres in Westmeath, the total coming to 28,713 acres valued at £15,717. The *Irish Times* found an old photograph in 2016 and wrote the following about the 8th Earl, who appeared in the snap.

> Our man, however, is the eighth earl: William Cecil James Philip John Paul Howard, better known as Billy Wicklow, star of Dublin literary circles, author of a number of books on theology and a familiar figure in certain drinking establishments around Dublin city centre. While at Oxford he was known as Cracky Clonmore and was a friend of Evelyn Waugh and John Betjeman. He

had also been banned from his own home in Wicklow, thanks to his predilection for going to Mass with the help. It's all very *Brideshead Revisited* – but this was Ireland, or at least Dublin, in the 1960s.

The title was first created in 1793 for Alice Howard, Dowager Viscountess Wicklow. She was the daughter of William Forward, an MP for Donegal in the Irish House of Commons. Her husband was the Bishop of Elphin, styled Right Reverend Robert Howard, Lord Bishop of Elphin. The dead Viscount's first title had been Baron Clonmore in Carlow. The 4th Earl had been the Lord Lieutenant of Wicklow between 1831 and 1869.

In 1951 the 8th Earl sold the family estate and home to the Irish Government. The home was the beautiful Shelton Abbey near Arklow. It was subsequently used as an open prison.

The 5th Marquis of Waterford, John Henry De La Poer MP, of Curraghmore in Waterford, had 26,035 acres in Wicklow in 1876 valued at £4,620 about £388,080 in modern money. The Beresford marquisate is not very old as such things go, having been created in 1789, a promotion from a previous Barony in 1786. No small cause of the promotion was the vast acreage the family had obtained, not just in Waterford but all over Ireland. In the 1876 Returns the family name occurs no fewer than 14 time, in 9 counties, including being missed several times as with the 1876 holder of the title, who had land in Kilkenny 406 acres, Cavan 305 acres, Kildare 55 acres. The Wicklow acreage at 26,055 acres is included. His combined holdings of 66,684 acres had a valuation of £32,752.

Because this is one of the surviving great estates, with the current 9th Marquis, Henry Nicholas de la Poer Beresford in residence at Curraghmore, there are a number of points to note. The 9th Marquis, unlike the incumbent in 1976, the 5th Marquis, was educated at Harrow but, like the 5th Marquis, his father, the 8th Marquis, served in the poshest and most expensive regiment in the British Army, the Life Guards. Service in that particular regiment also provided close proximity to the Crown, as the function of the officers of the regiment is to protect the blood royal, with their own lives if necessary.

After his first wife died in 1873, a year later the 5th Marquis married a daughter of the Duke of Beaufort, whose own estate ran to over 51,000 acres in the west of England. The 5th Marquis also sat as an MP, was Lord Lieutenant of the County, and was Master of the Buckhounds, a ministerial appointment in Government. The website for Curraghmore claims that the Beresfords arrived in England with William the Bastard, a claim the Beresford Family Society is unable to substantiate as yet (but they are working on it). However, look at the fifth entry for this county, Count Edmund de la Poer, and this is where there does appear to be a link to the Norman occupation of England.

Viscount Powerscourt of Enniskerry in County Wicklow had 11,729 acres in Wexford with a valuation of £4,453 in 1876.

See page 409.

The 6th Earl Fitzwilliam, William Wentworth Fitzwilliam of Coolattin Park, Shilleleagh, owned 89,891 acres in Wexford in 1876 valued at £46,444 about £3,901,296 in modern money. The Earl Fitzwilliam was the thirty-fifth largest landowner in Great Britain in 1876, but ranked much higher in terms of income. He was outranked in the income stakes by just five Dukes – Westminster excluded because his London acres were missed from the tally. Fitzwilliam's full property portfolio is set out in Bateman. Aside from the 89,895 acres in Wicklow, he owned 22,192 in Yorkshire, 881 acres in Northampton, 533 acres in Cambridge, 308 acres in Derby, 75 acres in Huntingdon 17 acres in Lincoln, 1,532 acres in Kildare and 325 acres in Wexford. The total was 115,743 acres, valued at £138,801.

Bateman marks the Earl with a Gothic cross, indicating that he had held land since the time of Henry VII in an unbroken male line. The peerage became extinct in 1979. The name indicates a Norman origin but the creation of the family as one of the greatest landowners in nineteenth-century Great Britain is first recorded in Yorkshire when Sir John Fitzwilliam of Sprotborough married Margaret Clarell, the daughter of Thomas Clarell of Aldwark, whose family were of Norman origin. The first connections with Ireland were Elizabethan. Sir William Fitzwilliam was Lord Deputy in Ireland from 1571 to 1575, a post obtained by having supervised the execution of Mary Queen of Scots on her half-sister Elizabeth's warrant in 1558. He came back to Ireland between 1588 and 1594. Sir William's grandfather had been Sheriff of London, though not Mayor. He was close enough to the money, however, to be able to buy the Milton Hall estate at Peterborough in 1502. The Fitzwilliam man in Ireland arrived rich, landed, royally connected and with blood on his hands.

The next big acquisition of land occurred when the newly minted Earl married Lady Anne Watson-Wentworth, daughter of Thomas Watson-Wentworth, 1st Marquess of Rockingham, and sister of Charles Watson-Wentworth, 2nd Marquess of Rockingham. He was succeeded by his son, the 4th Earl.

In 1766 Rockingham became Prime Minister. Here is what Wikipedia writes about that ministry, which only lasted a year.

The First Rockingham ministry headed by the Marquess of Rockingham served between 1765 and 1766 during the reign of George III. It is often referred to as the only government ever to have been made up almost entirely of members of the Jockey Club – Rockingham being a prominent patron and follower of the turf. Rockingham was noted for his ignorance of foreign affairs, and his Ministry failed to reverse the growing isolation of Britain within Europe. The Ministry fell in 1766 and was replaced by one headed by William Pitt. There was a 2nd Rockingham Ministry in 1781 but it ended with the death of Rockingham, in post. The 4th Earl inherited his uncle Rockingham's estate, including the North Yorkshire estate of Wentworth –Woodhouse, sometimes described as the largest house ever built in England. And he came back to Ireland as the Lord Lieutenant.

After the death of the 10th Earl in 1979, Wentworth Woodhouse was sold. But the lands, at about 80,000 acres, and the town of Malton in North Yorkshire were retained by the family. So were the acres at Milton Hall, perhaps 50,000 acres in all. The estate at Bourne Park near Canterbury, omitted in Bateman, passed into in the possession of the 8th Earl's daughter, the Lady Anne, Marchioness of Bristol, whose daughter, the Hon. Helena Anne, is the wife of the prominent Conservative politician and MP Jacob Rees-Mogg.

There is little in the public domain about what happened to the Irish acreage but the *Irish Times* in 2016 had a look at the history when the house at Coolattin was used for an auction.

After the Great Famine and the land clearances, an estimated 2,000 people emigrated from the estate to Canada and tens of thousands of Canadians can today trace their ancestry to Coolattin. By 1948, more than twenty years after Irish independence, Peter Wentworth-Fitzwilliam, the 8th Earl Fitzwilliam, still owned Coolattin. That summer, he died in an air crash in France, along with Kathleen 'Kick' Kennedy. Fitzwilliam was allegedly trying to divorce his wife in Wicklow and planning to marry the sister of future US President John F. Kennedy. Kennedy herself already had a separate connection to Ireland – she had married, four years earlier in 1944, William Cavendish, eldest son and heir to the 10th Duke of Devonshire, owner of Lismore Castle. But that marriage lasted just four months. Cavendish was killed while serving with the British Army in Belgium during the Second World War, leaving Kennedy widowed and titled Marchioness of Hartington. Fitzwilliam's widow, Olive, Countess Fitzwilliam (nee Plunket), a daughter of the Bishop of Meath, lived on in Coolattin until her death in 1975. The Coolattin estate and the contents of the house were subsequently sold.

Today, Coolattin House is owned by Coolattin Golf Club and overlooks the course.

Landowners of over 1,000 acres in Wicklow in 1876

		Acreage	Valuation 1876 (£)	Valuation Current (£)
1	Fitzwilliam, Earl, Coolatin Park, Shillelagh	89,891	46,444	3,901,296
2	Powerscourt, Viscount Lord, Powerscourt House, Enniskerry	36,693	8,890	746,760
3	Waterford, Marquess of, Curraghmore, Waterford	26,035	4,620	388,080
4	Wicklow, Earl of, Shelton Abbey, Arklow	22,103	10,763	904,092
5	Hugo, John Mandeville, Landscape	17,937	1,246	104,664
6	Caryfort, Earl of, Glenart Castle, Arklow	16,291	11,856	995,904
7	Downshire, Marquess of, Hillsborough, Co. Down	15,766	5,018	421,512
8	Meath, Earl of, Kilruddery, Bray, Co. Wicklow	14,717	6,011	504,924
9	Cunningham, Robert A. Gun, Mountkennedy	10,479	5,809	487,956
10	Moore, Joseph Scott, Kilbride Manor, Blessington	8,730	1,595	133,980
11	Kemmis, William, Ballinacor	8,041	1,436	120,624
12	Brady, Luke Reps, Limerick	5,837	587	49,308
13	Acton, Thomas, Westaston	4,845	2,729	229,236
14	Dick, Wm W.F., Humewood	4,770	2,534	212,856
15	Parnell, Charles S., Avondale, Rathdrum	4,678	1,245	104,580
16	Hutchison, Sir Edward S., Bray	4,471	1,202	100,968
17	Mining Co of Ireland, -	4,409	261	21,924
18	Synge, Francis, Glenmore, Ashford	4,298	1,825	153,300
19	Wade, Robert, Clonbraney	4,055	3,694	310,296
20	Whaley, Richard Wm, Whaley Abbey	3,956	1,919	161,196
21	Westby, William Jones, High Park	3,874	1,179	99,036
22	Grogan, William, Slaney Park	3,761	2,108	177,072
23	Bunbury, D. Tighe, Rosanna	3,459	2,538	213,192
24	Monck, Viscount, Charleville, Enniskerry	3,434	1,556	130,704

		Acreage	Valuation 1876 (£)	Valuation Current (£)
25	Byrne, Andrew William Reps, Croneybyrne, Rathdrum	3,202	842	70,728
26	Saunders, Robert S. Pratt, Saundersgrove	3,143	2,059	172,956
27	Bayley, Edward S., Ballyarthur	3,036	1,872	157,248
28	Kirkpatrick, Alex R., Donacomper	2,976	1,195	100,380
29	Bourne, Andrew, France	2,898	660	55,440
30	Paul, Sir Robert J. Bart, Ballyglan, Waterford	2,894	1,836	154,224
31	Radcliffe, Stephen Reps, In Chancery	2,847	760	63,840
32	Courtney, Richard H., Coolballintaggart, Moyne, Rathdrum	2,827	451	37,884
33	Fishbourne, Ed Eustace, Dublin	2,820	269	22,595
34	Bookey, Georgina, Derrybane	2,684	1,099	92,316
35	De Robeck, Baron of Gowran, Grange	2,638	1,654	138,936
36	Tottenham, Charles, Ballycurry	2,540	1,409	118,356
37	Tynte, Joseph Pratt, Tynte Park, Dunlavin	2,532	2,186	183,624
38	O'Byrne, William R., Cabinteely House	2,363	2,118	177,912
39	Esmonde, Sir John, Ballynastragh, Gorey	2,088	425	35,700
40	Pennefather, Edward, Rathsallagh	1,941	1,581	132,804
41	Heytesbury, Lord, 41 Eaton Place, London	1,902	1,162	97,608
42	La Touche, William Robert, Bellevue, Delgany	1,798	2,964	248,976
43	Mahony, David, Grangecow	1,769	1,243	104,412
44	Bookey, William T., Derrybane	1,745	267	22,248
45	Truell, Henry Pomeroy, Clonmannon	1,663	1,707	143,388
46	Dopping-Hepenstall R.A., Derrycassan, Granard	1,568	925	77,700
47	Greene, Francis Wm, Kilranalagh	1,559	837	70,308

		Acreage	Valuation 1876 (£)	Valuation Current (£)
48	Smith, Mrs E., Baltyboys, Blessington	1,558	460	38,640
49	M'Mahon, John, Donard	1,547	859	72,156
50	Barton, Thomas, Glendalough House	1,542	482	40,488
51	Carroll, Coote A., England	1,519	1,149	96,516
52	Smith, John Greydon, Baltyboys House, Blessington	1,518	1,090	91,560
53	Cogan, Rt Hon. W.R.F., Tinode, Co. Wicklow	1,506	294	24,696
54	Guinness, Benjamin Lee, Dublin	1,493	384	32,256
55	Heighton, William, Donard	1,475	564	47,376
56	Byrne, Peter Reps, Dublin	1,410	125	10,500
57	Hodgson, Henry, Ballyraine	1,402	256	21,504
58	Salkeld, Joseph, England	1,355	543	45,612
59	Radcliffe, William, -	1,353	523	43,932
60	Carroll, Henry, Ballinure	1,346	1,159	97,356
61	Keogh, George, Roundwood	1,319	470	39,480
62	Hudson, Richard Reps, -	1,294	345	28,980
63	Oliver, John, Cherrymount	1,291	869	72,996
64	Hudson, George Reps, -	1,291	342	28,728
65	Trinity College Provost and Fellows Dublin	1,287	408	34,272
66	Booth, George, Lara	1,250	229	19,236
67	Hodson, Sir George Bart, Holybrook, Bray	1,211	1,186	99,624
68	Hume, William, Humewood, Kilteagon	1,203	48	4,032
69	Calwell, Rev. Joseph, Aghaves, Brookborough	1,201	335	28,140
70	Ellis, Robert F., Sea Park	1,197	1,315	110,460
71	Snell, Thomas, Ballintomboy	1,178	25	2,100
72	Vavasour, William, -	1,175	194	16,296
73	Jones, Robert P., Woodside, Hacketstown	1,159	79	6,636
74	Aldborough, Earl of, Paris	1,156	803	67,452

		Acreage	Valuation 1876 (£)	Valuation Current (£)
75	Frizell. Charles, Castle Kevin, Annamoe	1,148	466	39,144
76	Graydon, Laurance, Toomon	1,148	441	37,044
77	Whitshed, Sir St Vincent Reps, Greystones, Delgany	1,142	1,356	113,904
78	Duckett, William, Ducketts Grove	1,096	880	73,920
79	Day, Rev. A. and Guinness Miss, Ballymanus, Aughrim	1,077	303	25,452
80	Scott, James E., Ballygannon	1,066	1,443	121,212
81	Drought, Rev. Thomas, Clonoulty, Cashel	1,064	381	32,004
82	Humphrey, Alexander, -	1,048	394	33,096
83	Butler, James, Dublin	1,029	773	64,932
84	Edge, John H., Monkstown	1,028	188	15,792
85	Sweetman, Patrick, Dublin	1,027	795	66,780
86	Nixon, Henry, Kilkenny	1,010	114	9,576
87	Revell, Wm Horton, Balleymoney	1,000	375	31,500

Landowners of over 1,000 acres in Wicklow in 1876 ranked by estimated rental income

		Acreage	Valuation 1876 (£)	Valuation Current (£)
1	Fitzwilliam, Earl, Coolatin Park, Shillelagh	89,891	46,444	3,901,296
2	Caryfort, Earl of, Glenart Castle, Arklow	16,291	11,856	995,904
3	Wicklow, Earl of, Shelton Abbey, Arklow	22,103	10,763	904,092
4	Powerscourt, Viscount Lord, Powerscourt House, Enniskerry	36,693	8,890	746,760
5	Meath, Earl of, Kilruddery, Bray, Co. Wicklow	14,717	6,011	504,924
6	Cunningham, Robert A. Gun, Mountkennedy	10,479	5,809	487,956
7	Downshire, Marquess of, Hillsborough, Co. Down	15,766	5,018	421,512

		Acreage	Valuation 1876 (£)	Valuation Current (£)
8	Waterford, Marquess of, Curraghmore, Waterford	26,035	4,620	388,080
9	Wade, Robert, Clonbraney	4,055	3,694	310,296
10	La Touche, William Robert, Bellevue, Delgany	1,798	2,964	248,976
11	Acton, Thomas, Westaston	4,845	2,729	229,236
12	Bunbury, D. Tighe, Rosanna	3,459	2,538	213,192
13	Dick, Wm W.F., Humewood	4,770	2,534	212,856
14	Tynte, Joseph Pratt, Tynte Park, Dunlavin	2,532	2,186	183,624
15	O'Byrne, William R., Cabinteely House	2,363	2,118	177,912
16	Grogan, William, Slaney Park	3,761	2,108	177,072
17	Saunders, Robert S. Pratt, Saundersgrove	3,143	2,059	172,956
18	Whaley, Richard Wm, Whaley Abbey	3,956	1,919	161,196
19	Bayley, Edward S., Ballyarthur	3,036	1,872	157,248
20	Paul, Sir Robert J. Bart, Ballyglan, Waterford	2,894	1,836	154,224

CONTEXT

This is largely a book of lists, but of internal Irish county lists. Ireland North with the UK, and South as the Republic, are two amongst 193 member states of the United Nations. It would seem only right then to close this final chapter by seeing where Ireland's landowners fit amongst the landowners of the Earth, starting with a list of Ireland's largest landowners. It is neither an exhaustive nor comprehensive list (the structure at the Land Registry and the cost of searches makes that impossible), but it is a list that shows the overall pattern of ownership as recorded in auction reports, farming and other lists, and by the media. It is printed here to encourage further research and further study of both patterns now and possible evolution into the future.

The non-Irish lists are given next. First, the UK land list of the ten largest landowners in the UK. This is pertinent in Ireland as the Queen is the legal owner of all land in Northern Ireland, a privilege she shares with the Irish State which owns all the land in the Republic.

Then the list of the ten largest landowners in the United States, several with Irish connections.

Next is the extraordinary Australian top ten land list where there is one farm that is bigger than the whole island of Ireland.

Finally, there is a section of the world's largest landowner list, compiled for this book. What it shows is the growing corporate ownership of land as capitalist China and Russia expand aggressively around the world. But it still shows that most of the world's acreage is in the ultimate ownership of monarchs, aristocrats and states. The minority owners of land are ordinary people – kept as far away as possible from actual ownership by bureaucratic structures, as bad in the USA as in China and Russia and nowhere quite as bad as the UK and its dominions where the feudal system prevails.

Table 1. Individual large landholders and cooperative holders of land in the Irish Republic and Northern Ireland 2021. List of 70 compiled between 2016 and 2021 from all sources.

	Name of landowner & County	Acreage	Source of information	Other comments
1	Coillte. The Forestry Commission of the Irish Republic. One of the largest integrated and profitable forestry estates outside Scandinavia	1,102,000	For this book. Coillte annual reports and accounts 2010–19	Coillte has been growing at about 10 per cent per annum in recent years.
2	The 26 dioceses of the Catholic Church in Ireland. 50 per cent of the dioceses, 13 in number, present no public accounts *FN	296,000 max 148,000 min Extremely conservative	Accounts of 11 dioceses. Suggests 148,000 acres. Est for other 13 is 148,000 acres	This is an average of dioceses and is conservative as fixed assets are not broken down, even in the accounts available
3	Bord na Mona. Irish Turf Board	200,000	For this book from the company. Annual report and accounts 2010-2018	This is a state-owned company heavily retrenching as turf is a rapidly disappearing resource.
4	Religious orders in Ireland. This is an average estimate taken from Orders whose holdings are known	120,000 Extremely conservative	Examination of various religious orders	This is an average of 175 orders out of over 375 and is conservative
5	The Forestry Service of Northern Ireland	80,000	For this book	The acreage of the Forestry Commission estate in Northern Ireland has been declining in recent years. Sales mostly
6	Glenveagh National Park (Estate) Donegal. The Irish State	41,000	For this book	One of the very rare gifts to the people of Ireland in the 1970s by Henry McIlhenny, a wealth American. The creator of the estate, Captain John George Adair from Laois, was one of the cruellest post-famine landlords

	Name of landowner & County	Acreage	Source of information	Other comments
7	Larry Goodman, farmer Co. Louth Branganstown Farms Ltd Ardee CAP Subsidies E413,000 to E 218,578	25,000 Est, perhaps double that	Local papers and visit	Larry Goodman is one of the most astute farmers/financiers in modern Ireland. Much of this land is leased or rented
8	Jack Marry (dcd) Louth	(25,000)	Local papers and personal visits.	Jack Marry was once the largest and best pig farmer in Ireland. He was early into the post-Communist east bloc with 50,000 acres leased in Poland. He was destroyed by the irresponsibility of the Irish banks in the 2008 bank crash
9	The National Trust in Northern Ireland. The Giants Causeway is the most popular National Trust site in the UK, attracting 690,000 visitors in 2020	21,887	For this book	The National Trust is an essentially English invention but is growing rapidly in Northern Ireland and recently added 1,000 acres at Castle Stuart
10	ESB Irish Electricity Board. Very reluctant to disclose acreage.	20,000	For this book. Annual reports and accounts 2010–18	Classic UK style reluctance to disclose acreage properly.
11	4th Baron O'Neill. A title in the peerage of the United Kingdom 1872 acreage 65,000. See WOBI. Shane's Castle County Antrim	15,000 In trust	For this book. WOBI	See note on trusts
12	5th Duke of Abercorn, family name Hamilton Tyrone. See WOBI 1872 acreage 60,000 Barons Court, County Tyrone	15,000 in trust Very conservative	For this book	The duke is married to an aunt of the 7th Duke of Westminster.

	Name of landowner & County	Acreage	Source of information	Other comments
13	7th Earl of Erne, family name Crichton. See WOBI. 1872 acreage 31,000 County Fermanagh. Estate managed by the National Trust. Castle and 1,900 acres held by the Crichton Trust	15,000 in trust	For this book	See note on trusts
14	9th Marquis of Downshire Estate. Family name Hill. See WOBI. Now based at Ripon in Yorkshire. 1872 Acreage 78,000 County Down	10,000 in Trust	For this book	See note on trusts
15	Blackwood family of Clandeboy Earl of Dufferin and Ava (extinct title) 18,000. See WOBI. County Down	10,000 in Trust	For this book	See note on trusts
16	Irish Dairy Board Cooperative. Many founders still hold shares. Now Ornua	10,000	For this book	Number 108 in the World 300 ranking of Cooperatives. May have 20,000 members
17	The UK Ministry of Defence in Northern Ireland	9,700	For this book	A once vast estate now down to acreage around Ballykelly RAF base and Ballykinlar Army base
18	Coolmore stud Tipperary. John Magnier	9,500	*Sunday Times* and local papers. *Irish Independent* wealthiest landowners	This is probably a huge underestimate. There are local O'Brien stables which are linked, and 7,000 acres in the US
19	12th Duke of Devonshire the family name is Cavendish. The duke no longer has a seat in the UK House of Lords. Lismore, Castle Waterford	8,000	*Sunday Times* and local papers. Visits.	This estate survived the Land Commission. The duke holds in trust 30,000 acres in the UK

	Name of landowner & County	Acreage	Source of information	Other comments
20	Cork Farmers Cooperative. A complex coop including North Cork Coop, Bandon Coop and others	8,000	Local papers	See note on Cooperative farms
21	9th Earl of Antrim, family name MacDonnell 1872 acreage 34,000. See WOBI. The estate is at Glenarm in Antrim and is family run. See WOBI	7,500	For this book	Like a lot of the residual aristocratic estates in Northern Ireland hard to estimate what's still in the trust.
22	Galway Farmers Cooperative. A complex mix of merged Coops including Arrabawn, Connaught Coop etc.	6,000	Local papers	The Galway Coops had many outlets and local marts.
23	Dobbs Acreage in 1872 5,000 Castle Dobbs County Antrim See WOBI	5,000 in trust	For this book	This is an old landed estate which is actively managed.
24	Grosvenor Estate Ely Court Fermanagh 1872 acreage 34,000. Parts of the estate sold to tenants in the late 1900s. See WOBI. County Fermanagh	5,000 in trust	For this book	After the Queen, the real largest landowner in the UK is the 7th Duke of Westminster, Hugh Grosvenor. However, much of the estate is abroad and all is in complex trusts
25	Mayo Cooperative Farmers. A true farming cooperative based on farmers Catal Lowry from Galway, David Boland from Roscommon, David and Ian Lamberton from Donegall and Timmy Quinn from Mayo	5,000	Local papers	Aurivo, an agri food company owned by former farmers has turnover of £446 million (2018). 1,000 shareholders and 10,000 members. Sells to 50 countries

	Name of landowner & County	Acreage	Source of information	Other comments
26	Dairygold Ltd. A true farm owned cooperative venture. Started in 1990. Limerick and Mitchelstown, County Cork	5,000	Annual accounts	Number 256 in the world 300 list of large cooperatives. Formed from smaller cooperatives
27	Sligo Farmers Cooperatives and markets	5,000	Local papers	Included with the Mayo and Midland Coop
28	Glanbia Addresses throughout Irish counties	4,000	Local papers and visit	Massive agri business founded by various farming cooperatives. Turnover £3.5 billion (2019) Number 98 in the world list of 300 top co operatives
29	Laois Farmers Cooperatives. Durrow, Donoughmore, and others	4,000	Local papers. Local knowledge. Visit	Associated with Glanbia, Glenbarrow. See Glenbia. Number 98 in the world top 300 cooperatives
30	9th Marquis of Waterford. Henry Beresford formerly the Earl of Tyrone. Curraghmore 1872 acreage 39,883 Land in Wicklow See WOBI Waterford	3,600	For this book	The 8th Marquis died in March 2015. He was a keen horseman and polo player and set up several local businesses. The current Marquis was a polo player. The family have lived at Curraghmore for 800 years
31	8th Earl Castle Stewart. Family name Stuart. Stuart Hall settled estates. 1872 acreage 32,615. See WOBI. County Tyrone	3,500	For this book	National Trust recently bought part of the Estate
32	Walter Furlong and family. Wexford and adjacent counties. Total of over E500,000 in CAP subsidies	3,500	Local papers and visit	This is a mix of leased and owned land. Owned 2,000 acres leased 1,500 with 22,000 acres in Argentina
33	Golden Vale Cooperative and related Companies Cork	3,000	Local and national papers	Originally founded by Tipperary and Cork Coop members

	Name of landowner & County	Acreage	Source of information	Other comments
34	VG Land holdings Whooley family Galway. Over E187,000 in CAP subsidies	3,000	Local and national papers	This is a family farming and fishing operation
35	Wexford Farmers Cooperatives and marts	3,000	Local papers	This cooperative has 2,500 shareholders almost all members.
36	Michael Smith Family Navan Co Meath Over E225,000 in CAP subsidy	2,500	Local and national papers.	Land is owned, leased and rented
37	Frank Joyce & Family Trim County Meath E213,000 CAP subsidies	2,500	Local and national papers	Land owned, leased and rented
38	Conroy Family, Portarlington Laois. CAP subsidy of E137,309	2,500	Local and national papers	Land owned, leased and rented
39	Jack and Jim Dobson Tyrone Large scale beef farming and processing. Dunbia brand	2,300	Local and national papers. Auction reports	Also known as Dawn Meat. Extensive land-holdings in Ireland, UK, Wales and Scotland
40	7th Earl of Caledon. Family name Alexander 1872 acreage 29,000 See WOBI. County Tyrone (7,500 in Tyrone orignally)	2,000	For this book	Famous military family, including WW2 commander who became Earl Alexander of Tunis
41	The Al Maktoum family. Owns 5 stud farms in Kildare and Tipperary Godolphin group E200,530 in CAP subsidies	2,000	This is a minimum estimate	Also owns stud farm in UK and USA

	Name of landowner & County	Acreage	Source of information	Other comments
42	Keating Family. Starting with a single Butcher's shop in Kilrush. County Clare This family farm business now has E1.5 billion turnover. Based in County Meath, Monaghan and in the UK.	2,000	This is a minimum estimate	The company has a range of brands Kepac being the best known. IT had extensive UK interests but these have now shifted to the US and China because of Brexit.
43	Irish Agricultural Wholesale Society. Now Aryzta. Huge multinational food company with roots in the Cooperatives of the nineteenth century Dublin	2,000	Local papers Auction and other reports	This vast enterprise grew, like so many other Irish businesses, from the cooperative movement. Now based in Dublin but with big operations in France and Switzerland
44	8th Marquis of Donegal Wexford. The original holding was 90,000 acres around Belfast, 100,000 acres in Donegall and 11,000 acres in Wexford. The family name is Chichester	2,000 in Trust for the Donegall estate	Local and national papers.	The current Marquis lives at Arthurstown in Wexford. His heir is the Earl of Belfast
45	Aga Khan racing stables Kildare	2,000	Stud list and local papers	All land held freehold
46	Opus Dei, an independent dioceses 'prelature'	2,000	Local reporting and some accounts	Charity commission Records not found
47	Church of Ireland Residual landholdings	2,000	In trusts of various kinds	The Church of Ireland has a structure of dioceses in both the Republic and Northern Ireland
48	O'Shea family farms Piltown, Kilkenny E229,633 CAP subsidy	2,000	Local papers	Land owned, leased and rented
49	Patrick Reynolds, Navan Meath CAP E260,805	2,000	Local papers	Land owned, leased and rented. Known as the Prince of Potatoes.

	Name of landowner & County	Acreage	Source of information	Other comments
50	McAuley Family Navan County Meath CAP E206,208	2,000	Local papers	Land owned, leased and rented
51	William Ahern Cashel Tipperary CAP Subsidy E197,118	2,000	Local and national papers	Land owned, leased and rented
52	Phoenix Park Dublin Irish Government	1,700	Local and national papers. Visit	This beautiful park is a much-loved Dublin recreation area
53	Park Farms Partnership Carlow CAP subsidy E220,564	1,500	Local and national papers. Auction reports	Not much public material on this organisation, save for the CAP subsidy
54	B & L Farms (unlimited) Belturbet Cavan CAP subsidy E208,178	1,300	Local and national paper. Auction and other reports	This farm enterprise is 'unlimited' which usually means large unencumbered assets
55	8th Earl of Longford. Family name Pakenham. Does not use title. Family estate in the Republic of Ireland	1,200	For this book	The Pakenham's had a long association with Ireland but are essentially Anglo Irish
56	Cistercian Abbey Roscrea Tipperary	1,200	Local and national papers	Prestigious school and widely admired farm
57	Thomas Codd Wexford CAP E245,358	1,200	Local papers	Land owned, leased and rented
58	4th Earl of Iveagh (Ned Guinness). Lives in Norfolk. Sold most of Irish estate to Irish Govt for £29 million. Major heir to Iveagh Trusts based in Switzerland	1,000	Minimum estimate Of residual Irish estate in trust	Owns 22,500 in UK in Norfolk

	Name of landowner & County	Acreage	Source of information	Other comments
59	Ronnie Wilson. Monaghan Mushrooms Tyholland, County Monaghan Teacher turned entrepreneur. Employs 3,500 people and sells 1,800 tons of mushrooms a week	1,000	*Sunday Times* Rich List	Minimum estimate of acreage
60	John Malone. American billionaire Largest private landowner in US, number 57 in world list	1,000	*Forbes, Irish Independent, Irish Times*	Main holdings are at Kiltegan in County Wicklow and Castlemartin in Kildare
61	Michael O'Leary, aggressive CEO of Ryanair. Gigginstown and Plantation Stud Kildare	1,000	Minimum estimate	May be moving.
62	Earl of Howth (Extinct title) Recently owned by Julian Gainsford St Lawrence, descendant Country Dublin	800	*Sunday Times* and local papers	Inherited estate. Estate sold to Tetrarch, an investment trust with land at Mount Juliet Estate in Kilkenny
63	Sir John Leslie Glasslough. Monaghan	800	Local papers and visit	An ancient estate on the border of the Republic and Northern Ireland
64	Queally Family Tramore Waterford CAP E199,118	800	Local papers	This may represent only unleased land
65	Lyons Family Dunboyne, County Meath. This is a US-Ireland agri-distilling business with 6,000 employees and customers in 120 countries	790	Local and national and other reports	Started by a distiller who set up a distiller at Dunboyne and in the Liberties in Dublin

	Name of landowner & County	Acreage	Source of information	Other comments
66	Musgrave Family Supervalue & Cenra. Budgens and Londis in UK. Now a huge £5 billion a year conglomerate it is dominated by the Musgrave family shareholdings	750	Local and national papers	The company was started in the 1800s by a Methodist family from Leitrim, who set up as commodity traders in Cork. Land in West Cork
67	Cork University Agricultural facility	750	Local and national papers	A world class Agricultural facility
68	Cyril Goode, Cattle Breeder in Wicklow CAP Subsidy E241,530	700	Local papers	Cyril Goode is a vet who breeds Simmental cattle
69	Rockwell College Tipperary	650	Local and national papers	Private school and large farm
70	O'Brien racing stud Kildare	650	Stud reports and local papers	Also land in Tipperary
71	Paul Carr, Letterkenny, Donegal CAP subsidy E221,510	450	Local and national papers	No other information on this farmer

The 10 largest landowners in the United Kingdom, excluding the Queen's overall feudal overlordship, which includes all of Northern Ireland.

Table 2. Top 10 largest landowners/land holdings in the UK in 2019.

	Name	Acres	Use
1	The Forestry Commission of England & Wales (and Scotland)	2,470,000 acres in 2001 down to 1,771,000 acres now. With 510,000 acres in England and Wales and 1.2 million acres in Scotland.	Forestry
2	The Ministry of Defence	Just over 1,049,796 acres down from over 1.1 million in 2001. There are a further 250,000 acres in Canada	Military training and farm leasing
3	Local Authorities	Between 993,000 in 2001 and 1,00,000 in 2020. Figures not accurately listed by Local Authorities.	Schools, hospitals, depots, some farms still

	Name	Acres	Use
4	National Trust	550,000 acres up from 400,000 acres in 2017	The biggest membership charity in the UK and Europe with a staggering 5.6 million members.
5	The Crown Estate	229,000 acres. In a 120-page annual report for 2016-2017, hugely distinguished by management terms and repetition, the Crown Estate fails anywhere to list its land assets. It admits to owning 229,000 rural acres, but not where. Wikipedia credits the Crown Estate with 1.9 million acres. This figure is possibly underestimating the amount of the UK foreshore owned by the Estate, which is 50 per cent, but the acreage is not specified by the Estate.	The Crown Estate is now the personal property of the Queen as of 2010. The estate includes farms, forests and has huge income from wayleaves across foreshore acreage
6	The Electricity Utilities	Between 200,000 and 300,000 acres in 2001 to about 200,000 now.	Electricity generation and transmission
7	Water Utilities	Between 200,000 and 300,000 acres from about 300,000 in 2001. This may be a serious underestimate	Water services
8	Network Rail	In 2001 British Rail had about 250,000 acres. About 200,000 acres now. Conservative	Rail services and a developing retail sector
9	The Duke of Buccleuch	In 2001 277,000 acres. There is a new duke but the acreage appears unchanged at about 277,000 acres.	Private estate in trust
10	The residual holdings of the National Coal Board	Reckoned at 320,000 acres in 2001. Probably less than 150,000 acres now.	Almost no coal mining but leases land for other uses

Table 3. The 10 largest individual landowners in the United States of America

	Name	Acres	Use
1	John Malone (in 2006 not even in top 10). Now also number 60 in the Irish list	2,200,000. *Forbes* 2020	Mixed
2	Ted Turner (in 2006 was number 1 with 1.8 million acres) Colorado, Florida, Georgia,	2,000,000 million. *Forbes* 2020	Mixed
3	Emmerson Family In 2006 number 3 with 1.5 million acres, mostly California	Sierra Pacific 1,870,000. *Forbes* in 2020	Ranching mixed use
4	Brad Kelly (in 2006 not in the top 10)	1,700,000. *Forbes* in 2020	Ranching mixed use
5	Reed Family Number 8 in 2006 with 770,000 acres mostly Washington State, California and Oregon	Went up to 1,300,000 now at 770,000 in *Forbes* 2020	Ranching mixed use
6	Irving family (in 2006 number 2 with 1.6 million acres) Canada and Maine	Went up to 1.2 million acres. 1,200,000 in *Forbes* 2020	Mixed with forestry leases
7	Singleton family (in 2006 number 4 with 1.2 million acres) New Mexico and California	1.1m million and 1,1,00,000 in *Forbes* 2020.	Mixed ranching and farming
8	King Family (in 2006 number 6 with 900,000 acres in Texas and Florida)	900,000 acres now 1,100,000 acres in *Forbes* 2020	Mixed ranching and farming
9	Stan Kroenke (in 2006, not in the list) Owns Arsenal F.C. Arizona Montana Wyoming and Canada	Went to 865,000 acres now 740,000 acres in *Forbes* 2020.	Mixed ranching and farming
10	Pingrees Family In 2006 number 5 with 960,000 acres mostly in Maine Massachusetts	830,000 acres. Still 830,000 acres in *Forbes* 2020.	Huge amount of forest

Not shown in this list is Jeff Bezos, the founder of Amazon and one of the three richest people in the world. He has been buying land for some time and is now reckoned to own about 420,000 acres according to *Forbes* magazine.

Context 437

Table 4. The largest farms of all. The Dominion of Australia
Top 10 largest ranch holdings and owners in Australia. 2017 including the largest farm holding in the world.

	Owner	Size	Use
1	Gina Reinhart and Shanghai CRED Mostly South Australia. Between 24 million and 27 million acres	20 stations 24 million acres, less about 5,000,000 acres leased for Australian defence, but plus Ms Reinhart's other holdings. Total about 22 million acres.	Cattle, about 185,000 head.
2	Clifton Hills. South Australia. Estimated at 4,200,000 acres, down from 7,000,000 acres	Owned by the Brook family until 1960. Now estimated at 4.2 million acres of an original 7,000,000.	Cattle
3	Alexandria Station (with the Mittlebah Station). Northern Territories Estimated 5,720,000 million acres	Owned by the North Australia Pastoral Company. 4,000,000 acres- with the Mittlebah Station added estimated at 5,720,000 acres	Cattle. 55,000 at the Alexandria station
4	Davenport Downs Station Queensland 3,730,000 million acres	Owned by Paraway since 2009. About 3,730,000 acres	Cattle
5	Home Valley Station Western Australia South Australia 3,500,000 acres	Owned by the Indigenous Land Corporation founded in 2004 to assist indigenous Australian people to acquire land. 3,500,000 acres	Cattle
6	Innamincka Station South Australia 3,350,000 acres	Was part of the S. Kidman holdings. Now presumed part of Gina Reinharts holdings. About 3,350,000 acres	Cattle
7	Wave Hill Station. Northern Territories 3,340,000 acres. Est	Once part of the Vesty Union Cold Storage company, about 800,000 acres were transferred to indigenous people in 1975, after an 11-year strike. Current size is about 3,340,000 acres but overall ownership unclear	Cattle
8	Marion Downs Station Queensland 3,000,000 acres	North Australian Pastoral Company which bought the holding in 1934. Current size is just over 3,000,000 acres	Cattle

	Owner	Size	Use
9	Brunette Downs Station Northern Territories 3,000,000 acres	Owned recently by the Australian Agricultural Company. About 3,000,000 acres	Cattle
10	Quinyambie Station South Australia 3,000,000 acres	Once part of the Kidman holdings this was sold to the Morgan and Wells family Moutooroo Pastoral Company in 2010. Size is about 3,000,000 acres.	Cattle, originally sheep

Table 5. The new world land list compiled for *Who Owns Ireland*. 2021

	Name	Country where land held	Holding in acres
1★	HM Elizabeth 11, UK Sovereign and Queen of Australia, New Zealand, Canada and 26 other territories, is the legal owner of all land in those places, including British Antarctica. Her government agencies are active dealers and mangers on her behalf, in land of all kinds.	UK, Canada, New Zealand, Australia and much of Antarctica. All these countries are monarchical, having a Queen as head of state	6,600,000,000 acres approximately
2★	The Russian state owns about 50 per cent of the land of Russia and deals actively in land especially forest land. The state/private division is very like the United States in percentages	Russia is a democracy with significant oligarchical influence, similar to the United States	2,447,266,384 acres out of 4,219,424,000 acres
3★	The People's Republic of China All land in China is owned by the state and held for the people. Land is now being let to families on leases of varying length. There is market on land in China, though limited.	China is a People's Republic and is a one-party Communist state that includes Tibet	1,288,400,000 acres
4★	The US Federal Government owns about 30 per cent of the United States and deals actively in farmland forestry and other real estate	The United States of America and territories The country is nominally a democracy, but, like Russia, is hugely influenced by financially wealthy oligarchs.	762,000,000 acres out of 2,423,884,160 acres

	Name	Country where land held	Holding in acres
5★	King of Harald V of Norway. The countries territories in Antarctica add enormously to his legal superiority as ruler	Kingdom of Norway and Antarctica	Total 712,276,253 acres Norway 80,002, 560 acres. Antarctica 617,000,000 and 15,130,240 acres in Svalbard
6★★	The resident community of people of Greenland. The country is an external territory of Denmark, but the land is held by the Greenland community of about 56,000 people. Former President Trump of the United States tried to buy the country from Denmark, not being aware of who the owners actually are. Ignorance of landownership is very widespread.	Greenland. Semi-independent but legally part of the Kingdom of Denmark	535,218,189 acres
7★	King Salaman of Saudi Arabia. The king holds all land from Allah on the basis of Islamic law and tradition.	Kingdom of Saudi Arabia	518,000,000 acres according to the World Bank. 530,000,000 acres according to the Saudi national statistics office
8★	The Aboriginal people of Australia as communal freeholders of the Crown	The Dominion of Australia. Head of state Queen Elizabeth II	247,000,000 acres out of Australia's 3,357,934,182 acres
9★	The Inuit, First Nation and Aboriginal Eskimo people of Canada. These are mainly 'pending rights' claims but are being successfully pursued so far.	The Dominion of Canada. Head of State Queen Elizabeth II	200,000,000 acres out of Canada's total acreage of 2,264,467,640 acres
10★	The Catholic Church. When first elected Pope, Francis I is understood to have been given a copy of *Who Owns the World* as a guide to the Church's land holdings, especially in Italy.	USA, South America, Italy & worldwide. The Catholic Church is a monarchy headed by the Pope and is a member of the UN with that status	178,751,000 acres. This is a very conservative estimate but is base on extensive research

	Name	Country where land held	Holding in acres
11★	King Maha Vajiralongkorn pf Thailand. The internal dynamics of the Thai constitution are medieval and hyper monarchical. The democracy of Thailand, self formed, is virtually excluded from the constitution.	Kingdom of Thailand	126,793,600 acres
12★	King Felipe VI of Spain. The transition from the facist regime of Franco is not complete where land is concerned. Much reform is needed to rationalise landownership for the democracy that Spain has become.	Kingdom of Spain	125,040,274 acres
13★	King Mohammed VI of Morocco. Land system is Islamic with the king holding the land in trust for the people from Allah. The regime is paternalistic and the king has a degree of popular support, but the landownership system is medieval	Kingdom of Morocco	113,354,880. King Mohammed also claims 62,300,160 acres of the Western Sahara, illegally invaded in 1975 then unlawfully annexed by Morocco in 1976
14★	King Carl XIV Gustav of Sweden Much of Swedish land is still held by aristocratic families. And there is growing leasing of forest land by corporate interests.	Kingdom of Sweden	111,188,480 acres
15★	Emperor Naruhito of Japan. The Macarthur constitution of Japan abolished aristocratic titles and later landholdings but left the feudal superiority of the Emperor intact.	Japan. Japan is a democracy whose head of state is the Emperor	93,372,160 Acres
16★	Malaysia. The Agong (King) Al Sultan Abdullah of Pahang and one of the 9 hereditary Sultans and Rajas of Johor, Kedah,Negeri Sembilan,Kelantan, Pahang,Perak,Perlis,Selangor and Terengagganu	The Kingdom of Malaysia	81,81,507,200 acres In Malaysia there is a mixture of British and of Islamic ownership. The feudal superior is the Agong (King)

	Name	Country where land held	Holding in acres
17★	Sultan Quaboos bin Said al Said of Oman. Held by the Sultan on the basis of Islamic Law.	The Sultanate of Oman	726,480,000 acres
18★	King Norodom Sihamoni of Cambodia	The Kingdom of Cambodia	44,734,720 acres
19★	King Gyanendra of Nepal until 2008 when the Hindu kingdom became a republic. The ultimate feudal superior still appears to be the former king	Nepal is a Republic with elements of monarchical rule	36,369,280 acres
20★★	Ms Gina Rinehart with Shanghai CRED	The Dominion of Australia	29,040,000 acres
21★	King Abdullah II of Jordan held under Islamic Law from Allah	The Kingdom of Jordan	22,076,800 acres
22★★	Zhongding Dairy and Severney Bur	China and Russia.	22,022,000 acres
23★	The 7 Sheikdoms of the United Arab Emirates. Held by the Sheiks under Islamic law	Abu Dhabi, Dubai, Sharjah, Ras-al-Khaimah, Fuhairah, Umm-al-Qaiwain Ajman	19,198,893 acres
24★	The Irish State in its first constitution of 1922 inherited the legal ownership of all land in the Republic from the UK Crown. That situation persists in the current Constitution.	The Republic of Ireland	17,367,632 acres
25★★	Joe Lewis (UK) Financier	Australia	16,940,000 acres
	Weyerhauser REIT (Real Estate Investment Trust)	USA	14,412,000
26★★	Machlachlan Family	Australia	13,915,000 acres
27★★	Guy Hands and Terra Firma (UK financier)	Australia	13,794,000 acres
28★★	Macquarie Bank Australia Best estimate as to acreage held under corporate identities	Australia	10,648,000 acres
29★	King Willem-Alexander of the Netherlands. One third of the constitution deals with the monarchy. Acreage here is the land he rules.	The Kingdom of the Netherlands	10,507,200 acres

	Name	Country where land held	Holding in acres
30★	King Jigme Khevar Namgyel Wangchuck (Druk Gyalop – Dragon King) of Bhutan. Rules under Buddhism law and traditions	The Kingdom of Bhutan	9,479,360 acres
31★★	Brook Family	Australia	8,470,000 acres
32★★	Brett-Blundy Family	Australia	8,228,000 acres
33★★	Macdonald Family	Australia	8,131,200 acres
34★★	Jeremy Bayard	Australia	7,937,600 acres
35★	King Philippe of Belgium. Constitution unclear on feudal superiority. Land ruled	The Kingdom of Belgium	7,543,680 acres
36★	King Letsie III of Lesotho. Land is held from the king according to African (Zulu) tribal laws and customs	The Kingdom of Lesotho	7,500,000 acres
37★★	Holmes A'Court Family	Australia	6,050,000 acres
38★★	Williams Family	Australia	5,808,000 acres
39★★	Hughes Family	Australia	5,445,000 acres
40★★	Handelsbanken	Sweden & Scandenavia	4,840,000 acres
41★★	Mondi Group	South Africa and Russia	4,840,000 acres
42★★	Oxenford Family	Australia	4,767,000 acres
43★	Emir Sabah al Ahmad al Jabr al Sabah of Kuwait. Land held according to Islamic Law.	The Emirate of Kuwait	4,403,00 acres
44★	King Mswati III of Swaziland. All land held by the king on traditional African customary basis	The Kingdom of Swaziland	4,290,560 acres
45★★	Angelini Family of Chile	Chile, Argentina, Brazil, Uruguay	3,872,000 acres
46★★	Menegazzo Family	Australia	3,872,000 acres
47★★	Acton Family	Australia	3,799,400 acres
48★★	Irving Family	The USA & Canada on Crown leases	3,146,000 acres
49★★	Robert McBride	Australia	3,146,000 acres
50★★	Allan Myers	Australia	2,855,600 acres
51★	Sheik Tamim bin Hamad al Thani	The Sheikdom of Quatar	2,826,240 acres

	Name	Country where land held	Holding in acres
52★★	Harris Family	Australia	2,662,000 acres
53★★	Brinkworth family	Australia	2,420,000 est acres
54★★	Matte Family	Chile, Argentina, Brazil	2,420,000 est acres
55★★	Ruslan Moldabekov with EBRD bank	Kazakhstan	2,420,000 est acres
56★★	Kerry Stokes currently buying 1,210,000 acres	Australia	2,400,000 acres
57★★	John Malone. Number 1 in US list and on Irish list	USA	2,257,000 acres Alt Forbes 2,200,000 acres
58★★	Andrew Twiggy Forrest	Australia	2,185,260 acres
59★★	Benneton Family (Italy)	Chile (Patagonia contested ownership	2,153,800 acres
60★★	UK Forestry Commission all parts.	UK. Ultimately all land is legally owned by the Crown. Elizabeth 11	2,065,019 acres
61★★	Andrei Verevski	Ukraine	1,960,200 est acres
62★★	Emmerson Family	USA	1,960,000 acres Alt 1,870,000 acres Forbes
63★★	Ted Turner	USA	1,920,000 acres Alt Forbes 2,000,000 acres
64★★	Potlatch REIT	USA	1,900,000 acres
65★★	Colin Ross	Australia	1,815,000 acres
66★★	Airat Khairullin	Russia	1,815,000 est acres
67★★	Luke Butler	Australia	1,783,540 acres
68★★	Ma Zingfa (China)	Australia	1,708,520 acres
69★★	Agro Centre Astana	Kazakhstan	1,694,000 acres
70★★	Ternator Sarch Co. (Finland)	Finland & Estonia	1,621,400 acres
71★★	Lee Family	Australia	1,604,460 acres
72★★	Oleg Bakhmatuk	Ukraine	1,582,680 acres
73★★	Consortium of investors (New Forest)	Australia. New Zealand	1,452,000 acres
74★	Sultan Hassanal Bolkiah of Brunei Land held on strict Islamic Law terms	The Sultanate of Brunei, with significant holdings elsewhere	1,424,640 acres

	Name	Country where land held	Holding in acres
75**	Eduardo Elsztain	Argentina, Brazil, Paraguay, Brazil	1,420,000 est acres
76**	Vasily Rozinov	Russia, Kazakhstan	1,415,000 est acres
77**	Stan Kroenke	USA	1,380,000 acres. Alt 740,000 Forbes
78**	Koch Bros (May have merged)	USA and Crown lease is Canada	1,311,640 acres
79**	Reed Family	USA	1,300,000 acres. Alt 770,000 Forbes
80**	Romeo Roxas Phillippens	Australia	1,282,600 acres
81**	Irving Family	USA	1,250,000 acres Alt 1,200,000 Forbes
82**	Young An Group	South Korea, mostly Australia	1,210,000 acres
83**	Igor Khudokomorov	Russia	1,161,600 acres
84**	Brad Kelley	USA	1,150,000 acres Alt 1,700,000 Forbes
85**	Logemann Family	Brazil	1,115,620 acres
86**	Bill Gunn	Australia	1,113,200 acres
87**	Coillte. The Irish Forestry Commission	Republic of Ireland	1,102,000
88**	Vadim Moshkevich	Russia	1,098,680 acres
89**	Vamintatarstan	Russia Tatarstan	1,074,680 acres
90**	UK Ministry of Defence (Excludes Canadian leases of 250,000 acres)	UK. All MoD land is Crown land legally.	1,039,000 acres
91**	Singleton Family	USA	1,028,500 acres Alt 1,110,000 Ares Forbes
92**	Craig Astill	Australia	987,630 acres
93**	Paddy Handbury	Australia	968,000 acres
94**	De Moraes Family	Brazil. South America	943,800 acres
95**	King and Lewis Family	USA	900,000 acres. Alt 911,215 acres Forbes

	Name	Country where land held	Holding in acres
96★★	Pingree Family	USA and Canada	830,000 acres Alt Forbes 830,000 acres
97★	The National Trust of England & Wales, Scotland and Northern Ireland	UK (England, Wales, Scotland and NI) Even freeholds are held from the Crown	785,000 acres (min)
98★★	Hewitt Family	Australia	726,000 acres
99★	Wilkes Brothers	USA	702,000 acres
100★	Grand Duke Henri of Luxembourg	The Grand Duchy Luxembourg	639,000 acres (min)
101★	Briscoe Family	USA	620,000 acres (min)
102★★	The Church of Jesus Christ of Latter Day Saints (Mormons)	USA	615,000 acres est (min)
103★★	Lyxes Family	USA	615,000 acres
104★	Duke of Westminster (UK based)	UK, Canada, USA, Ireland Australia	610,000 acres (min)
105★★	O'Connor Family	USA	587,700 acres
106★★	Ford Family	USA	580,000 acres (min)

APPENDIX

Ranks of the British and Irish peerage and Parliamentary Structures Between 1801 and the Present

The highest rank in the British and Irish Peerage is that of the Sovereign. The Sovereign is either a King or a Queen, and only the Sovereign can create or confer titles of honour such as peerages. The Sovereign is the 'font of all honour'.

After the Sovereign, the highest British title is that of Prince. It is confined to members of the Royal Family. At least one British peer, the Duke of Wellington, has a title as Prince of the Holy Roman Empire, but does not use it officially in the UK. The Holy Roman Empire is now, like the British Empire, a figment of historical imagination.

Other titles include:

Duke, with the female title of Duchess
Marquis and Marchioness
Earl and Countess
Viscount and Viscountess
Baron and Baroness – the courtesy title is Lord and Lady and is used to address members of the House of Lords in London
Baronet and Lady. A Baronet is an hereditary knight, with Bt after his name. The last creation of a Baronetcy was for Denis Thatcher, the husband of Margaret Thatcher, the former British Prime Minister. His son Mark is now Sir Mark Thatcher Bt.
Knight – a Sir or Dame and is for the lifetime of the holder only.

The importance of a title in the period covered by this book is that it conferred the right to sit in the upper house of the legislature or Parliaments then existing.

Between 1541 and 1801, the Kingdom of Ireland was united with the Kingdom of Great Britain via the two crowns. The Sovereign of the UK was the Lord of Ireland and its King or Queen. Ireland had a separate House of Commons and House of Lords in Dublin between 1541 and 1801, the year the Parliamentary unification of both countries became effective.

In January 1801 the Act of Union, which created the United Kingdom of Great Britain and Ireland, became effective. The Irish House of Commons closed and seats were created for Irish members of Parliament in London. Those Irish peers who had been granted new hereditary peerages in the UK peerage, obtained seats in the UK House of Lords.

From 1801 there were two types of peerage: that of Ireland and that of the UK. In 1801 the Irish House of Lords dissolved and the Irish peers lost their seats but not their titles. Some of the Irish peers were made peers of the new United Kingdom and some could sit in the House of Lords in London until 1999. That year most of the hereditary peers were finally ejected from the House of Lords, save for a residue of 90 who still have seats. It is the only legislature in the world that admits hereditary peers (or persons) into the process of law making. With the hereditary element it is the second largest legislature in the world, exceeded only by the People's National Congress of the Peoples Republic of China, with 2,980 members representing over 1.3 billion people. There are over 800 members of the British House of Lords, the majority of them holding their title as baron or baroness only for the lifetime of the holder. They are appointed by the Queen on the Prime Minister's recommendation. They have no representative function. The hereditary element do not represent any interest other than their own. They are the strangest anomaly in the legislatures of the planet.

In 1921 the 26 counties of Southern Ireland became a Free State under the British Crown. In 1949 the Free State became a republic and left the British Commonwealth. Members of the Irish Parliament, the Dail, are known as 'Deputies'. The only other title in Ireland is that of 'Senator', given to members of the upper house of the Dail. With the Irish Presidents permission Irish citizens may accept foreign titles. The late Peter Sutherland, former Attorney General of the Irish Republic, was a British knight, a 'sir'. The former Irish businesswoman Detta O'Cathain is a life baroness in the British House of Lords.

END NOTE

The main victims of the Irish banking crisis of 2008 were its family home owners, the little people who were finally getting a piece of land. About 90,000 are still stranded, in arrears, holding the irresponsible loans made them by irresponsible Irish banks. One reason for this is traceable back, in historic terms, to the landlords who held the entire country in chains from about the early 1600s. Key to the conduct of the landlords was their possession, in addition to all land, of government, police, army, courts – and information.

The Irish Government solved the banking crisis by placing the country in hock for about 64 billion Euros, payable by the Irish taxpayer over the next thirty or more years. What the Irish Government sat upon was information. Because it controlled the law, no actions were mounted by the State against the miscreants, some of whom were State officials. But no one else had adequate information to mount effective legal actions. Or Parliamentary action. The Dail failed the people as radically as had the landlords' parliaments in the nineteenth century. The ability of the citizens of the Republic, and to a lesser extent those of Northern Ireland, to protect themselves or to get compensation from the guilty parties was limited by the lack of information and a legal system that was as inimical to ordinary people as ever it was under the landlords.

On the night of 29 February 2008 the Irish Government gave a blanket guarantee for the debts of the failing Irish banks. In the inquiry into what happened, begun in 2014, six years after the crisis, no evidence emerged to show that the Government knew the scale of liability it was undertaking that night, or how it would repay the new debts it needed. That guarantee turned out to be €64 billion, about €18,000 per person in the Republic and about two-thirds of Irish GDP. The Irish taxpayer will still be paying this off thirty or forty years from now. The belated inquiry, which reported in 2015, has been described as an autopsy on a corpse long dead. If the corpse is the Irish taxpayer it is not quite so dead that the money cannot be extracted from it for years to come. The inquiry was an expensive and useless one, almost entirely because the Irish establishment delayed its start for six years. By then memories had dulled, evidence had vanished and the Fianna Fail government that had been responsible for much of the crisis in the first place was out of office. But the most outstanding characteristic of the inquiry was the failure to obtain relevant facts. During the crisis a moment occurred when it looked like the Irish public, as they had once done to a British Embassy in Dublin, were going to turn up and burn down the Dail.

If there is a record of what transpired the night the Irish Government took on the debts of the banks, and placed the country in hock for thirty or forty years, it has not been revealed to the people of the country. The powerlessness of the citizens, while not as absolute as under the landlords, proved just as complete.

SPECIAL BIBLIOGRAPHY

To understand the present and to predict the future, sometimes you have to deep dive the past, especially the less plumbed and murkier parts of it.

'Land Owners of Ireland', Return of Owners of Land (Dublin: HMSO, 20 April 1876)

This book relies substantially on the first edition, in the original, of the 'Land Owners of Ireland' (part of the UK Return of Owners of Land, 1872) compiled by the Local Government Board of Ireland, and published by its secretary, B. Banks, on 20 April 1876 in Dublin. It was printed by Alexander Thom, at 87 and 88 Abbey Street, Printer to the Queen's most excellent Majesty, for Her Majesty's Stationary Office. The volume was priced at 3 shillings and 6 pence, the modern equivalent of about 20 decimal pence, but more like £14 in real terms.

So, Why Start with the Return, a Document Published in 1876?

By starting in this manner this book sets a clear, factual 'start line' for landownership in the Republic of Ireland and, to a lesser extent, in Northern Ireland. This is important because very little use has been made by academics, Irish or others, of the Return, and because conceivably the most important record of how Ireland changed everything for its people by redistributing land from landlords to peasants is still a state secret after 138 years.

The Land Commission was founded in 1881, but followed the Landlord and Tenant Act 1870 and four subsequent acts. It was implicit in them. The key right in the first act, installed by John Bright MP who later provoked the creation of the Return of Landowners, set up a mortgage arrangement for tenants to buy their holdings with a government loan over thirty-five years at 5 per cent. This was used by less than 1,000 tenants from the original Act but ultimately became the mechanism by which almost all land was transferred from landlord to peasant in Ireland.

The secret files are the 8 million records of the Irish Land Commission from 1881 to 1999, held in a warehouse in Portlaois, County Laois under the Irish Official Secrets Act 1963 and earlier. There is an excellent article by John Grenham in the *Irish Times* of 23 September 2013 pointing out that the Land Commission records for Northern Ireland between 1881 and 1922 had been handed to the Public Records Office in Northern Ireland and are available to the public. This means that the Irish Official Secrets Act is only being applied to individuals in the Republic.

Starting as one of the most impoverished countries on earth, in the wake of the 'Great Famine' (*Gorta Mor*) of 1845 to 1850, that same Republic now ranks fourth in the world in terms of GDP per capita (see the Introduction to this book). It might be wise to work out how that happened. It happened to no other country on the planet in such a fashion, and hiding the records as state secrets does not help humanity much.

The Extraordinary Survey of Which the Irish Return Forms the Fourth and Final Volume

The overall survey to obtain the four volumes of the original Return for all four countries of the United Kingdom – England, Ireland, Scotland and Wales – was commenced in 1872 after a very short debate in the British House of Lords on 19 February that year, which probably lasted less than 40 minutes. The overall survey was based, separately, on each of the four countries of the core United Kingdom in that year.

Publication began with Scotland in 1874, in Edinburgh. The Return of Owners of Land for England and Wales appeared as two volumes and was published in London in 1875. The survey for Ireland was commenced in January 1873 on the orders of the Lord Lieutenant.

The four volumes of the complete Return run to over 2,000 pages. Officially, it was a Parliamentary paper of the United Kingdom Parliament. It is one of the largest Parliamentary documents ever published in Hansard, the official record of Parliament. It is available via the UK Parliamentary website at parliament.uk.

Comments by Historians

There is only one comment of significance between 1881 and 2001, and there is no meaningful historiography for the Return of Owners of Land, despite its scale and importance.

Professor Spring Rice, writing in 1970 in the Leicester University Press reprinting of an extract of the *Great Landowners of Great Britain and Ireland ...* made by John Bateman in 1873, described the Return as 'one of the most heroic of the Victorian's pioneering enterprises in statistical inquiry'.

In practice, the Return is not technically statistical, but wholly factual. Professor Spring speculated that if extracts were made from Bateman's book (or the Return) of land holdings between 1,000 acres and 2,000 acres, 'the result would be something like the complete population of England's nobility and gentry'. Obsessed with the nobility and gentry, as were most historians, even as late as 1970 Professor Spring failed to realise that if the facts in the Return were examined statistically, two key single facts would emerge – the scale of concentration of all landownership in a statistically tiny section of the population and the scale of complete landlessness amongst the rest of the population. These two facts are largely used as the basis on which to examine the change in landownership in Ireland since the time of the Return in 1876.

The change is historically of enormous significance. No such change, from aristocratic hereditary land holdings to an essentially peasant population, has occurred on this scale in any other country in the world. The success of the young Republic after 1922 was mostly celebrated as a political success, and not the basic economic transformation of a people and their prospects that it actually was. Perhaps to do so might have highlighted too clearly the way this new nation had been largely misgoverned by those who inherited the mantle of British imperialism and its monarchical landholdings, in the Free State and later, the Republic.

The Physical Return for Ireland as Printed: Basic Facts

The Return of Owners of Land of 1 acre and upwards is based on each of the thirty-two counties of the country, divided into their ancient provinces of Leinster, Munster, Connaught and Ulster. There are 325 pages in all, folio in size. There are summaries of ownership for each province. The landowners of over 1 acre are listed alphabetically, with their address, within each county.

The total number of landowners of over 1 acre in Ireland in 1876 was 32,164. There were a further 36,144 owners of less than an acre. The population of the country, which can be extracted from the population for each county, is not given in the summary, probably deliberately; it was about 4.9 million people. Inclusion of that figure would have shown that the number of landless people (not demographically adjusted) in Ireland in 1876 was about 99 per cent of the population. The Irish were absolutely, as shown by the British Parliament, a landless people.

The Return of Landowners for Ireland, 1876 (The US Genealogical Society Edition of 1988)

In 1988, the American Genealogical Publishing Co. Inc., at Baltimore, Maryland, published an A4 (reduced, but facsimile) copy of the Return of Owners of Land in Ireland from the original at Loyola University in New Orleans. The catalogue number is 87-81693 in the Library of Congress and the ISBN number is 0806312033. This is a valuable tool for researchers, but does not contain the record of the Parliamentary debate in the House of Lords in 1872 which launched the overall Return. And there are no notes to explain the Return documents themselves.

The Great Landowners of Great Britain and Ireland: A List of All Owners of Three Thousand Acres and Upwards, Worth £3,000 a Year, *by John Bateman FRGS (4th Edition, 1883)*

After the Return, *Who Owns Ireland* is dependent on this book, first published in 1876 and again in 1878, 1879 and finally in 1883. The edition used here is the final 1883 publication, in the original. The final 1883 edition included the addition of 1,320 owners of 2,000 acres and upwards in England, Scotland, Ireland and Wales, their acreage and income from land being culled from the Modern Domesday Book, along with their colleges, clubs and services. It is corrected in the vast majority of cases by the owners themselves.

The book is 533 pages long. It was printed in London by Harrison, 59 Pall Mall, SW, booksellers to Her Majesty and HRH, the Prince of Wales. The book is arranged alphabetically by the name of the landowner and contains names, addresses and biographical details. It is not arranged by county and does not align with the Return. The number of entries approximates to the somewhat (aporical) figure of 3,000 families, usually given for the inner British élite or Establishment.

Bateman is, in practice, the specific record of the British élite, a fact largely ignored by most British historians, perhaps because it includes facts like their acreage and income. There is extensive commentary and a fuller biography of John Bateman in the book, *Who Owns Britain and Ireland* (Canongate, 2001), pp.41–48.

Griffith's Valuation, 1847–64

Between 1847 and 1864, (Sir) Richard Griffith was responsible for carrying out the Primary Valuation of Tenements (generally referred to as Griffith's Valuation because of his role in the project). The aim of the valuation was to produce a uniform guide to the relative value of land throughout the whole of Ireland in order to decide liability to pay the Poor rate (for the support of the poor and destitute within each Poor Law union). The project required Griffith and a team of valuers to determine the value of every piece of land and property in the country enabling every occupiers' tax due to be assessed. The information they collated covering all 32 counties was compiled into over 300 volumes and published over a period of 17 years.

(findmypast.co.uk)

Griffith's Valuation, indexed with images in this database, is one of Ireland's premier genealogical resources, referencing approximately one million individuals who occupied property in Ireland between 1848 and 1864. Griffith's Valuation, or Primary Valuation of Ireland, was executed under the direction of Sir Richard Griffith to provide a basis for determining taxes. This involved establishing the value of all privately held lands and buildings in both rural and urban areas in order to figure a rental rate for each unit of property. The resulting survey was arranged by barony and civil parish, with an index to townlands appearing in each volume. The original volumes of the survey are held in the National Archives, Dublin, and Public Record Office, Belfast.

Griffith's Valuation is an invaluable reference for family historians with ancestors in Ireland in part because much census material from the nineteenth century has been lost. In effect, it is the only detailed guide to where in Ireland people lived in the mid-nineteenth century and what property they owned or leased. Griffith's Valuation serves as a census substitute for the years before, during, and after the Great Famine. Griffith's Valuation is also a valuable record of social and economic data and includes map reference numbers that can help researchers identify and perhaps locate property on Ordinance Survey maps created before the valuations took place.

Few other records can be used to identify an Irish ancestor's exact place of origin, and only Griffith's Valuation links an individual to a specific townland and civil parish. This is extremely important, since the first step in Irish genealogical research is to identify an ancestor's townland and civil parish, which can lead you to ecclesiastical parish records of births and marriages.

(ancestry.com)

Griffith's Valuation, described above for simplicity's sake from findmypast.co.uk and ancestry.com, is, in history terms, a work in progress. It was commenced in 1847, one of the worst years of the famine, and ended in 1864 while the country was still losing population as a result of the famine. It is largely based on leases and gives an essentially false picture of how concentrated landownership actually was. From Griffith's, it is impossible to make the link between ownership of land and the link to state power in Parliament, which the combination of the Return and Bateman makes possible. Griffith's is not a record of landowners to compare with the Return, therefore. Griffiths is also huge, whereas the Return is about landowners, in summary form and contained in a single volume. Ownership can be traced via Griffith's, but would be a monumental task which, in practice, is actually better accomplished with the Return. Properly understood and studied, however, Griffith's could be used to show how the first native Irish landholders began the creation of landownership, and of the Irish middle class, in embryonic form via leases.

The Aristocracy and the Landed Gentry

Burke's Landed Gentry (1871, 1906, 1921, 1952 and 1965–72). This invaluable source no longer appears in its original form. There is a publication, but so far only Scotland is covered.

Burke's Landed Gentry of Ireland (1958). Burke's first edition of the landed commoners of Great Britain, which included families with estates in Ireland, appeared in 1833. It was confined to families with landed estates, but without hereditary titles. The titled appeared in a companion volume called *Burke's Peerage and Knightage*. In advertising for the later editions in the mid-nineteenth century, the editors say that the names of over 100,000 people appear in the books. The full list would include the names of children, grandchildren, cousins and anyone else who might have a claim on the estate. The actual heads of families and the owners of the estates would have been little larger than the numbers given by Bateman for his 3,000 plus the *Great Landowners and Squires*, (3,817) in his closing tables from page 501 (1883 edition) onwards. Bateman, himself a large landowner, tags some of the entries with an 'S' to indicate a reliable claim to have owned the estate since the time of Henry VII (1485–1509). Most, if not all of the entrants in Burke's would have had a family crest or shield, issued by the College of Arms, in London, Edinburgh, Dublin, or possibly Cardiff. The authenticity of this element of the entry has always been under query since applications for a coat of arms were sometimes accompanied by a 'gratuity' and not always either checked or checkable. This comment gives a flavour of the situation, made by a later editor of Burke's, 'If everybody who claims to have come over with the Conqueror were right, William must have landed with 200,000 men-at-arms instead of about 12,000' (the scale of exaggeration is proportional to these two numbers).

The specific editions of *Burke's Landed Gentry* used in connection were the following:

1899 – This title was the first edition of Burke's popular *Landed Gentry* series which dealt exclusively with Ireland. As a consequence, it has great deal more detail about the Irish families included. While these families are all labelled 'landed gentry', the group is much larger than the traditional landlords, including those aspiring to this status from the professional, business and merchant classes. This still represents a fairly narrow group, though the family histories are very extensive, including widely diverging collateral lines, junior branches and in-laws. These related families are quite likely to have come from the general farming and artisan community. These genealogies were mostly compiled by the Irish Chief Herald of the time (titled the 'Ulster King of Arms') and are generally considered to be fairly reliable.

Burke's Peerage and Baronetage (1896, 1906). This book reappeared in 2000.

Cahill, Kevin, *Who Owns Britain (and Ireland)* (Edinburgh: Canongate, 2001, 2002). Contains significant sections on the history of Irish landownership, first details of the county holdings of the landed gentry and comments on the interlinked land history of Great Britain and Ireland.

Cahill, Kevin, *Who Owns the World* (Edinburgh: Mainstream Random House, 2006, 2nd edition 2007, later version by Hachette in New York in 2010). This book was an attempt to impose structure on what was known about landownership worldwide at the time. It sets out a methodology for examining landownership systematically and has notes, however brief, on the landownership systems in most of the world's 193 countries and territories.

Debrett's Peerage and Baronetage (London: Macmillan, 2011, 2000 and previous editions). This huge work is published every five years.

Original Source Books

McEwen, John, *Who Owns Scotland* (Edinburgh: 2nd Edition, Polygon, 1981). This was the first attempt to tackle landownership on a systematic basis, with acreages, in Scotland.

Wightman, Andy, *Who Owns Scotland* (Edinburgh: Canongate Books, 1996). Andy Wightman is currently a member of the Scottish Parliament (MSP). He maintains a website of Scottish landowners. His book, *The Poor Had No Lawyers* (Edinburgh: Barlinnie, 2010) addresses the issue of how the poor were kept from landownership in Scotland by the corrupt deployment of the law by those with the money to pay for the laws to be written, and then abused. It was much the same in Ireland.

Additional Source Books on Power and Politics Relating to Land

De Juvenel, Bertrand, *On Power*, also known as *On Sovereignty* (New York: Greenwood Press and Beacon Press, 1981 and earlier). This is one of the very few books ever written that analyses power itself.

Olson, Professor Mancur, *The Rise and Decline of Nations* (Yale University Press, 1986).

GENERAL BIBLIOGRAPHY

Ball, Michael, *Housing Policy and Economic Power* (London: Methuen, 1983).

Beard, Madeleine, *English Landed Society in the 20th Century* (London: Routledge, 1989).

Beckett, James Camlin, *The Making of Modern Ireland* (London: Faber & Faber, 1965).

Bedarida, Francois, *A Social History of England 1851–1990* (London: Taylor & Francis, 1991).

Beresford, Dr Philip, *The Sunday Times Book of the Rich* (London: Weidenfeld & Nicholson, 1990) with Irish entrants.

Brodrick, George C., *English Land and English Landlords* (New York: Augustus M. Kelley Inc., 1968), from an earlier edition in 1881, privately published in London.

Brown, Anthony Cave, *'C': The Secret Life of Sir Stewart Menzies, Spymaster to Winston Churchill* (London: MacMillan, 1987). One of the most extraordinary insights ever written about the minds and culture of the aristocratic landed class, Eton College and the power elite who were running Britain & Ireland.

Brown, Terence, *Ireland: A Social and Cultural History, 1922 to the Present* (London: Fontana Press/Collins Press, 1981).

Bryant, Arthur, *English Saga* (London: William Collins & Co., various editions 1963–77). Also published as *The Story of England*.

Cairnduff, Maureen (ed.), *Who's Who in Ireland: The Influential 1,000* (Dublin: Checkout Publications, 1999).

Callander, Robin, *How Scotland is Owned* (Edinburgh: Canongate, 1998).

Cannadine, David, *The Decline and Fall of the British Aristocracy* (USA: Yale University Press, 1990).

Cannadine, David, *Aspects of Aristocracy* (London: Viking/Penguin, 1998).

Carter, Harold, *The Study of Urban Geography* (London: Arnold, 4th edition, 1995).

Corti, Count Egon Caesar, *The Rise of the House of Rothschild* (London: Victor Gollancz, 1928).

Cramb, Auslan, *Who Owns Scotland Now* (Edinburgh: Mainstream Publishing, 1996).

D'Auvergne, M. Nelson, *Tarnished Coronets* (London: Werner Laurie, 2nd edition, 1937).

Davis, William, *The Rich: A New Study of the Species* (London: Sidgwick & Jackson, 1983).

De Smith, Stanley A., *Constitutional and Administrative Law*, edited by Harry Street and Rodney Brazier (London: Penguin Books, 1971).

De Tocqeville, Alexis, *Journeys to England and Ireland* (London: Faber & Faber, 1957).

Devonshire, Duchess of, *The Estate, a View from Chatsworth* (London: Macmillan, 1990).

Dooley, Terence, *The Land For the People: The Land Question in Independent Ireland* (Dublin: UCD Press, 2004).

Drucker, Peter, *The Age of Discontinuity* (New York: Harper & Row, 1968).
Evans, Sir Harold, *Good Times, Bad Times* (London: Atheneum, 1984).
Ferguson Niall, *The House of Rothschild*, two volumes (London: Penguin Books, 2000).
Field, Leslie, *Bendor: The Golden Duke of Westminster* (London: Weidenfeld & Nicholson, 1983).
George, Henry, *Progress and Poverty* (London: Hogarth Press, centenary edition, 1979; 1st edition, 1879).
Gill, Robin, *The Myth of the Empty Church* (London: SPCK, 1993).
Girouard, Mark, *The Victorian Country House* (London: Book Club Associates, 1979).
Girouard, Mark, *Life in the English Country House* (Yale University Press, 1984).
Graham, Ysenda Maxtone, *The Church Hesitant* (London: Hodder & Stoughton, 1993).
Graves, Charles, *Leather Armchairs The Chivas Regal Book of London Clubs* (London: Cassel, 1963). Many Irish landowners belonged to London clubs. There is a more recent edition of this book.
Guinness, Desmond, and William Ryan, *Irish Houses and Castles* (London: Thames & Hudson, 1971).
Guinness, Michele, *The Guinness Legend* (London: Hodder & Stoughton, 1990).
Guttsman, W.L. (ed.), *The English Ruling Class* (London: Weidenfeld & Nicholson, 1969).
Hallam, Elizabeth, *Domesday Book* (Thames & Hudson, 1986; 1st English version, 1086).
Hobhouse, Henry, *The Seeds of Change: Five Plants that Transformed Mankind* (London: Harper Trade, 1997). This includes the potato.
Hone, Nathanial J., *The Manor and Manorial Records* (London: Dutton, 1906).
Kennedy, Liam, *Unhappy the Land* (Dublin: Merrion Press, 2015). Challenges the story of Irish exceptional historical misery.
Kennedy, Paul, *Preparing for the 21st Century* (London, HarperCollins, 1993).
Lacey, Robert, *Aristocrats* (London: Hutchinson, 1983).
Lee, Joseph, J., *Ireland 1912–1985* (Cambridge University Press, 1989).
Lovell, Terry, *Number One Millbank: The Financial Fall of the Church of England* (London: HarperCollins, 1997).
Lundberg, Ferdinand, *The Rich and the Super Rich* (New York: Lyle Stuart Inc., 1968).
McEwen, John, *A Life in Forestry*, edited by Doris Hatvany (Perth: Perth & Kinross Libraries, 1998). John McEwen is the godfather of landownership studies. His life story is well worth reading.
Madge, Sidney, *The Domesday of Crown Lands* (London: Routledge, 1938).
Manthorpe, John, *Ten Chief Land Registrars* (London: The Land Registry, 1997).
Montgomery, Maureen E., *Gilded Prostitution: Status, Money and Transatlantic Marriages 1870–1914* (London: Routledge, 1989).

Montgomery, William Ernest, *The History of Land Tenure in Ireland* (Forgotten Books, 2019). This is a reprint of the Cambridge University Yorke prize-winning essay on land law for 1888 – historically interesting.

Moody, T.W., F.X. Martin, & Dermot Keogh (eds), *The Course of Irish History* (Dublin: Radio Telefis Eireann, 1978).

Moore, Barrington, *Social Origins of Dictatorship and Democracy: Lord and Peasant in the Making of the Modern World* (London: Penguin Books, 1966).

Newman, Peter, *The Canadian Establishment* (Toronto: McClelland & Stewart Ltd, 1975).

Olson, Mancur, *The Logic of Collective Action* (Harvard University Press, 1990).

Olson, Mancur, *Power and Prosperity* (New York: Basic Books, 2000).

Peel, J.H.B., *Peel's England* (Newton Abbott: David & Charles, 1977).

Picknett, Lynn, Clive Prince, and Stephen Prior, *Double Standards* (London: Little Brown, 2001). This book is included as a general 'caution' about the British and Irish Establishment's willingness to falsify the historic record, which both have probably done with the records of landownership.

Pixley, Francis, *The History of the Baronetage* (London: Duckworth, 1900).

Poirteir, Cathal, *Famine Echoes* (Dublin: Gill & Macmillan, 1995).

Rossmore, Lord, *Things I Can Tell: Recollections of an Irish Landowner* (London: Eveleigh Nash, 1912).

Ruoff, T.B.F., *HM Land Registry 1862–1962. A Centenary History* (London: Land Registry, 1962).

Sampson, Anthony, *Anatomy of Britain* (London: Hodder & Stoughton, 1962 and subsequent editions).

Schama, Simon, *A History of Britain* (London: BBC Worldwide, 2002) from the TV series, especially Part 3: 'Britain from 1776 to 2000'.

Scott, John, *The Upper Classes: Property and Privilege in Britain* (London: Macmillan, 1982).

Short, Brian, and Mick Reed, *Landownership and Society in Edwardian Britain* (University of Sussex, 1987).

Sinclair, C., *The Lost Land: Land Use Changes in England 1945–1990* (Council for the Protection of Rural England, 1992). This is a somewhat obscure lobby group, specialising in the protection of nostalgia and memories of a Britain in which the lord was secure in his castle and the peasants sat at the gate, landless.

Smith, Goldwyn, *A Constitutional and Legal History of England* (New York: Dorset Press, 1990).

Stephenson, Tom, *Forbidden Land: The Struggle for Access to Mountain and Moorland*, edited by Anne Holt (Manchester University Press, 1988).

Taylor, Richard Norton, *Whose Land is it Anyway?* (Wellingborough: Turnstone Press, 1982). This was one of the most important recent books on the extraordinary misdistribution of land in the UK. It is indicative that Richard Taylor, a senior correspondent at the *Guardian* newspaper, could not get a mainstream publisher in London to take the book.

Thorold, Peter, *The London Rich* (London: Viking, 1999). Some of them were Irish landowners.
Wightman, Andy, *Land Reform, Politics, Power and the Public Interest* (Edinburgh: Friends of John McEwen, 1999 – the McEwen lecture on land tenure in Scotland).
Woodham-Smith, Cecil, *The Great Hunger: Ireland 1845–1849* (London: Penguin, 1991, earlier editions by Hamish Hamilton, London, 1962, and by Penguin in 1999 and later). This is the definitive account of the Irish Famine.
Wormell, Peter, *Anatomy of Agriculture* (London: Harrap, 1978).
Wright-Mills, C., *The Power Elite* (New York: Oxford University Press, 1956).
Wylie, J.C.W., *Irish Land Law* (London: Bloomsbury Professional, 2010 and 2013). Professor Wylie was a UK consultant to the Irish Law Reform Commission's attempts to reform Irish land law between 2001 and 2009. The reforms were a failure and reinforced historic structural failures by endorsing them; ignoring, as ever, either the lessons of history or their effects. The reforms failed to address the secrecy in which original deeds and documents remain held, failed to simplify the system and failed to take real advantage of technology advances.
Yardley, Michael, *Sandhurst: A Documentary* (London: Harrap, 1987).
Young, Hugo, *One of Us* (London: Macmillan, 1990).

Periodicals, Yearbooks, Newspapers and Special Editions

Daily Mail: Britain's landowners published in 2000.
Estates Gazette: The journal of the estate and land business profession, published weekly in London by Reed Business. This is an indispensable source, together with the Valuation Offices' reports of the Republic and the UK, to land values past and present. It was first published in 1858.
Forbes Magazine (USA): The billionaires published annually 1995 to 2019.
Irish Examiner: Now a part of the Independent group. Originally published as the Cork Examiner. Excellent farming and property information. Consulted regularly for this book.
Irish Independent: The Republic's largest-selling newspaper has excellent property and farming information.
Irish Times: published in Dublin, the Irish 'paper of record' has excellent property information and farming news.
'Land and Liberty' published by the *Georgist* magazine.
Mail on Sunday, 'Rich Report 2000 and 2001', edited by Rachel Oldroyd and Rodney Gilchrist.
The Observer, 'Young Rich', published in 1999 and 2000.
OECD: The Organisation for Economic Co-operation and Development, in Paris. Produces valuable economic reports on individual countries. The reports on Ireland, the UK, China and India were consulted for information on the changes in GDP per head. This part of the book is incomplete, as the basic information suggested much more extensive study for which time and resources ran out.
Properties of the National Trust (in Northern Ireland): an annual publication.

Sunday Times 'Rich Lists': published from 1989 and ongoing, with a special Irish supplement. The founding editor of the *Sunday Times* 'Rich List' was Dr Philip Beresford (who retired in 2017). The 'Rich Lists', compiled from hard factual sources, including company records in Companies House in the UK and the Republic of Ireland, is a wholly unique record of the rich and how they accumulate their wealth. Most academics do not understand the hard sources for the 'Rich List' records and there is no academic record of the rich of either the Republic of Ireland or of the United Kingdom to match the *Sunday Times* list.

Sunday Times, 'Richest of the Rich from 1066 to 2000': compiled and edited by Dr Philip Beresford and Professor W.D. Rubenstein. (Kevin Cahill was a researcher on the 1st edition in 1989 and Dr Beresford's assistant editor on the 1990 and 1991 editions.)

'Richest 200 Women in the World', *Eurobusiness Magazine*, edited by Kevin Cahill (June 2000).

'Richest 250 Women in the UK (and Ireland)' in *BusinessAge Magazine*, edited by Kevin Cahill (1992).

'Richest 400 Europeans', *Eurobusiness Magazine*, edited by Kevin Cahill (1999).

'Richest 500 individuals on the UK Stock Exchange', *BusinessAge Magazine*, edited by Kevin Cahill (1993).

'Richest 500 people in the UK', *BusinessAge Magazine*, edited by Tom Rubython (1993 and 1994).

'Richest 500 people in the UK, including Ireland', *BusinessAge Magazine*, edited by Kevin Cahill.

For international landholders for the concluding chapter:
The Business Insider (Australia)
Farm Weekly (Australia)
The Land Report (USA).
The Irish Farmers Journal is the Irish weekly farming newspaper, sold mainly in Ireland. It is the largest-selling farming newspaper in the country with a circulation of over 60,000 a week in 2018. It is published every Sunday. It employs ninety people and is owned by the Agricultural Trust, which also owns *The Irish Field*. This is one of the most indispensable sources of information on land sales and markets in rural Ireland, where all the land actually is. This paper's archives are worth a book or more, all on their own.

Government and Official Sources

All the main government services in the Irish Republic and Northern Ireland have websites. Most function reasonably well but are not equipped to answer questions about the historic background or detailed structure of landownership in either parts of the island. The work of the pre-1922 Land Commission in Northern Ireland and its successors after partition are little studied. The Land Commission records in the Republic are held, from 1870 to the present, in a warehouse in

Portlaois, Co. Laois and are inaccessible, governed by the Irish Official Secrets Act 1963.

Central Statistical Office, Dublin and devolved offices.

Coillte: This is the Irish State Forestry body and is the largest single landowner in the Irish Republic at Dublin Road, Newtownmountkennedy, Co. Wicklow.

Department of Agriculture, Environment and Rural Affairs, Belfast, Northern Ireland.

Department of Agriculture, Food and Marine, Kildare St, Dublin.

Government Information Office, Dublin.

Land Registry of Northern Ireland is part of the Department of Finance and is located at 7 Lanyon Place, Belfast, BT1 3LP.

Land Registry of the Republic of Ireland: Now known as the Property Registration Authority, at 7 Chancery Street, Smithfield, Dublin 7. There is also a Registry of Deeds at Henrietta Place, Inns Quay, Dublin. The original deeds and documents of title are not available to the public in the Irish system, which is otherwise computerised.

Northern Ireland Forestry Service: Based at Innishkeen House in Enniskillen, County Fermanagh.

Northern Ireland Office, Belfast and Northern Ireland Ministry of Finance.

Northern Ireland Public Records Office, Belfast.

Other Reference Sources

Burke's Landed Gentry, 1871, 1906, 1921, 1952 and 1965–1972. *Burke's Landed Gentry* is no longer published in this form.

Kelly, Kevin, *Europe's Elite 1,000* (London: Cadogan Publications, 1999).

Lord Belmont, aka Timothy William Ferres: This blogger from Belfast has more than 2.7 million visitors to his website. He writes, with humour, about an eclectic collection of subjects including the landed gentry and the peerage. Despite my own possession of over forty original copies of editions of Debrett's and Burke's across two centuries (see above), Timothy finds sources and details on landowners that were beyond my reach. When checked, he has always turned out to be accurate and correct. I use his information with his kind permission and compliment him on his extraordinary sources.

The Ancestor: Quarterly Review of Family History, Heraldry, Antiquity and History, Vols I–X (London: Archibald Constable & Co.).

Walford's County Families of the United Kingdom (1900 and other editions). In its day, probably the most accurate of these publications and includes the Irish families.

Who's Who: Specific editions consulted for Irish sources for this book are 1907, 1912, 1920, 1931, 1947, 1955, 1964, 1976, 1981, 1992, 1997, 1998, 1999 and 2000. *Who's Who* is published annually by A&C Black, now part of Bloomsbury Publishing, London.

ACKNOWLEDGMENTS

Firstly, I owe so much to so many I don't know where to begin thanking everyone. Secondly, this is not a standard for-the-book disclaimer; there are many and ferocious views about the Irish famine of 1845 to 1850. What I say in *Who Owns Ireland* is entirely my own opinions and neither directly or indirectly the view of those I thank for getting me this far in life, and to this book.

I'd like to thank my long dead parents for making sure that my brothers and sister and I got the best education they could provide for us in the Ireland of the time. They never saw my late brother Paul become a professor at an Italian university and a published poet in both English and Italian, and were long gone when my books appeared. They never saw what they paid for. I'd also like to thank my brother Michael and his family for their support and my sister Eibhlin and her husband Derek too, for support over the years.

Behind most writers is a secondary school where a special teacher, or two, probably set the course towards authorship. In my case at Rockwell College, Cashel, in County Tipperary, it was the late Father Aidan Lehane CSSP. But the man of books was Father Campbell CSSP. He taught 'off piste', on another planet from the official curriculum. I still remember borrowing his copy of Goncharov's *Oblomov*, a book about a man who never got out of bed.

Studying English at the then New University of Ulster I also took the 'off piste' route. Well, most of the books on the course were off piste the other way, Neanderthal. I only read nine of them. They seemed remote from English which is mostly spoken, rather than written, in common usage. I did the spoken bit at the *Irish Times* debating competition, but no course credits were available for the winners of the Demosthenes trophy that year.

This is a good moment to thank James Connolly SC, a barrister and Bencher at King's Inn's in Dublin, and our mutual friend Garrett Wren CA. Without James's help there would have been no *Irish Times* trophy and without Garrett's support over the years, probably no books at all. Whenever I see *Educating Rita*, which was filmed at Trinity College Dublin in James's old office at the Hist* I recall a night to truly remember: his inaugural as Auditor. Dissidents stormed the TCD dining hall where physical battle (albeit of the rugby scrum variety) instead of oral occurred. The dissidents then chained themselves to the railings around Parliament Square,

---

* The College Historical Society (CHS), often referred to as The Hist, is one of the two debating societies at Trinity College Dublin. It was established in 1770 (the other one, The Phil, was established in 1685) and is the oldest surviving undergraduate student society in the world. It was inspired by the club formed by the philosopher Edmund Burke during his own time in Trinity in 1747. It. James Connolly SC was the 204th Auditor of the Hist.

inside college gates. The Defence Minister, Paddy Cooney, a speaker, escaped out a latrine window. We got back to James's rooms in Botany Bay to find a *skian dubh* upright in the floor beneath the letter box. In the film Julie Walters holds up a copy of Ferlinghetti's *An Eye on the World,* a book of poetry that I have had for fifty years and still read most weeks or months. So, thanks Lawrence Ferlinghetti, who died recently aged 101.

The big thanks for my considering writing books about landownership goes to Dr Philip Beresford, the former founder and long-time editor of the *Sunday Times* Rich List. He assigned me 'old money' in Britain. This meant land, which turned out, in research terms, to be a whole 'new found land'. With further help from Philip, I discovered the lost second Domesday, the return of Owners of Land of 1872, via Bateman's *The Great Landowners of Great Britain and Ireland*, in the Ealing Public library.

To Philip and his wife Della, the former Management Education Editor of the *Financial Times*, I owe more than I can ever repay. And to the other mates from NUU, Andy Harley, Alison Dewar, and now Anne, Andy's wife. Thanks to Philip we have 'Zoomed' through the pandemic.

Over the years I received invaluable help from Michael Freeman and his family, formerly of the Irish Land Registry. The opportunity to re-present the Return of Owners of Land in Committee Room G of the House of Lords I owe to the later Professor the Lord Laird of Artigarvan FBCS, an Ulsterman. As was Paddy, later the Rt Hon the Lord Ashdown and Companion of Honour, who hired me as his researcher in the House of Commons in the 1980s. My campaign with him against American irregularities in the IT industry inspired my first normally published book, *Trade Wars*.

I am of course a journalist, I think the words 'to boot' applies. There are many I'd like to thank but who, as valued sources, might prefer anonymity. The Saltees and their Banrion will never be forgotten, however. Nor a day at Grinsing near Vienna. The glasses were a quarter of a litre and too numerous to count. The rainstorm and lightening would have inspired Beethoven's 'Emperor', anew.

Those I can openly thank are my recent editor at *Computer Weekly* Bill Goodwin, hero of a seven-year battle to keep journalistic sources confidential, which he won In the European Court of Human Rights. And Fiona O'Cleirigh, chair of the London Freelance Branch of the NUJ for a number of years, and faithful friend in my legal adventures on the issue of mass surveillance. And Tony Gosling, Tif and Martin, of Community Radio Bristol FM. Robin Tatam, former submariner, former Chair of the South West RSA, has always supported this and earlier books.

Finally, there are the members of my family, who are listed in the dedication. First, Jane and Ian. Kay, who minds books as a director of Vancouver City Library. She and Jen surveyed Canada for *Who Owns the World*. Stella and Ed did much of the maths on American land for the same book. The grandchildren, Ivo and Arlo, have helped with IT averaging and stats for this book. Rona has taken a keen interest (she's 22 months old, but in our house you are never too young to start on a book). And my wife Ros, one of whose ancestors, Mrs Bennett, was the Jilly Cooper of her day. She was a rarity as a woman writing books in the 1790s, getting huge advances, and being published in Dublin, London and Paris.

Out at Beer Quarry caves, one of the UK's potentially most important prehistoric sites, there is Steve Rodgers, a man with 'second sight' about flint, mankind's only tool for millennia. And his family, Alice, Rene and Jayne. And our accountant Chris Wray at Colyton.

At The History Press, Ronan Colgan who commissioned the book, Alex Waite who completed the herculean task of editing it and Cynthia Hamilton who publicised it. A huge thanks.